ENGLISH-JAPANESE, JAPANESE-ENGLISH DICTIONARY OF COMPUTER AND DATA-PROCESSING TERMS

EI-WA—WA-EI
KONPYŪTA-DĒTA SHORI
YŌGO JITEN
英和-和英
コンピューター-データ処理
用語辞典

The MIT Press
Cambridge, Massachusetts
London, England

ENGLISH-JAPANESE, JAPANESE-ENGLISH DICTIONARY OF COMPUTER AND DATA-PROCESSING TERMS

EI-WA—WA-EI
KONPYŪTA-DĒTA SHORI
YŌGO JITEN
英和-和英
コンピューター-データ処理
用語辞典

Gene Ferber

This book was set in Optima and
Japanese Grotesk by Asco Trade
Typesetting Limited in Hong Kong,
and printed and bound by Halliday
Lithograph in the United States
of America.

Library of Congress Cataloging-in-
Publication Data

Ferber, Gene.
English-Japanese/Japanese-English
dictionary of computer and data-
processing terms = Ei-Wa Wa-Ei
konpyūta dēta shori yōgo jiten =
[Ei-Wa Wa-Ei konpyūta-dēta shori
yōgo jiten]/Gene Ferber.
p. cm.
ISBN 0-262-06114-7
1. Computers—Dictionaries.
2. Electronic data processing—
Dictionaries.   3. English language
—Dictionaries—Japanese.
4. Computers—Dictionaries—
Japanese.   5. Electronic data
processing—Dictionaries—
Japanese.   6. Japanese language—
Dictionaries—English.   I. Title.
II. Title: Ei-Wa Wa-Ei konpyūta
dēta shori yōgo jiten.
QA76.15.F47 1988
004'.03'956—dc19   88-1301
                    CIP

Special thanks to J. H. Ferber,
K. J. O'Neill, and D. A. Hytha,
whose expertise and continued
support have made this dictionary
possible.

PREFACE

This dictionary is designed primarily to help English-speaking engineers, computer and data-processing professionals, and marketing and sales executives working in Japan or dealing with their Japanese counterparts in the West. Western companies are beginning to train engineers and marketing staff in spoken Japanese in order to approach the Japanese market more efficiently; a knowledge of the Japanese terminology of one of the most important areas of technology could be a great asset to international companies specializing in the sale or purchase of computers and computer-related products.

The main advantage of this dictionary in this respect is the inclusion of romanized transcriptions of Japanese terms, thus facilitating communication for those with only a spoken knowledge of the Japanese language. In the English-Japanese section, each English term is followed by the romanized Japanese, then by the Japanese characters. In the Japanese-English section, the romanized Japanese words (*rōmaji*) are listed first, and roman alphabetical order is observed. This is to simplify reference by Western speakers of Japanese; the Japanese-English section can also be used by native speakers of Japanese who are familiar with both roman script and roman alphabetical order.

Another advantage is the exact romanized transcription of words borrowed from the English language and expressed in *katakana* form (Japanese characters used to represent the sounds of borrowed foreign words). For example, *konpyūta*, rather than *computer*, is the transcription given for コンピュータ. This is to facilitate Western recognition and reproduction of the katakana characters.

An apostrophe has been used in certain of the romanized words to clarify the reading and pronunciation of the Japanese characters. For example: *jun'i* ("sequence"), as opposed to *jūni* ("twelve").

In entries where a group of English words, rather than a single word, has been borrowed into the Japanese language and expressed in katakana form, the words are separated by a dot in the Japanese text. In the romanized version, a hyphen separates them. For example:

intafuēsu-messēji-purosessa
interface message processor
インタフェース・メッセージ・
プロセッサ

To my knowledge this dictionary is the only one of its kind. Japanese publications on the subject do not include the romanization of the Japanese characters, and they use the Japanese alphabetical order in the Japanese-English section. It is hoped that this work, organized with Western users in mind, will serve as a practical tool in their international dealings.

AUTHOR'S NOTE

Readers should be aware that a
specialized technical dictionary
cannot encompass all the words
and expressions pertaining to a
rapidly evolving technology. While
great care has been taken to list
as many terms as possible in the
present edition, there may be
oversights, and indeed imperfections.
The author therefore welcomes any
comments or suggestions from
users of this dictionary.

Such comments or suggestions
can be addressed to Gene Ferber,
c/o the computer science editor,
The MIT Press, 55 Hayward Street,
Cambridge, Massachusetts 02142,
United States of America.

ENGLISH-JAPANESE
EI-WA
英和

A

A Programming Language (APL)
Apuru; Eipiieru, puroguramingu gengo (APL)
アプル；エイ ピーエル；
プログラミング言語

abbreviation
shōryaku
省略

ABEND (abnormal end of task)
ABEND (tasuku no ijō shūryō)
タスクの異常終了

aberration
shūsa
収差

abnormal
fusei; ijō (na)
不正；異常（な）

abnormal end of task (ABEND)
tasuku no ijō shūryō (ABEND)
タスクの異常終了

abnormal function
fuseiki kansū
不正規関数

abnormal termination
ijō na shūryō
異常な終了

abnormality
ijō
異常

abort
abōto suru; hōki suru; uchikiru
アボートする；放棄する；
打ち切る

absolute address
zettai adoresu
絶対アドレス

absolute addressing
zettai adoresshingu;
zettai adoresu shitei
絶対アドレッシング；
絶対アドレス指定

absolute code
zettai kōdo
絶対コード

absolute coding
zettai kōdeingu
絶対コーディング

absolute element
zettai eremento
絶対エレメント

absolute error
zettai gosa
絶対誤差

absolute execution area
zettai jikkō ryō'iki
絶対実行領域

absolute expression
zettai hyōgen keishiki; zettai shiki
絶対表現形式；絶対式

absolute instruction
kikaigo meirei
機械語命令

absolute language
kikaigo
機械語

absolute loader
zettai rōda
絶対ローダ

absolute loader routine
zettai rōda-rūchin
絶対ローダ・ルーチン

absolute program loader
zettai puroguramu-rōda
絶対プログラム・ローダ

absolute programming
kikaigo puroguramingu
機械語プログラミング

absolute value
zettai chi
絶対値

absolute-value computer
zettai chi keisanki
絶対値計算機

absolute-value programming
zettai chi keikakuhō
絶対値計画法

abstract
chūshō (teki na)
抽象 （的な）

abstract machine
chūshō kikai
抽象機械

abstract object
chūshōteki taishō
抽象的対象

abstract symbol
chūshō kigō
抽象記号

abstraction
chūshō(ka)
抽象（化）

AC (alternating current)
AC (kōryū)
交流

AC dump
AC danpu (kōryū danpu)
AC ダンプ；交流ダンプ

AC power supply
AC dengen (kōryū dengen)
AC 電源；交流電源

acceleration
kasoku
加速

acceleration time
kasoku jikan
加速時間

acceptability
akuseputabiritei
アクセプタビリティ

acceptance inspection
ukeire kensa
受け入れ検査

acceptance test
ukeire shiken
受け入れ試験

accepting station
jushin tanmatsu
受信端末

acceptor
akuseputa
アクセプタ

access (noun)
akusesu; yobidashi
アクセス；呼び出し

access (verb)
akusesu suru; in'yō suru;
sanshō suru; yobidasu
アクセスする；引用する；
参照する；呼び出す

access arm
akusesu-āmu
アクセス・アーム

access control
akusesu seigyo
アクセス制御

access control key
akusesu seigyo kii
アクセス制御キー

access control lock
akusesu seigyo jō
アクセス制御錠

access control mechanism
akusesu seigyo kikō
アクセス制御機構

access control procedure
akusesu seigyo tetsuzuki
アクセス制御手続き

access control register
akusesu seigyo rejisuta
アクセス制御レジスタ

access control section
akusesu seigyo setsu
アクセス制御節

access control word (ACW)
akusesu seigyo go (ACW)
アクセス制御語

access controller
akusesu seigyo sōchi
アクセス制御装置

access function
akusesu kansū
アクセス関数

access key
akusesu-kii
アクセス・キー

access key organization
akusesu-kii hensei
アクセス・キー編成

access level
akusesu-reberu
アクセス・レベル

access line
akusesu-kaisen
アクセス回線

access management
akusesu kanri
アクセス管理

access mechanism
akusesu kikō
アクセス機構

access method
akusesu hō; akusesu hōshiki
アクセス法；アクセス方式

access mode
akusesu hōshiki; akusesu-mōdo
アクセス方式；
アクセス・モード

access path
akusesu keiro
アクセス経路

access permission
akusesu kyoka
アクセス許可

access range
akusesu han'i
アクセス範囲

access right
akusesu ken
アクセス権

access time
akusesu jikan; akusesu-taimu;
yobidashi jikan
アクセス時間；
アクセス・タイム；
呼び出し時間

accessibility
akusesu kanōsei
アクセス可能性

accessible
akusesu kanō
アクセス可能

accessing
akusesu; yobidashi
アクセス；呼び出し

accountable time
riyō kanō jikan; shiyō kanō jikan;
yūkō jikan
利用可能時間；使用可能時間；
有効時間

accounting
akaunteingu; kaikei; kakin
アカウンティング；会計；課金

accounting information
kaikei jōhō
会計情報

accounting machine
kaikeiki
会計機

accounting number
akaunteingu bangō
アカウンティング番号

accounting routine
kaikei rūchin
会計ルーチン

accounting system
kaikei shisutemu
会計システム

accounts processing
kakin shori
課金処理

accumulate
chikuseki suru; ruisan suru
蓄積する；累算する

accumulate in a system
shisutemu uchi ni chikuseki suru
システム内に蓄積する

accumulation
chikuseki; ruisan; tairyū
蓄積；累算；滞留

accumulator
akyumurēta; ruisanki
アキュムレータ；累算器

accumulator register
akyumurēta-rejisuta;
ruisanki rejisuta
アキュムレータ・レジスタ；
累算器レジスタ

accuracy
seikakudo
正確度

accuracy control
seikakudo seigyo
正確度制御

accuracy control character
seikakudo seigyo moji
正確度制御文字

accuracy control system
seikakudo seigyo shisutemu
正確度制御システム

ACK (acknowledgment)
ACK; akku (kōtei ōtō)
アック；肯定応答

acknowledgment (ACK)
kōtei ōtō (ACK; akku)
肯定応答；アック

acknowledgment character
kōtei ōtō moji
肯定応答文字

ACM (Association for Computing Machinery)
ACM (Amerika Keisanki Gakkai)
アメリカ計算機学会

acoustic coupler
onkyō kapura;
onkyō ketsugō sōchi
音響カプラ；音響結合装置

acoustic delay
chō'ompa chien
超音波遅延

acoustic delay line
chō'ompa chiensen
超音波遅延線

acoustic efficiency
onkyō kōka
音響効果

acoustic feedback
onkyō fuiidobakku
音響フィードバック

acoustic fidelity
onkyōteki chūjissei
音響的忠実性

acoustic memory
chō'ompa kioku
超音波記憶

acoustic signal
onkyō shingō
音響信号

acoustic storage
chō'ompa kioku
超音波記憶

acoustic store
chō'ompa kioku sōchi
超音波記憶装置

acoustics
onkyō
音響

acronym
akuronimu; ryakuseigo; tōjigo
アクロニム；略成語；頭辞語

ACS (autonomous control system)
ACS (jiritsu seigyo shisutemu)
自律制御システム

action
akushon; dōsa
アクション；動作

action cluster
akushon-kurasuta
アクション・クラスタ

action code
akushon-kōdo
アクション・コード

action command
akushon-komando
アクション・コマンド

action directive
akushon shiji
アクション指示

action entry
akushon-entori
アクション・エントリ

action stub
akushon-sutabu
アクション・スタブ

activate
katsudōka suru; katsuyōka suru;
kidō saseru
活動化する；活用化する；
起動させる

activation
katsuyōka; kidō
活用化；起動

active
akuteibu; jikkōchū no; katsudō;
kidōchū no; nōdō; shiyōchū no
アクティブ；実行中の；活動；
起動中の；能動；使用中の

active bank
shiyōkanō banku
使用可能バンク

active block
kidōchū no burokku
起動中のブロック

active display
akuteibu-deisupurei
アクティブ・ディスプレィ

active element
nōdō soshi
能動素子

active file
katsudō fuairu; shiyōchū no fairu
活動ファイル；
使用中のファイル

active job
jikkōchū no jyobu
実行中のジョブ

active program
jikkōchū no puroguramu;
katsudō puroguramu
実行中のプログラム；
活動プログラム

active state
akuteibu jōtai; dōsa jōtai
アクティブ状態；動作状態

active station
katsudō tanmatsu
活動端末

active system
akuteibu-shisutemu
アクティブ・システム

active task
akuteibu-tasuku; katsudō tasuku
アクティブ・タスク；
活動タスク

activity
akuteibitei; dōsa; katsudō;
katsudōsei; katsuyō; sagyō;
shiyō
アクティビティ；動作；活動；
活動性；活用；作業；使用；

activity identifier
akuteibitei shikibetsu mei
アクティビティ識別名

activity ratio
shiyōritsu
使用率

activity save area (ASA)
akuteibitei hokan'iki (ASA)
アクティビティ保管域

actual address
jitsu adoresu
実アドレス

actual argument
jitsu hikisū
実引き数

actual code
jitsu kōdo
実コード

actual coding
jitsu kōdeingu
実コーディング

actual decimal point
jissai no shōsūten
実際の小数点

actual instruction
jikkō meirei
実行命令

actual parameter
jitsu parameta
実パラメタ

actual parameter list
jitsu parameta no narabi
実パラメタの並び

actual parameter part
jitsu parameta bu
実パラメタ部

actual result
jitsu kekka
実結果

actual source
jitsu genshi
実原始

actuator
akuchuēta
アクチュエータ

ACU (arithmetic and control unit)
ACU (enzan seigyo sōchi)
演算制御装置

ACU (automatic calling unit)
ACU (jidō yobidashi sōchi)
自動呼び出し装置

ACW (access control word)
ACW (akusesu seigyo go)
アクセス制御語

A/D or A-D (analog-to-digital)
A/D (anarogu-deijitaru)
アナログ・ディジタル

A/D conversion (analog-to-digital conversion)
A/D henkan (anarogu-deijitaru henkan)
A／D変換; アナログ・ディジタル変換

A/D converter (analog-to-digital converter; ADC)
A/D henkanki; A/D konbāta (anarogu-deijitaru henkanki; anarogu-deijitaru-konbāta; ADC)
A／D変換器; A／Dコンバータ; アナログ・ディジタル変換器; アナログ・ディジタル・コンバータ

ADA (automatic data acquisition)
ADA (jidō dēta shūshū)
自動データ収集

adaptability
tekiōsei
適応性

adaptable
tekiō kanō
適応可能

adaptation
tekigō; tekiō
適合; 適応

adapter
adaputa
アダプタ

adaptive control
tekiō seigyo
適応制御

adaptive control system
tekiō seigyo shisutemu
適応制御システム

adaptive function
tekiō kinō
適応機能

adaptive response
tekiō ōtō
適応応答

adaptive routing
tekigō keiro sentaku
適合経路選択

adaptive structure
tekiō kōzō
適応構造

adaptive system
tekigō shisutemu; tekiō shisutemu
適合システム; 適応システム

ADC (analog-to-digital converter)
ADC (anarogu-deijitaru henkanki; Anarogu-deijitaru-konbāta)
アナログ・ディジタル変換器; アナログ・ディジタル・コンバータ

ADCCP (advanced data communication control procedure)
ADCCP (adobansudo-dēta tsūshin seigyo tejun)
アドバンス・データ通信制御手順

ADD (addition)
ADD (kasan)
加算

add (verb)
kasan suru
加算する

add-in board
ado-in-bōdo
アド・イン・ボード

add-in card
ado-in-kādo
アド・イン・カード

add-on
ado-on
アド・オン

add-on keyboard
ado-on-kiibōdo
アド・オン・キーボード

add-on memory
ado-on-memori
アド・オン・メモリ

add-on module
ado-on-mojyūru
アド・オン・モジュール

add time
kasan jikan
加算時間

add-to-memory
ado-tsū-memori
アド・ツー・メモリ

addend
kasū
加数

adder
adā; kasanki
アダー; 加算器

5

adder-subtracter
kagenzanki
加減算器

adder-subtracter execution
kagenzanki jikkō
加減算器実行

adder-subtracter execution time
kagenzanki jikkō jikan
加減算器実行時間

adder-subtracter instruction
kagenzanki meirei
加減算器命令

adding machine
kasanki
加算機

adding operator
kagen enzanshi
加減演算子

addition (ADD)
kasan (ADD)
加算

addition table
kasan hyō
加算表

additional
tsuika
追加

additional area
tsuika ryō'iki
追加領域

additional characters
tokushu moji; tsuika moji
特殊文字；追加文字

additional data storage
tsuika dēta kioku
追加データ記憶

additional drive
tsuika kudō kikō
追加駆動機構

additional file
tsuika fuairu
追加ファイル

additional item
tsuika kōmoku
追加項目

additional on-line data capacity
tsuika on-rain-dēta yōryō
追加オン・ライン・データ容量

additional record
tsuika rekōdo
追加レコード

additional storage
tsuika kioku
追加記憶

additional unit
tsuika sōchi
追加装置

address
adoresu; banchi
アドレス；番地

address assignment
adoresu shitei; adoresu wariate
アドレス指定；
アドレス割り当て

address bus
adoresu-basu
アドレス・バス

address calculation
adoresu keisan
アドレス計算

address check
adoresu kensa
アドレス検査

address component
adoresu kōsei yōso
アドレス構成要素

address computation
adoresu keisan
アドレス計算

address constant
adoresu teisū
アドレス定数

address conversion
adoresu henkan
アドレス変換

address-conversion table
adoresu henkan tēburu
アドレス変換テーブル

address counter
adoresu-kaunta
アドレス・カウンタ

address error
adoresu ayamari
アドレス誤り

address field
adoresu-fuiirudo
アドレス・フィールド

address format
adoresu keishiki
アドレス形式

address generator
adoresu-zenerēta
アドレス・ゼネレータ

address identifier
adoresu shikibetsushi
アドレス識別子

address key
adoresu-kii
アドレス・キー

address management
adoresu kanri
アドレス管理

address mapping
adoresu-mappingu
アドレス・マッピング

address modification
adoresu henkō;
adoresu shūshoku
アドレス変更；アドレス修飾

address modifier
adoresu henkōshi;
adoresu shūshokushi
アドレス変更子；
アドレス修飾子

address part
adoresu bu
アドレス部

address reference
adoresu sanshō
アドレス参照

address register
adoresu-rejisuta
アドレス・レジスタ

address selection
adoresu sentaku
アドレス選択

address space
adoresu kūkan
アドレス空間

address-space extension
adoresu kūkan kakuchō
アドレス空間拡張

address-space identifier
adoresu kūkan shikibetsushi
アドレス空間識別子

address-space management
adoresu kūkan kanri
アドレス空間管理

address stop
adoresu teishi
アドレス停止

address table
adoresu-tēburu
アドレス・テーブル

address track
adoresu-torakku
アドレス・トラック

address translation
adoresu henkan
アドレス変換

address translation table
adoresu henkan tēburu
アドレス変換テーブル

addressability
adoresu shitei kanōsei
アドレス指定可能性

addressable
adoresu shitei kanō
アドレス指定可能

addressable point
adoresu (shitei) kanōten
アドレス（指定）可能点

addressing
adoresshingu; adoresu shitei
アドレッシング；アドレス指定

addressing mode
adoresshingu-mōdo
アドレッシング・モード

addressing system
adoresu shitei shisutemu
アドレス指定システム

adjust
chōsei suru
調整する

adjustable
seigō
整合

adjustment
chōsei; seigō
調整；整合

administrative data processing
jimu kanri dēta shori
事務管理データ処理

ADP (automatic data processing)
ADP (jidō dēta shori)
自動データ処理

**ADPS (automatic data processing
system)**
ADPS (jidō dēta shori shisutemu)
自動データ処理 システム

advance
adobansu
アドバンス

advance mode
adobansu-mōdo
アドバンス・モード

advanced (development)
kōdo; sentanteki
高度；先端的

advanced automation
sentanteki jidōka
先端的自動化

advanced automation system
sentanteki jidōka shisutemu
先端的自動化ツステム

advanced control
kōdo seigyo; sakimawari seigyo
高度制御；先回り制御

advanced control system
kōdo seigyo shisutemu;
sakimawari seigyo shisutemu
高度制御システム；
先回り制御システム

**advanced data communication
control procedure (ADCCP)**
adobansu-dēta tsūshin seigyo
tejun (ADCCP)
アドバンス・
データ通信制御手順

advanced information system(s)
kōdo jōhō shisutemu
高度情報システム

advanced system(s)
kōdo shisutemu
高度システム

advanced system development
kōdo shisutemu kaihatsu
高度システム開発

advanced system technology
kōdo shisutemu gijutsu
高度システム技術

AF (audio frequency)
AF (kachō shūhasū; onsei
shūhasū)
可聴周波数；音声周波数

AGC (automatic gain control)
AGC (jidō ritoku seigyo)
自動利得制御

agenda
ajienda
アジェンダ

aggregate expression
shūgō taishiki
集合体式

aggregate type
shūgōtai no kata
集合体の型

aggregation function
shūgō kansū
集合関数

AI (artificial intelligence)
AI (jinkō chinō)
人工知能

alarm
arāmu; keihō; keikoku
アラーム；警報；警告

alarm display
keihō hyōji; keikoku hyōji
警報表示；警告表示

alarm system
keihō shisutemu
警報システム

alarm tone
kachō keihō
可聴警報

algebra
daisū
代数

algebraic language
daisū shori gengo
代数処理言語

ALGOL (Algorithmic Language)
ALGOL (arugorizumikku gengo;
Arugoru; sampō gengo)
アルゴリズミック言語；
アルゴル；算法言語

algorithm
arugorizumu; sampō
アルゴリズム；算法

algorithm translation
arugorizumu hon'yaku
アルゴリズム翻訳

algorithmic
arugorizumikku; arugorizumuteki
アルゴリズミック；
アルゴリズム的

Algorithmic Language (ALGOL)
arugorizumikku gengo; Arugoru;
sampō gengo (ALGOL)
アルゴリズミック言語；
アルゴル；算法言語

algorithmic structure
arugorizumu kōzō
アルゴリズム構造

alias
betsumei
別名

alias description entry
betsumei kijutsukō
別名記述項

alias section
betsumei setsu
別名節

align
ichiawaseru
位置合わせる

alignment
ichiawase; seiretsu
位置合わせ；整列

alignment mark
ichiawase māku
位置合わせマーク

all-purpose computer
han'yō keisanki
汎用計算機

allocate
arokēto suru; wariateru;
waritsukeru
アロケートする；割り当てる；
割り付ける

allocation
arokēshon; haibun; wariate;
waritsuke
アロケーション；配分；
割り当て；割り付け

allocation routine
waritsuke rūchin
割り付けルーチン

allocator
arokēta
アロケータ

allowance
kyūyo
給与

alphabet
arufuabetto; eiji
アルファベット；英字

alphabetic
arufuabetto no; eiji
アルファベットの；英字

alphabetic character
eiji
英字

alphabetic code
eiji kōdo
英字コード

alphabetic string
eiji retsu
英字列

alphabetical
eiji
英字

alphabetical character
eiji
英字

alphameric
arufuamerikku; eisūji
アルファメリック；英数字

alphameric character
eisūji
英数字

alphameric code
arufuamerikku-kōdo; eisūji kōdo
アルファメリック・コード；
英数字コード

alpha-micro
arufua-maikuro
アルファ・マイクロ

alphanumeric
eisūji (no)
英数字（の）

alphanumeric character
eisūji
英数字

alphanumeric character set
eisūji setto
英数字セット

alphanumeric code
eisūji kōdo
英数字コード

alphanumeric coded character set
eisūji kōdo-setto
英数字コード・セット

alphanumeric data
eisūji dēta
英数字データ

alphanumeric data code
eisūji dēta-kōdo
英数字データ・コード

alphanumeric keyboard
eisūji kemban sōchi;
eisūji kiibōdo
英数字鍵盤装置；
英数字キーボード

alteration
henkō
変更

alteration switch
henkō(yō) suitchi
変更（用）スイッチ

alternate
daitai; kōgo
代替；交互

alternate device
daitai kiki
代替機器

alternate file
daitai fuairu
代替ファイル

alternate route
daitai keiro
代替経路

alternate routing
daitai keiro shitei
代替経路指定

alternate timer
daitai taima
代替タイマ

alternate track
daitai torakku
代替トラック

alternating current (AC)
kōryū (AC)
交流

alternative
daikō; daitai
代行；代替

alternative denial
hiteironriseki enzan
否定論理積演算

alternative receiving function
daikō jushin kinō
代行受信機能

alternative system
daitai shisutemu
代替システム

ALU (arithmetic and logic unit)
ALU (enzan ronri sōchi; sanjutsu
ronri kairo)
演算論理装置；算術論理回路

AM (amplitude modulation)
AM (shimpuku henchō)
振幅変調

A-M operation (automatic-manual operation)
A-M sōsa (jidō-shudō sōsa)
A-M 操作；
自動-手動操作

ambiguity
aimaisei
曖昧性

ambiguity error
aimaisei gosa
曖昧性誤差

ambiguous
aimai
曖昧

amelioration
kairyō
改良

amend
henkō suru
変更する

amendment
amendomento; henkō
アメンドメント；変更

amendment code
amendomento-kōdo
アメンドメント・コード

amendment file
amendomento-fuairu
アメンドメント・ファイル

amendment record
amendomento-rekōdo
アメンドメント・レコード

amendment tape
amendomento-tēpu
アメンドメント・テープ

American National Standards Institute (ANSI)
Amerika Kikaku Kyōkai (ANSI)
アメリカ規格協会

American Standard Code for Information Interchange (ASCII)
Jōhō Kōkan'yō Beikoku Hyōjun
Kōdo (ASCII)
情報交換用米国標準コード

amount of information
jōhō ryō
情報量

amplification
zōfuku
増幅

amplifier
anpu; zōfukuki
アンプ；増幅器

amplitude
shimpuku
振幅

amplitude control
shimpuku seigyo
振幅制御

amplitude distortion
shimpuku hizumi
振幅歪み

amplitude limiter
shimpuku seigenki
振幅制限器

amplitude limiting
shimpuku seigen
振幅制限

amplitude modulation (AM)
shimpuku henchō (AM)
振幅変調

analog
anarogu; sōjigata
アナログ；相似型

analog adder
anarogu kasanki
アナログ加算器

analog channel
anarogu-chaneru
アナログ・チャネル

analog comparator
anarogu-konparēta
アナログ・コンパレータ

analog computer
anarogu keisanki
アナログ計算機

analog data
anarogu-dēta
アナログ・データ

analog device
anarogu sōchi
アナログ装置

analog input
anarogu nyūryoku
アナログ入力

analog network
anarogu kairomō; anarogu-
nettowāku
アナログ回路網；
アナログ・ネットワーク

analog output
anarogu shutsuryoku
アナログ出力

analog representation
anarogu hyōgen
アナログ表現

analog signal
anarogu shingō
アナログ信号

analog to digital (A/D; A-D)
anarogu-deijitaru (A/D; A-D)
アナログ・ディジタル

analog-to-digital conversion
anarogu-deijitaru henkan
アナログ・ディジタル変換

analog-to-digital converter (A/D converter; ADC)
anarogu-deijitaru henkanki; anarogu-deijitaru-konbāta (A/D henkanki; A/D konbāta; ADC)
アナログ・ディジタル変換器；アナログ・ディジタル・コンバータ；A/D変換器；A/Dコンバータ

analysis
bunseki; kaiseki
分析；解析

analysis method
kaisekihō
解析法

analysis system
kaiseki shisutemu
解析システム

analyst
anarisuto; bunsekisha
アナリスト；分析者

analytic(al)
kaiseki
解析

analytical function
kaiseki kansū
解析関数

analytical function generator
kaiseki kansū zenerēta
解析関数ゼネレータ

analytical model
kaiseki moderu
解析モデル

analyzer
anaraiza; kaisekiki
アナライザ；解析器

AND
AND; ronriseki
AND；論理積

AND circuit
AND kairo; ronriseki kairo
AND回路；論理積回路

AND element
AND soshi; ronriseki soshi
AND素子；論理積素子

AND gate
AND gēto; ronriseki gēto
ANDゲート；論理積ゲート

AND operation
AND enzan; ronriseki enzan
AND演算；論理積演算

annotation
chūshaku
注釈

ANSI (American National Standards Institute)
ANSI (Amerika Kikaku Kyōkai)
アメリカ規格協会

answer
hentō; ōtō
返答；応答

answer tone
ōtō on
応答音

answerback
ansabakku; hentō
アンサバック；返答

answering
hentō
返答

AP (application program)
AP (apurikēshon-puroguramu; ōyō puroguramu)
アプリケーション・プログラム；応用プログラム

aperture card
apachua-kādo
アパチュア・カード

APL (A Programming Language)
APL (Apuru; Eipiieru; puroguramingu gengo)
アプル；エイピーエル；プログラミング言語

application
apurikēshon; ōyō; riyō; tekiyō; tsūyō
アプリケーション；応用；利用；適用；通用

application field
riyō bun'ya
利用分野

application method
riyō hōhō
利用方法

application package
apurikēshon-pakkēji
アプリケーション・パッケージ

application philosophy
apurikēshon-fuirosofui; ōyō shisō
アプリケーション・フィロソフィ；応用思想

application program (AP)
apurikēshon-puroguramu; ōyō puroguramu (AP)
アプリケーション・プログラム；応用プログラム

application study
ōyō kenkyū
応用研究

application system
ōyō shisutemu
応用システム

applications-oriented language
tokutei gyōmumuki gengo
特定業務向き言語

applications programmer
apurikēshon-puroguramа; ōyō puroguramа
アプリケーション・プログラマ；応用プログラマ

applied computer science
ōyō keisanki kagaku
応用計算機科学

applied data processing
ōyō dēta shori
応用データ処理

applied information technology
ōyō jōhō gijutsu
応用情報技術

applied management information system
ōyō kei'ei jōhō shisutemu
応用経営情報システム

applied operations research
ōyō operēshon-risāchi
応用オペレーション・リサーチ

applied systems research
ōyō shisutemu kenkyū
応用システム研究

approach
apurōchi; hōhō; hōshiki
アプローチ；方法；方式

approximation
kinji
近似

APT (automatic picture transmission)
APT (jidō sōga)
自動送画

arbitrary sequence computer
nin'i junjo keisanki
任意順序計算機

architecture
ākitekucha
アーキテクチャ

archival memory
ākaibaru-memori; hozon kioku
アーカイバル・メモリ；
保存記憶

archive
ākaibu; kiroku
アーカイブ；記録

archived file
ākaibu-fuairu
アーカイブ・ファイル

archiving
kiroku
記録

area
kioku (ryō')iki; ryō'iki
記憶（領）域；領域

area definition
kioku'iki teigi
記憶域定義

area search
ryō'iki tansaku
領域探索

argument
āgyumento; hikisū
アーギュメント；引き数

arithmetic and control unit (ACU)
enzan seigyo sōchi (ACU)
演算制御装置

arithmetic and logic unit (ALU)
enzan ronri sōchi; sanjutsu ronri kairo (ALU)
演算論理装置；算術論理回路

arithmetic check
sanjutsu kensa
算術検査

arithmetic circuit
enzan kairo
演算回路

arithmetic expression
sanjutsu shiki
算術式

arithmetic instruction
sanjutsu meirei
算術命令

arithmetic mean
sanjutsu heikin
算術平均

arithmetic operation
sanjutsu enzan
算術演算

arithmetic operator
sanjutsu enzanshi; sanjutsu sayōso
算術演算；算術作用素

arithmetic overflow
sanjutsu keta afure
算術桁溢れ

arithmetic register
enzan rejisuta
演算レジスタ

arithmetic shift
sanjutsu keta okuri; sanjutsu shifuto
算術桁送り；算術シフト

arithmetic statement
sanjutsu sutētomento
算術ステートメント

arithmetic subroutine
enzan saburūchin
演算サブルーチン

arithmetic sum
sanjutsu wa
算術和

arithmetic underflow
sanjutsu kaiketa afure
算術下位桁溢れ

arithmetic unit
enzan sōchi
演算装置

arrangement
hairetsu
配列

array
arei; hairetsu
アレイ；配列

array allocation
arei haibun; hairetsu haibun
アレイ配分；配列配分

array computer
arei-konpyūta
アレイ・コンピュータ

array declarator
hairetsu sengenshi
配列宣言子

array declarator statement
hairetsu sengenshi bun
配列宣言子文

array element
hairetsu yōso
配列要素

array language
hairetsu gengo
配列言語

array name
hairetsu mei
配列名

array partitioning
hairetsu bunkatsu
配列分割

array processing
arei shori
アレイ処理

array processor
arei-purosessa
アレイ・プロセッサ

array segment
hairetsu segumento
配列セグメント

arrival (of message)
chakushin
着信

arrival of message at terminal
tanmatsu ni chakushin
端末に着信

arrive (message)
chakushin suru
着信する

arrow diagram
yasenzu
矢線図

arrow key
yasen kii
矢線キー

artificial intelligence (AI)
jinkō chinō (AI)
人工知能

artificial language
jinkō gengo
人工言語

ASA (activity save area)
ASA (akuteibitei hokan'iki)
アクティビティ保管域

ascending order
shōjun
昇順

ASCII (American Standard Code for Information Interchange)
ASCII (Jōhō Kōkan'yō Beikoku Hyōjun Kōdo)
情報交換用米国標準コード

aspect ratio
asupekuto ritsu
アスペクト率

ASR (automatic send-receive set)
ASR (jidō sōjushin sōchi)
自動送受信装置

assemble
asenburu suru
アセンブルする

assembler
asenbura(-puroguramu)
アセンブラ（・プログラム）

assembler directive
asenbura shiji
アセンブラ指示

assembler source code
asenbura-sōsu-kōdo
アセンブラ・ソース・コード

assembling
asenburu; kumitate
アセンブル；組み立て

assembling system
kumitate shisutemu
組み立てシステム

assembling time
asenburu jikan
アセンブル時間

assembly
asenburi; kumitate
アセンブリ；組み立て

assembly code
asenburi-kōdo
アセンブリ・コード

assembly language
asenburi gengo
アセンブリ言語

assembly line
kumitate rain
組み立てライン

assembly list
asenburi-risuto
アセンブリ・リスト

assembly operation
asenburi sōsa
アセンブリ操作

assembly phase
asenburi-fuēzu
アセンブリ・フェーズ

assembly program
asenburi-puroguramu
アセンブリ・プログラム

assembly routine
asenburi-rūchin
アセンブリ・ルーチン

assembly time
asenburi jikan
アセンブリ時間

assertion language
hyōmei gengo
表明言語

assessment
hyōtei
評定

assign
asain suru; wariateru
アサインする；割り当てる

assignment
wariate
割り当て

assignment statement
dainyūbun
代入文

associated address
rensō adoresu
連想アドレス

association
ketsugō; rensō
結合；連想

Association for Computing Machinery (ACM)
Amerika Keisanki Gakkai (ACM)
アメリカ計算機学会

associative memory
rensō kioku
連想記憶

associative processor
rensō purosessa
連想プロセッサ

associative relation
rensō kankei
連想関係

associative retrieval
rensō kensaku
連想検索

associative storage
rensō kioku
連想記憶

associative store
rensō kioku sōchi
連想記憶装置

assumed decimal point
sōtei shita shōsūten
想定した小数点

astable
hiantei
非安定

asynchronous
hidō; hidōki; hidōkishiki
非同；非同期；非同期式

asynchronous circuit
hidōkishiki kairo
非同期式回路

asynchronous communication
hidōki tsūshin
非同期通信

asynchronous computer
hidōkishiki keisanki
非同期式計算機

asynchronous control
hidōki seigyo
非同期制御

asynchronous data transmission
hidōki dēta densō
非同期データ伝送

asynchronous device
hidōkishiki sōchi
非同期式装置

asynchronous mode
hidōki(shiki) mōdo
非同期(式)モード

asynchronous multiprogramming
hidōki maruchi-puroguramingu
非同期マルチ・プログラミング

asynchronous operation
hidōki sōsa
非同期操作

asynchronous processing
hidōki shori
非同期処理

asynchronous system
hidōki shisutemu; hidōkishiki
非同期システム; 非同期式

asynchronous transmission
hidōki densō
非同期伝送

asynchronous working
hidōki dōsa
非同期動作

attach
setsuzoku suru; tempu suru
接続する; 添付する

attached to ———
——— ni tempu
———に添付

attachment
setsuzoku kikō; tempu
接続機構; 添付

attention
atenshon
アテンション

attention interrupt
atenshon warikomi
アテンション割り込み

attention signal
atenshon shingō
アテンション信号

attenuation
gensui
減衰

attenuation distortion
gensui hizumi
減衰歪み

attenuation equalization
gensui tōka
減衰等化

attenuator
gensuiki
減衰器

attribute
zokusei
属性

audible alarm
kachō keihō
可聴警報

audio frequency (AF)
kachō shūhasū; onsei shūhasū
(AF)
可聴周波数; 音声周波数

audio response
onsei ōtō
音声応答

audio response unit
onsei ōtō sōchi
音声応答装置

auditing
kansa
監査

auditing system
kansa shisutemu
監査システム

audits
kansa
監査

augend
hikasū
被加数

autoabstract
jidō shōroku
自動抄録

autocall
jidō yobidashi
自動呼び出し

autocode
ōto-kōdo
オート・コード

autocoding
jidō kōdeingu; ōto-kōdeingu
自動コーディング;
オート・コーディング

autocorrelation
jiko sōkan
自己相関

autodraft
jidō seizu
自動製図

autofeed
ōto-fuiido
オート・フィード

autoindex
jidō sakuin
自動索引

autointerrupt
jidō warikomi
自動割り込み

autoloader
jidō rōda
自動ローダ

autolock
jidō rokku
自動ロック

automata
otōmata
オトーマタ

automated
jidōka
自動化

automated data analysis
jidōka dēta kaiseki
自動化データ解析

automated data collection system
jidōka dēta shūshū shisutemu
自動化データ収集システム

automated information system
jidōka jōhō shisutemu
自動化情報システム

automatic
jidō(teki na)
自動（的な）

automatic abstract
jidō shōroku
自動抄録

automatic answering
jidō ōtō; jidō hentō
自動応答; 自動返答

automatic assembling system
jidō kumitate shisutemu
自動組み立てシステム

13

automatic brightness control
jidō kido chōsetsu
自動輝度調節

automatic calling
jidō yobidashi
自動呼び出し

automatic calling equipment
jidō yobidashi sōchi
自動呼び出し装置

automatic calling unit (ACU)
jidō yobidashi sōchi (ACU)
自動呼び出し装置

automatic check
jidō kensa
自動検査

automatic closed-loop system
jidō tojita rūpu-shisutemu
自動閉じたループ・システム

automatic coding
jidō kōdeingu
自動コーディング

automatic computer
jidō keisanki
自動計算機

automatic control
jidō seigyo
自動制御

automatic data acquisition (ADA)
jidō dēta shūshū (ADA)
自動データ収集

automatic data processing (ADP)
jidō dēta shori (ADP)
自動データ処理

automatic data-processing equipment
jidō dēta shori sōchi
自動データ処理装置

automatic data-processing system (ADPS)
jidō dēta shori shisutemu (ADPS)
自動データ処理システム

automatic data processor
jidō dēta shori sōchi
自動データ処理装置

automatic data switching
jidō dēta kōkan
自動データ交換

automatic debugging
jidō debaggingu
自動デバッギング

automatic decision making
jidō ishi kettei
自動意思決定

automatic diagnosis
jidō shindan
自動診断

automatic diagnostic function
jidō shindan kinō
自動診断機能

automatic dialing
jidō daiaru
自動ダイアル

automatic dialing unit
jidō daiaru sōchi
自動ダイアル装置

automatic dictionary
jidō jisho
自動辞書

automatic disconnection
jidō setsudan
自動切断

automatic error correction
jidō ayamari teisei
自動誤り訂正

automatic error detection
jidō ayamari kenshutsu
自動誤り検出

automatic error detection and correction
jidō ayamari kenshutsu-teisei kinō
自動誤り検出‐訂正機能

automatic exchange
jidō kōkan
自動交換

automatic gain control (AGC)
jidō ritoku seigyo (AGC)
自動利得制御

automatic hardward dump
jidō hādouea-danpu
自動ハードウェア・ダンプ

automatic indexing
jidō sakuin
自動索引

automatic information organization system
jidō jōhō kōsei shisutemu
自動情報構成システム

automatic language translation
jidō gengo hon'yaku
自動言語翻訳

automatic line numbering
jidō gyōbangōka
自動行番号化

automatic-manual operation (A-M operation)
jidō-shudō sōsa (A-M sōsa)
自動‐手動操作；A-M操作

automatic picture transmission (APT)
jidō sōga (APT)
自動送画

automatic programming
jidō puroguramingu
自動プログラミング

automatic punch
jidō senkō
自動せん孔

automatic recognition
jidō ninshiki
自動認識

automatic repetition system
jidō rensō hōshiki
自動連送方式

automatic restart
jidō saishidō
自動再始動

automatic return mechanism
jidō fukki kikō
自動復帰機構

automatic send-receive set (ASR)
jidō sōjushin sōchi (ASR)
自動送受信装置

automatic sort
jidō bunrui
自動分類

automatic start
jidō shidō
自動始動

automatic stop
jidō teishi
自動停止

automatic test system
jidō shiken shisutemu
自動試験システム

automatic typesetting
jidō shokuji
自動植字

automatic voltage regulator (AVR)
jidō den'atsu chōseiki (AVR)
自動電圧調整器

automation
jidōka; otomēshon
自動化；オトメーション

automaton
otōmaton
オトーマトン

automechanism
jidō kikō
自動機構

automonitor
jidō monita
自動モニタ

autonomous
jiritsu
自律

autonomous capability
jiritsu keipabiritei
自律ケイパビリティ

autonomous computing
jiritsu keisan
自律計算

autonomous control system (ACS)
jiritsu seigyo shisutemu (ACS)
自律制御システム

autonomous system
jiritsu shisutemu
自律システム

autonomous working
jiritsu dōsa
自律動作

autoprogramming
jidō puroguramu
自動プログラム

autostart
jidō shidō
自動始動

auxiliary
hojo
補助

auxiliary equipment
hojo sōchi
補助装置

auxiliary memory
hojo kioku
補助記憶

auxiliary memory unit
hojo kioku sōchi
補助記憶装置

auxiliary operation
hojo sōsa
補助操作

auxiliary storage
hojo kioku
補助記憶

auxiliary store
hojo kioku sōchi
補助記憶装置

availability
abeirabiritei; kayōsei; riyō
kanōdo; shiyō kanōdo
アベイラビリティ；可用性；
利用可能度；使用可能度

availability criteria
abeirabiritei kijun
アベイラビリティ基準

availability ratio
abeirabiritei ritsu
アベイラビリティ率

available machine time
riyō kanō jikan;
shiyō kanō jikan
利用可能時間；使用可能時間

average
heikin
平均

average access time
heikin yobidashi jikan
平均呼び出し時間

average information content
heikin jōhō ryō
平均情報量

average operation time
heikin dōsa jikan;
heikin enzan jikan
平均動作時間；平均演算時間

average transmission speed
heikin densō sokudo
平均伝送速度

AVR (automatic voltage regulator)
AVR (jidō den'atsu chōseiki)
自動電圧調整器

B

back-end computer
kōchigata keisanki
後置型計算機

back-end processor
bakku-endo-puresessa;
kōchigata purosessa
バック・エンド・プロセッサ；
後置型プロセッサ

back substitution
kōtai dainyū
後退代入

background
bakkuguraundo; haikei
バックグラウンド；背景

background job
bakkuguraundo-jyobu;
haikei jyobu
バックグラウンド・ジョブ；
背景ジョブ

background processing
bakkuguraundo shori;
haikei shori
バックグラウンド処理；
背景処理

background program
bakkuguraundo-puroguramu;
haikei puroguramu
バックグラウンド・プログラム；
背景プログラム

backing storage
hojo kioku
補助記憶

backing storage device
hojo kioku sōchi
補助記憶装置

backing store
hojo kioku sōchi
補助記憶装置

backspace (BS)
bakkusupēsu; kōtai (BS)
バックスペース；後退

backspace character
kōtai moji
後退文字

backup
bakku-appu; hojo; ichiji(teki)
バック・アップ；補助；
一時(的)

backup copy
bakku-appu-kopii
バック・アップ・コピー

backup disk
bakku-appu-deisuku
バック・アップ・ディスク

backup file
bakku-appu-fuairu
バック・アップ・ファイル

backup memory
bakku-appu-memori; ichiji kioku
バック・アップ・メモリ；
一時記憶

backup program
bakku-appu-puroguramu
バック・アップ・プログラム

backup storage
bakku-appu-kioku; ichiji kioku
バック・アップ記憶；一時記憶

backup system
bakku-appu-shisutemu
バック・アップ・システム

backup unit
bakku-appu-sōchi
バック・アップ装置

Backus-Naur Form (BNF)
Bakkusu-Naua hō;
Bakkusu-Naua hyōkihō (BNF)
バックス・ナウア法；
バックス・ナウア表記法

backward channel
gyaku chaneru
逆チヤネル

backward printing
gyaku hōkō insatsu
逆方向印刷

backward read
gyaku yomi
逆読み

backward sort
gyaku bunrui
逆分類

BAL (basic-assembler language)
BAL (kihon asenbura gengo)
基本アセンブラ言語

balance check
baransu-chekku
バランス・チェック

BAM (basic access method)
BAM (kihon akusesu hōshiki)
基本アクセス方式

band
bando; tai'iki
バンド；帯域

band compression
tai'iki asshuku
帯域圧縮

band printer
bandoshiki insho sōchi
バンド式印書装置

bandwidth
bando haba; tai'iki haba
バンド幅；帯域幅

bank
banku
バンク

bar code
bā-kōdo
バー・コード

bar-code scanner
bā-kōdo yomitori sōchi
バー・コード読み取り装置

bar display
bā-deisupurei
バー・ディスプレイ

bar printer
bā inji sōchi; bā-purinta
バー印字装置；バー・プリンタ

barrel printer
entō inji sōchi
円筒印字装置

base
bēsu; kijun; kitei; tei
ベース；基準；基底；底

base address
bēsu-adoresu; kijun adoresu;
kitei adoresu
ベース・アドレス；
基準アドレス；基底アドレス

base address register
kijun adoresu-rejisuta;
kitei adoresu-rejisuta
基準アドレス・レジスタ；
基底アドレス・レジスタ

base band
bēsu-bando
ベース・バンド

base notation
kisū hyōkihō
基数表記法

base number
kisū
基数

base register (br)
bēsu-rejisuta; kijun rejisuta;
kitei rejisuta (br)
ベース・レジスタ；
基準レジスタ；基底レジスタ

based storage
kiteitsuki kioku'iki
基底付き記憶域

BASIC (Beginner's All-purpose Symbolic Instruction Code)
BASIC (Bēshikku)
ベーシック

basic access method (BAM)
kihon akusesu hōshiki (BAM)
基本アクセス方式

basic assembler
kihon asenbura
基本アセンブラ

basic-assembler language (BAL)
kihon asenbura gengo (BAL)
基本アセンブラ言語

basic block
bunsetsu
文節

basic cycle
kihon saikuru
基本サイクル

basic data word length
kihon dēta go chō
基本データ語長

basic direct access method (BDAM)
kihon chokusetsu akusesu
hōshiki (BDAM)
基本直接アクセス方式

basic external function
kihon gaibu kansū
基本外部関数

basic indexed sequential access method (BISAM)
kihon sakuin jun akusesu hōshiki (BISAM)
基本索引順アクセス方式

basic instruction
kihon meirei
基本命令

basic instruction set
kihon meirei setto
基本命令セット

basic linkage
kihon renketsu
基本連結

basic number
kisū
基数

basic operating system (BOS)
kihon operēteingu-shisutemu (BOS)
基本オペレーティング・システム

basic real constant
kihon jitsu teisū
基本実定数

basic sequential access method (BSAM)
kihon junji akusesu hōshiki (BSAM)
基本順次アクセス方式

basic solution
kiteikai
基底解

basic statement
kihonbun
基本文

basic symbol
kihon kigō
基本記号

basic telecommunications access method (BTAM)
kihon tsūshin akusesu hōshiki (BTAM)
基本通信アクセス方式

basic variable
kihon hensū
基本変数

basic word length
kihon go chō
基本語長

batch
batchi; ikkatsu
バッチ；一括

batch checking
ikkatsu chekku
一括チェック

batch job
batchi-jyobu; ikkatsu jyobu
バッチ・ジョブ；一括ジョブ

batch number
batchi bangō
バッチ番号

batch print
batchi insatsu; ikkatsu insatsu
バッチ印刷；一括印刷

batch printing
batchi insatsu; ikkatsu insatsu
バッチ印刷；一括印刷

batch processing
batchi shori; ikkatsu shori
バッチ処理；一括処理

batch program
batchi-puroguramu
バッチ・プログラム

batch total
batchi gōkei
バッチ合計

batch transmission
batchi densō; ikkatsu densō
バッチ伝送；一括伝送

battery
batteri; denchi
バッテリ；電池

battery backup
batteri-bakku-appu
バッテリ・バック・アップ

battery backup unit
batteri-bakku-appu sōchi
バッテリ・バック・アップ装置

battery-driven
denchi kudō
電池駆動

baud
bō
ボー

Baudot code
Bōdo-kōdo
ボード・コード

BCC (block check character)
BCC (burokku kensa moji)
ブロック検査文字

BCD (binary-coded decimal)
BCD (nishinka jisshin)
2進化10進

BCD code (binary-coded decimal code)
BCD kōdo (nishinka jisshin kōdo)
BCDコード；2進化10進コード

BCW (buffer control word)
BCW (baffua seigyo go)
バッファ制御語

BDAM (basic direct access method)
BDAM (kihon chokusetsu akusesu hōshiki)
基本直接アクセス方式

beam deflection
biimu henkō
ビーム偏向

beam lead
biimu-riido
ビーム・リード

beam lead device (BLD)
biimu-riido soshi (BLD)
ビーム・リード素子

Beginner's All-purpose Symbolic Instruction Code (BASIC)
Bēshikku (BASIC)
ベーシック

beginning of file label
fuairu hajime raberu
ファイル始めラベル

beginning of tape (BOT)
tēpu kaishi; tēpu no hajime; tēpu shitan
テープ開始；テープの始め；テープ始端

beginning-of-tape marker
tēpu kaishi māka; tēpu no hajime māka; tēpu shitan māka
テープ開始マーカ；テープの始めマーカ；テープ始端マーカ

beginning of text
tekisuto kaishi; tekisuto no hajime; tekisuto shitan
テキスト開始；テキストの始め；テキスト始端

behavior
kōdō; kyodō
行動；挙動

belt printer
berutoshiki purinta
ベルト式プリンタ

benchmark
benchimāku
ベンチマーク

benchmark problem
benchimāku mondai
ベンチマーク問題

benchmark program
benchimāku-puroguramu
ベンチマーク・プログラム

benchmark test
benchimāku-tesuto
ベンチマーク・テスト

bias
baiasu; katayori
バイアス；偏り

bias distortion
baiasu hizumi
バイアス歪み

bias error
baiasu ayamari
バイアス誤り

bidirectional flow
sōhōkō nagare
双方向流れ

bidirectional operation
sōhōkō sōsa
双方向操作

bidirectional printer
sōhōkō insho sōchi
双方向印書装置

bilinear
sōsenkei
双線形

bilinear system
sōsenkei shisutemu
双線形システム

biMOS (bipolar MOS)
baipōragata MOS
バイポーラ型MOS

binary
bainari; nichi; nishin; nishinsū
バイナリ；2値；2進；2進数

binary adder
nishin kasanki
2進加算器

binary arithmetic operation
nishin enzan; nishin sanjutsu enzan
2進演算；2進算術演算

binary Boolean operation
nishin Būru enzan
2進ブール演算

binary card
bainari-kādo; nishinsū kādo
バイナリ・カード；2進数カード

binary cell
nichi soshi
2値素子

binary character
nishin moji
2進文字

binary chop
bainari-choppu
バイナリ・チョップ

binary circuit
nishin kairo
2進回路

binary code
bainari-kōdo; nishin kōdo
バイナリ・コード；2進コード

binary-coded character
nishinka moji
2進化文字

binary-coded decimal (BCD)
nishinka jisshin (BCD)
2進化10進

binary-coded-decimal code (BCD code)
nishinka jisshin kōdo (BCD kōdo)
2進化10進コード；BCDコード

binary-coded-decimal notation
nishinka jisshinhō
2進化10進法

binary-coded-decimal representation
nishinka jisshin hyōjihō
2 進化10進表示法

binary-coded notation
nishinka hyōkihō
2 進化表記法

binary comparator
nishin hikaku kairo
2 進比較回路

binary comparison
nishin hikaku
2 進比較

binary counter
bainari-kaunta; nishin kaunta
バイナリ・カウンタ；
2 進カウンタ

binary digit (bit)
bainari-deijitto; nishin sūji (bitto)
バイナリ・ディジット；
2 進数字；ビット

binary element
nishin yōso
2 進要素

binary element string
nishin yōso retsu
2 進要素列

binary encoding
nishin enkōdeingu
2 進エンコーディング

binary form
nishinhō
2 進法

binary fraction
nishin shōsū
2 進小数

binary half-adder
nishin hankasanki
2 進半加算器

binary incremental representation
nishin zōbun hyōjihō
2 進増分表示法

binary integer
nishin seisū
2 進整数

binary loader
bainari-rōda
バイナリ・ローダ

binary logic
nichi ronri
2 値論理

binary logic element
nichi ronri soshi
2 値論理素子

binary notation
nishinhō
2 進法

binary number
nishinsū
2 進数

binary number system
nishinsū shisutemu
2 進数システム

binary numeral
nishinsū
2 進数

binary operation
nishin enzan
2 進演算

binary operator
nikō enzanshi
2 項演算子

binary point
(nishin) shōsūten
（2進）小数点

binary radix
nishin kisū
2 進基数

binary representation
nishin hyōgen; nishin hyōjihō;
nishinhō
2 進表現；2 進表示法；2 進法

binary search
nibun tansaku; nishin tansaku
二分探索；2 進探索

binary-search tree
nishin tansaku ju
2 進探索樹

binary signaling
nishin shingō
2 進信号

binary subtractor
nishin genzanki
2 進減算器

binary synchronous communication (BSC)
nishin dēta dōki tsūshin (BSC)
2 進データ同期通信

binary system
nishin shisutemu
2 進システム

binary-to-decimal conversion
nishin jisshin henkan
2 進10進変換

binary tree
nishin ju
2 進樹

binary unit
nishin tan'i
2 進単位

binary variable
nichi hensū; nishin hensū
2 値変数；2 進変数

binding
renketsu
連結

binomial
nikō
2 項

binomial distribution
nikō bumpu
2 項分布

bionics
baionikkusu
バイオニックス

bipolar
baipōra; ryōkyokusei
バイポーラ；両極性

bipolar MOS (biMOS)
baipōragata MOS
バイポーラ型MOS

bipolar pulse
ryōkyokusei parusu
両極性パルス

bipolar signal
ryōkyokusei shingō
両極性信号

bipolar technology
baipōra gijutsu
バイポーラ技術

biquinary
ni-go shin(hō); ni-go shinsū
2 - 5 進(法)；2 - 5 進数

biquinary code
ni-go shin(hō) fugō;
ni-go shin(hō) kōdo
2 - 5 進(法)符号；
2 - 5 進(法)コード

biquinary notation
ni-go shinhō
2 - 5 進法

biquinary number
ni-go shinsū
2 - 5 進数

BISAM (basic indexed sequential access method
BISAM (kihon sakuin jun akusesu hōshiki)
基本索引順アクセス方式

bistable
niantei; sōantei
二安定；双安定

bistable circuit
niantei kairo; sōantei kairo
二安定回路；双安定回路

bistable element
sōantei soshi
双安定素子

bistable trigger circuit
sōantei kairo;
sōantei toriga kairo
双安定回路；双安定トリガ回路

bit (binary digit)
bitto (bainari-deijitto; nishin sūji)
ビット；バイナリ・ディジット；
2 進数字

bit address
bitto-adoresu
ビット・アドレス

bit-addressable memory
bitto-adoresu kioku
ビット・アドレス記憶

bit combination
bitto-konbinēshon
ビット・コンビネーション

bit configuration
bitto kōsei
ビット構成

bit density
bitto mitsudo
ビット密度

bit error rate
bitto ayamari ritsu
ビット誤り率

bit line
bitto sen
ビット線

bit-oriented
bitto muki
ビット向き

bit pattern
bitto-patān
ビット・パターン

bit position
bitto ichi
ビット位置

bit pulse length
bitto-parusuchō
ビット・パルス長

bit rate
bitto densō sokudo; bitto ritsu
ビット伝送速度；ビット率

bit slice
bitto-suraisu
ビット・スライス

bit-slice microprocessor
bitto-suraisu-maikuropurosessa
ビット・スライス・マイクロプ
ロセッサ

bit stream
bitto-sutoriimu
ビット・ストリーム

bit string
bitto retsu; bitto-sutoringu
ビット列；ビット・ストリング

bit structure
bitto kōzō
ビット構造

bit synchronization
bitto dōki
ビット同期

bit table
bitto-tēburu
ビット・テーブル

bits per inch (bpi)
bitto/inchi (bpi)
ビット／インチ

bits per second (bps)
bitto/byō (bps)
ビット／秒

black box
burakku-bokkusu
ブラック・ボックス

blank
buranku; kūhaku
ブランク；空白

blank character
buranku moji; kūhaku moji
ブランク文字；空白文字

blank line
buranku gyō; kūhaku gyō
ブランク行；空白行

blank tape
buranku-tēpu; kūhaku tēpu
ブランク・テープ；空白テープ

BLD (beam lead device)
BLD (biimu-riido sōchi)
ビーム・リード装置

block
burokku
ブロック

block address
burokku-adoresu
ブロック・アドレス

block cancel character
burokku torikeshi moji
ブロック取り消し文字

block chart
burokku-chāto
ブロック・チャート

block check
burokku-chekku; burokku kensa
ブロック・チェック；
ブロック検査

block check character (BCC)
burokku kensa moji (BCC)
ブロック検査文字

block code
burokku-kōdo
ブロック・コード

block coding
burokku-kōdeingu
ブロック・コーディング

block count
burokku-kaunto; burokkusū
ブロック・カウント；
ブロック数

block data subprogram
shokichi settei fukupuroguramu
初期値設定副プログラム

block diagram
burokku-daiyaguramu;
burokku zu
ブロック・ダイヤグラム；
ブロック図

block error rate
burokku ayamari ritsu
ブロック誤り率

block gap
burokku kankaku
ブロック間隔

block graphics
burokku-gurafuikkusu
ブロック・グラフィックス

block header
burokku midashi
ブロック見出し

block ignore character
burokku torikeshi moji
ブロック取り消し文字

block initial statement
burokku no kaishi bun
ブロックの開始文

block length
burokku chō
ブロック長

block length indicator
burokku chō hyōshiki
ブロック長標識

block name
burokku mei
ブロック名

block number
burokku bangō
ブロック番号

block prefix
burokku settōgo
ブロック接頭語

block record
burokku-rekōdo
ブロック・レコード

block sequence indicator
burokku junjo hyōshiki
ブロック順序標識

block size
burokku-saizu
ブロック・サイズ

block sort
burokku bunrui; burokku-sōto
ブロック分類；
ブロック・ソート

block structure
burokku kōzō
ブロック構造

block terminal statement
bunsetsu no tanmatsu bun
文節の端末文

block transfer
burokku tensō
ブロック転送

blocked record
burokkuka rekōdo
ブロック化レコード

blocking
burokkingu; burokkuka
ブロッキング；ブロック化

blocking factor
burokkuka insū
ブロック化因数

blocking oscillator
burokkingu hasshinki
ブロッキング発振器

BNF (Backus-Naur Form)
BNF (Bakkusu-Naua hō; Bakkusu-
Naua hyōkihō)
バックス・ナウア法；
バックス・ナウア表記法

board
bōdo; kiban
ボード；基盤

board computer
bōdo-konpyūta
ボード・コンピュータ

Boolean add
Būru kasan; ronri kasan
ブール加算；論理加算

Boolean algebra
Būru daisū
ブール代数

Boolean expression
Būru enzanshiki; Būru ronrishiki
ブール演算式；ブール論理式

Boolean format
Būru shoshiki; ronri shoshiki
ブール書式；論理書式

Boolean function
Būru kansū
ブール関数

Boolean logic
Būru ronri
ブール論理

Boolean operation
Būru enzan
ブール演算

Boolean operator
Būru enzanshi
ブール演算子

Boolean variable
Būru hensū
ブール変数

boot
būto
ブート

boot-up
būto-appu
ブート・アップ

bootstrap
būtosutorappu
ブートストラップ

bootstrap circuit
būtosutorappu kairo
ブートストラップ回路

bootstrap loader
būtosutorappu-rōda
ブートストラップ・ローダ

bootstrap record
būtosutorappu-rekōdo
ブートストラップ・レコード

borrow
borō; kari
ボロー；借り

BOS (basic operating system)
BOS (kihon operēteingu-
shisutemu)
基本オペレーティング・
システム

BOT (beginning of tape)
BOT (tēpu kaishi; tēpu no hajime;
tēpu shitan)
テープ開始；テープの始め；
テープ始端

bottom-up approach
botomu-appu-apurōchi;
jōshōgata apurōchi
ボトム・アップ・アプローチ；
上昇型アプローチ

bottom-up parsing
jōshōgata kaiseki
上昇型解析

bound
baundo
バウンド

bound module
renketsuzumi mojyūru
連結済みモジュール

boundary
kyōkai
境界

boundary alignment
kyōkai awase
境界合わせ

boundary argument
kyōkai hikisū
境界引き数

boundary condition
kyōkai jōken
境界条件

boundary value
kyōkai chi
境界値

boundary value problem
kyōkai chi mondai
境界値問題

bpi (bits per inch)
bpi (bitto/inchi)
ビット／インチ

BPI (bytes per inch)
BPI (baito/inchi)
バイト／インチ

bps (bits per second)
bps (bitto/byō)
ビット／秒

BPS (bytes per second)
BPS (baito/byō)
バイト／秒

br (base register)
br (bēsu-rejisuta; kijun rejisuta;
kitei rejisuta)
ベース・レジスタ；
基準レジスタ；基底レジスタ

branch
bunki; buranchi
分岐；ブランチ

branch address
bunki adoresu; bunki banchi
分岐アドレス；分岐番地

branch and bound method
bunki gentei hō
分岐限定法

branch instruction
buranchi meirei; bunki meirei
ブランチ命令；分岐命令

branch off (verb)
bunki suru
分岐する

branch point
bunki pointo; bunkiten
分岐ポイント；分岐点

breadboard
bureddobōdo; jikken'yō mokei
ブレッドボード；実験用模型

break
chūdan
中断

breakdown
kōfu; koshō; shishō; shōgai
降伏；故障；支障；障害

breakpoint
burekku-pointo; kugiriten
ブレック・ポイント；区切り点

breakpoint halt
kugiriten teishi
区切り点停止

breakpoint instruction
burekku-pointo meirei;
kugiriten meirei
ブレック・ポイント命令；
区切り点命令

breakpoint switch
kugiriten suitchi
区切り点スイッチ

brightness
kido; meido
輝度；明度

British Standards (BS)
Eikoku Kōgyō Kikaku (BS)
英国工業規格

British Standards Institution (BSI)
Eikoku Kōgyō Kikaku Kyōkai (BSI)
英国工業規格協会

broadband
kōtai'iki
広帯域

broadcast
dōhō tsūshin
同報通信

brush sensing
burashi yomitori
ブラシ読み取り

brush sensor
burashi yomitori kikō
ブラシ読み取り機構

brush station
burashi kikō
ブラシ機構

BS (backspace)
BS (kōtai)
後退

BS (British Standards)
BS (Eikoku Kōgyō Kikaku)
英国工業規格

BSAM (basic sequential access method)
BSAM (kihon junji akusesu
hōshiki)
基本順次アクセス方式

BSC (binary synchronous communication)
BSC (nishin dēta dōki tsūshin)
２進データ同期通信

BSI (British Standards Institution)
BSI (Eikoku Kōgyō Kikaku Kyōkai)
英国工業規格協会

BTAM (basic telecommunications access method)
BTAM (kihon tsūshin akusesu hōshiki)
基本通信アクセス方式

bubble memory
jiki baburu kioku
磁気バブル記憶

bubble sort
baburu-sōto
バブル・ソート

bucket
baketto
バケット

buffer
baffua; kanshō
バッファ；緩衝

buffer area
baffua iki; kanshō ryō'iki
バッファ域；緩衝領域

buffer control
baffua seigyo
バッファ制御

buffer control word (BCW)
baffua seigyogo (BCW)
バッファ制御語

buffer gate
ronriwa gēto
論理和ゲート

buffer register
baffua-rejisuta
バッファ・レジスタ

buffer storage
baffua kioku; kanshō kioku
バッファ記憶；緩衝記憶

buffer store
baffua kioku sōchi;
kanshō kioku sōchi
バッファ記憶装置；
緩衝記憶装置

buffered
baffuatsuki
バッファ付き

buffered printer
baffuatsuki insho sōchi
バッファ付き印書装置

buffering
baffuaringu; kanshō shuhō
バッファリング；緩衝手法

buffering function
baffuaringu kinō
バッファリング機能

bug
bagu
バグ

build (a system) (verb)
kōchiku suru
構築する

building-block system
birudeingu-burokku hōshiki
ビルディング・ブロック方式

built-in
jidō; kumikomi; naizō
自動；組み込み；内蔵

built-in check
kumikomi kensa
組み込み検査

built-in control
kumikomi seigyo
組み込み制御

built-in function
kumikomi kansū; kumikomi kinō
組み込み関数；組み込み機能

bulk storage
baruku kioku; daiyōryō kioku
バルク記憶；大容量記憶

bundled package
bandoru-pakkēji
バンドル・パッケージ

bundling
bandoru sōsa
バンドル操作

burst
basuto
バスト

burst error
basuto ayamari
バスト誤り

burst mode
basuto hōshiki; basuto-mōdo
バスト方式；バスト・モード

burster
basuta
バスタ

bus
basu; bosen
バス；母線

business automation
bijinesu-otomēshon;
jimu jidōka
ビジネス・オトメーション；
事務自動化

business data processing
jimu (dēta) shori
事務（データ）処理

business machine
jimu kikai
事務機械

business management information system
bijinesu keiei jōhō shisutemu
ビジネス経営情報システム

business system
bijinesu-shisutemu; jimu shisutemu
ビジネス・システム；
事務システム

business system analysis
bijinesu-shisutemu kaiseki
ビジネス・システム解析

busy
shiyōchū
使用中

bypass
baipasu
バイパス

bypass record
baipasu-rekōdo
バイパス・レコード

byte
baito
バイト

byte address
baito-adoresu
バイト・アドレス

byte count
baito-kaunto
バイト・カウント

byte mode
baito hōshiki; baito-mōdo
バイト方式; バイト・モード

byte-oriented
baito muki
バイト向き

byte processing
baito shori
バイト処理

bytes per inch (BPI)
baito/inchi (BPI)
バイト / インチ

bytes per second (BPS)
baito/byō (BPS)
バイト / 秒

C

cable
kēburu
ケーブル

cable attached to ———
——— ni tempu suru kēburu
———に添付するケーブル

cache memory
kyasshu-memori
キャッシュ・メモリ

CAD (computer-aided design)
CAD (keisanki enjo sekkei;
keisanki en'yō sekkei; keisanki
riyō sekkei)
計算機援助設計;
計算機援用設計;
計算機利用設計

**CADA (computer-assisted data
analysis)**
CADA (keisanki josei dēta
kaiseki)
計算機助成データ解析

**CADCAM (computer-aided
design−computer-aided
manufacture)**
CADCAM (keisanki enjo sekkei−
keisanki enjo seizō; keisanki
en'yō sekkei−keisanki en'yō
seizō; keisanki riyō sekkei−
keisanki riyō seizō)
計算機援助設計-
計算機援助製造;
計算機援用設計-
計算機援用製造;
計算機利用設計-
計算機利用製造

CAI (computer-aided instruction)
CAI (keisanki enjo gakushū;
keisanki en'yō gakushū; keisanki
riyō gakushū)
計算機援助学習;
計算機援用学習;
計算機利用学習

**CAI language (computer-aided
instruction language)**
CAI'yō gengo
(keisanki enjo gakushū gengo;
keisanki en'yō gakushū gengo;
keisanki riyō gakushū gengo)
CAI用言語
計算機援助学習言語;
計算機援用学習言語;
計算機利用学習言語

CAL (computer-assisted learning)
CAL (keisanki en'yō gakushū;
keisanki josei gakushū; keisanki
riyō gakushū)
計算機援用学習;
計算機助成学習;
計算機利用学習

calculate
keisan suru
計算する

calculation
keisan
計算

calculation key
keisan kii
計算キー

calculator
keisanki
計算器

calendar clock
karenda-kurokku
カレンダ・クロック

call
kōru; yobidashi
コール; 呼び出し

call-back
kōru-bakku
コール・バック

call by name
namaekae
名前変え

call by quantity
ryōtori
量取り

call by reference
banchi tori
番地取り

call by result
kekka tori
結果取り

call by value
ataitori
値取り

call directing
atesaki shitei
宛先指定

call-directing code (CDC)
atesaki shitei kōdo (CDC)
宛先指定コード

call instruction
kōru meirei; yobidashi meirei
コール命令；呼び出し命令

call word
yobidashi go
呼び出し語

called station
hiko kyoku
被呼局

calling
yobidashi
呼び出し

calling indicator
hiko hyōji; yobidashi hyōji
被呼表示；呼び出し表示

calling list
yobidashi risuto
呼び出しリスト

calling program
yobidashi puroguramu
呼び出しプログラム

calling sequence
yobidashi keiretsu
呼び出し系列

calling station
kiko kyoku
起呼局

CAM (computer-aided manufacturing)
CAM (keisanki enjo seizō; keisanki en'yō seizō; keisanki riyō seizō)
計算機援助製造；
計算機援用製造；
計算機利用製造

CAM (content-addressable memory)
CAM (rensō kioku)
連想記憶

CAN (cancel)
CAN (torikeshi)
取り消し

cancel (CAN)
torikeshi (CAN)
取り消し

cancel (*verb*)
torikesu
取り消す

cancel character
torikeshi moji
取り消し文字

cancel indicator
torikeshi hyōji
取り消し表示

cancellation
kaijo; torikeshi
解除；取り消し

capability
keipabiritei; kinō
ケイパビリティ；機能

capability mechanism
keipabiritei kikō
ケイパビリティ機構

capability rating index
keipabiritei hyōtei shisū
ケイパビリティ評定指数

capacitor
kondensa
コンデンサ

capacitor storage
kondensa kioku
コンデンサ記憶

capacitor store
kondensa kioku sōchi
コンデンサ記憶装置

capacity
nōryoku; shūyō; yōryō
能力；収容；容量

capacity expansion
yōryō kakuchō
容量拡張

capacity expansion problem
yōryō kakuchō mondai
容量拡張問題

capacity planning
yōryō keikaku
容量計画

capacity utility function
yōryō kōyō kansū
容量効用関数

capstan
kyapusutan
キャプスタン

card
kādo
カード

card code
kādo-kōdo
カード・コード

card column
kādo no keta
カードの桁

card deck
kādo-dekku
カード・デック

card design
kādo sekkei
カード設計

card edge
kādo no fuchi
カードの縁

card face
kādo-fuēsu; kado no omote
ガード・フェース；カードの表

card feed
kādo-fuiido; kādo okuri
カード・フィード；カード送り

card field
kādo-fuiirudo; kādo ran
カード・フィールド；カード欄

card file
kādo-fuairu
カード・ファイル

card format
kādo keishiki
カード形式

card gauge
kādo-gēji
カード・ゲージ

25

card hopper
kādo-hoppa
カード・ホッパ

card image
kādo-imēji
カード・イメージ

card input
kādo nyūryoku
カード入力

card jam
kādo-jyamu
カード・ジャム

card leading edge
kādo no zen'en
カードの前縁

card matching
kādo no tsukiawase
カードの突き合わせ

card punch (CP)
kādo senkō sōchi; kādo senkōki (CP)
カードせん孔装置;
カードせん孔機

card punching
kādo senkō
カードせん孔

card reader (CR)
kādo yomitori sōchi; kādo yomitoriki (CR)
カード読み取り装置;
カード読み取り機

card row
kādo-rō
カード・ロー

card sorter
kādo bunruiki; kādo-sōta
カード分類機; カード・ソータ

card stacker
kādo-sutakka
カード・スタッカ

card systems
kādo-shisutemu
カード・システム

card-to-disk
kādo-deisuku
カード・ディスク

card-to-disk conversion
kādo-deisuku henkan
カード・ディスク変換

card-to-disk converter
kādo-deisuku henkanki
カード・ディスク変換器

card-to-tape
kādo-tēpu
カード・テープ

card-to-tape conversion
kādo-tēpu henkan
カード・テープ変換

card-to-tape converter
kādo-tēpu henkanki
カード・テープ変換器

card trailing edge
kādo no kōen
カードの後縁

card verifier
kādo kenkōki
カード検孔機

card verifying
kādo kenkō
カード検孔

card weight
kādo osae
カード押さえ

cards per minute (CPM)
kādo/fun (CPM)
カード / 分

carriage
kami okuri kikō
紙送り機構

carriage control
kami okuri seigyo
紙送り制御

carriage control tape
kami okuri seigyo tēpu
紙送り制御テープ

carriage return (CR)
fukki; kaigyō fukki (CR)
復帰; 改行復帰

carriage-return character
fukki moji
復帰文字

carrier
hansōha; kyaria
搬送波; キャリア

carrier detector
kyaria kenshutsu
キャリア検出

carrier system
hansō shisutemu;
kyaria-shisutemu
搬送システム;
キャリア・システム

carry
keta age; kyari
桁上げ; キャリ

carry-complete signal
keta age kanryō shingō
桁上げ完了信号

carry digit
kyari-deijitto
キャリ・ディジット

carry indicator
keta age hyōjishi
桁上げ表示子

carry time
keta age jikan
桁上げ時間

carrying case
keitaiyō kēsu
携帯用ケース

cartridge
kātorijji
カートリッジ

cartridge disk
kātorijji-deisuku
カートリッジ・ディスク

cartridge magnetic tape (CRMT)
kātorijji jiki tēpu (CRMT)
カートリッジ磁気テープ

cartridge reader
kātorijji yomitori sōchi
カートリッジ続み取り装置

cascade control
kasukēdo seigyo
カスケード制御

cascade sort
kasukēdo bunrui
カスケード分類

cascaded carry
kasukēdoshiki keta age
カスケード式桁上げ

case shift
dan shifuto
段シフト

case statement
kēsu-sutētomento
ケース・ステートメント

cassette
kasetto
カセット

cassette drive
kasetto-doraibu
カセット・ドライブ

cassette handler
kasetto sōchi
カセット装置

cassette magnetic tape (CMT)
kasettogata jiki tēpu (CMT)
カセット型磁気テープ

cassette recorder
kasetto-rekōda
カセット・レコーダ

casual user
ichijiteki yūza
一時的ユーザ

catalog
katarogu
カタログ

category
kōrui
項類

catenated search
rensa tansaku
連鎖探索

cathode-ray tube (CRT)
inkyokusenkan (CRT)
陰極線管

cathode-ray-tube memory (CRT memory)
inkyokusenkan kioku (CRT kioku)
陰極線管記憶；CRT記憶

cathode-ray-tube visual display unit (CRT visual display unit)
inkyokusenkan hyōji sōchi (CRT hyōji sōchi)
陰極線管表示装置；CRT表示装置

CAW (channel address word)
CAW (chaneru-adoresu go; chaneru-adoresu-wādo)
チャネル・アドレス語；チャネル・アドレス・ワード

CBL (computer-based learning)
CBL (keisanki bēsu gakushū; keisanki riyō gakushū)
計算機ベース学習；計算機利用学習

CBT (computer-based training)
CBT (keisanki bēsu kunren; keisanki riyō kunren)
計算機ベース訓練；計算機利用訓練

CC (condition code)
CC (kondeishon-kōdo)
コンディション・コード

CCB (command control block)
CCB (komando seigyo burokku; shirei seigyo burokku)
コマンド制御ブロック；指令制御ブロック

CCD (charge-coupled device)
CCD (denka ketsugō soshi)
電荷結合素子

CCE (communication control equipment)
CCE (tsūshin seigyo sōchi)
通信制御装置

CCP (communication control program)
CCP (tsūshin seigyo puroguramu)
通信制御プログラム

CCR (communication control routine)
CCR (tsūshin seigyo rūchin)
通信制御ルーチン

CCU (communication control unit)
CCU (tsūshin seigyo sōchi)
通信制御装置

CCW (channel command word)
CCW (chaneru shirei go; chaneru shirei wādo)
チャネル指令語；チャネル指令ワード

CCW (command control word)
CCW (shirei seigyo go)
指令制御語

CDC (call-directing code)
CDC (atesaki shitei kōdo)
宛先指定コード

CDL (computer design language)
CDL (keisanki sekkei'yō gengo)
計算機設計用言語

CE (custom engineer)
CE (hoshu'in)
保守員

cell
seru
セル

central computer
chūō keisanki
中央計算機

central control unit
chūō seigyo sōchi
中央制御装置

central operation processing unit
chūō enzan shori sōchi
中央演算処理装置

central processing unit (CPU)
chūō shori sōchi (CPU)
中央処理装置

central processor
chūō shori sōchi
中央処理装置

central station
chūō kyoku
中央局

central system
chūō shisutemu
中央システム

central terminal
chūō tanmatsu sōchi
中央端末装置

centralization
shūchūka
集中化

centralized
shūchū(gata)
集中（型）

centralized computer network
shūchūgata konpyūta-nettowāku
集中型コンピュータ・ネットワーク

centralized control
shūchū seigyo
集中制御

27

centralized data processing
shūchū dēta shori
集中データ処理

centralized data-processing system
shūchū dēta shori shisutemu
集中データ処理システム

centralized information structure
shūchū jōhō kōzō
集中情報構造

centralized information system
shūchū jōhō shisutemu
集中情報システム

centralized operation
shūchū sōsa
集中操作

centralized system
shūchū hōshiki
集中方式

centrally located computer
shūchūgata konpyūta
集中型コンピュータ

chad
chado; senkō kuzu
チャド；せん孔くず

chain
chein; rensa
チェイン；連鎖

chain code
chein-kōdo; rensa kōdo
チェイン・コード；連鎖コード

chain printer
cheinshiki insatsu sōchi
チェイン式印刷装置

chained command
rensa shirei
連鎖指令

chained file
rensa fuairu
連鎖ファイル

chained list
rensa risuto
連鎖リスト

chained record
rensa rekōdo
連鎖レコード

chaining
rensa
連鎖

chaining address
rensa adoresu
連鎖アドレス

chaining check
rensa chekku
連鎖チェック

chaining overflow
rensa afure
連鎖溢れ

chaining search
rensa tansaku
連鎖探索

change
henkō
変更

change bit
henkō bitto
変更ビット

change dump
henkō'iki danpu
変更域ダンプ

channel
chaneru; tsūshinro
チャネル；通信路

channel address
chaneru-adoresu
チャネル・アドレス

channel address field
chaneru-adoresu-fuiirudo
チャネル・アドレス・
フィールド

channel address register
chaneru-adoresu-rejisuta
チャネル・アドレス・レジスタ

channel address word (CAW)
chaneru-adoresu go;
chaneru-adoresu-wādo (CAW)
チャネル・アドレス語；
チャネル・アドレス・ワード

channel busy
chaneru shiyōchū
チャネル使用中

channel capacity
chaneru yōryō
チャネル容量

channel command
chaneru shirei
チャネル指令

channel command code
chaneru shirei kōdo
チャネル指令コード

channel command register
chaneru shirei rejisuta
チャネル指令レジスタ

channel command word (CCW)
chaneru shirei go;
chaneru shirei wādo (CCW)
チャネル指令語；
チャネル指令ワード

channel control
chaneru seigyo
チャネル制御

channel control check
chaneru seigyo chekku
チャネル制御チェック

channel control register
chaneru seigyo rejisuta
チャネル制御レジスタ

channel control unit
chaneru seigyo sōchi
チャネル制御装置

channel control word
chaneru seigyo go
チャネル制御語

channel data check
chaneru-dēta-chekku
チャネル・データ・チェック

channel end
chaneru shūryō
チャネル終了

channel interface
chaneru-intafuēsu
チャネル・インタフェース

channel interrupt
chaneru warikomi
チャネル割り込み

channel load
chaneru fuka
チャネル負荷

channel priority feature
chaneru yūsen kikō
チャネル優先機構

channel program
chaneru-puroguramu
チャネル・プログラム

channel scheduler
chaneru-sukejyūra
チャネル・スケジューラ

channel status byte
chaneru jōtai baito
チャネル状態バイト

channel status word (CSW)
chaneru jōtai go (CSW)
チャネル状態語

channel synchronizer
chaneru dōki sōchi
チャネル同期装置

channel-to-channel
chanerukan
チャネル間

channel-to-channel adapter
chanerukan adaputa
チャネル間アダプタ

character
kyarakuta; moji
キャラクタ；文字

character-addressable
kyarakuta-adoresukanō
キャラクタ・アドレス可能

character block
kyarakuta-burokku
キャラクタ・ブロック

character boundary
moji kyōkai
文字境界

character change
moji henkō
文字変更

character check
moji kensa
文字検査

character code
kyarakuta-kōdo; moji kōdo
キャラクタ・コード；
文字コード

character count
moji kaunto
文字カウント

character deletion
moji sakujo
文字削除

character density
moji mitsudo
文字密度

character display
kyarakuta-deisupurei; moji hyōji
キャラクタ・ディスプレィ；
文字表示

character emitter
kyarakuta-emitta
キャラクタ・エミッタ

character encoding
kyarakuta-enkōdeingu;
moji kōdoka
キャラクタ・エンコーディング；
文字コード化

character error
goji
誤字

character error rate
goji ritsu
誤字率

character expression
moji shiki
文字式

character fill
moji jūten
文字充てん

character generator
moji hasseiki
文字発生器

character insertion
moji sōnyū
文字挿入

character key
kyarakuta-kii
キャラクタ・キー

character manipulation
moji shori
文字処理

character-oriented
moji muki
文字向き

character parity
kyarakuta-paritei; moji paritei
キャラクタ・パリティ；
文字パリティ

character outline
moji rinkaku
文字輪郭

character picture
moji pikucha
文字ピクチャ

character pitch
moji kankaku
文字間隔

character position
moji ichi
文字位置

character printer
kyarakuta-purinta
キャラクタ・プリンタ

character processing
moji shori
文字処理

character reader
moji yomitori sōchi
文字読み取り装置

character recognition
moji ninshiki
文字認識

character set
kyarakuta-setto; moji no kumi;
moji setto
キャラクタ・セット；
文字の組み；文字セット

character space
moji kankaku
文字間隔

character string
moji retsu
文字列

character subset
moji sabusetto
文字サブセット

character synchronization
moji dōki
文字同期

characteristic
tokusei
特性

characteristic distortion
tokusei hizumi
特性歪み

characteristic impedance
tokusei inpiidansu
特性インピーダンス

characteristics
tokusei
特性

characters per inch (cpi)
moji/inchi (cpi)
文字／インチ

characters per second (cps)
moji/byō (cps)
文字／秒

charge-coupled device (CCD)
denka ketsugō soshi (CCD)
電荷結合素子

charge transfer device (CTD)
denka tensō soshi (CTD)
電荷転送素子

chart
chāto; kōshi; zu
チャート；格子；図

chart recorder
chāto-rekōda
チャート・レコーダ

check
chekku; kensa
チェック；検査

check bit
chekku-bitto; kensa bitto
チェック・ビット；検査ビット

check box
chekku-bokkusu
チェック・ボックス

check character
kensa moji
検査文字

check digit
kensa sūji
検査数字

check-digit calculation
kensa sūji keisan
検査数字計算

check-digit verification
kensa sūji kenshō
検査数字検証

check indicator
chekku-injikēta
チェック・インジケータ

check sum
chekku-samu; kensa gōkei
チェック・サム；検査合計

check symbol
kensa kigō
検査記号

check system
kensa hōshiki
検査方式

checking feature
kensa kinō
検査機能

checking program
kensa puroguramu
検査プログラム

checking routine
kensa rūchin
検査ルーチン

checkout routine
chekku-auto-rūchin
チェック・アウト・ルーチン

checkout scanning
chekku-auto sōsa
チェック・アウト走査

checkpoint
chekku-pointo
チェック・ポイント

checkpoint dump
chekku-pointo-danpu
チェック・ポイント・ダンプ
．

checkpoint record
chekku-pointo-rekōdo
チェック・ポイント・レコード

checkpoint restart
chekku-pointo saishidō
チェック・ポイント再始動

checkpoint routine
chekku-pointo-rūchin
チェック・ポイント・ルーチン

Chinese character
kanji
漢字

Chinese-character printer
kanji purinta
漢字プリンタ

chip
chippu
チップ

chip socket
chippu-soketto
チップ・ソケット

chip tray
chippu hako
チップ箱

CIM (computer input microfilming; computer input on microfilm)
CIM (konpyūta nyūryoku maikurofuirumu)
コンピュータ入力マイクロフィルム

cipher
angō
暗号

ciphertext
angōbun
暗号文

CIR (current instruction register)
CIR (karento meirei rejisuta)
カレント命令レジスタ

circuit
kairo; kaisen
回路；回線

circuit analysis
kairo kaiseki
回路解析

circuit board
kairo bōdo; kaisen bōdo
回路ボード；回線ボード

circuit breaker
kaiheiki
開閉器

circuit grade
kaisen no shurui
回線の種類

circuit interface
kaisen intafuēsu
回線インタフェース

circuit load
kaisen fuka
回線負荷

circuit logic
kairo ronri
回路論理

circuit protection device
kaisen hogo sōchi
回線保護装置

circuit-switched network
kaisen kōkanmō
回線交換網

circuit switching
kaisen kōkan
回線交換

circular shift
junkan shifuto
循環シフト

circulating memory
junkan kioku
循環記憶

circulating register
junkan rejisuta
循環レジスタ

circulating storage
junkan kioku
循環記憶

clamp
kuranpu
クランプ

clamping circuit
kuranpu kairo
クランプ回路

classification
ruibetsu; shubetsu
類別；種別

classify
ruibetsu suru
類別する

clause
ku
句

clear
kuria; shōkyo
クリア；消去

clear (verb)
kuria suru; shōkyo suru;
zero ni suru
クリアする；消去する；
ゼロにする

clear instruction
shōkyo meirei
消去命令

clipper
kurippu kairo
クリップ回路

clipping
kurippingu
クリッピング

clipping circuit
kurippu kairo
クリップ回路

clock
kokuji sōchi; kurokku
刻時装置；クロック

clock frequency
kurokku shūhasū
クロック周波数

clock generator
kurokku-zenerēta
クロック・ゼネレータ

clock pulse
kokuji parusu; kurokku-parusu
刻時パルス；クロック・パルス

clock rate
kurokku-reito; kurokku sokudo
クロック・レイト；
クロック速度

clock register
kokuji rejisuta
刻時レジスタ

clock scan
kokuji sōsa
刻時走査

clock service
kurokku-sābisu
クロック・サービス

clock signal
kurokku shingō
クロック信号

clock signal generator
kurokku shingō hasshinki
クロック信号発振器

clock table
kurokku-tēburu
クロック・テーブル

clock track
kurokku-torakku
クロック・トラック

closed array
tojita hairetsu
閉じた配列

closed loop
tojita rūpu
閉じたループ

closed-loop system
tojita rūpu-shisutemu
閉じたループ・システム

closed routine
tojita rūchin
閉じたルーチン

closed shop
kurozudo-shoppu
クロズド・ショップ

closed-shop programming
kurozudo-shoppu-
puroguramingu
クロズド・ショップ・
プログラミング

closed subroutine
tojita saburūchin
閉じたサブルーチン

closed system
tojita shisutemu
閉じたシステム

closure
heisa; heishi
閉鎖；閉止

cluster
kurasuta
クラスタ

cluster control
kurasuta seigyo
クラスタ制御

clustering
kurasutaringu
クラスタリング

CMI (computer-managed instruction)
CMI (keisanki kanri kyōiku)
計算機管理教育

CML (computer-managed learning)
CML (keisanki kanri gakushū)
計算機管理学習

CML (current mode logic)
CML (denryū mōdo ronri)
電流モード論理

CMOS (complementary metal oxide semiconductor)
CMOS (sōhogata mosu)
相補型モス; 相補型MOS

CMT (cassette magnetic tape)
CMT (kasettogata jiki tēpu)
カセット型磁気テープ

CMT interface board
CMT intafuēsu-bōdo
CMTインタフェース・ボード

COAX (coaxial cable)
COAX (dōkei kēburu)
同軸ケーブル

coaxial cable (COAX)
dōkei kēburu (COAX)
同軸ケーブル

COBOL (Common Business-Oriented Language)
COBOL (Koboru)
コボル; COBOL

COBOL character
Koboru moji
コボル文字

code
fugō; kōdo
符号; コード

code book
kōdo-bukku
コード・ブック

code check
kōdo-chekku
コード・チェック

code conversion
kōdo henkan
コード変換

code converter
kōdo henkanki
コード変換器

code distance
kōdo kyori
コード距離

code element
kōdo yōso
コード要素

code extension character
kōdo kakuchō moji
コード拡張文字

code image
kōdo-imēji
コード・イメージ

code image read
kōdo-imēji yomitori
コード・イメージ読み取り

code set
kōdo-setto
コード・セット

code table
fugō hyō; kōdo hyō
符号表; コード表

code translation
kōdo hon'yaku
コード翻訳

code value
kōdo chi
コード値

coded character
fugōka moji
符号化文字

coded character set
fugōka moji setto
符号化文字セット

coded decimal
fugōka jisshinsū; kōdoka jisshinsū
符号化10進数; コード化10進数

coded decimal notation
fugōka jisshinhō; kōdoka jisshinhō
符号化10進法; コード化10進法

coded program
fugōka puroguramu
符号化プログラム

coded representation
fugōka hyōji
符号化表示

coder
kōda
コーダ

coding
fugōka; kōdeingu; kōdoka
符号化; コーディング; コード化

coding line
kōdeingu gyō
コーディング行

coding sheet
kōdeingu yōshi
コーディング用紙

coding system
kōdo taikei
コード体系

coding theory
fugōka riron
符号化理論

coding unit
kōdeingu-yunitto
コーディング・ユニット

coefficient
keisū
係数

coincidence
itchi
一致

coincidence circuit
itchi kairo
一致回路

coincidence duration
itchi jikan
一致時間

coincidence gate
itchi gēto
一致ゲート

cold start
korudo-sutāto
コルド・スタート

cold-type system (CTS)
korudo-taipu-shisutemu (CTS)
コルド・タイプ・システム

collate
shōgō suru
照合する

collating
shōgō
照合

collating operation
shōgō sōsa
照合操作

collating sequence
shōgō junjo
照合順序

collator
shōgōki
照合機

collector
korekuta
コレクタ

color
iro; karā
色；カラー

color code
iro kōdo; karā-kōdo
色コード；カラー・コード

color coding
iro kōdeingu; karā-kōdeingu
色コーディング；
カラー・コーディング

color decoder
karā-dekōda
カラー・デコーダ

color display
karā-deisupurei
カラー・ディスプレィ

column
jūretsu; karamu; keta
縦列；カラム；桁

column binary
karamu-bainari
カラム・バイナリ

column indicator
keta hyōjiki
桁表示器

COM (computer output microfilming; computer output on microfilm)
COM (konpyūta shutsuryoku maikurofuirumu)
コンピュータ出力マイクロフィルム

COM output
COM shutsuryoku
COM出力

COM recorder
COM rekōda
COMレコーダ

combination
kumiawase
組み合わせ

combinational circuit
kumiawase kairo
組み合わせ回路

combinational logic
kumiawase ronri
組み合わせ論理

combined database
tōgō dētabēsu
統合データベース

combined file
nyūshutsuryoku kyōyō fuairu
入出力共用ファイル

command
komando; shiji; shirei
コマンド；指示；指令

command address
shirei adoresu
指令アドレス

command chaining
shirei rensa
指令連鎖

command code
shirei kōdo
指令コード

command control block (CCB)
shirei seigyo burokku (CCB)
指令制御ブロック

command control word (CCW)
shirei seigyo go (CCW)
指令制御語

command interrupt
shirei warikomi
指令割り込み

command language
komando gengo; shirei gengo
コマンド言語；指令言語

command mode
shirei mōdo
指令モード

command processing
shirei shori
指令処理

command pulse
shirei parusu
指令パルス

command rejection
shirei kyohi
指令拒否

command retry
shirei saishikō
指令再試行

comment
chūshaku
注釈

comment field
chūshaku ran
注釈欄

comment line
chūshaku gyō
注釈行

common area
kyōtsū iki
共通域

common block
kyōtsū burokku
共通ブロック

Common Business-Oriented Language (COBOL)
Koboru (COBOL)
コボル

common carrier
denshin denwa kaisha; hansōha kyōdō
電信電話会社；搬送波共同

common code
kyōtsū kōdo
共通コード

common expression
kyōtsū shiki
共通式

common field
kyōtsū fuiirudo
共通フィールド

common language
kyōtsū gengo
共通言語

common segment
kyōtsū segumento
共通セグメント

common storage area
kyōtsū kioku ryō'iki
共通記憶領域

common subexpression
kyōtsū bubun shiki
共通部分式

common subroutine
kyōtsū saburūchin
共通サブルーチン

common user network
kyōtsū yūza-nettowāku
共通ユーザ・ネットワーク

common variable
kyōtsū hensū
共通変数

communication
densō; kōshin; renraku; tsūshin
電送；交信；連絡；通信

communication auxiliary equipment
tsūshin hojo sōchi
通信補助装置

communication board
tsūshin bōdo
通信ボード

communication buffer
tsūshin'yō baffua
通信用バッファ

communication card
tsūshin kādo
通信カード

communication channel
tsūshin chaneru; tsūshinro
通信チャネル；通信路

communication console
tsūshin seigyo taku
通信制御卓

communication control
tsūshin seigyo
通信制御

communication control character
tsūshin seigyo moji
通信制御文字

communication control equipment (CCE)
tsūshin seigyo sōchi (CCE)
通信制御装置

communication control program (CCP)
tsūshin seigyo puroguramu (CCP)
通信制御プログラム

communication control routine (CCR)
tsūshin seigyo rūchin (CCR)
通信制御ルーチン

communication control unit (CCU)
tsūshin seigyo sōchi (CCU)
通信制御装置

communication controller
tsūshin seigyo sōchi
通信制御装置

communication device
tsūshin sōchi
通信装置

communication element
tsūshin eremento
通信エレメント

communication equipment
tsūshin setsubi
通信設備

communication facilities
tsūshin setsubi
通信設備

communication facility
tsūshin kinō
通信機能

communication function
tsūshin kinō
通信機能

communication interrupt
tsūshin warikomi
通信割り込み

communication line
tsūshin kaisen
通信回線

communication link
tsūshin rinku
通信リンク

communication network
tsūshinmō
通信網

communication path
tsūshin keiro
通信経路

communication-processing system
tsūshin shori shisutemu
通信処理システム

communication processor (CP)
tsūshin'yō purosessa (CP)
通信用プロセッサ

communication satellite
tsūshin eisei
通信衛星

communication science
tsūshin kagaku
通信科学

communication server
tsūshin'yō sāba
通信用サーバ

communication software
tsūshin'yō sofutouea
通信用ソフトウェア

communication speed
tsūshin sokudo
通信速度

communication system
tsūshin shisutemu
通信システム

communication terminal
tsūshin tanmatsu (sōchi)
通信端末（装置）

communication theory
tsūshin riron
通信理論

communications
tsūshin
通信

communications adapter
tsūshin'yō adaputa
通信用アダプタ

communications control adapter
tsūshin seigyo adaputa
通信制御アダプタ

communications interface
tsūshin'yō intafuēsu
通信用インタフェース

communications language
tsūshin gengo
通信言語

communications processor
tsūshin'yō shori sōchi
通信用処理装置

communications software
tsūshin'yō sofutouea
通信用ソフトウェア

communications terminal
tsūshin'yō tanmatsu
通信用端末

compaction
asshuku
圧縮

compandor
asshinki
圧伸器

comparator
hikakuki
比較器

comparator check
hikaku kensa
比較検査

compare
hikaku suru
比較する

comparing (of data)
hikaku (dēta no)
比較（データの）

comparing unit
hikaku kikō
比較機構

comparison
hikaku
比較

comparison expression
hikaku shiki
比較式

compatibility
gokansei; konpateibiritei
互換性；コンパティビリティ

compatibility check
gokansei kensa
互換性検査

compatible
gokansei ga aru; tekigō
互換性がある；適合

compensation
hoshō; kyūyo
補償；給与

compilation
hon'yaku; konpairēshon
翻訳；コンパイレーション

compilation error
hon'yaku ayamari; konpairēshon
ayamari
翻訳誤り；コンパイレーション誤り

compilation run
konpairēshon-ran
コンパイレーション・ラン

compilation time
hon'yaku jikan; konpairu jikan
翻訳時間；コンパイル時間

compile
konpairu suru
コンパイルする

compile time
hon'yaku jikan; konpairu jikan
翻訳時間；コンパイル時間

compiler
konpaira
コンパイラ

compiler-compiler
konpaira-konpaira
コンパイラ・コンパイラ

compiler directing statement
hon'yaku shiji meirei
翻訳指示命令

compiler generator
konpaira-zenerēta
コンパイラ・ゼネレータ

compiler language
konpaira gengo
コンパイラ言語

compiler optimization
konpaira ni yoru saitekika
コンパイラによる最適化

compiling
konpairingu
コンパイリング

compiling computer
konpairingu keisanki
コンパイリング計算機

compiling system
konpairingu-shisutemu
コンパイリング・システム

complement
hosū
補数

complement base
hosū no soko
補数の底

complement on nine
kyū no hosū
9の補数

complement on one
ichi no hosū
1の補数

complement on ten
jū no hosū
10の補数

complementary
hosū; sōhogata; sōhoteki
補数；相補型；相補的

complementary circuit
sōhogata kairo
相補型回路

complementary controller
sōhogata seigyo sōchi
相補型制御装置

**complementary metal oxide
semiconductor (CMOS)**
sōhogata mosu (CMOS)
相補型MOS；相補型モス

complementary operation
hosū enzan
補数演算

complementary operator
hosū enzanshi
補数演算子

complementary programming
sōhoteki puroguramingu
相補的プログラミング

complementer
hosū kairo; hosūki
補数回路；補数器

complete carry
zen keta age
全桁上げ

completion
kanryō; kansei; shūryō
完了；完成；終了

complex
fukuso
複素

complex constant
fukuso teisū
複素定数

complex data
fukuso dēta
複素データ

complex interval
fukuso kukan
複素区間

complex number
fukuso sū
複素数

complex numeral expression
fukuso sūkei
複素数形

component
buhin; konponento; kōsei yōso
部品；コンポーネント；構成要素

composite algorithm
fukugō hō
複合法

composite design
fukugō sekkei
複合設計

composite distribution
fukugō bumpu
複合分布

composite file
fukugō fuairu
複合ファイル

composite gain
fukugō ritoku
複合利得

composite part
fukugō buhin
複合部品

composite video
konpojitto-bideo
コンポジット・ビデオ

compound condition
fukugō jōken
複合条件

compound expression
fukugō shiki
複合式

compound mode
fukugō mōdo
複合モード

compound statement
fukugō bun
複合文

compress mode
asshuku mōdo
圧縮モード

compressed code
asshuku kōdo
圧縮コード

compression
asshuku
圧縮

compressor
asshukuki
圧縮器

computability
keisan kanōsei
計算可能性

computable
keisan kanō
計算可能

computation
keisan
計算

computation sequence
keisan junjo
計算順序

computational
keisangata
計算型

compute
keisan suru
計算する

computer
keisanki; konpyūta
計算機；コンピュータ

computer-aided design (CAD)
keisanki enjo sekkei;
keisanki en'yō sekkei;
keisanki riyō sekkei (CAD)
計算機援助設計；
計算機援用設計；
計算機利用設計

**computer-aided design–
computer-aided manufacture
(CADCAM)**
keisanki enjo sekkei–keisanki
enjo seizō; keisanki en'yō
sekkei–keisanki en'yō seizō;
keisanki riyō sekkei–keisanki riyō
seizō (CADCAM)
計算機援助設計-
計算機援助製造；
計算機援用設計-
計算機援用製造；
計算機利用設計-
計算機利用製造

computer-aided instruction (CAI)
keisanki enjo gakushū;
keisanki en'yō gakushū;
keisanki riyō gakushū (CAI)
計算機援助学習；
計算機援用学習；
計算機利用学習

**computer-aided instruction
language (CAI language)**
keisanki enjo gakushū gengo;
keisanki en'yō gakushū gengo;
keisanki riyō gakushū gengo
(CAI'yō gengo)
計算機援助学習言語；
計算機援用学習言語；
計算機利用学習言語
CAI用言語

**computer-aided manufacturing
(CAM)**
keisanki enjo seizō;
keisanki en'yō seizō;
keisanki riyō seizō (CAM)
計算機援助製造；
計算機援用製造；
計算機利用製造

computer animation
konpyūta-animēshon
コンピュータ・アニメーション

computer application
keisanki ōyō; keisanki riyō
計算機応用；計算機利用

computer application system
keisanki riyō shisutemu
計算機利用システム

computer architecture
konpyūta-ākitekucha
コンピュータ・アーキテクチャ

computer art
konpyūta-āto
コンピュータ・アート

**computer-assisted data analysis
(CADA)**
keisanki josei dēta kaiseki
(CADA)
計算機助成データ解析

computer-assisted data evaluation
keisanki josei dēta hyōka
計算機助成データ評価

computer-assisted learning (CAL)
keisanki en'yō gakushū;
keisanki josei gakushū;
keisanki riyō gakushū (CAL)
計算機援用学習;
計算機助成学習;
計算機利用学習

computer-assisted teaching
keisanki en'yō kyōiku;
keisanki josei kyōiku;
keisanki riyō kyōiku
計算機援用教育;
計算機助成教育;
計算機利用教育

computer-based
keisanki bēsu; keisanki riyō
計算機ベース; 計算機利用

computer-based automation
keisanki bēsu jidōka
計算機ベース自動化

computer-based communication system
keisanki bēsu tsūshin shisutemu
計算機ベース通信システム

computer-based conference system
keisanki bēsu kaigi shisutemu
計算機ベース会議システム

computer-based consultant system
keisanki bēsu-konsarutanto-
shisutemu
計算機ベース・コンサルタント・
システム

computer-based control
keisanki bēsu seigyo
計算機ベース制御

computer-based control and communication system
keisanki bēsu seigyo-tsūshin
shisutemu
計算機ベース制御-
通信システム

computer-based information and control system
keisanki bēsu jōhō-seigyo
shisutemu
計算機ベース情報-
制御システム

computer-based learning (CBL)
keisanki bēsu gakushū;
keisanki riyō gakushū (CBL)
計算機ベース学習;
計算機利用学習

computer-based learning system
keisanki bēsu gakushū
shisutemu; keisanki riyō gakushū
shisutemu
計算機ベース学習システム;
計算機利用学習システム

computer-based management system
keisanki bēsu kanri shisutemu
計算機ベース管理システム

computer-based production control system
keisanki bēsu seisan kanri
shisutemu
計算機ベース生産管理システム

computer-based training (CBT)
keisanki bēsu kunren;
keisanki riyō kunren (CBT)
計算機ベース訓練;
計算機利用訓練

computer-based training system
keisanki bēsu kunren shisutemu
計算機ベース訓練システム

computer bureau
konpyūta-byūrō
コンピュータ・ビューロー

computer code
keisanki kōdo; konpyūta-kōdo
計算機コード; コンピュータ・
コード

computer complex
keisanki fukugōtai
計算機複合体

computer configuration
keisanki kōsei
計算機構成

computer control
keisanki seigyo
計算機制御

computer-controlled
keisanki seigyo (no)
計算機制御(の)

computer-dependent language
keisanki izon gengo
計算機依存言語

computer design language (CDL)
keisanki sekkei'yō gengo (CDL)
計算機設計用言語

computer graphics
konpyūta-gurafuikkusu
コンピュータ・グラフィックス

computer graphics simulation
konpyūta-gurafuikkusu-
shimyurēshon
コンピュータ・グラフィックス・
シミュレーション

computer hobbyist
konpyūta-hobiisuto
コンピュータ・ホビースト

computer information
keisanki jōhō
計算機情報

computer information support system
keisanki jōhō shien shisutemu
計算機情報支援システム

computer information system
keisanki jōhō shisutemu
計算機情報システム

computer input microfilming; computer input on microfilm (CIM)
konpyūta nyūryoku
maikurofuirumu (CIM)
コンピュータ入力マイクロフィ
ルム

computer installation
keisanki setchi
計算機設置

computer instruction
keisanki meirei
計算機命令

computer language
keisanki gengo
計算機言語

computer learning
keisanki gakushū
計算機学習

computer-managed instruction (CMI)
　keisanki kanri kyōiku (CMI)
　計算機管理教育

computer-managed learning (CML)
　keisanki kanri gakushū (CML)
　計算機管理学習

computer model
　keisanki moderu
　計算機モデル

computer network
　keisanki nettowāku; keisankimō
　計算機ネットワーク；計算機網

computer networking technology
　keisanki nettowāku gijutsu
　計算機ネットワーク技術

computer operation
　keisanki sōsa
　計算機操作

computer operator
　keisanki sōsa'in;
　konpyūta-operēta
　計算機操作員；
　コンピュータ・オペレータ

computer-oriented language
　keisankimuki gengo
　計算機向き言語

**computer output microfilming;
computer output on microfilm
(COM)**
　konpyūta shutsuryoku
　maikurofuirumu (COM)
　コンピュータ出力マイクロフィ
　ルム

**computer performance evaluation
(CPE)**
　keisanki seinō hyōka (CPE)
　計算機性能評価

computer procedure flowchart
　keisanki tetsuzuki nagarezu
　計算機手続き流れ図

computer program
　keisanki puroguramu
　計算機プログラム

computer-related
　keisanki kanren
　計算機関連

computer-related science
　keisanki kanren kagaku
　計算機関連科学

computer run
　jikkō; konpyūta-ran
　実行；コンピュータ・ラン

computer run chart
　konpyūta-ran-chāto
　コンピュータ・ラン・チャート

computer science
　keisanki kagaku
　計算機科学

computer security
　kimitsu hogo
　機密保護

computer simulation
　keisanki shimyurēshon
　計算機シミュレーション

computer system
　keisanki shisutemu
　計算機システム

computer utility
　konpyūta-yūteiritei
　コンピュータ・ユーティリティ

computer word
　go; keisanki wādo; wādo
　語；計算機ワード；ワード

computerized
　keisankika
　計算機化

**computerized decision-making
system**
　keisankika ishi kettei shisutemu
　計算機化意思決定システム

computerized information
　keisankika jōhō
　計算機化情報

computerized information system
　keisankika jōhō shisutemu
　計算機化情報システム

**computerized management
information system**
　keisankika kei'ei jōhō shisutemu
　計算機化経営情報システム

computerware
　konpyūtauea
　コンピュータウェア

computing
　enzan; keisan
　演算；計算

computing error
　keisan gosa
　計算誤差

computing speed
　enzan sokudo
　演算速度

computing time
　enzan jikan
　演算時間

concatenate
　renketsu suru
　連結する

concatenated data set
　renketsu dēta-setto
　連結データ・セット

concatenation
　renketsu
　連結

concatenation character
　renketsu moji
　連結文字

concatenation expression
　renketsu shiki
　連結式

concatenation operator
　renketsu enzanshi
　連結演算子

concept
　gainen
　概念

conceptual
　gainen
　概念

conclusion
　shūketsu
　終結

concordance
　yōgo sakuin
　用語索引

concurrent
　(dōji) heikō no
　(同時)並行の

concurrent design
heikō sekkei
並行設計

concurrent operation
(dōji) heikō dōsa
（同時）並行動作

concurrent processing
dōji shori; heikō shori
同時処理；並行処理

condensed information
asshuku jōhō
圧縮情報

condition
jōken
条件

condition code (CC)
jōken kōdo; kondeishon-kōdo (CC)
条件コード；コンディション・コード

condition entry
jōken entori
条件エントリ

condition indicator
jōken hyōshiki
条件標識

condition name
jōken mei
条件名

condition register
jōken rejisuta
条件レジスタ

condition stub
jōken sutabu
条件スタブ

conditional
jōken; jōkentsuki
条件；条件付き

conditional assembly instruction
jōkentsuki asenburi meirei
条件付きアセンブリ命令

conditional branch
jōkentsuki bunki
条任付き分岐

conditional branch instruction
jōkentsuki bunki meirei
条件付き分岐命令

conditional expression
jōken shiki
条件式

conditional jump
jōkentsuki tobikoshi
条件付き飛び越し

conditional jump instruction
jōkentsuki tobikoshi meirei
条件付き飛び越し命令

conditional register
jōken rejisuta
条件レジスタ

conditional statement
jōken bun; jōken meirei
条件文；条件命令

conditional transfer
jōkentsuki tobikoshi
条件付き飛び越し

conditional transfer instruction
jōkentsuki tobikoshi meirei
条件付き飛び越し命令

conditional variable
jōken hensū
条件変数

conditions of application
riyō jittai
利用実態

conditions of use
shiyō jōken
使用条件

conferencing
kaigi
会議

configuration
kōsei
構成

congestion
heisoku; konsatsu
閉塞；混雑

connect
setsuzoku suru
接続する

connect time
setsuzoku jikan
接続時間

connectable
setsuzokukanō
接続可能

connection
setsuzoku
接続

connection cable
setsuzokuyō kēburu
接続用ケーブル

connection interface
ichi kenshutsuki; kenshutsu intafuēsu
位置検出器；検出インタフェース

connective
ketsugōshi; renketsugo
結合子；連結語

connectivity
renketsusei
連結性

connector
ketsugōshi; konekuta
結合子；コネクタ

connector pin
konekuta-pin
コネクタ・ピン

consecutive
renzoku
連続

consecutive file
renzoku fuairu
連続ファイル

consecutive number
renzoku bangō
連続番号

consecutive processing
renzoku shori
連続処理

consecutive storage
renzoku kioku
連続記憶

conservation
tairyū
滞留

consistency
itchi
一致

console
konsoru; seigyotaku; sōsataku
コンソル；制御卓；操作卓

console display
sōsataku hyōji sōchi
操作卓表示装置

console message
sōsataku messēji
操作卓メッセージ

console panel
sōsa ban
操作盤

console unit
seigyo taku; sōsa taku
制御卓; 操作卓

constant (*noun*)
teisū
定数

constant ratio code
teiritsu kōdo
定率コード

constant value control
teichi seigyo
定値制御

content(s)
naiyō
内容

content-addressable memory (CAM)
rensō kioku (CAM)
連想記憶

content-addressable store
rensō kioku sōchi
連想記憶装置

content-independent address
naiyō dokuritsu adoresu
内容独立アドレス

contents analysis
naiyō bunseki
内容分析

contents retrieval
naiyō kensaku
内容検索

contents supervision
naiyō kanshi
内容監視

contention
kontenshon
コンテンション

context
bummyaku
文脈

context editing
bummyaku henshū
文脈編集

context-free
bummyaku jiyū
文脈自由

context-free grammar
bummyaku jiyū bumpō
文脈自由文法

context-free language
bummyaku jiyū gengo
文脈自由言語

context searching
bummyaku tansaku
文脈探索

context-sensitive
bummyaku izon
文脈依存

context-sensitive grammar
bummyaku izon bumpō
文脈依存文法

context-sensitive language
bummyaku izon gengo
文脈依存言語

contiguous
ichiren
一連

continuation
keizoku
継続

continuation column
keizoku hyōji keta
継続表示桁

continuation line
ato no gyō; keizoku gyō
あとの行; 継続行

continuous
renzoku
連続

continuous action
renzoku dōsa
連続動作

continuous distribution
renzoku bumpu
連続分布

continuous information
renzoku jōhō
連続情報

continuous information source
renzoku jōhō gen
連続情報源

continuous operation
renzoku sōsa
連続操作

continuous processing
renzoku shori
連続処理

continuous processing system
renzoku shori shisutemu
連続処理システム

continuous record
renzoku rekōdo
連続レコード

continuous running
renzoku unten
連続運転

continuous stationery
renzoku inji yōshi; renzoku insatsushi
連続印字用紙; 連続印刷紙

continuous system
renzoku shisutemu
連続システム

continuous system simulation
renzoku shisutemu-shimyurēshon
連続システム・
シミュレーション

contour line
tōkō sen
等高線

contour map
tōkō senzu
等高線図

contract programming
keiyaku puroguramingu
契約プログラミング

contrast
kontorasuto
コントラスト

control (*noun*)
kanri; kanshi; seigyo
管理; 監視; 制御

control (*verb*)
kanshi suru; seigyo suru
監視する；制御する

control abstraction
seigyo chūshōka
制御抽象化

control algorithm
seigyo arugorizumu
制御アルゴリズム

control block
seigyo burokku
制御ブロック

control break
seigyo no kireme
制御の切れ目

control bus
seigyo basu
制御バス

control card
seigyo kādo
制御カード

control character
seigyo moji
制御文字

control circuit
seigyo kairo
制御回路

control command
seigyo shirei
制御指令

control computer
seigyo'yō keisanki
制御用計算機

control counter
seigyo kaunta
制御カウンタ

control desk
seigyo taku
制御卓

control error
seigyo hensa
制御偏差

control field
seigyo fuiirudo
制御フィールド

control flow
seigyo no nagare
制御の流れ

control format
seigyo shoshiki
制御書式

control function
seigyo kinō
制御機能

control hierarchy
seigyo kaisō
制御階層

control hole
seigyo senkō
制御せん孔

control information
seigyo jōhō
制御情報

control instruction
seigyo meirei
制御命令

control instruction register
seigyo meirei rejisuta
制御命令レジスタ

control interface
seigyo intafuēsu
制御インタフェース

control key
seigyo kii
制御キー

control level
seigyo reberu
制御レベル

control loop
seigyo rūpu
制御ループ

control mechanism
seigyo kikō
制御機構

control mode
seigyo mōdo
制御モード

control operation
seigyo sōsa
制御操作

control panel
seigyo ban; sōsa ban
制御盤；操作盤

control procedure
seigyo tetsuzuki
制御手続き

control processor
seigyo purosessa
制御プロセッサ

control program
seigyo puroguramu
制御プログラム

control program for microprocessors (CP/M)
maikuropurosessa'yō seigyo puroguramu (CP/M)
マイクロプロセッサ用制御プログラム

control punch
seigyo senkō
制御せん孔

control register
seigyo rejisuta
制御レジスタ

control routine
seigyo rūchin
制御ルーチン

control section
seigyo setsu
制御節

control sequence
seigyo shiikensu
制御シーケンス

control signal
seigyo shingō
制御信号

control statement
seigyo bun
制御文

control station
seigyo kyoku; seigyo tanmatsu
制御局；制御端末

control storage
seigyo kioku
制御記憶

control storage for system
shisutemu'yō seigyo kioku
システム用制御記憶

control storage for user
yūza'yō seigyo kioku
ユーザ用制御記憶

control store
seigyo kioku sōchi
制御記憶装置

41

control structure
seigyo kōzō
制御構造

control system
seigyo shisutemu
制御システム

control system operation
seigyo shisutemu sōsa
制御システム操作

control technique
seigyo gihō
制御技法

control terminal
seigyo tanmatsu (sōchi)
制御端末（装置）

control transfer
seigyo ikō
制御移行

control unit (CU)
seigyo sōchi; seigyo yunitto (CU)
制御装置；制御ユニット

control word
seigyo go; seigyo wādo
制御語；制御ワード

controlled system
seigyo taishō
制御対象

controlled variable
seigyo ryō
制御量

controller
seigyo sōchi
制御装置

conventional
kyūrai no
旧来の

convergence
shūsoku
収束

conversational
kaiwa(gata); taiwa(gata)
会話(型)；対話(型)

conversational compiler
kaiwagata konpaira
会話型コンパイラ

conversational language
kaiwagata gengo
会話型言語

conversational mode
kaiwa mōdo; kaiwagata mōdo
会話モード；会話型モード

conversational processing
kaiwagata shori
会話型処理

conversational utility
kaiwagata yūteiritei
会話型ユーティリティ

conversion
henkan; ikō
変換；移行

conversion code
henkan kigō
変換記号

conversion program
henkan puroguramu
変換プログラム

convert (verb)
henkan suru
変換する

convert feature
henkan kikō
変換機構

converter
henkanki; konbāta
変換器；コンバータ

converting
henkan
変換

coordinate (math.)
zahyō
座標

coordinate grid
zahyō kōshi
座標格子

coordinate system
zahyō kei
座標系

coordination
kyōchō
協調

coprocessor
kopurosessa
コプロセッサ

coroutine
korūchin
コルーチン

copy (verb)
fukusha suru; kopii suru;
tenki suru
複写する；コピーする；
転記する

copy library
fukusha raiburari
複写ライブラリ

copy module
fukusha mojyūru
複写モジュール

core
jishin; koa
磁心；コア

core array
jishin arei
磁心アレイ

core dump
koa-danpu
コア・ダンプ

core image
koa-imēji
コア・イメージ

core memory
jishin kioku
磁心記憶

core plane
koa-purein
コア・プレイン

core storage
jishin kioku
磁心記憶

core store
jishin kioku sōchi
磁心記憶装置

correction
hosei; shūsei; teisei
補正；修正；訂正

corrective maintenance
shūri hoshu
修理保守

correlation
sōkan
相関

correlation analysis
sōkan kaiseki
相関解析

corrupted data
hason sareta dēta
破損されたデータ

corruption of data
dēta no hason
データの破損

cost
hiyō; kosuto
費用；コスト

cost analysis
hiyō bunseki
費用分析

cost-effective
hiyō yūkō
費用有効

cost-effectiveness
hiyō yūkōsei
費用有効性

cost information
hiyō jōhō
費用情報

cost minimization
hiyō saishōka
費用最小化

cost-performance
hiyō-seinō; kosuto-pafuōmansu
費用性能；コスト・
パフォーマンス

cost reduction
hiyō teigen
費用低減

count
kaunto
カウント

counter
kaunta; keisūki
カウンタ；計数器

coupler
kapura
カプラ

coupling
ketsugō
結合

courier font
kūrie-fuonto
クーリエ・フォント

courseware
kōsuea
コースウェア

CP (card punch)
CP (kādo senkō sōchi; kādo senkōki)
カードせん孔装置；
カードせん孔機

CP (communication processor)
CP (tsūshin'yō purosessa)
通信用プロセッサ

CPE (computer performance evaluation)
CPE (keisanki seinō hyōka)
計算機性能評価

cpi (characters per inch)
cpi (moji/inchi)
文字／インチ

CPM (cards per minute)
CPM (kādo/fun)
カード／分

cpm (characters per minute)
cpm (moji/fun)
文字／分

CPM (critical-path method)
CPM (genkai keiro hō; kurichikaru-pasu hō)
限界経路法；クリチカル・
パス法

CP/M (control program for microprocessors)
CP/M (maikuropurosessa'yō seigyo puroguramu)
マイクロプロセッサ用制御
プログラム

cps (characters per second)
cps (moji/byō)
文字／秒

CPU (central processing unit)
CPU (chūō shori sōchi)
中央処理装置

CPU scheduler
CPU sukejūra
CPUスケジューラ

CR (card reader)
CR (kādo yomitori sōchi; kādo yomitoriki)
カード読み取り装置；
カード読み取り機

CR (carriage return)
CR (fukki; kaigyō fukki)
復帰；改行復帰

crash
shōtotsu
衝突

CRC (cyclic redundancy check)
CRC (junkai jōchō kensa)
巡回冗長検査

creation
sakusei
作成

creative system
sōzō shisutemu
創造システム

crippled mode operation
koshō mōdo dōsa
故障モード動作

criterion
kijun
基準

critical
kiken; kurichikaru
危険；クリチカル

critical path
genkai keiro;
kurichikaru-pasu
限界経路；クリチカル・パス

critical-path method (CPM)
genkai keiro hō;
kurichikaru-pasu hō (CPM)
限界経路法；
クリチカル・パス法

critical region
kiken ryō'iki
危険領域

critical section
kiken chi'iki
危険地域

CRMT (cartridge magnetic tape)
CRMT (kātorijji jiki tēpu)
カートリッジ磁気テープ

cross assembler
kurosu-asenbura
クロス・アセンブラ

cross-check
kurosu-chekku
クロス・チェック

cross compiler
kurosu-konpaira
クロス・コンパイラ

cross-correlation
sōgo sōkan
相互相関

cross-reference
sōgo sanshō
相互参照

cross-reference list
sōgo sanshō hyō
相互参照表

cross-reference table
sōgo sanshō hyō
相互参照表

cross talk
rōwa
漏話

CRT (cathode-ray tube)
CRT (inkyokusenkan)
CRT；陰極線管

CRT memory (cathode-ray-tube memory)
CRT kioku (inkyokusenkan kioku)
CRT記憶；陰極線管記憶

CRT visual display unit (cathode-ray-tube visual display unit)
CRT hyōji sōchi (inkyokusenkan hyōji sōchi)
CRT表示装置；
陰極線管表示装置

cryptographic technique
angō shuhō
暗号手法

cryptography
angōhō
暗号法

cryptology
angōgaku
暗号学

CSW (channel status word)
CSW (chaneru jōtai go)
チャネル状態語

CTD (charge transfer device)
CTD (denka tensō soshi)
電荷転送素子

CTS (cold-type system)
CTS (korudo-taipu-shisutemu)
コルド・タイプ・システム

CU (control unit)
CU (seigyo yunitto)
制御ユニット

cumulative
ruiseki
累積

cumulative indexing
ruiseki sakuintsuke
累積索引付け

cumulative percentage
ruiseki ritsu
累積率

cumulative remainder
ruiseki saritsu
累積差率

current (electricity)
denryū
電流

current (present)
genzai
現在

current amplification factor
denryū zōfuku ritsu
電流増幅率

current instruction register (CIR)
karento meirei rejisuta (CIR)
カレント命令レジスタ

current mode logic (CML)
denryū mōdo ronri (CML)
電流モード論理

current position
genzai ichi
現在位置

current record
genzai rekōdo
現在レコード

cursor
ichi hyōji kikō; kāsoru
位置表示機構；カーソル

cursor addressing
kāsoru-adoresu shitei
カーソル・アドレス指定

cursor key
kāsoru-kii
カーソル・キー

cursor position
kāsoru no ichi
カーソルの位置

curve
kyokusen
曲線

curve detection
kyokusen kenshutsu
曲線検出

curve-pattern
kyokusen patān
曲線パターン

curve-pattern compaction
kyokusen patān asshuku
曲線パターン圧縮

curved line
kyokusen
曲線

custom engineer (CE)
hoshu'in (CE)
保守員

custom LSI
kasutamu LSI
カスタムLSI

custom program
kasutomu-puroguramu
カスタム・プログラム

cut off (*verb*)
setsudan suru
切断する

cybernetic control
saibaneteikku seigyo
サイバネティック制御

cybernetic system
saibaneteikku-shisutemu
サイバネティック・システム

cybernetics
saibaneteikkusu
サイバネティックス

cycle
dankai; saikuru; shūki
段階；サイクル；周期

cycle check
saikuru-chekku; shūki kensa
サイクル・チェック；周期検査

cycle count
saikuru-kaunto
サイクル・カウント

cycle counter
saikuru-kaunta
サイクル・カウンタ

cycle index
saikuru-indekkusu
サイクル・インデックス

cycle time
saikuru jikan; saikuru-taimu
サイクル時間；サイクル・
タイム

cycle timer
saikuru-taima
サイクル・タイマ

cycles per second
saikuru/byō
サイクル／秒

cyclic code
junkai fugō
巡回符号

cyclic redundancy check (CRC)
junkai jōchō kensa (CRC)
巡回冗長検査

cyclic redundancy check character
junkai jōchō kensa moji
巡回冗長検査文字

cyclic shift
junkan keta okuri; junkan shifuto
循環桁送り；循環シフト

cyclic storage
junkan kioku
循環記憶

cyclic structure
junkanteki kōzō
循環的構造

cylinder
shirinda
シリンダ

cylinder operation
shirinda sōsa
シリンダ操作

cylinder overflow
shirinda afure
シリンダ溢れ

cylinder overflow area
shirinda afure'iki
シリンダ溢れ域

cypher
angō
暗号

D

DA (differential analyzer)
DA (bibun kaisekiki)
微分解析器

D/A (digital-to-analog)
D/A (deijitaru-anarogu)
ディジタル・アナログ

D/A conversion (digital-to-analog conversion)
D/A henkan (deijitaru-anarogu henkan)
Ｄ／Ａ変換；ディジタル・
アナログ変換

D/A converter (digital-to-analog converter)
D/A henkanki; D/A konbāta (deijitaru-anarogu henkanki; deijitaru-anarogu konbāta)
Ｄ／Ａ変換器；Ｄ／Ａコンバータ；
ディジタル・アナログ変換器；
ディジタル・アナログ・
コンバータ

DAC (digital-to-analog converter)
DAC (deijitaru-anarogu henkanki; deijitaru-anarogu-konbāta)
ディジタル・アナログ変換器；
ディジタル・アナログ・
コンバータ

dagger operation
dagā-operēshon
ダガー・オペレーション

daisychain
deijii-chein
ディジー・チェイン

daisywheel printer
deijii-hoiiru-purinta
ディジ・ホイール・プリンタ

DAM (direct-access method)
DAM (chokusetsu akusesu hōshiki)
直接アクセス方式

damping
gensui
減衰

damping oscillation
gensui shindō
減衰振動

damping time
gensui jikan
減衰時間

DASD (direct-access storage device)
DASD (chokusetsu akusesu kioku sōchi)
直接アクセス記憶装置

DAT (dynamic address translator)
DAT (dōteki adoresu henkanki)
動的アドレス変換器

data
dēta; ichi jōhō; shiryō
データ；位置情報；資料

data abstraction
dēta chūshōka
データ抽象化

data acquisition
dēta shūshū
データ収集

data acquisition and control system
dēta shūsū-seigyo shisutemu
データ収集-制御システム

data acquisition system
dēta shūshū shisutemu
データ収集システム

data adapter unit
dēta-adaputa sōchi
データ・アダプタ装置

data address
dēta-adoresu
データ・アドレス

data administration
dēta kanri
データ管理

data administrator
dēta kanrisha
データ管理者

data array
dēta hairetsu
データ配列

data attribute
dēta zokusei
データ属性

data buffer
dēta-baffua
データ・バッファ

data bus
dēta-basu
データ・バス

data bus enable (DBE)
dēta-basu-enēburu (DBE)
データ・バス・エネーブル

data capacity
dēta yōryō
データ容量

data capture
dēta kiroku; dēta-kyapucha
データ記録;
データ・キャプチャ

data capture utility
dēta kiroku yūteiritei
データ記録ユーティリティ

data card
dēta-kādo
データ・カード

data carrier
dēta-kyarya
データ・キャリャ

data cell
dēta-seru
データ・セル

data cell drive
dēta-seru sōchi
データ・セル装置

data center
dēta-senta
データ・センタ

data chaining
dēta rensa
データ連鎖

data channel
dēta-chaneru
データ・チャネル

data channel multiplexer
dēta-chaneru-maruchipurekusa
データ・チャネル・
マルチプレクサ

data check
dēta-chekku; dēta kensa
データ・チェック; データ検査

data cleaning
dēta tenken
データ点検

data code
dēta-kōdo
データ・コード

data coding
dēta fugōka; dēta-kōdeingu;
dēta-kōdoka
データ符号化; データ・
コーディング; データ・コード化

data collection
dēta shūshū
データ収集

data collection system
dēta shūshū shisutemu
データ収集システム

data communication control
dēta tsūshin seigyo
データ通信制御

data communication equipment
dēta tsūshin kiki
データ通信機器

data communication subsystem (DCS)
dēta tsūshin sōchi (DCS)
データ通信装置

data communication system
dēta tsūshin shisutemu
データ通信システム

data communication terminal
dēta tsūshin tanmatsu (sōchi)
データ通信端末（装置）

data communication unit
dēta tsūshin sōchi
データ通信装置

data communications
dēta tsūshin
データ通信

data communications exchange
dēta tsūshin kōkan
データ通信交換

data compaction
dēta asshuku
データ圧縮

data compression
dēta asshuku
データ圧縮

data consistency
dēta seigōsei
データ整合性

data constellation
dēta gun
データ群

data control
dēta seigyo
データ制御

data control block (DCB)
dēta seigyo burokku (DCB)
データ制御ブロック

data control unit
dēta seigyo sōchi
データ制御装置

data conversion
dēta henkan
データ変換

data conversion feature
dēta henkan kinō
データ変換機能

data corruption
dēta hason
データ破損

data definition
dēta teigi
データ定義

data definition statement
dēta teigi sutētomento
データ定義ステートメント

data delimiter
dēta-derimita
データ・デリミタ

data description
dēta kijutsu
データ記述

data description attribute
dēta kijutsu zokusei
データ記述属性

data description entry
dēta kijutsu kōmoku
データ記述項目

data description language (DDL)
dēta kijutsu gengo (DDL)
データ記述言語

data dictionary
dēta jisho
データ辞書

data-directed input/output
dētagata nyūshutsuryoku
データ型入出力

data directory
dēta-dairekutori
データ・ディレクトリ

data display
dēta-deisupurei; dēta hyōji
データ・ディスプレィ；
データ表示

data display unit
dēta hyōji sōchi
データ表示装置

data division
dēta bu
データ部

data element
dēta yōso
データ要素

data encryption
dēta angōka
データ暗号化

data entry
dēta-entori; dēta nyūryoku
データ・エントリ；データ入力

data entry keyboard
dēta nyūryoku kemban sōchi
データ入力鍵盤装置

data entry machine
dēta nyūryoku kiki
データ入力機器

data entry switch
dēta nyūryoku suitchi
データ入力スイッチ

data error
dēta ayamari
データ誤り

data exchange
dēta kōkan
データ交換

data file
dēta-fuairu
データ・ファイル

data file compaction
dēta-fuairu asshuku
データ・ファイル圧縮

data flow
dēta nagare
データ流れ

data flow analysis
dēta nagare bunseki
データ流れ分析

data flow diagram
dēta nagare zu
データ流れ図

data flowchart
dēta nagare zu
データ流れ図

data format
dēta keishiki; dēta shoshiki
データ形式；データ書式

data format item
dēta keishiki kōmoku;
dēta shoshiki kōmoku
データ形式項目；データ書式項目

data gathering
dēta shūshū
データ収集

data handling
dēta shori
データ処理

data hierarchy
dēta kaisō
データ階層

data independence
dēta dokuritsu
データ独立

data input
dēta nyūryoku
データ入力

data input area
dēta nyūryoku ryōiki
データ入力領域

data input station
dēta nyūryoku sutēshon
データ入力ステーション

data inscriber
dēta kirokuki
データ記録器

data integrity
dēta kanzensei
データ完全性

data interchange
dēta chūkei
データ中継

data item
dēta kōmoku
データ項目

data item validation
dēta kōmoku kenshō
データ項目検証

data language
dēta gengo
データ言語

data layout
dēta keishiki
データ形式

data length
dēta chō
データ長

data link
dēta-rinku
データ・リンク

data link control
dēta-rinku seigyo
データ・リンク制御

data link escape (DLE)
densō seigyo kakuchō (DLE)
伝送制御拡張

data link escape character
densō seigyo kakuchō moji
伝送制御拡張文字

data list
dēta-risuto
データ・リスト

data logger
dēta-roga
データ・ロガ

data logging
dēta-rogingu
データ・ロギング

data loss
dēta datsuraku; dēta sonshitsu
データ脱落；データ損失

data maintenance
dēta hoshu
データ保守

data management
dēta kanri
データ管理

data management common code
dēta kanri kyōtsū kōdo
データ管理共通コード

data management define table
dēta kanri teigi tēburu
データ管理定義テーブル

data management routine (DMR)
dēta kanri rūchin (DMR)
データ管理ルーチン

data management system (DMS)
dēta kanri shisutemu (DMS)
データ管理システム

data manipulation
dēta sōsa
データ操作

data manipulation language (DML)
dēta sōsa gengo (DML)
データ操作言語

data map
dēta-mappu
データ・マップ

data materialization
dēta jittaika
データ実体化

data medium
dēta baitai
データ媒体

data migration
dēta isō
データ移送

data mobility
dēta idōsei
データ移動性

data mode
dēta-mōdo
データ・モード

data model
dēta-moderu
データ・モデル

data module
dēta-mojyūru
データ・モジュール

data-name
dēta mei
データ名

data organization
dēta hensei
データ編成

data origination
dēta-orijinēshon
データ・オリジネーション

data path
dēta keiro
データ経路

data pen
dēta-pen
データ・ペン

data plotter
dēta-purotta
データ・プロッタ

data preparation
dēta jumbi
データ準備

data processing (DP)
dēta shori (DP)
データ処理

data-processing center (DPC)
dēta shori senta (DPC)
データ処理センタ

data-processing equipment
dēta shori kiki
データ処理機器

data-processing operation
dēta shori dōsa; dēta shori sōsa
データ処理動作;
データ処理操作

data-processing system
dēta shori shisutemu
データ処理システム

data processor
dēta shori sōchi
データ処理装置

data protection
dēta hogo
データ保護

data record
dēta-rekōdo
データ・レコード

data recorder
dēta kirokuki; dēta-rekōda
データ記録器;
データ・レコーダ

data recording
dēta kiroku; dēta-rekōdeingu
データ記録;
データ・レコーディング

data reduction
dēta seiri
データ整理

data reduction center (DRC)
dēta seiri senta (DRC)
データ整理センタ

data representation
dēta hyōgen
データ表現

data restructuring
dēta saikōsei
データ再構成

data retrieval
dēta kensaku
データ検索

data security
dēta kimitsu hogo
データ機密保護

data segment
dēta-segumento
データ・セグメント

data semantics
dēta imiron
データ意味論

data service
dēta-sābisu
データ・サービス

data set (DS)
dēta-setto (DS)
データ・セット

data set allocation
dēta-setto haibun
データ・セット配分

data set control block (DSCB)
dēta-setto seigyo burokku (DSCB)
データ・セット制御ブロック

data set label
dēta-setto-raberu
データ・セット・ラベル

data set organization
dēta-setto hensei
データ・セット編成

data set ready (DSR)
dēta-setto-redei (DSR)
データ・セット・レディ

data sharing
dēta kyōyū
データ共有

data sheet
dēta yōshi
データ用紙

data signaling rate
dēta shingō sokudo
データ信号速度

data sink
dēta-shinku
データ・シンク

data source
dēta gen
データ源

data staging
dēta dankaika
データ段階化

data statement
dēta bun
データ文

data station
dēta-sutēshon; dēta tanmatsu
データ・ステーション；
データ端末

data storage
dēta kioku
データ記憶

data structure
dēta kōzō
データ構造

data structure choice
dēta kōzō sentaku
データ構造選択

data structure diagram
dēta kōzō zu
データ構造図

data sublanguage
dēta jun gengo
データ準言語

data submodel
dēta-sabu-moderu
データ・サブ・モデル

data subset
dēta-sabu-setto
データ・サブ・セット

data switching
dēta kōkan
データ交換

data system(s)
dēta-shisutemu
データ・システム

data tablet
dēta-taburetto
データ・タブレット

data tape
dēta-tēpu
データ・テープ

data terminal
dēta tanmatsu (sōchi)
データ端末（装置）

data terminal equipment
dēta tanmatsu kiki
データ端末機器

data terminal ready (DTR)
dēta tanmatsu sōchi redei (DTR)
データ端末装置レディ

data test
dēta-tesuto
データ・テスト

data track
dēta-torakku
データ・トラック

data transfer
dēta tensō
データ転送

data transfer channel
dēta tsūshinro
データ通信路

data transfer rate
dēta tensō sokudo
データ転送速度

data transfer speed
dēta tensō sokudo
データ転送速度

data translation
dēta henkan
データ変換

data transmission
dēta densō
データ伝送

data transmission circuit
dēta densō kaisen
データ伝送回線

data transmission efficiency
dēta densō koritsu
データ伝送効率

data transmission network
dēta densō nettowāku
データ伝送ネットワーク

data transmission system
dēta densō shisutemu
データ伝送システム

data transmission unit
dēta densō sōchi
データ伝送装置

data transmission utilization ratio
yūkō dēta densō ritsu
有効データ伝送率

data type
dēta no kata; dēta-taipu
データの型；データ・タイプ

data unit
dēta tan'i
データ単位

data unit control
dēta tan'i seigyo
データ単位制御

data validation
dēta datō kensa
データ妥当検査

data verification
dēta kensa
データ検査

data-verifying program
dēta kensa puroguramu
データ検査プログラム

data vetting
dēta kensa
データ検査

data word
dēta go
データ語

databank
dētabanku
データバンク

database
dētabēsu
データベース

database administrator
dētabēsu kanrisha
データベース管理者

database approach
dētabēsu-apurōchi
データベース・アプローチ

database control system (DBCS)
dētabēsu seigyo shisutemu
(DBCS)
データベース制御システム

49

database description
dētabēsu kijutsu
データベース記述

database exception condition
dētabēsu reigai jōken
データベース例外条件

database identifier
dētabēsu ichi'imei
データベース一意名

database key
dētabēsu-kii
データベース・キー

database language
dētabēsu gengo
データベース言語

database machine
dētabēsu kikai
データベース機械

database management
dētabēsu kanri
データベース管理

database management system (DBMS)
dētabēsu kanri shisutemu (DBMS)
データベース管理システム

database portability
dētabēsu ishokusei
データベース移植性

database procedure
dētabēsu tetsuzuki
データベース手続き

database status indicator
dētabēsu jōtai shijishi
データベース状態指示子

database structure
dētabēsu kōzō
データベース構造

database support
dētabēsu-sapōto
データベース・サポート

database system
dētabēsu-shisutemu
データベース・システム

datapen reader
dētapen-riida
データペン・リーダ

dB (decibel)
dB (deshiberu)
デシベル

DBCS (database control system)
DBCS (dētabēsu seigyo shisutemu)
データベース制御システム

DBE (data bus enable)
DBE (dēta-basu-enēburu)
データ・バス・エネーブル

DBMS (database management system)
DBMS (dētabēsu kanri shisutemu)
データベース管理システム

DC (device control)
DC (sōchi seigyo)
装置制御

DC (direct current)
DC (chokuryū)
直流

DC amplifier (direct-current amplifier)
DC zōfukuki (chokuryū zōfukuki)
DC増幅器；直流増幅器

DC regulated circuit (direct-current regulated circuit)
DC teiden'atsu kairo (chokuryū teiden'atsu kairo)
DC定電圧回路；
直流定電圧回路

DCB (data control block)
DCB (dēta seigyo burokku)
データ制御ブロック

DCS (data communication subsystem)
DCS (dēta tsūshin sōchi)
データ通信装置

DCTL (direct-coupled transistor logic)
DCTL (chokketsugata toranjisuta ronri)
直結型トランジスタ論理

DD (double density)
DD (bai mitsudo)
倍密度

DDA (digital differential analyzer)
DDA (keisūgata bibun kaisekiki)
計数型微分解析器

DDC (direct digital control)
DDC (chokusetsu deijitaru seigyo)
直接ディジタル制御

DDE (direct data entry)
DDE (chokusetsu dēta nyūryoku)
直接データ入力

DDL (data description language)
DDL (dēta kijutsu gengo)
データ記述言語

DDP (distributed data processing)
DDP (bunsangata dēta shori)
分散型データ処理

DDX (digital data exchange)
DDX (deijitaru-dēta kōkanmō)
ディジタル・データ交換網

dead time
deddo-taimu
デッド・タイム

deadlock
deddorokku
デッドロック

deblock
hiburokkuka suru
非ブロック化する

deblocking
hiburokkuka
非ブロック化

debug
debaggu suru; tenaosu
デバッグする；手直す

debugging
debagginngu; tenaoshi
デバッギング；手直し

debugging aid
debagginngu-eido
デバッギング・エイド

debugging routine
debagginngu-rūchin
デバッギング・ルーチン

decay
gensui
減衰

decay time
gensui jikan
減衰時間

decentralization
bunsanka
分散化

decentralized
bunsangata
分散型

decentralized computer
bunsangata keisanki;
bunsangata konpyūta
分散型計算機;
分散型コンピュータ

decentralized computer network
bunsangata keisankimō;
bunsangata konpyūta-nettowāku
分散型計算機網;
分散型コンピュータ・
ネットワーク

decentralized control
bunsangata seigyo
分散型制御

decentralized data processing
bunsangata dēta shori
分散型データ処理

decentralized information system
bunsangata jōhō shisutemu
分散型情報システム

decentralized processing
bunsangata dēta shori
分散型データ処理

decentralized structure
bunsangata kōzō
分散型構造

decentralized unit
bunsangata sōchi
分散型装置

decibel (dB)
deshiberu (dB)
デジベル

decimal
jisshin(hō)
10進(法)

decimal address
jisshin adoresu
10進アドレス

decimal arithmetic
jisshin enzan
10進演算

decimal arithmetic function
jisshin enzan kikō
10進演算機構

decimal code
jisshin kōdō
10進コード

decimal counter
jisshin kaunta
10進カウンタ

decimal digit
jisshin sūji
10進数字

decimal feature
jisshin enzan kikō
10進演算機構

decimal normalization
jisshin seikika
10進正規化

decimal notation
jisshin hō
10進法

decimal number
jisshin sū
10進数

decimal number format
jisshin sū shoshiki
10進数書式

decimal number system
jisshin hō
10進法

decimal numeral
jisshin sū
10進数

decimal numeration system
jisshin hō
10進法

decimal operation
jisshin enzan
10進演算

decimal operator
jisshin enzanshi
10進演算子

decimal overflow
jisshin keta afure
10進桁溢れ

decimal overflow exception
jisshin keta afure reigai
10進桁溢れ例外

decimal point
(jisshin) shōsūten
（10進）小数点

decimal radix
jisshin kisū
10進基数

decimal system
jisshin hō
10進法

decimal-to-binary conversion
jisshin-nishin henkan
10進-2進変換

decision
deshijon; handan; hantei; kettei
デシジョン；判断；判定；決定

decision analysis
kettei kaiseki
決定解析

decision box
handan kigō
判断記号

decision control
kettei seigyo
決定制御

decision criteria
kettei kijun
決定基準

decision element
ronri soshi
論理素子

decision feedback system
hantei kikan hōshiki
判定帰還方式

decision instruction
handan meirei
判断命令

decision level
shikibetsu reberu
識別レベル

decision making
ishi kettei
意思決定

decision-making capability
ishi kettei kinō
意思決定機能

decision-making process
ishi kettei katei
意思決定過程

decision-making strategy
ishi kettei senryaku
意思決定戦略

decision-making system
ishi kettei shisutemu
意思決定システム

decision-making theory
ishi kettei riron
意思決定理論

decision mechanism
kettei kikō
決定機構

decision process
kettei katei
決定過程

decision strategy
kettei senryaku
決定戦略

decision support system (DSS)
ishi kettei shien shisutemu (DSS)
意思決定支援システム

decision symbol
handan kigō
判断記号

decision table
deshijon-tēburu; kettei hyō
デシジョン・テーブル；決定表

decision theory
kettei riron
決定理論

deck
dekku
デック

declaration
sengen
宣言

declarative macroinstruction
sengen makuro meirei
宣言マクロ命令

declarative statement
sengen bun
宣言文

declarator
sengenshi
宣言子

decode
dekōdo suru; fukugō suru;
kaidoku suru; kaisetsu suru
デコードする；復号する；
解読する；解説する

decode cycle
dekōdo-saikuru
デコード・サイクル

decoder
dekōda; fukugōki; kaidokuki
デコーダ；復号器；解読器

decoding
dekōdeingu; fukugō;
kaidoku; kaisetsu
デコーディング；復号；
解読；解説

decoding circuit
dekōdeingu kairo;
dekōdeingu kaisen
デコーディング回路；
デコーディング回線

decollate
bunri suru
分離する

decollator
bunriki; dekorēta
分離器；デコレータ

decouple
genketsugō suru
減結合する

decoupling
genketsugō
減結合

decrement
dekuremento; gembun
デクレメント；減分

dedicated
sen'yō
専用

dedicated computer
sen'yō keisanki
専用計算機

dedicated line
sen'yō kaisen
専用回線

dedicated system
sen'yō shisutemu
専用システム

default (*noun*)
shōryakuji kaishaku
省略時解釈

default assumption
shōryakuji kaishaku
省略時解釈

default option
shōryakuji opushon
省略時オプション

default value
shōryakuji no atai
省略時の値

defect (*noun*)
kekkan
欠陥

defective
kekkan no aru
欠陥のある

deferred
chien; sueoki
遅延；据え置き

deferred entry
sueoki iriguchi
据え置き入り口

deferred exit
sueoki deguchi
据え置き出口

deferred update
chien kōshin
遅延更新

define
kakutei suru; kitei suru;
teigi suru
確定する；規定する；定義する

define constant statement
teisū teigi bun
定数定義文

define storage statement
kioku'iki teigi bun
記憶域定義文

defined
kakutei; kitei; teigi(sumi)
確定；規定；定義（済み）

defined instruction
teigisumi meirei
定義済み命令

definition
kakutei; kitei; teigi
確定；規定；定義

deflection
henkō
偏向

deflection circuit
henkō kairo
偏向回路

deflection plate
henkō ban
偏向板

deformation
henkei
変形

degeneracy
shukutai
縮退

degenerate
shukutai (shita)
縮退（した）

degradation
retsuka; seinōteika
劣化；性能低下

degradation factor
seinōteika insū
性能低下因数

delay (*noun*)
chien; okure
遅延；遅れ

delay circuit
chien kairo
遅延回路

delay distortion
chien hizumi
遅延歪み

delay element
chien soshi
遅延素子

delay equalization
chien tōka
遅延等化

delay equalizer
chien tōkaki
遅延等化器

delay factor
chien inshi
遅延因子

delay flip-flop
chien furippu-furoppu
遅延フリップ・フロップ

delay line
chien sen
遅延線

delay line clock
chien sen kurokku
遅延線クロック

delay line store
chien sen kioku sōchi
遅延線記憶装置

delay memory
chien kioku
遅延記憶

delay time
chien jikan
遅延時間

delay unit
chien sōchi
遅延装置

delayed
chien; taiji
遅延；待時

delayed response
chien ōtō
遅延応答

delayed time system
taiji hōshiki
待時方式

delayed transaction
taiji toranzakushon
待時トランザクション

delegation
i'nin
委仕

delete
masshō suru; sakujo suru
抹消する；消除する

delete character
masshō moji
抹消文字

deletion
masshō; sakujo
抹消；削除

delimit
kugiru; kyōkai shitei suru
区切る；境界指定する

delimiter
kugiri kigō; kugiri moji
区切り記号；区切り文字

delimiter macroinstruction
kyōkai makuro meirei
境界マクロ命令

delimiter statement
kugiri sutētomento
区切りステートメント

delivery (of message)
sōtatsu
送達

delta
deruta
デルタ

delta modulation
deruta henchō
デルタ変調

delta signal
deruta shingō
デルタ信号

demand (*noun*)
demando; yōkyū
デマンド；要求

demand mode
demando-mōdo
デマンド・モード

demand paging
yōkyūji pējingu
要求時ページング

demand processing
demando shori
デマンド処理

demarcation
bunkai
分界

demarcation point
bunkai ten
分界点

demodulation
fukuchō
復調

demodulator
fukuchōki
復調器

demonstration
jisshō
実証

denary notation
nishin hō
2進法

density
mitsudo
密度

dependence
jūzoku
従属

dependence list
jūzoku risuto
従属リスト

dependent
jūzoku
従属

dependent segment
jūzoku segumento
従属セグメント

dependent variable
jūzoku hensū
従属変数

depletion
deipuriishon
ディプリーション

depletion MOS (D-MOS)
deipuriishon MOS (D-MOS)
ディプリーションMOS

depletion type
deipuriishon gata
ディプリーション型

deposit (verb)
hozon suru
保存する

depress (keys)
asshuku suru
圧縮する

dequeue
dekyū
デキュー

derivation
dōshutsu
導出

derivative action
bibun dōsa
微分動作

derivative time
bibun jikan
微分時間

derived data item
hasei dēta kōmoku
派生データ項目

derived record
hasei rekōdo
派生レコード

descending order
kōjun
降順

description
kijutsu
記述

descriptive parameter
kijutsuteki parameta
記述的パラメタ

descriptor
kijutsushi
記述子

deserializer
heichokuretsu kōkan kairo
並直列交換回路

design (noun)
sekkei
設計

design automation
sekkei jidōka
設計自動化

design objective
sekkei mokuteki
設計目的

design philosophy
sekkei shisō
設計思想

design theory
sekkei riron
設計理論

designational expression
ikisaki shiki
行き先式

designator
shijishi
指示子

desk checking
takujōgata kensa
卓上型検査

desk-top computer
takujōgata keisanki
卓上型計算機

destination
atesaki; ikisaki; densō saki;
nyūryoku saki
宛先；行き先；伝送先；入力先

destination address
ikisaki adoresu
行き先アドレス

destination code
atesaki kōdo
宛先コード

destination station
atesaki sutēshon
宛先ステーション

destruction
hakai
破壊

destructive
hakai
破壊

destructive addition
hakai kasan
破壊加算

destructive reading
hakai yomidashi
破壊読み出し

destructive readout (DRO)
hakai yomidashi (DRO)
破壊読み出し

destructive storage
hakai kioku
破壊記憶

destructive test
hakai shiken
破壊試験

destructive testing
hakai shiken
破壊試験

detail card
meisai kādo
明細カード

detail file
meisai fuairu
明細ファイル

detail record
meisai rekōdo
明細レコード

detail tape
meisai tēpu
明細テープ

detailed
shōsai
詳細

detect
kempa suru; kenshutsu suru
検波する; 検出する

detecting code
kenshutsu fugō
検出符号

detection
kempa; kenshutsu; tanchi
検波; 検出; 探知

detection circuit
kenshutsu kairo
検出回路

detection system
kenshutsu hōshiki
検出方式

detector
kenshutsuki; tanchiki
検出器; 探知器

deterministic
kakutei(teki); ketteisei
確定(的); 決定性

deterministic language
ketteisei gengo
決定性言語

deterministic model
kakuteiteki moderu
確定的モデル

deterministic process
kakuteiteki katei
確定的過程

deterministic retrieval
kakuteiteki kensaku
確定的検索

deterministic simulation
kakuteiteki shimyurēshon
確定的シミュレーション

deterministic system
kakuteiteki shisutemu
確定的システム

development
kaihatsu
開発

deviation
hensa; ukai
偏差; 迂回

deviation line
ukaisen
迂回線

device
debaisu; sōchi
デバイス; 装置

device adapter
sōchi adaputa
装置アダプタ

device address
sōchi adoresu
装置アドレス

device allocation
sōchi wariate
装置割り当て

device busy
sōchi shiyōchū
装置使用中

device control (DC)
sōchi seigyo (DC)
装置制御

device control character
sōchi seigyo moji
装置制御文字

device correspondence table
sōchi tai'ōhyō
装置対応表

device dependence
sōchi izon
装置依存

device diagnostic program
sōchi shindan puroguramu
装置診断プログラム

device identification
sōchi shikibetsu
装置識別

device identifier
sōchi shikibetsushi
装置識別子

device independence
sōchi dokuritsu
装置独立

device-independent
sōchi dokuritsu
装置独立

device-independent access method
sōchi dokuritsu akusesu hōshiki
装置独立アクセス方式

device inoperable
sōchi dōsa funō
装置動作不能

device media control language (DMCL)
sōchi baitai seigyo gengo (DMCL)
装置媒体制御言語

device number
sōchi bangō
装置番号

device status word
sōchi jōtai go
装置状態語

device type
sōchi taipu
装置タイプ

Dewey decimal classification
Deyūi jisshin bunruihō
デューイ10進分類法

DI (diode)
DI (daiōdo)
ダイオード

diagnosis
shindan
診断

diagnostic check
shindan kensa
診断検査

diagnostic function test
kinō shindan tesuto
機能診断テスト

diagnostic program
shindan puroguramu
診断プログラム

diagnostic routine
shindan rūchin
診断ルーチン

diagnostic search
shindan tansaku
診断探索

diagnostic system
shindan shisutemu
診断システム

diagnostic test
shindan tesuto
診断テスト

diagnostics
shindan
診断

diagram
daiyaguramu; zu; zuhyō
ダイヤグラム；図；図表

dial
daiaru
ダイアル

dial terminal
daiaru tanmatsu sōchi
ダイアル端末装置

dialing
daiaringu; daiaru yobidashi
ダイアリング；ダイアル呼び出し

dialing adapter
daiaringu-adaputa
ダイアリング・アダプタ

dialing device
daiaru sōchi
ダイアル装置

dialing mode
daiaru-mōdo
ダイアル・モード

dialogue
taiwa
対話

dibit
sō bitto
双ビット

dichotomizing search
nibun tansaku
二分探索

dichotomy
nibunhō
二分法

dictionary
jisho
辞書

difference
sa
差

differential
bibun; sabun; sadō
微分；差分；差動

differential amplifier
sadō zōfukuki
差動増幅器

differential analyzer
bibun kaisekiki
微分解析器

differential signal
sabun shingō
差分信号

differentiating
bibun
微分

differentiating amplifier
bibun zōfukuki
微分増幅器

differentiating circuit
bibun kairo
微分回路

differentiation
bibun
微分

differentiation circuit
bibun kairo
微分回路

differentiator
bibun kairo; bibunki
微分回路；微分器

diffusion
kakusan
拡散

digit
deijitto; keta; sūji
ディジット；桁；数字

digit compression
keta asshuku
桁圧縮

digit position
keta ichi; sūji ichi
桁位置；数字位置

digit punch
sūji senkō
数字せん孔

digit select character
sūji sentaku moji
数字選択文字

digital
deijitaru; keisūgata
ディジタル；計数型

digital circuit
deijitaru kairo
ディジタル回路

digital clock
deijitaru-kurokku
ディジタル・クロック

digital communication
deijitaru tsūshin
ディジタル通信

digital computer
deijitaru keisanki;
keisūgata keisanki
ディジタル計算機；
計数型計算機

digital data
deijitaru-dēta
ディジタル・データ

digital data exchange (DDX)
deijitaru-dēta kōkanmō (DDX)
ディジタル・データ交換網

digital data processor
deijitaru-dēta shori sōchi
ディジタル・データ処理装置

digital differential analyzer (DDA)
keisūgata bibun kaisekiki (DDA)
計数型微分解析器

digital display
deijitaru-deisupurei; sūji hyōji
ディジタル・ディスプレィ；
数字表示

digital electronic computer
deijitaru denshi keisanki
ディジタル電子計算機

digital filter
deijitaru-fuiruta
ディジタル・フィルタ

digital input
deijitaru nyūryoku
ディジタル入力

digital input/output
deijitaru nyūshutsuryoku
ディジタル入出力

digital logic
sūji ronri
数字論理

digital model
deijitaru-moderu
ディジタル・モデル

56

digital output
deijitaru shutsuryoku
ディジタル出力

digital output adapter
deijitaru shutsuryoku adaputa
ディジタル出力アダプタ

digital output control
deijitaru shutsuryoku seigyo
ディジタル出力制御

digital plotter
deijitaru-purotta
ディジタル・プロッタ

digital recording
deijitaru-rekōdo
ディジタル・レコード

digital representation
deijitaru hyōgen
ディジタル表現

digital signal
deijitaru shingō
ディジタル信号

digital simulation
deijitaru-shimyurēshon
ディジタル・シミュレーション

digital switching
deijitaru kōkan
ディジタル交換

digital system
deijitaru-shisutemu
ディジタル・システム

digital-to-analog conversion
deijitaru-anarogu henkan
ディジタル・アナログ変換

digital-to-analog converter (D/A converter)
deijitaru-anarogu henkanki;
deijitaru-anarogu-konbāta
(D/A henkanki; D/A konbāta)
ディジタル・アナログ変換器;
ディジタル・アナログ・
コンバータ; D/A変換器;
D/Aコンバータ

digitization
deijitaruka; keisūka
ディジタル化; 計数化

digitize
deijitaruka suru; keisūka suru
ディジタル化する; 計数化する

digitized
keisūka
計数化

digitized signal
deijitaruka shingō
ディジタル化信号

digitizer
deijitaiza
ディシタイザ

DIL (dual-in-line)
DIL (deyuaru-in-rain)
デュアル・イン・ライン

DIL switch (dual-in-line switch)
DIL suitchi (deyuaru-in-rain-suitchi)
DILスイッチ; デュアル・
イン・ライン・スイッチ

dimension
jigen
次元

dimension attribute
jigen zokusei
次元属性

dimension statement
jigen meireibun
次元命令文

diode (DI)
daiōdo (DI)
ダイオード

diode function generator
daiōdo kansū hasseiki
ダイオード関数発生器

diode gate
daiōdo-gēto
ダイオード・ゲート

diode logic
daiōdo ronri
ダイオード論理

diode matrix
daiōdo-matorikkusu
ダイオード・マトリックス

diode-transistor logic (DTL)
daiōdo-toranjisuta ronri (DTL)
ダイオード・トランジスタ論理

DIP (dual-in-line package)
DIP (deyuaru-in-rain-pakkēji)
デュアル・イン・ライン・
パッケージ

direct access
chokusetsu akusesu
直接アクセス

direct-access device
chokusetsu akusesu sōchi
直接アクセス装置

direct-access file
chokusetsu akusesu-fuairu
直接アクセス・ファイル

direct-access memory
chokusetsu akusesu-memori
直接アクセス・メモリ

direct-access method (DAM)
chokusetsu akusesu hōshiki
(DAM)
直接アクセス方式

direct-access storage
chokusetsu kioku
直接記憶

direct-access storage device (DASD)
chokusetsu akusesu kioku sōchi
(DASD)
直接アクセス記憶装置

direct-access store
chokusetsu kioku sōchi
直接記憶装置

direct address
chokusetsu adoresu
直接アドレス

direct address instruction
chokusetsu adoresu meirei
直接アドレス命令

direct address relocation
chokusetsu adoresu saihaichi
直接アドレス再配置

direct addressing
chokusetsu adoresu shitei
直接アドレス指定

direct code
chokusetsu kōdo
直接コード

direct coding
chokusetsu kōdeingu
直接コーディング

direct control
chokusetsu seigyo
直接制御

direct control microprogram
chokusetsu seigyo maikuro-puroguramu
直接制御マイクロ・プログラム

direct-coupled transistor logic (DCTL)
chokketsugata toranjisuta ronri (DCTL)
直結型トランジスタ論理

direct current (DC)
chokuryū (DC)
直流

direct current amplifier (DC amplifier)
chokuryū zōfukuki (DC zōfukuki)
直流増幅器；D/C増幅器

direct data display
chokusetsu dēta-deisupurei
直接データ・ディスプレィ

direct data entry (DDE)
chokusetsu dēta nyūryoku (DDE)
直接データ入力

direct data set
chokusetsu dēta-setto
直接データ・セット

direct digital control (DDC)
chokusetsu deijitaru seigyo (DDC)
直接ディジタル制御

direct index
chokusetsu sakuin
直接索引

direct input
chokusetsu nyūryoku
直接入力

direct insert
chokusetsu sōnyū
直接挿入

direct insert routine
chokusetsu sōnyū rūchin
直接挿入ルーチン

direct insert subroutine
chokusetsu sōnyū saburūchin
直接挿入サブルーチン

direct instruction
chokusetsu meirei
直接命令

direct location mode
chokusetsu rokēshon-mōdo
直接ロケーション・モード

direct memory access (DMA)
chokusetsu akusesu (DMA)
直接アクセス

direct memory access method
chokusetsu akusesu hōshiki
直接アクセス方式

direct mode
chokusetsu mōdo
直接モード

direct organization
chokusetsu hensei
直接編成

direct output
chokusetsu shutsuryoku
直接出力

direct search
chokusetsu tansaku
直接探索

direction
hōkō
方向

directive
shiji
指示

directory
dairekutori; tōrokubo
ダイレクトリ；登録簿

directory management
dairekutori kanri
ダイレクトリ管理

disable
shiyō kinshi
使用禁止

disabling
shiyō kinshi
使用禁止

disassembler
gyaku asenbura
逆アセンブラ

disc. *See* disk.

disconnect
kirihanasu; setsudan suru
切り離す；切断する

disconnect mode
setsudan mōdo
切断モード

disconnect signal
setsudan shingō
切断信号

disconnection
kirihanashi; setsudan
切り離し；切断

discrete component
kobetsu buhin
個別部品

discrete data
risanteki dēta
離散的データ

discrete event
risanteki jishō
離散的事象

discrete event simulation
risanteki jishō shimyurēshon
離散的事象シミュレーション

discrete part
kobetsu buhin
個別部品

discrete representation
risanteki hyōgen
離散的表現

discrete simulation
risanteki shimyurēshon
離散的シミュレーション

discrimination
shikibetsu
識別

discrimination circuit
shikibetsu kairo
識別回路

discrimination instruction
handan meirei
判断命令

discrimination level
shikibetsu reberu
識別レベル

discriminator
deisukuriminēta
ディスクリミネータ

disintegration
kaihen
壊変

disk *or* **disc**
deisuku
ディスク

disk-based operating system (DOS)
deisuku-operēteingu-shisutemu
(DOS)
ディスク・オペレーティング・
システム

disk cable
deisuku-kēburu
ディスク・ケーブル

disk cartridge
deisuku-kātorijji
ディスク・カートリッジ

disk drive
deisuku-doraibu;
deisuku kudō kikō
ディスク・ドライブ;
ディスク駆動機構

disk dump
deisuku-danpu
ディスク・ダンプ

disk file
deisuku-fuairu
ディスク・ファイル

disk file organization
deisuku-fuairu hensei
ディスク・ファイル編成

disk librarian
deisuku-raiburarian
ディスク・ライブラリアン

disk library
deisuku-raiburari
ディスク・ライブラリ

disk operating system (DOS)
deisuku-operēteingu-shisutemu
(DOS)
ディスク・オペレーティング・
システム

disk-oriented system
deisukushiki shisutemu
ディスク式システム

disk pack
deisuku-pakku
ディスク・パック

disk-resident system
deisuku-rejidento-shisutemu
ディスク・レジデント・システム

disk sort
deisuku-sōto; deisuku bunrui
ディスク・ソート; ディスク分類

disk storage
deisuku kioku
ディスク記憶

disk unit
deisuku kudō kikō;
deisuku-yunitto
ディスク駆動機構;
ディスク・ユニット

diskette
deisuketto
ディスケット

dispatch (*verb*)
deisupatchi suru; shimei suru
ディスパッチする; 指名する

dispatcher
deisupatcha
ディスパッチャ

dispatching
shimei
指名

dispatching priority
shimei jun'i
指名順位

dispersed processing units
bunsangata shori sōchi
分散型処理装置

displacement
hen'i
変位

display (*noun*)
deisupurei; hyōji; hyōji sōchi
ディスプレィ; 表示; 表示装置

display code
deisupurei-kōdo
ディスプレィ・コード

display console
deisupurei-konsoru;
hyōji sōsataku
ディスプレィ・コンソル;
表示操作卓

display control
hyōji seigyo
表示制御

display density
hyōji mitsudo
表示密度

display information
hyōji jōhō
表示情報

display mode
hyōji mōdo
表示モード

display panel
hyōji paneru
表示パネル

display screen
hyōji gamen
表示画面

display terminal
hyōji'yō tanmatsu (sōchi)
表示用端末 (装置)

display tube
hyōji kan
表示管

display unit
deisupurei sōchi; hyōji sōchi
ディスプレィ装置; 表示装置

displayed warning
hyōji keihō
表示警報

distance
kyori
距離

distort
hizumu
歪む

distorted
hizumi
歪み

distorted information
hizumi jōhō
歪み情報

distortion
hizumi
歪み

distortion rate
hizumi ritsu
歪み率

distributed
bunsangata
分散型

distributed control
bunsangata seigyo
分散型制御

distributed data processing (DDP)
bunsangata dēta shori (DDP)
分散型データ処理

distributed function
bunsangata kinō
分散型機能

distributed information system
bunsangata jōhō shisutemu
分散型情報システム

distributed processing
bunsangata dēta shori
分散型データ処理

distributed processing system
bunsangata dēta shori shisutemu
分散型データ処理システム

distributed system
bunsangata shisutemu
分散型システム

distribution (of messages)
hō
報

disturbance
bōgai; gairan
妨害; 外乱

divide
bunkatsu suru
分割する

dividend
josū
除数

divider
bunshūki
分周器

dividing
bunshū
分周

division (operation)
josan
除算

division (part)
bu
部

DLE (data link escape)
DLE (densō seigyo kakuchō)
伝送制御拡張

DMA (direct memory access)
DMA (chokusetsu akusesu)
直接アクセス

DMCL (device media control language)
DMCL (sōchi baitai seigyo gengo)
装置媒体制御言語

DML (data manipulation language)
DML (dēta sōsa gengo)
データ操作言語

D-MOS (depletion MOS)
D-MOS (deipuriishon MOS)
ディプリーションMOS

DMR (data management routine)
DMR (dēta kanri rūchin)
データ管理ルーチン

DMS (data management system)
DMS (dēta kanri shisutemu)
データ管理システム

do-nothing instruction
mudōsa meirei
無動作命令

document
bunsho; dokyumento; shorui
文書; ドキュメント; 書類

document analysis form
bunsho bunseki hyō
文書分析表

document processor
bunsho shori sōchi
文書処理装置

document reader
dokyumento-riida
ドキュメント・リーダ

document retrieval
dokyumento kensaku
ドキュメント検索

documentation
bunsho; bunshoka;
dokyumentēshon
文書; 文書化;
ドキュメンテーション

documentation system
dokyumentēshon-shisutemu
ドキュメンテーション・
システム

domain
ryō'iki
領域

domain movement
ryō'iki idō
領域移動

dormant state
kyūshi jōtai
休止状態

DOS (disk-based operating system; disk operating system)
DOS (deisuku-operēteingu-shisutemu)
ディスク・オペレーティング・
システム

dot
dotto
ドット

dot cycle
dotto shūki
ドット周期

dot generation
dotto seisei
ドット生成

dot matrix
dotto-matorikkusu
ドット・マトリックス

dot matrix character
dotto-matorikkusu moji
ドット・マトリックス文字

dot matrix printer
dotto-matorikkusu-purinta
ドット・マトリックス・
プリンタ

dot method
dotto hōshiki
ドット方式

dot pattern
dotto-patān
ドット・パターン

dot pattern generator
dotto-patān hasseiki
ドット・パターン発生器

dot pitch
dotto-pitchi
ドット・ピッチ

dot printer
dotto-purinta;
dottoshiki insho sōchi
ドット・プリンタ;
ドット式印書装置

double address
ni adoresu
2アドレス

double buffering
nijū baffuaringu;
nijū kanshō shuhō
二重バッファリング;
二重緩衝手法

double current
fukuryū
複流

double current transmission
fukuryū densō
複流伝送

double density (DD)
bai (kiroku) mitsudo (DD)
倍（記録）密度

double-density disk
bai mitsudo deisuku
倍密度ディスク

double error
nijū ayamari
二重誤り

double-length number
nibai chōsū
二倍長数

double-length register
bai chō rejisuta
倍長レジスタ

double-length word
bai chō go
倍長語

double precision
bai seido; nibai seido
倍精度；二倍精度

double-precision arithmetic
nibai seido enzan
二倍精度演算

double-precision number
bai seido sū
倍精度数

double pulse
bai parusu; daburu-parusu
倍パルス；ダブル・パルス

double-pulse reading
daburu-parusu yomi
ダブル・パルス読み

double-pulse recording
bai parusu kiroku hōshiki
倍パルス記録方式

double punching
nijū senkō
二重せん孔

double word
daburu-wādo
ダブル・ワード

download
daunrōdo
ダウンロード

downloading
daunrōdeingu
ダウンローディング

downtime
daun-taimu; koshō jikan;
kyūshi jikan
ダウン・タイム；故障時間；
休止時間

DP (data processing)
DP (dēta shori)
データ処理

DP (dynamic programming)
DP (dōteki keikakuhō)
動的計画法

DPC (data processing center)
DPC (dēta shori senta)
データ処理センタ

DRC (data reduction center)
DRC (dēta seiri senta)
データ整理センタ

drift
dorifuto
ドリフト

drive
doraibu; kudō kikō
ドライブ；駆動機構

drive pulse
kudō parusu
駆動パルス

DRO (destructive readout)
DRO (hakai yomidashi)
破壊読み出し

drop-in
doroppo-in
ドロッポ・イン

drop-out
doroppo-auto
ドロッポ・アウト

drum
doramu; jiki doramu
ドラム；磁気ドラム

drum-oriented system
doramushiki shisutemu
ドラム式システム

drum plotter
doramushiki purotta
ドラム式プロッタ

drum printer
doramushiki insho sōchi
ドラム式印書装置

drum storage
jiki doramu kioku
磁気ドラム記憶

dry run
kijō kensa
机上検査

DS (data set)
DS (dēta-setto)
データ・セット

DSCB (data set control block)
DSCB (dēta-setto seigyo burokku)
データ・セット制御ブロック

DSR (data set ready)
DSR (dēta-setto-redei)
データ・セット・レディ

DSS (decision support system)
DSS (ishi kettei shien shisutemu)
意思決定支援システム

DTL (diode-transistor logic)
DTL (daiōdo-toranjisuta ronri)
ダイオード・トランジスタ論理

DTR (data terminal ready)
DTR (dēta tanmatsu sōchi redei)
データ端末装置レディ

dual
deyuaru; sōtai
デュアル；双対

dual channel
deyuaru-chaneru
デュアル・チャネル

dual control
nijū seigyo
二重制御

dual flexible disk drive
deyuaru-furekishiburu-deisuku
kudō kikō
デュアル・フレキシブル・
ディスク駆動機構

dual-in-line (DIL)
deyuaru-in-rain (DIL)
デュアル・イン・ライン

dual-in-line package (DIP)
deyuaru-in-rain-pakkēji (DIP)
デュアル・イン・ライン・
パッケージ

dual-in-line switch (DIL switch)
deyuaru-in-rain-suitchi (DIL
suitchi)
デュアル・イン・ライン・スイッチ;
DILスイッチ

dual index mode
deyuaru-indekkusu-mōdo
デュアル・インデックス・
モード

dual mode
deyuaru-mōdo
デュアル・モード

dual operation
sōtai enzan
双対演算

dual processor
deyuaru-purosessa
デュアル・プロセッサ

dual system
deyuaru-shisutemu
デュアル・システム

dummy
damii; giji
ダミー; 疑似

dummy activity
giji akuteibitei
疑似アクティビティ

dummy argument
damii-āgyumento
ダミー・アーギュメント

dummy entry
giji nyūryoku
疑似入力

dummy instruction
damii meirei
ダミー命令

dummy statement
kūbun
空文

dump (noun)
danpu
ダンプ

dump (verb)
danpu suru
ダンプする

dump analysis
danpu kaiseki
ダンプ解析

dump check
danpu kensa
ダンプ検査

dumping
danpingu
ダンピング

duodecimal
jūnishin(hō)
12進 (法)

duodecimal number
jūnishin sū
12進数

duplex
deyupurekkusu; nijū
デュプレックス; 二重

duplex channel
nijū tsūshinro
二重通信路

duplex communication system
nijū tsūshin hōshiki
二重通信方式

duplex line
nijū kaisen
二重回線

duplex operation
deyupurekkusu-operēshon
デュプレックス・
オペレーション

duplex system
deyupurekkusu-shisutemu;
nijū shisutemu
デュプレックス・システム;
二重システム

duplex transmission
nijū densō
二重伝送

duplicate (verb)
fukusei suru
複製する

duplicate label
nijū teigi raberu
二重定義ラベル

duplication
fukusei
複製

duplication check
nijū kensa
二重検査

durability
taikyūsei
耐久性

duration
jikan; jizoku jikan
時間; 持続時間

during transmission
sōshin tochū
送信途中

duty
eki
役

dyadic Boolean operation
nikō Būru enzan
2項ブール演算

dyadic Boolean operator
nikō Būru enzanshi
2項ブール演算子

dyadic operation
nikō enzan
2項演算

dynamic
dainamikku; dōteki
ダイナミック; 動的

dynamic address translation (DAT)
dōteki adoresu henkan (DAT)
動的アドレス変換

dynamic allocation
dōteki wariate
動的割り当て

dynamic buffering
dōteki baffuaringu
動的バッファリング

dynamic characteristics
dōtokusei
動特性

dynamic circuit
dainamikku kairo; dōteki kairo
ダイナミック回路；動的回路

dynamic control
dōteki seigyo
動的制御

dynamic debugging tool
dainamikku-debaggingu-tsūru
ダイナミック・デバッギング・
ツール

dynamic device reconfiguration
dōteki sōchi saikōsei
動的装置再構成

dynamic dump
dōteki danpu
動的ダンプ

dynamic flip-flop
dōteki furippu-furoppu
動的フリップ・フロップ

dynamic memory allocation
dōteki kioku'iki wariate
動的記憶域割り当て

dynamic model
dōteki moderu
動的モデル

dynamic parameter
dōteki parameta
動的パラメタ

dynamic program loading
dōteki puroguramu-rōdeingu
動的プログラム・ローディング

dynamic program relocation
dōteki puroguramu saihaichi
動的プログラム再配置

dynamic programming (DP)
dōteki keikakuhō (DP)
動的計画法

dynamic RAM
dainamikku RAM
ダイナミックRAM

dynamic register
dōteki rejisuta
動的レジスタ

dynamic relocation
dōteki saihaichi
動的再配置

dynamic resource allocation
dōteki shigen haibun
動的資源配分

dynamic restructuring
dōteki saikōsei
動的再構成

dynamic stop
dainamikku-sutoppu
ダイナミック・ストップ

dynamic storage
dōteki kioku
動的記憶

dynamic storage allocation
dōteki kioku'iki wariate
動的記憶域割り当て

dynamic store
dōteki kioku sōchi
動的記憶装置

dynamic structure
dōteki kōzō
動的構造

dynamic subroutine
dōteki saburūchin
動的サブルーチン

E

each-pass own code (EPOC)
iichi-pasu-oun-kōdo (EPOC)
イーチ・パス・オウン・コード

EAM (electrical accounting machine)
EAM (denkishiki kaikeiki)
電気式会計機

EAROM (electrically alterable read-only memory)
EAROM (denkiteki saikakikomi ROM)
電気的再書き込みROM

EBAM (electron beam addressed memory)
EBAM (denshi biimu-memori)
電子ビーム・メモリ

EBCDIC (extended binary coded decimal interchange code)
EBCDIC (kakuchō nisshinka jisshin kōdo)
拡張2進化10進コード

EBM (end-of-block marker)
EBM (burokku owari māka; burokku shūketsu māka)
ブロック終りマーカ；
ブロック終結マーカ

EBR (electron beam recording)
EBR (denshi biimu kiroku)
電子ビーム記録

ECAP (electronic circuit analysis program)
ECAP (denshi kairo kaiseki puroguramu)
電子回路解析プログラム

ECB (event control block)
ECB (jishō seigyo burokku)
事象制御ブロック

ECC (error-correcting code)
ECC (ayamari teisei fugō)
誤り訂正符号

echo
ekō; hankyō
エコー；反響

echo check
ekō-chekku; hankyō kensa
エコー・チェック；反響検査

echo checking system
ekō-chekku hōshiki
エコー・チェック方式

echo suppressor
ekō yokuseiki; hankyō yokuseiki
エコー抑制器；反響抑制器

ECL (emitter-coupled logic)
ECL (emitta ketsugōgata ronri)
エミッタ結合型論理

ECMA (European Computer Manufacturers' Association)
ECMA (Ōshū Denshi Keisanki Seizō Gyōsha Kyōkai)
欧州電子計算機製造業者協会

edge
ejji; hashi; tansen
エッジ；端；端線

edge card
ejji-kādo
エッジ・カード

edge connector
ejji-konekuta
エッジ・コネクタ

edge detection
tansen kenshutsu
端線検出

edge-punched card
ejji-kādo; ejji senkō kādo
エッジ・カード；
エッジせん孔カード

edit
henshū suru
編集する

edit control character
henshū seigyo moji
編集制御文字

edit-directed input/output
edeittogata nyūshutsuryoku
EDIT型入出力

edit-directed transmission
henshū shiji densō
編集指示伝送

edit mode
henshū mōdo
編集モード

edit program
henshū puroguramu
編集プログラム

edit routine
henshū rūchin
編集ルーチン

editing
henshū
編集

editing character
henshū'yō moji
編集用文字

editing function
henshū kinō
編集機能

editing sign control character
henshu'yō fugō
編集用符号

editing symbol
henshu'yō kigō
編集用記号

editor
edeita; henshū puroguramu
エディタ；編集プログラム

EDP (electronic data processing)
EDP (denshi dēta shori; denshishiki dēta shori)
電子データ処理；
電子式データ処理

EDPM (electronic data-processing machine)
EDPM (denshi dēta shori kikai)
電子データ処理機械

EDPS (electronic data-processing system
EDPS (denshi dēta shori shisutemu)
電子データ処理システム

EDS (exchangeable disk store)
EDS (kōkankanō deisuku kioku sōchi)
交換可能ディスク記憶装置

EEPROM (electrically erasable programmable read-only memory)
EEPROM (denkiteki shōkyokanō puroguramukanō ROM)
電気的消去可能プログラム
可能ROM

EEROM (electrically erasable read-only memory)
EEROM (denkiteki shōkyokanō ROM)
電気的消去可能ROM

effective address
jikkō adoresu; yūkō adoresu
実行アドレス；有効アドレス

effective data transfer rate
yūkō dēta tensō sokudo
有効データ転送速度

effective gain
jikkō ritoku
実行利得

effective instruction
jikkō meirei
実行命令

effective order
jikkō junjo; jikkō meirei
実行順序；実行命令

effective speed
jikkō sokudo
実行速度

effective system
yūkō shisutemu
有効システム

effective time
jikkō jikan
実行時間

effectiveness
yūkō
有効

effector
efuekuta
エフェクタ

efficiency
kōritsu
効率

EFM (end-of-field marker)
EFM (fuiirudo owari māka)
フィールド終りマーカ

EIA (Electronic Industries Association)
EIA (Denshi Kōgyō Kai)
電子工業会

eigenvalue
koyū chi
固有値

eight-bit alphameric code
hachi bitto eisūji kōdo
8ビット英数字コード

eight-level code
hachi tan'i kōdo
8 単位コード

eighty-column card
hachijū ran kādo
80欄カード

either-OR
hōganteki ronriwa
包含的論理和

either-OR operation
hōganteki ronriwa enzan
包含的論理和

ejection
hajikidashi
弾き出し

elapsed time
keika jikan
経過時間

elapsed timer
keika taima
経過タイマ

electric accounting machine (EAM)
denkishiki kaikeiki (EAM)
電気式会計機

electric cable
denryoku kēburu
電力ケーブル

electric power failure
dengen ijō
電源異常

electric power supply
dengen
電源

electrical engineering
denki kōgaku
電気工学

electrically alterable read-only memory (EAROM)
denkiteki saikakikomi ROM (EAROM)
電気的再書き込みROM

electrically erasable read-only memory (EEROM)
denkiteki shōkyokanō ROM (EEROM)
電気的消去可能ROM

electrically programmable read-only memory (EPROM)
denkiteki puroguramukanō ROM (EPROM)
電気的プログラム可能ROM

electron beam addressed memory (EBAM)
denshi biimu-memori (EBAM)
電子ビーム・メモリ

electron beam recording (EBR)
denshi biimu kiroku (EBR)
電子ビーム記憶

electronic
erekutoronikkusu; denshi; denshishiki
エレクトロニックス；電子；
電子式

electronic automatic exchange
denshi kōkan
電子交換

electronic circuit
denshi kairo
電子回路

electronic circuit analysis program (ECAP)
denshi kairo kaiseki puroguramu (ECAP)
電子回路解析プログラム

electronic computer
denshi keisanki
電子計算機

electronic computer system
denshi keisanki shisutemu
電子計算機システム

electronic control system
denshi seigyo shisutemu
電子制御システム

electronic counter
denshi kaunta
電子カウンタ

electronic data processing (EDP)
denshi dēta shori;
denshishiki dēta shori (EDP)
電子データ処理；
電子式データ処理

electronic data-processing machine (EDPM)
denshi dēta shori kikai (EDPM)
電子データ処理機械

electronic data-processing system (EDPS)
denshi dēta shori shisutemu (EDPS)
電子データ処理システム

electronic device
denshi sōchi
電子装置

electronic differential analyzer
denshi bibun kaisekiki
電子微分解析器

electronic file
denshi fairu
電子ファイル

electronic filing
denshi fairingu
電子ファイリング

Electronic Industries Association (EIA)
Denshi Kōgyō Kai (EIA)
電子工業会

electronic information exchange system
denshi jōhō kōkan shisutemu
電子情報交換システム

electronic information-processing system
denshi jōhō shori shisutemu
電子情報処理システム

electronic information system
denshi jōhō shisutemu
電子情報システム

electronic mail
denshi yūbin
電子郵便

electronic method
denshi hōhō
電子方法

electronic office
erekutoronikkusu-ofuisu
エレクトロニックス・オフィス

electronic printer
denshi insho sōchi;
denshi purinta
電子印書装置；電子プリンタ

electronic switch
denshi suitchi
電子スイッチ

electronic switching system
denshi kōkan shisutemu
電子交換システム

electronics
denshi; denshi kōgyō;
erekutoronikkusu
電子；電子工業；
エレクトロニックス

electrophotographic printer
denshi shashinshiki insho sōchi
電子写真式印書装置

electrophotography
denshi shashin
電子写真

electrostatic printer
seidenshiki insho sōchi;
seidenshiki purinta
静電式印書装置；
静電式プリンタ

electrostatic storage
seidenshiki kioku
静電式記憶

element
eremento; soshi; yōso
エレメント；素子；要素

element error rate
eremento ayamari ritsu
エレメント誤り率

element file
eremento-fuairu
エレメント・ファイル

elementary divisor
tan'inshi
単因子

elementary item
kihon kōmoku
基本項目

elementary item posting
kihon kōmoku tenki
基本項目転記

elementary operation
kihon sōsa
基本操作

eleven punch
jūichi senkō
11せん孔

eliminate
jokyo suru
除去する

elimination
jokyo
除去

EM (end of medium)
EM (baitai no owari; baitai
shūtan)
媒体の終り；媒体終端

embedded computer
umekomi keisanki
埋め込み計算機

embedded computer system
umekomi keisanki shisutemu
埋め込み計算機システム

emboss
enbosu suru
エンボス

embossment
enbosumento
エンボスメント

emergency
kinkyū
緊急

emergency action
kinkyū dōsa
緊急動作

emergency maintenance
kinkyū hoshu
緊急保守

emergency shutdown
kinkyū teishi
緊急停止

emergency signal
kinkyū shingō
緊急信号

emitter
emitta
エミッタ

emitter-coupled logic (ECL)
emitta ketsugōgata ronri (ECL)
エミッタ結合型論理

emitter follower
emitta-fuōrowa
エミッタ・フォーロワ

emitter-follower diode transistor logic
emitta-fuōrowa-daiōdo-
toranjisuta ronri
エミッタ・フォーロワ・
ダイオード・トランジスタ・
論理

emitter-follower logic circuit
emitta-fuōrowa ronri kairo
エミッタ・フォーロク論理回路

EMOS (enhancement MOS)
enhansumentogata MOS
エンハンスメント型MOS

empty file
kū fuairu
空ファイル

empty medium
kū baitai
空媒体

empty set
kū shūgō
空集合

empty string
kū sutoringu
空ストリング

emulation
emyurēshon
エミュレーション

emulator
emyurēta
エミュレータ

emulator program
emyurēta-puroguramu
エミュレータ・プログラム

enable
enēburu; kakikomi kyoka;
shiyōkanō
エネーブル；書き込み許可；
使用可能

enable ring
kakikomi kyoka ringu
書き込み許可リング

enabled
shiyōkanō
使用可能

enabling
shiyōkanō; yūkōka
使用可能；有効化

enabling signal
shiyōkanō shingō
使用可能信号

encode
fugōka suru; kōdoka suru
符号化する；コード化する

encode table
enkōdo-tēburu
エンコード・テーブル

encoder
enkōda; fugōki
エンコーダ；符号器

encoding
fugōka; kōdoka
符号化；コード化

encryption
angōka
暗号化

end
endo; shūketsu; shūryō; shūshi;
shūtan
エンド；終結；終了；終止；終端

end-around carry
junkan keta age
循環桁上げ

end-around shift
junkan keta idō
循環桁移動

end column
shūshi keta
終止桁

end file record
fuairu shūryō kiroku
ファイル終了記録

END line
endo gyō
エンド行

end mark
endo-māku
エンド・マーク

end of block (EOB)
burokku no owari;
burokku shūketsu (EOB)
ブロックの終り；ブロック終結

end-of-block marker (EBM)
burokku owari māka;
burokku shūketsu māka (EBM)
ブロック終りマーカ；
ブロック終結マーカ

end of data
dēta no owari
データの終り

end-of-data marker
dēta owari māka
データ終りマーカ

end of field
fuiirudo no owari
フィールドの終り

end-of-field marker (EFM)
fuiirudo owari māka (EFM)
フィールド終りマーカ

end of file (EOF)
fuairu no owari (EOF)
ファイルの終り

end-of-file label
fuairu owari raberu
ファイル終りラベル

end-of-file marker
fuairu owari māka
ファイル終りマーカ

end of job (EOJ)
jyobu no owari; jyobu shūryō
(EOJ)
ジョブの終り；ジョブ終了

end of medium (EM)
baitai shūtan (EM)
媒体終端

end-of-medium character
baitai shūtan moji
媒体終端文字

end of message (EOM)
messēji no owari;
messēji shūketsu (EOM)
メッセージの終り；
メッセージ終結

end of record
rekōdo no owari
レコードの終り

end-of-record marker (ERM)
rekōdo owari māka (ERM)
レコード終りマーカ

end-of-record word
rekōdo owari go
レコード終り語

end of reel
riiru no owari; riiru shūtan
リールの終り；リール終端

end of run
ran owari; ran shūryō
ラン終り；ラン終了

end of tape (EOT)
tēpu no owari; tēpu shūtan
(EOT)
テープの終り；デープ終端

end-of-tape marker
tēpu owari māka;
tēpu shūtan māka
テープ終りマーカ；
テープ終端マーカ

end-of-tape warning
tēpu shūtan yokoku
テープ終端予告

end of task
tasuku no owari; tasuku shūryō
タスクの終り；タスク終了

end of text (ETX)
tekisuto shūketsu (ETX)
テキスト終結

end-of-text character
tekisuto shūketsu moji
テキスト終結文字

end of transmission (EOT)
densō shūketsu (EOT)
伝送終結

end-of-transmission block (ETB)
densō burokku shūketsu (ETB)
伝送ブロック終結

**end-of-transmission block
character**
densō burokku shūketsu moji
伝送ブロック終結文字

end-of-transmission character
densō shūketsu moji
伝送終結文字

end of volume (EOV)
boryūmu no owari (EOV)
ボリュームの終り

end-of-volume label
boryūmu owari raberu
ボリューム終りラベル

end-to-end acknowledgment
shūtankan kakunin
終端間確認

end user
endo-yūza; saishū riyōsha
エンド・ユーザ; 最終利用者

engaged (line)
heisoku
閉塞

enhance
enhansu suru; kyōchō suru
エンハンスする; 強調する

enhancement
enhansumento; kyōchō
エンハンスメント; 強調

enhancement MOS (EMOS)
enhansumentogata MOS (EMOS)
エンハンスメント型MOS

ENQ (enquiry)
ENQ (toiawase)
問い合わせ

enquiry (ENQ)
kensaku; shōkai; toiawase (ENQ)
検索; 照会; 問い合わせ

enquiry character
toiawase moji
問い合わせ文字

enquiry station
shōkai'yō tanmatsu
照会用端末

enquiry system
toiawase shisutemu
問い合わせシステム

enquiry terminal
shōkai'yō tanmatsu
照会用端末

enquiry utility
toiawase yūteiritei
問い合わせユーティリティ

enter
nyūryoku suru
入力する

enter key
nyūryoku kii
入力キー

enter mode
nyūryoku mōdo
入力モード

entry
entori; iriguchi; kijutsukō; kinyū;
kōmoku; nyūryoku
エントリ; 入り口; 記述項;
記入; 項目; 入力

entry buffer
kinyū baffua
記入バッファ

entry conditions
iriguchi jōken
入り口条件

entry name
iriguchi mei
入り口名

entry point
iriguchi ten
入り口点

entry sequence
nyūryoku jun
入力順

enumeration
retsukyohō
列挙法

environment
kankyō
環境

environment clause
kankyō ku
環境句

environment division
kankyō bu
環境部

environment specification
kankyō shiyō
環境仕様

environmental test
kankyō shiken
環境試験

EOB (end of block)
EOB (burokku no owari; burokku
shūketsu)
ブロックの終り; ブロック終結

EOF (end of file)
EOF (fuairu no owari)
ファイルの終り

EOJ (end of job)
EOJ (jyobu no owari; jyobu
shūryō)
ジョブの終り; ジョブ終了

EOM (end of message)
EOM (messēji no owari; messēji
shūketsu)
メッセージの終り;
メッセージ終結

EOT (end of tape)
EOT (tēpu no owari; tēpu shūtan)
テープの終り; テープ終端

EOT (end of transmission)
EOT (densō shūketsu)
伝送終結

EOV (end of volume)
EOV (boryūmu no owari)
ボリュームの終り

epitaxy
epitakushi
エピタクシ

EPOC (each-pass own code)
EPOC (iichi-pasu-oun-kōdo)
イーチ・パス・オウン・コード

EPROM (erasable programmable read-only memory)
EPROM (shōkyokanō
puroguramukanō ROM)
消去可能プログラム可能ROM

EQ (equivalence)
EQ (tōka)
等価

EQ gate (equivalence gate)
EQ gēto (tōka gēto)
EQゲート; 等価ゲート

equal indicator
tōchi hyōjishi
等値表示子

equalization
tōka
等化

equalizer
tōkaki
等化器

equipment
kiki; sōbi; sōchi
機器; 装備; 装置

equipment check
kiki kensa; sōchi kensa
機器検査; 装置検査

equipment compatibility
kiki (no) gokansei
機器の互換性

equipment failure
kiki koshō
機器故障

equivalence (EQ)
dōchi; dōka; tōka (EQ)
同値；同価；等価

equivalence gate (EQ gate)
tōka gēto (EQ gēto)
等価ゲート；EQゲート

equivalent binary digit
tōka nishin sūji
等価2進数字

ER (executive request)
ER (eguzekuteibu-rikuesuto)
エグゼクティブ・リクエスト

erasable
shōkyokanō
消去可能

erasable programmable read-only memory (EPROM)
shōkyokanō puroguramukanō ROM (EPROM)
消去可能プログラム可能ROM

erasable storage
shōkyokanō kioku
消去可能記憶

erase
massatsu suru; masshō suru; shōkyo suru
抹殺する；抹消する；消去する

erase character
shōkyo moji
消去文字

erase head
shōkyo heddo
消去ヘッド

erasing device
shōkyoki
消去器

erasure
masshō
抹消

ERB (extent request block)
ERB (ekusutento yōkyū burokku)
エクステント要求ブロック

ERM (end-of-record marker)
ERM (rekōdo owari māka)
レコード終りマーカ

erroneous
ayamari
誤り

erroneous block
ayamari burokku
誤りブロック

error
ayamari; erā; gosa
誤り；エラー；誤差

error analysis
ayamari kaiseki
誤り解析

error check
erā-chekku; ayamari kensa
エラー・チェック；誤り検査

error checking
ayamari kensa
誤り検査

error checking and correction
ayamari kensa-teisei
誤り検査-訂正

error-checking and correction system
ayamari kensa-teisei shisutemu
誤り検査-訂正システム

error-checking code
ayamari kensa fugō
誤り検査符号

error code
ayamari kōdo
誤りコード

error condition
ayamari jōtai
誤り状態

error control
ayamari seigyo
誤り制御

error-control character
ayamari seigyo moji
誤り制御文字

error-control system
ayamari seigyo hōshiki
誤り制御方式

error-correcting code (ECC)
ayamari teisei fugō (ECC)
誤り訂正符号

error-correcting routine
ayamari teisei rūchin
誤り訂正ルーチン

error-correcting system
ayamari teisei hōshiki
誤り訂正方式

error correction
ayamari teisei
誤り訂正

error-detecting code
ayamari kenshutsu fugō
誤り検出符号

error-detecting code system
ayamari kenshutsu fugō hōshiki
誤り検出符号方式

error-detecting routine
ayamari kenshutsu rūchin
誤り検出ルーチン

error-detecting system
ayamari kenshutsu hōshiki
誤り検出方式

error detection
ayamari kenshutsu
誤り検出

error detection and correction
ayamari kenshutsu-teisei
誤り検出-訂正

error detection and correction device
ayamari kenshutsu-teisei kikō
誤り検出-訂正機構

error detection and correction function
ayamari kenshutsu-teisei kinō
誤り検出-訂正機能

error diagnostics
ayamari shindan
誤り診断

error-diagnostics code
ayamari shindan kōdo
誤り診断コード

error estimation
gosa suitei
誤差推定

error flag
ayamari hyōshiki
誤り標識

error-free
ayamari hassei nai
誤り発生ない

error frequency
ayamari hindo
誤り頻度

error-handling routine
ayamari shori rūchin
誤り処理ルーチン

error indicator
ayamari hyōshiki
誤り標識

error list
erā-risuto
エラー・リスト

error message
ayamari messēji; erā-messēji
誤りメッセージ;
エラー・メッセージ

error probability
ayamari kakuritsu
誤り確率

error procedure
ayamari tejun
誤り手順

error range
ayamari han'i
誤り範囲

error rate
ayamari ritsu
誤り率

error recovery
ayamari kaifuku
誤り回復

error-recovery routine
ayamari kaifuku rūchin
誤り回復ルーチン

error report
erā-ripōto
エラー・リポート

error routine
ayamari rūchin; erā-rūchin
誤りルーチン;
エラー・ルーチン

error signal
ayamari shingō; erā shingō
誤り信号; エラー信号

error warning
ayamari keihō
誤り警報

ESC (escape)
ESC (kakuchō)
拡張

escape (ESC)
kakuchō (ESC); menseki
拡張; 免責

escape character
kakuchō moji
拡張文字

escape procedure
menseki tetsuzuki
色責手続き

estimation
suitei
推定

ETB (end-of-transmission block)
ETB (densō burokku shūketsu)
伝送ブロック終結

ETX (end of text)
ETX (tekisuto shūketsu)
テキスト終結

European Computer Manufacturers' Association (ECMA)
Ōshū Denshi Keisanki Seizō Gyōsha Kyōkai (ECMA)
欧洲電子計算機製造業者協会

evaluation
hyōka
評価

evaluation of expression
shiki no hyōka
式の評価

evaluation system
hyōka shisutemu
評価システム

even check
gūsū kensa
偶数検査

even-odd check
kigū kensa
奇偶検査

even parity
gūsū paritei
偶数パリティ

even-parity check
gūsū paritei-chekku
偶数パリティ・チェック

event
ibento; jishō
イベント; 事象

event control block (ECB)
jishō seigyo burokku (ECB)
事象制御ブロック

event scanning
jishō sōsa
事象走査

event-scanning mechanism
jishō sōsa kikō
事象走査機構

event sequence
jishō shiikensu
事象シーケンス

event simulation
jishō shimyurēshon
事象シミュレーション

event variable
jishō hensū
事象変数

exception
reigai
例外

exception principle system
reigai hōshiki
例外方式

exception reporting
reigai hōkoku
例外報告

exchange
kōkan; kōkankyoku
交換; 交換局

exchange buffering
kōkan kanshō hōshiki
交換緩衝方式

exchange register
kōkan rejisuta
交換レジスタ

exchange service
kōkan sābisu
交換サービス

exchange system
kōkan hōshiki
交換方式

exchangeable disk
kōkankanō deisuku
交換可能ディスク

exchangeable disk store (EDS)
kōkankanō deisuku kioku sōchi
(EDS)
交換可能ディスク記憶装置

exchangeable magnetic disk
kōkankanō jiki deisuku
交換可能磁気ディスク

exclusion
haita
排他

exclusion operation
haitateki enzan
排他的演算

exclusive
haitateki
排他的

exclusive control
haitateki seigyo
排他的制御

exclusive-NOR (XNOR)
haitateki hitei ronriwa;
haitateki NOR (XNOR)
排他的否定論理和;
排他的NOR; XNOR

exclusive-NOR circuit (XNOR circuit)
haitateki hitei ronriwa kairo;
haitateki NOR kairo (XNOR kairo)
排他的否定論理和回路;
排他的NOR回路; XNOR回路

exclusive-OR (XOR)
haitateki OR; haitateki ronriwa
(XOR)
排他的OR; 排他的論理和;
XOR

exclusive-OR circuit (XOR circuit)
haitateki OR kairo; haitateki
ronriwa kairo (XOR kairo)
排他的OR回路;
排他的論理和回路; XOR回路

exclusive-OR element (XOR element)
haitateki OR soshi; haitateki
ronriwa soshi (XOR soshi)
排他的OR素子;
排他的論理和素子; XOR素子

exclusive-OR gate (XOR gate)
haitateki OR gēto; haitateki
ronriwa gēto (XOR gēto)
排他的ORゲート;
排他的論理和ゲート;
XORゲート

exclusive-OR operation (XOR operation)
haitateki OR enzan; haitateki
ronriwa enzan (XOR enzan)
排他的OR演算;
排他的論理和演算; XOR演算

exclusive reference
haitateki sanshō
排他的参照

exclusive segment
haitateki segumento
排他的セグメント

executable
jikkō(kanō)
実行 （可能）

executable program
jikkōkanō puroguramu
実行可能プログラム

executable statement
jikkō bun
実行文

executable unit
jikkō tan'i
実行単位

execute
jikkō suru
実行する

execute statement
jikkō seigyo bun
実行制御文

execution
jikkō; meirei jikkō
実行; 命令実行

execution area
jikkō ryō'iki
実行領域

execution cycle
jikkō dankai; jikkō saikuru;
meirei jikkō dankai
実行段階; 実行サイクル;
命令実行段階

execution error
jikkō ayamari
実行誤り

execution phase
meirei jikkō dankai
命令実行段階

execution step
jikkō suteppu
実行ステップ

execution time
jikkō jikan
実行時間

executive
eguzekuteibu; kanshi
エグゼクティブ; 監視

executive program
kanshi puroguramu
監視プログラム

executive request (ER)
eguzekuteibu-rikuesuto (ER)
エグゼクティブ・リクェスト

executive routine
eguzekuteibu-rūchin
エグゼクティブ・ルーチン

executive system
eguzekuteibu-shisutemu;
kanshi shisutemu
エグゼクティブ・システム;
監視システム

exhaustive search
zensū tansaku
全数探索

existence
sonzai
存在

existence verification
sonzai kenshō
存在検証

exit
deguchi
出口

exit address
deguchi adoresu
出口アドレス

exit point
deguchi ten
出口点

exit routine
deguchi rūchin
出口ルーチン

expander
shinchōki
伸長器

expansion
kakuchō; shinchō
拡張；伸長

expansion feature
kakuchō kikō
拡張機構

expansion interface
kakuchō intafuēsu
拡張インタフェース

expected response
kitai ōtō
期待応答

expected value
kitai chi
期待値

expert system
ekkusupāto-shisutemu
エックスパート・システム

explicit address
meishi adoresu
明示アドレス

explicit declaration
meishi sengen
明示宣言

exponent
shisū
指数

exponent overflow
shisū keta afure; shisū ōbafurō
指数桁溢れ；指数オーバフロー

exponent part
shisū bu
指数部

exponent underflow
shisū ka'i keta afure;
shisū andafurō
指数下位桁溢れ；
指数アンダフロー

exponential distribution
shisū bumpu
指数分布

exponential function
shisū kansū
指数関数

exponentiation
shisūka
指数化

expression
hyōgen; keishiki; shiki
表現；形式；式

expression constant
sūshiki teisū
数式定数

extended
kakuchō
拡張

extended BASIC
kakuchō BASIC
拡張BASIC

extended binary coded decimal interchange code (EBCDIC)
kakuchō nisshinka jisshin kōdo (EBCDIC)
拡張2進化10進コード

extended control
kakuchō seigyo
拡張制御

extended language
kakuchō gengo
拡張言語

extended precision
kakuchō seido
拡張精度

extended storage
kakuchō kioku
拡張記憶

extensible
kakuchōkanō
拡張可能

extensible language
kakuchōkanō gengo
拡張可能言語

extension
kakuchō
拡張

extension sort
kakuchō bunrui; kakuchō sōto
拡張分類；拡張ソート

extension unit
kakuchō tan'i; kakuchō yunitto
拡張単位；拡張ユニット

extent
ekusutento
エクステント

extent request block (ERB)
ekusutento yōkyū burokku (ERB)
エクステント要求ブロック

extent table
ekusutento-tēburu
エクステント・テーブル

external
gaibu
外部

external attribute
gaibu zokusei
外部属性

external control
gaibu seigyo
外部制御

external definition
gaibu teigi
外部定義

external definition record
gaibu teigi rekōdo
外部定義レコード

external entry point
gaibu iriguchi ten
外部入り口点

external environment information
gaibu kankyō jōhō
外部環境情報

external function
gaibu kansū
外部関数

external function reference
gaibu kansū in'yō
外部関数引用

external interrupt
gaibu warikomi
外部割り込み

external interrupt status word
gaibu warikomi jōta go
外部割り込み状態語

external medium
gaibu baitai
外部媒体

external merge
gaibu kumiawase
外部組み合わせ

external name
gaibu mei
外部名

external procedure
gaibu tetsuzuki
外部手続き

external program parameter
gaibu puroguramu-parameta
外部プログラム・パラメタ

external reference
gaibu sanshō
外部参照

external reference record
gaibu sanshō rekōdo
外部参照レコード

external schema
gaibu sukiima
外部スキーマ

external signal
gaibu shingō
外部信号

external sort
gaibu bunrui
外部分類

external storage
gaibu kioku
外部記憶

external store
gaibu kioku sōchi
外部記憶装置

external subroutine
gaibu saburūchin
外部サブルーチン

external symbol
gaibu kigō
外部記号

external synchronization
gaibu dōki
外部同期

extract
chūshutsu
抽出

extract function
chūshutsu kinō
抽出機能

extract instruction
chūshutsu meirei
抽出命令

extract operation
chūshutsu sōsa
抽出操作

F

F (format)
F (fuōmatto; keishiki; shoshiki;
yōshiki)
フォーマット；形式；書式；
様式

face
fuēsu; jitai
フェース；字体

face bonding
fuēsu-bondeingu
フェース・ボンディング

face change character
jitai henkō moji
字体変更文字

face-down bonding
fuēsu-daun-bondeingu
フェース・ダウン・ボンディング

face-down feed
ura okuri
裏送り

face-up feed
omote okuri
表送り

facilities management
kikō kanri; setsubi kanri; shisetsu
kanri
機構管理；設備管理；施設管理

facility
kikō; kinō; setsubi; shisetsu
機構；機能；設備；施設

facsimile (FAX)
fuakushimiri; mosha densō (FAX)
ファクシミリ；模写電送

fact
jijitsu; jikō
事実；事項

fact retrieval
jijitsu kensaku; jikō kensaku
事実検索；事項検索

factor
inshi; insū; yō'in
因子；因数；要因

factor analysis
inshi bunseki
因子分析

factoring
bunkai
分解

factual information
jijitsu jōhō
事実情報

fade in
fuēdo-in
フェード・イン

fade out
fuēdo-auto
フェード・アウト

fail-safe
fueiru-sēfu
フェイル・セーフ

fail-safe design
fueiru-sēfu sekkei
フェイル・セーフ設計

fail-safe procedure
fueiru-sēfu tejun;
fueiru-sēfu tetsuzuki
フェイル・セーフ手順;
フェイル・セーフ手続き

fail-safe system
fueiru-sēfu-shisutemu
フェイル・セーフ・システム

fail-soft
fueiru-sofuto
フェイル・ソフト

fail-soft system
fueiru-sofuto-shisutemu
フェイル・ソフト・システム

failure
jiko; koshō
事故; 故障

failure identification
koshō shikibetsu
故障識別

failure mechanism
koshō kikō
故障機構

failure minimization
koshō saishōka
故障最小化

failure of ———; failure to ———
——— funō
——— 不能

failure probability
koshō kakuritsu
故障確率

failure rate
koshō ritsu
故障率

fall time
tachisagari jikan
立ち下り時間

false
ayamari; Itsuwari
誤り; 偽り

false code
itsuwari kōdo
偽りコード

fan-in
fuan-in; ronri nyūryoku
ファン・イン; 論理入力

fan-out
fuan-auto; ronri shutsuryoku
ファン・アウト; 論理出力

fan-out free
ronri shutsuryoku nai
論理出力ない

fast access
kōsoku akusesu;
kōsoku yobidashi
高速アクセス; 高速呼び出し

fast-access memory
kōsoku kioku
高速記憶

fast-access storage
kōsoku kioku
高速記憶

fast Fourier transform (FFT)
kōsoku Fūrie henkan (FFT)
高速フーリェ変換

fast line
kōsoku sen
高速線

fatal error
chimeiteki ayamari
致命的誤り

fault
ayamari; ijō; jiko;
kekkan; koshō; shōgai
誤り; 異常; 事故;
欠陥; 故障; 障害

fault detectability
koshō kenchisei
故障検知性

fault detection
shōgai kenshutsu
障害検出

fault finding
koshō hakken
故障発見

fault isolation
koshō bunri
故障分離

fault location
koshō hakken
故障発見

fault location problem
koshō hakken mondai
故障発見問題

fault monitoring
koshō seigyo
故障制御

fault redundancy
koshō jōchō(do)
故障冗長（度）

fault time
koshō jikan
故障時間

fault tolerance
koshō kyoyō
故障許容

fault-tolerant system
koshō kyoyō shisutemu
故障許容システム

faulty
ijō (na); jiko
異常(な); 事故

faulty message
ijō dembun; jiko dembun
異常電文; 事故電文

FAX (facsimile)
FAX (fuakushimiri; mosha densō)
ファクシミリ; 模写電送

FCB (file control block)
FCB (fuairu seigyo burokku)
ファイル制御ブロック

FCC (Federal Communications Commission) (USA)
FCC (Beikoku Rempō Tsūshin
I'inkai)
米国連邦通信委員会

FCT (file control table)
FCT (fairu seigyo tēburu)
ファイル制御テーブル

FD (floppy disk)
FD (furoppi-deisuku)
フロッピ・ディスク

FD (full duplex)
FD (zen nijū)
全二重

FDM (finite difference method)
FDM (yūgen sabumpō)
有限差分法

FDM (frequency division multiplexing; frequency division multiplexer)
FDM (shūhasū bunkatsu tajū hōshiki; shūhasū bunkatsu tajū hōshiki sōchi)
周波数分割多重方式;
周波数分割多重方式装置

FDOS (floppy-disk operating system)
FDOS (furoppi-deisuku-operēteingu-shisutemu)
フロッピ・ディスク・
オペレーティング・システム

FDX (full duplex)
FDX (zen nijū)
全二重

FE (format effector)
FE (shoshiki seigyo moji)
書式制御文字

feasibility study
fuiijibiritei kenkyū;
jitsugenkanōsei kentō
フィージビリティ研究;
実現可能性検討

feature
kikō; kinō; tokuchō
機構; 機能; 特徴

Federal Communications Commission (FCC) (USA)
Beikoku Rempō Tsūshin I'inkai (FCC)
米国連邦通信委員会

Federal Information Processing Standards (FIPS) (USA)
Beikoku Rempō Jōhō Shori Hyōjun (FIPS)
米国連邦情報処理標準

feed (noun)
fuiido; okuri
フィード; 送り

feed (verb)
okuru
送る

feed error
okuri ayamari
送り誤り

feed forward
fuiido-fuōwādo; seihōkō okuri
フィード・フォーワード;
正方向送り

feed forward control
fuiido-fuōwādo seigyo
フィード・フォーワード制御

feed holes
okuri ana
送り孔

feed hopper
fuiido-hoppa; okuri hoppa
フィード・ホッパ; 送りホッパ

feed pitch
fuiido-pitchi; okuri kankaku
フィード・ピッチ; 送り間隔

feed rate
fuiido sokudo; okuri sokudo
フィード速度; 送り速度

feedback
fuiidobakku; kikan
フィードバック; 帰還

feedback control
fuiidobakku seigyo
フィードバック制御

feedback loop
fuiidobakku-rūpu
フィードバック・ループ

feedback system
fuiidobakku-shisutemu;
kikan hōshiki
フィードバック・システム;
帰還方式

FEM (finite element method)
FEM (yūgen yōso hō)
有限要素法

FEP (front-end processor)
FEP (furonto-endo-purosessa)
フロント・エンド・プロセッサ

ferrite
fueraito
フェライト

ferrite core
fueraito jishin; fueraito-koa
フェライト磁心;
フェライト・コア

ferrite rod
fueraito-roddo
フェライト・ロッド

FET (field effect transistor technology)
FET (denkai kōka toranjisuta gijutsu)
電界効果トランジスタ技術

fetch (noun)
fuetchi; toridashi
フェッチ; 取り出し

fetch (verb)
fuetchi suru; toridasu
フェッチする; 取り出す

fetch cycle
meirei toridashi dankai
命令取り出し段階

fetch-execute
meirei toridashi-jikkō
命令取り出し-実行

fetch-execute cycle
meirei toridashi-jikkō dankai
命令取り出し-実行段階

fetch protection
toridashi bōshi
取り出し防止

fetch time
meirei toridashi jikan
命令取り出し時間

FF (form feed)
FF (shoshiki okuri)
書式送り

FFT (fast Fourier transform)
FFT (kōsoku Fūrie henkan)
高速フーリェ変換

fiber optics
fuaiba-oputeikkusu
ファイバ・オプティックス

fiber-optics transmission
fuaiba-oputeikkusu densō
ファイバ・オプティックス伝送

Fibonacci search
Fuibonatchi tansaku
フィボナッチ探索

Fibonacci series
Fuibonatchi sūretsu
フィボナッチ数列

fiche
fuisshu
フィッシュ

field
fuiirudo; ran
フィールド; 欄

field check
fuiirudo-chekku
フィールド・チェック

field control
fuiirudo seigyo
フィールド制御

field control check
fuiirudo seigyo chekku
フィールド制御チェック

field definition
fuiirudo teigi
フィールド定義

field descriptor
fuiirudo kijutsushi
フィールド記述子

field-developed program
fuiirudo kaihatsu puroguramu
フィールド開発プログラム

field effect transistor technology (FET)
denkai kōka toranjisuta gijutsu (FET)
電界効果トランジスタ技術

field length
fuiirudo chō; fuiirudo no nagasa
フィールド長; フィールドの長さ

field selection
fuiirudo sentaku
フィールド選択

field separator
ran kugiri
欄区切り

field sequence
fuiirudo-shiikensu
フィールド・シーケンス

FIFO (first-in first-out)
FIFO (saki ire saki dashi)
先入れ先出し

fifth-generation computer
daigo sedai keisanki
第五世代計算機

FIGS (figure shift)
FIGS (sūji shifuto)
数字シフト

figure
sūji
数字

figure shift (FIGS)
sūji shifuto (FIGS)
数字シフト

file
fuairu
ファイル

file access method
fuairu-akusesu-mōdo
ファイル・アクセス・モード

file activity ratio
fuairu shiyō ritsu
ファイル使用率

file amendment
fuairu henkō
ファイル変更

file analysis
fuairu bunseki
ファイル分析

file analysis form
fuairu bunsekihyō
ファイル分析表

file archive
fuairu-ākaibu; fuairu hozon
ファイル・アーカイブ;
ファイル保存

file attribute
fuairu zokusei
ファイル属性

file cleanup
fuairu kōshin
ファイル更新

file consolidation
fuairu tōgō
ファイル統合

file contents
fuairu naiyō
ファイル内容

file control
fuairu seigyo
ファイル制御

file control block (FCB)
fuairu seigyo burokku (FCB)
ファイル制御ブロック

file control table
fuairu seigyo tēburu
ファイル制御テーブル

file conversion
fuairu henkan
ファイル変換

file converter
fuairu-konbāta
ファイル・コンバータ

file coupling
fuairu ketsugō
ファイル結合

file declaration statement
fuairu sengen bun
ファイル宣言文

file definition name
fuairu teigi mei
ファイル定義名

file description
fuairu kijutsu
ファイル記述

file description entry
fuairu kijutsu kōmoku
ファイル記述項目

file descriptor
fuairu kijutsushi
ファイル記述子

file designation
fuairu shitei
ファイル指定

file dumping
fuairu danpu; fuairu hakidashi
ファイル・ダンプ;
ファイル掃き出し

file header
fuairu midashi
ファイル見出し

file header label (HDR)
fuairu midashi raberu (HDR)
ファイル見出しラベル

file header label group
fuairu midashi raberu gun
ファイル見出しラベル群

file identification
fuairu shikibetsu
ファイル識別

file identifier
fuairu shikibetsumei
ファイル識別名

file index
fuairu-indekkusu
ファイル・インデックス

file inquiry
fuairu kensaku
ファイル検索

file label
fuairu-raberu
ファイル・ラベル

file layout
fuairu reiauto; fuairu sekkei;
fuairu yōshiki
ファイル・レイアウト；
ファイル設計；
ファイル様式

file loading
fuairu-rōdeingu
ファイル・ローディング

file maintenance
fuairu hoshu; fuairu iji
ファイル保守；ファイル維持

file management
fuairu kanri
ファイル管理

file management system
fuairu kanri shisutemu
ファイル管理システム

file name
fuairu mei
ファイル名

file organization
fuairu hensei
ファイル編成

file overflow
fuairu-ōbafurō
ファイル・オーバフロー

file partitioning
fuairu kubunka
ファイル区分化

file print
fuairu-purinto
ファイル・プリント

file processing
fuairu shori
ファイル処理

file protection
fuairu hogo
ファイル保護

file protection ring
fuairu hogo ringu
ファイル保護リング

file reconstitution
fuairu fukkyū; fuairu fukugen
ファイル復旧；ファイル復元

file record specification
fuairu-rekōdo shiyō
ファイル・レコード仕様

file recovery
fuairu kaifuku
ファイル回復

file reference
fuairu in'yō; fuairu sanshō
ファイル引用；ファイル参照

file retention period
fuairu hozon kikan
ファイル保存期間

file scan
fuairu sōsa
ファイル走査

file search
fuairu tansaku
ファイル探索

file security
fuairu hogo
ファイル保護

file separator (FS)
fuairu bunri moji (FS)
フアイル分離文字

file sequence
fuairu junjo
ファイル順序

file sequence number
fuairu junjo bangō
ファイル順序番号

file server
fuairu-sāba
ファイル・サーバ

file set
fuairu-setto
ファイル・セット

file set identifier
fuairu-setto shikibetsumei
ファイル・セット識別名

file sharing
fuairu kyōyō; fuairu-sheāringu
ファイル共用；
ファイル・シェアーリング

file specification form
fuairu shijisho
ファイル指示書

file structure
fuairu kōzō
ファイル構造

file support
fuairu-sapōto
ファイル・サポート

file trailer label
fuairu atogaki raberu
ファイル後書きラベル

file trailer label group
fuairu atogaki raberu gun
ファイル後書きラベル群

file transfer
fuairu tensō
ファイル転送

file transfer utility
fuairu tensō yūteiritei
ファイル転送ユーティリティ

file update
fuairu kōshin
ファイル更新

file updating
fuairu kōshin
ファイル更新

filestore
fuairu kioku sōchi; fuairusutōa
ファイル記憶装置；
ファイルストーア

filing
fuairingu
ファイリング

filing system
fuairingu-shisutemu
ファイリング・システム

fill
jūten
充てん

fill character
jūten moji
充てん文字

film
fuirumu; maku
フィルム；膜

film reader
fuirumu yomitori sōchi
フィルム読み取り装置

film recorder
fuirumu kiroku sōchi
フィルム記録装置

film scanner
fuirumu sōsa kikō
フィルム走査機構

FILO (first-in last-out)
FILO (saki ire ato dashi)
先入れ後出し

filter
fuiruta
フィルタ

finite automaton
yūgen otōmaton
有限オートマトン

finite difference method (FDM)
yūgen sabumpō (FDM)
有限差分法

finite element method (FEM)
yūgen yōso hō (FEM)
有限要素法

finite state
yūgen jōtai
有限状態

finite-state language
yūgen jōtai gengo
有限状態言語

finite-state machine
yūgen jōtai kikai
有限状態機械

FIPS (Federal Information Processing Standards) (USA)
FIPS (Beikoku Rempō Jōhō Shori Hyōjun)
米国連邦情報処理標準

firmware
fuāmuuea
ファームウェア

first-generation computer
daiichi sedai keisanki
第一世代計算機

first-in first-out (FIFO)
sakiire sakidashi (FIFO)
先入れ先出し

first-in last-out (FILO)
sakiire atodashi (FILO)
先入れ後出し

first-level address
dai'ichi reberu-adoresu
第一レベル・アドレス

first-level definition
dai'ikkai no teigi
第一階の定義

first operand
dai'ichi operando
第一オペランド

first order
ichiji
一次

first-order control
ichiji seigyo
一次制御

first-order subroutine
ichiji saburūchin
一次サブルーチン

first-order system
ichiji shisutemu
一次システム

first-pass own code (FPOC)
fuasuto-pasu-oun-kōdo (FPOC)
ファスト・パス・オウン・コード

five-level code
go tan'i fugō
5単位符号

fixed-block length
kotei burokku chō
固定ブロック長

fixed-clock time control
teikankaku jikan seigyo hōshiki
定間隔時間制御方式

fixed-command control
teichi seigyo
定値制御

fixed connector
kotei konekuta
固定コネクタ

fixed data name
kimatta dēta mei
決まったデータ名

fixed decimal point
kotei jisshin shōsūten
固定10進小数点

fixed disk
kotei deisuku
固定ディスク

fixed-disk store
kotei deisuku kioku sōchi
固定ディスク記憶装置

fixed field
kotei fuiirudo
固定フィールド

fixed-fixed block
kotei-kotei burokku
固定固定ブロック

fixed format
kotei keishiki
固定形式

fixed-format message
kotei keishiki messēji
固定形式メッセージ

fixed head
kotei heddo
固定ヘッド

fixed-head disk
kotei heddo-deisuku
固定ヘッド・ディスク

fixed-head storage
kotei heddo kioku
固定ヘッド記憶

fixed length
koteichō
固定長

fixed-length field
kotei chō fuiirudo
固定長フィールド

fixed-length format
kotei chō keishiki
固定長形式

fixed-length record
kotei chō rekōdo
固定長レコード

fixed-length word
kotei chō go
固定長語

fixed memory
kotei kioku
固定記憶

fixed point
kotei shōsūten
固定小数点

fixed-point arithmetic
kotei shōsūten enzan
固定小数点演算

fixed-point binary
kotei shōsūten nishinsū
固定小数点2進数

fixed-point computer
kotei shōsūten hōshiki keisanki
固定小数点方式計算機

fixed-point integer
kotei shōsūten seisū
固定小数点整数

fixed-point notation
kotei shōsūten hyōkihō
固定小数点表記法

fixed-point number
kotei shōsūten sū
固定小数点数

fixed-point part
shōsūbu
小数部

fixed-point representation
kotei shōsūten hyōji
固定小数点表示

fixed-point representation system
kotei shōsūten hyōkihō
固定小数点表記法

fixed-point value
kotei shōsūten chi
固定小数点値

fixed-radix notation
kotei kisū hyōkihō
固定基数表記法

fixed routine
kotei rūchin
固定ルーチン

fixed storage
kotei kioku
固定記憶

fixed-variable
kotei-kahen
固定-可変

fixed-variable length
kotei-kahen chō
固定-可変長

fixed-variable-length field
kotei-kahen chō fuiirudo
固定-可変長フィールド

fixed word length
kotei go chō
固定語長

fixed-word-length computer
kotei go chō keisanki
固定語長計算機

flag
furaggu; hyōshiki
フラッグ；標識

flag bit
furagu-bitto
フラッグ・ビット

flat cable
furatto-kēburu
フラット・ケーブル

flat pack
furatto-pakku
フラット・パック

flat package
furatto-pakkēji
フラット・パッケージ

flat screen
furatto-sukuriin
フラット・スクリーン

flatbed plotter
heimen purotta
平面プロッタ

flexible disk
furekishiburu-deisuku
フレキシブル・ディスク

flexible-disk recorder
furekishiburu-deisuku-rekōda
フレキシブル・ディスク・
レコーダ

flexible-disk unit
furekishiburu-deisuku sōchi
フレキシブル・ディスク装置

flexidisk
furekishiburu-deisuku
フレキシブル・ディスク

flip-flop
furippu-furoppu
フリップ・フロップ

floating address
fudō adoresu
浮動アドレス

floating character
fudō moji
浮動文字

floating head
fudō heddo
浮動ヘッド

floating point (FP)
fudō shōsūten (FP)
浮動小数点

floating-point arithmetic
fudō shōsūten enzan
浮動小数点演算

floating-point base
fudō shōsūten kisū
浮動小数点基数

floating-point computer
fudō shōsūten hōshiki keisanki
浮動小数点方式計算機

floating-point constant
fudō shōsūten teisū
浮動小数点定数

floating-point notation
fudō shōsūten hyōkihō
浮動小数点表記法

floating-point number
fudō shōsūten sū
浮動小数点数

floating-point operations per second (FLOPS)
fudō shōsūten enzan/byō
(FLOPS)
浮動小数点演算／秒

floating-point package (FPP)
fudō shōsūten pakkēji (FPP)
浮動小数点パッケージ

floating-point radix
fudō shōsūten kisū
浮動小数点基数

floating-point register (fr)
fudō shōsūten rejisuta (fr)
浮動小数点レジスタ

floating-point representation
fudō shōsūten hyōji
浮動小数点表示

floating-point routine
fudō shōsūten rūchin
浮動小数点ルーチン

floating replacement character
fudō okikae moji
浮動置き換え文字

floor stand
furoa-sutando
フロア・スタンド

floppy disk
furoppi-deisuku
フロッピ・ディスク

floppy-disk operation system (FDOS)
furoppi-deisuku-operēteingu-shisutemu (FDOS)
フロッピ・ディスク・
オペレーティング・システム

FLOPS (floating-point operations per second)
FLOPS (fudō shōsūten enzan/byō)
浮動小数点演算／秒

flow (noun)
furō; nagare
フロー; 流れ

flow analysis
nagare kaiseki
流れ解析

flow control
nagare seigyo
流れ制御

flow diagram
nagare zu
流れ図

flow direction
nagare no muki
流れの向き

flow line
nagare sen
流れ線

flow network
nagare nettowāku
流れネットワーク

flow system
nagare shisutemu
流れシステム

flowchart
nagarezu
流れ図

flowchart connector
nagarezu ketsugōshi
流れ図結合子

flowchart symbols
nagarezu kigō
流れ図記号

flowcharting
furōchāteingu; nagarezu sakusei
フローチャーティング;
流れ図作成

fluctuation
hendō; jitta
変動; ジッタ

fluorescence
keikō
蛍光

flux
jisoku
磁束

flux density
jisoku mitsudo
磁束密度

flux transition
jisoku hanten
磁束反転

flying head
fudō heddo
浮動ヘッド

flying-spot scanner
furaingu-supotto sōsa kikō
フライング・スポット走査機構

FM (frequency modulation)
FM (shūhasū henchō)
周波数変調

FM data recorder
FM dēta-rekōda
FMデータ・レコーダ

follow-up control
tsuijū seigyo
追従制御

font
fuonto; jitai
フォント; 字体

font change character
jitai henkan moji
字体変換文字

footprint
ashiato
足跡

FOR statement
kurikaeshi bun
繰り返し文

forbidden character code
kinshi moji fugō
禁止文字符号

forbidden combination
kinshi kumiawase
禁止組み合わせ

forecasting
yosoku
予測

forecasting technique
yosoku gihō
予測技法

foreground
fuoaguraundo; zenkei
フォアグラウンド; 前景

foreground job
fuoaguraundo-jyobu;
zenkei jyobu
フォアグラウンド・ジョブ;
前景ジョブ

foreground processing
zenkei shori
前景処理

foreground program
fuoaguraundo-puroguramu;
zenkei puroguramu
フォアグラウンド・プログラム;
前景プログラム

foreign (non-Japanese) language
gaikokugo
外国語

foreign (non-Japanese) language system extension (FSX)
gaikokugo shisutemu kakuchō (FSX)
外国語システム拡張

form (document)
fuōmu; shoshiki; yōshi
フォーム；書式；用紙

form (expression; shape)
hyōgen; keishiki; keitai; shiki
表現；形式；形態；式

form advance
shoshiki okuri
書式送り

form control
shoshiki seigyo
書式制御

form feed (FF)
shoshiki okuri (FF)
書式送り

form feed character
shoshiki okuri moji
書式送り文字

form of application
riyō keitai
利用形態

form stacker
fuōmu-sutakka; renzoku yōshi ukedai
フォーム・スタッカ；連結用紙受け台

form stop
fuōmu-sutoppu
フォーム・ストップ

formal
keishiki
形式

formal definition
keishiki teigi
形式定義

formal language
keishiki gengo
形式言語

formal logic
keishiki ronri
形式論理

formal parameter
kari parameta
仮パラメタ

formal specification
keishiki shiyō
形式仕様

format (F)
fuōmatto; keishiki; shoshiki; yōshiki (F)
フォーマット；形式；書式；様式

format chart
yōshiki zu
様式図

format code
shoshiki kōdo
書式コード

format control
shoshiki seigyo
書式制御

format control card
shoshiki seigyo kādo
書式制御カード

format description
shoshiki kijutsu
書式記述

format effector (FE)
shoshiki seigyo moji (FE)
書式制御文字

format item
keishiki kōmoku
形式項目

format specification
shoshiki shiyō
書式仕様

formatted
shoshiki tsuki; teiyōshiki
書式付き；定様式

formatted data
teiyōshiki dēta
定様式データ

formatted display
teiyōshiki hyōji
定様式表示

formatted message
teiyōshiki messēji
定様式メッセージ

formatted READ statement
shoshikitsuki riido bun
書式付きREAD文

formatted WRITE statement
shoshikitsuki raito bun
書式付きWRITE文

formatting
shoshiki sakusei; shoshiki tsuke
書式作成；書式付け

formula manipulation
sūshiki shori
数式処理

formula manipulation language
sūshiki shori gengo
数式処理言語

Formula Translation (FORTRAN)
Fuōtoran (FORTRAN)
フォートラン

FORTH
fuōsu
フォース

FORTRAN (Formula Translation)
FORTRAN (Fuōtoran)
フォートラン

forward channel
junhōkō chaneru
順方向チャネル

forward direction
junhōkō
順方向

forward read
jun yomi
順読み

forward reading
jun yomi
順読み

forward sort
jun bunrui
順分類

forward space
mae okuri
前送り

four-address
yon adoresu
4アドレス

four-address instruction
yon adoresu meirei
4 アドレス命令

four-plus-one address
yon purasu ichi adoresu
4 ＋ 1 アドレス

four-wire channel
yonsenshiki tsūshinro
4 線式通信路

four-wire circuit
yonsenshiki kaisen
4 線式回線

four-wire system
yonsenshiki
4 線式

Fourier transform
Fūrie henkan
フーリェ変換

fourth-generation computer
daiyon sedai keisanki
第四世代計算機

FP (floating point)
FP (fudō shōsūten)
浮動小数点

FPP (floating-point package)
FPP (fudō shōsūten pakkēji)
浮動小数点パッケージ

fr (floating-point register)
fr (fudō shōsūten rejisuta)
浮動小数点レジスタ

fraction
shōsū
小数

fractional part
shōsūbu
小数部

fragmentation
bunkatsu; dampenka
分割；断片化

frame
furēmu
フレーム

frame count error
furēmu-kaunto-erā
フレーム・カウント・エラー

frame synchronization
furēmu dōki
フレーム同期

framing
furēmu shiji
フレーム指示

framing bit
furēmu shiji bitto
フレーム指示ビット

free access
furii-akusesu
フリー・アクセス

free form
jiyū keishiki
自由形式

free format
furii-fuōmatto; jiyū shoshiki
フリー・フォーマット；
自由書式

free-standing
yukauegata
床上型

free-standing drive
yukauegata kudō kikō
床上型駆動機構

free storage
furii kioku
フリー記憶

frequency
hindo; kaisū; shūhasū
頻度；回数；周波数

frequency band
shūhasū tai'iki
周波数帯域

frequency discrimination
shūhasū bembetsu
周波数弁別

frequency division multiplexer (FDM)
shūhasū bunkatsu tajū hōshiki sōchi (FDM)
周波数分割多重方式装置

frequency division multiplexing (FDM)
shūhasū bunkatsu tajū hōshiki (FDM)
周波数分割多重方式

frequency modulation (FM)
shūhasū henchō (FM)
周波数変調

frequency response
shūhasū ōtō
周波数応答

frequency shift
shūhasū hen'i
周波数変位

frequency shift keying (FSK)
shūhasū hen'i hōshiki (FSK)
周波数変位方式

friction
masatsu
摩擦

friction feed
masatsu okuri
摩擦送り

friction speed
masatsu sokudo
摩擦速度

front end
furonto-endo; zenchi
フロント・エンド；前置

front-end processor (FEP)
furonto-endo-purosessa (FEP)
フロント・エンド・プロセッサ

front-end system
zenchi shisutemu
前置システム

front panel (of console)
furonto-paneru
フロント・パネル

FS (file separator)
FS (fuairu bunri moji)
ファイル分離文字

FSK (frequency shift keying)
FSK (shūhasū hen'i hōshiki)
周波数変位方式

FSX (foreign [non-Japanese] language system extension)
FSX (gaikokugo shisutemu kakuchō)
外国語システム拡張

full adder
zen kasanki
全加算器

full duplex (FDX)
zen nijū (FDX)
全二重

full-duplex channel
zen nijū tsūshinro
全二重通信路

full-duplex communication
zen nijū tsūshin
全二重通信

full-duplex system
zen nijū hōshiki
全二重方式

full-duplex transmission
zen nijū densō
全二重伝送

full-read pulse
zen sentaku yomidashi parusu
全選択読み出しパルス

full subtracter
zen genzanki
全減算器

full word
zen go
全語

function (arithmetic)
kansū
関数

function (feature)
eki; kanō; kiki; kikō; kinō; sābisu
役; 可能; 機器; 機構; 機能;
サービス

function code
kiki seigyo kōdo
機器制御コード

function diagram
kinō zu
機能図

function element
kinō soshi
機能素子

function evaluation
kansū hyōka
関数評価

function generator
kansū hassei puroguramu;
kansū hasseiki
関数発生プロクラム;
関数発生器

function key
kinō kii
機能キー

function part
sōsa bu
操作部

function punch
seigyo senkō
制御せん孔

function space
kansū kūkan
関数空間

function subprogram
kansū sabupuroguramu
関数サブプログラム

function table
kansū hyō; kansū tēburu;
kinō hyō; kinō tēburu
関数表; 関数テーブル;
機能表; 機能テーブル

functional block
kinō burokku
機能ブロック

functional character
kinō kyarakuta
機能キャラクタ

functional dependence
kansū izon
関数依存

functional design
kinō sekkei
機能設計

functional device
kinō debaisu
機能デバイス

functional diagram
kinō zu
機能図

functional information
kinō jōhō
機能情報

functional information system
kinō jōhō shisutemu
機能情報システム

functional macroinstruction
kinō makuro meirei
機能マクロ命令

functional objective
kinō mokuteki
機能目的

functional symbol
ronri kigō
論理記号

functional system
kinō shisutemu
機能システム

functional test
kinō tesuto
機能テスト

functionality
kinōsei
機能性

futuristic information
shōrai jōhō
将来情報

G

G (giga-)
G (giga-)
ギガ

gain
ritoku
利得

game
gēmu
ゲーム

game theory
gēmu riron
ゲーム理論

gang punch
shūdan senkō
集団せん孔

gap
gyappu; kankaku
ギャップ; 間隔

gap scatter
gyappu no baratsuki
ギャップのばらつき

garbage
fuyō jōhō; gābejji
不要情報; ガーベッジ

garbage collection
gābejji-korekushon
ガーベッジ・コレクション

garbage-in garbage-out (GIGO)
gābejji-in-gābejji-auto (GIGO)
ガーベッジ・イン・ガーベッジ・
アウト; ギゴ

gate
gēto
ゲート

gate circuit
gēto kairo
ゲート回路

gate control
gēto seigyo
ゲート制御

gate matrix
gēto-matorikkusu
ゲート・マトリックス

gate pulse
gēto-parusu
ゲート・パルス

gateway
gētouei
ゲートウェイ

gateway computer
gētouei-konpyūta
ゲートウェイ・コンピュータ

gather write
shūgō kakidashi
集合書き出し

gathering (of data)
(dēta) shūshū
(データ)収集

Gaussian pulse
Gausugata parusu
ガウス型パルス

GCR (group-coded recording)
GCR (gurūpu-kōdeiddo-
rekōdeingu)
グループ・コーディッド・
レコーディング

GD (graphic display)
GD (gurafuikku-deisupurei; zukei
hyōji)
グラフィック・ディスプレイ;
図形表示

general communication system
ippan tsūshin shisutemu
一般通信システム

general format
ippan keishiki
一般形式

general information
ippan jōhō
一般情報

general information network
ippan jōhō nettowāku
一般情報ネットワーク

general interface
han'yō intafuēsu
汎用インタフェース

general poll
ikkatsu pōru
一括ポール

general-purpose
han'yō
汎用

general-purpose computer
han'yō keisanki;
han'yō konpyūta
汎用計算機; 汎用コンピュータ

general-purpose computer system
han'yō keisanki shisutemu
汎用計算機システム

general-purpose integrated system
han'yō sōgō shisutemu
汎用総合システム

general-purpose interface
han'yō intafuēsu
汎用インタフェース

general-purpose operating system
han'yō operēteingu-shisutemu
汎用オペレーティング・
システム

general-purpose program
han'yō puroguramu
汎用プログラム

general-purpose register
han'yō rejisuta
汎用レジスタ

general-purpose simulation
han'yō shimyurēshon
汎用シミュレーション

general-purpose simulation system (GPSS)
han'yō shimyurēshon-shisutemu
(GPSS)
汎用シミュレーション・
システム

general register (gr)
han'yō rejisuta (gr)
汎用レジスタ

general system
ippan shisutemu
一般システム

general-use
han'yō
汎用

generalization
ippanka
一般化

generalized
han'yō; ippanka
汎用; 一般化

generalized information system (GIS)
han'yō jōhō shisutemu; ippanka jōhō shisutemu (GIS)
汎用情報システム；
一般化情報システム

generalized routine
han'yō rūchin
汎用ルーチン

generalized sort-merge program
han'yō bunrui-kumiawase puroguramu
汎用分類-組み合わせプログラム

generate
hassei suru; seisei suru
発生する；生成する

generated
seisei
生成

generated address
seisei adoresu
生成アドレス

generating
seisei
生成

generating function
bokansū; seisei kansū; seisei takōshiki
母関数；生成関数；生成多項式

generating program
seisei puroguramu
生成プログラム

generating routine
seisei rūchin
生成ルーチン

generation
sedai; seisei
世代；生成

generation data group
sedaibetsu dēta-gurūpu
世代別データ・グループ

generation number
sedai bangō
世代番号

generation routine
seisei rūchin
生成ルーチン

generation system
sedai hōshiki; seisei hōshiki
世代方式；生成方式

generation technique
sedai gihō; sedai hō; seisei gihō; seisei hō
世代技法；世代法；生成技法；生成法

generation version number
sedai kōshin bangō
世代更新番号

generator
hasseiki; seisei puroguramu; zenerēta
発生器；生成プログラム；ゼネレータ

generic
sōshō(teki)
総称(的)

generic constant
ippan no teisū
一般の定数

generic data
sōshō(teki) dēta
総称(的)データ

generic name
sōshō mei
総称名

generic procedure
sōshō(teki) tetsuzuki
総称(的)手続き

GET
GET
GET

get into (an error gets into a system)
konnyū suru (erā ga shisutemu ni konnyū suru)
混入する
（エラーがシステムに混入する）

Gibson mix
Gibuson-mikkusu
ギブソン・ミックス

giga-(G)
giga-(G)
ギガ

gigacycle
giga-saikuru
ギガ・サイクル

GIGO (garbage-in garbage-out)
GIGO (gābejji-in-gābejji-auto)
ギゴ；ガーベッジ・イン・ガーベッジ・アウト

GIS (generalized information system)
GIS (han'yō jōhō shisutemu; ippanka jōhō shisutemu)
汎用情報システム；
一般化情報システム

global
gurōbaru; tai'iki (no; teki)
グローバル；大域(の；的)

global flow analysis
tai'ikiteki nagare kaiseki
大域的流れ解析

global optimization
tai'ikiteki saitekika
大域的最適化

global processor
tai'ikiteki purosessa
大域的プロセッサ

global set symbol
gurōbaru-setto kigō
グローバル・セット記号

global variable
gurōbaru hensū; tai'ikiteki hensū
グローバル変数；大域的変数

glossary
yōgojiten; yōgoshū
用語辞典；用語集

GO TO
GO TO (goto; tobikoshi)
GO TO；ゴト；飛び越し

GO TO statement
GO TO bun; tobikoshi bun
GO TO文；飛び越し文

golfball
gōfubōru
ゴフボール

golfball printer
gōfubōru-purinta
ゴフボール・プリンタ

gothic font
goshikku-fuonto
ゴシック・フォント

GPSS (general-purpose simulation system)
GPSS (han'yō shimyurēshon-shisutemu)
汎用シミュレーション・システム

gr (general register)
gr (han'yō rejisuta)
汎用レジスタ

graceful degradation
koshō mōdo dōsa
故障モード動作

gramping
guranpu sōsa
グランプ操作

grand-scale IC
chōdai kibo shūseki kairo
超大規模集積回路

grand-scale integration (GSI)
chōdai kibo shūsekika (GSI)
超大規模集積化

grandfather file
sofu fuairu
祖父ファイル

graph
gurafu; sakuzu
グラフ；作図

graph algorithm
gurafu riron
グラフ理論

graph manipulation
gurafu shori
グラフ処理

graph plotter
gurafu-purotta; sakuzu purotta
グラフ・プロッタ；
作図プロッタ

graph structure
gurafu kōzō
グラフ構造

graphic
gurafuikku; zukei
グラフィック；図形

graphic board
gurafuikku-bōdo
グラフィック・ボード

graphic character
zukei moji
図形文字

graphic data
gurafuikku-dēta; zukei dēta
グラフィック・データ；
図形データ

graphic data display
gurafuikku-dēta-deisupurei;
zukei hyōji
グラフィック・データ・
ディスプレィ；図形表示

graphic data display unit
zukei hyōji sōchi
図形表示装置

graphic data processing
gurafuikku-dēta shori;
zukei dēta shori
グラフィック・データ処理；
図形データ処理

graphic display (GD)
gurafuikku-deisupurei;
zukei hyōji (GD)
グラフィック・ディスプレィ；
図形表示

graphic display control
gurafuikku-deisupurei seigyo;
zukei hyōji seigyo
グラフィック・
ディスプレィ制御；
図形表示制御

graphic display program
zukei hyōji puroguramu
図形表示プログラム

graphic display unit
zukei hyōji sōchi
図形表示装置

graphic form
zukei
図形

graphic indicator
gurafuikku hyōshiki
グラフィック標識

graphic language
gurafuikkusu'yō gengo;
zukei (shori) gengo
グラフィックス用言語；
図形(処理)言語

graphic manipulation
gurafuikkusu shori
グラフィックス処理

graphic output
zukei shutsuryoku
図形出力

graphic output unit
zukei shutsuryoku sōchi
図形出力装置

graphic panel
gurafuikku-paneru
グラフィック・パネル

graphic planning system
gurafuikkusu keikaku shisutemu
グラフィックス計画システム

graphic symbol
zukigō
図記号

graphic system
gurafuikku-shisutemu
グラフィック・システム

graphical
gurafuikku; zukei
グラフィック；図形

graphical display
gurafuikku-deisupurei
グラフィック・ディスプレィ

graphical output
zukei shutsuryoku
図形出力

graphics
gurafuikkusu; zukei
グラフィックス；図形

graphics board
gurafuikkusu-bōdo
グラフィックス・ボード

graphics card
gurafuikkusu-kādo
グラフィックス・カード

graphics display
gurafuikkusu-deisupurei
グラフィックス・ディスプレィ

graphics operating system
gurafuikkusu-operēteingu-shisutemu
グラフィックス・
オペレーティング・システム

graphics processing
zukei shori
図形処理

graphics system
gurafuikkusu-shisutemu
グラフィックス・システム

graphics system design
gurafuikkusu-shisutemu sekkei
グラフィックス・システム設計

graphics tablet
gurafuikkusu-taburetto
グラフィックス・タブレット

graphics terminal
gurafuikkusu shori tanmatsu
sōchi; zukei shori tanmatsu
sōchi
グラフィックス処理端末装置;
図形処理端末装置

Gray code
Gurei-kōdo
グレイ・コード

green display
guriin-deisupurei
グリーン・ディスプレィ

grid
kōshi
格子

grid control
kōshi seigyo
格子制御

group
gun; gurūpu
群; グループ

group carry
gurūpu keta age
グループ桁上げ

group check
gurūpu kensa
グループ検査

group classification
gurūpu bunrui
グループ分類

group classification code
gurūpu bunrui kōdo
グループ分類コード

group code
gun fugō
群符号

group-coded recording (GCR)
gurūpu-kōdeiddo-rekōdeingu
(GCR)
グループ・コーディッド・
レコーディング

group delay
gun chien
群遅延

group indicate
gurūpu hyōji
グループ表示

group item
gurūpu kōmoku
グループ項目

group library
gurūpu-raiburari
グループ・ライブラリ

group mark
gurūpu-māku
グループ・マーク

group marker
gurūpu-māka
グループ・マーカ

group name
gurūpu mei
グループ名

group number
gurūpu bangō
グループ番号

group printing
gurūpu insatsu; gurūpu-purinto
グループ印刷; グループ・
プリント

group record
gurūpu-rekōdo
グループ・レコード

group separator (GS)
gurūpu bunri moji (GS)
グループ分離文字

group theory
gun ron
群論

grouped
gurūpu(ka)
グループ(化)

grouped messages
gurūpu(ka) dembun
グループ(化)電文

grouped records
gurūpu(ka) rekōdo
グループ(化)レコード

grouping
gurūpuka
グループ化

GS (group separator)
GS (gurūpu bunri moji)
グループ分離文字

GSI (grand-scale integration)
GSI (chōdai kibo shūsekika)
超大規模集積化

guard digit
hogo keta
保護桁

guard mode
hogo mōdo
保護モード

guard signal
hogo shingō
保護信号

guide
gaido
ガイド

guide edge
gaido-ejji
ガイド・エッジ

guide margin
gaido-mājin
ガイド・マージン

gulp
garupu
ガルプ

Gunn diode
Gan daiōdo
ガン・ダイオード

Gunn effect
Gan kōka
ガン効果

H

H (high)
H (kō'i; kō reberu)
高位；高レベル

hacker
hakka
ハッカ

hacking
hakkingu
ハッキング

half adder
han kasanki
半加算器

half duplex (HDX)
han nijū (HDX)
半二重

half-duplex channel
han nijū tsūshinro
半二重通信路

half-duplex communication system
han nijū tsūshin shisutemu
半二重通信システム

half-duplex transmission (HDX)
han nijū densō (HDX)
半二重伝送

half subtracter
han gensanki
半減算器

half word
hāfu-wādo; han go
ハーフ・ワード；半語

half-write pulse
han sentaku kakikomi parusu
半選択書き込みパルス

halt
teishi
停止

halt instruction
teishi meirei
停止命令

Hamming code
Hamingu-kōdo
ハミング・コード

Hamming distance
Hamingu kyori
ハミング距離

hand-operated
shudō(shiki)
手動(式)

hand-operated calculator
shudō keisanki
手動計算器

hand punch
hando-panchi;
shudōshiki senkōki
ハンド・パンチ；
手動式せん孔機

hand-written
tekaki
手書き

hand-written character recognition
tekaki moji ninshiki
手書き文字認識

hand-written numeral recognition
tekaki sūji ninshiki
手書き数字認識

handle (_verb_)
handoru suru
ハンドルする

handler
handora
ハンドラ

handling
handoringu
ハンドリング

handling time
handoringu jikan
ハンドリング時間

handshake
akushu; shoki setsuzoku
握手；初期接続

handshaking
akushu; shoki setsuzoku tejun
握手；初期接続手順

hang-up
teishi
停止

hard copy
hādo-kopii
ハード・コピー

hard-copy log
hādo-kopii-rogu
ハード・コピー・ログ

hard disk (HD)
hādo-deisuku (HD)
ハード・ディスク

hard-disk connector
hādo-deisuku-konekuta
ハード・ディスク・コネクタ

hard-disk interface card
hādo-deisuku-intafuēsu-kādo
ハード・ディスク・
インタフェース・カード

hard-sectored disk
hādo-sekuta-deisuku
ハード・セクタ・ディスク

hard-sectoring
hādo-sekutoringu
ハード・セクトリング

hard system
hādo-shisutemu
ハード・システム

hard-wired
haisen
配線

hard-wired logic
haisen ronri
配線論理

hardware
hādouea; kanamono
ハードウェア；金物

hardware character generation
hādouea moji seisei
ハードウェア文字生成

hardware check
hādouea-chekku; hādouea kensa
ハードウェア・チェック；
ハードウェア検査

hardware configuration
hādouea kōsei
ハードウェア構成

hardware control
hādouea seigyo
ハードウェア制御

hardware description
hādouea kijutsu
ハードウェア記述

hardware management
hādouea kanri
ハードウェア管理

hardware multiply/divide
hādouea jōjosan
ハードウェア乗除算

hardware representation
kanamono hyōgen
金物表現

hardware-software configuration
hādouea-sofutouea kōsei
ハードウェア・
ソフトウェア構成

hash
hasshu
ハッシュ

hash coding
hasshu-kōdeingu
ハッシュ・コーディング

hash table
hasshu-tēburu
ハッシュ・テーブル

hash total
hasshu gōkei
ハッシュ合計

hashing
hasshingu
ハッシング

hazard
hazādo
ハザード

hazard analysis
hazādo kaiseki
ハザード解析

hazard control
hazādo seigyo
ハザード制御

hazard elimination
hazādo haijo
ハザード排除

hazard rate
hazādo ritsu
ハザード率

HCI (human-computer interface)
HCI (ningen-keisanki intafuēsu)
人間-計算機インタフェース

HD (hard disk)
HD (hādo-deisuku)
ハード・ディスク

HDLC (high-level data link control)
HDLC (haireberu-dēta-rinku seigyo; kōreberu-dēta-rinku seigyo)
ハイレベル・データ・
リンク制御; 高レベル・データ・
リンク制御

HDR (file header label)
HDR (fuairu midashi raberu)
ファイル見出しラベル

HDX (half duplex; half-duplex transmission)
HDX (han nijū; han nijū densō)
半二重, 半二重伝送

head
heddo
ヘッド

head crash
heddo shōtotsu
ヘッド衝突

head gap
heddo-gyappu; heddo kankaku
ヘッド・ギャップ; ヘッド間隔

head positioning
heddo ichi settei
ヘッド位置設定

header
hedda; midashi
ヘッダ; 見出し

header block
midashi burokku
見出しブロック

header card
midashi kādo
見出しカード

header cell
midashi seru
見出しセル

header entry
midashi kōmoku
見出し項目

header label
midashi raberu
見出しラベル

header record
midashi rekōdo
見出しレコード

header table
midashi tēburu
見出しテーブル

heading
heddeingu; midashi
ヘッディング; 見出し

heading line
midashi gyō
見出し行

heat conduction
netsudendō
熱伝導

heat conduction analysis
netsudendō kaiseki
熱伝導解析

hertz (Hz)
herutsu (Hz)
ヘルツ

heterogeneous
ishitsu (no)
異質(の)

heuristic
hakken(teki)
発見(的)

heuristic approach
hakkenteki apurōchi
発見的アプローチ

heuristic program
hakkenteki puroguramu
発見的プログラム

heuristic search
hakkenteki tansaku
発見的探索

heuristics
hakken
発見

HEX (hexadecimal notation)
HEX (jūrokushin hō)
16進法

hexadecimal
jūrokushin
16進

hexadecimal address
jūrokushin adoresu
16進アドレス

hexadecimal code
jūrokushin kōdo
16進コード

hexadecimal digit
  jūrokushin sūji
  16進数字

hexadecimal notation (HEX)
  jūrokushin hō (HEX)
  16進法

hexadecimal number
  jūrokushin sū
  16進数

hexadecimal number system
  jūrokushin hō
  16進法

hexadecimal numeral
  jūrokushin sū
  16進数

hexadecimal representation
  jūrokushin hō
  16進法

hexadecimal value
  jūrokushin chi
  16進値

hidden
  in
  陰

hidden data
  in dēta
  陰データ

hidden line
  insen
  陰線

hidden-line removal
  insen jokyo
  陰線除去

hidden-surface removal
  inmen jokyo
  陰面除去

hierarchical classification
  kaisō bunrui
  階層分類

hierarchical computer
  kaisō keisanki
  階層計算機

hierarchical storage
  kaisō kioku
  階層記憶

hierarchical structure
  kaisō kōzō
  階層構造

hierarchy
  kaisō
  階層

hierarchy of operators
  enzanshi jun'i
  演算子順位

hierarchy system
  kaisō shisutemu
  階層システム

high (H)
  kō'i; kō reberu (H)
  高位；高レベル

high-capacity internal storage
  daiyōryō naibu kioku
  大容量内部記憶

high-level data link control (HDLC)
  haireberu-dēta-rinku seigyo;
  kōreberu-dēta-rinku seigyo
  (HDLC)
  ハイレベル・データ・
  リンク制御；高レベル・データ・
  リンク制御

high-level data link control procedure
  haireberu-dēta-rinku seigyo
  tejun; kōreberu-dēta-rinku seigyo
  tejun
  ハイレベル・データ・
  リンク制御手順；高レベル・
  データ・リンク制御手順

high-level decision making
  kōreberu ishi kettei
  高レベル意思決定

high-level language
  kōreberu gengo; kōsuijun gengo
  高レベル言語；高水準言語

high-level-language machine
  kōsuijun gengo kikai
  高水準言語機械

high-order end
  saisatan
  最左端

high reliability
  kōshinraido; kōshinraisei
  高信頼度；高信頼性

high resolution
  kōkaizōdo
  高解像度

high-resolution graphics
  kōkaizōdo zukei
  高解像度図形

high speed
  kōsoku(do)
  高速（度）

high-speed access
  kōsoku akusesu
  高速アクセス

high-speed bus
  kōsoku bosen
  高速母線

high-speed carry
  kōsoku keta age
  高速桁上げ

high-speed memory
  kōsoku kioku
  高速記憶

high-speed printer
  kōsoku insho sōchi
  高速印書装置

high-speed processing
  kōsoku shori
  高速処理

high-speed storage
  kōsoku kioku
  高速記憶

high-threshold logic (HTL)
  kōshikiichi ronri (HTL)
  高敷居値論理

highway
  haiuei
  ハイウェイ

hit rate
  fuairu shiyōritsu
  ファイル使用率

hobbyist
  hobiisuto
  ホビースト

hold (*verb*)
  hoji; hōrudo; horyū (suru)
  保持；ホールド；保留（する）

hold file
  hōrudo-fuairu
  ホールド・ファイル

hold instruction
  hoji meirei
  保持命令

hold queue
horyū machigyōretsu
保留待ち行列

hold signal
horyū shingō
保留信号

holding
hoji
保持

holding circuit
hoji kairo
保持回路

holding register
hoji rejisuta
保持レジスタ

holding time
horyū jikan
保留時間

hole
ana; hōru; senkō
孔; ホール; せん孔

hole count check
senkōsū kensa
せん孔数検査

hole count error
senkōsū ayamari
せん孔数誤り

hole pattern
senkō patān
せん孔パターン

hole sort
hōru-sōto
ホール・ソート

Hollerith card
Horerisu-kādo
ホレリス・カード

Hollerith code
Horerisu-kōdo
ホレリス・コード

Hollerith constant
moji teisū
文字定数

Hollerith field descriptor
moji ran kijutsushi
文字欄記述子

Hollerith type
mojigata
文字型

holographic memory
horogurafuikku kioku
ホログラフィック記憶

holography
horogurafui
ホログラフィ

home address
hōmu-adoresu
ホーム・アドレス

home computer
hōmu-konpyūta
ホーム・コンピュータ

home electronics
hōmu-erekutoronikkusu
ホーム・エレクトロニックス

home mode
hōmu-mōdo
ホーム・モード

home position
hōmu-pojishon
ホーム・ポジション

home record
hōmu-rekōdo
ホーム・レコード

homeostasis
homeosutashisu
ホメオスタシス

homogeneity
dōshitsu
同質

homogeneous
dōshitsu no
同質の

hopper
hoppa
ホッパ

horizontal
suihei(gata); suijun
水平(型); 水準

horizontal check
suihei kensa
水平検査

horizontal Chinese characters
suijun kanji
水準漢字

horizontal feed
suihei okuri
水平送り

horizontal format
suihei shoshiki
水平書式

horizontal microprogram
suiheigata maikuropuroguramu
水平型マイクロプログラム

horizontal parity
suihei kigū; suihei paritei
水平奇偶; 水平パリティ

horizontal parity check
suihei kigū kensa;
suihei paritei-chekku
水平奇偶検査;
水平パリティ・チェック

horizontal scanning
suihei sōsa
水平走査

horizontal tabulation (HT)
suihei tabu (HT)
水平タブ

horizontal tabulation character (HT)
suihei tabu moji (HT)
水平タブ文字

host
hosuto; jōi; oya
ホスト; 上位; 親

host computer
jōi keisanki; jōi konpyūta
hosuto-konpyūta
上位計算機;上位コンピュータ;
ホスト・コンピュータ

host CPU
jōi CPU
上位CPU

host language
jōi gengo; oya gengo
上位言語; 親言語

host language database
oya gengo dētabēsu
親言語データベース

host preparation facility
jōi shisutemu jumbi kinō
上位システム準備機能

host processing
hosuto-purosesshingu
ホスト・プロセッシング

host processor
hosuto-purosessa
ホスト・プロセッサ

host system
hosuto-shisutemu; jōi shisutemu;
oya shisutemu
ホスト・システム；
上位システム；親システム

housekeeping
dantori; hausukiipingu; jumbi
段取り；ハウスキーピング；
準備

housekeeping operation
dantori sōsa; hausukiipingu sōsa;
jumbi sōsa
段取り操作；
ハウスキーピング操作；準備操作

housekeeping routine
hausukiipingu-rūchin;
jumbi rūchin
ハウスキーピング・ルーチン；
準備ルーチン

HSI (human-system interface)
HSI (ningen-shisutemu-
intafuēsu)
人間−システム・
インタフェース

**HT (horizontal tabulation;
horizontal tabulation character)**
HT (suihei tabu; suihei tabu moji)
水平タブ；水平タブ文字

HTL (high-threshold logic)
HTL (kōshikiichi ronri)
高敷居値論理

hub
habu
ハブ

human-computer interface (HCI)
ningen-keisanki intafuēsu
(HCI)
人間−計算機インタフェース

human-system interface (HSI)
ningen-shisutemu-intafuēsu
(HSI)
人間−システム・
インタフェース

hunting
hanteingu; ranchō
ハンティング；乱調

hybrid
haiburiddo; konsei
ハイブリッド；混成

hybrid channel
haiburiddo-chaneru
ハイブリッド・チャネル

hybrid circuit
haiburiddo kairo; konsei kairo
ハイブリッド回路；混成回路

hybrid coil
haiburiddo-koiru
ハイブリッド・コイル

hybrid computer
haiburiddo keisanki;
haiburiddo-konpyūta
ハイブリッド計算機；
ハイブリッド・コンピュータ

hybrid IC
haiburiddo IC; konsei IC
ハイブリッドIC；混成IC

hybrid integrated circuit
konsei shūseki kairo
混成集積回路

hybrid interface
haiburiddo-intafuēsu
ハイブリッド・インタフェース

hybrid model
haiburiddo-moderu
ハイブリッド・モデル

hybrid package
haiburiddo jissō; konsei jissō
ハイブリッド実装；混成実装

hybrid system
haiburiddo-shisutemu
ハイブリッド・システム

hyperresolution
chōbunkai
超分解

hysteresis
hisuterishisu
ヒステリシス

hysteresis loop
hisuterishisu-rūpu
ヒステリシス・ループ

hysteresis loss
hisuterishisu son
ヒステリシス損

Hz (hertz)
Hz (herutsu)
ヘルツ

I

IACK (interrupt acknowledge signal)
IACK (warikomi kōtei ōtō shingō)
割り込み肯定応答信号

IAR (instruction address register)
IAR (meirei adoresu-rejisuta)
命令アドレス・レジスタ

IAS (immediate-access storage; immediate-access store)
IAS (sokuji akusesu kioku; sokuji akusesu kioku sōchi)
即時アクセス記憶;
即時アクセス記憶装置

IBG (interblock gap)
IBG (burokkukan kankaku)
ブロック間間隔

IC (integrated circuit)
IC (shūseki kairo)
集積回路

IC socket
IC soketto
IC ソケット

ICA (International Communications Association)
ICA (Kokusai Tsūshin Kyōkai)
国際通信協会

ICC (International Computation Center)
ICC (Kokusai Keisan Senta)
国際計算センタ

ICM (integrated circuit memory)
ICM (shūseki kairo kioku)
集積回路記憶

icon *or* ikon
aikon
アイコン

ID (identification)
ID (shikibetsu)
識別

ID (industrial dynamics)
ID (indasutoriaru-dainamikkusu)
インダストリアル・
ダイナミックス

IDCS (interactive distribution control system)
IDCS (intarakuteibu-deisutoribyūshon seigyo shisutemu)
インタラクティブ・ディストリ
ビューション制御システム

ideal system
risōteki shisutemu
理想的システム

identification (ID)
shikibetsu (ID)
識別

identification address
shikibetsu adoresu
識別アドレス

identification code
shikibetsu kōdo
識別コード

identification division
midashi bu
見出し部

identification number
shikibetsu bangō
識別番号

identifier
ichi'i mei; namae; shikibetsushi
一意名; 名前; 識別子

identify
shikibetsu suru
識別する

identify (an error; a problem)
kenshutsu suru
謙出する

identity
midashi
見出し

IDF (intermediate distributing frame)
IDF (chūkan tanshiban)
中間端子盤

idle character
asobi moji
遊び文字

idle communications mode
asobi tsūshin mōdo
遊び通信モード

idle time
asobi jikan
遊び時間

IDP (integrated data processing)
IDP (shūchū dēta shori; sōgō dēta shori)
集中データ処理;
総合データ処理

IDPS (integrated data-processing system)
IDPS (shūchū dēta shori shisutemu; sōgō dēta shori shisutemu)
集中データ処理システム;
総合データ処理システム

IE (industrial engineering)
IE (indasutoriaru-enjiniaringu)
インダストリアル・
エンジニアリング

IEC (International Electrotechnical Commission)
IEC (Kokusai Denki Hyōjun Kaigi)
国際電気標準会議

IEEE (Institute of Electrical and Electronic Engineers)
IEEE (Denki Denshi Gakkai)
電気電子学会

IF statement
bubun jōken bun
部分条件文

IF THEN
ifu-zen; gan'i
IF-THEN; 含意

IFAC (International Federation for Automatic Control)
IFAC (Kokusai Jidō Seigyo Rengō)
国際自動制御連合

IFIP (International Federation for Information Processing)
IFIP (Kokusai Jōhō Shori Rengō)
国際情報処理連合

IGDM (illegal guard mode)
IGDM (iriigaru-gādo-mōdo)
イリーガル・ガード・モード

ignore character
torikeshi moji
取り消し文字

ignore gate
hitei gēto
否定ゲート

ikon *or* icon
aikon
アイコン

illegal
ihō; iriigaru
違法; イリーガル

illegal character
ihō moji
違法文字

illegal code
ihō kōdo
違法コード

illegal command
ihō komando
違法コマンド

illegal guard mode (IGDM)
iriigaru-gādo-mōdo (IGDM)
イリーガル・ガード・モード

illegal instruction
ihō meirei
違法命令

illegal operation
ihō sōsa; iriigaru-operēshon
違法操作；イリーガル・
オペレーション

image
eizō; gazō; imēji
映像；画像；イメージ

image analysis
gazō kaiseki
画像解析

image data
imēji-dēta
イメージ・データ

image enhancement
imēji-enhansumento
イメージ・エンハンスメント

image mode
imēji-mōdo
イメーシ・モード

image processing
eizō shori; gazō shori;
imēji shori
映像処理；画像処理；
イメージ処理

image-processing system
imēji shori shisutemu
イメージ処理システム

image scanner
imēji sōsa kikō; imēji-sukyana
イメージ走査機構；
イメージ・スキャナ

image scanning
imēji sōsa
イメージ走査

image sensor
imēji-sensa
イメージ・センサ

immediate access
sokuji akusesu
即時アクセス

immediate-access storage (IAS)
sokuji akusesu kioku (IAS)
即時アクセス記憶

immediate-access store (IAS)
sokuji akusesu kioku sōchi (IAS)
即時アクセス記憶装置

immediate address
sokuchi adoresu
即値アドレス

immediate addressing
sokuchi adoresu shitei
即値アドレス指定

immediate AND
sokuchi endo
即値 AND

immediate command
sokuji shirei
即時指令

immediate control
sokuji seigyo
即時制御

immediate data
sokuchi dēta
即値データ

immediate instruction
sokuchi meirei
即値命令

immediate operand
sokuchi operando
即値オペランド

immediate operation
sokuji sōsa
即時操作

immediate processing
sokuji shori
即時処理

immediate skip
sokuji sukippu
即時スキップ

immediate status
sokuji sutētasu
即時ステータス

immediately accessible
chokusetsu akusesu kanō
直接アクセス可能

IMP (interface message processor)
IMP (intafuēsu-messēji-purosessa)
インタフェース・メッセージ・
プロセッサ

impact
inpakuto; shōgeki
インパクト；衝撃

impact evaluation
inpakuto hyōka
インパクト評価

impact line dot printer
inpakuto-rain-dotto-purinta
インパクト・ライン・ドット・
プリンタ

impact printer
inpakuto-purinta;
shōgekishiki insho sōchi
インパクト・プリンタ；
衝撃式印書装置

impedance
inpiidansu
インピーダンス

imperative macro
jikkōgata makuro
実行型マクロ

imperative macroinstruction
jikkōgata makuro meirei
実行型マクロ命令

imperative statement
mujōken meirei
無条件命令

implementation
jitsugen
実現

implementation feasibility study
jitsugen kanōsei kentō
実現可能性検討

implementation planning
jitsugen keikaku
実現計画

implementor
sakuseisha
作成者

implication
gan'i
含意

implication gate
naigan gēto
内含ゲート

implicit
ammoku no; in
暗黙の；陰

implicit address
ammoku no adoresu
暗黙のアドレス

implicit declaration
ammoku no sengen
暗黙の宣言

implicit instruction
ammoku no meirei
暗黙の命令

implicit pointer
in pointa
陰ポインタ

impulse
inparesu
インパレス

impulse response
inparesu ōtō
インパレス応答

IMS (information management system)
IMS (jōhō kanri shisutemu)
情報管理システム

in-house
in-hausu
イン・ハウス

in-line
in-rain
イン・ライン

in-line procedure
in-rain tejun
イン・ライン手順

in-line processing
in-rain shori
イン・ライン処理

in-line subroutine
in-rain-saburūchin
イン・ライン・サブルーチン

in-line system
in-rain-shisutemu
イン・ライン・システム

inactive
hikatsudō; kyūshichū
非活動；休止中

inactive file
kyūshichū fuairu
休止中ファイル

inactive line
hikatsudō kaisen
非活動回線

inactive program
hikatsudō puroguramu
非活動プログラム

inactive station
hikatsudō tanmatsu
非活動端末

incidence matrix
setsuzoku gyōretsu
接続行列

incident
jiko
事故

inclusion gate
naihō gēto
内包ゲート

inclusive NOR
hōganteki NOR
包含的NOR

inclusive NOR circuit
hōganteki NOR kairo
包含的NOR回路

inclusive OR
hōganteki OR; hōganteki ronriwa
包含的OR；包含的論理和

inclusive OR circuit
hōganteki OR kairo;
hōganteki ronriwa kairo
包含的OR回路；
包含的論理和回路

inclusive OR operation
hōganteki OR enzan;
hōganteki ronriwa enzan
包含的OR演算；
包含的論理和演算

incoming message
jushin dembun
受信電文

incomplete code
mikan kōdo
未完コード

incomplete message
mikan messēji
未完メッセージ

incomplete routine
mikan rūchin
未完ルーチン

inconnector
iriketsugōshi
入り結合子

inconsistency
mujun
矛盾

increment
zōbun
増分

incremental
inkurimentaru; zōbun
インクリメンタル；増分

incremental binary representation
zōbun nishin hyōjihō
増分2進表示法

incremental compaction
zōbun asshuku
増分圧縮

incremental compiler
inkurimentaru-konpaira
インクリメンタル・コンパイラ

incremental computer
zōbun keisanki
増分計算機

incremental dump
inkurimentaru-danpu
インクリメンタル・ダンプ

incremental integrator
zōbun sekibunki
増分積分器

incremental plotter
inkurimentaru-purotta
インクリメンタル・プロッタ

incremental recorder
inkurimentaru-rekōda
インクリメンタル・レコーダ

incremental representation
zōbun hyōjihō
増分表示法

incremental vector
zōbun bekuta
増分ベクタ

indentation
jisage
字下げ

independent
dokuritsu; tandoku (no)
独立；単独 (の)

independent control system
tandoku seigyo shisutemu
単独制御システム

independent procedure
dokuritsu tejun
独立手順

independent utility
dokuritsu yūteiritei
独立ユーティリティ

independent utility program
dokuritsu yūteiritei-puroguramu
独立ユーティリティ・
プログラム

independent variable
dokuritsu hensū
独立変数

index
indekkusu; sakuin; shihyō
インデックス；索引；指標

index data item
shihyō dēta kōmoku
指標データ項目

index domain
sakuin ryō'iki
索引領域

index file
indekkusu-fuairu
インデックス・ファイル

index item
sakuin kōmoku
索引項目

index map
sakuin chizu
索引地図

index modification
shihyō henkō
指標変更

index name
shihyō mei
指標名

index parameter
shihyō parameta
指標パラメタ

index part
shihyō bu
指標部

index register
shihyō rejisuta
指標レジスタ

index sequential
sakuin junji
索引順次

index sequential access
sakuin junji akusesu
索引順次アクセス

index sequential access disk
sakuin junji akusesu-deisuku
索引順次アクセス・ディスク

index sequential structure
sakuin junji kōzō
索引順次構造

index structure
sakuin kōzō
索引構造

index table
sakuin hyō
索引表

index variable
shihyō hensū
指標変数

index word
shihyō go
指標語

indexed
indekkusu(do); sakuintsuki
インデックス (ド)；索引付き

indexed address
sakuintsuki adoresu;
shihyōtsuki adoresu
索引付きアドレス；
指標付きアドレス

indexed addressing
sakuintsuki adoresu shitei
索引付きアドレス指定

indexed data item
shihyōtsuki dēta kōmoku
指標付きデータ項目

indexed file
sakuintsuki fuairu
索引付きファイル

indexed grammar
indekkusu bumpō
インデックス文法

indexed language
indekkusu gengo
インデックス言語

indexed sequential access method (ISAM)
sakuin junji akusesu hōshiki (ISAM)
索引順次アクセス方式

indexed sequential data set
sakuin junji dēta-setto
索引順次データ・セット

indexed sequential file
sakuin junji fuairu
索引順次ファイル

indexed sequential file management system (ISFMS)
sakuin junji fuairu kanri shisutemu (ISFMS)
索引順次ファイル管理システム

indexed sequential organization
sakuin junji hensei
索引順次編成

indexed set
sakuintsuki oyako shūgō
索引付き親子集合

indexing
indekkusshingu; sakuintsuke;
shihyōtsuke
インデックッシング；索引付け；
指標付け

indicate
hyōji suru; shiji suru
表示する；指示する

indicating device
hyōji kiki
表示機器

indicating function
hyōji kinō
表示機能

indication
hyōji; hyōmei; shiji
表示；表明；指示

indicative abstract
shijiteki shōroku
指示的抄録

indicator
hyōji kikō; hyōjishi; hyōshiki
表示機構；表示子；標識

indicator lamp
hyōji ranpu
表示ランプ

indicator register
hyōji rejisuta
表示レジスタ

indirect address
kansetsu adoresu
間接アドレス

indirect addressing
kansetsu adoresu shitei
間接アドレス指定

indirect control
kansetsu seigyo
間接制御

indirect instruction
kansetsu meirei
間接命令

indirect output
kansetsu shutsuryoku
間接出力

individual message
kobetsu dembun
個別電文

industrial automation
kōgyō otomēshon;
sangyō otomēshon
工業オトメーション；
産業オトメーション

industrial automation system
kōgyō otomēshon-shisutemu;
sangyō otomēshon-shisutemu
工業オトメーション・システム；
産業オトメーション・システム

industrial computer
kōgyō'yō keisanki;
sangyō'yō keisanki
工業用計算機；産業用計算機

industrial computer system
kōgyō'yō keisanki shisutemu;
sangyō'yō keisanki shisutemu
工業用計算機システム；
産業用計算機システム

industrial data processing
kōgyō'yō dēta shori;
sangyō'yō dēta shori
工業用データ処理；
産業用データ処理

industrial engineering (IE)
indasutoriaru-enjiniaringu (IE)
インダストリアル・
エンジニアリング

industrial information system
kōgyō'yō jōhō shisutemu;
sangyō'yō jōhō shisutemu
工業用情報システム；
産業用情報システム

industrial system
kōgyō'yō shisutemu;
sangyō'yō shisutemu
工業用システム・
産業用システム

ineffective time
mukō jikan
無効時間

inference
suiron
推論

infinite loop
mugen rūpu
無限ループ

infinite-pad method
mugen pado hōshiki
無限パド方式

infix notation
infuikkusu hyōkihō
インフィックス表記法

informatics
infuomachikkusu
インフォマチックス

information
ichi jōhō; jōhō
位置情報；情報

information bit
jōhō bitto
情報ビット

information channel
jōhō tsūshinro
情報通信路

information collection
jōhō shūshū
情報収集

information content
jōhō ryō
情報量

information control
jōhō seigyo
情報制御

information-control system
jōhō seigyo shisutemu
情報制御システム

information destination
jōhō ikisaki
情報行き先

information display
jōhō hyōji
情報表示

information display unit
jōhō hyōji sōchi
情報表示装置

information evaluation
jōhō hyōka
情報評価

information feedback
jōhō fuiidobakku; jōhō kikan
情報フィードバック；情報帰還

information feedback system
jōhō kikan hōshiki
情報帰還方式

information flag
jōhō hyōshiki
情報標識

information flow
jōhō nagare
情報流れ

information flow analysis
jōhō nagare kaiseki
情報流れ解析

information flow control
jōhō nagare seigyo
情報流れ制御

information flowchart
jōhō nagarezu
情報流れ図

information integration
jōhō tōgō
情報統合

information interchange
jōhō kōkan
情報交換

information item
jōhō kōmoku
情報項目

information loss
jōhō sonshitsu
情報損失

information management system (IMS)
jōhō kanri shisutemu (IMS)
情報管理システム

information network
jōhō nettowāku; jōhōmō
情報ネットワーク；情報網

information network control
jōhō nettowāku seigyo
情報ネットワーク制御

information processing
jōhō shori
情報処理

information-processing center
jōhō shori senta
情報処理センタ

information-processing language
jōhō shori gengo
情報処理言語

information-processing load
jōhō shori ryō
情報処理量

Information Processing Society of Japan
Jōhō Shori Gakkai (Nihon)
情報処理学会(日本)

information-processing system
jōhō shori shisutemu
情報処理システム

information processor
jōhō shori sōchi
情報処理装置

information protection
jōhō hogo
情報保護

information resource
jōhō shigen
情報資源

information retrieval (IR)
jōhō kensaku (IR)
情報検索

information retrieval system
jōhō kensaku shisutemu
情報検索システム

information science
jōhō kagaku
情報科学

information selection
jōhō sentaku
情報選択

information separator (IS)
jōhō bunri moji (IS)
情報分離文字

information source
jōhō gen
情報源

information storage
jōhō chikuseki
情報蓄積

information storage and retrieval (IS/R)
jōhō chikuseki-kensaku (IS/R)
情報蓄積-検索

information structure
jōhō kōzō
情報構造

information support system
jōhō shien shisutemu
情報支援システム

information synthesis
jōhō gōsei
情報合成

information system
jōhō shisutemu
情報システム

information systems science
jōhō shisutemu kagaku
情報システム科学

information technology (IT)
jōhō gijutsu (IT)
情報技術

information theory
jōhō riron
情報理論

information transfer
jōhō dentatsu
情報伝達

information transmission
jōhō densō
情報伝送

inhibit
inhibitto; kinshi; yokushi (suru)
インヒビット；禁止；
抑止(する)

inhibit circuit
yokushi kairo
抑止回路

inhibit gate
yokushi gēto
抑止ゲート

inhibit line
inhibitto-rain; yokushi sen
インヒビット・ライン；抑止線

inhibit pulse
yokushi parusu
抑止パルス

inhibiting signal
kinshi shingō
禁止信号

initial
kaishi; shoki
開始；初期

initial condition
shoki jōken
初期条侎

initial failure
shoki koshō
初期故障

initial instructions
shoki meirei
初期命令

initial line
kaishi gyō
開始行

initial load
shoki rōdo
初期ロード

initial mode
shoki mōdo
初期モード

initial program loader (IPL)
shoki puroguramu-rōda (IPL)
初期プログラム・ローダ

initial program loading
shoki puroguramu-rōdeingu
初期プログラム・ローディング

initial statement
kaishi bun
開始文

initial value
shoki chi
初期値

initialization
shoki settei; shokichi settei
初期設定；初期値設定

initialization mode
shoki settei mōdo
初期設定モード

initialize
shoki settei suru; shokichi settei
suru
初期設定する；初期値設定する

initiating task
kaishi tasuku
開始タスク

initiator
kaishi puroguramu
開始プログラム

initiator/terminator
kaishi puroguramu–shūshi
puroguramu
開始プログラム–終止プログラム

ink
inku
インク

ink jet printer
inku-jietto-purinta
インク・ジェット・プリンタ

ink mist printer
inku-misuto-purinta
インク・ミスト・プリンタ

ink reflectance
inku no hansharitsu
インクの反射率

ink ribbon
inku-ribon
インク・リボン

ink ribbon cartridge
inku-ribon-kātorijji
インク・リボン・カートリッジ

ink smudge
inku no hamidashi
インクのはみ出し

ink squeeze-out
inku no kasure
インクのかすれ

ink uniformity
inku no kin'itsusei
インクの均一性

inoperable
dōsa funō
動作不能

input (*noun*)
nyūryoku
入力

input (*verb*)
nyūryoku suru
入力する

input area
nyūryoku iki
入力域

input block
nyūryoku burokku
入力ブロック

input blocking factor
nyūryoku burokkuka insū
入力ブロック化因数

input buffer
nyūryoku baffua
入力バッファ

input channel
nyūryoku chaneru
入力チャネル

input complement
nyūryoku hosū
入力補数

input control
nyūryoku seigyo
入力制御

input control unit
nyūryoku seigyo sōchi
入力制御装置

input data
nyūryoku dēta
入力データ

input data validation
nyūryoku dēta kenshō
入力データ検証

input device
nyūryoku kiki; nyūryoku sōchi
入力機器；入力装置

input element
nyūryoku eremento
入力エレメント

input hopper
nyūryoku hoppa
入力ホッパ

input instruction
nyūryoku meirei
入力命令

input job stream
nyūryoku jyobu-sutoriimu
入力ジョブ・ストリーム

input keyboard
nyūryoku kiibōdo
入力キーボード

input layout
nyūryoku haichi;
nyūryoku reiauto
入力配置；入力レイアウト

input magazine
nyūryoku magajin
入力マガジン

input medium
nyūryoku baitai
入力媒体

input/output (I/O)
nyūshutsuryoku (I/O)
入出力

input/output area
nyūshutsuryoku ryŏ'iki
入出力領域

input/output buffers
nyūshutsuryoku baffua
入出力バッファ

input/output bus
nyūshutsuryoku basu
入出力バス

input/output channel
nyūshutsuryoku chaneru
入出力チャネル

input/output chip
nyūshutsuryoku chippu
入出力チップ

input/output command
nyūshutsuryoku shirei
入出力指令

input/output control
nyūshutsuryoku seigyo
入出力制御

input/output control signal
nyūshutsuryoku seigyo shingō
入出力制御信号

input/output control system (IOCS)
nyūshutsuryoku seigyo
shisutemu (IOCS)
入出力制御システム

input/output control unit
nyūshutsuryoku seigyo sōchi
入出力制御装置

input/output controller
nyūshutsuryoku seigyo sōchi
入出力制御装置

input/output data
nyūshutsuryoku dēta
入出力データ

input/output device
nyūshutsuryoku sōchi
入出力装置

input/output equipment
nyūshutsuryoku kiki
入出力機器

input/output file
nyūshutsuryoku fuairu
入出力ファイル

input/output instruction
nyūshutsuryoku meirei
入出力命令

input/output interface
nyūshutsuryoku intafuēsu
入出力インタフェース

input/output interruption
nyūshutsuryoku warikomi
入出力割り込み

input/output list
nyūshutsuryoku narabi
入出力並び

input/output medium
nyūshutsuryoku baitai
入出力媒体

input/output module (IOM)
nyūshutsuryoku mojyūru (IOM)
入出力モジュール

input/output operation
nyūshutsuryoku sōsa
入出力操作

input/output port
nyūshutsuryoku pōto
入出力ポート

input/output port buffer
nyūshutsuryoku pōto-baffua
入出力ポート・バッファ

input-output procedure
nyūshutsuryoku tetsuzuki
入出力手続き

input-output processing
nyūshutsuryoku shori
入出力処理

input-output processor (IOP)
nyūshutsuryoku shori sōchi (IOP)
入出力処理装置

input/output register
nyūshutsuryoku rejisuta
入出力レジスタ

input/output relationship
nyūshutsuryoku kankei
入出力関係

input/output restrictions
nyūshutsuryoku seigen
入出力制限

input/output routine
nyūshutsuryoku rūchin
入出力ルーチン

input/output section
nyūshutsuryoku sekushon
入出力セクション

input/output statement
nyūshutsuryoku bun
入出力文

input-output system
nyūshutsuryoku shisutemu
入出力システム

input/output terminal
nyūshutsuryoku tanmatsu (sōchi)
入出力端末（装置）

input/output typewriter
nyūshutsuryoku taipuraita
入出力タイプライタ

input/output unit
nyūshutsuryoku sōchi
入出力装置

input procedure
nyūryoku tetsuzuki
入力手続き

input processing
nyūryoku shori
入力処理

input program
nyūryoku puroguramu
入力プログラム

input queue
nyūryoku machigyōretsu
入力待ち行列

input routine
nyūryoku rūchin
入力ルーチン

input signal
nyūryoku shingō
入力信号

input source
nyūryoku gen
入力源

input specification
nyūryoku shiyō
入力仕様

input specification sheet
nyūryoku shiyōsho
入力仕様書

input state
nyūryoku jōtai
入力状態

input stream
nyūryoku nagare;
nyūryoku sutoriimu
入力流れ；入力ストリーム

input-to-output approach
nyūryoku-shutsuryoku apurōchi
入力-出力アプローチ

input unit
nyūryoku sōchi
入力装置

input variable
nyūryoku hensū
入力変数

input work queue
nyūryoku sagyō machigyōretsu
入力作業待ち行列

inquiry
shōkai; toiawase
照会；問い合わせ

inquiry station
shōkai'yō tanmatsu (sōchi);
toiawase tanmatsu (sōchi)
照会用端末(装置)；
問い合わせ端末(装置)

inquiry system
toiawase shisutemu
問い合わせシステム

inquiry unit
shōkai sōchi; toiawase sōchi
照会装置；問い合わせ装置

inscriber
kirokuki; moji inji sōchi
記録機；文字印字装置

insert (verb)
sōnyū suru
挿入する

inserted record
sōnyū rekōdo
挿入レコード

insertion
sōnyū
挿入

insertion sequence
sōnyū no retsu
挿入の列

insertion sort
sōnyūhō bunrui
挿入法分類

insignificant
ka'i no
下位の

insignificant data
ka'i no dēta
下位のデータ

insignificant digit
ka'i no sūji
下位の数字

inspection
kensa
検査

inspection error
kensa ayamari
検査誤り

inspection routine
kensa tejun
検査手順

instability
fuantei
不安定

install
setchi suru
設置する

installation
setchi
設置

installation date
setchi kijitsu
設置期日

**Institute of Electrical and
Electronic Engineers (IEEE)**
Denki Denshi Gakkai (IEEE)
電気電子学会

instruction
meirei; shiji; shirei
命令；指示；指令

instruction address
meirei adoresu
命令アドレス

instruction address register (IAR)
meirei adoresu-rejisuta (IAR)
命令アドレス・レジスタ

instruction bank
meirei banku
命令バンク

instruction code
meirei kōdo
命令コード

instruction counter
meirei kaunta
命令カウンタ

instruction cycle
meirei saikuru
命令サイクル

instruction decode
meirei dekōdo; meirei kaidoku
命令デコード；命令解読

instruction decoder
meirei dekōda
命令デコーダ

instruction execution
meirei jikkō
命令実行

instruction execution cycle
meirei jikkō saikuru
命令実行サイクル

instruction execution time
meirei jikkō jikan
命令実行時間

instruction fetch
meirei fuetchi; meirei toridashi
命令フェッチ；命令取り出し

instruction fetch cycle
meirei fuetchi saikuru;
meirei toridashi saikuru
命令フェッチ・サイクル；
命令取り出しサイクル

instruction field
meirei fuiirudo
命令フィールド

instruction format
meirei keishiki
命令形式

instruction length
meirei chō
命令長

instruction length code
meirei chō kōdo
命令長コード

instruction manual
kaisetsusho; setsumeisho;
shijisho
解説書；説明書；指示書

instruction number
meirei sū
命令数

instruction overlap
meirei chōfuku
命令重複

instruction part
meirei bu
命令部

instruction phase
meirei dankai
命令段階

instruction prefetch
meirei sakitori
命令先取り

instruction-processing unit
meirei shori sōchi
命令処理装置

instruction register (ir)
meirei rejisuta (ir)
命令レジスタ

instruction repertoire
meirei repātori
命令レパートリ

instruction set
meirei setto
命令セット

instruction set processor (ISP)
meirei setto-purosessa (ISP)
命令セット・プロセッサ

instruction time
meirei jikan
命令時間

instruction word
meirei go
命令語

instrumentation
keisoku
計測

instrumentation analysis
keisoku bunseki
計測分析

instrumentation control interface card
keisoku seigyo intafuēsu-kādo
計測制御インタフェース・
カード

instrumentation control interface module
keisoku seigyo intafuēsu-mojyūru
計測制御インタフェース・
モジュール

instrumentation system
keisoku shisutemu
計測システム

instrumentation technology
keisoku kōgaku
計測工学

insulator
zetsuentai
絶縁体

integer
seisū
整数

integer arithmetic
seisū enzan
整数演算

integer attribute
seisū zokusei
整数属性

integer BASIC
seisū BASIC
整数 BASIC

integer constant
seiteisū
整定数

integer division
seisū bu
整数部

integer programming
seisū keikakuhō
整数計画法

integer type
seisūgata
整数型

integer variable
seihensū
整変数

integral control
sekibun seigyo
積分制御

integral control action
sekibun seigyo dōsa
積分制御動作

integral equation
sekibun hōteishiki
積分方程式

integral number
seisū
整数

integrated
shūchū; ;shūseki; sōgō; tōgō
集中; 集積; 総合; 統合

integrated circuit (IC)
shūseki kairo (IC)
集積回路

integrated circuit memory (ICM)
shūseki kairo kioku (ICM)
集積回路記憶

integrated communication adapter
tsūshin tōgō adaputa
通信統合アダプタ

integrated computer system
sōgō keisanki shisutemu
総合計算機システム

integrated data processing (IDP)
shūchū dēta shori (IDP);
sōgō dēta shori
集中データ処理;
総合データ処理

integrated data-processing system (IDPS)
shūchū dēta shori shisutemu (IDPS);
sōgō dēta shori shisutemu
集中データ処理システム;
総合データ処理システム

integrated data system
shūchū dēta-shisutemu;
sōgō dēta-shisutemu
集中データ・システム;
総合データ・システム

integrated database
shūchū dētabēsu; sōgō dētabēsu
集中データベース;
総合データベース

integrated disk
tōgō(gata) deisuku
統合(型)ディスク

integrated disk unit
tōgō(gata) deisuku sōchi
統合(型)ディスク装置

integrated emulation
tōgō emyurēshon
統合エミュレーション

integrated emulator
tōgō emyurēta
統合エミュレータ

integrated file adapter
fuairu tōgō adaputa
ファイル統合アダプタ

integrated file structure
fuairu tōgō kōzō
ファイル統合構造

integrated general register
shūchū han'yō rejisuta
集中汎用レジスタ

integrated information system
sōgō jōhō shisutemu
総合情報システム

**integrated management
information system**
shūchū kei'ei jōhō shisutemu;
sōgō kei'ei jōhō shisutemu
集中経営情報システム;
総合経営情報システム

integrated office system
sōgō ofuisu-shisutemu
総合オフィス・システム

integrated software
tōgō(gata) sofutouea
統合(型)ソフトウエア

integrated system
sōgō shisutemu
総合システム

integrating circuit
sekibun kairo
積分回路

integration
integurēshon; sekibun; shūseki;
shūsekika; tōgōka
インテグレーション; 積分;
集積; 集積化; 統合化

integrator
sekibunki
積分器

integrity
hozen; kanzensei
保全; 完全性

intelligence
chinō
知能

intelligent
chinō; interijiento
知能; インテリジェント

intelligent terminal
chinō tanmatsu (sōchi);
interijiento tanmatsu (sōchi)
知能端末(装置);
インテリジェント端末(装置)

interaction
intarakushon; sōgokankei;
sōgokanren; sōgosayō; taiwa
インタラクション; 相互関係;
相互関連; 相互作用; 対話

interactive
intarakuteibu; kaiwagata;
sōgokankei; sōgokanren;
sōgosayō; taiwagata
インタラクティブ; 会話型;
相互関係; 相互関連; 相互作用;
対話型

**interactive distribution control
system (IDCS)**
intarakuteibu-deisutoribyūshon
seigyo shisutemu (IDCS)
インタラクティブ・ディスド
リビューション制御システム

interactive graphics
kaiwagata gurafuikkusu;
kaiwagata zukei; taiwagata
gurafuikkusu; taiwagata zukei;
taiwashiki gurakuikkusu
会話型グラフィックス;
会話型図形;
対話型グラフィックス;
対話型図形;
対話式グラフィックス

interactive information system
kaiwagata jōhō shisutemu
会話型情報システム

interactive language
kaiwagata gengo
会話型言語

interactive method
sōgosayō hōshiki; taiwa hōshiki
相互作用方式; 対話方式

interactive mode
sōgosayō mōdo; taiwa mōdo
相互作用モード; 対話モード

interactive processing
kaiwagata shori
会話型処理

interactive processor
kaiwagata purosessa
会話型プロセッサ

interactive programming
kaiwagata puroguramingu
会話型プログラミング

interactive system
kaiwagata shisutemu;
sōgosayō shisutemu
会話型システム;
相互作用システム

interactive task
kaiwagata tasuku
会話型タスク

interactive terminal
kaiwagata tanmatsu (sōchi)
会話型端末(装置)

interblock gap (IBG)
burokkukan kankaku (IBG)
ブロック間間隔

intercepting
daikōjushin
代行受信

interchange
chūkei; kōkan
中継; 交換

interchange circuit
chūkei kairo
中継回路

interchangeability
kōkan kanōsei
交換可能性

interchangeable
kōkankanō
交換可能

interconnected
sōgoketsugō; sōgosetsuzoku
相互結合; 相互接続

interconnecting
sōgoketsugō; sōgosetsuzoku
相互結合; 相互接続

103

interconnecting activities
sōgoketsugō akuteibitei
相互結合アクティビティ

interconnecting elements
sōgoketsugō eremento
相互結合エレメント

interconnecting network
sōgoketsugō nettowāku
相互結合ネットワーク

interconnection
sōgoketsugō; sōgosetsuzoku
相互結合；相互接続

interface
intafuēsu
インタフェース

interface board
intafuēsu-bōdo
インタフェース・ボード

interface card
intafuēsu-kādo
インタフェース・カード

interface computer
intafuēsu keisanki
インタフェース計算機

interface control
intafuēsu seigyo
インタフェース制御

interface control check
intafuēsu seigyo chekku
インタフェース制御チェック

interface message processor (IMP)
intafuēsu-messēji-purosessa (IMP)
インタフェース・メッセージ・
プロセッサ

interface module
intafuēsu-mojyūru
インタフェース・モジュール

interface routine
intafuēsu-rūchin
インタフェース・ルーチン

interface termination
intafuēsu shūtan
インタフェース終端

interface unit
intafuēsu-yunitto
インタフェース・ユニット

interfacing logic
intafuēshingu ronri
インタフェーシング論理

interference
bōgai
妨害

interference detection
bōgai kenshutsu
妨害検出

interference detection system
bōgai kenshutsu shisutemu
妨害検出システム

interfile relationship
fuairukan kankei
ファイル間関係

interleave
intariibu suru
インタリーブする

interlock
intarokku
インタロック

intermediate
chūkan
中間

intermediate-access storage
chūkan akusesu kioku
中間アクセス記憶

intermediate block check
chūkan burokku-chekku
中間ブロック・チェック

intermediate distributing frame (IDF)
chūkan tanshiban (IDF)
中間端子盤

intermediate document
chūkan dokyumento
中間ドキュメント

intermediate frequency
chūkan shūhasū
中間周波数

intermediate language
chūkan gengo
中間言語

intermediate output file
chūkan shutsuryoku fuairu
中間出力ファイル

intermediate storage
chūkan kioku
中間記憶

intermediate total
chūkan gōkei
中間合計

intermittent
kanketsu
間欠

intermittent action
kanketsu dōsa
間欠動作

intermittent error
kanketsu ayamari
間欠誤り

internal
nai; naibu; naizō
内；内部；内蔵

internal clocking
naibu kurokku
内部クロック

internal code
naibu kōdo
内部コード

internal company network
shanaimō
社内網

internal drive
naibu doraibu; naizō doraibu
内部ドライブ；内蔵ドライブ

internal environment information
naibu kankyō jōhō
内部環境情報

internal function register
naibu kinō rejisuta
内部機能レジスタ

internal interrupt
naibu warikomi
内部割り込み

internal interrupt system
naibu warikomi shisutemu
内部割り込みシステム

internal memory
naibu kioku
内部記憶

internal name
naibu mei
内部名

internal procedure
naibu tetsuzuki
内部手続き

internal register
naibu rejisuta
内部レジスタ

internal ROM
naizō ROM
内蔵ROM

internal sort
naibu bunrui
内部分類

internal storage
naibu kioku
内部記憶

internal store
naibu kioku sōchi
内部記憶装置

internal working memory
naibu sagyōyō kioku
内部作業用記憶

internally stored program
naibu kioku sareta puroguramu;
naibu puroguramu
内部記憶されたプログラム；
内部プログラム

**International Electrotechnical
Commission (IEC)**
Kokusai Denki Hyōjun Kaigi (IEC)
国際電気標準会議

**International Federation for
Automatic Control (IFAC)**
Kokusai Jidō Seigyo Rengō (IFAC)
国際自動制御連合

**International Federation for
Information Processing (IFIP)**
Kokusai Jōhō Shori Rengō (IFIP)
国際情報処理連合

**International Organization for
Standardization; International
Standards Organization (ISO)**
Kokusai Hyōjunka Kikō (ISO)
国際標準化機構

**International Telecommunication
Union (ITU)**
Kokusai Denki Tsūshin Rengō
(ITU)
国際電気通信連合

interpolation
hokan
補間

interpolation circuit
hokan kairo
補間回路

interpolator
hokan kairo
補間回路

interpret
hon'yaku suru; kaishaku suru;
tsūyaku suru
翻訳する；解釈する；通訳する

interpreter
hon'yakuki; intapurita;
tsūyaku rūchin
翻訳器；インタプリタ；
通訳ルーチン

interpreting
hon'yaku; tsūyaku
翻訳；通訳

interpretive
intapuriteibu; kaishaku; tsūyaku
インタプリティブ；解釈；通訳

interpretive code
tsūyaku kōdo
通訳コード

interpretive programming
tsūyaku puroguramingu
通訳プログラミング

interpretive routine
kaishaku rūchin; tsūyaku rūchin
解釈ルーチン；通訳ルーチン

interprocessor buffer
purosessakan baffua
プロセッサ間バッファ

interprogram communication
puroguramukan renraku
プログラム間連絡

interrecord gap (IRG)
rekōdokan kankaku (IRG)
レコード間間隔

interrelated
sōgokankei; sōgokanren
相互関係；相互関連

interrogation
kensaku; toiawase
検索；問い合わせ

interrogation terminal
kensaku tanmatsu (sōchi)
検索端末(装置)

interrogator
toiawase sōchi
問い合わせ装置

interrupt
chūdan suru; warikomu
中断する；割り込む

**interrupt acknowledge signal
(IACK)**
warikomi kōtei ōtō shingō (IACK)
割り込み肯定応答信号

interrupt action
warikomi dōsa
割り込み動作

interrupt analysis
warikomi kaiseki
割り込み解析

interrupt condition
warikomi jōken
割り込み条件

interrupt control
warikomi seigyo
割り込み制御

interrupt control state
warikomi seigyo jōtai
割り込み制御状態

interrupt counter
warikomi kaunta
割り込みカウンタ

interrupt enable
warikomi kanō
割り込み可能

interrupt function
warikomi kinō
割り込み機能

interrupt handler
warikomi shori rūchin
割り込み処理ルーチン

interrupt inhibit
warikomi kinshi
割り込み禁止

interrupt I/O
warikomi I/O
割り込みI/O

interrupt initialization procedure
warikomi shokika tejun
割り込み初期化手順

interrupt level
warikomi reberu
割り込みレベル

interrupt lockout
warikomi rokku-auto
割り込みロック・アウト

interrupt mask
warikomi masuku
割り込みマスク

interrupt priority
warikomi yūsendo
割り込み優先度

interrupt priority signal
warikomi yūsen kyoka shingō
割り込み優先許可信号

interrupt request (IRQ)
warikomi yōkyu (IRQ)
割り込み要求

interrupt signal
warikomi shingō
割り込み信号

interrupt source
warikomi gen
割り込み原

interrupt time
warikomi jikan
割り込み時間

interruptible state
warikomikanō jōtai
割り込み可能状態

interruption
chūdan; chūdan teishi; warikomi
中断；中断停止；割り込み

interruption code
warikomi kōdo
割り込みコード

interruption handling routine
warikomi shori rūchin
割り込み処理ルーチン

interruption level
warikomi reberu
割り込みレベル

interruption pending
warikomi machi
割り込み待ち

interruption queue
warikomi machigyōretsu
割り込み待ち行列

interruption request (IRQ)
warikomi yōkyū (IRQ)
割り込み要求

interruption request signal
warikomi yōkyū shingō
割り込み要求信号

interruption routine
warikomi rūchin
割り込みルーチン

interruption status word
warikomi jōtai go
割り込み状態語

interruption subroutine
warikomi saburūchin
割り込みサブルーチン

intersection
intasekushon; kōsa;
kyōtsū bubun
インタセクション；交差；
共通部分

intersection gate
kyōtsū bubun gēto
共通部分ゲート

intersystem communication
shisutemukan tsūshin
システム間通信

interval
intabaru; kankaku; kukan
インタバル；間隔；区間

interval arithmetic
kukan enzan
区間演算

interval timer
kankaku keiji kikō
間隔計時機構

interval timer interruption
kankaku keiji kikō warikomi
間隔計時機構割り込み

intervention (from operator)
kainyū (operēta no)
介入(オペレータの)

intervention required
kainyū yōkyū
介入要求

intrinsic function
kumikomi kansū
組み込み関数

invalid
futō; mukō
不当；無効

invalid data
futō dēta
不当データ

invalid key
futō kii
不当キー

invalid name
futō namae
不当名前

invalid punch
futō senkō
不当せん孔

invalid sequence
futō junjo
不当順序

inventory control
zaiko kanri
在庫管理

inventory information system
zaiko jōhō shisutemu
在庫情報システム

inventory planning
zaiko keikaku
在庫計画

inverse sequence
gyaku junjo
逆順序

inversion
hanten
反転

invert (*verb*)
hanten suru
反転する

inverted AND (NAND)
hiteiseki (NAND)
否定積

inverted AND circuit (NAND circuit)
hiteiseki kairo; NAND kairo
否定積回路；NAND回路

inverted AND element (NAND element)
hiteiseki soshi; NAND soshi
否定積素子；NAND 素子

inverted AND gate (NAND gate)
hiteiseki gēto; NAND gēto
否定積ゲート；NAND ゲート

inverted AND operation (NAND operation)
hiteiseki enzan; NAND enzan
否定積演算；NAND 演算

inverted file
gyaku fairu
逆ファイル

inverted OR (NOR)
hiteiwa (NOR)
否定和

inverted OR circuit (NOR circuit)
hiteiwa kairo; NOR kairo
否定和回路；NOR 回路

inverted OR element (NOR element)
hiteiwa soshi; NOR soshi
否定和表子；NOR 表子

inverted OR gate (NOR gate)
hiteiwa gēto; NOR gēto
否定和ゲート；NOR ゲート

inverted OR operation (NOR operation)
hiteiwa enzan; NOR enzan
否定和演算；NOR 演算

inverter
inbāta
インバータ

I/O (input/output)
I/O (nyūshutsuryoku)
入出力

IOCS (input/output control system)
IOCS (nyūshutsuryoku seigyo shisutemu)
入出力制御システム

IOM (input/output module)
IOM (nyūshutsuryoku mojyūru)
入出力モジュール

IOP (input-output processor)
IOP (nyūshutsuryoku shori sōchi)
入出力処理装置

IPL (initial program loader)
IPL (shoki puroguramu-rōda)
初期プログラム・ローダ

IR (information retrieval)
IR (jōhō kensaku)
情報検索

ir (instruction register)
ir (meirei rejisuta)
命令レジスタ

IRG (interrecord gap)
IRG (rekōdokan kankaku)
レコード間間隔

IRQ (interrupt request; interruption request)
IRQ (warikomi yōkyū)
割り込み要求

IS (information separator)
IS (jōhō bunri moji)
情報分離文字

ISAM (indexed sequential access method)
ISAM (sakuin junji akusesu hōshiki)
索引順次アクセス方式

ISFMS (indexed sequential file management system)
ISFMS (sakuin junji fairu kanri shisutemu)
索引順次ファイル管理システム

ISI mode
ISI mōdo
ISI モード

island
airando
アイランド

island code
airando-kōdo
アイランド・コード

ISO (International Organization for Standardization; International Standards Organization)
ISO (Kokusai Hyōjunka Kikō)
国際標準化機構

ISO code
ISO kōdo
ISO コード

ISO recommendation
ISO suisen kikakuan
ISO 推選規格案

isolate (*verb*)
bunri suru
分離する

isolated locations
koritsu kioku ichi
孤立記憶位置

isolation
koritsu
孤立

ISP (instruction set processor)
ISP (meirei setto-purosessa)
命令セット・プロセッサ

IS/R (information storage and retrieval)
IS/R (jōhō chikuseki-kensaku)
情報蓄積-検索

issue a number
hatsuban suru; tsūban ga tsukeru
発番する；通番が付ける

IT (information technology)
IT (jōhō gijutsu)
情報技術

italic font
itarikku-fuonto
イタリック・フォント

item
kōmoku
項目

iterate
hampuku suru; kurikaesu
反復する；繰り返す

iteration
hampuku; kurikaeshi
反復；繰り返し

iterative
hampuku; kurikaeshi
反復；繰り返し

ITU (International Telecommunication Union)
ITU (Kokusai Denki Tsūshin Rengō)
国際電気通信連合

jack
jyakku
ジャック

jack panel
jyakku-paneru;
jyakkugata haisenban
ジャック・パネル;
ジャック型配線盤

jack plug
jyakku-puragu
ジャック・プラグ

jam
jyamu
ジャム

jam detection
jyamu kenshutsu
ジャム検出

jam detection device
jyamu kenshutsu sōchi
ジャム検出装置

Japan Information Processing Development Center (JIPDEC)
Nihon Jōhō Shori Kaihatsu Kyōkai (JIPDEC)
日本情報処理開発協会

Japanese characters
kana
仮名

Japanese Electronic Industry Development Association (JEIDA)
Nihon Denshi Kōgyō Shinkō Kyōkai (JEIDA)
日本電子工業振興協会

Japanese Industrial Standards (JIS)
Nihon Kōgyō Hyōjun Kikaku (JIS)
日本工業標準規格

Japanese Industrial Standards Committee (JISC)
Nihon Kōgyō Hyōjun Chōsakai (JISC)
日本工業標準調査会

Japanese-language information system (NIS)
Nihongo jōhō shisutemu (NIS)
日本語情報システム

Japanese-language line printer (NLP)
Nihongo rain-purinta (NLP)
日本語ライン・プリンタ

Japanese-language serial printer (NSP)
Nihongo shiriaru-purinta (NSP)
日本語シリアル・プリンタ

Japanese-language word processor (NWP)
Nihongo wādo-purosessa (NWP)
日本語ウード・プロセッサ

JCB (job control block)
JCB (jyobu seigyo burokku)
ジョブ制御ブロック

JCL (job control language)
JCL (jyobu seigyo gengo)
ジョブ制御言語

JEIDA (Japanese Electronic Industry Development Association)
JEIDA (Nihon Denshi Kōgyō Shinkō Kyōkai)
日本電子工業振興協会

JIPDEC (Japan Information Processing Development Center)
JIPDEC (Nihon Jōhō Shori Kaihatsu Kyōkai)
日本情報処理開発協会

JIS (Japanese Industrial Standards)
JIS (Nihon Kōgyō Hyōjun Kikaku)
日本工業標準規格

JIS keyboard
JIS kiibōdo
JIS キーボード

JISC (Japanese Industrial Standards Committee)
JISC (Nihon Kōgyō Hyōjun Chōsakai)
日本工業標準調査会

jitter
jitta
ジッタ

job
jyobu
ジョブ

job abort
jyobu no hōki
ジョブの放棄

job accounting
jyobu kaikei
ジョブ会計

job accounting routine
jyobu kaikei rūchin
ジョブ会計ルーチン

job control
jyobu seigyo
ジョブ制御

job control block (JCB)
jyobu seigyo burokku (JCB)
ジョブ制御ブロック

job control language (JCL)
jyobu seigyo gengo (JCL)
ジョブ制御言語

job control program
jyobu seigyo puroguramu
ジョブ制御プログラム

job control statement
jyobu seigyo bun;
jyobu seigyo sutētomento
ジョブ制御文;
ジョブ制御ステートメント

job deck
jyobu-dekku
ジョブ・デック

job entry
jyobu nyūryoku
ジョブ入力

job file
jyobu-fuairu
ジョブ・ファイル

job file index
jyobu-fuairu no sakuin
ジョブ・ファイルの索引

job flow
jyobu nagare
ジョブ流れ

job flow control
jyobu nagare seigyo
ジョブ流れ制御

job library
jyobu-raiburari
ジョブ・ライブラリ

job logging
jyobu-rogingu
ジョブ・ロギング

job management
jyobu kanri
ジョブ管理

job mix
jyobu-mikkusu
ジョブ・ミックス

job-oriented terminal
tokutei gyōmuyō tanmatsu
(sōchi)
特定業務用端末（装置）

job priority
jyobu yūsen jun'i
ジョブ優先順位

job queue
jyobu machigyōretsu
ジョブ待ち行列

job scheduler
jyobu-sukejyūra
ジョブ・スケジューラ

job scheduling
jyobu-sukejyūringu
ジョブ・スケジューリング

job shop operation
jyobu-shoppu-operēshon
ジョブ・ショップ・
オペレーション

job shop scheduling
jyobu-shoppu-sukejyūringu
ジョブ・ショップ・
スケジューリング

job shop simulation
jyobu-shoppu-shimyurēshon
ジョブ・ショップ・
シミュレーション

job stack
jyobu-sutakku
ジョブ・スタック

job statement
jyobu-sutētomento
ジョブ・ステートメント

job step
jyobu-suteppu
ジョブ・ステップ

job stream
jyobu nagare; jyobu-sutoriimu
ジョブ流れ；
ジョブ・ストリーム

job time limit
jyobu-taimu-rimitto
ジョブ・タイム・リミット

joint assembly
ketsugō asenburi
結合アセンブリ

journal
jyānaru
ジャーナル

journal printing
jyānaru insatsu
ジャーナル印刷

journal roll reader
jyānaru-rōru-riida
ジャーナル・ロール・リーダ

joy stick
jyoi-suteikku
ジョイ・スティック

judgment
handan
判断

judgment function
handan kinō
判断機能

judgment time
handan jikan
判断時間

jump
tobikoshi
飛び越し

jump instruction
tobikoshi meirei
飛び越し命令

junction
setsugō
接合

junction diode
setsugō daiōdo
接合ダイオード

junction transistor
setsugō toranjisuta
接合トランジスタ

justification
chōsei; ichi chōsei; soroe;
tsume; yose
調整；位置調整；揃え；
詰め；寄せ

justify
chōsei suru; ichi o chōsei suru;
soroeru; tsumeru; yoseru
調整する；位置を調整する；
揃える；詰める；寄せる

K

k (kilo-) (10³ or 1,000)
k (kiro-) (10³ or 1,000)
k；キロ

K (kilo-) (2¹⁰ or 1,024)
K (kiro-) (2¹⁰ or 1,024)
K；キロ

kana (Japanese characters)
kana
仮名

kanji (Chinese characters)
kanji
漢字

kanji printer
kanji purinta
漢字プリンタ

kanji teleprinter
kanji denshin injiki;
kanji terepurinta
漢字電信印字機；
漢字テレプリンタ

Kb (kilobit)
Kb (Kbitto; kirobitto)
Kb；Kビット；キロビット

KB (kilobyte)
KB (kirobaito)
KB；キロバイト

KB/s (kilobytes per second)
KB/s (kirobaito/byō)
KB/s；キロバイト／秒

kernel
kaku
核

key
kii
キー

key abbreviation
kii no ryakujika
キーの略字化

key area
midashi ryō'iki
見出し領域

key argument
kii-āgyumento
キー・アーギュメント

key arrangement
kii hairetsu
キー配列

key break
kii ware
キー割れ

key click
kii-kurikka
キー・クリッカ

key depression
kii asshuku
キー圧縮

key entry
kii-entori
キー・エントリ

key entry area
kii-entori iki
キー・エントリ域

key field
kii-fuiirudo
キー・フィールド

key generation
kii seisei
キー生成

key in (*verb*)
kii-in suru
キー・インする

key memory
kii-memori
キー・メモリ

key number
kii sū
キー数

key pulse
kii-parusu
キー・パルス

key punch
kemban senkōki; kii-panchi
鍵盤せん孔機; キー・パンチ

key rollover
kii-rōōba
キー・ローオーバ

key sequence
kii jun
キー順

key station
kii-sutēshon
キー・ステーション

key-to-cassette
kii-tsū-kasetto
キー・ツー・カセット

key-to-disk
kii-tsū-deisuku
キー・ツー・ディスク

key-to-disk unit
kii-tsū-deisuku sōchi
キー・ツー・ディスク装置

key-to-diskette
kii-tsū-deisuketto
キー・ツー・ディスケット

key–to–floppy disk
kii-tsū-furoppi-deisuku
キー・ツー・フロッピ・
ディスク

key-to-tape
kii-tsū-tēpu
キー・ツー・テープ

key transformation
kii henkan
キー変換

key verify
kii kenkō
キー検孔

keyboard
kemban; kiibōdo
鍵盤; キーボード

keyboard accounting machine
kiibōdo kaikeiki
キーボード会計機

keyboard connector
kiibōdo-konekuta
キーボード・コネクタ

keyboard data
kiibōdo-dēta
キーボード・データ

keyboard display
kemban hyōji sōchi
鍵盤表示装置

keyboard entry
kemban nyūryoku
鍵盤入力

keyboard inquiry
kemban toiawase
鍵盤問い合わせ

keyboard perforator
kemban senkōki
鍵盤せん孔機

keyboard printer
kemban insatsu sōchi
鍵盤印刷装置

keyboard punch
kemban senkōki
鍵盤せん孔機

keyboard send/receive (KSR)
kemban sōjushin (KSR)
鍵盤送受信

keyboard send/receive device
kemban sōjushin sōchi
鍵盤送受信装置

keying
taken
打鍵

keypad
kiipaddo
キーパッド

keyword
kiiwādo
キーワード

keyword in context (KWIC)
kuikku (KWIC)
クイック

keyword out of context (KWOC)
kuokku (KWOC)
クオック

kilo- (k) (10³ or 1,000)
kiro- (k) (10^3 or 1,000)
キロ; k

kilo- (K) (2¹⁰ or 1,024)
kiro- (K) (2^{10} or 1,024)
キロ; K

kilobaud
kirobō
キロボー

kilobit (Kb)
Kbitto; kirobitto (Kb)
K ビット; キロビット

kilobyte (KB)
kirobaito (KB)
キロバイト

kilobytes per second (KB/s)
kirobaito/byō (KB/s)
キロバイト / 秒

kilocycle
kirosaikuru
キロサイクル

knowledge
chishiki
知識

knowledge base
chishiki bēsu
知識ベース

knowledge-based
chishiki bēsu
知識ベース

knowledge-based system
chishiki bēsu-shisutemu
知識ベース・システム

knowledge engineering
chishiki kōgaku
知識工学

known information
kichi jōhō
既知情報

known structure
kichi kōzō
既知構造

KSR (keyboard send/receive)
KSR (kemban sōjushin)
鍵盤送受信

KWIC (keyword in context)
KWIC (kuikku)
クイック；KWIC

KWIC index
KWIC indekkusu
クイック・インデックス；
KWIC インデックス

KWOC (keyword out of context)
KWOC (kuokku)
クオック；KWOC

L

LA (laboratory automation)
LA (raboratori-otomēshon)
ラボラトリ・オトメーション

label
nafuda; raberu
名札；ラベル

label check
raberu-chekku; raberu kensa
ラベル・チェック；ラベル検査

label constant
raberu teisū
ラベル定数

label field
raberu ran
ラベル欄

label group
raberu gun; raberu-gurūpu
ラベル群；ラベル・グループ

label handling
raberu shori
ラベル処理

label-handling routine
raberu shori rūchin
ラベル処理ルーチン

label identifier
raberu shikibetsushi
ラベル識別子

label number
raberu bangō
ラベル番号

label record
raberu-rekōdo
ラベル・レコード

label routine
raberu-rūchin
ラベル・ルーチン

label set
raberu-setto
ラベル・セット

label standard level
raberu hyōjun reberu
ラベル標準レベル

label variable
raberu hensū
ラベル変数

labeled
raberutsuki
ラベル付き

laboratory automation (LA)
raboratori-otomēshon (LA)
ラボラトリ・オトメーション

lace punch
rēsu senkō
レースせん孔

laced card
rēsu-kādo
レース・カード

lag
okure
遅れ

LAN (local-area network)
LAN (kigyōnai jōhō tsūshinmō)
企業内情報通信網

language
gengo
言語

language analysis
gengo bunseki
言語分析

language complexity
gengo no fukusatsusei
言語の複雑性

language construction
gengo kōchiku
言語構築

language conversion
gengo henkan
言語変換

language conversion program
gengo henkan puroguramu
言語変換プログラム

language definition
gengo teigi
言語定義

language form
gengo keishiki
言語形式

language generation
gengo seisei
言語生成

language level
gengo suijun
言語水準

language processing
gengo shori
言語処理

language processor
gengo shori puroguramu
言語処理プログラム

language recognition
gengo ninshiki
言語認識

language statement
gengo sutētomento
言語ステートメント

language theory
gengo riron
言語理論

language translation
gengo hon'yaku
言語翻訳

language translator
gengo hon'yaku puroguramu
言語翻訳プログラム

language type
gengo keishiki
言語形式

large capacity
dai yōryō
大容量

large-capacity storage (LCS)
dai yōryō kioku (LCS)
大容量記憶

large scale
dai kibo
大規模

large-scale integrated circuit
dai kibo shūseki kairo
大規模集積回路

large-scale integration (LSI)
dai kibo shūsekika (LSI)
大規模集積化

large-scale network
dai kibo nettowāku
大規模ネットワーク

large-scale system
dai kibo shisutemu
大規模システム

laser memory
rēza-memori
レーザ・メモリ

laser printer
rēza-purinta
レーザ・プリンタ

laser recording
rēza-kiroku
レーザ記録

last-in first-out (LIFO)
atoire sakidashi (LIFO)
後入れ先出し

last pass
rasuto-pasu
ラスト・パス

last-pass own code (LPOC)
rasuto-pasu-oun-kōdo (LPOC)
ラスト・パス・オウン・コード

latency
machi jikan
待ち時間

latency time
kaiten machi jikan;
yobidashi jikan
回転待ち時間；呼び出し時間

layout
haichi; reiauto; yōshiki
配置；レイアウト；様式

layout character
shoshiki seigyo moji
書式制御文字

layout design
haichi sekkei
配置設計

layout planning
haichi keikaku
配置計画

LCB (line control block)
LCB (kaisen seigyo burokku)
回線制御ブロック

LCD (liquid-crystal display)
LCD (ekishō deisupurei)
液晶ディスプレィ

LCS (large-capacity storage)
LCS (dai yōryō kioku)
大容量記憶

LDB (logical database)
LDB (ronriteki dētabēsu)
論理的データベース

lead time
senkō jikan
先行時間

leading character
senkō moji
先行文字

leading edge
zen'en
前縁

leading graphics
senkō moji
先行文字

learner
gakushūsha
学習者

learning
gakushū
学習

learning machine
gakushū kikai
学習機械

learning system
gakushū shisutemu
学習システム

leased line
sen'yō kaisen; sen'yō sen
専用回線；専用線

leased-line network
sen'yō kaisenmō
専用回線網

leasing
riishingu
リーシング

least significant bit (LSB)
saikai no bitto (LSB)
最下位のビット

least significant character (LSC)
saikai no moji (LSC)
最下位の文字

least significant digit (LSD)
saikai no sūji (LSD)
最下位の数字

LED (light-emitting diode)
LED (hakkō daiōdo)
発光ダイオード

LED display
LED deisupurei
LEDディスプレィ

left justify
hidari tsume; hidari yose
左詰め；左寄せ

left shift
hidari shifuto
左シフト

length
nagasa
長さ

length factor
nagasa no keisū
長さの係数

letter (character)
eiji; moji
英字；文字

letter shift (LTRS)
eiji shifuto (LTRS)
英字シフト

level
reberu; suijun
レベル；水準

level diagram
reberu-daiyaguramu
レベル・ダイヤグラム

level indicator
reberu hyōshiki
レベル標識

level number
reberu bangō
レベル番号

level shift
reberu-shifuto
レベル・シフト

level shifter
reberu-shifuta
レベル・シフタ

LF (line feed)
LF (kaigyō)
改行

librarian
raiburarian
ライブラリアン

librarian program
raiburarian-puroguramu
ライブラリアン・プログラム

library
raiburari
ライブラリ

library control
raiburari seigyo
ライブラリ制御

library editor
raiburari henshū puroguramu
ライブラリ編集プログラム

library file
raiburari-fuairu
ライブラリ・ファイル

library file designator
raiburari-fuairu shijishi
ライブラリ・ファイル指示子

library function
raiburari kansū
ライブラリ関数

library maintenance
raiburari hoshu
ライブラリ保守

library management
raiburari kanri
ライブラリ管理

library name
raiburari mei
ライブリ名

library of data
dēta no raiburari
データのライブラリ

library program
raiburari-puroguramu
ライブラリ・プログラム

library routine
raiburari-rūchin
ライブラリ・ルーチン

library software
raiburari-sofutouea
ライブラリ・ソフトウェア

library structure
raiburari kōzō
ライブラリ構造

library subroutine
raiburari-saburūchin
ライブラリ・サブルーチン

library tape
raiburari-tēpu
ライブラリ・テープ

library update
raiburari kōshin
ライブラリ更新

life span
jumyō
寿命

LIFO (last-in first-out)
LIFO (atoire sakidashi)
後入れ先出し

light-emitting diode (LED)
hakkō daiōdo (LED)
発光ダイオード

light guide
raito-gaido
ライト・ガイド

light pen
raito-pen
ライト・ペン

light-pen connector
raito-pen-konekuta
ライト・ペン・コネクタ

light-pen interface
raito-pen-intafuēsu
ライト・ペン・インタフェース

light up (verb)
tentō suru
点灯する

limit
rimitto; seigen
リミット；制限

limit check
rimitto-chekku
リミット・チェック

limiter
rimitta
リミッタ

line (communication)
kaisen; rain; sen
回線；ライン；線

line (text)
gyō; rain
行；ライン

line adapter
kaisen adaputa
回線アダプタ

line analysis
kaisen bunseki
回線分析

line control
kaisen seigyo
回線制御

line control block (LCB)
kaisen seigyo burokku (LCB)
回線制御ブロック

113

line deletion
gyō masshō
行抹消

line detection
kaisendan kenshutsu
回線断検出

line editor
rain-edeita
ライン・エディタ

line feed (LF)
kaigyō (LF); rain okuri
改行; ライン送り

line group
kaisen gurūpu
回線グループ

line impedance
kaisen inpiidansu
回線インピーダンス

line indicator
gyō hyōji
行表示

line interface
kaisen intafuēsu
回線インタフェース

line load
kaisen fuka
回線負荷

line number
gyō bangō
行番号

line printer (LP)
gyō inji sōchi; rain-purinta (LP)
行印字装置; ライン・プリンタ

line printing
gyō insatsu
行印刷

line protection
kaisen hogo
回線保護

line protection device
kaisen hogo sōchi
回線保護装置

line segment
rain-segumento
ライン・セグメント

line spacing
gyō okuri
行送り

line speed
kaisen sokudo
回線速度

line-switched network
kaisen kōkanmō
回線交換網

line switching
kaisen kōkan
回線交換

line-switching system
kaisen kōkan shisutemu
回線交換システム

line terminal
kaisen shūtan sōchi
回線終端装置

linear
senkei
線形

linear circuit
senkei kairo
線形回路

linear equalization
senkei tōka
線形等化

linear equation
senkei hōteishiki
線形方程式

linear list
senkei risuto
線形リスト

linear optimization
senkei saitekika
線形最適化

linear programming (LP)
senkei keikakuhō (LP)
線形計画法

linear selection
senkei sentaku
線形選択

linear structure
senkei kōzō
線形構造

lines per minute (LPM)
gyō/fun (LPM)
行／分

link
renkei; renketsu; rinku
連係; 連結; リンク

link address
renketsu adoresu; rinku-adoresu
連係アドレス;
リンク・アドレス

link editor
renkei henshū puroguramu;
renketsu henshū puroguramu
連係編集プログラム;
連結編集プログラム

link information
renkei jōhō; renketsu jōhō
連係情報; 連結情報

link library
renkei raiburari;
renketsu raiburari
連係ライブラリ;
連結ライブラリ

link loader
rinku-rōda
リンク・ローダ

linkage
renkei; renketsu; rinkēji
連係; 連結; リンケージ

linkage editor
renkei henshū puroguramu;
renketsu henshū puroguramu
連係編集プログラム;
連結編集プログラム

linkage name
renkei mei; renketsu mei
連係名; 連結名

linked list
rinkuto-risuto
リンクト・リスト

linked subroutine
rinkuto-saburūchin
リンクト・サブルーチン

linker
rinka
リンカ

liquid crystal
ekishō
液晶

liquid-crystal display (LCD)
ekishō deisupurei (LCD)
液晶ディスプレィ

LISP (list-processing language)
LISP (risuto shori gengo)
リスト処理言語

list (*noun*)
　hyō; risuto
　表；リスト

list compacting
　risuto asshuku
　リスト圧縮

list-directed input/output
　risutokei nyūshutsuryoku
　リスト形入出力

list-directed transmission
　risuto shiji densō
　リスト指示伝送

list editor
　risuto henshū puroguramu
　リスト編集プログラム

list generation
　risuto seisei
　リスト生成

list manipulation language
　risuto shori gengo
　リスト処理言語

list moving
　risuto idō
　リスト移動

list processing
　risuto shori
　リスト処理

list-processing language (LISP)
　risuto shori gengo (LISP)
　リスト処理言語 (LISP)

list representation
　risuto hyōgen
　リスト表現

list scheduling
　risuto-sukejyūringu
　リスト・スケジューリング

list structure
　risuto kōzō
　リスト構造

listing
　risuteingu; sahyō
　リスティング；作表

literal constant
　riteraru teisū
　リテラル定数

literal operand
　riteraru-operando
　リテラル・オペランド

literals
　chokuteisū; riteraru
　直定数；リテラル

live operation
　katsudō sōsa
　活動操作

live run
　katsudō unten
　活動運転

live testing
　katsudō shiken
　活動試験

liveware
　raibuuea
　ライブウエア

LOAD (load)
　LOAD (fuka; rōdo)
　負荷；ロード

load (LOAD)
　fuka; rōdo (LOAD)
　負荷；ロード

load analysis
　fuka bunseki
　負荷分析

load-and-go
　rōdo-ando-gō
　ロード・アンド・ゴー

load density
　fuka mitsudo
　負荷密度

load distribution
　fuka bunsan
　負荷分散

load module
　rōdo-mojyūru
　ロード・モジュール

load point
　rōdo-pointo
　ロード・ポイント

load-point indicator
　rōdo-pointo hyōshiki
　ロード・ポイント標識

load-point marker
　rōdo-pointo-māka
　ロード・ポイント・マーカ

load sharing
　rōdo-shearingu
　ロード・シェアリング

loader
　rōda
　ローダ

loading
　rōdeingu
　ローディング

loading instruction
　rōdo meirei
　ロード命令

loading routine
　rōdo rūchin
　ロード・ルーチン

local
　kōnai; kyokushoteki; rōkaru
　構内；局所的；ローカル

local-area network (LAN)
　kigyōnai jōhō tsūshinmō (LAN)
　企業内情報通信網

local control
　kyoku'ikinai seigyo
　局域内制御

local mode
　rōkaru-mōdo
　ローカル・モード

local operation
　kōnai sōsa
　構内操作

local processing
　kyoku'ikinai shori; rōkaru shori
　局域内処理；ローカル処理

local processor
　kyokushoteki shori sōchi;
　rōkaru shori sōchi
　局所的処理装置；
　ローカル処理装置

local station
　kōnai tanmatsu
　構内端末

local storage
　kyokubu kioku
　局部記憶

local storage register
　kyokubu kioku rejisuta
　局部記憶レジスタ

local terminal
　kōnai tanmatsu (sōchi)
　構内端末（装置）

local test
rōkaru-tesuto
ローカル・テスト

local variable
kyokushoteki sūchi hensū
局所的数値変数

locality
kyokushosei
局所性

locate
ichi shitei
位置指定

locate (*verb*)
ichi o shitei suru
位置を指定する

locate mode
ichi shitei mōdo
位置指定モード

location
basho; ichi; kioku ichi; rokēshon
場所; 位置; 記憶位置;
ロケーション

location counter
(kioku) ichi kaunta
(記憶)位置カウンタ

locator
rokēta
ロケータ

locator qualifier
rokēta shūshokushi
ロケータ修飾子

lock
rokku
ロック

lock key
rokku-kii
ロック・キー

lock list
rokku-risuto
ロック・リスト

lock mode
rokku-mōdo
ロック・モード

lock option
rokku-opushon
ロック・オプション

lockout
rokku-auto
ロック・アウト

lockout procedure
rokku-auto tejun
ロック・アウト手順

log
kiroku; rogu
記録; ログ

log in
rogu-in
ログ・イン

log off
rogu-ofu
ログ・オフ

log on
rogu-on
ログ・オン

log out
rogu-auto
ログ・アウト

logarithm
taisū
対数

logger
roga
ロガ

logging
rogingu
ロギング

logging-in
rogingu-in
ロギング・イン

logging-out
rogingu-auto
ロギング・アウト

logic
ronri
論理

logic analysis
ronri bunseki
論理分析

logic analyzer
ronri anaraiza
論理アナライザ

logic circuit
ronri kairo
論理回路

logic design
ronri sekkei
論理設計

logic diagram
ronri zu
論理図

logic element
ronri soshi
論理素子

logic function
ronri kansū
論理関数

logic gate
ronri gēto
論理ゲート

logic information system
ronri jōhō shisutemu
論理情報システム

logic instruction
ronri meirei
論理命令

logic network
ronri nettowāku
論理ネットワーク

logic operation
ronri enzan
論理演算

logic seeking
ronri tansaku
論理探索

logic shift
ronri keta okuri; ronri shifuto
論理桁送り; 論理シフト

logic symbols
ronri kigō
論理記号

logic system
ronri shisutemu
論理システム

logic system design
ronri shisutemu sekkei
論理システム設計

logic unit
ronri(teki) sōchi
論理(的)装置

logic variable
ronri hensū
論理変数

logical
ronri(teki)
論理(的)

logical add
ronri wa
論理和

logical address
ronri adoresu
論理アドレス

logical block
ronri burokku
論理ブロック

logical circuit
ronri kairo
論理回路

logical comparison
ronri hikaku
論理比較

logical connectives
ronri ketsugōshi
論理結合子

logical constant
ronri teisū
論理定数

logical data
ronri dēta
論理データ

logical data independence
ronriteki dēta no dokuritsu
論理的データの独立

logical database (LDB)
ronriteki dētabēsu (LDB)
論理的データベース

logical design
ronri sekkei
論理設計

logical device number
ronri(teki) sōchi bangō
論理(的)装置番号

logical difference
ronri sa
論理差

logical element
ronri soshi
論理素子

logical entity
ronri kōseitai
論理構成体

logical error
ronri ayamari; ronri erā
論理誤り; 論理エラー

logical expression
ronri shiki
論理式

logical factor
ronri inshi
論理因子

logical file
ronri fuairu
論理ファイル

logical flowchart
ronri nagarezu
論理流れ図

logical function
ronri kansū
論理関数

logical IF statement
ronri IF bun
論理 IF 文

logical instruction
ronri meirei
論理命令

logical I/O control system
ronriteki nyūshutsuryoku seigyo shisutemu
論理的入出力制御システム

logical judgment
ronri handan
論理判断

logical name
ronri mei
論理名

logical operand
ronri operando
論理オペランド

logical operation
ronri enzan
論理演算

logical operator
ronri enzanshi; ronri sayōso
論理演算子; 論理作用素

logical port
ronri pōto
論理ポート

logical primary
ronri ichijishi
論理一次子

logical product
ronri seki
論理積

logical record
ronri rekōdo
論理レコード

logical shift
ronri keta okuri; ronri shifuto
論理桁送り; 論理シフト

logical sum
ronri wa
論理和

logical table
ronri hyō
論理表

logical type
ronri gata
論理型

logical unit
ronri(teki) sōchi; ronri tan'i
論理(的)装置; 論理単位

logical unit name
ronri(teki) sōchi mei
論理(的)装置名

logical unit number
ronri(teki) sōchi bangō
論理(的)装置番号

logical unit table
ronri(teki) sōchi tēburu
論理(的)装置テーブル

logical value
ronri chi
論理値

logical variable
ronri hensū
論理変数

long-precision floating point
chō seido fudō shōsūten
長精度浮動小数点

long word
chō go
長語

longitudinal check
suihei kensa
水平検査

117

longitudinal parity
suihei paritei
水平パリティ

longitudinal parity check (LPC)
suihei paritei kensa (LPC)
水平パリティ検査

longitudinal redundancy check (LRC)
suihei jōchō kensa (LRC)
水平冗長検査

longitudinal redundancy check character
suihei jōchō kensa moji
水平冗長検査文字

look up
rukku-appu; sanshō; tansaku
ルック・アップ; 参照; 探索

look-up operation
tansaku sōsa
探索操作

look-up table
rukku-appu-tēburu;
sanshō'yō tēburu
ルック・アップ・テーブル;
参照用テーブル

loop
rūpu
ループ

loop box
rūpu-bokkusu
ループ・ボックス

loop checking
hensō shōgō
返送照合

loop-checking system
hensō shōgō hōshiki
返送照合方式

loop counter
rūpu-kaunta
ループ・カウンタ

loop network
rūpu-nettowāku
ループ・ネットワーク

loss of data
dēta no datsuraku;
dēta no sonshitsu
データの脱落; データの損失

loss of information
jōhō no datsuraku;
jōhō no sonshitsu
情報の脱落; 情報の損失

low frequency
tei shūha
低周波

low indicator
tei chi hyōjishi
低値表示子

low level
tei reberu; tei suijun
低レベル; 低水準

low-level code
tei reberu-kōdo
低レベル・コード

low-level language
tei reberu gengo;
tei suijun gengo
低レベル言語; 低水準言語

low-order digit
saitei'i no sūji
最低位の数字

low-order end
saiutan
最右端

low-order memory
tei banchi kioku ryō'iki
低番地記憶領域

low-order storage
tei banchi kioku ryō'iki
低番地記憶領域

low speed
tei soku(do)
低速(度)

lower paper feed
kabu kami okuri
下部紙送り

LP (line printer)
LP (gyō inji sōchi; rain-purinta)
行印字装置; ライン・プリンタ

LP (linear programming)
LP (senkei keikakuhō)
線形計画法

LPC (longitudinal parity check)
LPC (suihei paritei kensa)
水平パリティ検査

LPM (lines per minute)
LPM (gyō/fun)
行 / 分

LPOC (last-pass own code)
LPOC (rasuto-pasu-oun-kōdo)
ラスト・パス・オウン・コード

LRC (longitudinal redundancy check)
LRC (suihei jōchō kensa)
水平冗長検査

LSB (least significant bit)
LSB (saikai no bitto)
最下位のビット

LSC (least significant character)
LSC (saikai no moji)
最下位の文字

LSD (least significant digit)
LSD (saikai no sūji)
最下位の数字

LSI (large-scale integration)
LSI (dai kibo shūsekika)
大規模集積化

LTRS (letter shift)
LTRS (eiji shifuto)
英字シフト

M

m (milli-)
m (miri-)
ミリ

MAC (multiaccess computer)
MAC (tajū akusesu keisanki)
多重アクセス計算機

machine
kikai; mashin
機械；マシン

machine address
kikaigo adoresu
機械語アドレス

machine-aided
kikai enjo
機械援助

machine-aided cognition
kikai enjo ninchi
機械援助認知

machine check
kikai chekku
機械チェック

machine-check interruption
kikai chekku warikomi
機械チェック割り込み

machine code
kikai kōdo
機械コード

machine configuration
kikai kōsei
機械構成

machine control
kikai seigyo
機械制御

machine cycle
kikai saikuru
機械サイクル

machine decision
kikai ishi kettei
機械意思決定

machine dependence
kikai izon
機械依存

machine-dependent
kikai izon
機械依存

machine description language
kikai kijutsu go
機械記述語

machine error
kikai ayamari
機械誤り

machine independence
kikai kara dokuritsu
機械から独立

machine-independent
kikai kara dokuritsu
機械から独立

machine instruction
kikaigo meirei
機械語命令

machine intelligence
kikai chinō
機械知能

machine language
kikai gengo; kikaigo
機械言語；機械語

machine-language coding
kikaigo kōdeingu
機械語コーディング

machine learning
kikai gakushū
機械学習

machine logic
kikai ronri
機械論理

machine malfunction
kikai godōsa
機械誤動作

machine monitoring
kikai seigyo
機械制御

machine operation
kikai sōsa
機械操作

machine operator
kikai sōsain
機械操作員

machine-oriented language
kikai muki gengo
機械向き言語

machine program
kikai puroguramu
機械プログラム

machine-readable medium
kikai kadoku baitai
機械可読媒体

machine-sensible
kikai kadoku
機械可読

machine-sensible form
kikai kadoku hō
機械可読法

machine-sensible information
kikai kadoku jōhō
機械可読情報

machine translation
kikai hon'yaku
機械翻訳

machine word
kikai go
機械語

macroassembler
makuro-asenbura
マクロ・アセンブラ

macroassembly
makuro-asenburi
マクロ・アセンブリ

macroassembly program
makuro-asenburi-puroguramu
マクロ・アセンブリ・
プログラム

macrocall
makuro-kōru; makuro yobidashi
マクロ・コール；
マクロ呼び出し

macrocode
makuro-kōdo
マクロ・コード

macrocoding
makuro-kōdeingu
マクロ・コーディング

macrocommand
makuro-komando; makuro shirei
マクロ・コマンド；マクロ指令

macrocontrol
makuro seigyo
マクロ制御

macrocontrol statement
makuro seigyo bun
マクロ制御文

macrodeclaration
makuro sengen
マクロ宣言

macrodefinition
makuro teigi
マクロ定義

macrodiagnostics
makuro shindan
マクロ診断

macrodirectory
makuro-dairekutori
マクロ・ダイレクトリ

macroelement
makuro yōso
マクロ要素

macroexpansion
makuro tenkai
マクロ展開

macrogenerating program
makuro seisei puroguramu
マクロ生成プログラム

macrogeneration
makuro seisei
マクロ生成

macrogenerator
makuro seisei puroguramu
マクロ生成プログラム

macroinstruction
makuro meirei
マクロ命令

macrolanguage
makuro gengo
マクロ言語

macrolibrary
makuro-raiburari
マクロ・ライブラリ

macroprocessor
makuropurosessa
マクロプロセッサ

macroprogram
makuropuroguramu
マクロプログラム

macroprogramming
makuropuroguramingu
マクロプログラミング

macroprototype
makuro genkei
マクロ原型

magnetic
jiki; jishin
磁気; 磁心

magnetic backing store
jiki hojo kioku sōchi
磁気補助記憶装置

magnetic bubble
jiki baburu
磁気バブル

magnetic card
jiki kādo
磁気カード

magnetic-card memory
jiki kādo kioku
磁気カード記憶

magnetic-card storage
jiki kādo kioku
磁気カード記憶

magnetic-card unit
jiki kādo sōchi
磁気カード装置

magnetic character
jiki moji
磁気文字

magnetic-character reader (MCR)
jiki moji yomitori sōchi (MCR)
磁気文字読み取り装置

magnetic-character reader/sorter
jiki moji yomitori-bunruiki
磁気文字読み取り-分類機

magnetic-character recognition (MCR)
jiki moji ninshiki (MCR)
磁気文字認識

magnetic core
jiki koa
磁気コア

magnetic-core matrix
jiki koa-matorikkusu
磁気コア・マトリックス

magnetic-core memory
jiki koa kioku; jishin kioku
磁気コア記憶; 磁心記憶

magnetic-core storage
jiki koa kioku; jishin kioku
磁気コア記憶; 磁心記憶

magnetic delay line
jiki chien sen
磁気遅延線

magnetic disk
jiki deisuku
磁気ディスク

magnetic-disk pack
jiki deisuku-pakku
磁気ディスク・パック

magnetic-disk storage
jiki deisuku kioku
磁気ディスク記憶

magnetic-disk unit
jiki deisuku sōchi
磁気ディスク装置

magnetic domain
jiku
磁区

magnetic drum
jiki doramu
磁気ドラム

magnetic-drum storage
jiki doramu kioku
磁気ドラム記憶

magnetic-drum unit
jiki doramu sōchi
磁気ドラム装置

magnetic file
jiki fuairu
磁気ファイル

magnetic film
jiki fuirumu
磁気フィルム

magnetic head
jiki heddo
磁気ヘッド

magnetic ink
jiki inku
磁気インク

magnetic-ink character
jiki inku moji
磁気インク文字

magnetic-ink character encoding
jiki inku moji fugōka;
jiki inku moji kōdoka
磁気インク文字符号化;
磁気インク文字コード化

magnetic-ink character inscriber
jiki inku moji kirokuki
磁気インク文字記録機

magnetic-ink character reader (MICR)
jiki inku moji yomitori sōchi (MICR)
磁気インク文字読み取り装置

magnetic-ink character recognition (MICR)
jiki inku moji ninshiki (MICR)
磁気インク文字認識

magnetic-ink character sorter
jiki inku moji bunruiki
磁気インク文字分類機

magnetic-ink character verification
jiki inku moji kenshō
磁気インク文字検証

magnetic language
jiki gengo
磁気言語

magnetic media
jishin baitai
磁心媒体

magnetic medium
jishin baitai
磁心媒体

magnetic memory
jiki kioku
磁気記憶

magnetic stripe
jiki sutoraipu
磁気ストライプ

magnetic tape (MT)
jiki tēpu (MT)
磁気テープ

magnetic tape cassette
jiki tēpu-kasetto
磁気テープ・カセット

magnetic tape cassette handler
jiki tēpu-kasetto sōchi
磁気テープ・カセット装置

magnetic tape cassette unit
jiki tēpu-kasetto sōchi
磁気テープ・カセット装置

magnetic-tape code
jiki tēpu-kōdo
磁気テープ・コード

magnetic-tape deck
jiki tēpu-dekku
磁気テープ・デック

magnetic-tape drive
jiki tēpu kudō kikō
磁気テープ駆動機構

magnetic-tape encoder
jiki tēpu-enkōda
磁気テープ・エンコーダ

magnetic-tape handler
jiki tēpu sōchi
磁気テープ装置

magnetic-tape label
jiki tēpu-raberu
磁気テープ・ラベル

magnetic-tape storage
jiki tēpu kioku
磁気テープ記憶

magnetic-tape unit (MTU)
jiki tēpu sōchi (MTU)
磁気テープ装置

magnetic thin film
jiki haku maku
磁気薄膜

magnetic thin film memory
jiki haku maku kioku
磁気薄膜記憶

magnetic thin film storage
jiki haku maku kioku
磁気薄膜記憶

magnetic wire store
jiki waiya kioku sōchi
磁気ワイヤ記憶装置

magnetically encoded output
jiki fugōki shutsuryoku
磁気符号器出力

magnitude
shimpuku; zettaichi
振幅；絶対値

magnitude comparison
shimpuku hikaku
振幅比較

magnitude transition
shimpuku sen'i
振幅遷移

main board
shu bōdo
主ボード

main control
shu seigyo
主制御

main control unit
shu seigyo sōchi
主制御装置

main features (of equipment)
tokuchō
特徴

main file
shu fuairu
主ファイル

main internal memory
shu kioku
主記憶

main internal memory unit
shu kioku sōchi
主記憶装置

main memory
mein-memori; shu kioku
メイン・メモリ；主記憶

main processor
shu purosessa
主プロセッサ

main program
shu puroguramu
主プログラム

main routine
shu rūchin
主ルチン

main storage
shu kioku('iki; ryō'iki)
主記憶（域；領域）

main storage dump
shu kioku'iki danpu
主記憶域ダンプ

main store
shu kioku sōchi
主記憶装置

main system
shu shisutemu
主システム

main task
shu tasuku
主タスク

mainframe
hontai; meinfurēmu(-konpyūta)
本体；メインフレーム
（・コンピュータ）

mainframe micro
meinfurēmu-maikuro
メインフレーム・マイクロ

maintainability
hoshusei; hozensei
保守性；保全性

maintenance
iji; hoshu; tairyū
維持；保守；滞留

maintenance contract
hoshu keiyaku
保守契約

maintenance program
hoshu(yō) puroguramu
保守(用)プログラム

maintenance routine
hoshu rūchin
保守ルーチン

maintenance service
hoshu sābisu
保守サービス

maintenance system
hoshu shisutemu
保守システム

maintenance time
hoshu jikan
保守時間

majority
tasūketsu
多数決

majority decision element
tasūketsu soshi
多数決素子

majority element
tasūketsu soshi
多数決素子

majority logic
tasūketsu ronri
多数決論理

majority operation
tasūketsu enzan
多数決演算

malfunction
godōsa
誤動作

malfunction location
godōsa ichi
誤動作位置

malfunction warning
godōsa keihō
誤動作警報

man-machine
ningen-kikai
人間-機械

man-machine interaction
ningen-kikai sōgokankei
人間-機械相互関係

man-machine interface (MMI)
ningen-kikai intafuēsu (MMI)
人間-機械インタフェース

man-machine system
ningen-kikai shisutemu
人間-機械システム

management
kanri; kei'ei
管理；経営

management by exception
reigai kanri
例外管理

management information
kei'ei jōhō
経営情報

management information system (MIS)
kei'ei jōhō (kanri) shisutemu (MIS)
経営情報(管理)システム

management-oriented
kei'ei muki
経営向き

management support system
kei'ei sapōto-shisutemu
経営サポート・システム

manipulation
shori
処理

manned
yūjin
有人

manned operation
yūjin dōsa
有人動作

mantissa
kasū
仮数

manual (instruction book)
kaisetsusho; setsumeisho; shijisho
解説書；説明書；指示書

manual (≠automatic)
manyuaru; shu; shudō (no)
マニュアル；手；手動(の)

manual backup
shudō bakku-appu
手動バック・アップ

manual closed-loop system
shudō tojita rūpu-shisutemu
手動閉じたループ・システム

manual control
shudō seigyo
手動制御

manual input
shudō nyūryoku
手動入力

manual input register
shudō nyūryoku rejisuta
手動入力レジスタ

manual input unit
shudō nyūryoku sōchi
手動入力装置

manual method
shudō hōhō
手動方法

manual mode
shudōteki mōdo
手動的モード

manual operation
shu sōsa; shudō sōsa
手操作；手動操作

manual system
shudō shisutemu
手動システム

map (noun)
mappu; shazō
マップ；写像

map (verb)
shazō suru
写像する

map register (mr)
mappu-rejisuta (mr)
マップ・レジスタ

mapping
mappingu; shazō
マッピング；写像

mapping division
shazō bu
写像部

mapping function
mappingu kinō
マッピング機能

mapping system
mappingu-shisutemu
マッピング・システム

MAR (memory address register)
MAR (kioku adoresu-rejisuta)
記憶アドレス・レジスタ

margin
genkai
限界

marginal check
genkai kensa
限界検査

mark
māku
マーク

mark card
māku-kādo
マーク・カード

mark encoding
māku-enkōdeingu; māku fugōka;
māku-kōdoka
マーク・エンコーディング；
マーク符号化；
マーク・コード化

mark hold
māku-hōrudo
マーク・ホールド

mark reader
māku yomitori sōchi
マーク読み取り装置

mark reading
māku yomitori
マーク読み取り

mark-reading station
māku yomitori kikō
マーク読み取り機構

mark sense
māku-sensu
マーク・センス

mark-sensed card
māku-sensu-kādo
マーク・センス・カード

mark sensing
māku-senshingu; māku yomitori
マーク・センシング；
マーク読み取り

mark-sensing card
māku yomitori kādo
マーク読み取りカード

mark-sensing punch
māku yomitori senkōki
マーク読み取りせん孔機

mark verification
māku kensa; māku kenshō
マーク検査；マーク検証

marker
hyōshiki; māka
標識；マーカ

mask
masuku
マスク

mask alignment
masuku awase
マスク合わせ

mask bit
masuku-bitto
マスク・ビット

mask register
masuku-rejisuta
マスク・レジスタ

masked ROM
masuku ROM
マスク ROM

masked state
masuku jōtai
マスク状態

mass data
dairyō dēta; masu-dēta
大量データ；マス・データ

mass storage
dai kioku; daiyōryō kioku
大記憶；大容量記憶

mass-storage control system
dai kioku kanri shisutemu
大記憶管理システム

mass-storage device
daiyōryō kioku sōchi
大容量記憶装置

mass-storage record
dai kioku rekōdo
大記憶レコード

mass-storage system
daiyōryō kioku shisutemu
大容量記憶システム

mass-storage unit
daiyōryō kioku sōchi
大容量記憶装置

master
kihon; masuta; shu
基本；マスタ；主

master card
kihon kādo; masuta-kādo
基本カード；マスタ・カード

master clock
masuta-kurokku; shu kokuji kikō
マスタ・クロック；主刻時機構

master control program
masuta seigyo puroguramu
マスタ制御プログラム

master file
kihon fuairu; masuta-fuairu
基本ファイル；
マスタ・ファイル

master file directory
masuta-fuairu-dairekutori
マスタ・ファイル・
ダイレクトリ

master group
shu gun
主群

master instruction tape (MIT)
masuta-insutorakushon-tēpu
(MIT)
マスタ・インストラクション・
テープ

master menu
masuta-menyū
マスタ・メニュー

master record
masuta-rekōdo
マスタ・レコード

master routine
shu rūchin
主ルーチン

master scheduler
masuta-sukejyūra
マスタ・スケジューラ

master/slave system
masuta/surēbu-shisutemu
マスタ／スレーブ・システム

master station
masuta-sutēshon; shu tanmatsu
マスタ・ステーション；主端末

master tape
masuta-tēpu
マスタ・テープ

match (*verb*)
tsukiawaseru
突き合わせる

match key
tsukiawase kii
突き合わせキー

matching (of data)
tsukiawase (dēta no)
突き合わせ（データの）

mathematical analysis
sūri kaiseki
数理解析

mathematical check
sūgakuteki kensa
数学的検査

mathematical model
sūgakuteki moderu
数学的モデル

mathematical programming (MP)
sūri keikakuhō (MP)
数理計画法

mathematical software
sūchi keisan'yō sofutouea
数値計算用ソフトウェア

matrix
gyōretsu; matorikkusu
行列；マトリックス

matrix analysis
matorikkusu kaiseki
マトリックス解析

matrix display
matorikkusu-deisupurei
マトリックス・ディスプレィ

matrix matching
matorikkusu-matchingu
マトリックス・マッチング

matrix printer
matorikkusu-purinta
マトリックス・プリンタ

matrix representation
gyōretsu hyōgen
行列表現

matrix storage
matorikkusu kioku
マトリックス記憶

maximum block length
saidai burokku chō
最大ブロック長

maximum capacity
saidai yōryō
最大容量

maximum communication speed
saidai tsūshin sokudo
最大通信速度

maximum load
saidai fuka
最大負荷

maximum printing speed
saidai insatsu sokudo
最大印刷速度

Mb (megabit)
Mb (megabitto)
メガビット

MB (megabyte)
MB (megabaito)
メガバイト

MBR (memory buffer register)
MBR (kioku baffua-rejisuta)
記憶バッファ・レジスタ

MCR (magnetic-character reader)
MCR (jiki moji yomitori sōchi)
磁気文字読み取り装置

MCR (magnetic-character recognition)
MCR (jiki moji ninshiki)
磁気文字認識

mean
heikin
平均

mean access time
heikin akusesu jikan
平均アクセス時間

mean information content
heikin jōhō ryō
平均情報量

mean time between failures (MTBF)
heikin koshō kankaku (MTBF)
平均故障間隔

mean time between maintenance (MTBM)
heikin hoshu kankaku (MTBM)
平均保守間隔

mean time to diagnosis (MTTD)
shindan made no heikin jikan (MTTD)
診断までの平均時間

mean time to failure (MTTF)
heikin shoki koshō jikan (MTTF)
平均初期故障時間

mean time to repair (MTTR)
heikin shūfuku jikan (MTTR)
平均修復時間

measure (*verb*)
sokutei suru
測定する

measurement
sokudo
測度

mechanical
kikai
機械

mechanical method
kikai hōhō
機械方法

mechanical translation
kikai hon'yaku
機械翻訳

mechanistic system
kikaiteki shisutemu
機械的システム

mechanization
kikaika
機械化

mechanization problem
kikaika mondai
機械化問題

media
baitai
媒体

medium
baitai
媒体

medium conversion
baitai henkan
媒体変換

medium-scale integrated circuit
chū kibo shūseki kairo
中規模集積回路

medium-scale integration (MSI)
chū kibo shūsekika (MSI)
中規模集積化

megabit (Mb)
megabitto (Mb)
メガビット

megabyte (MB)
megabaito (MB)
メガバイト

megahertz (MHz)
megaherutsu (MHz)
メガヘルツ

member
ko; menba
子；メンバ

member condition
ko no jōken
子の条件

member record
ko rekōdo
子レコード

memory
kioku (sōchi); memori
記憶(装置)；メモリ

memory access
akusesu
アクセス

memory address register (MAR)
kioku adoresu-rejisuta (MAR)
記憶アドレス・レジスタ

memory allocation
kioku wariate
記憶割り当て

memory area
kioku iki; kioku ryō'iki
記憶域；記憶領域

memory board
kioku bōdo
記憶ボード

memory buffer register (MBR)
kioku rejisuta (MBR)
記憶レジスタ

memory capacity
kioku yōryō
記憶容量

memory card
kioku kādo
記憶カード

memory cell
kioku seru
記憶セル

memory compaction
kioku asshuku
記憶圧縮

memory constitution
kioku'iki hensei
記憶域編成

memory contention
kioku'iki sōdatsu
記憶域争奪

memory-controlled
kioku seigyo no
記憶制御の

memory cycle
kioku saikuru; memori-saikuru
記憶サイクル；
メモリ・サイクル

memory data register
kioku dēta-rejisuta
記憶データ・レジスタ

memory dump
memori-danpu
メモリ・ダンプ

memory error
kioku ayamari
記憶誤り

memory-error indicator
kioku ayamari hyōjishi
記憶誤り表示子

memory hierarchy
kioku kaisō
記憶階層

memory interference
kioku'iki shōtotsu
記憶域衝突

memory interleave
memori-intariibu
メモリ・インタリーブ

memory location
kioku basho
記憶場所

memory lockout
kioku'iki rokku-auto
記憶域ロック・アウト

memory management
kioku'iki kanri
記憶域管理

memory map
kioku chizu; memori-mappu
記憶地図；メモリ・マップ

memory-mapped I/O
memori-mappudo I/O
メモリ・マップドI/O

memory mapping
kioku mappingu; kioku shazō
記憶マッピング；記憶写像

memory module
kioku mojyūru
記憶モジュール

memory overlays
memori-ōbarei
メモリ・オーバレイ

memory protect(ion)
kioku hogo
記憶保護

memory register
kioku rejisuta
記憶レジスタ

memory-resident operating system
kioku jōchū operēteingu-
shisutemu
記憶常駐オペレーティング・
システム

memory size
kioku yōryō
記憶容量

memory support
kioku shien
記憶支援

125

memory support system
kioku shien shisutemu;
memori-sapōto-shisutemu
記憶支援システム;
メモリ・サポート・システム

memory switching system
kioku kōkan shisutemu
記憶交換システム

memory system
kioku hōshiki; kioku sōchi
記憶方式; 記憶装置

memory usage accounting
kioku'iki shiyō ni tai suru kakin
記憶域使用に対する課金

menu
menyū; mokuroku
メニュー; 目録

menu-driven software
menyū kudōgata sofutouea
メニュー駆動型ソフトウェア

menu selection
menyū sentaku
メニュー選択

mercury contact relay
suigin setten rirē
水銀接点リレー

mercury delay line
suigin chien sen
水銀遅延線

mercury storage
suigin kioku
水銀記憶

mercury-wetted relay
suigin setten keidenki
水銀接点継電器

merge (noun)
kumiawase; māji
組み合わせ; マージ

merge (verb)
kumiawaseru; māji suru
組み合わせる; マージする

merge pass
kumiawase pasu; māji-pasu
組み合わせパス; マージ・パス

merge-sort
kumiawase-bunrui; māji-sōto
組み合わせ-分類;
マージ・ソート

merging
heigō; kumiawase
併合; 組み合わせ

mesial
hanchi
半値

mesial point
hanchi ten
半値点

message
dembun; messēji
電文; メッセージ

message control program
messēji seigyo puroguramu
メッセージ制御プログラム

message destination
dembun ikisaki
電文行き先

message dispatch
dembun hasshin
電文発信

message editing
messēji henshū
メッセージ編集

message flow
dembun no nagare
電文の流れ

message numbering
dembun tsūban
電文通番

message operation
dembun sōsa
電文操作

message parity
messēji-paritei
メッセージ・パリティ

message processing
messēji-shori
メッセージ処理

message processing program
messēji shori puroguramu
メッセージ処理プログラム

message queuing
messēji machigyōretsu
メッセージ待ち行列

message reception
(dembun) jushin
（電文）受信

message retransmission
dembun saisō
電文再送

message routing
messēji keiro shitei
メッセージ経路指定

message segment
messēji-segumento
メッセージ・セグメント

message source
messēji gen
メッセージ源

message switching
messēji kōkan
メッセージ交換

message switching system
messēji kōkan shisutemu
メッセージ交換システム

metal-oxide semiconductor (MOS)
mosu (MOS)
モス

metal-oxide semiconductor field effect transistor technology (MOSFET)
mosu denkai kōka toranjisuta gijutsu (MOSFET)
モス電界効果トランジスタ技術

metal-oxide semiconductor IC
mosu IC; MOSgata IC
モスIC; MOS型IC;
モス型IC

metal-oxide semiconductor integrated circuit
mosu shūseki kairo
モス集積回路

metal-oxide semiconductor ROM
mosu ROM; MOSgata ROM
モスROM; MOS型ROM;
モス型ROM

metal-oxide semiconductor transistor (MOST)
mosu-toranjisuta (MOST)
モス・トランジスタ

metalangue
chōgengo
超言語

metalinguistic formula
chōgengo shiki
超言語式

metalinguistic variable
chōgengo hensū
超言語変数

method
hō; hōhō; hōshiki
法; 方法; 方式

methodology
hōhōron
方法論

MHz (megahertz)
MHz (megaherutsu)
メガヘルツ

MICR (magnetic-ink character reader)
MICR (jiki inku moji yomitori sōchi)
磁気インク文字読み取り装置

MICR (magnetic-ink character recognition)
MICR (jiki inku moji ninshiki)
磁気インク文字認識

micro-
chōkogata; maikuro
超小形; マイクロ

microassembly
chōkogata kumitate
超小形組み立て

microcassette
maikuro-kasetto
マイクロ・カセット

microcircuit
maikuro kairo
マイクロ回路

microcode
maikuro-kōdo
マイクロ・コード

microcommand
maikuro meirei
マイクロ命令

microcomponent
chōkogata kōsei bubun
超小形構成部分

microcomputer
maikuro-konpyūta
マイクロ・コンピュータ

microcontroller
maikuro-kontorōra
マイクロ・コントローラ

microdiagnostics
maikuro shindan
マイクロ診断

microdrive
maikuro-doraibu
マイクロ・ドライブ

microdrive cartridge
maikuro-doraibu-kātorijji
マイクロ・ドライブ・カートリッジ

microelectronic system
chōkogata denshi hōshiki
超小形電子方式

microelectronics
chōkogata denshi kōgaku
超小形電子工学

microelement
chōkogata soshi
超小形素子

microfiche
maikurofuisshu
マイクロフィッシュ

microfiche viewer
maikurofuisshu hyōjiki
マイクロフィッシュ表示器

microfilm
maikurofuirumu
マイクロフイルム

micro−floppy disk
maikuro-furoppi-deisuku
マイクロ・フロッピ・ディスク

microinstruction
maikuro meirei
マイクロ命令

micromainframe
maikuro-meinfurēmu
マイクロ・メインフレーム

micromainframe link
maikuro-meinfurēmu-rinku
マイクロ・メインフレーム・リンク

micromarket
maikuro-māketto
マイクロ・マーケット

microminiaturization
maikuro kogataka
マイクロ小形化

micromodule
maikuro-mojyūru
マイクロ・モジュール

micromodule technique
maikuro-mojyūru gijutsu
マイクロ・モジュール技術

microoperation
maikuro sōsa
マイクロ操作

micro-OS
maikuro OS
マイクロOS

microprocessor
maikuropurosessa
マイクロプロセッサ

microprocessor unit (MPU)
maikuropurosessa sōchi (MPU)
マイクロプロセッサ装置

microprogram
maikuropuroguramu
マイクロプログラム

microprogramming
maikuropuroguramingu
マイクロプログラミング

microsecond
maikuro byō
マイクロ秒

microstructure
chōkogata kōzō
超小形構造

microswitch
maikuro-suitchi
マイクロ・スイッチ

microwave
maikuro nami
マイクロ波

micro−word length
maikuro gochō
マイクロ語長

MIL (military specifications) (USA)
MIL (beigun kikaku) (USA)
米軍規格

military specifications (MIL) (USA)
beigun kikaku (MIL) (USA)
米軍規格

milli- (m)
miri- (m)
ミリ

127

millisecond (ms)
miribyō (ms)
ミリ秒

millisecond speed range
miribyō sokudo haba
ミリ秒速度幅

miniaturization
kogataka
小形化

minicomputer
mini-konpyūta
ミニ・コンピュータ

minidisk
mini-deisuku
ミニ・ディスク

minidiskette
mini-deisuketto
ミニ・ディスケット

mini−floppy disk
mini-furoppi-deisuku
ミニ・フロッピ・ディスク

minimal
saishō
最小

minimax approximation
mini-makkusu kinji
ミニ・マックス近似

minimax method
mini-makkusu hō
ミニ・マックス法

minimicro
minimaikuro-konpyūta
ミニマイクロ・コンピュータ

minimum
saishō
最小

minimum access code
saishō akusesu-kōdo;
saishō yobidashi kōdo
最小アクセス・コード；
最小呼び出しコード

minimum access coding
saishō akusesu-kōdeingu;
saishō yobidashi kōdeingu
最小アクセス・コーディング；
最小呼び出しコーディング

minimum area
saishō ryō'iki
最小領域

minimum block length
saishō burokku chō
最小ブロック長

minimum communication speed
saishō tsūshin sokudo
最小通信速度

minimum cost
saishō hiyō
最小費用

minimum delay code
saishō chien kōdo
最小遅延コード

minimum distance code
saishō kyori kōdo
最小距離コード

minimum latency code
saishō machijikan kōdo
最小待ち時間コード

minimum latency coding
saishō machijikan kōdeingu
最小待ち時間コーディング

minimum time
saitan jikan
最短時間

minor control change
tei'i no seigyo henkō
低位の制御変更

minor cycle
shōshūki
小周期

minuend
higensū
被減数

MIP (mixed integer programming)
MIP (kongō seisū keikakuhō)
混合整数計画法

MIS (management information system)
MIS (kei'ei jōhō kanri shisutemu;
kei'ei jōhō shisutemu)
経営情報管理システム；
経営情報システム

misfeed
okuri ayamari
送り誤り

misinformation
gojōhō
誤情報

mismatch
fuitchi
不一致

misoperation
gosōsa
誤操作

misoperation detection
gosōsa kenshutsu
誤操作検出

misoperation detection function
gosōsa kenshutsu kinō
誤操作検出機能

MIT (master instruction tape)
MIT (masuta-insutorakushon-tēpu)
マスタ・インストラクション・テープ

mixed-base notation
kongō kisū hyōkihō
混合基数表記法

mixed-base numeration system
kongō kisū hyōkihō
混合基数表記法

mixed integer programming (MIP)
kongō seisū keikakuhō (MIP)
混合整数計画法

mixed mode
kongō mōdo
混合モード

mixed-mode operation
kongō enzan
混合演算

mixed radix
kongō kisū
混合基数

mixed-radix notation
kongō kisū hyōkihō
混合基数表記法

mixed-type arithmetic expression
kongō sanjutsu shiki
混合算術式

MMI (man-machine interface)
MMI (ningen-kikai intafuēsu)
人間-機械インタフェース

mnemonic code
kanryaku kioku kōdo
簡略記憶コード

mnemonic instruction code
kanryaku meirei kōdo
簡略命令コード

mnemonic name
kanryaku mei
簡略名

mnemonic operation codes
kanryaku meirei kōdo
簡略命令コード

mnemonic symbol
kanryaku kioku kigō
簡略記憶記号

mnemonics
kanryaku kiokugō
簡略記憶号

mobile
idōshiki
移動式

mode
hōshiki; mōdo
方式；モード

mode bit
hōshiki bitto
方式ビット

mode compatibility
hōshiki gokansei; mōdo gokansei
方式互換性；モード互換性

model
kata; moderu
型／形；モデル

model-building language
moderu kōsei gengo
モデル構成言語

model-running language
moderu jikkō gengo
モデル実行言語

modeling package
moderingu-pakkēji
モデリング・パッケージ

modem (modulator-demodulator)
henfukuchō sōchi; modemu
変復調装置；モデム

modifiability
shūseikanōsei
修正可能性

modification
henkō; shūsei(ka); shūshoku(ka)
変更；修正(化)；修飾(化)

modification level
shūsei reberu
修正レベル

modified address
shūseika adoresu
修正化アドレス

modifier
henkōshi; shūshoku
変更子；修飾

modifier bit
shūshoku bitto
修飾ビット

modifier register
shihyō rejisuta
指標レジスタ

modify (verb)
henkō suru; shūshoku suru
変更する；修飾する

modular
mojyūra
モジューラ

modular computer system
mojyūra keisanki shisutemu
モジューラ計算機システム

modular design
mojyūra sekkei
モジューラ設計

modular programming
mojyūra-puroguramingu
モジューラ・プログラミング

modular structure
mojyūra kōzō
モジューラ構造

modular system
mojyūra-shisutemu
モジューラ・システム

modular system control
mojyūra-shisutemu seigyo
モジューラ・システム制御

modular system program
mojyūra-shisutemu-puroguramu
モジューラ・システム・
プログラム

modularity
mojyūrasei
モジューラ性

modularization
mojyūraka
モジューラ化

modulation
henchō
変調

modulation rate
henchō sokudo
変調速度

modulator
henchō sōchi
変調装置

modulator-demodulator (modem)
henfukuchō sōchi; modemu
変復調装置；モデム

module
mojyūru
モジュール

module for general use
han'yō mojyūru
汎用モジュール

module name
mojyūru mei
モジュール名

module structure
mojyūru kōzō
モジュール構造

modulo
mojyūro
モジューロ

modulo arithmetic
mojyūro enzan
モシューロ演算

modulo _n_ check
mojyūro _n_ kensa
モジューロn検査

modulo _n_ counter
mojyūro _n_ kaunta
モジューロnカウンタ

modulo _n_ residue
mojyūro _n_ jōyo
モジューロn剰余

monadic
tankō
単項

monadic Boolean operator
tankō Būru enzanshi
単項ブール演算子

monadic operation
tankō enzan
単項演算

monadic operator
tankō enzanshi
単項演算子

monitor (noun)
kanshi puroguramu; monita
監視プログラム；モニタ

monitor (verb)
kanshi suru
監視する

monitor code
kanshi kōdo
監視コード

monitor interrupt
kanshi puroguramu warikomi
監視プログラム割り込み

monitor mode
kanshi mōdo
監視モード

monitor printer
kanshi'yō insho sōchi
監視用印書装置

monitor routine
kanshi rūchin; monita-rūchin
監視ルーチン；
モニタ・ルーチン

monitor station
kanshi tanmatsu
監視端末

monitor system
kanshi shisutemu;
monita-shisutemu
監視システム；
モニタ・システム

monitoring
kanri; kanshi; kanshi seigyo;
seigyo
管理；監視；監視制御；制御

monitoring program
kanshi puroguramu
監視プログラム

monitoring system
kanshi shisutemu
監視システム

monochrome
monokuro
モノクロ

monolithic
monorishikku
モノリシック

monolithic integrated circuit
monorishikku shūseki kairo
モノリシック集積回路

monolithic programming
monorishikku-puroguramingu
モノリシック・プログラミング

monostable
tan'antei
単安定

monostable circuit
tan'antei kairo
単安定回路

monostable element
tan'antei soshi
単安定素子

monostable multivibrator
tan'antei maruchibaiburēta
単安定マルチバイブレータ

monostable trigger circuit
tan'antei kairo;
tan'antei toriga kairo
単安定回路；単安定トリガ回路

MOS (metal-oxide semiconductor)
MOS (mosu)
モス

MOSFET (metal-oxide semiconductor field effect transistor technology)
MOSFET (mosu denkai kōka toranjisuta gijutsu)
モス電界効果トランジスタ技術

MOST (metal-oxide semiconductor transistor)
MOST (mosu-toranjisuta)
モス・トランジスタ

most significant bit (MSB)
saijōi no bitto (MSB)
最上位のビット

most significant character (MSC)
saijōi no moji (MSC)
最上位の文字

most significant digit (MSD)
saijōi no sūji (MSD)
最上位の数字

mother board
mazā-bōdo; shu bōdo
マサー・ボード；主ボード

mouse
mausu
マウス

mouse connector
mausu-konekuta
マウス・コネクタ

mouse-driven
mausu-doriiben
マウス・ドリーベン

mouse interface
mausu-intafuēsu
マウス・インタフェース

mouse set
mausu-setto
マウス・セット

movable
idōshiki
移動式

movable head
idōshiki heddo
移動式ヘッド

move (verb)
idō suru
移動する

move instruction
idō meirei
移動命令

move mode
idō mōdo
移動モード

moving average
idō heikin
移動平均

moving target
idō mokuhyō
移動目標

MP (mathematical programming)
MP (sūri keikakuhō)
数理計画法

MP/M
MP/M
MP／M

MPU (microprocessor unit)
MPU (maikuropurosessa sōchi)
マイクロプロセッサ装置

mr (map register)
mr (mappu-rejisuta)
マップ・レジスタ

ms (millisecond)
ms (miribyō)
ミリ秒

MSB (most significant bit)
MSB (saijō'i no bitto)
最上位のビット

MSC (most significant character)
MSC (saijō'i no moji)
最上位の文字

MSD (most significant digit)
MSD (saijō'i no sūji)
最上位の数字

MSI (medium-scale integration)
MSI (chū kibo shūsekika)
中規模集積化

MT (magnetic tape)
MT (jiki tēpu)
磁気テープ

MTBF (mean time between failures)
MTBF (heikin koshō kankaku)
平均故障間隔

MTBM (mean time between maintenance)
MTBM (heikin hoshu kankaku)
平均保守間隔

MTTD (mean time to diagnosis)
MTTD (shindan made no heikin jikan)
診断までの平均時間

MTTF (mean time to failure)
MTTF (heikin shoki koshō jikan)
平均初期故障時間

MTTR (mean time to repair)
MTTR (heikin shūfuku jikan)
平均修復時間

MTU (magnetic-tape unit)
MTU (jiki tēpu sōchi)
磁気テープ装置

multi-
fuku; fukusū; maruchi; ta; tajū
複; 複数; マルチ; 多; 多重

multiaccess
maruchi-akusesu; tajū yobidashi
マルチ・アクセス;
多重呼び出し

multiaccess computer (MAC)
tajū akusesu keisanki (MAC)
多重アクセス計算機

multiaccess system
maruchi-akusesu-shisutemu;
tajū yobidashi shisutemu
マルチ・アクセス・システム;
多重呼び出しシステム

multiaddress
fukusū adoresu
複数アドレス

multiaddress instruction
fukusū adoresu meirei
複数アドレス命令

multiaddress message
fukusū adoresu-messēji
複数アドレス・メッセージ

multibus
maruchi-basu
マルチ・バス

multichannel
tachaneru
多チャネル

multichip
maruchi-chippu
マルチ・チップ

multicomputer system
fukugō keisanki shisutemu
複合計算機システム

multicriteria
takijun
多基準

multicycle sort
fuku saikuru bunrui
複サイクル分類

multidimensional
tajigen
多次元

multidimensional system
tajigen shisutemu
多次元システム

multidrop
bunki (no)
分岐(の)

multifield
fukusū ran
複数欄

multifield index
fukusū ran sakuin
複数欄索引

multifile
fukusū fuairu
複数ファイル

multifile volume
fukusū fuairu-boryūmu
複数ファイル・ボリューム

multifunction
takinō; tanō
多機能; 多能

multifunction board
takinō bōdo
多機能ボード

multifunction card
takinō kādo
多機能カード

multifunctional
takinōteki
多機能的

multijob
maruchi-jyobu; tajū jyobu
マルチ・ジョブ; 多重ジョブ

multijob operation
maruchi-jyobu-operēshon;
tajū jyobu sōsa
マルチ・ジョブ・
オペレーション;
多重ジョブ操作

multijob scheduling
tajū jyobu-sukejyūringu
多重ジョブ・スケジューリング

multilayer
tasō
多層

multilayer printed circuit board
tasō insatsu haisen kiban
多層印刷配線基板

multilength arithmetic
tabaichō enzan
多倍長演算

multilength number
tabaichō sū
多倍長数

multilength working
tabaichō shori
多倍長処理

multilevel
tajū reberu; takaisō
多重レベル；多階層

multilevel address
tajū reberu-adoresu
多重レベル・アドレス

multilevel computer
tajū reberu keisanki
多重レベル計算機

multilevel index
takaisō sakuin
多階層索引

multilevel planning
tajū reberu keikaku
多重レベル計画

multilevel structure
tajū reberu kōzō
多重レベル構造

multilevel system
tajū reberu-shisutemu
多重レベル・システム

multilinked list
tajū renketsu risuto
多重連結リスト

multiloop
tajū rūpu
多重ループ

multiobjective
tamokuteki
多目的

multipage
maruchi-pēji
マルチ・ページ

multiperson control
taninsū seigyo
多人数制御

multiphase
fukusū fuēzu
複数フェーズ

multiplate disc
maruchi-pureito-deisuku
マルチ・プレイト・ディスク

multiple
fukusū; tajū
複数；多重

multiple access
tajū akusesu; tajū yobidashi
多重アクセス；多重呼び出し

multiple address
fukusū adoresu
複数アドレス

multiple-address code
fukusū adoresu-kōdo
複数アドレス・コード

multiple-address instruction
fukusū adoresu meirei
複数アドレス命令

multiple-assignment statement
tajū dainyūbun
多重代入文

multiple closure
tajū heisa
多重閉鎖

multiple declaration
tajū sengen
多重宣言

multiple error
tajū ayamari
多重誤り

multiple file
fukusū fairu
複数ファイル

multiple-length number
tabaichō sū
多倍長数

multiple line
fukusū kaisen
複数回線

multiple objective
tamokuteki
多目的

multiple precision
tabai seido
多倍精度

multiple-precision arithmetic
tabai seido enzan
多倍精度演算

multiple processing
tajū shori
多重処理

multiple processing system
tajū shori shisutemu
多重処理システム

multiple punch(ing)
tajū senkō
多重せん孔

multiple-request
tajū yōkyū
多重要求

multiple statement
tajū sutētomento
多重ステートメント

multiple terminals
tajū tanmatsu
多重端末

multiple track
tajū torakku
多重トラック

multiple-track error
tajū torakku ayamari
多重トラック誤り

multiple-use card
tamokuteki kādo
多目的カード

multiplex
maruchipurekusu
マルチプレクス

multiplex adapter
maruchipurekusu-adaputa
マルチプレクス・アダプタ

multiplex mode
maruchipurekusu-mōdo;
tajū hōshiki
マルチプレクス・モード；
多重方式

multiplex operation
tajū sōsa
多重操作

multiplexer (MUX)
maruchipurekusa;
tajū hōshiki sōchi (MUX)
マルチプレクサ；多重方式装置

multiplexer channel
maruchipurekusa-chaneru;
tajū chaneru
マルチプレクサ・チャネル；
多重チャネル

multiplexer mode
maruchipurekusa-mōdo
マルチプレクサ・モード

multiplexing
tajū hōshiki; tajūka
多重方式；多重化

multiplicand
hijōsū
被乗数

multiplication
jōzan
乗算

multiplier
jōsū
乗数

multiplier factor
jōsū
乗数

multiply
jōzan suru
乗算する

multipoint
bunki (no); maruchi-pointo
分岐(の)；マルチ・ポイント

multipoint circuit
bunki kairo
分岐回路

multipoint line
bunki kaisen
分岐回線

multipoint network
bunki nettowāku
分岐ネットワーク

multipoint operation
bunki sōsa
分岐操作

multipoint system
bunki hōshiki
分岐方式

multiprecision arithmetic
tabai seido enzan
多倍精度演算

multiprocess synchronization
tajū purosesu dōki
多重プロセス同期

multiprocessing
tajū shori
多重処理

multiprocessing system
tajū shori shisutemu
多重処理システム

multiprocessor
maruchi-purosessa;
tajū purosessa
マルチ・プロセッサ；
多重プロセッサ

multiprocessor system
maruchi-purosessa-shisutemu;
tajū purosessa-shisutemu
マルチ・プロセッサ・システム；
多重プロセッサ・システム

multiprogramming
maruchi-puroguramingu;
tajū puroguramingu
マルチ・プログラミング；
多重プログラミング

multiprogramming operations
tajū puroguramingu dōsa;
tajū puroguramingu sōsa
多重プログラミング動作；
多重プログラミング操作

multiprogramming system
tajū puroguramingu-shisutemu
多重プログラミング・システム

multipurpose
tanō
多能

multiqueue
tajū machigyōretsu
多重待ち行列

multireel
fukusū riiru
複数リール

multireel file
fukusū riiru-fuairu
複数リール・ファイル

multiring file
fukū ringu-fuairu
複リング・ファイル

multispeed
tasokudo
多速度

multistage
tadankai
多段階

multistate
tajū jōtai
多重状態

multistation
maruchi-sutēshon
マルチ・ステーション

multisystem
fukusū shisutemu; tajū shisutemu
複数システム；多重システム

multisystem operation
tajū shisutemu sōsa
多重システム操作

multitask
maruchi-tasuku; tajū tasuku
マルチ・タスク；多重タスク

multitask operation
tajū tasuku sōsa
多重タスク操作

multiunit
fukusū yunitto
複数ユニット

multiuser
maruchi-yūza
マルチ・ユーザ

multiuser system
maruchi-yūza-shisutemu
マルチ・ユーザ・システム

multivariable
tahensū
多変数

multivibrator
maruchibaiburēta
マルチバイブレータ

multivolume
fukusū boryūmu
複数ボリューム

multivolume file
fukusū boryūmu-fuairu
複数ボリューム・ファイル

multiway access
tahōkō akusesu
多方向アクセス

multiway conversion
tahōkō henkan
多方向変換

mutual exclusion
sōgo haijo
相互排除

mutual information
sōgo jōho
相互情報

mutual recursion
 sōgo kaiki
 相互回帰

MUX (multiplexer)
 MUX (maruchipurekusa; tajū
 hōshiki sōchi)
 マルチプレクサ；多重方式装置

Mylar
 Maira
 マイラ

N

n-**adic operation**
 n kō enzan
 n 項演算

n-**ary relation**
 n kō kankei
 n 項関係

N-channel metal-oxide
semiconductor (NMOS)
 N-chaneru MOS (NMOS)
 N チャネル MOS

n-**core-per-bit storage**
 n koa/bittoshiki kioku
 n コア / ビット式記憶

n-**level address**
 n-reberu-adoresu
 n レベル・アドレス

n-**level logic**
 n-reberu ronri
 n レベル論理

NAK (negative acknowledgment)
 NAK; nakku (hitei ōtō)
 ナック；否定応答

name
 mei; namae; shikibetsumei
 名；名前；識別名

name field
 namae fuiirudo
 名前フィールド

named common block
 namaetsuki kyōtsū burokku
 名前付き共通ブロック

named constant
 namaetsuki teisū
 名前付き定数

NAND (inverted AND; negative
AND; NOT AND)
 NAND (hiteiseki; hitei AND;
 hiteironriseki)
 否定積; 否定AND; 否定論理積

NAND circuit
 hiteironriseki kairo; hiteiseki
 kairo; NAND kairo
 否定論理積回路；否定積回路；
 NAND 回路

NAND element
 hiteironriseki soshi; hiteiseki
 soshi; NAND soshi
 否定論理積素子；否定積素子；
 NAND 素子

NAND gate
 hiteironriseki gēto; hiteiseki gēto;
 NAND gēto
 否定論理積ゲート；
 否定積ゲート；
 NAND ゲート

NAND operation
 hiteironriseki enzan; hiteiseki
 enzan; NAND enzan
 否定論理積演算；否定積演算；
 NAND 演算

nano-
 nano-
 ナノ

nanoprocessor
 nanopurosessa
 ナノプロセツサ

nanosecond (ns)
 nanobyō (ns)
 ナノ秒

nanosecond speed range
 nanobyō sokudo haba
 ナノ秒速度幅

narrative
 bun; chūshaku
 文；注釈

narrow band
 kyōtai'iki
 狭帯域

narrower term
 ka'i gainen
 下位概念

National Bureau of Standards (NBS)
(USA)
 Beikoku Hyōjun Kyoku (NBS)
 米国標準局

natural function generator
 shizen kansū zenerēta
 自然関数ゼネレータ

natural language
 shizen gengo
 自然言語

natural law function generator
 shizen kansū zenerēta
 自然関数ゼネレータ

natural logarithm
 shizen taisū
 自然対数

natural number
shizen sū
自然数

natural sequence
shizen junjo
自然順序

NBS (National Bureau of Standards) (USA)
NBS (Beikoku Hyōjun Kyoku)
米国標準局

NC (numerical control)
NC (sūchi seigyo)
数値制御

NCU (network control unit)
NCU (nettowāku seigyo sōchi)
ネットワーク制御装置

NDRO (nondestructive readout)
NDRO (hihakai yomidashi)
非破壊読み出し

NDRO storage
hihakai yomidashi kioku
非破壊読み出し記憶

NDU (network data unit)
NDU (nettowāku-dēta tan'i)
ネットワーク・データ単位

negate
hitei suru
否定する

negation
hitei
否定

negative
fu; fusei; hitei
負; 負性; 否定

negative acknowledgment (NAK)
hitei ōtō (NAK; nakku)
否定応答; ナック

negative acknowledgment character
hitei ōtō moji
否定応答文字

negative feedback (NFB)
fukikan (NFB)
負帰還

negative logic
furonri
負論理

negative pole
inkyoku
陰極

negative resistance
fusei teikō
負性抵抗

negator
hitei soshi
否定素子

neither-NOR
hitei ronriwa
否定論理和

neither-NOR operation
hitei ronriwa enzan
否定論理和演算

NEQ (nonequivalence)
NEQ (futōka)
不等価

NEQ element (nonequivalence element)
NEQ soshi (futōka soshi)
NEQ 素子; 不等価素子

NEQ gate (nonequivalence gate)
NEQ gēto (futōka gēto)
NEQ ゲート; 不等価ゲート

nest
ireko; nesuto
入れ子; ネスト

nest relation
ireko kankei
入れ子関係

nested structure
ireko kōzō
入れ子構造

nesting
ireko; nesuteingu
入れ子; ネスティング

nesting loop
ireko rūpu
入れ子ループ

nesting store
ireko kioku sōchi
入れ子記憶装置

nesting subroutine
ireko saburūchin
入れ子サブルーチン

net time
shōmi jikan
正味時間

network
kairomō; kaisenmō; mō; nettowāku
回路網; 回線網; 網; ネットワーク

network address
nettowāku-adoresu
ネットワーク・アドレス

network analog
nettowāku-anarogu
ネットワーク・アナログ

network analysis
nettowāku kaiseki
ネットワーク解析

network analyzer
nettowāku-anaraiza; nettowāku kaisekiki
ネットワーク・アナライザ; ネットワーク解析器

network control
nettowāku seigyo
ネットワーク制御

network control unit (NCU)
nettowāku seigyo sōchi (NCU)
ネットワーク制御装置

network data unit (NDU)
nettowāku-dēta tan'i (NDU)
ネットワーク・データ単位

network operator
kaisenmō sōsain
回線網操作員

network programming
nettowāku-puroguramingu
ネットワーク・プログラミング

network structure
nettowāku kōzō
ネットワーク構造

network system
nettowāku-shisutemu
ネットワーク・システム

neutral transmission
tanryūshiki densō
単流式伝送

new-line character (NL)
kaigyō fukki moji (NL)
改行復帰文字

next pointer
seihōkō pointa
正方向ポインタ

NFB (negative feedback)
NFB (fukikan)
負帰還

nibble
niburu
ニブル

nickel delay line
nikkeru chien sen
ニッケル遅延線

nine's complement
kyū no hosū
9 の補数

nine-track magnetic tape
kyū torakku jiki tēpu
9 トラック磁気テープ

nines check
kyūjōyo kensa
9 剰余検査

ninety-column card
kyūjū ran kādo
90欄カード

NIP (nucleus initialization program)
NIP (chūkaku shoki settei puroguramu)
中核初期設定プログラム

NIS (Japanese-language information system)
NIS (Nihongo jōhō shisutemu)
日本語情報システム

NL (new-line character)
NL (kaigyō fukki moji)
改行復帰文字

NLP (Japanese-language line printer)
NLP (Nihongo rain-purinta)
日本語ライン・プリンタ

NMOS (N-channel metal-oxide semiconductor)
NMOS (N-chaneru MOS)
N-チャネル MOS

no-address instruction
muadoresu meirei
無アドレス命令

no connection
setsuzoku nai
接続ない

no op (no operation)
no-opu (mudōsa)
ノ・オプ；無動作

no-op instruction
mudōsa meirei; no-opu meirei
無動作命令；ノ・オプ命令

no operation (no op)
mudōsa (no-opu)
無動作；ノ・オプ

no record found
rekōdo nai
レコードない

node
nōdo
ノード

noise
noizu; zatsuon
ノイズ；雑音

noise factor
noizu yō'in
ノイズ要因

noise figure
zatsuon shisū
雑音指数

noise generator
zatsuon hasseiki
雑音発生器

noise killer
noizu bōshiki
ノイズ防止器

noise margin
zatsuon yoyū
雑音余裕

noise ratio
noizu ritsu
ノイズ率

noise suppression
zatsuon yokuatsu
雑音抑圧

noiseless
zatsuon no nai
雑音のない

noisy
zatsuon no aru
雑音のある

noisy mode
noizu-mōdo
ノイズ・モード

nominal speed
meimoku sokudo
名目速度

nonaddressable memory
adoresutsuke funō kioku
アドレス付け不能記憶

non-Chinese character
hikanji
非漢字

noncomputational
hikeisangata
非計算型

noncontiguous item
dokuritsu kōmoku
独立項目

noncontiguous working storage
dokuritsu sagyō basho
独立作業場所

nondedicated
hisen'yō
非専用

nondedicated terminal
hisen'yō tanmatsu (sōchi)
非専用端末(装置)

nondestructive readout (NDRO)
hihakai yomidashi (NDRO)
非破壊続み出し

nondestructive readout memory
hihakai yomidashi kioku
非破壊読み出し記憶

nondeterminacy
hiketteisei
非決定性

nondeterministic programming
hiketteiteki keikakuhō
非決定的計画法

nondeterministic system
hiketteisei shisutemu
非決定性システム

nonequivalence (NEQ)
futōka (NEQ)
不等価

nonequivalence element (NEQ element)
futōka soshi (NEQ soshi)
不等価素子；NEQ 素子

nonequivalence gate (NEQ gate)
futōka gēto (NEQ gēto)
不等価ゲート；NEQ ゲート

nonerasable
shōkyo funō
消去不能

nonerasable storage
shōkyo funō kioku
消去不能記憶

nonexclusive
hihaitateki
非排他的

nonexecutable
hijikkō; jikkō funō
非実行；実行不能

nonexecutable instruction
hijikkō meirei
非実行命令

nonexecutable program
jikkō funō puroguramu
実行不能プログラム

nonexecutable statement
hijikkō bun
非実行文

nonimpact printer
hishōgekishiki inji sōchi
非衝撃式印字装置

nonlinear
hisenkei
非線形

nonlinear circuit
hisenkei kairo
非線形回路

nonlinear equalization
hisenkei tōka
非線形等化

nonlinear network
hisenkei nettowāku
非線形ネットワーク

nonlinear optimization
hisenkei saitekika
非線形最適化

nonlinear programming
hisenkei keikakuhō
非線形計画法

nonlocal
hikyokushoteki
非局所的

nonlocal variable
hikyokushoteki sūchi hensū
非局所的数値変数

nonmaskable interrupt
masuku fukanō warikomi
マスク不可能割り込み

nonoperation instruction
mudōsa meirei
無動作命令

non-packed-mode terminal
hipakettogata tanmatsu
非パケット型端末

nonprint
inji yokusei
印字抑制

nonprivilege instruction
hitokken meirei
非特権命令

nonprocedural
hitejun(teki); hitetsuzuki
非手順(的)；非手続き

nonprocedural language
hitejunteki gengo;
hitetsuzuki muki gengo
非手順的言語；
非手続き向き言語

nonrelocatable
saihaichi funō
再配置不能

nonresident
hijōchū
非常駐

nonresident routine
hijōchū rūchin
非常駐ルーチン

nonreturn to zero (NRZ)
hizero fukki; hizero modori (NRZ)
非ゼロ復帰；非ゼロ戻り

nonreturn-to-zero change recording
hizero fukki henka kiroku hōshiki
非ゼロ復帰変化記録方式

nonreturn-to-zero inverted (NRZI)
NRZI hōshiki (NRZI)
NRZI 方式

nonreturn-to-zero mark recording
hizero fukki māku kiroku hōshiki
非ゼロ復帰マーク記録方式

nonreturn-to-zero recording
hizero fukki kiroku hōshiki
非ゼロ復帰記録方式

nonreusable
saishiyō funō
再使用不能

nonshareable
kyōyō funō
共用不能

nonstandard
hihyōjun; hyōjungai
非標準；標準外

nonthreshold logic (NTL)
hishikii chi ronri (NTL)
非敷居値論理

nonvolatile
fukihassei; jikyū
不揮発性；持久

nonvolatile memory
fukihassei kioku; jikyū kioku
不揮発性記憶；持久記憶

NOR (inverted OR) (neither-nor; NOT OR)
NOR (hiteiwa) (hitei OR; hiteironriwa)
否定和；否定 OR；否定論理和

NOR circuit (inverted OR circuit)
hiteiwa kairo; NOR kairo
否定和回路；NOR 回路

NOR element (inverted OR element)
hiteiwa soshi; NOR soshi
否定和素子；NOR 素子

NOR gate (inverted OR gate)
hiteiwa gēto; NOR gēto
否定和ゲート；NOR ゲート

NOR operation (inverted OR operation)
hiteiwa enzan; NOR enzan
否定和演算；NOR 演算

normal
seijō; seiki; tsūjō
正常；正規；通常

normal answer
seijō ōtō
正常応答

normal behavior
seijō kyodō
正常挙動

normal direction flow
seihōkō no nagare
正方向の流れ

normal flow
tsūjō nagare
通常流れ

normal form
seiki gata
正規型

normal function
seiki kansū
正規関数

normal mode
tsūjō mōdo
通常モード

normal response
seijō ōtō; tsūjō ōtō
正常応答；通常応答

normal termination
seijō shūryō
正常終了

normalization
seikika
正規化

normalize
seikika suru
正規化する

NOT-AND (NAND; negative AND)
NOT-AND (hitei AND;
hiteironriseki)
否定 AND；否定論理積

NOT-AND circuit
hiteironriseki kairo;
NOT-AND kairo
否定論理積回路；
NOT-AND 回路

NOT-AND element
hiteironriseki soshi;
NOT-AND soshi
否定論理積素子；
NOT-AND 素子

NOT-AND gate
hiteironriseki gēto;
NOT-AND gēto
否定論理積ゲード；
NOT-AND ゲート

NOT-AND operation
hiteironriseki enzan;
NOT-AND enzan
否定論理積演算；
NOT-AND 演算

NOT circuit
hitei kairo; NOT kairo
否定回路；NOT 回路

NOT element
hitei soshi; NOT soshi
否定素子；NOT 素子

NOT gate
hitei gēto; NOT gēto
否定ゲート；NOT ゲート

NOT operation
hitei enzan; NOT enzan
否定演算；NOT 演算

NOT-OR
hiteironriwa
否定論理和

NOT-OR operation
hiteironriwa enzan
否定論理和演算

notation
hyōkihō; kijihō
表記法；記示法

notational system
kigō shiki
記号式

nought state
zero jōtai
ゼロ状態

NRZ (nonreturn to zero)
NRZ (hizero fukki; hizero modori;
NRZ hōshiki)
非ゼロ復帰；非ゼロ戻り；
NRZ 方式

NRZI (nonreturn-to-zero inverted)
NRZI (NRZI hōshiki)
NRZI 方式

ns (nanosecond)
ns (nanobyō)
ナノ秒

NSP (Japanese-language serial printer)
NSP (Nihongo shiriaru-purinta)
日本語シリアル・プリンタ

NTL (nonthreshold logic)
NTL (hishikii chi ronri)
非敷居値論理

nucleus
chūkaku
中核

nucleus initialization program (NIP)
chūkaku shoki settei
puroguramu (NIP)
中核初期設定プログラム

NUL (null)
NUL (kūhaku)
空白

null (NUL)
kara; kū; kūhaku (NUL)
空；空；空白

null character
kūhaku moji
空白文字

null data area
kū dēta'iki
空データ域

null file
kū fuairu
空ファイル

null set
kū shūgō
空集合

null string
kū retsu
空列

number
ban; bangō; sū
番；番号；数

number attribute
sū zokusei
数属性

number cruncher
sū no kurancha
数のクランチャ

number representation
sū no hyōgen
数の表現

number representation system
kisūhō
記数法

number sign
bangō kigō
番号記号

number system
kisūhō
記数法

numeral
sū; sūji
数; 数字

numeration system
kisūhō
記数法

numeric
sūchi; sūji
数値; 数字

numeric character
sūji
数字

numeric character set
sūji setto
数字セット

numeric code
sūji kōdo
数字コード

numeric coding
sūji kōdeingu
数字コーディング

numeric data
sūji dēta
数字データ

numeric data processor
sūji dēta-purosessa;
sūji dēta shori sōchi
数字データ・プロセッサ;
数字データ処理装置

numeric digit
sūji
数字

numeric display
sūji deisupurei
数字ディスプレィ

numeric field
sūji fuiirudo
数字フィールド

numeric item
sūji kōmoku
数字項目

numeric keyboard
sūji kemban kikō
数字鍵盤機構

numeric keypad
sūchi kiipaddo
数値キーパッド

numeric punching
sūji senkō
数字せん孔

numeric representation
sū no hyōgen; sūhyōji
数の表現; 数表示

numeric shift
sūji shifuto
数字シフト

numeric value
sūchi
数値

numeric word
sūji go
数字語

numerical
sūchi; sūji
数値; 数字

numerical analysis
sūchi kaiseki
数値解析

numerical character
sūji
数字

numerical control (NC)
sūchi seigyo (NC)
数値制御

numerical data processor
sūchi dēta-purosessa;
sūchi dēta shori sōchi
数値データ・プロセッサ;
数値データ処理装置

numerical pad
sūchi paddo
数値パッド

NWP (Japanese-language word processor)
NWP (Nihongo wādo-purosessa)
日本語ワード・プロセッサ

O

O and M (organization and methods)
O and M (soshiki-hōshiki)
O and M; O アンド M;
組織-方式

OA (office automation)
OA (ofuisu-otomēshon)
オフィス・オトメーション

object code
mokuteki kōdo
目的コード

object computer
jikkōyō keisanki;
mokuteki keisanki
実行用計算機；目的計算機

object language
mokuteki gengo
目的言語

object language program
mokuteki gengo puroguramu
目的言語プログラム

object machine
mokuteki kikai
目的機械

object module
mokuteki mojyūru
目的モジュール

object program
mokuteki puroguramu
目的プログラム

object record
taishō rekōdo
対象レコード

object routine
mokuteki rūchin
目的ルーチン

object time
jikkōji
実行時

objective
mokuteki
目的

objective function
mokuteki kansū
目的関数

observation
kansoku
観測

observation matrix
kansoku gyōretsu
観測行列

obsolescence
chimpuka
陳腐化

obsolete
chimpu na
陳腐な

O/C (open collector)
O/C (ōpun-korekuta)
オープン・コレクタ

occurrence
shutsugen
出現

OCR (optical character reader)
OCR (kōgakushiki moji yomitori
sōchi)
光学式文字続み取り装置

OCR (optical character recognition)
OCR (kōgakushiki moji ninshiki)
光学式文字認識

octal
hasshin
8 進

octal constant
hasshin teisū
8 進定数

octal digit
hasshin sūji
8 進数字

octal field description
hasshin ran kijutsu
8 進欄記述

octal notation
hasshin hō
8 進法

octal number
hasshin sū
8 進数

octal number system
hasshin hō
8 進法

odd check
kisū kensa
奇数検査

odd-even check
kigū kensa
奇偶検査

odd parity
kisū paritei
奇数パリティ

odd parity check
kisū paritei kensa
奇数パリティ検査

OEM (original equipment manufacturer)
OEM (aite sakishōhyō seizō
kaisha)
相手先商標製造会社

off
ofu
オフ

off-hook
ofu-hukku
オフ・フック

off-line
hichokketsu; ofu-rain
非直結；オフ・ライン

off-line control
ofu-rain seigyo
オフ・ライン制御

off-line data transmission
ofu-rain-dēta densō
オフ・ライン・データ伝送

off-line equipment
ofu-rain kiki; ofu-rain sōchi
オフ・ライン機器；
オフ・ライン装置

off-line feature
ofu-rain kikō; ofu-rain kinō
オフ・ライン機構；
オフ・ライン機能

off-line operation
ofu-rain dōsa; ofu-rain sōsa
オフ・ライン動作；
オフ・ライン操作

off-line processing
ofu-rain shori
オフ・ライン処理

off-line storage
ofu-rain kioku
オフ・ライン記憶

off-line system
ofu-rain-shisutemu
オフ・ライン・システム

off-line working
ofu-rain dōsa
オフ・ライン動作

off-lining
hichokketsu; ofu-rainingu
非直結；オフ・ライニング

off-punch
ofu senkō
オフせん孔

office automation (OA)
ofuisu-otomēshon (OA)
オフィス・オトメーション

office computer
gyōmu keisanki; ofuisu-konpyūta
業務計算機；
オフィス・コンピュータ

offset
ofusetto
オフセット

offset stacker
ofusetto-sutakka
オフセット・スタッカ

OFT (optical fiber tube)
OFT (hikari fuaiba kan)
光ファイバ管

OLRT (on-line real time)
OLRT (on-rain-riaru-taimu)
オン・ライン・リアル・タイム

OLRT operation (on-line real-time operation)
OLRT sōsa (on-rain-riaru-taimu sōsa)
オン・ライン・リアル・
タイム操作；OLRT操作

OLRT system (on-line real-time system)
OLRT shisutemu (on-rain-riaru-taimu-shisutemu)
オン・ライン・リアル・タイム・
システム；OLRTシステム

OMR (optical mark reader)
OMR (kōgakushiki māku yomitori sōchi)
光学式マーク読み取り装置

OMR (optical mark recognition)
OMR (kōgakushiki māku ninshiki)
光学式マーク認識

on
on
オン

on-demand system
sokuji kaitō shisutemu
即時回答システム

on-hook
on-hukku
オン・フック

on-line
chokketsu; on-rain
直結；オン・ライン

on-line central file
on-rain chūō fuairu
オン・ライン中央ファイル

on-line communication
on-rain tsūshin
オン・ライン通信

on-line communication system
on-rain tsūshin shisutemu
オン・ライン通信システム

on-line computing
on-rain keisan hōshiki
オン・ライン計算方式

on-line control
on-rain seigyo
オン・ライン制御

on-line data acquisition
on-rain-dēta shūshū
オン・ライン・データ収集

on-line data entry
on-rain-dēta nyūryoku
オン・ライン・データ入力

on-line data gathering
on-rain-dēta shūshū
オン・ライン・データ収集

on-line data transmission
on-rain-dēta densō
オン・ライン・データ伝送

on-line debugging
on-rain-debaggingu
オン・ライン・デバッギング

on-line diagnosis
on-rain shindan
オン・ライン診断

on-line equipment
on-rain kiki; on-rain sōchi
オン・ライン機器；
オン・ライン装置

on-line information
on-rain jōhō
オン・ライン情報

on-line information retrieval
on-rain jōhō kensaku
オン・ライン情報検索

on-line interrogation
on-rain kensaku;
on-rain toiawase
オン・ライン検索；
オン・ライン問い合わせ

on-line operation
on-rain dōsa
オン・ライン動作

on-line processing
on-rain shori
オン・ライン処理

on-line real time (OLRT)
on-rain-riaru-taimu (OLRT)
オン・ライン・リアル・タイム

on-line real-time operation (OLRT operation)
on-rain-riaru-taimu sōsa (OLRT sōsa)
オン・ライン・リアル・
タイム操作；OLRT操作

on-line real-time system (OLRT system)
on-rain-riaru-taimu-shisutemu (OLRT shisutemu)
オン・ライン・リアル・タイム・
システム；OLRTシステム

on-line storage
on-rain kioku
オン・ライン記憶

on-line system
on-rain-shisutemu
オン・ライン・システム

on-line tape punch
on-rain-tēpu panchi
オン・ライン・テープ・パンチ

on-line terminal
on-rain tanmatsu (sōchi)
オン・ライン端末（装置）

on-line testing
on-rain shiken;
on-rain-tesuteingu
オン・ライン試験；
オン・ライン・テスティング

on-line working
on-rain dōsa
オン・ライン動作

on-off action
on-ofu dōsa
オン・オフ動作

on-off control
on-ofu seigyo
オン・オフ制御

on-off system
on-ofu-shisutemu
オン・オフ・システム

on-site
on-saito
オン・サイト

ON unit
ON-yunitto
ONユニット

one address
ichi adoresu
1アドレス

one-address code
ichi adoresu-kōdo
1アドレス・コード

one-address instruction
ichi adoresu meirei
1アドレス命令

one-ahead addressing
ichi sakitori adoresu shitei
1先取りアドレス指定

**one-chip central processing unit
(one-chip CPU)**
wan-chippu CPU
ワン・チップCPU

one-chip computer
wan-chippu-konpyūta
ワン・チップ・コンピュータ

one-digit adder
ichisūji kasanki
1数字加算器

one drive
ichi doraibu
1ドライブ

one-for-one
ichi tai ichi
1対1

one level
ichi reberu
1レベル

one-level address
ichi reberu-adoresu
1レベル・アドレス

one-level storage
ichi reberu kioku
1レベル記憶

one-level store
ichi reberu kioku sōchi
1レベル記憶装置

one-level subroutine
ichi reberu-saburūchin
1レベル・サブルーチン

one-plus-one address
ichi purasu ichi adoresu
1＋1アドレス

one-plus-one address instruction
ichi purasu ichi adoresu meirei
1＋1アドレス命令

one-shot multivibrator
wan-shotto-maruchibaiburēta
ワン・ショット・
マルチバイブレータ

one-shot operation
tampatsu sōsa
単発操作

one state
ichi jōtai
1状態

one-to-one assembler
ichi tai ichi asenbura
1対1アセンブラ

one-to-one translator
ichi tai ichi hon'yakuki
1対1翻訳器

one way
ichi hōkō
一方向

one-way communication
ichi hōkō tsūshin
一方向通信

one's complement
ichi no hosū
1の補数

OP-amp (operational amplifier)
enzan zōfukuki
演算増幅器

op code (operation code)
opu-kōdo; meirei kōdo
オプ・コード；命令コード

open
hiraita; kai; ōpun
開いた；開；オープン

open (a file) (verb)
kaisetsu suru (fairu o)
開設する（ファイルを）

open circuit
hiraita kairo
開いた回路

open collector (O/C)
ōpun-korekuta (O/C)
オープン・コレクタ

open end
ōpun-endo
オープン・エンド

open-ended
kakuchōkanō
拡張可能

open-ended design
kakuchōkanō sekkei
拡張可能設計

open loop
kai rūpu; ōpun-rūpu
開ループ；オープン・ループ

open-loop control
kai rūpu seigyo
開ループ制御

open-loop system
kai rūpu-shisutemu
開ループ・システム

open routine
ōpun-rūchin
オープン・ルーチン

open-shop
ōpun-shoppu
オープン・ショップ

open-shop programming
ōpun-shoppu-puroguramingu
オープン・ショップ・
プログラミング

open subprogram
hiraita fukupuroguramu
開いた副プログラム

open subroutine
hiraita saburūchin;
ōpun-saburūchin
開いたサブルーチン；
オープン・サブルーチン

open system
hiraita shisutemu
開いたシステム

operand
enzansū; operando
演算数；オペランド

operand addressing
operando shitei
オペランド指定

operand field
operando-fuiirudo; operando ran
オペランド・フィールド；
オペランド欄

operand length
operando no nagasa
オペランドの長さ

operand part
operando bu
オペランド部

operate
shikō suru; sōsa suru
施工する；操作する

operating instructions
dōsa shirei
動作指令

operating line
sōsa sen
操作線

operating mode
operēteingu-mōdo
オペレーディング・モード

operating ratio
dōsa ritsu; kadō ritsu
動作率；稼動率

operating state
sadō jōtai
作動状態

operating station
shikō kasho; sōsa taku
施工箇所；操作卓

operating system (OS)
operēteingu-shisutemu (OS)
オペレーティング・システム

operating system firmware
operēteingu-shisutemu-
fuāmuuea
オペレーティング・システム・
ファームウエア

operating time
dōsa jikan; kadō jikan
動作時間；稼動時間

operating unit
operēteingu-yunitto;
shikō kasho
オペレーティング・ユニット；
施工箇所

operation (action)
dōsa; kadō; operēshon;
sadō; sagyō; sōsa; unten
動作；稼動；オペレーション；
作動；作業；操作；運転

operation (math)
enzan; operēshon
演算；オペレーション

operation code (op code)
meirei kōdo (opu-kōdo)
命令コード；オプ・コード

operation cycle
enzan saikuru; dōsa saikuru
演算サイクル；動作サイクル

operation decoder
meirei dekōda; meirei kaidokuki
命令デコーダ；命令解読器

operation field
meirei fuiirudo; meirei ran
命令フィールド；命令欄

operation manual
sōsa kaisetsusho; sōsa
setsumeisho; sōsa shijisho
操作解説書；操作説明書；
操作指示書

operation part
meirei bu
命令部

operation planning
operēshon keikaku
オペレーション計画

operation register
operēshon-rejisuta
オペレーション・レジスタ

operation speed
enzan sokudo
演算速度

operation time
enzan jikan
演算時間

operational
sōsakanō
操作可能

operational amplifier (OP-amp)
enzan zōfukuki
演算増幅器

operational flowchart
sōsa nagarezu
操作流れ図

operational planning
operēshon keikaku
オペレーション計画

operational planning information
operēshon keikaku jōhō
オペレーション計画情報

operational semantics
enzanjō no imi
演算上の意味

operations analysis
operēshon kaiseki
オペレーション解析

operations per minute
enzan/fun
演算/分

operations research (OR)
operēshon-risāchi (OR)
オペレーション・リサーチ

operator
enzanshi; operēta; sōsain
演算子；オペレータ；操作員

operator command
operēta shirei; sōsain shirei
オペレータ指令；操作員指令

143

operator console
operēta-konsoru; seigyo taku;
sōsa kemban; sōsataku
オペレータ・コンソル；制御卓；
操作鍵盤；操作卓

operator control
operēta seigyo; sōsain seigyo
オペレータ制御；操作員制御

operator control panel
sōsa seigyoban
操作制御盤

operator error
operēta-erā
オペレータ・エラー

operator ID
sōsain ID
操作員 ID

operator identity card
sōsain shikibetsu kādo
操作員識別カード

operator part
meirei bu
命令部

operator precedence
enzanshi no yūsen jun'i
演算子の優先順位

operator's access code
sōsain akusesu-kōdo
操作員アクセス・コード

operator's control panel
operēta seigyoban;
sōsain seigyoban
オペレータ制御盤；
操作員制御盤

operator's guide
operēta-gaido
オペレータ・ガイド

operator's intervention
sōsain kainyū
操作員介入

optical
hikari; kōgakushiki
光；光学式

optical bar-code reader
kōgaku bā-kōdo yomitori sōchi
光学バー・コード読み取り装置

optical character
kōgakushiki moji
光学式文字

optical character encoding
kōgakushiki moji fugōka;
kōgakushiki moji kōdoka
光学式文字符号化；
光学式文字コード化

optical character reader (OCR)
kōgakushiki moji yomitori sōchi
(OCR)
光学式文字読み取り装置

optical character recognition (OCR)
kōgakushiki moji ninshiki (OCR)
光学式文字認識

optical character verification
kōgakushiki moji kenshō
光学式文字検証

optical disk
kōgakushiki deisuku
光学式ディスク

optical fiber
hikari fuaiba
光ファイバ

optical fiber tube (OFT)
hikari fuaiba kan (OFT)
光ファイバ管

optical mark
kōgakushiki māku
光学式マーク

optical mark encoding
kōgakushiki māku fugōka;
kōgakushiki māku kōdoka
光学式マーク符号化；
光学式マーク・コード化

optical mark reader (OMR)
kōgakushiki māku yomitori sōchi
(OMR)
光学式マーク読み取り装置

optical mark reading
kōgakushiki māku yomitori
光学式マーク読み取り

optical mark recognition (OMR)
kōgakushiki māku ninshiki (OMR)
光学式マーク認識

optical memory system
kōgakushiki kioku shisutemu
光学式記憶システム

optical reader
kōgakushiki yomitori sochi
光学式読み取り装置

optical scanner
kōgakushiki sōsa kikō
光学式走査機構

optical scanning
kōgakushiki sōsa
光学式走査

optical type font
kōgaku taipu-fuonto
光学タイプ・フォント

optimal
saiteki
最適

optimal control
saiteki seigyo
最適制御

optimal solution
saitekikai
最適解

optimization
saitekika
最適化

optimization program
saitekika puroguramu
最適化プログラム

optimization strategy
saitekika senryaku
最適化戦略

optimization technique
saitekika gihō
最適化技法

optimize
saitekika suru
最適化する

optimizing compiler
saitekika konpaira
最適化コンパイラ

optimizing control
saitekika seigyo
最適化制御

optimum
saiteki
最適

optimum code
saiteki kōdo
最適コード

optimum coding
saiteki kōdeingu
最適コーディング

optimum control
saiteki seigyo
最適制御

optimum programming
saiteki keikakuhō;
saiteki puroguramingu
最適計画法; 最適プログラミング

option
nin'i sentaku; opushon
任意選択; オプション

option card
opushon kādo
オプション・カード

optional
nin'i; nin'i sentaku; opushon;
opushonaru
任意; 任意選択; オプション;
オプショナル

optional command
opushon meirei
オプション命令

optional feature
nin'i sentaku kikō; nin'i sentaku
kinō; opushonaru kikō;
opushonaru kinō
任意選択機構; 任意選択機能;
オプショナル機構;
オプショナル機能

optional function
opushonaru kinō; sentaku kinō
オプショナル機能; 選択機能

optional label
nin'i raberu
任意ラベル

optional module
nin'i mojyūru
任意モジュール

optional stop instruction
nin'i teishi meirei;
opushonaru teishi meirei
任意停止命令;
オプショナル停止命令

optional terminal
nin'i no tanmatsu (sōchi)
任意の端末(装置)

optoelectronics
oputo-erekutoronikkusu
オプト・エレクトロニックス

OR (operations research)
OR (operēshon-risāchi)
オペレーション・リサーチ

OR
OR; ronriwa
OR; 論理和

OR circuit
OR kairo; ronriwa kairo
OR回路; 論理和回路

OR element
OR soshi; ronriwa soshi
OR素子; 論理和素子

OR ELSE
haitateki ronriwa
排他的論理和

OR gate
OR gēto; ronriwa gēto
ORゲート; 論理和ゲート

OR operation
OR enzan; ronriwa enzan
OR演算; 論理和演算

order (command) (*noun*)
meirei; shirei
命令; 指令

order (sequence) (*noun*)
jun'i; junjo
順位; 順序

order of precedence
yūsen jun'i
優先順位

ordering
hairetsu
配列

ordinary message (≠urgent message)
tsūjō no dembun
通常の電文

organic system
yūkitai shisutemu
有機体システム

organization
hensei; soshiki
編成; 組織

organization and methods (O and M)
soshiki-hōshiki (O and M)
組織-方式; OアンドM;
O and M

organization file
hensei fuairu
編成ファイル

organization structure
hensei kōzō
編成構造

orientation
orientēshon
オリエンテーション

oriented
muki
向き

origin
gen; kiten
原; 基点

original
genshi; honrai (no)
原始; 本来(の)

original data
genshi shiryō
原始資料

original document
genshi bunsho
原始文書

original equipment manufacturer (OEM)
aite saki shōhyō seizō kaisha (OEM)
相手先商標製造会社

original terminal
honrai no tanmatsu (sōchi)
本来の端末(装置)

originating
honrai no
本来の

originator
orijinēta
オリジネータ

orphan
koritsu shita dēta
孤立したデータ

OS (operating system)
OS (operēteingu-shisutemu)
オペレーティング・システム

145

oscillating
　　hasshin; oshirēteingu
　　発振; オシレーティング

oscillating sort
　　oshirēteingu bunrui
　　オシレーティング分類

oscillator
　　hasshinki; oshirēta
　　発振器; オシレータ

oscilloscope
　　oshirosukopu
　　オシロスコプ

out connector
　　shutsu ketsugōshi
　　出結合子

out device
　　shutsuryoku sōchi
　　出力装置

output (*noun*)
　　shutsuryoku
　　出力

output (*verb*)
　　shutsuryoku suru
　　出力する

output area
　　shutsuryoku iki;
　　shutsuryoku ryō'iki
　　出力域; 出力領域

output block
　　shutsuryoku burokku
　　出力ブロック

output blocking factor
　　shutsuryoku burokkuka insū
　　出力ブロック化因数

output break
　　shutsuryoku chūdan
　　出力中断

output buffer
　　shutsuryoku baffua
　　出力バッファ

output bus
　　shutsuryoku basu
　　出力バス

output channel
　　shutsuryoku chaneru
　　出力チャネル

output data
　　shutsuryoku dēta
　　出力データ

output device
　　shutsuryoku sōchi
　　出力装置

output efficiency
　　shutsuryoku kōritsu
　　出力効率

output element
　　shutsuryoku soshi
　　出力素子

output file
　　shutsuryoku fuairu
　　出力ファイル

output format
　　shutsuryoku yōshiki
　　出力様式

output format specification
　　shutsuryoku (yōshiki) shiyōgaki
　　出力(様式)仕様書き

output journal
　　shutsuryoku jyānaru
　　出力ジャーナル

output layout
　　shutsuryoku reiauto
　　出力レイアウト

output medium
　　shutsuryoku baitai
　　出力媒体

output procedure
　　shutsuryoku tetsuzuki
　　出力手続き

output processing
　　shutsuryoku shori
　　出力処理

output program
　　shutsuryoku puroguramu
　　出力プログラム

output punch
　　shutsuryoku senkōki
　　出力せん孔機

output queue
　　shutsuryoku machigyōretsu
　　出力待ち行列

output routine
　　shutsuryoku rūchin
　　出力ルーチン

output signal
　　shutsuryoku shingō
　　出力信号

output specifications
　　shutsuryoku shitei
　　出力指定

output stacker
　　shutsuryoku sutakka
　　出力スタッカ

output-to-input approach
　　shutsunyūryoku apurōchi;
　　shutsunyūryoku hōhō
　　出入力アプローチ; 出入力方法

output typewriter
　　shutsuryoku taipuraita
　　出力タイプライダ

output unit
　　shutsuryoku sōchi
　　出力装置

output variable
　　shutsuryoku hensū
　　出力変数

output work queue
　　shutsuryoku sagyō
　　machigyōretsu
　　出力作業待ち行列

overall system
　　zentai shisutemu
　　全体システム

overflow
　　afure; ōbafurō
　　溢れ; オーバフロー

overflow address
　　afure adoresu
　　溢れアドレス

overflow area
　　afure iki
　　溢れ域

overflow indicator
　　afure hyōshiki
　　溢れ標識

overflow record
　　afure rekōdo
　　溢れレコード

overflow register
　　afure rejisuta
　　溢れレジスタ

P

overflow test
afure tesuto
溢れテスト

overhead
ōbaheddo
オーバヘッド

overhead bit
ōbaheddo-bitto
オーバヘッド・ビット

overhead time
ōbaheddo-taimu
オーバヘッド・タイム

overintegration
ōbaintegurēshon
オーバインテグレーション

overlap
heikō
並行

overlap processing
heikō shori
並行処理

overlay
ōbarei
オーバレイ

overlay load module
ōbarei-rōdo-mojyūru
オーバレイ・ロード・
モジュール

overlay program
ōbarei-puroguramu
オーバレイ・プログラム

overlay segment
ōbarei-segumento
オーバレイ・セグメント

overlay structure
ōbarei kōzō
オーバレイ構造

overlay supervisor
ōbarei kanshi puroguramu
オーバレイ監視プログラム

overload
kafuka
過負荷

overload monitor
kafuka kanshi
過負荷監視

overloading
kafuka
過負荷

overpunch
ōbapanchi
オーバパンチ

overrun
ōbaran
オーバラン

overseas telecommunications
kaigai no tsūshin
海外の通信

overwrite
kakinaosu; kasanegaku
書き直す；重ね書く

overwriting
kakinaoshi; kasanegaki
書き直し；重ね書き

own code
oun-kōdo
オウン・コード

own coding
oun-kōdeingu
オウン・コーディング

own coding routine
oun-kōdeingu-rūchin
オウン・コーディング・ルーチン

owner
oya; shoyūsha
親；所有者

owner-coupled set
oyako ketsugō shūgō
親子結合集合

owner identifier
shoyūsha shikibetsumei
所有者識別名

owner pointer
oya pointa
親ポインタ

owner record
oya rekōdo
親レコード

**p-channel metal-oxide
semiconductor**
p-chaneru MOS
P-チャネルMOS

p-channel MOS
p-chaneru MOS
P-チャネルMOS

pack
pakku
パック

package
jissō; pakkēji
実装；パッケージ

package program
pakkēji-puroguramu
パッケージ・プログラム

packaging capacity
jissō yōryō
実装容量

packaging density
jissō mitsudo
実装密度

packed decimal
pakku jisshinsū
パック10進数

packed-mode terminal
pakettogata tanmatsu (sōchi)
パケット型端末(装置)

packet
paketto
パケット

packet assembly/disassembly (PAD)
paketto kumitate/bunkai (PAD)
パケット組み立て／分解

packet switching
paketto kōkan
パケット交換

packet-switching network
paketto kōkanmō
パケット交換網

packing
pakkingu
パッキング

packing density
kiroku mitsudo
記録密度

PAD (packet assembly/disassembly)
PAD (paketto kumitate/bunkai)
パケット組み立て / 分解

pad (*noun*)
paddo; umekomi
パッド；埋め込み

pad (*verb*)
paddo suru; umekomu
パッドする；埋め込む

pad character
umekomi moji
埋め込み文字

padding
paddeingu; umekomi sōsa
パッデング；埋め込み操作

page
pēji
ページ

page address
pēji-adoresu
ページ・アドレス

page fault
pēji fuzai; pēji shōgai
ページ不在；ページ障害

page fault frequency (PFF)
pēji shōgai hindo (PFF)
ページ障害頻度

page footer
pēji ashigaki
ページ脚書き

page footing
pēji ashigaki
ページ脚書き

page frame
pēji waku
ページ枠

page header
pēji midashi
ページ見出し

page heading
pēji atamagaki
ページ頭書き

page-in
pēji-in
ページ・イン

page number
pēji bangō
ページ番号

page-out
pēji-auto
ページ・アウト

page overflow
pēji afure
ページ溢れ

page printer
pēji insho sōchi
ページ印書装置

page reader
pēji yomitori sōchi
ページ読み取り装置

page size
pēji-saizu
ページ・サイズ

page table
pēji-tēburu
ページ・テーブル

paging
pējingu
ページング

paging algorithm
pējingu-arugorizumu
ページング・アルゴリズム

paging device
pējingu sōchi
ページング装置

paging machine
pējingu kikai
ページング機械

paging rate
pējingu ritsu
ページング率

paging system
pējingu-shisutemu
ページング・システム

paging technique
pējingu gihō
ページング技法

PAM (pulse amplitude modulation)
PAM (parusu shimpuku henchō)
パルス振幅変調

panel
ban; paneru
盤；パネル

panel display
paneru-deisupurei
パネル・ディスプレイ

panic dump
panikku-danpu
パニック・ダンプ

paper feed
kami okuri
紙送り

paper feed mechanism
kami okuri kikō
紙送り機構

paper jam
yōshi no jyamu
用紙のジャム

paper jam detection
yōshi no jyamu kenshutsu
用紙のジャム検出

paper jam detector
yōshi no jyamu kenshutsu kikō
用紙のジャム検出機構

paper loop
kami tēpu-rūpu
紙テープ・ループ

"paper low" indicator
yōshi fusoku hyōji
用紙不足表示

paper-roll holder
rōru kami horuda
ロール紙ホルダ

paper size
yōshi sumpō
用紙寸法

paper tape
kami tēpu
紙テープ

paper-tape code
kami tēpu-kōdo
紙テープ・コード

paper-tape loop
kami tēpu-rūpu
紙テープ・ループ

paper-tape punch (PTP)
kami tēpu-panchi; kami tēpu
senkō sōchi; kami tēpu senkōki
(PTP)
紙テープ・パンチ；
紙テープせん孔装置；
紙テープせん孔機

paper-tape reader (PTR)
kami tēpu yomitoriki;
kami tēpu yomitori sōchi (PTR)
紙テープ続み取り機;
紙テープ続み取り装置

paper-tape unit
kami tēpu sōchi
紙テープ装置

paper-tape verifier
kami tēpu kenkōki
紙テープ検孔機

paper-tape verifying
kami tēpu kenkō
紙テープ検孔

paper throw
kami tobashiokuri
紙飛ばし送り

paragraph
bunsetsu; danraku
文節; 段落

paragraph header
danraku midashi
段落見出し

paragraph name
danraku mei
段落名

parallel
heikō; heiretsu
並行; 並列

parallel access
heiretsu akusesu
並列アクセス

parallel adder
heiretsu kasanki
並列加算器

parallel addition
heiretsu kasan
並列加算

parallel arithmetic
heiretsu enzan
並列演算

parallel computer
heiretsushiki keisanki
並列式計算機

parallel control
heiretsu seigyo
並列制御

parallel data transmission
heiretsu dēta densō
並列データ伝送

parallel machine
heikō (shori) kikai
並行(処理)機械

parallel merging
heikō heigō
並行併合

parallel-mode transmission
heikō mōdo densō
並行モード伝送

parallel operation
heikō sōsa; heiretsu sōsa
並行操作; 並列操作

parallel processing
heikō shori; heiretsu shori
並行処理; 並列処理

parallel programming
heikō puroguramingu
並行プログラミング

parallel running
heikō unten
並行運転

parallel search
heikō tansaku; heiretsu tansaku
並行探索; 並列探索

parallel search storage
heiretsu tansaku kioku
並列探索記憶

parallel storage
heiretsu kioku
並列記憶

parallel system
heiretsu shisutemu
並列システム

parallel transmission
heiretsu densō
並列伝送

parallelism detection
heikō shori kenshutsu
並行処理検出

parameter
baikai; parameta
媒介; パラメタ

parameter card
parameta-kādo
パラメタ・カード

parameter-driven
parameta kudōgata
パラメタ駆動型

parameter table
parameta-tēburu
パラメタ・テーブル

parameter word
parameta go
パラメタ語

parametric language
parametagata gengo
パラメタ型言語

parametron
parametoron
パラメトロン

parent
oya
親

parity
kigū; paritei
奇偶; パリティ

parity bit
kigū kensa bitto; paritei-bitto
奇偶検査ビット;
パリティ・ビット

parity check
kigū kensa; paritei-chekku
奇偶検査; パリティ・チェック

parity error
kigū kensa ayamari; paritei-erā
奇偶検査誤り; パリティ・エラー

parse
operando kaiseki; pāzu
オペランド解析; パーズ

parse tree
pāzu ki
パーズ木

parser
pāza
パーザ

parser construction
pāza kōchiku
パーザ構築

parser generator
pāza-zenerēta
パーザ・ゼネレータ

parsing
pāshingu
パーシング

parsing table
pāshingu-tēburu
パーシング・テーブル

part
bu
部

partial carry
bubun keta age
部分桁上げ

partial match
bubunteki itchi
部分的一致

partial product
bubun seki
部分積

partial redundancy
bubun jōchōdo
部分冗長度

partial sum
bubun wa
部分和

partial system failure
bubunteki shisutemu koshō
部分的システム故障

partial word
bubun go
部分語

partition
kubun; kukaku
区分；区画

partitioned
kubun
区分

partitioned data set
kubun dēta-setto
区分データ・セット

partitioned file
kubun fuairu
区分ファイル

partitioned organization
kubun hensei
区分編成

partitioning
kubunka
区分化

PASCAL
Pasukaru
Pascal；パスカル

pass
pasu
パス

passive
judō
受動

passive circuit
judō kairo
受動回路

passive element
judō soshi
受動素子

passive station
judō tanmatsu
受動端末

passive system
judō shisutemu
受動システム

password
aikotoba; aikotoba; pasuwādo
合い言葉；合い詞；パスワード

password security protection
aikotoba kimitsu hogo
合い言葉機密保護

patch
patchi
パッチ

patch panel
patchi-paneru
パッチ・パネル

patchboard
haisenban
配線盤

path
keiro; pasu
経路；パス

path analysis
keiro kaiseki
経路解析

path compression
pasu asshuku
パス圧縮

path control
keiro seigyo
経路制御

path length
keiro no nagasa
経路の長さ

path structure
keiro kōzō
経路構造

pattern
patān
パターン

pattern analysis
patān kaiseki
パターン解析

pattern control
patān seigyo
パターン制御

pattern display
patān-deisupurei
パターン・ディスプレイ

pattern recognition
patān ninshiki
パターン認識

pattern system
patān-shisutemu
パターン・システム

pattern theory
patān riron
パターン理論

pause
ichiji teishi
一時停止

pause instruction
ichiji teishi meirei
一時停止命令

PC (personal computer)
PC (pāsokon; pāsonaru-konpyūta)
パーソコン；パーソナル・コンピュータ

PC (printed circuit)
PC (insatsu haisen kairo)
印刷配線回路

PCB (printed circuit board)
PCB (insatsu haisenban; purinto kiban)
印刷配線板；プリント基板

PCB (program communication block)
PCB (puroguramu renraku burokku)
プログラム連絡ブロック

PCM (pulse code modulation)
PCM (parusu fugō henchō)
パルス符号変調

PCM (punch-card machine)
PCM (kādo senkō sōchi; kādo senkōki)
カードせん孔装置；
カードせん孔機

PCS (punch-card system)
PCS (senkō kādo-shisutemu)
せん孔カード・システム

PDU (port data unit)
PDU (pōto-dēta tan'i)
ポート・データ単位

PE (phase encoding)
PE (isō kōdoka hōshiki; PE hōshiki)
位相コード化方式；PE方式

peak data transfer rate
piiku-dēta tensō sokudo
ピーク・データ転送速度

peak load
piiku fuka
ピーク負荷

peak to peak (P-P)
hakōchi; piikupiiku (P-P)
波高値；ピークピーク

peak-to-peak magnitude
piikupiiku shimpuku
ピークピーク振幅

peak-to-peak value
piikupiiku chi
ピークピーク値

peek (PEEK)
piiku (PEEK)
ピーク

PEEK (peek)
PEEK (Piiku)
ピーク

peek-a-boo check
shikaku senkō kensa
視覚せん孔検査

pen plotter
pen-purotta
ペン・プロッタ

perforate
senkō suru
せん孔する

perforated paper tape
senkō kami tēpu
せん孔紙テープ

perforated tape
senkō tēpu
せん孔テープ

perforation
senkō
せん孔

perforation rate
senkō sokudo
せん孔速度

perforator
senkō sōchi; senkōki
せん孔装置；せん孔機

performance
seinō
性能

performance evaluation
seinō hyōka
性能評価

performance test
seinō shiken
性能試験

period
shūki
周期

periodic
shūki(teki)
周期(的)

periodic disturbance
shūkiteki gairan
周期的外乱

periodic pulse train
shūkiteki parusu retsu
周期的パルス列

peripheral control unit
shūhen seigyo sōchi
周辺制御装置

peripheral device
shūhen kiki; shūhen sōchi
周辺機器；周辺装置

peripheral equipment
shūhen kiki; shūhen sōchi
周辺機器；周辺装置

peripheral interface
shūhen intafuēsu
周辺インタフェース

peripheral interface channel
shūhen intafuēsu-chaneru
周辺インタフェース・チャネル

peripheral-limited
shūhen kiki ni yoru seigen
周辺機器による制限

peripheral LSI chip
shūhen LSI chippu
周辺LSIチップ

peripheral transfer
shūhen sōchikan dēta tensō
周辺装置間データ転送

peripheral unit
shūhen sōchi
周辺装置

peripherals
shūhen kiki; shūhen sōchi
周辺機器；周辺装置

peripherals control
shūhen kiki seigyo
周辺機器制御

permanent
eikyū; eizoku; jōchū
永久；永続；常駐

permanent error
eikyū ayamari
永久誤り

permanent file
eizoku fuairu
永続ファイル

permanent memory
kotei kioku
固定記憶

permanent segment
jōchū segumento
常駐セグメント

permanent storage
kotei kioku
固定記憶

permanent virtual circuit (PVC)
aite kotei setsuzoku (PVC)
相手固定接続

151

personal
kojin; pāsonaru; shiyō
個人; パーソナル; 私用

personal code
kojin kōdo
個人コード

personal computer (PC)
pāsokon; pāsonaru-konpyūta
(PC)
パーソコン;
パーソナル・コンピュータ

personal computer picture
pāsokon gamen
パーソコン画面

personal CP/M
pāsonaru CP/M
パーソナル CP／M

personal identification device (PID)
kojin shikibetsu sōchi (PID)
個人識別装置

personal identification number (PIN)
kojin shikibetsu bangō;
PIN bangō (PIN)
個人識別番号; PIN 番号

personalization
kojinka
個人化

personalized database system
kojinka dētabēsu-shisutemu
個人化データベース・システム

PERT (program evaluation and review technique)
PERT (pāto; puroguramu hyōka-kanri gihō)
PERT; パート;
プログラム評価-管理技法

PFB (positive feedback)
PFB (seikikan)
正帰還

PFC (port flow control)
PFC (pōto nagare seigyo)
ポート流れ制御

PFF (page fault frequency)
PFF (pēji shōgai hindo)
ページ障害頻度

phase
dankai; fuēzu; isō
段階; フェーズ; 位相

phase diagram
dankaizu
段階図

phase distortion
isō hizumi
位相歪み

phase encoding (PE)
isō kōdoka hōshiki; PE hōshiki
(PE)
位相コード化方式; PE 方式

phase error
fuēzu-erā
フェーズ・エラー

phase-locked loop
fuēzu-rokku-rūpu
フェーズ・ロック・ループ

phase modulation
isō henchō
位相変調

phase name
fuēzu mei
フェーズ名

phase table
fuēzu-tēburu
フェーズ・テーブル

photocell
hikari denkan
光電管

photodetector
hikari kenshutsu kikō
光検出機構

photodiode
fuoto-daiōdo
フォト・ディオード

photoelectric reader
kōdenshiki yomitori sōchi
光電式読み取り装置

photoetching
fuoto-etchingu
フォト・エッチング

photographic storage
shashin kioku
写真記憶

photographic typesetting
shashin shokuji
写真植字

photographic typesetting equipment
shashin shokujiki
写真植字機

physical block
butsuriteki burokku
物理的ブロック

physical data
butsuriteki dēta
物理的データ

physical data independence
butsuriteki dēta no dokuritsu
物理的データの独立

physical device
butsuriteki sōchi
物理的装置

physical device number
butsuriteki sōchi bangō
物理的装置番号

physical file
butsuri fuairu
物理ファイル

physical input/output control system (PIOCS)
butsuriteki nyūshutsuryoku seigyo shisutemu (PIOCS)
物理的入出力制御システム

physical record
butsuri rekōdo
物理レコード

physical unit
butsuriteki sōchi
物理的装置

physical unit block (PUB)
butsuriteki sōchi burokku (PUB)
物理的装置ブロック

physical unit table
butsuriteki sōchi tēburu
物理的装置テーブル

PI (programmed instruction)
PI (puroguramu gakushū)
プログラム学習

picosecond (ps)
pikobyō (ps)
ピコ秒

pictorial pattern recognition
gazō patān ninshiki
画像パターン認識

picture
gamen; gazō; pikucha
画面；画像；ピクチャ

picture check
pikucha kensa
ピクチャ検査

picture data
pikucha-dēta
ピクチャ・データ

picture element
gaso
画素

picture processing
gazō shori; pikucha shori
画像処理；ピクチャ処理

picture recording
rokuga
録画

PID (personal identification device)
PID (kojin shikibetsu sōchi)
個人識別装置

piecewise linear approximation
kubunteki senkei kinji
区分的線形近似

piezoelectric effect
atsudenkōka
圧電効果

piezoresistance
atsuteikō
圧抵抗

piggyback system
pigibakku-shisutemu
ピギバック・システム

pilot model
pairotto-moderu
パイロット・モデル

pilot system
pairotto-shisutemu
パイロット・システム

PIN (personal identification number)
PIN (kojin shikibetsu bangō; PIN bangō)
個人識別番号；PIN 番号

pin
pin
ピン

pin feed
pin-fuiido
ピン・フィード

pin header
pin-hedda
ピン・ヘッダ

pinboard
pinbōdo
ピンボード

pinch-off
pinchi-ofu
ピンチ・オフ

pinch roller
pinchi-rōra
ピンチ・ローラ

pincushion distortion
itomakigata hizumi
糸巻型歪み

PIOCS (physical input/output control system)
PIOCS (butsuriteki nyūshutsuryoku seigyo shisutemu)
物理的入出力制御システム

pipeline system
paipu-rain-shisutemu
パイプ・ライン・システム

piracy
tōsaku
盗作

pitch
kankaku; pitchi
間隔；ピッチ

pivot operation
pibotto enzan
ピボット演算

pivoting
pibotto enzan
ピボット演算

pixel
gaso; pikuseru
画素；ピクセル

place of interruption
tochū
途中

planning
keikaku
計画

planning decision
keikaku kettei
計画決定

planning information
keikaku jōhō
計画情報

planning model
keikaku moderu
計画モデル

planning science
keikaku kagaku
計画科学

planning strategy
keikaku senryaku
計画戦略

planning system
keikaku shisutemu
計画システム

platen
puraten
プラテン

PL/M (program language for microcomputers)
PL/M (maikurokonpyūta'yō puroguramingu gengo)
マイクロコンピュータ用プログラミング言語

PL/1 (programming language/one)
PL/1 (puroguramingu gengo/ichi)
プログラミング言語/1；PL/1

PLOT (plotter)
PLOT (purotta)
プロッタ

plot (*verb*)
sakuzu suru
作図する

plotter (PLOT)
purotta; sakuzu sōchi (PLOT)
プロッタ；作図装置

plotting board
sakuzu ban
作図盤

plug compatible
puragu gokansei
プラグ互換性

plug-in
puragu-in; sashikomishiki
プラグ・イン；さし込み式

153

plug-in system
puragu-in hōshiki
プラグ・イン方式

plug-in terminal
puragu-in tanshi
プラグ・イン端子

plug-in unit
puragu-in-yunitto;
sashikomishiki buhin
プラグ・イン・ユニット；
さし込み式部品

plugboard
haisenban
配線盤

PM (preventive maintenance)
PM (yobō hoshu)
予防保守

PMOS (p-channel metal-oxide semiconductor; p-channel MOS)
PMOS (p-chaneru MOS)
p-チャネルMOS

point (*verb*)
hyōji suru
表示する

point of contact
setten
接点

point of sale (POS)
posu (POS)
ポス

point-of-sale terminal (POS terminal)
posu tanmatsu sōchi (POS tanmatsu sōchi)
ポス端末装置；POS端末装置

point-to-point system
nichitenkan hōshiki;
pointo tai pointo hōshiki
二地点間方式；
ポイント対ポイント方式

point-to-point transmission
nichitenkan densō
二地点間伝送

pointer
pointa
ポインタ

pointer array
pointa-arei
ポインタ・アレイ

pointer data
pointa-dēta
ポインタ・データ

pointer variable
pointa hensū
ポインタ変数

pointing device
hyōji kishin
表示器針

POKE (poke)
POKE (pōku)
ポーク

poke (POKE)
pōku (POKE)
ポーク

Polish notation
Pōrando kihō
ポーランド記法

poll
pōru
ポール

polling
pōringu
ポーリング

polling list
pōringu-risuto
ポーリング・リスト

polyphase sort
porifuēzu bunrui
ポリフェーズ分類

pop
poppu
ポップ

port
pōto
ポート

port data unit (PDU)
pōto-dēta tan'i (PDU)
ポート・データ単位

port flow control (PFC)
pōto nagare seigyo (PFC)
ポート流れ制御

port presentation service (PPS)
pōto teiji sābisu (PPS)
ポート提示サービス

portability
ishokusei; keitaisei
移植性；携帯性

portable
ishoku; keitai('yō)
移植；携帯(用)

portable data medium
keitai'yō dēta baitai
携帯用データ媒体

portable remote terminal
keitai'yō tanmatsu (sōchi)
携帯用端末(装置)

POS (point of sale)
POS (posu)
ポス

POS terminal (point-of-sale terminal)
POS tanmatsu sōchi (posu tanmatsu sōchi)
ポス端末装置；POS端末装置

position
ichi
位置

position control
ichi seigyo
位置制御

position indicator
ichi hyōshiki
位置標識

position setting
ichi settei
位置設定

position setting descriptor
ichi settei kijutsushi
位置設定記述子

positional notation
kuraidori kisūhō
位取り記数法

positional parameter
tei'ichi parameta
定位置パラメタ

positional representation
kuraidori kisūhō
位取り記数法

positioning
ichikime
位置決め

positioning control
ichikime seigyo
位置決め制御

positioning control system
ichikime seigyo shisutemu
位置決め制御システム

positioning error
ichikime gosa
位置決め誤差

positioning time
ichikime jikan
位置決め時間

positive
kōteiteki
肯定的

positive acknowledgment
kōtei ōtō
肯定応答

positive feedback (PFB)
seikikan (PFB)
正帰還

positive logic
seironri
正論理

postamble block
posutoanburu-burokku
ポストアンブル・ブロック

postedit
jigo henshū
事後編集

postmortem
jigo bunseki
事後分析

postmortem dump
jigo bunseki danpu
事後分析ダンプ

postmortem routine
jigo bunseki rūchin
事後分析ルーチン

postprocessor
posuto-purosessa
ポスト・プロセッサ

postread station
posuto-riido-sutēshon
ポスト・リード・ステーション

potential result
yosō kekka
予想結果

power
dengen; denryoku; dōryoku
電源；電力；動力

power capacity
dengen yōryō
電源容量

power control
dengen seigyo
電源制御

power distribution system
denryoku haibun sōchi; haidenki
電力配分装置；配電機

power fail recovery
dengen ijō kaifuku;
dengen ijō saikaishi
電源異常回復；電源異常再開始

power failure
dengen ijō
電源異常

power level
denryoku reberu
電力レベル

power line
dōryoku sen
動力線

power line cable
dōryoku sen kēburu
動力線ケーブル

power source
denryoku gen
電力源

power supply
dengen
電源

power switch
dengen suitchi
電源スイッチ

power transistor
denryoku toranjisuta
電力トランジスタ

power unit
dengen sōchi; denryoku sōchi
電源装置；電力装置

P-P (peak to peak)
P-P (hakōchi; piiku-piiku)
波高値；ピーク・ピーク

PPS (port presentation service)
PPS (pōto teiji sābisu)
ポート提示サービス

practical application
ōyō
応用

preamble block
purianburu-burokku
プリアンブル・ブロック

preassigned memory
puri-asain-memori
プリ・アサイン・メモリ

precedence
jun'i; yūsen jun'i; yūsen junjo;
yūsendo
順位；優先順位；優先順序；
優先度

precedence function
senkō kansū; yūsendo kansū
先行関数；優先度関数

precedence level
jun'i reberu
順位レベル

precedence table
yūsen jun'i tēburu
優先順位テーブル

precision
seido
精度

predefined
kitei; teigisumi
既定；定義済み

predefined instruction
teigisumi meirei
定義済み命令

predefined period
teigisumi jiki
定義済み時期

predefined processing
teigisumi shori
定義済み処理

preemption
kyōsei haijo
強制排除

preference
senkō; yorigonomi
先行；選り好み

prefetch
sakitori
先取り

prefix
settō
接頭

prefix notation
settō hyōkihō
接頭表記法

prefix operator
settō enzanshi
接頭演算子

preformatted
teiyōshiki
定様式

preliminary
yobi
予備

preliminary design
yobi sekkei
予備設計

prelist
puri-risuto
プリ・リスト

PREP (preparation)
PREP (maeshori)
前処理

preparation (PREP)
maeshori (PREP); jumbi
前処理；準備

preparation symbol
jumbi kigō
準備記号

preprepared program
zensettei puroguramu
前設定プログラム

preprinted
jizen insatsu
事前印刷

preprinted form
jizen insatsu yōshi
事前印刷用紙

preprocessor
puri-purosessa
プリ・プロセッサ

prepunch
jizen senkō
事前せん孔

prerequisite
zentei
前提

preselection
sentaku sakiyomi
選択先読み

presentation
teishi
提示

preset
puri-setto; zensettei
プリ・セット；前設定

preset parameter
puri-setto-parameta
プリ・セット・パラメタ

presetting
zensettei
前設定

prevent
yobō suru
予防する

prevention
yobō
予防

preventive maintenance (PM)
yobō hoshu (PM)
予防保守

primary console
shu sōsataku
主操作卓

primary CPU
ichiji CPU
一次 CPU

primary key
kihon kii
基本キー

primary station
ichiji kyoku
一次局

primary storage
ichiji kioku
一次記憶

primary store
ichiji kioku sōchi
一次記憶装置

primary system
shu shisutemu
主システム

primary track
shu torakku
主トラック

prime number generation
sosū seisei
素数生成

primitive
purimiteibu
プリミティブ

primitive resolution
meirei bunkai
命令分解

print
inji; insatsu; insho; purinto
印字；印刷；印書；プリント

print area
insho'iki
印書域

print contrast ratio
insatsu senmeido
印刷鮮明度

print control character
insatsu seigyo moji
印刷制御文字

print control unit
insatsu seigyo sōchi
印刷制御装置

print file
insho fuairu
印書ファイル

print hammer
inji hamma
印字ハンマ

print head
inji heddo; purinto-heddo
印字ヘッド；プリント・ヘッド

print image
insho imēji
印書イメージ

print line
insatsu gyō; insho gyō
印刷行；印書行

print position
insatsu ichi; insho ichi
印刷位置；印書位置

print queue
insatsu machigyōretsu
印刷待ち行列

print server
purinto-sāba
プリント・サーバ

print station
insatsu kikō; purinto-sutēshon
印刷機構；
プリント・ステーション

print wheel
inji hoiiru; purinto-hoiiru
印字ホイール；
プリント・ホイール

print wire
inji waiya; purinto-waiya
印字ワイヤ；プリント・ワイヤ

printable group
insatsu shūdan
印刷集団

printed circuit (PC)
insatsu haisen kairo (PC)
印刷配線回路

printed circuit board (PCB)
insatsu haisenban; purinto kiban
(PCB)
印刷配線板；プリント基板

printed form
jizen insatsu yōshi
事前印刷用紙

printed output
inji shutsuryoku;
insatsu shutsuryoku
印字出力；印刷出力

printer
inji sōchi; insatsu sōchi;
insho sōchi; purinta
印字装置；印刷装置；
印書装置；プリンタ

printer attachment
inji sōchi setsuzoku kikō;
inji sōchi tempu
印字装置接続機構；
印字装置添付

printer cable
purinta-kēburu
プリンタ・ケーブル

printer connector
purinta-konekuta
プリンタ・コネクタ

printer interface
purinta-intafuēsu
プリンタ・インタフェース

printer keyboard
purinta-kiibōdo
プリンタ・キーボード

printing
insatsu
印刷

printing card proof punch
insatsu senkōki
印刷せん孔機

printing card punch
insatsu senkōki
印刷せん孔機

printing format
insatsu yōshiki
印刷様式

printing head
inji heddo
印字ヘッド

printing machine
insatsuki
印刷機

printing paper
insatsushi
印刷紙

printing speed
insatsu sokudo
印刷速度

printout
inji shutsuryoku; insatsu
shutsuryoku; purinto-auto
印字出力；印刷出力；
プリント・アウト

priority
    to have priority over ———
yūsen; yūsen jun'i; yūsendo
——— yori yūsen sareru
優先；優先順位；優先度
———より優先される

priority communication
yūsen dembun; yūsen tsūshin
優先電文；優先通信

priority indicator
yūsen hyōshiki
優先標識

priority interrupt
yūsen warikomi
優先割り込み

priority level
yūsen jun'i; yūsen reberu
優先順位；優先レベル

priority number
yūsen bangō
優先番号

priority processing
yūsen shori
優先処理

priority retrieval
yūsen kensaku
優先検索

priority scheduler
yūsen sukejyūra
優先スケジューラ

priority scheduling
yūsen sukejyūringu
優先スケジューリング

priority service
yūsen sābisu
優先サービス

privacy
kimitsu
機密

privacy key
kimitsu kii
機密キー

privacy lock
kimitsu jō
機密錠

privacy lock procedure
kimitsu jō tetsuzuki
機密錠手続き

privacy of data
dēta no kimitsu
データの機密

private
sen'yō; sen'yū; shisetsu; shiyō
専用；専有；私設；私用

private file
sen'yū fuairu
専有ファイル

private library
sen'yū raiburari; shiyō raiburari
専有／私用ライブラリ

private line
sen'yō kaisen
専用回線

private line service
sen'yō kaisen sābisu
専用回線サービス；

privately owned communication network
shisetsu tsūshinmō
私設通信網

privately owned line
shisetsu kaisen
私設回線

privileged access
tokkenteki akusesu
特権的アクセス

privileged instruction
tokken meirei
特権命令

privileged mode
tokken mōdo
特権モード

privileged operation
tokken sōsa
特権操作

privileged operation exception
tokken meirei reigai
特権命令例外

privileged user
tokken yūza
特権ユーザ

probabilistic algorithm
kakuritsuteki arugorizumu
確率的アルゴリズム

probabilistic automaton
kakuritsu otōmaton
確率オートマトン

probabilistic system
kakuritsuteki shisutemu
確率的システム

probability
kakuritsu
確率

probability check
kakuritsu kensa
確率検査

probability density function
kakuritsu mitsudo kansū
確率密度関数

probability theory
kakuritsu ron
確率論

probe
purōbu
プローブ

problem
mondai
問題

problem analysis
mondai bunseki
問題分析

problem control
mondai seigyo
問題制御

problem definition
mondai teigi
問題定義

problem description
mondai kijutsu
問題記述

problem diagnosis
mondai shindan
問題診断

problem evaluation
mondai hyōka
問題評価

problem identification
mondai shikibetsu
問題識別

problem location
mondai hakken
問題発見

problem-oriented language
mondai muki gengo
問題向き言語

problem program
mondai puroguramu
問題プログラム

problem solving
mondai kaiketsu
問題解決

problem state
mondai jōtai
問題状態

problem statement analysis
mondai kijutsu bunseki
問題記述分析

problem statement dialogue
mondai kijutsu kaiwa
問題記述会話

procedural language
tejun gengo; tetsuzukigata gengo
手順言語；手続き型言語

procedure
tejun; tetsuzuki
手順；手続き

procedure analysis
tejun bunseki
手順分析

procedure chart
tetsuzuki chāto
手続きチャート

procedure declaration
tetsuzuki no sengen
手続きの宣言

procedure definition
tetsuzuki teigi
手続き定義

procedure division
tetsuzuki bu
手続き部

procedure function
tetsuzuki kansū
手続き関数

procedure identifier
tetsuzuki mei
手続き名

procedure name
tetsuzuki mei
手続き名

procedure narrative
tetsuzuki bun;
tetsuzuki chūshaku
手続き文；手続き注釈

procedure-oriented language
tejunmuki gengo
手順向き言語

procedure return
tetsuzuki modori
手続き戻り

procedure statement
tetsuzuki bun
手続き文

procedure subprogram
tetsuzuki fukupuroguramu
手続き副プログラム

procedure type
tetsuzuki taipu
手続きタイプ

process (noun)
katei
過程

process (verb)
shori suru
処理する

process bound
purosesu-baundo; shori seiyaku
プロセス・バウンド; 処理制約

process chart
purosesu-chāto;
purosesu nagarezu
プロセス・チャート;
プロセス流れ図

process computer
purokon; purosesu-konpyūta
プロコン;
プロセス・コンピュータ

process control
purosesu seigyo
プロセス制御

process control computer
purosesu seigyo keisanki
プロセス制御計算機

process input/output (process I/O)
purosesu nyūshutsuryoku
(purosesu I/O)
プロセス入出力; プロセスI/O

process input/output unit (process I/O unit)
purosesu nyūshutsuryoku sōchi
(purosesu I/O sōchi)
プロセス入出力装置;
プロセスI/O装置

process synchronization
purosesu dōki
プロセス同期

processed data
shori sareta dēta
処理されたデータ

processed information
shori sareta jōhō
処理された情報

processing
shori (sōsa)
処理(操作)

processing capability
shori kinō
処理機能

processing equipment
shori kiki; shori sōchi
処理機器; 処理装置

processing limits
shori genkai
処理限界

processing load
shori fuka
処理負荷

processing program
shori puroguramu
処理プログラム

processing routine
shori rūchin
処理ルーチン

processing speed
shori sokudo
処理速度

processing system
shori shisutemu
処理システム

processing technique(s)
shori gihō; shori hōhō
処理技法; 処理方法

processing time
shori jikan
処理時間

processing unit
shori sōchi
処理装置

processor
purosessa; shori sōchi
プロセッサ; 処理装置

processor bound
purosessa-baundo
プロセッサ・バウンド

processor call statement
purosessa yobidashi seigyobun
プロセッサ呼び出し制御文

processor chips
purosessa-chippu
プロセッサ・チップ

processor control console
purosessa seigyotaku
プロセッサ制御卓

processor sharing
purosessa kyōyū
プロセッサ共有

processor state register (PSR)
purosessa jōtai rejisuta (PSR)
プロセッサ状態レジスタ

product
purodakuto; seki
プロダクト; 積

production
seisan; seisei
生産; 生成

production control
seisan kanri
生産管理

production language
seisei gengo
生成言語

production line
seisan rain
生産ライン

production line monitoring
seisan rain kanri
生産ライン管理

production run
homban unten
本番運転

production system
seisan shisutemu
生産システム

production test
homban tesuto
本番テスト

production time
seisan jikan
生産時間

profile
purofuairu
プロファイル

program
puroguramu
プログラム

159

program address counter
puroguramu-adoresu-kaunta
プログラム・アドレス・カウンタ

program analysis
puroguramu kaiseki
プログラム解析

program behavior
puroguramu no kōdō
プログラムの行動

program body
puroguramu hontai
プログラム本体

program card
puroguramu-kādo
プログラム・カード

program certification
puroguramu kenshō
プログラム検証

program check
puroguramu-chekku
プログラム・チェック

program communication block (PCB)
puroguramu renraku burokku (PCB)
プログラム連絡ブロック

program comparison
puroguramu hikaku
プログラム比較

program compatibility
puroguramu no gokansei
プログラムの互換性

program composition
puroguramu sakusei
プログラム作成

program comprehension
puroguramu rikai
プログラム理解

program control
puroguramu seigyo
プログラム制御

program control data
puroguramu seigyo dēta
プログラム制御データ

program-controlled interrupt
puroguramu seigyo ni yoru warikomi
プログラム制御による割り込み

program correctness
puroguramu no seitōsei
プログラムの正当性

program counter
puroguramu-kaunta
プログラム・カウンタ

program crash
puroguramu-kurasshi
プログラム・クラッシ

program definition
puroguramu teigi
プログラム定義

program description
puroguramu kijutsu
プログラム記述

program design
puroguramu sekkei
プログラム設計

program development time
puroguramu kaihatsu jikan
プログラム開発時間

program documentation
puroguramu bunshoka
プログラム文書化

program editing
puroguramu henshū
プログラム編集

program efficiency
puroguramu kōritsu
プログラム効率

program evaluation and review technique (PERT)
pāto; puroguramu hyōka-kanri gihō (PERT)
パート; プログラム評価-管理技法

program exception
puroguramu reigai
プログラム例外

program exception interrupt
puroguramu reigai warikomi
プログラム例外割り込み

program execution
puroguramu no jikkō
プログラムの実行

program file
puroguramu-fuairu
プログラム・ファイル

program flowchart
puroguramu nagarezu
プログラム流れ図

program generator
puroguramu-zenerēta
プログラム・ゼネレータ

program identifier
puroguramu mei
プログラム名

program input
puroguramu nyūryoku
プログラム入力

program instruction
puroguramu meirei
プログラム命令

program interrupt(ion)
puroguramu warikomi
プログラム割り込み

program language
puroguramu gengo
プログラム言語

program language for microcomputers (PL/M)
maikurokonpyuta'yō puroguramingu gengo (PL/M)
マイクロコンピュータ用プログラミング言語

program library
puroguramu-raiburari
プログラム・ライブラリ

program linkage
puroguramu-rinkēji
プログラム・リンケージ

program listing
puroguramu-risuto
プログラム・リスト

program load
puroguramu-rōdo
プログラム・ロード

program loader
puroguramu-rōda
プログラム・ローダ

program lock register
puroguramu-rokku-rejisuta
プログラム・ロック・レジスタ

program loop
puroguramu-rūpu
プログラム・ループ

program maintenance
puroguramu hoshu
プログラム保守

program manipulation
puroguramu shori
プログラム処理

program mix
puroguramu-mikkusu
プログラム・ミックス

program modeling
puroguramu-moderuka
プログラム・モデル化

program modification
puroguramu henkō
プログラム変更

program module
puroguramu-mojyūru
プログラム・モジュール

program monitor
puroguramu-monita
プログラム・モニタ

program name
puroguramu mei
プログラム名

program optimization
puroguramu saitekika
プログラム最適化

program overlay
puroguramu -ōbarei
プログラム・オーバレイ

program package
puroguramu-pakkēji
プログラム・パッケージ

program parameter
puroguramu-parameta
プログラム・パラメタ

program part
puroguramu bubun
プログラム部分

program pause
puroguramu ichiji teishi
プログラム一時停止

program preparation
puroguramu jumbi
プログラム準備

program priority
puroguramu yūsen jun'i;
puroguramu yūsendo
プログラム優先順位;
プログラム優先度

program register
puroguramu-rejisuta
プログラム・レジスタ

program restructuring
puroguramu saikōsei
プログラム再構成

program segment
puroguramu-segumento
プログラム・セグメント

program semantics
puroguramu no imiron
プログラムの意味論

program sheet
puroguramu yōshi
プログラム用紙

program specification
puroguramu shiyō
プログラム仕様

program standards
puroguramu hyōjun
プログラム標準

program statement analysis
puroguramu bun kaiseki
プログラム文解析

program status register
puroguramu jōtai rejisuta
プログラム状態レジスタ

program status word (PSW)
puroguramu jōtai go (PSW)
プログラム状態語

**program status word register
(PSWR)**
puroguramu jōtai go rejisuta
(PSWR)
プログラム状態語レジスタ

program step
puroguramu-suteppu
プログラム・ステップ

program switch
puroguramu-suitchi
プログラム・スイッチ

program synchronization
puroguramu dōki
プログラム同期

program tape
puroguramu-tēpu
プログラム・テープ

program test
puroguramu-tesuto
プログラム・テスト

program transformation
puroguramu henkan
プログラム変換

program unit
puroguramu tan'i
プログラム単位

program validation
puroguramu no datōsei kensa
プログラムの妥当性検査

program verification
puroguramu no kenshō
プログラムの検証

programmable information
puroguramukanō jōhō
プログラム可能情報

programmable multiplexer
puroguramukanō
maruchipurekusa
プログラム可能マルチプレクサ

**programmable read-only memory
(programmable ROM; PROM)**
puroguramukanō yomidashi
sen'yō kioku; puroguramukanō
yomitori sen'yō kioku (PROM)
プログラム可能読み出し
専用記憶;
プログラム可能読み取り
専用記憶

**programmable ROM
(programmable read-only memory;
PROM)**
puroguramukanō yomidashi
sen'yō kioku; puroguramukanō
yomitori sen'yō kioku (PROM)
プログラム可能読み出し
専用記憶;
プログラム可能読み取り
専用記憶

161

programmed check
puroguramu ni yoru kensa
プログラムによる検査

programmed dump
puroguramudo-danpu
プログラムド・ダンプ

programmed halt
puroguramu ni yoru teishi
プログラムによる停止

programmed instruction (PI)
puroguramu gakushū (PI);
puroguramu meirei
プログラム学習;
プログラム命令

**programmed input/output
(programmed I/O)**
puroguramudo nyūshutsuryoku
(puroguramudo I/O)
プログラムド入出力;
プログラムドI/O

programmed learning
puroguramu gakushū
プログラム学習

programmed logic
puroguramudo ronri
プログラムド論理

programmed switch
puroguramudo-suitchi
プログラムド・スイッチ

programmer
purogurama
プログラマ

**programmer-defined
macroinstruction**
puroguroma teigi makuro meirei
プログラマ定義マクロ命令

programming
keikakuhō; puroguramingu
計画法; プログラミング

programming environment
puroguramingu kankyō
プログラミング環境

programming error
puroguramingu ayamari
プログラミング誤り

programming flow diagram
puroguramingu nagarezu
プログラミング流れ図

programming flowchart
puroguramingu nagarezu
プログラミング流れ図

programming language
puroguramingu gengo
プログラミング言語

programming module
puroguramingu-mojyūru
プログラミング・モジュール

programming primitive
puroguramingu kihon meirei
プログラミング基本命令

programming standards
puroguramingu hyōjun
プログラミング標準

programming system
puroguramingu-shisutemu
プログラミング・システム

programming technique
puroguramingu gihō
プログラミング技法

project
keikaku
計画

projection
tōsha
投射

**PROM (programmable read-only
memory; programmable ROM)**
PROM (puroguramukanō
yomidashi sen'yō kioku;
puroguramukanō yomitori sen'yō
kioku)
プログラム可能読み出し
専用記憶;
プログラム可能読み取り
専用記憶

PROM programmer
PROM puroguramu
PROM プログラマ

prompt (*noun*)
puronputo
プロンプト

prompting
puronputeingu
プロンプティング

proof list
purūfu-risuto
プルーフ・リスト

propagate
dempa suru
伝播する

propagated error
dempa ayamari
伝播誤り

propagation
dempa
伝播

propagation delay
dempa chien
伝播遅延

propagation delay time
dempa chien jikan
伝播遅延時間

propagation path
dempa keiro
伝播経路

propagation time
dempa jikan
伝播時間

proper string
kigō no kihonretsu
記号の基本列

proper subset
shinbubun shūgō
真部分集号

property
tokusei
特性

property sort
tokusei bunrui
特性分類

property value
zokusei chi
属性値

property value set
zokusei chi shūgō
属性値集合

proportional control action
hirei seigyo dōsa
比例制御動作

proprietary program
shoyūken o shuchō dekiru
puroguramu
所有権を主張できるプログラム

proprietary software
shoyūken o shuchō dekiru
sofutouea
所有権を主張できるソフトウ
エア

protect
hogo suru; yobō suru
保護する；予防する

protected
hogo sareta
保護された

protected data
hogo sareta dēta
保護されたデータ

protected field
hogo sareta fuiirudo
保護されたフィールド

protected location
hogo iki; hogo kioku (ryō)iki
保護域；保護記憶(領)域

protected record
hogo sareta rekōdo
保護されたレコード

protecting device
hogo sōchi
保護装置

protecting mechanism
hogo kikō
保護機構

protection
hogo; yobō
保護；予防

protection character
hogo moji
保護文字

protection key
hogo kii
保護キー

protective ground
hoan'yō setchi
保安用接地

protocol
kiyaku; purotokoru
規約；プロトコル

prototype
genkei; purototaipu
原型；プロトタイプ

ps (picosecond)
ps (pikobyō)
ピコ秒

pseudo-
giji
疑似

pseudo−assembly language
giji asenburi gengo
疑似アセンブリ言語

pseudocode
giji kōdo
疑似コード

pseudoinstruction
giji meirei
疑似命令

pseudo-operation
giji sōsa
疑似操作

pseudorandom codes
giji randamu kōdo
疑似ランダム・コード

pseudorandom numbers
giji ransū
疑似乱数

**pseudorandom sequence of
numbers**
giji ransū retsu
疑似乱数列

pseudoregister
giji rejisuta
疑似レジスタ

pseudovariable
giji hensū
疑似変数

PSR (processor state register)
PSR (purosessa jōtai rejisuta)
プロセッサ状態レジスタ

PSW (program status word)
PSW (puroguramu jōtai go)
プログラム状態語

**PSWR (program status word
register)**
PSWR (puroguramu jōtai go
rejisuta)
プログラム状態語レジスタ

PTP (paper-tape punch)
PTP (kami tēpu-panchi; kami
tēpu senkō sōchi; kami tēpu
senkōki)
紙テープ・パンチ；
紙テープせん孔装置；
紙テープせん孔機

PTR (paper-tape reader)
PTR (kami tēpu yomitoriki; kami
tēpu yomitori sōchi)
紙テープ読み取り機；
紙テープ読み取り装置

PUB (physical unit block)
PUB (butsuriteki sōchi burokku)
物理的装置ブロック

public data network
kōshū dēta mō
公衆データ網

public file
kyōyū fuairu
共有ファイル

pull-out disk
puru-auto-deisuku
プル・アウト・ディスク

pull-out disk unit
puru-auto-deisuku sōchi
プル・アウト・ディスク装置

pulse
parusu
パルス

pulse advance
parusu no susumi
パルスの進み

pulse amplitude
parusu shimpuku
パルス振幅

pulse amplitude modulation (PAM)
parusu shimpuku henchō (PAM)
パルス振幅変調

pulse base
parusu-bēsu
パルス・ベース

pulse base center point
parusu-bēsu chūōten
パルス・ベース中央点

pulse base distortion
parusu-bēsu hizumi
パルス・ベース歪み

pulse base magnitude
parusu-bēsu shimpuku
パルス・ベース振幅

pulse center point
parusu chūōten
パルス中央点

pulse code modulation (PCM)
parusu fugō henchō (PCM)
パルス符号変調

pulse delay time
parusu no okure
パルスの遅れ

pulse duration
parusu haba
パルス幅

pulse duration distortion
parusu haba hizumi
パルス幅歪み

pulse duration modulation
parusu haba henchō
パルス幅変調

pulse fall time
parusu tachisagari jikan
パルス立ち下り時間

pulse forming
parusu keisei
パルス形成

pulse-forming circuit
parusu keisei kairo
パルス形成回路

pulse frequency modulation
parusu shūhasū henchō
パルス周波数変調

pulse generator
parusu hasseiki
パルス発生器

pulse length
parusu haba
パルス幅

pulse length distortion
parusu haba hizumi
パルス幅歪み

pulse length modulation
parusu haba henchō
パルス幅変調

pulse magnitude
parusu shimpuku
パルス振幅

pulse magnitude fluctuation
parusu shimpuku jitta
パルス振幅ジッタ

pulse magnitude jitter
parusu shimpuku jitta
パルス振幅ジッタ

pulse modulation
parusu henchō
パルス変調

pulse number modulation
parusu sūhenchō
パルス数変調

pulse phase modulation
parusu isō henchō
パルス位相変調

pulse position
parusu ichi
パルス位置

pulse position modulation
parusu ichi henchō
パルス位置変調

pulse regeneration
parusu saisei
パルス再生

pulse regeneration circuit
parusu saisei kairo
パルス再生回路

pulse repetition frequency
parusu kurikaeshi shūhasū
パルス繰り返し周波数

pulse repetition frequency fluctuation
parusu kurikaeshi shūhasū jitta
パルス繰り返し周波数ジッタ

pulse repetition frequency jitter
parusu kurikaeshi shūhasū jitta
パルス繰り返し周波数ジッタ

pulse repetition period
parusu kurikaeshi shūki
パルス繰り返し周期

pulse repetition period fluctuation
parusu kurikaeshi shūki jitta
パルス繰り返し周期ジッタ

pulse repetition period jitter
parusu kurikaeshi shūki jitta
パルス繰り返し周期ジッタ

pulse repetition rate
parusu kurikaeshi ritsu
パルス繰り返し率

pulse response
parusu ōtō
パルス応答

pulse rise time
parusu tachiagari jikan
パルス立ち上り時間

pulse separation
parusu kankaku
パルス間隔

pulse separation distortion
parusu kankaku hizumi
パルス間隔歪み

pulse shape
parusu kei
パルス形

pulse shaping
parusu seikei
パルス整形

pulse shaping circuit
parusu seikei kairo
パルス整形回路

pulse time modulation
parusu jihenchō
パルス時変調

pulse top
parusu-toppu
パルス・トップ

pulse top center point
parusu-toppu chūōten
パルス・トップ中央点

pulse top distortion
parusu-toppu hizumi
パルス・トップ歪み

pulse top magnitude
parusu-toppu shimpuku
パルス・トップ振幅

pulse train
parusu retsu
パルス列

pulse waveform
parusu hakei
パルス波形

pulse width
parusu haba
パルス幅

pulse width distortion
parusu haba hizumi
パルス幅歪み

punch (*noun*)
panchi; senkō sōchi; senkōki
パンチ；せん孔装置；せん孔機

punch (*verb*)
panchi suru; senkō suru
パンチする；せん孔する

punch-card machine (PCM)
kādo senkō sōchi; kādo senkōki
(PCM)
カードせん孔装置；
カードせん孔機

punch operator
panchi-operēta
パンチ・オペレータ

punch position
senkō ichi
せん孔位置

punch queue
senkō machigyōretsu
せん孔待ち行列

punch rate
senkō sokudo
せん孔速度

punch station
senkō kikō
せん孔機構

punched card
senkō kādo
せん孔カード

punched-card code
senkō kādo-kōdo
せん孔カード・コード

punched-card interpreter
senkō kādo-intapurita
せん孔カード・インタプリタ

punched-card processing
senkō kādo shori
せん孔カード処理

punched-card reader
senkō kādo yomitori sōchi;
senkō kādo yomitoriki
せん孔カード読み取り装置；
せん孔カード読み取り機

punched-card system (PCS)
senkō kādo-shisutemu (PCS)
せん孔カード・システム

punched-card verifier
senkō kādo kenkōki
せん孔カード検孔機

punched-card verifying
senkō kādo kenkō
せん孔カード検孔

punched output
senkō shutsuryoku
せん孔出力

punched tag
senkō tagu
せん孔タグ

punched tape
senkō tēpu
せん孔テープ

puncher
pancha; senkō sōchi; senkōki
パンチャ；せん孔装置；せん孔機

punching
panchingu; senkō sōsa
パンチング；せん孔操作

punching machine
pancha; senkō sōchi; senkōki
パンチャ；せん孔装置；せん孔機

punching positions
senkō ichi
せん孔位置

punctuation
kutō
句読

punctuation character
kutō moji
句読文字

punctuation mark
kutō kigō; kutōten
句読記号；句読点

pure binary notation
jun nishin hō
純2進法

pure binary numeration system
jun nishin kisūhō
純2進記数法

push
oshi; pusshu
押し；プッシュ

push down (*verb*)
atoire sakidashi suru
後入れ先出しする

push-down list
atoire sakidashi hyō
後入れ先出し表

push-down method
atoire sakidashi hōshiki
後入れ先出し方式

push-down stack
atoire sakidashi sutakku
後入れ先出しスタック

push-down storage
atoire sakidashi kioku
後入れ先出し記憶

push-down store
atoire sakidashi kioku sōchi
後入れ先出し記憶装置

push up (*verb*)
sakiire sakidashi suru
先入れ先出しする

push-up list
sakiire sakidashi hyō
先入れ先出し表

push-up method
sakiire sakidashi hōshiki
先入れ先出し方式

push-up storage
sakiire sakidashi kioku
先入れ先出し記憶

push-up store
sakiire sakidashi kioku sōchi
先入れ先出し記憶装置

PVC (permanent virtual circuit)
PVC (aite kotei setsuzoku)
相手固定接続

Q

Q-A (question and answer)
Q-A (shitsumon-kaitō)
質問-回答

QCB (queue control block)
QCB (machigyōretsu seigyo burokku)
待ち行列制御ブロック

QISAM (queued indexed sequential-access method)
QISAM (taiki sakuin junji akusesu hōshiki)
待機索引順次アクセス方式

QP (quadratic programming)
QP (niji keikakuhō)
二次計画法

QSAM (queued sequential-access method)
QSAM (taiki junji akusesu hōshiki)
待機順次アクセス方式

QTAM (queued telecommunications access method)
QTAM (taiki tsūshin akusesu hōshiki)
待機通信アクセス方式

quad in line
kuoddo-in-rain
クオッド・イン・ライン

quadrant
shibun kukan
四分区間

quadratic programming (QP)
niji keikakuhō (QP)
二次計画法

quadratic selection
niji sentaku hōshiki
二次選択方式

quadrature
kyūsekihō
求積法

quadruple-length register
yonbaichō rejisuta
四倍長レジスタ

qualified name
shūshoku sareta namae
修飾された名前

qualifier
shūshokushi
修飾子

qualitative
teiseiteki
定性的

qualitative information
teiseiteki jōhō
定性的情報

quality
hinshitsu
品質

quality assurance
hinshitsu hoshō
品質保証

quality control
hinshitsu kanri
品質管理

quality information system
hinshitsu jōhō shisutemu
品質情報システム

quality system
hinshitsu shisutemu
品質システム

quantitative
teiryōteki
定量的

quantitative information
teiryōteki jōhō
定量的情報

quantity
ryō
量

quantization
ryōshika
量子化

quantize
ryōshika suru
量子化する

quantize distortion
ryōshika hizumi
量子化歪み

quantize error
ryōshika gosa
量子化誤差

quantize noise
ryōshika zatsuon
量子化雑音

quantum
ryōshi
量子

quartet
yonbitto-baito
4ビット・バイト

quartz crystal
suishō
水晶

query
shitsumon; toiawase
質問；問い合わせ

query-answering system
toiawase ōtō shisutemu
問い合わせ応答システム

query formation
shitsumon keishikika
質問形式化

query processing
toiawase shori
問い合わせ処理

question
shitsumon
質問

question and answer (Q-A)
shitsumon-kaitō (Q-A)
質問-回答

question-and-answer system
shitsumon-kaitō shisutemu
質問-回答システム

queue
gyōretsu; machigyōretsu
行列；待ち行列

queue control
machigyōretsu seigyo
待ち行列制御

queue control block (QCB)
machigyōretsu seigyo burokku (QCB)
待ち行列制御ブロック

queued access
taiki akusesu
待機アクセス

queued access method
taiki akusesu hōshiki
待機アクセス方式

queued indexed sequential-access method (QISAM)
taiki sakuin junji akusesu hōshiki (QISAM)
待機索引順次アクセス方式

queued sequential-access method (QSAM)
taiki junji akusesu hōshiki (QSAM)
待機順次アクセス方式

queued telecommunications access method (QTAM)
taiki tsūshin akusesu hōshiki (QTAM)
待機通信アクセス方式

queuing
gyōretsu; machiawase; machigyōretsu
行列; 待ち合わせ; 待ち行列

queuing list
machigyōretsu risuto
待ち行列リスト

queuing network
machigyōretsu nettowāku
待ち行列ネットワーク

queuing system
machigyōretsu shisutemu
待ち行列システム

queuing theory
machiawase riron
待ち合わせ理論

quick-access memory
kuikku-akusesu-memori
クィック・アクセス・メモリ

quick look
kuikku-rukku
クィック・ルック

quick response time
kōsoku ōtō jikan
高速応答時間

quick start
kuikku-sutāto
クィック・スタート

QUICKTRAN
QUICKTRAN
QUICKTRAN

quinary
goshinhō
5進法

quintet
gobitto-baito
5ビット・バイト

quotient
akinai
商

quotient register
shō rejisuta
商レジスタ

QWERTY keyboard
QWERTY kiibōdo
QWERTY キーボード

R

r (register)
r (rejisuta)
レジスタ

raceway
rēsuuei
レースウェイ

rack
rakku
ラック

rack type
rakkugata
ラック型

radix
kisū
基数

radix complement
kisū no hosū
基数の補数

radix conversion
kisū henkan
基数変換

radix-minus-one complement
kisū mainasu ichi no hosū
基数マイナス1の補数

radix notation
kisū hyōkihō
基数表記法

radix numeration system
kisū hyōkihō
基数表記法

radix point
kiten; shōsūten
基点; 小数点

radix sort
kisūhō bunrui
基数法分類

RAM (random-access memory)
RAM (randamu-akusesu kioku; randamu-akusesu-memori)
ランダム・アクセス記憶;
ランダム・アクセス・メモリ

RAM board
RAM bōdo
RAM ボード

RAM chip
RAM chippu
RAM チップ

ramp
keisha; ranpu
傾斜; ランプ

ramp nonlinearity
keisha hichokusen hizumi;
ranpu hichokusen hizumi
傾斜非直線歪み;
ランプ非直線歪み

ramp response
ranpu ōtō
ランプ応答

RAMPS (resource allocation in multiple-project scheduling)
RAMPS (ranpusu)
ランプス

random
ran; randamu
乱; ランダム

random access
chokusetsu akusesu;
ran akusesu; ran yobidashi;
randamu-akusesu;
sokuji yobidashi
直接アクセス; 乱アクセス;
乱呼び出し; ランダム・
アクセス; 即時呼び出し

random-access device
randamu-akusesu sōchi
ランダム・アクセス装置

random-access file
chokusetsu akusesu fuairu;
ran akusesu-fuairu;
randamu-akusesu-fuairu;
sokuji yobidashi fuairu
直接アクセス・ファイル;
乱アクセス・ファイル;
ランダム・アクセス・ファイル;
即時呼び出しファイル

random-access memory (RAM)
randamu-akusesu kioku;
randamu-akusesu-memori (RAM)
ランダム・アクセス記憶;
ランダム・アクセス・メモリ

random-access storage
randamu-akusesu kioku
ランダム・アクセス記憶

random data
ran dēta
乱データ

random enquiry
ran toiawase
乱問い合わせ

random file
ran hensei fuairu; randamu-fuairu
乱編成ファイル;
ランダム・ファイル

random number(s)
ransū
乱数

random-number generation
ransū hassei
乱数発生

random-number generator
ransū hasseiki
乱数発生器

random-number sequence
ransū hairetsu
乱数配列

random organization
ran hensei
乱編成

random processing
randamu shori
ランダム処理

random pulse train
randamu-parusu retsu
ランダム・パルス列

random retrieval
randamu kensaku
ランダム検索

random scan
randamu sōsa
ランダム走査

random search
randamu tansaku
ランダム探索

random-walk method
randamu-uōku hō
ランダム・ウォーク方

randomizing
randamuka
ランダム化

randomly accessible
ran akusesu kanō;
randamu-akusesu kanō
乱アクセス可能;
ランダム・アクセス可能

range
haba; han'i; reinji
幅; 範囲; レインジ

range check
han'i kensa; reinji-chekku
範囲検査; レインジ・チェック

range finder
han'i chōseiki
範囲調整器

rank
hairetsu; jun'i
配列; 順位

ranking
jun'itsuke
順位付け

raster
rasuta
ラスタ

raster display
rasuta hyōji sōchi
ラスタ表示装置

raster plotter
rasuta-purotta
ラスタ・プロッタ

raster scan
rasuta sōsa
ラスタ走査

raster scanning
rasuta sōsa
ラスタ走査

rate
hiritsu; ritsu
比率; 率

rated
teikaku
定格

rated speed
teikaku sokudo
定格速度

ratio
hiritsu; kaisū; ritsu
比率; 回数; 率

ratio control
hiritsu seigyo
比率制御

rational number
yūrisū
有理数

raw data
genshi dēta; nama dēta
原始データ；生データ

RB (return to bias)
RB (RB hōshiki)
RB方式

RC (remote concentrator)
RC (rimōto-konsentorēta)
リモート・コンセントレータ

read (*verb*)
yomu; yomidasu; yomitoru
読む；読み出す；読み取る

read-around ratio
yomitorikanō kaisū
読み取り可能回数

read-back check
yomitori chekku
読み取りチェック

read cycle time
yomitori saikuru-taimu
読み取りサイクル・タイム

read error
yomitori ayamari
読み取り誤り

read head
yomitori heddo
読み取りヘッド

read instruction
yomitori meirei
読み取り命令

read-only (RO)
yomidashi sen'yō;
yomitori sen'yō (RO)
読み出し専用；読み取り専用

read-only chip
yomidashi sen'yō chippu
読み出し専用チップ

read-only memory (ROM)
kotei kioku; rōmu;
yomidashi sen'yō kioku;
yomitori sen'yō kioku (ROM)
固定記憶；ローム；
読み出し専用記憶；
読み取り専用記憶

read-only memory chip
ROM chippu
ROMチップ

read-only storage (ROS)
kotei kioku;
yomidashi sen'yō kioku;
yomitori sen'yō kioku (ROS)
固定記憶；読み出し専用記憶；
読み取り専用記憶

read-only storage unit
kotei kioku sōchi
固定記憶装置

read-only store
kotei kioku sōchi
固定記憶装置

read pulse
yomidashi parusu
読み出しパルス

read rate
yomitori sokudo
読み取り速度

read statement
yomibun; yomidashi bun;
yomitori bun
読み文；読み出し文；
読み取り文

read station
yomitori kikō
読み取り機構

read-write (R-W)
yomikaki; yomitori kakikomi
(R-W)
読み書き；読み取り書き込み

read-write channel
yomitori kakikomi chaneru
読み取り書き込みチャネル

read-write check
yomikaki kensa
読み書き検査

read-write head
yomikaki heddo
読み書きヘッド

read-write memory
yomikaki kioku;
yomitori kakikomi kioku
読み書き記憶；
読み取り書き込み記憶

read-write protection
yomitori kakikomi hogo
読み取り書き込み保護

reader
riida; yomitori sōchi
リーダ；読み取り装置

reading
yomidashi; yomitori
読み出し；読み取り

readout
riido-auto; yomidashi
リード・アウト；読み出し

ready
redei; sadōkanō
レディ；作動可能

ready condition
redei jōtai; sadōkanō jōtai
レディ状態；作動可能状態

ready for receiving
chakushinka
着信可

ready for sending
sōshinka
送信可

ready status
redei jōtai
レディ状態

ready status word
redei jōtai go
レディ状態語

real address
jitsu adoresu
実アドレス

real constant
jitsu teisū
実定数

real interval
jitsu kukan
実区間

real number
jissū
実数

real storage
jitsu kioku('iki)
実記憶（域）

real time
jitsu jikan; riaru-taimu
実時間；リアル・タイム

real-time clock (RTC)
jitsu jikan tokei;
riaru-taimu-kurokku (RTC)
実時間時計;
リアル・タイム・クロック

real-time computer
jitsu jikan keisanki;
riaru-taimu-konpyūta
実時間計算機;
リアル・タイム・コンピュータ

real-time control
jitsu jikan seigyo
実時間制御

real-time information processing
jitsu jikan jōhō shori
実時間情報処理

real-time input
jitsu jikan nyūryoku
実時間入力

real-time job
jitsu jikan jyobu
実時間ジョブ

real-time operating system
jitsu jikan operēteingu-
shisutemu; riaru-taimu-
operēteingu-shisutemu
実時間オペレーティング・
システム; リアル・タイム・
オペレーティング・システム

real-time operation
jitsu jikan dōsa; riaru-taimu dōsa
実時間動作; リアル・タイム動作

real-time OS (real-time operating system)
jitsu jikan OS; riaru-taimu OS
実時間OS; リアル・タイムOS

real-time output
jitsu jikan shutsuryoku
実時間出力

real-time processing
jitsu jikan shori; riaru-taimu shori
実時間処理; リアル・タイム処理

real-time simulation
jitsu jikan shimyurēshon
実時間シミュレーション

real-time system
jitsu jikan shisutemu;
riaru-taimu-shisutemu
実時間システム;
リアル・タイム・システム

real variable
jitsu hensū
実変数

realization
jitsugen
実現

reallocation
saihaibun
再配分

realm
ryō'iki
領域

realm data item
ryō'iki dēta kōmoku
領域データ項目

realm description entry
ryō'iki kijutsukō
領域記述項

realm name
ryō'iki mei
領域名

realm section
ryō'iki setsu
領域節

reblock
saiburokkuka
再ブロック化

reblocking
saiburokkuka
再ブロック化

reboot
riibūto
リーブート

recall factor
saigenritsu
再現率

receive
chakushin suru; jushin suru;
uketoru
着信する; 受信する; 受け取る

receive interrupt
jushin chūdan
受信中断

receive interruption
jushin chūdan
受信中断

receive mode
jushin mōdo
受信モード

receive-only
jushin sen'yō
受信専用

received data
jushin dēta
受信データ

receiver (equipment)
jushinki
受信機

receiver (person)
chakushinsha
着信者

receiver signal element timing
jushin shingō eremento-taimingu
受信信号エレメント・
タイミング

receiving
chakushin; jushin; uketori
着信; 受信; 受け取り

receiving station
chakushin tanmatsu;
jushin tanmatsu
着信端末; 受信端末

receiving terminal
chakushin tanmatsu sōchi;
jushin tanmatsu sōchi
着信端末装置; 受信端末装置

receptor
juyōki
受容器

reciprocal distribution
sōhan bumpu
相反分布

recognition
ninshiki
認識

reconcile
chōsei suru
調整する

reconciliation
chōsei
調整

reconfiguration
saikōsei
再構成

reconstitution (of files)
fukugen
復元

record (*noun*)
kiroku; rekōdo
記録；レコード

record (*verb*)
kiroku suru; rekōdo suru
記録する；レコードする

record block
rekōdo-burokku
レコード・ブロック

record blocking
rekōdo-burokkuka
レコード・ブロック化

record checking
rekōdo kensa
レコード検査

record count
rekōdo-kaunto
レコード・カウント

record description
rekōdo kijutsu
レコード記述

record description entry
rekōdo kijutsukō
レコード記述項

record entry
rekōdo kijutsukō
レコード記述項

record format
rekōdo keishiki
レコード形式

record gap
rekōdo kankaku
レコード間隔

record identification
rekōdo shikibetsu
レコード識別

record key
rekōdo-kii
レコード・キー

record layout
rekōdo-reiauto; rekōdo yōshiki
レコード・レィアウト；
レコード様式

record length
rekōdo chō
レコード長

record length indicator
rekōdo chō hyōshiki
レコード長標識

record mark
rekōdo-māku
レコード・マーク

record name
rekōdo mei
レコード名

record occurrence
rekōdo-okarensu
レコード・オカレンス

record-oriented transmission
rekōdo densō
レコード伝送

record position
rekōdo haichi
レコード配置

record release
rekōdo kaihō
レコード解放

record segment
rekōdo-segumento
レコード・セグメント

record selection
rekōdo sentaku
レコード選択

record separator (RS)
rekōdo bunri moji (RS)
レコード分離文字

record sequence own code
rekōdo-shiikensu-oun-kōdo
レコード・シーケンス・
オウン・コード

record size
rekōdo-saizu
レコード・サイズ

record subentry
rekōdo fukukijutsukō
レコード副記述項

recorder
rekōda; kirokuki
レコーダ；記録機

recording
kiroku
記録

recording density
kioku mitsudo; kiroku mitsudo
記憶密度；記録密度

recording head
kiroku heddo
記録ヘッド

recording medium
kiroku baitai
記録媒体

recording tape
kiroku'yō tēpu
記録用テープ

recording track
kiroku torakku
記録トラック

recoverability
kaifukusei
回復性

recoverable
kaifukukanō; kaifukusei
回復可能；回復性

recoverable error
kaifukukanō ayamari
回復可能誤り

recovery
kaifuku
回復

recovery management
kaifuku kanri
回復管理

recovery management support (RMS)
kaifuku kanri sapōto (RMS)
回復管理サポート

recovery point
kaifuku ten
回復点

recovery procedure
kaifuku tejun
回復手順

171

rectangular pulse
hōkei parusu; kukei parusu
方形パルス；矩形パルス

rectangular pulse duration
kukei parusu haba
矩形パルス幅

rectification
seiryū
整流

rectifier
seiryūki
整流器

recursion
hampuku
反復

recursive
saiki; saikiteki
再帰；再帰的

recursive call
saiki yobidashi
再帰呼び出し

recursive definition
saikiteki teigi
再帰的定義

recursive function
saikiteki kansū
再帰的関数

recursive program
saikiteki puroguramu
再帰的プログラム

recursive routine
saikiteki rūchin
再帰的ルーチン

recursive subroutine
saikiteki saburūchin
再帰的サブルーチン

red tape
reddo-tēpu
レッド・テープ

red-tape operation
reddo-tēpu sōsa
レッド・テープ操作

redefinition
saiteigi
再定義

redesign
saisekkei
再設計

reduction
kangen; seiri henshū
還元；整理編集

reduction ratio
kangen ritsu
還元率

redundancy
jōchō(do)
冗長（度）

redundancy check
jōchō kensa
冗長検査

redundancy code
jōchō fugō
冗長符号

redundancy system
jōchō hōshiki
冗長方式

redundant
jōchō
冗長

redundant bit
jōchō bitto
冗長ビット

redundant character
jōchō moji
冗長文字

redundant code
jōchō fugō
冗長符号

redundant computation
jōchō keisan
冗長計算

redundant data
jōchō dēta
冗長データ

redundant information
jōchō jōhō
冗長情報

redundant system
jōchō shisutemu
冗長システム

reel
riirū
リール

reel number
riiru bangō
リール番号

reenterable
sainyūkanō
再入可能

reenterable load module
sainyūkanō rōdo-mojyūru
再入可能ロード・モジュール

reenterable program
sainyūkanō puroguramu
再入可能プログラム

reentrant
sainyūkanō
再入可能

reentrant code
sainyūkanō kōdo
再入可能コード

reentrant processor (REP)
sainyūkanō purosessa (REP)
再入可能プロセッサ

reentrant program
sainyūkanō puroguramu
再入可能プログラム

reentrant routine
sainyūkanō rūchin
再入可能ルーチン

reentry
sainyū
再入

reentry point
sainyūten
再入点

reevaluation
saihyōka
再評価

refer
in'yō suru
引用する

reference
in'yō; kijun; refuarensu; sanshō
引用；基準；レファレンス；参照

reference code
sanshō kōdo
参照コード

reference edge
kijun'en
基準縁

reference field
kijun jikai
基準磁界

reference file
sanshō fuairu
参照ファイル

reference input
kijun nyūryoku
基準入力

reference key
refuarensu-kii
レファレンス・キー

reference language
kijun gengo
基準言語

reference level
kijun reberu
基準レベル

reference noise
kijun noizu
基準ノイズ

reference number
refuarensu tsūban
レファレンス通番

reference volume
kijun onryō
基準音量

reference waveform
kijun hakei
基準波形

refinement
senren
洗練

reflectance
hansha
反射

reflectance ratio
hansha ritsu
反射率

reflected binary code
kōban nishin kōdo
交番2進コード

reflection
hansha
反射

reflection coefficient
hansha keisū
反射係数

reflective mark
hansha māku
反射マーク

reflective marker
hansha māka
反射マーカ

refresh
rifuresshu
リフレッシュ

refresh cycle
rifuresshu-saikuru
リフレッシュ・サイクル

refresh rate
rifuresshu-rēto
リフレッシュ・レート

refreshed display
rifuresshu-deisupurei
リフレッシュ・ディスプレィ

refreshing
rifuresshingu; saisei
リフレッシング；再生

regeneration
kioku saisei; saisei
記憶再生；再生

regeneration period
saisei shūki
再生周期

regenerative reading
saisei yomidashi
再生読み出し

regenerative storage
saisei kioku
再生記憶

regenerative store
saisei kioku sōchi
再生記憶装置

regenerative track
saisei torakku
再生トラック

region
ku'iki; ryō'iki
区域；領域

region partitioning
ryō'iki kukakuka
領域区画化

regional address
ku'ikinai adoresu
区域内アドレス

register (r)
chisūki; rejisuta (r)
置数器；レジスタ

register assignment
rejisuta wariate
レジスタ割り当て

register length
rejisuta chō
レジスタ長

register memory
rejisuta kioku
レジスタ記憶

register set
rejisuta-setto
レジスタ・セット

register transfer
rejisuta tensō
レジスタ転送

registration
ichikime; kanyū; tōroku
位置決め；加入；登録

regression
kaiki
回帰

regression analysis
kaiki bunseki
回帰分析

regression curve
kaiki kyokusen
回帰曲線

regular
seisoku
正則

regular expression
seisoku hyōgen
正則表現

regular language
seisoku gengo
正則言語

regulate
chōsei suru
調整する

regulating
chōsei
調整

reject
kyohi; rijiekuto
拒否；リジェクト

reject function
rijiekuto kinō
リジェクト機能

173

rejection
kyohi
拒否

related term
kanren gainengo
関連概念語

relation
hikaku;kankei; kanren; rirēshon
比較;関係;関連;リレーション

relation character
hikaku moji
比較文字

relation condition
hikaku jōken
比較条件

relation test
hikaku tesuto
比較テスト

relational
hikakushiki; kankei; kanren;
rirēshonaru(gata)
比較式;関係;関連;
リレーショナル（型）

relational algebra
kankei daisū
関係代数

relational calculus
kankei enzan
関係演算

relational database
kanren dētabēsu
関連データベース

relational expression
kankei shiki
関係式

relational operator
hikaku sayōso; kankei enzanshi
比較作用素;関係演算子

relational structure
kankei kōzō
関係構造

relative
sōtai
相対

relative address
sōtai adoresu
相対アドレス

relative addressing
sōtai adoresu shitei
相対アドレス指定

relative code
sōtai kōdo
相対コード

relative coding
sōtai kōdeingu
相対コーディング

relative data
sōtai dēta
相対データ

relative error
sōtai gosa
相対誤差

relative file
sōtai fuairu; sōtai hensei fuairu
相対ファイル;相対編成ファイル

relative indexing
sōtai shihyōtsuke
相対指標付け

relative key
sōtai kii
相対キー

relative operator
hikaku enzanshi
比較演算子

relative organization
sōtai hensei
相対編成

relative programming
sōtai puroguramingu
相対プログラミング

relative record number
sōtai rekōdo ban
相対レコード番

relay
keidenki; rirē
継電器;リレー

relaxation oscillator
shichō hasshinki
し張発振器

release
kaihō; ririisu
解放;リリース

relevance ratio
tekigō ritsu
適合率

reliability
shinraido; shinraisei
信頼度;信頼性

reliability analysis
shinraisei kaiseki
信頼性解析

reliability assessment
shinraisei hyōtei
信頼性評定

reliable
shinrai(sei)
信頼（性）

reload
sairōdo
再ロード

reloading time
sairōdeingu jikan
再ローディング時間

relocatability
saihaichikanōsei
再配置可能性

relocatable
rirokētaburu; saihaichikanō
リロケータブル;再配置可能

relocatable address
saihaichikanō adoresu
再配置可能アドレス

relocatable area
saihaichikanō iki
再配置可能域

relocatable code
saihaichikanō kōdo
再配置可能コード

relocatable element
rirokētaburu-eremento;
saihaichikanō eremento
リロケータブル・エレメント;
再配置可能エレメント

relocatable expression
saihaichikanō shiki
再配置可能式

relocatable library
saihaichikanō raiburari
再配置可能ライブラリ

relocatable loader
saihaichikanō rōda
再配置可能ローダ

relocatable name
saihaichikanō mei
再配置可能名

relocatable program
saihaichikanō puroguramu
再配置可能プログラム

relocatable program loader
saihaichikanō puroguramu-rōda
再配置可能プログラム・ローダ

relocatable routine
saihaichikanō rūchin
再配置可能ルーチン

relocatable symbol
saihaichikanō kigō
再配置可能記号

relocate
rirokēto suru; saihaichi suru
リロケートする；再配置する

relocation
rirokēshon; saihaichi
リロケーション；再配置

relocation dictionary
saihaichi deikushonari
再配置ディケショナリ

relocation record
saihaichi rekōdo
再配置レコード

relocation register
rirokēshon-rejisuta
リロケーション・レジスタ

remainder
jōyo; rimeinda
剰余；リメインダ

remainder check
jōyo chekku; rimeinda-chekku
剰余チェック；
リメインダ・チェック

remark
chū
注

remote
enkaku(chi); rimōto
遠隔(地)；リモート

remote access
enkaku akusesu
遠隔アクセス

remote-access computer system
enkaku akusesu keisanki
shisutemu
遠隔アクセス計算機システム

remote batch
enkaku batchi; rimōto-batchi
遠隔バッチ；リモート・バッチ

remote batch processing
enkakuchi batchi shori;
rimōto-batchi shori
遠隔地バッチ処理；
リモート・バッチ処理

remote batch terminal
rimōto-batchi tanmatsu
リモート・バッチ端末

remote communication facility
enkaku tsūshin kinō
遠隔通信機能

remote communication unit
enkaku tsūshin sōchi
遠隔通信装置

remote computer
enkaku keisanki
遠隔計算機

remote computer system
enkaku keisanki shisutemu
遠隔計算機システム

remote computing
enkaku keisan (shori)
遠隔計算（処理）

remote computing system
enkaku keisan (shori) shisutemu
遠隔計算（処理）システム

remote concentrator (RC)
rimōto-konsentorēta (RC)
リモート・コンセントレータ

remote console
enkaku sōsataku
遠隔操作卓

remote control
enkaku seigyo
遠隔制御

remote control function
enkaku seigyo kinō
遠隔制御機能

remote controller
enkaku seigyo sōchi
遠隔制御装置

remote data processing
enkakuchi dēta shori
遠隔地データ処理

remote data processor
enkaku(chi) dēta shori sōchi
遠隔（地）データ処理装置

remote debugging
enkaku debaggingu
遠隔デバッギング

remote format
enkaku keishiki; enkaku shoshiki
遠隔形式；遠隔書式

remote inquiry
enkaku shōkai; enkaku toiawase
遠隔照会；遠隔問い合わせ

remote inquiry unit
enkaku shōkai sōchi
遠隔照会装置

remote job entry (RJE)
enkaku jyobu nyūryoku (RJE)
遠隔ジョブ入力

remote location
enkaku tanmatsu
遠隔端末

remote operating unit
enkaku operēteingu sōchi
遠隔オペレーティング装置

remote operation
enkaku sōsa
遠隔操作

remote station
enkaku kyoku; enkaku tanmatsu
遠隔局；遠隔端末

remote system
enkaku shisutemu
遠隔システム

remote terminal
enkaku tanmatsu sōchi
遠隔端末装置

remote unit
rimōto sōchi
リモート装置

remote workstation
enkaku sagyō kyoku;
enkaku sagyō tanmatsu
遠隔作業局；遠隔作業端末

removable disk
torihazushikanō deisuku
取り外し可能ディスク

removable disk pack
torihazushikanō deisuku-pakku
取り外し可能ディスク・パック

remove (*verb*)
jokyo suru; torihazusu
除去する；取り外す

reorganization
saihensei
再編成

reorganize
saihensei suru
再編成する

REP (reentrant processor)
REP (sainyūkanō purosessa)
再入可能プロセッサ

repair
shūri
修理

repair delay time
shūri chien jikan
修理遅延時間

repair time
shūri jikan
修理時間

repairable
kashūri
可修理

repeat (*noun*)
hampuku; kurikaeshi
反復；繰り返し

repeat (*verb*)
kurikaesu
繰り返す

repeat count
hampukusū
反復数

repeat counter
kurikaeshi kaunta
繰り返しカウンタ

repeat function
kurikaeshi kinō
繰り返し機能

repeat instruction
kurikaeshi meirei
繰り返し命令

repeat operation
kurikaeshi enzan; kurikaeshi sōsa
繰り返し演算；繰り返し操作

repeatability
kurikaeshisei; saigensei
繰り返し性；再現性

repeating group
kurikaeshi shūdan
繰り返し集団

repeating item
kurikaeshi kōmoku
繰り返し項目

repetition
hampuku; kurikaeshi
反復；繰り返し

repetition instruction
hampuku meirei;
kurikaeshi meirei
反復命令；繰り返し命令

repetitive
hampuku; kurikaeshi
反復；繰り返し

repetitive operation
kurikaeshi enzan; kurikaeshi sōsa
繰り返し演算；繰り返し操作

replace
okikaeru; torikaeru
置き換える；取り替える

replacement
okikae; torikae
置き換え；取り替え

replacement problem
torikae mondai
取り替え問題

report
hōkoku(sho); ripōto
報告(書)；リポート

report description form
hōkokusho kijutsu yōshi
報告書記述用紙

report file
hōkoku fuairu
報告ファイル

report generation
hōkokusho sakusei
報告書作成

report generator
hōkokusho sakusei puroguramu
報告書作成プログラム

report layout
hōkokusho no yōshiki
報告書の様式

report program
ripōto-puroguramu
リポート・プログラム

report program generator (RPG)
hōkokusho sakusei puroguramu;
ripōto-puroguramu-zenerēta
(RPG)
報告書作成プログラム・
リポート・プログラム・
ゼネレータ

report section
hōkokusho setsu
報告書節

report writer feature
hōkokusho sakusei kinō
報告書作成機能

representation
hyōgen; hyōji; hyōki
表現；表示；表記

reproduce
fukusei suru; fukusha suru
複製する；複写する

reproducing punch
fukusha senkōki
複写せん孔機

reprogrammability
saipuroguramuka
再プログラム化

reprogrammable
saipuroguramukanō
再プログラム可能

request
yōkyū; shiyōkyū
要求；旨要求

request repeat system
saisōteisei hōshiki
再送訂正方式

request repeat system by interference detection
bōgai kenshutsu saisōteisei hōshiki
妨害検出再送訂正方式

request repeat system with error-detecting code
kenshutsu fugō saisōteisei hōshiki
検出符号再送訂正方式

request to send
sōshin yōkyū
送信要求

requesting
shiyōkyū; yōkyū
旨要求；要求

requesting terminal
shiyōkyū tanmatsu sōchi
旨要求端末装置

requirement(s)
yōken; yōkyū
要件；要求

requirements analysis
yōkyū bunseki
要求分析

requirements definition
yōkyū teigi
要求定義

requirements engineering
yōkyū teigi gijutsu
要求定義技術

requirements language
yōkyū gengo
要求言語

requirements specification
yōkyū shiyō
要求仕様

reread
saiyomitori
再読み取り

rerouting
keiro saishitei
経路再指定

rerun
riran; saijikkō
リラン；再実行

rerun point
saijikkōten; riran-pointo
再実行点；リラン・ポイント

rerun routine
saijikkō rūchin
再実行ルーチン

rescue dump
resukyū-danpu
レスキュー・ダンプ

rescue point
saikaiten
再開点

research
kenkyū
研究

reserve (*verb*)
yoyaku suru
予約する

reserved word
yoyaku go
予約語

reset
risetto (suru)
リセット（する）

reset key
risetto-kii
リセット・キー

reset pulse
risetto-parusu
リセット・パルス

resident
jōchū
常駐

resident area
jōchū iki
常駐域

resident control program
jōchū seigyo puroguramu
常駐制御プログラム

resident element
jōchū eremento
常駐エレメント

resident loader
jōchū rōda
常駐ローダ

resident module
jōchū mojyūru
常駐モジュール

resident routine
jōchū rūchin
常駐ルーチン

resident supervisor program
jōchū kanshi puroguramu
常駐監視プログラム

residual
minogashi
見逃し

residual error
minogashi ayamari
見逃し誤り

residual error rate
minogashi ayamari ritsu
見逃し誤り率

residue
jōyo
剰余

residue check
jōyo kensa
剰余検査

resistor
teikō
抵抗

resistor transistor logic (RTL)
teikō toranjisuta ronri (RTL)
抵抗トランジスタ論理

resolution
bunkainō; kaizōdo
分解能；解像度

resource
shigen
資源

resource allocation
shigen haibun
資源配分

resource allocation in multiple-project scheduling (RAMPS)
ranpusu (RAMPS)
ランプス

resource management
shigen kanri
資源管理

resource planning
shigen keikaku
資源計画

resource sharing
shigen kyōyō
資源共用

response
ōtō
応答

response time
ōtō jikan
応答時間

restart
saikaishi; saishidō
再開始；再始動

restart conditions
saishidō jōken
再始動条件

restart instruction
saishidō meirei
再始動命令

restore
fukugen suru
復元する

restrict
seigen suru
制限する

restricted use
gentei shiyō
限定使用

restriction
seigen
制限

restructuring
saikōsei
再構成

restructuring technique
saikōsei gijutsu
再構成技術

result
kekka
結果

resume transmission
sōshin o zokkō suru
送信を続行する

retention period
hozon kikan
保存期間

retransmission
saisō
再送

retrieval
kensaku
検索

retrieval function
kensaku kinō
検索機能

retrieve
kensaku suru
検索する

retry
saishikō
再試行

return
fukki; modori
復帰；戻り

return address
modori adoresu
戻りアドレス

return-address instruction
modori adoresu meirei
戻りアドレス命令

return code
modori kōdo
戻りコード

return-code register
modori kōdo-rejisuta
戻りコード・レジスタ

return instruction
fukki meirei; modori meirei
復帰命令；戻り命令

return key
modori kii
戻りキー

return mechanism
fukki kikō
復帰機構

return to bias (RB)
RB hōshiki (RB)
RB方式

return-to-bias recording
RB kiroku; RB rekōdeingu
RB記録；RBレコーディング

return to zero (RZ)
RZ hōshiki; zero fukki;
zero modori
RZ方式；ゼロ復帰；ゼロ戻り

return-to-zero mark (RZM)
zero fukki māku;
zero modori māku (RZM)
ゼロ復帰マーク；
ゼロ戻りマーク

reusability
saishiyōkanōsei
再使用可能性

reusable
saishiyōkanō
再使用可能

reusable program
saishiyōkanō puroguramu
再使用可能プログラム

reusable routine
saishiyōkanō rūchin
再使用可能ルーチン

reverse
gyaku; ribāsu
逆；リバース

reverse channel
gyaku chaneru
逆チャネル

reverse direction
gyaku hōkō
逆方向

reverse-direction flow
gyaku hōkō no nagare
逆方向の流れ

reverse indicator
ribāsu hyōji
リバース表示

reverse operation
gyaku sōsa
逆操作

reverse Polish (RP)
gyaku Pōrando kihō (RP)
逆ポーランド記法

reverse video
ribāsu-bideo
リバース・ビデオ

reverse voltage
gyaku den'atsu
逆電圧

reversibility
kagyakusei
可逆性

reversible
kagyaku(sei)
可逆（性）

reversible counter
kagyaku kaunta; ryōhōkō kaunta
可逆カウンタ；両方向カウンタ

revise
kaitei suru
改訂する

revised
kaitei
改訂

revision
kaitei
改訂

revision number
kaitei bangō
改訂番号

rewind (*noun*)
makimodoshi
巻戻し

rewind (*verb*)
makimodosu
巻戻す

rewind time
makimodoshi jikan
巻戻し時間

rewrite (*verb*)
saikakikomi
再書き込み

ribbon
ribon
リボン

ribbon cable
ribon-kēburu
リボン・ケーブル

right justify
migi tsume; migi yose
右詰め；右寄せ

right shift
migi shifuto
右シフト

ring counter
kanjō keisūki; ringu-kaunta
環状計数機；リング・カウンタ

ring network
ringu-nettowāku
リング・ネットワーク

ring shift
junkan keta idō; ringu-shifuto
循環桁移動；リング・シフト

ring structure
kanjō kōzō; ringu kōzō
環状構造；リング構造

ripple
hakyū
波及

rise time
tachiagari jikan
立ち上り時間

RJE (remote job entry)
RJE (enkaku jyobu nyūryoku)
遠隔ジョブ入力

RMS (recovery management support)
RMS (kaifuku kanri sapōto)
回復管理サポート

RO (read-only)
RO (yomidashi sen'yō; yomitori sen'yō)
読み出し専用；読み取り専用

rod memory
roddo-memori
ロッド・メモリ

rogue value
rōgu chi
ローグ値

role
yakuwari
役割り

role indicator
kinō hyōjishi
機能表示子

role name
yakumemei
役目名

roll back
rōru-bakku
ロール・バック

roll in
rōru-in
ロール・イン

roll out
rōru-auto
ロール・アウト

roll paper feed
rōru yōshi okuri
ロール用紙送り

roll paper feeder
rōru yōshi okuri kikō
ロール用紙送り機構

ROM (read-only memory)
ROM (kotei kioku; rōmu; yomidashi sen'yō kioku; yomitori sen'yō kioku)
固定記憶；ローム；
読み出し専用記憶；
読み取り専用記憶

ROM cartridge
ROM kātorijji
ROMカートリッジ

roman character
rōmaji
ローマ字

root phase
rūto-fuēzu
ルート・フェーズ

root segment
rūto-segumento
ルート・セグメント

ROS (read-only storage)
ROS (kotei kioku; yomidashi sen'yō kioku; yomitori sen'yō kioku)
固定記憶；読み出し専用記憶；
読み取り専用記憶

rotate
kaiten suru
回転する

rotation
kaiten
回転

round down (*verb*)
kirisuteru
切り捨てる

round off (*verb*)
marumeru
丸める

round-off error
marume gosa
丸め誤差

round up (*verb*)
kiriageru
切り上げる

rounding
marume
丸め

rounding down
kirisute
切り捨て

rounding error
marume gosa
丸め誤差

rounding off
marume
丸め

rounding up
kiriage
切り上げ

route
keiro
経路

routine
rūchin; tejun
ルーチン；手順

routine maintenance
rūchin hoshu
ルーチン保守

routine name
tejun mei
手順名

routing
keiro sentaku; keiro shitei
経路選択；経路指定

routing control (RTC)
keiro seigyo (RTC)
経路制御

row
gyō
行

row-binary card
gyō nishin kādo
行 2 進カード

row-by-row reading
yokoyomi
横読み

RP (reverse Polish)
RP (gyaku Pōrando kihō)
逆ポーランド記法

RPG (report program generator)
RPG (hōkokusho sakusei
puroguramu; ripōto-
puroguramu-zenerēta)
報告書作成プログラム；
リポート・プログラム・
ゼネレータ

RS (record separator)
RS (rekōdo bunri moji)
レコード分離文字

RTC (real-time clock)
RTC (jitsu jikan tokei; riaru-
taimu-kurokku)
実時間時計；
リアル・タイム・クロック

RTC (routing control)
RTC (keiro seigyo)
経路制御

RTL (resistor transistor logic)
RTL (teikō toranjisuta ronri)
抵抗トランジスタ論理

run
jikkō; ran; unten
実行；ラン；運転

run chart
jikkō nagarezu; ran-chāto
実行流れ図；ラン・チャート

run duration
jikkō jikan
実行時間

run phase
jikkō dankai
実行段階

run stream
ran-sutoriimu
ラン・ストリーム

run-time
jikkōji; ran-taimu
実行時；ラン・タイム

run-time error
jikkōji ayamari; ran-taimu-erā
実行時誤り；
ラン・タイム・エラー

run-time software
jikkōji sofutouea
実行時ソフトウェア

run-time statistics
jikkōji tōkei
実行時統計

run-time system
jikkōji shisutemu;
ran-taimu-shisutemu
実行時システム；
ラン・タイム・システム

run timer
ran-taima
ラン・タイマ

run-timer support package
ran-taima-sapōto-pakkēji
ラン・タイマ・サポート・
パッケージ

run unit
ran-yunitto
ラン・ユニット

running phase
jikkō dankai
実行段階

running state
jikkō jōtai
実行状態

running time
jikkō jikan
実行時間

running-time counter
jikkō jikan kaunta
実行時間カウンタ

R-W (read-write)
R-W (yomikaki; yomitori
kakikomi)
読み書き；読み取り書き込み

RZ (return to zero)
RZ (RZ hōshiki; zero fukki; zero
modori)
RZ 方式；ゼロ復帰；ゼロ戻り

RZM (return-to-zero mark)
RZM (zero fukki māku; zero
modori māku)
ゼロ復帰マーク；
ゼロ戻りマーク

RZM method
RZM hōshiki
RZM 方式

S

s (second)
s (byō)
秒

s-earth
shingō'yō setchi; tsūshin'yō āsu
信号用接地；通信用アース

safe
anzen (na)
安全（な）

safe design
anzen sekkei
安全設計

safe environment
anzen kankyō
安全環境

safety
anzen
安全

safety analysis
anzen kaiseki
安全解析

safety control
anzen seigyo
安全制御

safety control system
anzen seigyo shisutemu
安全制御システム

safety device
anzen sōchi
安全装置

safety function
anzen kinō
安全機能

safety mechanism
anzen kikō
安全機構

safety optimization
anzen saitekika
安全最適化

safety signal
anzen shingō
安全信号

safety stock
anzen zaiko
安全在庫

safety system
anzen shisutemu
安全システム

sag
sagu
サグ

SAI (subarchitecture interface)
SAI (sabu-ākitekucha-intafuēsu)
サブ・アーキテクチャ・
インタフェース

SAM (sequential-access method)
SAM (junji akusesu hōshiki)
順次アクセス方式

sample
hyōhon; sanpuru
標本；サンプル

sample and hold (S/H)
hyōhon oyobi hoji (S/H)
標本及び保持

sample hold
hyōhon hoji
標本保持

sample mean
hyōhon heikin
標本平均

sampled data control
sanpuruchi dēta seigyo
サンプル値データ制御

sampled value
hyōhonchi
標本値

sampling
hyōhonka; sanpuringu
標本化；サンプリング

sampling circuit
hyōhonka kairo
標本化回路

sampling frequency
hyōhonka shūhasū
標本化周波数

sampling period
sanpuringu shūki
サンプリング周期

sampling pulse
hyōhonka parusu
標本化パルス

sampling rate
hyōhonka ritsu
標本化率

satellite
eisei; sateraito
衛星；サテライト

satellite communication
eisei tsūshin
衛星通信

satellite computer
eisei keisanki; sateraito-konpyūta
衛星計算機；
サテライト・コンピュータ

satellite processor
eisei shori sōchi;
sateraito-purosessa
衛星処理装置；
サテライト・プロセッサ

satellite station
sateraito-sutēshon
サテライト・ステーション

satellite system
sateraito-shisutemu
サテライト・システム

saturated
hōwagata
飽和型

saturation
hōwa
飽和

save area
hokan'iki
保管域

SAW (surface acoustic waves)
SAW (hyōmen danseiha)
表面弾性波

sawtooth pulse
nokogirigata parusu
のこぎり型パルス

SBASIC (Structured BASIC)
SBASIC (Sutorakuchādo-Bēshikku)
ストラクチャード・ベーシック

SBC (single-board computer)
SBC (shinguru-bōdo-konpyūta)
シングル・ボード・コンピュータ

scale
kibo; kijunka; kuraidori; sukēru
規模；基準化；位取り；スケール

scale factor
bai ritsu; kijunka insū
倍率; 基準化因数

scale modifier
sukēru henkōshi
スケール変更子

scaling
kijunka; kuraidori
基準化; 位取り

scan (*noun*)
sōsa
走査

scan (*verb*)
sōsa suru
走査する

scan method
sōsa hōhō
走査方法

scan table
sōsa tēburu
走査テーブル

scanner
sōsa kikō; sōsaki; sukyāna
走査機構; 走査器; スキャーナ

scanning
sōsa
走査

scanning operation
sōsa sōsa
走査操作

scanning rate
sōsa sokudo
走査速度

scanning spot
sōsasen
走査線

scanning time
sōsa jikan
走査時間

scatter
bunsan
分散

scatter-load
bunsan rōdo
分散ロード

scatter-read
bunsan yomitori
分散読み取り

schedule
keikaku; sukejyūru; yotei
計画; スケジュール; 予定

scheduled
keikaku
計画

scheduled maintenance
keikaku hoshu
計画保守

scheduler
sukejyūra
スケジューラ

scheduling
sukejyūringu
スケジューリング

scheduling algorithm
sukejyūringu-arugorizumu
スケジューリング・アルゴリズム

scheduling model
sukejyūringu-moderu
スケジューリング・モデル

schema
gairyaku; sukiima
概略; スキーマ

schema chart
koyū dēta kōzō kijutsuzu;
sukiima zu
固有データ構造記述図;
スキーマ図

schema entry
koyū dēta kōzō kijutsukō;
sukiima kō
固有データ構造記述項;
スキーマ項

schema name
koyū dēta kōzō kijutsumei;
sukiima mei
固有データ構造記述名;
スキーマ名

schematic
gairyaku
概略

Schmitt circuit
Shumitto kairo
シュミット回路

Schmitt trigger circuit
Shumitto-toriga kairo
シュミット・トリガ回路

Schottky diode
Shottokii-daiōdo
ショットキー・ダイオード

Schottky transistor logic (STL)
Shottokii-toranjisuta ronri (STL)
ショットキー・トランジスタ論理

scientific calculation
kagaku keisan
科学計算

scientific computer
kagaku'yō keisanki
科学用計算機

scientific data processing
kagakuteki dēta shori
科学的データ処理

scientific information system
kagakuteki jōhō shisutemu
科学的情報システム

scientific instruction set
kagaku keisan meirei setto
科学計算命令セット

scientific language
kagaku'yō gengo
科学用言語

scientific management
kagakuteki kanri
科学的管理

scientific system
kagaku'yō shisutemu
科学用システム

scope
yūkō han'i
有効範囲

SCR (sequence control register)
SCR (chikuji seigyo rejisuta)
逐次制御レジスタ

scrambling
sukuranburingu
スクランブリング

scratch file
sukuratchi-fuairu
スクラッチ・ファイル

scratch pad
sukuratchi-paddo
スクラッチ・パッド

scratch pad memory
sukuratchi-paddo-memori
スクラッチ・パッド・メモリ

scratch tape
sukuratchi-tēpu
スクラッチ・テープ

screen
hyōji gamen; hyōjimen; sukuriin
表示画面；表示面；スクリーン

screen dump
sukuriin-danpu
スクリーン・ダンプ

screen editor
sukuriin-edeita
スクリーン・エディタ

screen turtle
sukuriin-tātaru
スクリーン・タータル

screening
sukuriiningu
スクリーニング

screening test
sukuriiningu-tesuto
スクリーニング・テスト

scroll
gamen idō; sukurōru
画面移動；スクロール

scrolling
gamen idō; sukōringu
画面移動；スコーリング

SCW (segment control word)
SCW (segumento seigyo go)
セグメント制御語

SD (single density)
SD (ichi mitsudo)
一密度

SDDL (stored-data definition language)
SDDL (kakunō dēta teigi gengo)
格納データ定義言語

SDI (selective dissemination of information)
SDI (jōhō no sentaku haifu)
情報の選択配布

SDLC (synchronous data link control)
SDLC (dōkishiki dēta-rinku seigyo)
同期式データ・リンク制御

SE (systems engineer)
SE (shisutemu-enjinia)
システム・エンジニア

search
tansaku
探索

search argument
tansaku insū
探索引数

search cycle
tansaku shūki
探索周期

search key
tansaku kii
探索キー

search-key lock
tansaku kii-rokku
探索キー・ロック

search memory
rensō kioku
連想記憶

search method
tansaku hōhō
探索方法

search strategy
tansaku senryaku
探索戦略

search time
tansaku jikan
探索時間

searching
tansaku
探索

seasonal variation
kisetsu hendō
季節変動

second (s)
byō (s); daini
秒；第二；第2

second-generation computer
daini sedai keisanki
第二世代計算機

second-order subroutine
niji saburūchin
二次サブルーチン

secondary
dainikai no; fuku; hojo; niji
第二階の；副；補助；二次

secondary index organization
niji sakuin hensei
二次索引編成

secondary indicator
hojo hyōjishi
補助表示子

secondary-level definition
dainikai no teigi
第二階の定義

secondary memory
hojo kioku
補助記憶

secondary reference tape
fuku hyōjun tēpu
副標準テープ

secondary source
sekando-sōsu
セカンド・ソース

secondary station
niji kyoku
二次局

secondary storage
hojo kioku; niji kioku
補助記憶；二次記憶

secondary store
hojo kioku sōchi; niji kioku sōchi
補助記憶装置；二次記憶装置

section
bu; sekushon; setsu
部；セクション；節

section header
sekushon midashi
セクション見出し

section name
sekushon mei
セクション名

sector
sekuta
セクタ

sector address
sekuta-adoresu
セクタ・アドレス

sector mode
sekuta-mōdo
セクタ・モード

sector queuing
sekuta machigyōretsu
セクタ待ち行列

183

sectoring
sekutoringu
セクトリング

security
kimitsu hogo
機密保護

security class
kimitsu no dankai
機密の段階

security protection
kimitsu hoji
機密保持

seek
motomeru; shiiku
求める；シーク

seek area
shiiku ryō'iki
シーク領域

seek separation
shiiku bunri
シーク分離

seek time
shiiku jikan
シーク時間

segment
bubun; kubun; segumento
部分；区分；セグメント

segment control word (SCW)
segumento seigyo go (SCW)
セグメント制御語

segment name
kubun mei; segumento mei
区分名；セグメント名

segment number
kubun bangō; segumento bangō
区分番号；セグメント番号

segment search argument (SSA)
segumento tansaku insū (SSA)
セグメント探索引数

segmentation
segumentēshon
セグメンテーション

segmented program
kubun puroguramu;
segumento-puroguramu
区分プログラム；
セグメント・プログラム

seizing signal
kidō shingō
起動信号

select (*verb*)
sembetsu suru; sentaku suru;
sentei suru
選別する；選択する；選定する

select receive
jushin sentaku
受信選択

select transmit
sōshin sentaku
送信選択

selecting
sembetsu; sentaku; sentei; shitei
選別；選択；選定；指定

selecting ability
sentaku kinō; serekuteingu kinō
選択機能；セレクティング機能

selection
sembetsu; sentaku; sentei
選別；選択；選定

selection check
sentaku kensa
選択検査

selection control
sentaku seigyo
選択制御

selection sort
sentakuhō bunrui
選択法分類

selection switch
sembetsu suitchi; sentaku suitchi
選別スイッチ；選択スイッチ

selective
sembetsu; sentaku(teki); shitei
選別；選択(的)；指定

selective calling
sentaku yobidashi
選択呼び出し

selective dissemination of information (SDI)
jōhō no sentaku haifu (SDI)
情報の選択配布

selective dump
shitei'iki danpu
指定域ダンプ

selective information retrieval (SIR)
sentakuteki jōhō kensaku (SIR)
選択的情報検索

selective listing
sentaku sahyō
選択作表

selective search
sentakuteki tansaku
選択的探索

selective stacker
sembetsu sutakka
選別スタッカ

selective trace
sentakuteki tsuiseki
選択的追跡

selectivity
sentakusei
選択性

selector
serekuta
セレクタ

selector channel
sentaku chaneru;
serekuta-chaneru
選択チャネル；
セレクタ・チャネル

self-actuated
jiryoku
自力

self-adapting
jiko tekiō
自己適応

self-adjusting
jiko chōsei
自己調整

self-checking
jiko kensa
自己検査

self-checking code
jiko kensa kōdo
自己検査コード

self-checking number
jiko kensa bangō
自己検査番号

self-checking number generator
jiko kensa bangō hassei kikō
自己検査番号発生機構

self-checking numeral
jiko kensa bangō
自己検査番号

self-checking system
jiko kensa hōshiki
自己検査方式

self-correcting
jiko teisei
自己訂正

self-correcting system
jiko teisei hōshiki
自己訂正方式

self-defining
jiko teigi
自己定義

self-defining term
jiko teigi kō
自己定義項

self-defining value
jiko teigi chi
自己定義値

self-describing
jiko kijutsu
自己記述

self-description
jiko kijutsusei
自己記述性

self-diagnosis
jiko shindan
自己診断

self-diagnostics
jiko shindan
自己診断

self-embedding
jiko umekomi
自己埋め込み

self-initialize
jiko shokika
自己初期化

self-load
jiko yomikomi
自己読み込み

self-loading
jiko rōdeingu
自己ローディング

self-maintenance
jiko hozen; jiko iji
自己保全；自己維持

self-maintaining
jiko iji
自己維持

self-monitoring
jiko kanshi
自己監視

self-operating
jiryoku
自力

self-organizing
jiko hensei
自己編成

self-organizing system
jiko hensei shisutemu
自己編成システム

self-regulating
jiko chōsei
自己調整

self-regulating system
jiko chōsei shisutemu
自己調整システム

self-relative address
jiko sōtai adoresu
自己相対アドレス

self-relative addressing
jiko sōtai adoresu shitei
自己相対アドレス指定

self-relocatable
jiko saihaichikanō
自己再配置可能

self-relocation
jiko saihaichi
自己再配置

self-repair
jiko shūfuku
自己修復

self-resetting loop
jiko risetto-rūpu
自己リセット・ループ

self-stabilization
jiko anteika
自己安定化

self-triggering program
jiko shidō puroguramu
自己始動プログラム

self-tuning
jiko dōchō
自己同調

semantic
imi(teki); imiron(teki);
semanteikku
意味(的)；意味論(的)；
セマンティック

semantic analysis
imironteki kaiseki
意味論的解析

semantic data independence
imiteki dēta dokuritsusei
意味的データ独立性

semantic evaluation
imironteki hyōka
意味論的評価

semantic generation
imi seisei
意味生成

semantic matrix
semanteikku-matorikkusu
セマンティック・マトリックス

semantic memory
imi memori
意味メモリ

semantic net
imi ketsugōmō
意味結合網

semantic preference
imijō no senkō
意味上の選好

semantic representation
imironteki hyōgen
意味論的表現

semantics
imi; imiron; semanteikkusu
意味；意味論；
セマンティックス

semaphore
udegi shingō
腕木信号

semiautomatic
hanjidō
半自動

semiautomatic control
hanjidō seigyo
半自動制御

semiautomatic switching center
hanjidō kōkan kyoku
半自動交換局

185

semiconductor
handōtai
半導体

semiconductor integrated circuit (SIC)
handōtai shūseki kairo (SIC)
半導体集積回路

semiconductor memory
handōtai kioku
半導体記憶

semiconductor rectifier
handōtai seiryūki
半導体整流器

send
hasshin suru; okuridasu;
sōshin suru
発信する；送り出す；送信する

sender
hasshinsha
発信者

sending
hasshin; okuridashi; sōshin
発信；送り出し；送信

sending terminal
hasshin tanmatsu (sōchi)
発信端末（装置）

sense (*verb*)
kenshutsu suru; sensu suru
検出する；センスする

sense amplifier
sensu-anpu; sensu zōfukuki
センス・アンプ；センス増幅器

sense byte
sensu-baito
センス・バイト

sense data
sensu-dēta
センス・データ

sense line
yomidashi sen
読み出し線

sense station
sensu kikō
センス機構

sense switch
sensu-suitchi
センス・スイッチ

sense wire
sensu-waiya
センス・ワイヤ

sensitivity
kando
感度

sensor
kenshutsuki; sensa
検出器；センサ

sensor-based computer
sensa-bēsu keisanki
センサ・ベース計算機

sentinel
hyōji; hyōshiki; mihari
表示；標識；見張り

separate (*verb*)
bunri suru
分離する

separate assembly
kobetsu asenburi
個別アセンブリ

separate compilation
bunri konpairēshon
分離コンパイレーション

separation
bunri
分離

separator
bunri fugō; bunri kigō; bunri moji
分離符号；分離記号；分離文字

septet
nanabitto-baito
7ビット・バイト

sequence
bunrui; chikuji; ichiren; jun;
junjo; shiikensu
分類；逐次；一連；順；
順序；シーケンス

sequence check
junjo kensa
順序検査

sequence checking
junjo kensa
順序検査

sequence code
junjo kōdo
順序コード

sequence control
chikuji seigyo; junjo seigyo
逐次制御；順序制御

sequence control counter
chikuji seigyo keisūki
逐次制御計数器

sequence control register (SCR)
chikuji seigyo rejisuta (SCR)
逐次制御レジスタ

sequence error
junjo ayamari
順序誤り

sequence number
ichiren bangō; tōshi bangō
一連番号；通し番号

sequencer
shiikensa
シーケンサ

sequencing
jun'itsuke; junjotsuke
順位付け；順序付け

sequencing key
jun'itsuke kii
順位付けキー

sequential
chikuji; jun; junji; junjo
逐次；順；順次；順序

sequential access
jun(ji) akusesu; jun(ji) yobidashi
順(次)アクセス；
順(次)呼び出し

sequential-access disk
jun(ji) akusesu-deisuku
順(次)アクセス・ディスク

sequential-access file
jun(ji) akusesu-fuairu
順(次)アクセス・ファイル

sequential-access memory
chikuji akusesu kioku;
jun(ji) akusesu kioku
逐次アクセス記憶；
順(次)アクセス記憶

sequential-access method (SAM)
jun(ji) akusesu hōshiki (SAM)
順(次)アクセス方式

sequential-access storage
jun(ji) akusesu kioku
順(次)アクセス記憶

sequential addressing
jun(ji) adoresu shitei
順(次)アドレス指定

sequential circuit
junjo kairo
順序回路

sequential computer
junji shori keisanki
順次処理計算機

sequential control
chikuji seigyo; junji seigyo
逐次制御; 順次制御

sequential data set
jun(ji) dēta-setto
順(次)データ・セット

sequential file
chikuji hensei fuairu;
jun(ji) hensei fuairu
逐次編成ファイル;
順(次)編成ファイル

sequential flow
jun nagare
順流れ

sequential list
jun risuto
順リスト

sequential list structure
jun risuto kōzō
順リスト構造

sequential logic
junjo ronri
順序論理

sequential logic element
junjo ronri soshi
順序論理素子

sequential logical circuit
junjo ronri kairo
順序論理回路

sequential operation
junji dōsa
順次動作

sequential processing
chikuji shori
逐次処理

sequential programming
chikuji puroguramingu
逐次プログラミング

sequential retrieval
junji kensaku
順次検索

sequential scheduler
chikuji sukejyūra; junji sukejyūra
逐次スケジューラ;
順次スケジューラ

sequential scheduling
chikuji sukejyūringu;
junji sukejyūringu
逐次スケジューリング;
順次スケジューリング

sequential scheduling system
chikuji sukejyūringu-shisutemu;
junji sukejyūringu-shisutemu
逐次スケジューリング・
システム;
順次スケジューリング・システム

sequential structure
jun kōzō
順構造

sequential-type transmission
chikujidōsagata densō
逐次動作型伝送

serial
chikuji; chokuretsu; renzoku;
shiriaru
逐次; 直列; 連続; シリアル

serial access
chokuretsu akusesu;
chikuji akusesu
直列アクセス; 逐次アクセス

serial-access file
chikuji akusesu-fuairu;
chokuretsu akusesu-fuairu
逐次アクセス・ファイル;
直列アクセス・ファイル

serial-access memory; serial-access storage
chikuji akusesu kioku;
chokuretsu akusesu kioku
逐次アクセス記憶;
直列アクセス記憶

serial arithmetic
chokuretsu enzan
直列演算

serial code
chokuretsu kōdo; tōshi kōdo
直列コード; 通しコード

serial computer
chokuretsushiki keisanki
直列式計算機

serial computer system
chokuretsushiki keisanki
shisutemu
直列式計算機システム

serial count
chokuretsu hōshiki kaunto
直列方式カウント

serial dot printer
shiriaru-dotto-purinta
シリアル・ドット・プリンタ

serial file processing
chikujishiki fuairu shori
逐次式ファイル処理

serial input/output interface (SIO)
chokuretsu nyūshutsuryoku
intafuēsu (SIO)
直列入出力インタフェース

serial number
ichiren bangō; renzokuban;
tōshi bangō
一連番号; 連続番; 通し番号

serial operation
chikuji sōsa; chokuretsu sōsa
逐次操作; 直列操作

serial organization
chokuretsu hensei
直列編成

serial-parallel addition
chokuheiretsu kasan
直並列加算

serial-parallel conversion
chokuheiretsu henkan
直並列変換

serial-parallel converter
chokuheiretsu henkan kairo
直並列変換回路

serial-parallel multiplication
chokuheiretsu jōzan
直並列乗算

serial printer
chikuji insho sōchi;
shiriaru-purinta
逐次印書装置;
シリアル・プリンタ

serial processing
chikuji shori
逐次処理

serial read
chikuji yomitori
逐次読み取り

serial read/punch
chikuji yomitori-senkōki
逐次読み取り-せん孔機

serial storage
chokuretsushiki kioku
直列式記憶

serial transfer
chokuretsu tensō
直列転送

serial transmission
chokuretsu densō
直列伝送

serialization
chokuretsuka
直列化

serialize
chokuretsuka suru
直列化する

serially reusable
chikuji saishiyōkanō
逐次再使用可能

serially reusable program
chikuji saishiyōkanō puroguramu
逐次再使用可能プログラム

serially reusable routine
chikuji saishiyōkanō rūchin
逐次再使用可能ルーチン

series
renzoku; shiriizu
連続；シリーズ

service bit
sābisu-bitto
サービス・ビット

service processor (SVP)
sābisu-purosessa (SVP)
サービス・プロセッサ

service program
sābisu-puroguramu
サービス・プログラム

service routine
sābisu-rūchin
サービス・ルーチン

service time
sābisu jikan
サービス時間

serviceability
shiyōkanōsei
使用可能性

serviceable
shiyōkanō
使用可能

serviceable time
shiyōkanō jikan
使用可能時間

servo
sābo
サーボ

servo integrator
sābo sekibunki
サーボ積分器

servo system
sābo-shisutemu
サーボ・システム

servomechanism
sābo kikō
サーボ機構

servomultiplier
sābo jōzanki
サーボ乗算器

session
sesshon
セッション

session control
sesshon seigyo
セッション制御

set (*noun*)
oyako shūgō; setto; shūgō
親子集合；セット；集合

set (*verb*)
settei suru; setto suru
設定する；セットする

set control key
setto seigyo kii
セット制御キー

set description
setto kijutsu
セット記述

set description entry
oyako shūgō kijutsukō;
setto kijutsukō
親子集合記述項；セット記述項

set entry
oyako shūgōkō
親子集合項

set identification
setto shikibetsu
セット識別

set identifier
setto shikibetsushi
セット識別子

set location counter
setto-rokēshon-kaunta
セット・ロケーション・カウンタ

set member
setto-menba
セット・メンバ

set membership
oyako kankei
親子関係

set name
setto mei
セット名

set occurrence
setto-okarensu
セット・オカレンス

set off (*verb*)
hassei suru
発生する

set operation
shūgō sōsa
集合操作

set-ordering criteria
oyako shūgō junjo kijun
親子集合順序基準

set owner
setto-ouna
セット・オウナ

set point
mokuhyōchi
目標値

set pulse
setto-parusu
セット・パルス

set section
oyako shūgō setsu; setto setsu
親子集合節；セット節

set selection
oyako shūgō sentaku
親子集合選択

set selection criteria
setto sentaku kijun
セット選択基準

set subentry
oyako shūgō fukukijutsukō
親子集合副記述項

set theory
shūgōron
集合論

setting
settei
設定

setup
setto-appu
セット・アップ

setup diagram
setto-appu-daiyaguramu
セット・アップ・ダイヤグラム

setup time
jumbi jikan; setto-appu jikan
準備時間；セット・アップ時間

seven-segment display
nana segumento-deisupurei
7セグメント・ディスプレィ

seven-track magnetic tape
nana torakku jiki tēpu
7トラック磁気テープ

sexadecimal
jūrokushin
16進

sexadecimal digit
jūrokushin sūji
16進数字

sexadecimal notation
jūrokushin hō
16進法

sexadecimal number
jūrokushin sū
16進数

sexadecimal numeral
jūrokushin sū
16進数

sextet
rokubitto-baito
6ビット・バイト

SG (signal ground)
SG (shingō'yō setchi; tsūshin'yō
āsu)
信号用接地；通信用アース

S/H (sample and hold)
S/H (hyōhon oyobi hoji)
標本及び保持

shading
in'ei
陰影

shadow printing
shadou insatsu
シャドウ印刷

shadow recording
shadou kiroku
シャドウ記録

shape
keijō
形状

shape code
keijō kōdo
形状コード

shape synthesis
keijō gōsei
形状合成

shape table
keijō tēburu
形状テーブル

shareable
kyōyōkanō
共用可能

shareable device
kyōyōkanō sōchi
共用可能装置

shared address
kyōyō adoresu
共用アドレス

shared control unit
kyōyō seigyo sōchi
共用制御装置

shared file
kyōyō fuairu
共用ファイル

shared input/output device
kyōyō nyūshutsuryoku sōchi
共用入出力装置

shared logic
kyōyō ronri
共用論理

shared main storage
kyōyō shu kioku
共用主記憶

shared memory
kyōyō kioku'iki
共用記憶域

shared processor
kyōyō purosessa
共用プロセッサ

shared resources
kyōyō shigen
共用資源

shared storage
kyōyō kioku
共用記憶

shared subchannel
kyōyō sabuchaneru
共用サブチャネル

shared system
kyōyō shisutemu
共用システム

shared terminal
kyōyō tanmatsu (sōchi)
共用端末（装置）

sheet
shiito; yōshi
ツート；用紙

sheet feeder
shiito-fuiida; yōshi okuri kikō
シート・フィーダ；
用紙送り機構

shift
idō; keta idō; keta okuri;
okuri; shifuto
移動；けた移動；けた送り；
送り；シフト

shift code
shifuto-kōdo
シフト・コード

shift count
keta idō sū; shifuto-kaunto
けた移動数；シフト・カウント

189

shift counter
keta idō kaunta; shifuto-kaunta
けた移動カウンタ;
シフト・カウンタ

shift-in (SI)
shifuto-in (SI)
シフト・イン

shift-in character (SI character)
shifuto-in moji (SI moji)
シフト・イン文字; SI文字

shift instruction
keta idō meirei
けた移動命令

shift key
shifuto-kii
シフト・キー

shift-out (SO)
shifuto-auto (SO)
シフト・アウト

shift-out character (SO character)
shifuto-auto moji (SO moji)
シフト・アウト文字; SO文字

shift pulse
shifuto-parusu
シフト・パルス

shift register
okuri rejisuta; shifuto-rejisuta
送りレジスタ; シフト・レジスタ

short block
tan burokku
短ブロック

short precision
tan seido
短精度

shortest route
saitan keiro
最短経路

shortest-route problem
saitan keiro mondai
最短経路問題

shutdown
shadan; unten teishi
遮断; 運転停止

SI (shift-in)
SI (shifuto-in)
シフト・イン

SI character (shift-in character)
SI moji (shifuto-in moji)
SI文字; シフト・イン文字

SIC (semiconductor integrated circuit)
SIC (handōtai shūseki kairo)
半導体集積回路

side effect
fukusayō
副作用

sideband
sokuhatai
側波帯

sight check
shikaku kensa;
shikaku senkō kensa
視覚検査; 視覚せん孔検査

sign
fugō; seifu fugō; shingō
符号; 正負符号; 信号

sign bit
fugō bitto
符号ビット

sign character
fugō moji
符号文字

sign condition
fugō jōken
符号条件

sign-control flip-flop
fugō seigyo furippu-furoppu
符号制御フリップ・フロップ

sign digit
fugō keta sūji
符号桁数字

sign magnitude
fugō zettaichi
符号絶対値

sign magnitude notation
fugō zettaichi hyōkihō
符号絶対値表記法

sign off
sain-ofu
サイン・オフ

sign on
sain-on
サイン・オン

sign position
fugō ichi; fugō keta
符号位置; 符号桁

sign propagation
fugō dempa
符号伝播

sign test
fugō tesuto
符号テスト

signal
shingō
信号

signal cable
shingōsen kēburu
信号線ケーブル

signal detection
shingō kenshutsu
信号検出

signal distance
shingō kyori
信号距離

signal ground (SG)
shingō'yō setchi; tsūshin'yō āsu (SG)
信号用接地; 通信用アース

signal level
shingō reberu
信号レベル

signal parameter
shingō parameta
信号パラメタ

signal quality detector
shingō hinshitsu kenshutsuki
信号品質検出器

signal recognition
shingō shikibetsu
信号識別

signal regeneration
shingō saisei
信号再生

signal-to-noise ratio (S/N)
shingō tai zatsuon hi (S/N)
信号対雑音比

signaling system
shingō hōshiki
信号方式

signed binary
fugōtsuki nishinsū
符号付き２進数

signed constant
fugōtsuki teisū
符号付き定数

signed field
fugōtsuki fuiirudo
符号付きフィールド

signed integer
fugōtsuki seisū
符号付き整数

signed term
fugōtsuki kō
符号付き項

significance
omomi; yūisei
重み；有意性

significance start character
yūkō keta kaishi moji
有効桁開始文字

significant
jōi no; yūi no; yūkō
上位の；有意の；有効

significant conditions
yūi jōtai
有意状態

significant data
jōi no dēta
上位のデータ

significant digit
yūkō sūji
有効数字

significant-digit arithmetic
yūkō sūji enzan
有効数字演算

significant error
yūi ayamari
有意誤り

significant event
yūi jishō
有意事象

significant figure
yūkō sūji
有効数字

significant instant
yūi shunkan
有意瞬間

significant interval
yūi kankaku
有意間隔

significant part
yūkō bubun
有効部分

silicon
shirikon
シリコン

silicon chip
shirikon-chippu
シリコン・チップ

silicon diode
shirikon-daiōdo
シリコン・ダイオード

silicon disk
shirikon-deisuku
シリコン・ディスク

silicon on sapphire (SOS)
shirikon-on-safuaia (SOS)
シリコン・オン・サファイア

silk-screening
shiruku-sukuriiningu
シルク・スクリーニング

simple absolute expression
tanjun zettai shiki
単純絶対式

simple arithmetic expression
tanjun enzan shiki
単純演算式

simple Boolean expression
tanjun ronrishiki
単純論理式

simple buffering
tanjun baffuaringu;
tanjun kanshō shuhō
単純バッファリング；
単純緩衝手法

simple condition
tanjun jōken
単純条件

simple conditional expression
tanjun jōken shiki
単純条件式

simple expression
tanjun shiki
単純式

simple name
tanjun mei
単純名

simple sequence structure
tanjun junjo kōzō
単純順序構造

simple statement
tanjun sutētomento
単純ステートメント

simple structure
tanjun kōzō
単純構造

simple system
tanjun shisutemu
単純システム

simple variable
tanjun hensū
単純変数

simplex
shinpurekkusu; tankō; tanshin
シンプレックス；単向；単信

simplex channel
tanshin tsūshinro
単信通信路

simplex circuit
tanshin kaisen
単信回線

simplex communication
tanshin tsūshin
単信通信

simplex communication system
tanshin tsūshin shisutemu
単信通信システム

simplex method
shinpurekkusu hōhō
シンプレックス方法

simplex operation
shinpurekkusu-operēshon
シンプレックス・オペレーション

simplex system
shinpurekkusu-shisutemu
シンプレックス・システム

simplex transmission
tanshin densō
単信伝送

simplification
tanjunka
単純化

simulate
shimyurēto suru
シミュレートする

simulated attention
shimyurēteddo-atenshon
シミュレーテッド・アテンション

simulation
shimyurēshon
シミュレーション

simulation executive
shimyurēshon-eguzekuteibu
シミュレーション・エグゼクティブ

simulation language
shimyurēshon gengo
シミュレーション言語

simulation model
shimyurēshon-moderu
シミュレーション・モデル

simulator
shimyurēta
シミュレータ

simulator program
shimyurēta-puroguramu
シミュレータ・プログラム

simulator routine
shimyurēta-rūchin
シミュレータ・ルーチン

simultaneity
dōjisei
同時性

simultaneous
dō; dōji
同; 同時

simultaneous access
dōji akusesu
同時アクセス

simultaneous carry
dōji keta age
同時桁上げ

simultaneous distribution of grouped messages
messēji-gurūpu dōhō
メッセージ・グループ同報

simultaneous distribution of messages
messēji dōhō
メッセージ同報

simultaneous distribution of single and grouped messages
messēji issei dōhō
メッセージ一斉同報

simultaneous distribution of single messages
kobetsu messēji dōhō
個別メッセージ同報

simultaneous DMA (simultaneous direct memory access)
dōji DMA
同時DMA

simultaneous operation
dōji sōsa
同時操作

simultaneous processing
dōji shori
同時処理

simultaneous search
dōji tansaku
同時探索

simultaneous transmission
dōji densō
同時伝送

single
kobetsu; shinguru; tan'itsu
個別; シングル; 単一

single-access mechanism
tan'itsu akusesu kikō
単一アクセス機構

single address
ichi adoresu; tan'itsu adoresu
1アドレス; 単一アドレス

single-address instruction
ichi adoresu meirei;
tan'itsu adoresu meirei
1アドレス命令;
単一アドレス命令

single-board computer (SBC)
shinguru-bōdo-konpyūta (SBC)
シングル・ボード・コンピュータ

single chip
ichi chippu
1チップ

single current
tanryū
単流

single-current transmission
tanryūshiki densō
単流式伝送

single density (SD)
ichi mitsudo (SD)
一密度

single-density disk
ichi mitsudo deisuku
一密度ディスク

single error
tan'itsu ayamari
単一誤り

single flexible disk drive
ichi furekishiburu-deisuku kudō kikō
一フレキシブル・
ディスク駆動機構

single-job scheduling
tan'itsu jyobu-sukejyūringu
単一ジョブ・スケジューリング

single precision
tanseido
単精度

single pulse
tan'itsu parusu
単一パルス

single reel
tan'itsu riiru
単一リール

single-shot operation
shinguru-shotto sōsa
シングル・ショット操作

single sideband (SSB)
tansoku hatai (SSB)
単側波帯

single-sideband modulation
tansoku hatai henchō
単側波帯変調

single-sideband transmission
tansoku hatai densō
単側波帯伝送

single-step operation
shinguru-suteppu sōsa
シングル・ステップ操作

single track
tan'itsu torakku
単一トラック

single unit
tan'itsu yunitto
単一ユニット

single-volume file
tan'itsu boryūmu-fuairu
単一ボリューム・ファイル

singular set
tan'itsu oyako shūgō
単一親子集合

singular value analysis
toku'i chi kaiseki
特異値解析

SIO (serial input/output interface)
SIO (chokuretsu nyūshutsuryoku intafuēsu)
直列入出力インタフェース

SIR (selective information retrieval)
SIR (sentakuteki jōhō kensaku)
選択的情報検索

six-bit alphameric code
roku bitto eisūji kōdo
6ビット英数字コード

size
ōkisa; saizu
大きさ；サイズ

skeletal code
honegumi kōdo
骨組みコード

skeleton
honegumi
骨組み

skeleton structure diagram
katakōzō zu
型構造図

skew
sukyū
スキュー

skip
sukippu
スキップ

skip flag
sukippu hyōshiki
スキップ標識

skip instruction
sukippu meirei
スキップ命令

slack
asobi
遊び

slack byte
asobi baito
遊びバイト

slave tape unit
jūtēpu sōchi
従テープ装置

slice
suraisu
スライス

slice level
suraisu-reberu
スライス・レベル

slicer
suraisa
スライサ

slicing circuit
suraisu kairo
スライサ回路

slot
surotto
スロット

slow
teisoku(do)
低速（度）

slow response time
teisoku ōtō jikan
低速応答時間

small-scale integrated circuit (SSIC)
shō kibo shūseki kairo (SSIC)
小規模集積回路

small-scale integration (SSI)
shō kibo shūsekika (SSI)
小規模集積化

smart terminal
chinō tanmatsu (sōchi)
知能端末（装置）

smooth
heikatsu
平滑

smoothing
heikatsuka
平滑化

S/N (signal-to-noise ratio)
S/N (shingō tai zatsuon hi)
信号対雑音比

snapshot
sunappu-shotto
スナップ・ショット

snapshot display
sunappu-shotto-deisupurei
スナップ・ショット・ディスプレイ

snapshot dump
sunappu-shotto-danpu
スナップ・ショット・ダンプ

snapshot program
sunappu-shotto-puroguramu
スナップ・ショット・プログラム

SO (shift-out)
SO (shifuto-auto)
シフト・アウト

SO character (shift-out character)
SO moji (shifuto-auto moji)
SO文字；シフト・アウト文字

SOB (start of block)
SOB (burokku kaishi)
ブロック開始

soft copy
sofuto-kopii
ソフト・コピー

soft keyboard
sofuto-kiibōdo
ソフト・キーボード

soft-sectored
sofuto-sekuta
ソフト・セクタ

soft-sectored disk
sofuto-sekuta-deisuku
ソフト・セクタ・ディスク

soft-sectoring
sofuto-sekutoringu
ソフト・セクトリング

soft system
sofuto-shisutemu
ソフト・ツステム

software
sofutouea
ソフトウェア

software control
sofutouea seigyo
ソフトウェア制御

software description
sofutouea kijutsu
ソフトウェア記述

193

software design
sofutouea sekkei
ソフトウェア設計

software development
sofutouea kaihatsu
ソフトウェア開発

software engineering
sofutouea kōgaku
ソフトウェア工学

software house
sofutouea-hausu
ソフトウェア・ハウス

software instrumentation
sofutouea keisoku
ソフトウェア計測

software integration
sofutouea tōgō
ソフトウェア統合

software integration test
sofutouea tōgō tesuto
ソフトウェア統合テスト

software maintenance
sofutouea hoshu
ソフトウェア保守

software measurement
sofutouea sokutei
ソフトウェア測定

software package
sofutouea-pakkēji
ソフトウェア・パッケージ

software science
sofutouea kagaku
ソフトウェア科学

software system
sofutouea-shisutemu
ソフトウェア・システム

software tool
sofutouea-tsūru
ソフトウェア・ツール

SOH (start of heading)
SOH (heddeingu kaishi)
ヘッディング開始

solicited key-in
ōtōgata kii-in
応答型キー・イン

solid-logic technology
kotai ronri gijutsu
固体論理技術

solid-state circuit
kotai kairo
固体回路

solid-state component
kotai soshi
固体素子

solid-state computer
kotai kairo keisanki
固体回路計算機

solid-state device
kotai sōchi
固体装置

solution
kaiketsu
解決

sonic delay line
chō'ompa chiensen
超音波遅延線

SOP (standard operating procedure)
SOP (hyōjun sōsa tejun)
標準操作手順

sort (noun)
bunrui; jun'i; sōto
分類；順位；ソート

sort (verb)
bunrui suru; sōto suru
分類する；ソートする

sort blocking factor
bunrui burokkuka insū
分類ブロック化因数

sort control item
jun'i seigyo kōmoku
順位制御項目

sort control key
jun'i seigyo kii
順位制御キー

sort key
bunrui kii
分類キー

sort-merge
bunrui-kumiawase
分類-組み合わせ

sort-merge program
bunrui-kumiawase puroguramu
分類-組み合わせプログラム

sort operation
bunrui sōsa
分類操作

sort program
bunrui puroguramu;
sōto-puroguramu
分類プログラム；
ソート・プログラム

sort utility
sōto-yūteiritei
ソート・ユーティリティ

sorted file
bunruizumi fuairu
分類済みファイル

sorter
bunruiki; sōta
分類機；ソータ

sorting
bunrui
分類

sorting utility
bunrui yūteiritei
分類ユーティリティ

SOS (silicon on sapphire)
SOS (shirikon-on-safuaia)
シリコン・オン・サファイア

sound board
saundo-bōdo
サウンド・ボード

sound synthesizer
oto gōseiki
音合成器

source
genshi; sōsu
原始；ソース

source card
genshi kādo
原始カード

source code
genshi kōdo; sōsu-kōdo
原始コード；ソース・コード

source coding
genshi kōdeingu
原始コーディング

source computer
genshi konpyūta
原始コンピュータ

source control statement
genshi seigyo bun
原始制御文

source data
genshi dēta
原始データ

source deck
genshi dekku
原始デック

source document
genshi shorui
原始書類

source language
genshi gengo
原始言語

source library
genshi raiburari
原始ライブラリ

source module
genshi mojyūru
原始モジュール

source program
genshi puroguramu
原始プログラム

source record
genshi rekōdo
原始レコード

source recording
genshi rekōdo sakusei
原始レコード作成

source routine
genshi rūchin
原始ルーチン

source statement
genshi sutētomento
原始ステートメント

SP (space character)
SP (kankaku moji)
間隔文字

space
akiryō'iki; kankaku; kūkan;
supēsu
空き領域; 間隔; 空間; スペース

space allocation
akiryō'iki wariate
空き領域割り当て

space allocation routine
akiryō'iki wariate rūchin
空き領域割り当てルーチン

space area
akiryō'iki
空き領域

space character (SP)
kankaku moji (SP)
間隔文字

space extension
kūkan kakuchō
空間拡張

space key
supēsu-kii
スペース・キー

space sharing
kūkan bunkatsu
空間分割

spacing
kankaku
間隔

span
supan
スパン

spanned file
supando-fuairu
スパンド・ファイト

spanned record
supando-rekōdo
スパンド・レコード

spanning indicator
supan shijishi
スパン指示子

spare tape
yobi tēpu
予備テープ

sparse matrix
sogyōretsu; supāsu-matorikkusu
疎行列; スパース・マトリックス

special characters
tokushu moji
特殊文字

special control character
tokushu seigyo moji
特殊制御文字

special equipment
tokushu na sōchi
特殊な装置

special feature
tokushu kikō
特殊機構

special function
tokushu kinō
特殊機能

special line
tokusen
特線

special-purpose computer
sen'yō keisanki
専用計算機

special register
tokushu rejisuta
特殊レジスタ

**specially written program
(≠package)**
sen'yō puroguramu
専用プログラム

specific
tokutei; tokuyū
特定; 特有

specific address
tokuyū adoresu
特有アドレス

specific code
tokuyū kōdo
特有コード

specification
shitei; shiyō(gaki)
指定; 仕様（書き）

specification language
shiyō kijutsu gengo
仕様記述言語

specification sheet
shitei yōshi
指定用紙

specification statement
sengen bun
宣言文

specification subprogram
shoki chisettei fukupuroguramu
初期値設定副プログラム

speech
onsei
音声

speech generation
onsei hassei
音声発生

speech generation device
onsei hasseiki
音声発生器

speech processing
onsei shori
音声処理

speech recognition
onsei ninshiki
音声認識

speech synthesis
onsei gōsei
音声合成

speech synthesizer
onsei gōseiki
音声合成器

speech understanding
onsei rikai
音声理解

speed
sokudo
速度

speed enhancement
sokudo zōka
速度増加

speed enhancer
sokudo zōka kikō
速度増加機構

speed of input
nyūryoku sokudo
入力速度

speed of output
shutsuryoku sokudo
出力速度

speed range
sokudo haba; sokudo han'i
速度幅；速度範囲

splicer
suparaisa
スプライサ

splicing
suparaishingu
スプライシング

spline
supurain
スプライン

spline function
supurain kinō
スプライン機能

split (*verb*)
bunkatsu suru
分割する

split-control field
bunkatsu seigyo fuiirudo
分割制御フィールド

split-word operation
bubungo enzan
部分語演算

spool
supūru
スプール

spool-in
supūru-in
スプール・イン

spool-out
supūru-auto
スプール・アウト

spooling
supūringu
スプーリング

spot punch
supotto-panchi
スポット・パンチ

spreadsheet
kan'i
簡易

spreadsheet program
kan'i puroguramu
簡易プログラム

sprocket holes
okuri ana
送り孔

sputtering
supattaringu
スパッタリング

square wave
hōkeiha
方形波

SSA (segment search argument)
SSA (segumento tansaku insū)
セグメント探索引数

SSB (single sideband)
SSB (tansoku hatai)
単測波帯

SSI (small-scale integration)
SSI (shō kibo shūsekika)
小規模集積化

SSIC (small-scale integrated circuit)
SSIC (shō kibo shūseki kairo)
小規模集積回路

stability
anteido; anteisei
安定路；安定性

stable
anteisei
安定性

stack
sutakku
スタック

stack allocation
sutakku haibun
スタック配分

stack indicator
sutakku hyōjishi
スタック表示子

stack machine
sutakku kikai
スタック機械

stack pointer
sutakku-pointa
スタック・ボインタ

stacked job processing
renzokushiki jyobu shori
連続式ジョブ処理

stacked memory
sutakku-memori
スタック・メモリ

stacker
sutakka
スタッカ

staircase
kaidanha
階段波

stall
kinō teishi
機能停止

stand-alone
dokuritsu(gata)
独立(型)

stand-alone computer
dokuritsu(gata) keisanki
独立(型)計算機

stand-alone console
dokuritsu(gata) sōsataku
独立(型)操作卓

stand-alone machine
dokuritsu(gata) kikai
独立(型)機械

stand-alone processing system
dokuritsu(gata) shori shisutemu
独立(型)処理システム

stand-alone program
dokuritsu(gata) puroguramu
独立(型)プログラム

stand-alone system
dokuritsu(gata) shisutemu
独立(型)システム

stand-alone type
dokuritsugata
独立型

standard
hyōjun; junkyo
標準；準拠

standard attachment
hyōjun tempu
標準添付

standard characters
hyōjun moji
標準文字

standard command
hyōjun meirei
標準命令

standard data format
hyōjun dēta keishiki
標準データ形式

standard deviation
hyōjun hensa
標準偏差

standard disk unit
hyōjun deisuku sōchi
標準ディスク装置

standard equipment
hyōjun sōbi
標準装備

standard feature
hyōjun kikō
標準機構

standard file
hyōjun fuairu
標準ファイル

standard form
hyōjun gata
標準型

standard format
hyōjun keishiki; hyōjun shoshiki
標準形式；標準書式

standard function
hyōjun kinō
標準機能

standard input/output interface
hyōjun nyūshutsuryoku intafuēsu
標準入出力インタフェース

standard instruction set
hyōjun meirei setto
標準命令セット

standard interface
hyōjun intafuēsu
標準インタフェース

standard keyboard
hairetsu junkyo no kiibōdo
配列準拠のキーボード

standard label
hyōjun raberu
標準ラベル

standard layout
hyōjun haichi
標準配置

standard operating procedure (SOP)
hyōjun sōsa tejun (SOP)
標準操作手順

standard package
hyōjun pakkēji
標準パッケージ

standard procedure
hyōjun tetsuzuki
標準手続き

standard reference tape
hyōjun jiki tēpu
標準磁気テープ

standard routine
hyōjun rūchin
標準ルーチン

standard subroutine
hyōjun saburūchin
標準サブルーチン

standard system tape
hyōjun shisutemu-tēpu
標準システム・テープ

standard tape
hyōjun tēpu
標準テープ

standard unit of accounting (SUA)
hyōjun kakin tan'i (SUA)
標準課金単位

standard unit of processing (SUP)
hyōjun shori tan'i (SUP)
標準処理単位

standardization
hyōjunka
標準化

standardize
hyōjunka suru
標準化する

standby
taiki
待機

standby area
taiki ryō'iki
待機領域

standby machine
taiki kikai
待機機械

standby processing
taiki shori
待機処理

standby redundancy
taiki jōchō
待機冗長

standby system
taiki shisutemu
待機システム

standby time
taiki jikan
待機時間

star network
seijōgata nettowāku
星状型ネットワーク

start
kaishi; kidō; shidō; sutāto
開始；起動；始動；スタート

start address
kaishi adoresu
開始アドレス

197

start bit
sutāto-bitto
スタート・ビット

start button
kidō botan
起動ボタン

start element
sutāto-eremento
スタート・エレメント

start interval
sutāto-bitto-taimu
スタート・ビット・タイム

start key
kidō kii
起動キー

start of block (SOB)
burokku kaishi (SOB)
ブロック開始

start of heading (SOH)
heddeingu kaishi (SOH)
ヘッディング開始

start-of-heading character
heddeingu kaishi moji
ヘッディング開始文字

start of message
messēji kaishi
メッセージ開始

start of text (STX)
tekisuto kaishi (STX)
テキスト開始

start-of-text character
tekisuto kaishi moji
テキスト開始文字

start pulse
sutāto-parusu
スタート・パルス

start signal
kaishi shingō
開始信号

start-stop
chōho; kidō-teishi
調歩; 起動-停止

start-stop supervision
chōho kanshi
調歩監視

start-stop synchronous system
chōho dōkishiki
調歩同期式

start-stop system
chōhoshiki
調歩式

start-stop time
kidō-teishi jikan
起動-停止時間

start-stop transmission
chōhoshiki densō
調歩式伝送

starter system
kidō shisutemu
起動システム

starting time
kidō jikan
起動時間

state
jōtai
状態

state diagram
jōtai zu
状態図

state transition diagram
jōtai sen'i zu
状態遷移図

statement
bun; meireibun; sutētomento
文; 命令文; ステートメント

statement bracket
bun no kakko
文の括弧

statement identifier
bun shikibetsushi
文識別子

statement label
bun no bangō
文の番号

statement name
bun mei
文名

statement number
bun bangō
文番号

statement prefix
bunsettōgo
文接頭語

static
seiteki
静的

static allocation
seiteki arokēshon
静的アロケーション

static circuit
seiteki kairo
静的回路

static dump
seiteki danpu
静的ダンプ

static RAM
seiteki RAM
静的RAM

static relocation
seiteki saihaichi
静的再配置

static storage
seiteki kioku
静的記憶

static store
seiteki kioku sōchi
静的記憶装置

static system
seiteki shisutemu
静的システム

staticize
seishika suru
静止化する

staticizer
seishika kikō
静止化機構

station
kasho; kikō; kyoku; sutēshon;
tanmatsu
箇所; 機構; 局; ステーション;
端末

stationary
teijō
定常

stationary information source
teijō jōhō gen
定常情報源

stationary state
teijō jōtai
定常状態

stationery
inji yōshi; insatsushi
印字用紙; 印刷紙

statistical
tōkeiteki
統計的

statistics
tōkei
統計

status
jōtai; sutētasu
状態；ステータス

status flag
jōtai hyōshiki
状態標識

status indicator
jōtai hyōshiki
状態標識

status information
jōtai jōhō
状態情報

status inquiry
jōtai toiawase
状態問い合わせ

status report
jōtai hōkoku
状態報告

status switching
jōtai kirikae
状態切り換え

status word
jōtai go
状態語

steady
teijō
定常

steering committee
seigyo i'inkai
制御委員会

step
kaidan; suteppu
階段；ステップ

step by step
suteppu-bai-suteppu
ステップ・バイ・ステップ

step-by-step operation
suteppu-bai-suteppu sōsa
ステップ・バイ・ステップ操作

step-by-step system
suteppu-bai-suteppu hōshiki
ステップ・バイ・ステップ方式

step counter
suteppu-kaunta
ステップ・カウンタ

step response
suteppu ōtō
ステップ応答

STL (Schottky transistor logic)
STL (Shottokii-toranjisuta ronri)
ショットキー・トランジスタ論理

stochastic decision process
kakuritsuteki kettei katei
確率的決定過程

stochastic process
kakuritsu katei
確率過程

stochastic programming
kakuritsuteki keikakuhō
確率的計画法

stochastic retrieval
kakuritsuteki kensaku
確率的検索

stochastic simulation
kakuritsuteki shimyurēshon
確率的シミュレーション

stock
zaiko
在庫

stock control
zaiko kanri
在庫管理

stop
sutoppu; teishi
ストップ；停止

stop bit
sutoppu-bitto
ストップ・ビット

stop code
sutoppu-kōdo
ストップ・コード

stop element
sutoppu-eremento
ストップ・エレメント

stop instruction
teishi meirei
停止命令

stop interval
sutoppu-bitto-taimu
ストップ・ビット・タイム

stop key
teishi kii
停止キー

stop pulse
sutoppu-parusu
ストップ・パルス

stop signal
teishi shingō
停止信号

stop time
teishi jikan
停止時間

storage
chikuseki; hozon; kioku (sōchi)
蓄積；保存；記憶（装置）

storage allocation
kioku('iki) wariate;
kioku('iki) waritsuke
記憶（域）割り当て；
記憶（域）割り付け

storage area
kioku iki; kioku ryō'iki
記憶域；記憶領域

storage attribute
kioku zokusei
記憶属性

storage block
kioku burokku
記憶ブロック

storage capacity
kioku yōryō
記憶容量

storage control
kioku seigyo
記憶制御

storage cycle
kioku saikuru
記憶サイクル

storage cycle time
kioku saikuru jikan
記憶サイクル時間

storage device
kioku sōchi
記憶装置

storage dump
kioku danpu
記憶ダンプ

storage element
kioku soshi
記憶素子

storage equipment
kioku sōchi
記憶装置

storage key
kioku kii
記憶キー

storage location
kioku basho
記憶場所

storage map
kioku wariatezu
記憶割り当て図

storage medium
kioku baitai
記憶媒体

storage operation
kioku sōsa
記憶操作

storage protection
kioku('iki) hogo
記憶(域)保護

storage protection feature
kioku hogo kikō
記憶保護機構

storage protection key
kioku hogo kii
記憶保護キー

storage reclaim
kioku'iki sairiyō
記憶域再利用

storage register
kioku rejisuta
記憶レジスタ

storage space
kioku kūkan
記憶空間

storage speed
kioku sokudo
記憶速度

storage stack
kioku sutakku
記憶スタック

storage system
kioku hōshiki
記憶方式

storage unit
kioku sōchi
記憶装置

store (*noun*)
kioku sōchi
記憶装置

store (*verb*)
chikuseki suru; kioku suru
蓄積する；記憶する

store-and-forward switching
chikuseki kōkan
蓄積交換

store cycle
kioku saikuru
記憶サイクル

store cycle time
kioku saikuru-taimu
記憶サイクル・タイム

store location
kioku ichi
記憶位置

stored data
kioku dēta
記憶データ

stored data definition language (SDDL)
kakunō dēta teigi gengo (SDDL)
格納データ定義言語

stored program
naibu puroguramu;
naizō puroguramu;
puroguramu kiokushiki;
puroguramu naizōshiki
内部プログラム；
内蔵プログラム；
プログラム記憶式；
プログラム内蔵式

stored-program computer
puroguramu naizōshiki keisanki
プログラム内蔵式計算機

storing
chikuseki; kioku
蓄積；記憶

straight-insertion sort
chokusetsu sōnyū bunrui
直接挿入分類

straight-line coding
chokusenteki kōdeingu
直線的コーディング

strategic planning information
senryaku keikaku jōhō
戦略計画情報

strategy
senryaku
戦略

stream
sutoriimu
ストリーム

stretch
hikinobasu
引き伸す

stretching
hikinobashi
引き伸し

string
renshi; retsu; sutoringu
連系；列；ストリング

string data
sutoringu-dēta
ストリング・データ

string functions
retsu kansū
列関数

string manipulation
sutoringu shori
ストリング処理

string processing
kigōretsu shori; sutoringu shori
記号列処理；ストリング処理

string representation
kigōretsu hyōgen
記号列表現

string sort
sutoringu-sōto
ストリング・ソート

strobe
sutorōbu
ストローブ

strobe pulse
sutorōbu-parusu
ストローグ・パルス

strobing circuit
sutorōbu kairo
ストローブ回路

stroke
sutorōku
ストローク

stroke center line
sutorōku chūshin sen
ストローク中心線

stroke edge
sutorōku fuchi
ストローク縁

stroke method
sutorōku hōshiki
ストローク方式

stroke width
sutorōku haba
ストローク幅

structural
kōzō(teki)
構造（的）

structural analysis
kōzō kaiseki
構造解析

structural data
kōzō(teki) dēta
構造(的)データ

structural data relationships
kōzō(teki) dēta kankei
構造(的)データ関係

structural design
kōzō sekkei
構造設計

structure
kōzō
構造

structure diagram
kōzō zu
構造図

structure division
kōzō bu
構造部

structure expression
kōzō shiki
構造式

structured
kōzōka
構造化

Structured BASIC (SBASIC)
Sutorakuchādo-Bēshikku
(SBASIC)
ストラクチャード・ベーシック

structured programming
kōzōka puroguramingu
構造化プログラミング

structured walkthrough
kōzōka uōkusurū
構造化ウオークスルー

structuring
kōzōka
構造化

stub
sutabu
スタブ

STX (start of text)
STX (tekisuto kaishi)
テキスト開始

SUA (standard unit of accounting)
SUA (hyōjun kakin tan'i)
標準課金単位

SUB (substitute character)
SUB (okikae moji)
置き換え文字

subarchitecture interface (SAI)
sabu-ākitekucha-intafuēsu (SAI)
サブ・アーキテクチャ・
インタフェース

subchannel
sabu-chaneru
サブ・チャネル

subentry
fuku kijutsukō
副記述項

subfunction
fuku kinō
副機能

subitem
bubun kōmoku
部分項目

subject
shutai
主体

subnetwork
sabu-nettowāku
サブ・ネットワーク

suboptimization
bubun saitekika
部分最適化

subprogram
fuku puroguramu;
sabu-puroguramu
副プログラム；サブ・プログラム

subroutine
sabu-rūchin
サブ・ルーチン

subroutine call
sabu-rūchin yobidashi
サブ・ルーチン呼び出し

subroutine library
sabu-rūchin-raiburari
サブ・ルーチン・ライブラリ

subroutine subprogram
sabu-rūchin-sabu-puroguramu
サブ・ルーチン・サブ・プログラム

subschema
sabu-sukiima
サブ・スキーマ

subschema description entry
kobetsu dēta kōzō kijutsukō;
sabu-sukiima kijutsukō
個別データ構造記述項；
サブ・スキーマ記述項

subschema entry
kobetsu dēta kōzō kijutsukō;
sabu-sukiima kijutsukō
個別データ構造記述項；
サブ・スキーマ記述項

subschema name
kobetsu dēta kōzō kijutsumei;
sabu-sukiima mei
個別データ構造記述名；
サブ・スキーマ名

subschema section
kobetsu dēta kōzō kijutsusetsu;
sabu-sukiima setsu
個別データ構造記述節；
サブ・スキーマ節

subscriber
kanyūsha
加入者

subscriber's line
kanyūsen
加入線

subscript
soeji
添え字

subscript-bound
soeji iki
添え字域

subscript expression
soeji shiki
添え字式

subscript list
soeji risuto
添え字リスト

subscripted
soejitsuki
添え字付き

subscripted variable
soejitsuki hensū
添え字付き変数

subscription
kanyū
加入

subset
sabusetto
サブセット

substitute
chikan; daiyō; okikae
置換；代用；置き換え

substitute character (SUB)
okikae moji (SUB)
置き換え文字

substitution
okikae
置き換え

substitution method
okikae hōhō
置き換え方法

substrate
kiban
基板

substring
bubunretsu; sabusutoringu
部分列；サブストリング

subsystem
sabu-shisutemu
サブ・システム

subtask
sabu-tasuku
サブ・タスク

subtracter
genzanki
減算器

subtraction
genzan
減算

successive approximation
chikuji hikaku
逐次比較

suite
kumi
組

sum
gōkei; wa
合計；和

sum check
gōkei kensa
合計検査

summary
yōyaku
要約

summary card
gōkei kādo
合計カード

summary punch
gōkei senkō
合計せん孔

summation check
gōkei kensa
合計検査

SUP (standard unit of processing)
SUP (hyōjun shori tan'i)
標準処理単位

super-
chō-
超

supercomputer
sūpa-konpyūta
スーパ・コンピュータ

superimposed
chōjō; sūpainpōzu
重畳；スーパインポーズ

superimposed board
sūpainpōzu-bōdo
スーパインポーズ・ボード

superimposed circuit
chōjō kairo
重畳回路

superimposed unit
sūpainpōzu-yunitto
スーパインポーズ・ユニット

superior print
jōihan
上位版

superscript
kataji
肩字

supersmall
chōko
超小

supervisor (equipment)
kanshi puroguramu; sūpabaiza
監視プログラム；スーパバイザ

supervisor (person)
kanshi sōsain; sūpabaiza
監視操作員；スーパバイザ

supervisor call
sūpabaiza yobidashi
スーパバイザ呼び出し

supervisor call instruction
sūpabaiza kōru meirei;
sūpabaiza yobidashi meirei
スーパバイザ・コール命令；
スーパバイザ呼び出し命令

supervisor mode
sūpabaiza-mōdo
スーパバイザ・モード

supervisor register
sūpabaiza-rejisuta
スーパバイザ・レジスタ

supervisor state
sūpabaiza jōtai
スーパバイザ状態

supervisory character
kanshi moji
監視文字

supervisory control system
kanshi shisutemu
監視システム

supervisory program
kanshi puroguramu
監視プログラム

supervisory routine
kanshi rūchin
監視ルーチン

supervisory system
kanshi shisutemu
監視システム

supplementary information
hojū jōhō
補充情報

support
sapōto; shien
サポート；支援

support resources
shien shigen
支援資源

support software
shien sofutouea
支援ソフトウェア

support system
sapōto-shisutemu;
shien shisutemu
サポート・システム；
支援システム

support utility
sapōto-yūteiritei
サポート・ユーティリティ

suppress
yokusei suru
抑制する

suppression
yokusei
抑制

surface
hyōmen
表面

surface acoustic waves (SAW)
hyōmen danseiha (SAW)
表面弾性波

surface disk
hyōmen deisuku
表面ディスク

surface plot
hyōmen purotto
表面プロット

SVP (service processor)
SVP (sābisu-purosessa)
サービス・プロセッサ

swap in
suwappu-in
スワップ・イン

swap out
suwappu-auto
スワップ・アウト

swapping
suwappingu
スワッピング

switch
kirikae; suitchi
切り換え；スイッチ

switch list
suitchi-risuto
スイッチ・リスト

switch over (*verb*)
kirikaeru
切り換える

switch statement
suitchi-sutētomento
スイッチ・ステートメント

switched circuit
kōkan kaisenmō
交換回線網

switched line
kōkan kaisen
交換回線

switched-message network
messēji kōkanmō
メッセージ交換網

switched network
kōkanmō
交換網

switched-network control
kōkanmō seigyo
交換網制御

switching
kirikae; kōkan; suitchingu
切り換え；交換；スイッチング

switching center (exchange)
kōkankyoku
交換局

switching device
kōkan kikō
交換機構

switching diode
suitchingu-daiōdo
スイッチング・ダイオード

switching speed
kirikae sokudo
切り換え速度

switching theory
kōkan riron
交換理論

switching time
kirikae jikan
切り換え時間

symbiont
shinbionto
シンビオント

symbiont control
shinbionto seigyo
シンビオント制御

symbol
kigō
記号

symbol manipulation
kigō shori
記号処理

symbol manipulation language
kigō shori gengo
記号処理言語

symbol table
kigō hyō
記号表

symbolic address
kigō adoresu
記号アドレス

symbolic addressing
kigō adoresu shitei
記号アドレス指定

symbolic code
kigō kōdo
記号コード

symbolic coding
kigō kōdeingu
記号コーディング

symbolic instruction
kigō meirei
記号命令

symbolic language
kigō gengo
記号言語

symbolic logic
kigō ronri
記号論理

symbolic manipulation
kigō shori
記号処理

symbolic name
kigō mei
記号名

symbolic operand
kigō operando
記号オペランド

symbolic programming
kigō puroguramingu
記号プログラミング

symbolic representation
kigō hyōgen
記号表現

symbolic string
kigō sutoringu
記号ストリング

SYN (synchronous idle)
SYN (dōki shingō)
同期信号

synchronization
dōki; dōkika
同期；同期化

synchronization error
dōki gosa
同期誤差

synchronization pulse
dōki parusu
同期パルス

synchronize
dōki(ka) suru
同期(化)する

synchronizer
dōki sōchi
同期装置

synchronizing pulse
dōki parusu
同期パルス

synchronous
dōki(shiki)
同期(式)

synchronous circuit
dōki(shiki) kairo
同期(式)回路

synchronous communication
dōki tsūshin
同期通信

synchronous computer
dōkishiki keisanki
同期式計算機

synchronous data link control (SDLC)
dōkishiki dēta-rinku seigyo (SDLC)
同期式データ・リンク制御

synchronous idle (SYN)
dōki shingō (SYN)
同期信号

synchronous machine
dōki(shiki) kikai
同期(式)機械

synchronous mode
dōki mōdo
同期モード

synchronous operation
dōki dōsa; dōki sōsa
同期動作；同期操作

synchronous processing
dōki shori
同期処理

synchronous processing system
dōki shori shisutemu
同期処理システム

synchronous system
dōki shisutemu; dōkihōshiki; dōkishiki; dōshiki
同期システム；同期方式；同期式；同式

synchronous system communication
dōki shisutemu tsūshin
同期システム通信

synchronous transmission
dōki densō
同期伝送

syntax
kōbun
構文

syntax analysis
kōbun kaiseki
構文解析

syntax diagram
kōbun kaisekizu
構文解析図

syntax error
kōbun ayamari
構文誤り

synthesis
gōsei
合成

synthesis procedure
gōsei tejun
合成手順

synthesis technique
gōsei gihō
合成技法

synthetic address
gōsei adoresu
合成アドレス

synthetic language
gōsei gengo
合成言語

synthetic voice
gōsei gengo
合成言語

SYSGEN (systems generation)
SYSGEN (shisutemu seisei)
システム生成

SYSPOOL (system temporary storage pool)
SYSPOOL (shisutemu jō no ichiji kioku'iki)
システム上の一時記憶域

system
hōshiki; shiki; shisutemu; soshiki; taikei
方式；式；システム；組織；体系

system access
shisutemu-akusesu
システム・アクセス

system adaptability
shisutemu tekiōsei
システム適応性

system analysis
shisutemu bunseki
システム分析

system application
shisutemu ōyō
システム応用

system architecture
shisutemu-ākitekucha
システム・アーキテクチャ

system assessment
shisutemu hyōtei
システム評定

system autonomy
shisutemu jiritsusei
システム自律性

system capacity
shisutemu yōryō
システム容量

system characteristics
shisutemu tokusei
システム特性

system chart
shisutemu-chāto
システム・チャート

system check
shisutemu-chekku
システム・チェック

system code
shisutemu-kōdo
システム・コード

system component
shisutemu-konponento;
shisutemu kōsei kiki
システム・コンポネント;
システム構成機器

system composition
shisutemu kōsei
システム構成

system composition diagram
shisutemu kōsei zu
システム構成図

system configuration
shisutemu kōsei
システム構成

system console
shisutemu sōsataku
システム操作卓

system control
shisutemu seigyo
システム制御

system control panel
shisutemu seigyo ban
システム制御盤

system controller
shisutemu seigyo sōchi
システム制御装置

system cost
shisutemu hiyō
システム費用

system data
shisutemu-dēta
システム・データ

system data file format
shisutemu-dēta-fuairu keishiki
システム・データ・ファイル形式

system default
shisutemu shōryakuji kaishaku
システム省略時解釈

system definition
shisutemu teigi
システム定義

system demonstration
shisutemu jisshō
システム実証

system description
shisutemu kijutsu
システム記述

system description language
shisutemu kijutsu gengo
システム記述言語

system design
shisutemu sekkei
システム設計

system design engineering
shisutemu sekkei kōgaku
システム設計工学

system development
shisutemu kaihatsu
システム開発

system down
shisutemu-daun
システム・ダウン

system dump
shisutemu-danpu
システム・ダンプ

system efficiency
shisutemu kōritsu
システム効率

system element
shisutemu-eremento
システム・エレメント

system error
shisutemu gosa
システム誤差

system evaluation
shisutemu hyōka
システム評価

system failure
shisutemu koshō
システム故障

system flowchart
shisutemu nagarezu
システム流れ図

system format
shisutemu keishiki
システム形式

system function
shisutemu kinō
システム機能

system function diagram
shisutemu kinō zu
システム機能図

system goal
shisutemu mokuhyō
システム目標

system hierarchy
shisutemu kaisō
システム階層

system house
shisutemu-hausu
システム・ハウス

system implementation
shisutemu jitsugen
システム実現

system initialization
shisutemu shoki settei;
shisutemu shokika
システム初期設定;
システム初期化

system initialization program
shisutemu shoki settei
puroguramu; shisutemu shokika
puroguramu
システム初期設定プログラム;
システム初期化プログラム

system input device
shisutemu nyūryoku sōchi
システム入力装置

system installation
shisutemu setchi
システム設置

system integration
shisutemu tōgō
システム統合

system integrity
shisutemu hozen
システム保全

system language
shisutemu gengo
システム言語

system layout
shisutemu haichi
システム配置

system library
shisutemu-raiburari
システム・ライブラリ

system life cycle
shisutemu no jumyō;
shisutemu-raifu-saikuru
システムの寿命；
システム・ライフ・サイクル

system loader
shisutemu-rōda
システム・ローダ

system log
shisutemu keika kiroku
システム経過記録

system logic
shisutemu ronri
システム論理

system macroinstruction
shisutemu-makuro meirei
システム・マクロ命令

system maintenance
shisutemu hozen; shisutemu iji
システム保全；システム維持

system management
shisutemu kanri
システム管理

system mechanism
shisutemu kikō
システム機構

system model
shisutemu-moderu
システム・モデル

system modification
shisutemu henkō
システム変更

system monitor
shisutemu-monita
システム・モニタ

system network architecture
shisutemu-nettowāku-ākitekucha
システム・ネットワーク・
アーキテクチャ

system objective
shisutemu mokuteki
システム目的

system operator
shisutemu sōsain
システム操作員

system optimization
shisutemu saitekika
システム最適化

system outline
shisutemu gairyaku;
shisutemu rinkaku
システム概略；システム輪郭

system output device
shisutemu shutsuryoku sōchi
システム出力装置

system package
shisutemu-pakkēji
システム・パッケージ

system performance
shisutemu seinō
システム性能

system planning
shisutemu keikaku
システム計画

system productivity
shisutemu seisansei
システム生産性

system program
shisutemu-puroguramu
システム・プログラム

system prototype
shisutemu genkei
システム原型

system recovery time
shisutemu kaifuku jikan
システム回復時間

system-related
shisutemu kanren
システム関連

system reliability
shisutemu shinraisei
システム信頼性

system requirements
shisutemu yōkyū
システム要求

system reset
shisutemu-risetto
システム・リセット

system residence
shisutemu jōchū
システム常駐

system residence volume
shisutemu jōchū boryūmu
システム常駐ボリューム

system-resident device
shisutemu jōchū sōchi
システム常駐装置

system-resident disk pack
shisutemu jōchū deisuku-pakku
システム常駐ディスク・パック

system-resident executive program
shisutemu jōchū kanshi
puroguramu
システム常駐監視プログラム

system-resident storage
shisutemu jōchū kioku
システム常駐記憶

system-resident volume
shisutemu jōchū boryūmu
システム常駐ボリューム

system resources
shisutemu shigen
システム資源

system response
shisutemu ōtō
システム応答

system response time
shisutemu ōtō jikan
システム応答時間

system restart
shisutemu saishidō
システム再始動

system safety
shisutemu anzen
システム安全

system scope
shisutemu han'i
システム範囲

system security
shisutemu anzen hoshu
システム安全保守

system shutdown
shisutemu unten teishi
システム運転停止

system simulation
shisutemu-shimyurēshon
システム・シミュレーション

system slowdown
shisutemu gensoku
システム減速

system software
shisutemu-sofutouea
システム・ソフトウェア

system specification
shisutemu shiyō
システム仕様

system structure
shisutemu kōzō
システム構造

system study
shisutemu kentō
システム検討

system supervisor
shisutemu-sūpabaiza
システム・スーパバイザ

system support
shisutemu-sapōto;
shisutemu shien
システム・サポート；
システム支援

system tape
shisutemu-tēpu
システム・テープ

system temporary storage pool (SYSPOOL)
shisutemu jō no ichiji kioku'iki (SYSPOOL)
システム上の一時記憶域

system test
shisutemu-tesuto
システム・テスト

system throughput
shisutemu shoriryō
システム処理量

system tuning
shisutemu chōsei;
shisutemu dōchō
システム調整；システム同調

system verification
shisutemu kensa
システム検査

system versatility
shisutemu tagei
システム多芸

systematic
keitōteki
系統的

systematic error
keitō gosa
系統誤差

systems analysis
shisutemu bunseki
システム分析

systems analyst
shisutemu-anarisuto;
shisutemu bunsekisha
システム・アナリスト；
システム分析者

systems compatibility
shisutemu gokansei
システム互換性

systems design
shisutemu sekkei
システム設計

systems designer
shisutemu sekkeisha
システム設計者

systems engineer (SE)
shisutemu-enjinia (SE)
システム・エンジニア

systems engineering
shisutemu kōgaku;
shisutemu kōgyō
システム工学；システム工業

systems generation (SYSGEN)
shisutemu seisei (SYSGEN)
システム生成

systems implementation
shisutemu no jitsugen;
shisutemu sakusei
システムの実現；システム作成

systems implementation language
shisutemu sakusei gengo
システム作成言語

systems maintenance
shisutemu iji
システム維持

systems methodology
shisutemu hōhōron
システム方法論

systems-oriented
shisutemu muki
システム向き

systems programmer
shisutemu-purogurama
システム・プログラマ

systems programming
shisutemu-puroguramingu
システム・プログラミング

systems software
shisutemu-sofutouea
システム・ソフトウェア

systems theory
shisutemu riron
システム理論

T

TA (technology assessment)
TA (tekunoroji-asesumento)
テクノロジ・アセスメント

TAB (tabulation)
TAB (ran okuri; seihyō;
shūkeihyō; tabu; tabyurēshon)
欄送り；製表；集計表；タブ；
タブュレーション

tab file
tabu-fuairu
タブ・ファイル

tab position
tabu setteiten
タブ設定点

tab spacing
ran okuri kankaku
欄送り間隔

table
hyō; tēburu
表；テーブル

table-driven compiler
tēburu kudōgata konpaira
テーブル駆動型コンパイラ

table-driven program
tēburu kudōgata puroguramu
テーブル駆動型プログラム

table element
tēburu yōso
テーブル要素

table look-at
tēburu chokusetsu sakuin
テーブル直接索引

table lookup
sakuhyō; tēburu sakuin
索表；テーブル索引

table lookup instruction
tēburu sakuin meirei
テーブル索引命令

table search
tēburu kensaku
テーブル検索

tablet
taburetto
タブレット

tabular language
tabyura gengo
タビュラ言語

tabulate
seihyō suru
製表する

tabulation (TAB)
ran okuri; seihyō; shūkeihyō;
tabu; tabyurēshon (TAB)
欄送り；製表；集計表；
タブ；タビュレーション

tabulation mark
seihyō kigō
製表記号

tabulation spacing
ran okuri kankaku
欄送り間隔

tabulator
seihyōki
製表機

tactical control information
senjutsu seigyo jōhō
戦術制御情報

tag
hyōshiki; tagu
標識；タグ

tag card
tagu-kādo
タグ・カード

tag format
tagu keishiki
タグ形式

tag marker
tagu senkōki
タグせん孔機

tag reader
tagu-riida; tagu yomitori senkōki
タグ・リーダ；
タグ読み取りせん孔機

tag sort
tagu bunrui; tagu-sōto
タグ分類；タグ・ソート

tag system
tagu-shisutemu
タグ・システム

take-up reel
tēpu makitori riiru
テープ巻き取りリール

tally
warifu
割り符

tandem
tandemu
タンデム

tandem operation
tandemu sōsa
タンデム操作

tandem processor
tandemu-purosessa
タンデム・プロセッサ

tandem system
tandemu-shisutemu
タンデム・システム

tape
tēpu
テープ

tape block
tēpu-burokku
テープ・ブロック

tape cartridge
tēpu-kātorijji
テープ・カートリッジ

tape cassette
tēpu-kasetto
テープ・カセット

tape channel
tēpu-chaneru
テープ・チャネル

tape code
tēpu-kōdo
テープ・コード

tape code selection switch
tēpu-kōdo sembetsu suitchi;
tēpu-kōdo sentaku suitchi
テープ・コード選別スイッチ；
テープ・コード選択スイッチ

tape-controlled carriage
tēpu seigyoshiki kyarijji
テープ制御式キャリッジ

tape deck
tēpu sōchi
テープ装置

tape drive
tēpu kudō kikō
テープ駆動機構

tape dump
tēpu-danpu
テープ・ダンプ

tape feed
tēpu okuri
テープ送り

tape file
tēpu-fairu
テープ・ファイル

tape format
tēpu keishiki
テープ形式

tape label
tēpu-raberu
テープ・ラベル

tape-labeling system (TLS)
tēpu-raberu-shisutemu (TLS)
テープ・ラベル・システム

tape library
tēpu-raiburari
テープ・ライブラリ

tape mark (TM)
tēpu-māku (TM)
テープ・マーク

tape marker
tēpu-māka
テープ・マーカ

tape-operating system (TOS)
tēpu-operēteingu-shisutemu
(TOS)
テープ・オペレーティング・システム

tape punch
tēpu-panchi; tēpu senkōki
テープ・パンチ；テープせん孔機

tape punch attachment
tēpu-panchi setsuzoku kikō
テープ・パンチ接続機構

tape reader
tēpu yomitori sōchi
テープ読み取り装置

tape reel
tēpu-riiru
テープ・リール

tape sort
tēpu bunrui; tēpu-sōto
テープ分類；テープ・ソート

tape station
tēpu-sutēshon
テープ・ステーション

tape streamer
tēpu-sutoriima
テープ・ストリーマ

tape swap
tēpu-suwappu
テープ・スワップ

tape-to-card conversion
tēpu-kādo henkan
テープ・カード変換

tape-to-card converter
tēpu-kādo henkanki
テープ・カード変換器

tape-to-tape conversion
tēpu-tēpu henkan
テープ・テープ変換

tape-to-tape converter
tēpu-tēpu henkanki
テープ・テープ変換器

tape transport
tēpu kudō kikō
テープ駆動機構

tape unit
jiki tēpu sōchi
磁気テープ装置

tape verifier
tēpu kenkōki
テープ検孔機

tape verifying
tēpu kenkō
テープ検孔

tapping
tōchō
盗聴

target
mokuhyō; mokuteki; tāgetto
目標；目的；ターゲット

target computer
mokuteki keisanki
目的計算機

target configuration
tāgetto-konfuigyurēshon
ターゲット・コンフィギュレーション

target data item
mokuhyō dēta kōmoku
目標データ項目

target identification
mokuhyō shikibetsu
目標識別

target language
mokuteki gengo
目的言語

target phase
tāgetto dankai
ターゲット段階

target program
mokuteki puroguramu
目的プログラム

task
tasuku
タスク

task analysis
tasuku kaiseki
タスク解析

task completion
tasuku kansei
タスク完成

task control
tasuku seigyo
タスク制御

task control block (TCB)
tasuku seigyo burokku (TCB)
タスク制御ブロック

task definition
tasuku teigi
タスク定義

task description
tasuku kijutsu
タスク記述

task dispatch
tasuku shimei
タスク技名

task dispatcher
tasuku shimei puroguramu
タスク技名プログラム

task identification
tasuku shikibetsu
タスク識別

task initiation
tasuku kaishi
タスク開始

task management
tasuku kanri
タスク管理

task priority
tasuku yūsen jun'i
タスク優先順位

209

task queue
tasuku machigyōretsu
タスク待ち行列

task selection
tasuku sentaku
タスク選択

task sequence
tasuku-shiikensu
タスク・レーケンス

TC (transmission control)
TC (densō seigyo)
伝送制御

TCAM (telecommunications access method)
TCAM (tsūshin akusesu hōshiki)
通信アクセス方式

TCB (task control block)
TCB (tasuku seigyo burokku)
タスク制御ブロック

TCU (transmission control unit)
TCU (densō seigyo sōchi)
伝送制御装置

TDG (test data generator)
TDG (tesuto-dēta seisei puroguramu)
テスト・データ生成プログラム

TDL (translation definition language)
TDL (henkan teigi gengo)
変換定義言語

TDM (time-division multiplexing)
TDM (jibunkatsu tajū hōshiki)
時分割多重方式

TDMA (time-division multiple access)
TDMA (jibunkatsu tajū akusesu)
時分割多重アクセス

TE (trailing end)
TE (shūtan)
終端

technical
gijutsu(teki)
技術 (的)

technical control
gijutsuteki seigyo
技術的制御

technical information
gijutsu jōhō
技術情報

technical information processing system
gijutsu jōhō shori shisutemu
技術情報処理システム

technical specifications
gijutsu shiyō
技術仕様

technical standards
gijutsu hyōjun
技術標準

technology
gijutsu; tekunoroji
技術; テクノロジ

technology assessment (TA)
tekunoroji-asesumento (TA)
テクノロジ・アセスメント

telecommunication(s)
tsūshin
通信

telecommunication facility
tsūshin kinō
通信機能

telecommunication line
tsūshin kaisen
通信回線

telecommunication network
tsūshinmō
通信網

telecommunication system
tsūshin shisutemu
通信システム

telecommunications access method (TCAM)
tsūshin akusesu hōshiki (TCAM)
通信アクセス方式

teleconferencing
terekanfuerenshingu
テレカンフェレンシング

telegraphic communication
denshin
電信

telemeter
teremēta
テレメータ

telemetering
enkaku sokutei; teremētaringu
遠隔測定; テレメータリング

teleprinter
denshin injiki; terepurinta
電信印字機; テレプリンタ

teleprinter exchange (TELEX)
terekkusu; teretaipu kōkan (TELEX)
テレックス; テレタイプ交換

teleprocessing
terepurosesshingu
テレプロセッシング

teleputer
terepyūta
テレピュータ

telesoftware
teresofutouea
テレソフトウェア

teletex
teretekkusu
テレテックス

teletext
teretekisuto
テレテキスト

teletype
denshin injiki; teretaipu
電信印字機; テレタイプ

teletypewriter
teretaipuraita
テレタイプライタ

teletypewriter exchange service (TWX)
teretaipuraita kōkan sābisu (TWX)
テレタイプライタ交換サービス

television (TV)
terebi (TV)
テレビ

teleworker
terewāka
テレワーカ

TELEX (teleprinter exchange)
terekkusu; teretaipu kōkan; TELEX
テレックス; テレタイプ交換; TELEX

temperature
ondo
温度

template
tenpurēto
テンプレート

template-matching
tenpurēto tsukiawase
テンプレート突き合わせ

temporary
ichiji(teki)
一時(的)

temporary file
ichiji(teki) fuairu
一時(的)ファイル

temporary memory
ichijiteki kioku
一時的記憶

temporary register
ichiji rejisuta
一時レジスタ

temporary storage
ichiji(teki) kioku
一時(的)記憶

temporary variable
ichiji(teki) hensū
一時(的)変数

ten's complement
jū no hosū
10の補数

term
kō
項

terminal
shūtan (sōchi); tāminaru;
tanmatsu (sōchi); tanshi
終端(装置); ターミナル;
端末(装置); 端子

terminal board
haisenban; tanmatsu bōdo
配線盤; 端末ボード

terminal control
tanmatsu seigyo
端末制御

terminal control unit
tanmatsu sōchi
端末装置

terminal equipment
tanmatsu kiki
端末機器

terminal keyboard
haisenban; tanmatsu kiibōdo
配線盤; 端末キーボード

terminal management
tanmatsu kanri
端末管理

terminal screen
tāminaru-sukuriin
ターミナル・スクリーン

terminal symbol
shūtan kigō
終端記号

terminal user
tanmatsu riyōsha; tanmatsu yūza
端末利用者; 端末ユーザ

terminated line
shūtan senro
終端線路

termination
shūketsu; shūryō
終結; 終了

termination environment
shūtan ryō'iki
終端領域

ternary
sanshin
3進

ternary incremental representation
sanshin zōbun hyōjihō
3進増分表示法

ternary notation
sanshin hō
3進法

test (*noun*)
kensa; shiken; tesuto
検査; 試験; テスト

test (*verb*)
tamesu
試す

test board
shiken ban
試験盤

test case
tesuto-kēsu
テスト・ケース

test conditions
tesuto jōken
テスト条件

test data
tesuto-dēta
テスト・データ

test data generator (TDG)
tesuto-dēta seisei puroguramu
(TDG)
テスト・データ生成プログラム

test mode
tesuto-mōdo
テスト・モード

test pack
tesuto-pakku
テスト・パック

test procedure
shiken tejun
試験手順

test program
tesuto-puroguramu
テスト・プログラム

test run
tesuto-ran
テスト・ラン

test tool
tesuto-tsūru
テスト・ツール

testing
shiken; tesuteingu
試験; テスティング

text
bunsho; hombun; tekisuto
文書; 本文; テキスト

text compression
tekisuto asshuku
テキスト圧縮

text editing
tekisuto henshū
テキスト編集

text editor
tekisuto-edeita;
tekisuto henshū puroguramu
テキスト・エディタ;
テキスト編集プログラム

text indicator
tekisuto hyōji
テキスト表示

text processing
bunsho shori; tekisuto shori
文書処理；テキスト処理

theoretical
riron(teki)
理論(的)

theoretical design
rironteki sekkei
理論的設計

theoretical system
rironteki shisutemu
理論的システム

theory
riron
理論

theory of computation
keisan riron
計算理論

theory of graphs
gurafu riron
グラフ理論

thermal printer
kannetsushiki insho sōchi
感熱式印書装置

thermal resistance
netsuteikō
熱抵抗

thermistor
sāmisuta
サーミスタ

thermoelectric effect
netsuden kōka
熱電効果

thick film
atsu maku
厚膜

thick-film integrated circuit
atsu maku shūseki kairo
厚膜集積回路

thin film
haku maku
薄膜

thin-film integrated circuit
haku maku shūseki kairo
薄膜集積回路

thin-film memory
jisei hakumaku kioku
磁性薄膜記憶

thin-film storage
jisei hakumaku kioku
磁性薄膜記憶

third-generation computer
daisan sedai keisanki
第三世代計算機

thrashing
surasshingu
スラッシング

threaded code
surededdo-kōdo
スレデッド・コード

threaded list
tsunagi risuto
つなぎリスト

three-address
san adoresu
3アドレス

three-address instruction
san adoresu meirei
3アドレス命令

three-plus-one address
san purasu ichi adoresu
3＋1アドレス

threshold
iki; shikiichi
閾；敷居値

threshold element
shikiichi soshi
敷居値素子

threshold level
shikiichi
敷居値

threshold logic
shikiichi ronri
敷居値論理

throughput
shori nōryoku; shoriryō;
surūputto
処理能力；処理量；スループット

thyristor
sairisuta
サイリスタ

tight coupling
kōketsugō
硬結合

tilt
chiruto
チルト

time
jikan; taimu
時間；タイム

time allocation
jikan waritsuke
時間割り付け

time base
jikan bēsu
時間ベース

time chart
taimu-chāto
タイム・チャート

time constant
jiteisū
時定数

time delay
(jikan) okure
(時間)遅れ

time dependence
jikan izon
時間依存

time-dependent
jikan izon
時間依存

time-division multiple access (TDMA)
jibunkatsu tajū akusesu (TDMA)
時分割多重アクセス

time-division multiplex communication
jibunkatsu tajū tsūshin
時分割多重通信

time-division multiplexer
jibunkatsu tajū sōchi
時分割多重装置

time-division multiplexing (TDM)
jibunkatsu tajū hōshiki (TDM)
時分割多重方式

time independence
jikan dokuritsu
時間独立

time-independent
jikan dokuritsu
時間独立

212

time interval
jikan kankaku
時間間隔

time lag
(jikan) okure
（時間）遅れ

time out
taimu-auto
タイム・アウト

time series
jikeiretsu
時系列

time series analysis
jikeiretsu kaiseki
時系列解析

time-share
jibunkatsu suru
時分割する

time-shared input/output system
jibunkatsu nyūshutsuryoku
shisutemu
時分割入出力システム

time sharing
jibunkatsu; taimu-shiearingu
時分割；タイム・シェアリング

time-sharing monitor system
jibunkatsu monita-shisutemu
時分割モニタ・システム

time-sharing option (TSO)
jibunkatsu opushon (TSO)
時分割オプション

time-sharing system (TSS)
jibunkatsu shisutemu; taimu-
shiearingu-shisutemu (TSS)
時分割システム；タイム・
シェアリング・システム

time slice
taimu-suraisu
タイム・スライス

time slicing
taimu-suraishingu
タイム・スライシング

time-slicing value
taimu-suraisu no chi
タイム・スライスの値

time variable
jihen
時変

time-varying
jihen
時変

timer
keijikikō; taima (kikō)
計時機構；タイマ（機構）

timer control
taima seigyo
タイマ制御

timer/counter
taima-kaunta
タイマ・カウンタ

timer interrupt
taima warikomi
タイマ割り込み

timer processing
taima shori
タイマ処理

timer service
taima-sābisu
タイマ・サービス

timing
taimingu
タイミング

timing chart
taimingu-chāto
タイミング・チャート

timing error
taimingu-erā
タイミング・エラー

timing pulse
taimingu-parusu
タイミング・パルス

timing track
taimingu-torakku
タイミング・トラック

Tiny BASIC
Taini BASIC; Taini-Bēshikku
タイニBASIC；
タイニ・ベージック

tip
chippu
チップ

title
hyōdai
表題

title format
hyōdai no shoshiki
表題の書式

TLS (tape labeling system)
TLS (tēpu-raberu-shisutemu)
テープ・ラベル・システム

TM (tape mark)
TM (tēpu-māku)
テープ・マーク

TN (transport network)
TN (tensō nettowāku)
転送ネットワーク

TNC (transport-network control)
TNC (tensō nettowāku seigyo)
転送ネットワーク制御

toggle
toguru
トグル

toggle flip-flop
toguru-furippu-furoppu
トグル・フリップ・フロップ

toggle switch
toguru-suitchi
トグル・スイッチ

token
tōken
トークン

tolerance
kyoyō genkai
許容限界

tool
kōgu
工具

top-down approach
kakōgata apurōchi;
toppu-daun-apurōchi
下降型アプローチ；
トップ・ダウン・アプローチ

top-down design
kakōgata sekkei;
toppu-daun sekkei
下降型設計；トップ・ダウン設計

top-down parsing
kakōgata kaiseki
下降型解析

topology
toporojii
トポロジー

213

TOS (tape-operating system)
TOS (tēpu-operēteingu-
shisutemu)
テープ・オペレーティング・システム

total (sum)
gōkei
合計

total information
tōtaru jōhō
トータル情報

total information system
tōtaru jōhō shisutemu
トータル情報システム

total precedence
taishō jun'i
対称順位

total system
tōtaru-shisutemu
トータル・システム

total systems approach
tōtaru-shisutemu-apurōchi
トータル・システム・アプローチ

touch-sensitive device
oshi kando sōchi;
tatchikando sōchi
押し感度装置; タッチ感度装置

touch-tone dialing
oshi botan-daiaru hōshiki
押しボタン・ダイアル方式

touchpad
oshipado
押しパド

tournament
tōnamento
トーナメント

tournament selection
tōnamento sentaku hōshiki
トーナメト選択方式

tournament sort
tōnamento sentakuhō bunrui
トーナメント選択法分類

trace
torēsu; tsuiseki
トレース; 追跡

trace mode
tsuiseki mōdo
追跡モード

trace program
tsuiseki puroguramu
追跡プログラム

trace table
tsuiseki tēburu
追跡テーブル

traceability
torēsabiritei
トレーサビリティ

tracer
torēsa; tsuiseki puroguramu
トレーサ; 追跡プログラム

tracing program
tsuiseki puroguramu
追跡プログラム

tracing routine
tsuiseki rūchin
追跡ルーチン

track
torakku
トラック

track address
torakku-adoresu
トラック・アドレス

track condition table
torakku jōken tēburu
トラック条件テーブル

track hold
torakku hogo
トラック保護

track overflow
torakku afure
トラック溢れ

track pitch
torakku kan no kyori
トラック間の距離

track recording density
senkiroku mitsudo
線記録密度

track selection
torakku sentaku
トラック選択

tracking
torakkingu
トラッキング

tracking error
torakkingu-erā
トラッキング・エラー

tracking system
tsuiseki shisutemu
追跡システム

tractor feed
torakuta-fuiido
トラクタ・フィード

traffic
kōtsū; tsūshinryō
交通; 通信量

traffic control
kōtsū seigyo
交通制御

traffic intensity
koryō
呼量

trailer
atogaki; torēra
後書き; トレーラ

trailer label
atogaki raberu
後書きラベル

trailer record
atogaki rekōdo
後書きレコード

trailing edge
kōen
後縁

trailing end (TE)
shūtan (TE)
終端

train printer
rain-purinta
ライン・プリンタ

training
kunren
訓練

transaction
gyōmu no jikkō; toranzakushon;
torihiki
業務の実行; トランザクション;
取り引き

transaction card
toranzakushon-kādo;
torihiki kādo
トランザクション・カード;
取り引きカード

transaction data
toranzakushon-dēta
トランザクション・データ

transaction-driven processing
toranzakushon shori
トランザクション処理

transaction file
toranzakushon-fuairu;
torihiki fuairu
トランザクション・ファイル；
取り引きファイル

transaction processing
toranzakushon shori
トランザクション処理

transaction record
toranzakushon-rekōdo
トランザクション・レコード

transceiver
toranshiiba
トランシーバ

transcribe
tenki suru; tensha suru
転記する；転写する

transcription
tenki; tensha
転記；転写

transducer
henkanki
変換器

transfer (*noun*)
dentatsu; tensō
伝達；転送

transfer (*verb*)
tensō suru
転送する

transfer check
tensō kensa
転送検査

transfer control
tensō seigyo
転送制御

transfer-control procedure
tensō seigyo tejun
転送制御手順

transfer impedance
dentatsu inpiidansu
伝達インピーダンス

transfer instruction
tensō meirei
転送命令

transfer operation
tensō sōsa
転送操作

transfer rate
tensō ritsu; tensō sokudo
転送率；転送速度

transfer time
tensō jikan
転送時間

transferable
tensōkanō
転送可能

transform (*verb*)
henkei suru
変形する

transformation
henkei
変形

transformer
henryūki
変流器

transient
hijōchū; kado
非常駐；過渡

transient area
hijōchū ryō'iki
非常駐領域

transient response
kado ōtō
過渡応答

transistor
toranjisuta
トランジスタ

transistor-transistor logic (TTL)
toranjisuta-toranjisuta ronri (TTL)
トランジスタ・トランジスタ論理

transition
sen'i
遷移

transition card
sen'i kādo
遷移カード

transition diagram
sen'i zu
遷移図

transition duration
sen'i jikan
遷移時間

transition table
sen'i tēburu
遷移 テーブル

translate
henkan suru; hon'yaku suru
変換する；翻訳する

translate duration
hon'yaku jikan
翻訳時間

translating algorithm
hon'yaku arugorizumu
翻訳アルゴリズム

translating program
hon'yaku puroguramu
翻訳プログラム

translating time
hon'yaku jikan
翻訳時間

translation
henkan; hon'yaku
変換；翻訳

translation definition language (TDL)
henkan teigi gengo (TDL)
変換定義言語

translator
hon'yakuki; toransurēta
翻訳器；トランスレータ

translator program
hon'yaku puroguramu
翻訳プログラム

translator writing system
toransurēta sakusei shisutemu
トランスレータ作成システム

transmission
denshin; densō; densō; sōjushin;
sōshin;
伝信；電送；伝送；送受信；
送信

during transmission
sōshin tochū
送信途中

transmission channel
densōro
伝送路

transmission circuit
densō kaisen
伝送回線

transmission control (TC)
densō seigyo (TC)
伝送制御

transmission control character
densō seigyo moji
伝送制御文字

transmission control unit (TCU)
densō seigyo sōchi (TCU)
伝送制御装置

transmission error
densō erā
伝送エラー

transmission facilities
densō setsubi
伝送設備

transmission interruption
sōshin chūdan
送信中断

transmission line
densō sen
伝送線

transmission loss
densō sonshitsu
伝送損失

transmission mode
densō hōshiki
伝送方式

transmission speed
densō sokudo
伝送速度

transmit
densō suru; sōshin suru
伝送する；送信する

transmitter
densōki; sōshinki; tsūshinki
伝送機；送信機；通信機

transmitter-receiver
sōjushin sōchi
送受信装置

transparent data
toransuparento-dēta
トランスパレント・データ

transparent mode
sokuōgata hōshiki
即応型方式

transport
isō; kudō kikō; tensō
移送；駆動機構；転送

transport mechanism
isō kikō
移送機構

transport network (TN)
tensō nettowāku (TN)
転送ネットワーク

transport network control (TNC)
tensō nettowāku seigyo (TNC)
転送ネットワーク制御

transport station
isō kikō
移送機構

trap
torappu; warikomi
トラップ；割り込み

traveling-wave tube (TWT)
shinkōhakan (TWT)
進行波管

tree
ki
木

tree-form language
ki kōzō gengo
木構造言語

tree structure
ki kōzō
木構造

trial
tameshi
試し

triangular
sankaku
三角

triangular pulse
sankaku parusu
三角パルス

trigger
toriga
トリガ

trigger circuit
toriga kairo
トリガ回路

trigger off (verb)
hassei suru
発生する

trigger pulse
toriga-parusu
トリガ・パルス

triggering
toriga
トリガ

triplet
sanbitto-baito
3ビット・バイト

troubleshooting
shōgai tankyū; shōgai tsuikyū
障害探究；障害追求

true binary notation
shin nishin hyōkihō
真2進表記法

true complement
shin no hosū
真の補数

truncated block
tan burokku
短ブロック

truncation
kirisute
切り捨て

truncation error
kirisute gosa
切り捨て誤差

trunk
toranku
トランク

trunk control
toranku seigyo
トランク制御

truth table
shinri chihyō
真理値表

TSO (time-sharing option)
TSO (jibunkatsu opushon)
時分割オプション

TSS (time-sharing system)
TSS (taimu-shiearingu-shisutemu)
タイム・シェアリング・システム

TTL (transistor-transistor logic)
TTL (toranjisuta-toranjisuta ronri)
トランジスタ・トランジスタ論理

tuning
chōsei; dōchō
調整；同調

turn off
tān-ofu
ターン・オフ

turn-off time
tān-ofu jikan
ターン・オフ時間

turn on
tān-on
ターン・オン

turn-on time
tān-on jikan
ターン・オン時間

turnaround document
tān-araundo-dokyumento
ターン・アラウンド・ドキュメント

turnaround time
tān-araundo jikan
ターン・アラウンド時間

turnkey operation
tān-kii sōsa
ターン・キー操作

turtle graphics
tātaru-gurafuikkusu
タータル・グラフルックス

TV (television)
TV (terebi)
テレビ

twelve-inch display
jūni inchi-deisupurei
12インチ・ディスプレィ

twelve punch
jūni senkō
12せん孔

twin check
tsui kensa
対検査

twisted pair
tsuisuto-pea
ツイスト・ベア

twister storage
tsuisuta kioku
ツイスタ記憶

two-address
ni adoresu
2アドレス

two-address instruction
ni adoresu meirei
2アドレス命令

two-dimensional storage
ni shigen kioku
2次元記憶

two-drive
ni doraibu
2ドライブ

two-drive recorder
ni doraibu-rekōda
2ドライブ・レコーダ

two-level subroutine
ni reberu-saburūchin
2レベル・サブルーチン

two-phase simplex method
ni dankai tantai hō
二段階単体法

two-plus-one address
ni purasu ichi adoresu
2＋1アドレス

two-state
ni jōtai
二状態

two-state variable
ni jōtai hensū
二状態変数

two-tape method
ni tēpu hōhō
2テープ方法

two-wire channel
nisenshiki chaneru
二線式チャネル

two-wire circuit
nisenshiki kaisen
二線式回線

two-wire system
nisen shiki
二線式

two's complement
ni no hosū
2の補数

TWT (traveling-wave tube)
TWT (shinkōhakan)
進行波管

TWX (teletypewriter exchange service)
TWX (teretaipu kōkan sābisu)
テレタイプ交換サービス

type
kata; taipu
型；タイプ

type bar
taipu-bā
タイプ・バー

type declaration
taipu sengen(bun)
タイプ宣言(文)

type font
katsu jikei
活字形

type in
taipu-in
タイプ・イン

type wheel
taipu-hoiiru
タイプ・ホイール

type wheel printer
taipu-hoiiru insho sōchi
タイプ・ホイール印書装置

typeface
jikei
字形

typesetting
shokuji
植字

typesetting system
shokuji shisutemu
植字システム

typewriter
taipuraita
タイプライタ

typewriter console
taipuraita sōsataku
タイプライタ操作卓

typewriter terminal
taipuraita-tāminaru
タイプライタ・ターミナル

U

UA (upper accumulator)
UA (jōi ruisanki)
上位累算器

UART (universal asynchronous receiver-transmitter)
UART (han'yō hidōki sōjushin kairo)
汎用非同期送受信回路

UCB (unit control block)
UCB (sōchi seigyo burokku)
装置制御ブロック

UDC (universal decimal classification)
UDC (kokusai jisshin bunruihō)
国際10進分類法

UHL (user header label)
UHL (riyōsha fuairu midashi raberu)
利用者ファイル見出しラベル

UHP (universal host processor)
UHP (yunibāsaru-hosuto-purosessa)
ユニバーサル・ホスト・プロセッサ

ULD (universal language definition)
ULD (fuhen gengo teigi)
普遍言語定義

ultrahigh frequency
chōtampa
超短波

ultrasonic
chō'ompa
超音波

ultrasonic bonding
chō'ompa bondeingu
超音波ボンディング

ultrasonic delay line
chō'ompa chiensen
超音波遅延線

ultrasonic memory
chō'ompa kioku
超音波記憶

ultrasonic storage
chō'ompa kioku
超音波記憶

ultrasonic wave
chō'ompa
超音波

ultrasonics
chō'ompa kōgaku
超音波工学

unary
tankō
単項

unary operation
tankō enzan
単項演算

unary operator
tankō enzanshi
単項演算子

unattended operation
mujin sōsa
無人操作

unbalanced error
fuheikō gosa
不平衡誤差

unblocked
hiburokkuka
非ブロック化

unblocked records
hiburokkuka rekōdo
非ブロック化レコード

unblocking
hiburokkuka
非ブロック化

unbundled package
anbandoru-pakkēji
アンバンドル・パッケージ

unbundling
anbandoringu
アンバンドリング

unconditional
mujōken
無条件

unconditional branch
mujōken bunki
無条件分岐

unconditional branch instruction
mujōken bunki meirei
無条件分岐命令

unconditional GO TO statement
mujōken GO TO bun
無条件GO TO文

unconditional jump
mujōken tobikoshi
無条件飛び越し

unconditional jump instruction
mujōken tobikoshi meirei
無条件飛び越し命令

unconditional statement
mujōken bun
無条件文

unconditional transfer
mujōken tensō;
mujōken tobikoshi
無条件転送；無条件飛び越し

unconditional transfer instruction
mujōken tobikoshi meirei
無条件飛び越し命令

unconnected
hiketsugō
非結合

unconnected terminal
hiketsugō tanmatsu (sōchi)
非結合端末（装置）

undefined
futei; miteigi
不定；未定義

undefined format
futei keishiki
不定形式

undefined instruction
miteigi meirei
未定義命令

undefined record
futei keishiki rekōdo
不定形式レコード

undefined symbol
miteigi kigō
未定義記号

under damping
anda-danpingu
アンダ・ダンピング

underflow
andafurō; kaiketa afure
アンダフロー；下位桁溢れ

underline
andarain
アンダライン

underpunch
andapanchi
アンダパンチ

undetected
minogashi
見逃し

undetected error
minogashi ayamari
見逃し誤り

undetected-error rate
minogashi ayamari ritsu
見逃し誤り率

unformatted
futei yōshiki; shoshiki nai
不定様式；書式ない

unformatted data
futei yōshiki dēta
不定様式データ

unformatted display
futei yōshiki hyōji
不定様式表示

unformatted message
futei yōshiki messēji
不定様式メッセージ

unformatted READ statement
shoshiki nai riido bun
書式ないREAD文

unformatted WRITE statement
shoshiki nai raito bun
書式ないWRITE文

unibus
yunibasu
ユニバス

unibus link
yunibasu renketsu;
yunibasu-rinku
ユニバス連結；ユニバス・リンク

unidirectional
tanhōkō
単方向

uniformity
kinissei; kinitsu
均一性；均一

union
gappei; ketsugō
合併；結合

unipolar
tankyokusei
単極性

unipolar pulse
tankyokusei parusu
単極性パルス

unipolar signal
tankyokusei shingō
単極性信号

uniprocessor
tan'itsu purosessa
単一プロセッサ

unit
sōchi; tan'i; yunitto
装置；単位；ユニット

unit (office; station)
kasho
箇所

unit control block (UCB)
sōchi seigyo burokku (UCB)
装置制御ブロック

unit control word
sōchi seigyo go
装置制御語

unit for counting computers
dai
台

unit impulse
tan'i inparusu
単位インパルス

unit impulse response
tan'i inparusu ōtō
単位インパルス応答

unit interval
tan'i kankaku
単位間隔

unit number
sōchi bangō
装置番号

unit of storage
baito
バイト

unit processor
tan'itsu purosessa
単一プロセッサ

unit record
yunitto-rekōdo
ユニット・レコード

unit record file
yunitto-rekōdo-fuairu
ユニット・レコード・ファイル

unit record routine
yunitto-rekōdo-rūchin
ユニット・レコード・ルーチン

unit separator (US)
yunitto bunri moji (US)
ユニット分離文字

unit step
tan'i suteppu
単位ステップ

unit step response
tan'i suteppu ōtō
単位ステップ応答

unit string
tan'i renshi; tan'i sutoringu
単位連糸；単位ストリング

United States of America Standards Code for Information Interchange (USASCII)
Jōhō Kōkan'yō Beikoku Hyōjun Kōdo (USASCII)
情報交換用米国標準コード

United States of America Standards Institute (USASI)
Beikoku Kikaku Kyōkai (USASI)
米国規格協会

universal
han'yō; kokusai(teki); yunibāsaru
汎用；国際(的)；ユニバーサル

universal asynchronous receiver-transmitter (UART)
han'yō hidōki sōjushin kairo (UART)
汎用非同期送受信回路

universal board
yunibāsaru-bōdo
ユニバーサル・ボード

universal character set
han'yō moji setto
汎用文字セット

universal decimal classification (UDC)
kokusai jisshin bunruihō (UDC)
国際10進分類法

universal host processor (UHP)
yunibāsaru-hosuto-purosessa (UHP)
ユニバーサル・ホスト・プロセッサ

universal instruction set
han'yō meirei setto
汎用命令セット

universal language definition (ULD)
fuhen gengo teigi (ULD)
普遍言語定義

universal module
yunibāsaru-mojyūru
ユニバーサル・モジュール

universal processing unit
han'yō shori sōchi
汎用処理装置

UNIX
UNIX; Yunikkusu
UNIX; ユニックス

unkeyed record
kii no nai rekōdo
キーのないレコード

unlabeled
nafuda no nai
名札のない

unlabeled basic statement
nafuda no nai kihon bun
名札のない基本文

unlabeled block
nafuda no nai burokku
名札のないフロック

unload
anrōdo
アンロード

unmanned
mujin
無人

unmanned operation
mujin sōsa
無人操作

unmanned station
mujin tanmatsu
無人端末

unmodified
hishūshoku
非修飾

unmodified instruction
hishūshoku meirei
非修飾命令

unpack
anpakku
アンパック

unpacked format
anpakku keishiki
アンパック形式

unprotected
muhogo
無保護

unrecoverable
kaifukufunō
回復不能

unrecoverable error
kaifukufunō ayamari
回復不能誤り

unrepairable
shūrifunō
修理不能

unsafe
fuanzen
不安全

unsigned
fugō nai
符号ない

unsigned binary
fugō nai nishinsū
符号ない2進数

unsigned integer
fugō nai seisū
符号ない整数

unsigned message
fugō nai messēji
符号ないメッセージ

unsolicited key-in
nin'igata kii-in
任意型キー・イン

unsolvable
kaiketsufunō
解決不能

unstable
fuantei
不安定

up time
shiyōkanō jikan
使用可能時間

update (*verb*)
kōshin suru
更新する

update number
kōshin bangō
更新番号

update routine
kōshin rūchin
更新ルーチン

update run
kōshin ran
更新ラン

updating
kōshin
更新

upper accumulator (UA)
jōi ruisanki (UA)
上位累算器

upper paper feed
jōbu kami okuri
上部紙送り

upward compatibility
appuwādo-konpateibiritei;
uwamuki no gokansei
アップワード・コンパティビリティ;
上向きの互換性

upward compatible
appuwādo-konpateiburu;
uwamuki no gokansei no
アップワード・コンパティブル;
上向きの互換性の

urgent
kinkyū; shikyū
緊急; 至急

urgent message
shikyū dembun
至急電文

usability
shiyosei
使用性

USASCII (USA Standards Code for Information Interchange)
USASCII (Jōhō Kōkan'yō Beikoku Hyōjun Kōdo)
情報交換用米国標準コード

USASI (USA Standards Institute)
USASI (Beikoku Kikaku Kyōkai)
米国規格協会

use
riyō; shiyō; yōto
利用; 使用; 用途

user
riyōsha; shiyōsha; yūza
利用者; 使用者; ユーザ

user-definable key
yūza teigikanō kii
ユーザ定義可能キー

user-defined character
yūza teigisumi moji
ユーザ定義済み文字

user documentation
yūza bunsho
ユーザ文書

user file
yūza-fuairu
ユーザ・ファイル

user-friendly system
riyōsha enjo shisutemu
利用者援助システム

user group
yūza-gurūpu
ユーザ・グループ

user header label (UHL)
riyōsha fuairu midashi raberu
(UHL)
利用者ファイル見出しラベル

user identification
yūza shikibetsu
ユーザ識別

user interface
yūza-intafēsu
ユーザ・インタフェース

user option
yūza-opushon
ユーザ・オプション

user-oriented system
riyōsha muki shisutemu
利用者向きシステム

user port
yūza-pōto
ユーザ・ポート

user priority
riyōsha yūsen jun'i
利用者優先順位

user profile
yūza-purofuairu
ユーザ・プロファイル

user program
yūza-puroguramu
ユーザ・プログラム

user terminal
yūza tanmatsu (sōchi)
ユーザ端末(装置)

user trailer label (UTL)
riyōsha atogaki raberu (UTL)
利用者後書きラベル

user volume header label
riyōsha boryūmu midashi
raberu
利用者ボリューム見出しラベル

utility
kōyō; yūteiritei
効用; ユーティリティ

utility processor
yūteiritei-purosessa
ユーティリティ・プロセッサ

utility program
yūteiritei-puroguramu
ユーティリティ・プログラム

utility routine
yūteiritei-rūchin
ユーティリティ・ルーチン

utilization ratio
shiyō ritsu
使用率

UTL (user trailer label)
UTL (riyōsha atogaki raberu)
利用者後書きラベル

V

v (volt)
v (boruto)
ボルト

vacuum
bakyūmu; shinkū
バキューム; 真空

vacuum column
bakyūmu-karamu
バキューム・カラム

vacuum evaporation
shinkū jōchaku
真空蒸着

vacuum tube
bakyūmu kan
バキューム管

VADR (virtual address)
VADR (kasō adoresu)
仮想アドレス

valid
datō
妥当

validation
datōsei kensa
妥当性検査

validation check
datōsei kensa
妥当性検査

validation program
datōsei kensa no puroguramu
妥当性検査のプログラム

validity
datōsei
妥当性

validity check
datōsei kensa
妥当性検査

value
atai; chi; kachi
値; 値; 価値

value analysis
kachi bunseki
価値分析

value part
atai no bu
値の部

value system
kachi shisutemu
価値システム

variable (*noun*)
(sūchi) hensū
（数値）変数

variable (*adjective*)
kahen
可変

variable address
kahen adoresu
可変アドレス

variable binding
kahen renketsu
可変連結

variable block length
kahen burokku chō
可変ブロック長

variable connector
kahen ketsugōshi
可変結合子

variable field
hensū fuiirudo
変数フィールド

variable fixed block
kahen kotei burokku
可変固定ブロック

variable format
kahen chō keishiki
可変長形式

variable frequency oscillator (VFO)
kahen shūhasū hasshinki (VFO)
可変周波数発振器

variable function generator
kahen kansū zenerēta
可変関数ゼネレータ

variable length
kahen chō
可変長

variable-length addressing
kahen chō adoresu shitei
可変長アドレス指定

variable-length data
kahen chō dēta
可変長データ

variable-length field
kahen chō fuiirudo
可変長フィールド

variable-length record
kahen chō rekōdo
可変長レコード

variable-length word
kahen chō go
可変長語

variable logic
kahen ronri
可変論理

variable name
hensu mei
変数名

variable point
kahen shōsūten
可変小数点

variable-point representation
kahen shōsūten hyōji
可変小数点表示

variable-point representation system
kahen shōsūten hyōji hō
可変小数点表示法

variable precision
kahen seido
可変精度

variable speed
kahen sokudo
可変速度

variable structure
kahen kōzō
可変構造

variable symbol
kahen kigō
可変記号

variable threshold logic (VTL)
kahen shikii chi ronri (VTL)
可変敷居値論理

variable-variable block
kahen-kahen burokku
可変-可変ブロック

variable word
kahen chō go
可変長語

variable word length
kahen go chō
可変語長

variance
bunsan
分散

variance analysis
bunsan bunseki
分散分析

varistor
barisuta
バリスタ

VC (virtual call)
VC (aite sentaku setsuzoku)
相手選択接続

VCO (voltage-controlled oscillator)
VCO (den'atsu seigyo hasshinki)
電圧制御発振器

VCR (videocassette recorder)
VCR (bideo-kasetto-rekōda)
ビデオ・カセット・レコーダ

VDL (Vienna definition language)
VDL (Uiinshiki teigi gengo)
ウイーン式定義言語

VDT (video display terminal)
VDT (bideo hyōji tanmatsu sōchi)
ビデオ表示端末装置

VDU (video display unit)
VDU (bideo hyōji sōchi; eizō hyōji sōchi)
ビデオ表示装置；映像表示装置

VDU (visual display unit)
VDU (hyōji sōchi; shikakuteki hyōji sōchi)
表示装置；視覚的表示装置

VDU signal
hyōji sōchi shingō
表示装置信号

VDU warning signal
hyōji sōchi keihō shingō
表示装置警報信号

vector
bekuta
ベクタ

vector computer
bekuta-konpyūta
ベクタ・コンピュータ

vector graphics
bekuta-gurafuikkusu
ベクタ・グラフィックス

vector mode
bekuta-mōdo
ベクタ・モード

vector-mode display unit
bekuta-mōdo hyōji sōchi
ベクタ・モード表示装置

Veitch diagram
Beichi zu
ベイチ図

velocity
sokudo
速度

Venn diagram
Ben zu
ベン図

VENUS (valuable and efficient network utility service)
biinasu; VENUS
ビーナス; VENUS

verbal response
onsei ōtō
音声応答

verification
kenkō; kensa; kenshō
検孔; 検査; 検証

verification process
kenshō katei
検証過程

verification technique
kenshō gihō
検証技法

verifier
kenkōki
検孔機

verify
kenkō suru; kensa suru; kenshō suru
検孔する; 検査する; 検証する

verifying
kenkō; kenshō
検孔; 検証

versatile
tageisei
多芸性

versatility
tagei
多芸

vertical
suichoku
垂直

vertical check
suichoku kensa
垂直検査

vertical feed
suichoku okuri
垂直送り

vertical format
suichoku shoshiki
垂直書式

vertical line
suichoku sen
垂直線

vertical parity check
suichoku kigū kensa
垂直奇偶検査

vertical redundancy check (VRC)
suichoku jōchō kensa (VRC)
垂直冗長検査

vertical scanning
suichoku sōsa
垂直走査

vertical synchronization
suichoku dōki
垂直同期

vertical tabulation (VT)
suichoku tabu (VT)
垂直タブ

vertical tabulation character (VT)
suichoku tabu moji (VT)
垂直タブ文字

very high frequency (VHF)
chōtampa (VHF)
超短波

very large scale integration (VLSI)
chōdai kibo shūsekika (VLSI)
超大規模集積化

VFO (variable frequency oscillator)
VFO (kahen shūhasū hasshinki)
可変周波数発振器

VHF (very high frequency)
VHF (chōtampa)
超短波

video
bideo
ビデオ

video conference
bideo-konfuerensu
ビデオ・コンフェレンス

video data
bideo-dēta
ビデオ・データ

video data terminal
bideo-dēta tanmatsu sōchi
ビデオ・データ端末装置

video detector
bideo-detekuta
ビデオ・デテクタ

video display terminal (VDT)
bideo hyōji tanmatsu sōchi (VDT)
ビデオ表示端末装置

video display unit (VDU)
bideo hyōji sōchi;
eizō hyōji sōchi (VDU)
ビデオ表示装置; 映像表示装置

video file
bideo-fuairu
ビデオ・ファイル

video game
bideo-gēmu
ビデオ・ゲーム

video information processing system
bideo jōhō shori shisutemu
ビデオ情報処理システム

video monitor
bideo-monita
ビデオ・モニタ

video processing unit
bideo shori sōchi
ビデオ処理装置

video RAM
bideo RAM
ビデオRAM

video screen
bideo hyōji sōchi
ビデオ表示装置

video signal
bideo shingō; eizō shingō
ビデオ信号; 映像信号

videocassette
bideo-kasetto
ビデオ・カセット

videocassette player
bideo-kasetto sōchi
ビデオ・カセット装置

videocassette recorder (VCR)
bideo-kasetto-rekōda (VCR)
ビデオ・カセット・レコーダ

videodisc
bideo-deisuku
ビデオ・ディスク

videodisc system
bideo-deisuku hōshiki
ビデオ・ディスク方式

videotape player
bideo-tēpu sōchi
ビデオ・テープ装置

videotape recorder
bideo-tēpu-rekōda
ビデオ・テープ・レコーダ

videotex
bideotekkusu
ビデオテックス

Vienna definition language (VDL)
Uiinshiki teigi gengo (VDL)
ウイーン式定義言語

viewdata
byūdēta
ビューデータ

VIP (visual information processor)
VIP (hyōji jōhō sōchi)
表示情報装置

virgin medium
mishiyō baitai
未使用媒体

virtual address (VADR)
kasō adoresu (VADR)
仮想アドレス

virtual address space
kasō adoresu kūkan
仮想アドレス空間

virtual addressing
kasō adoresu shitei
仮想アドレス指定

virtual call (VC)
aite sentaku setsuzoku (VC)
相手選択接続

virtual circuit
kasō kairo
仮想回路

virtual machine
kasō keisanki
仮想計算機

virtual machine philosophy
kasō keisanki shisō
仮想計算機思想

virtual machine technology
kasō keisanki gijutsu
仮想計算機技術

virtual memory
kasō kioku
仮想記憶

virtual operating system
kasō operēteingu-shisutemu
仮想オペレーティング・
システム

virtual result
kasō kekka
仮想結果

virtual route
kasō keiro
仮想経路

virtual storage
kasō kioku
仮想記憶

virtual storage access method (VSAM)
kasō kioku akusesu hōshiki (VSAM)
仮想記憶アクセス方式

virtual store
kasō kioku sōchi
仮想記憶装置

virtual telecommunications access method (VTAM)
kasō tsūshin akusesu hōshiki (VTAM)
仮想通信アクセス方式

visible-record computer (VRC)
hyōji rekōdo-konpyūta (VRC)
表示レコード・コンピュータ

visual detection
shikakuteki kenshutsu
視覚的検出

visual display
hyōji sōchi
表示装置

visual display output
hyōji sōchi shutsuryoku
表示装置出力

visual display unit (VDU)
hyōji sōchi; shikakuteki hyōji sōchi (VDU)
表示装置; 視覚的表示装置

visual information processing
shikaku jōhō shori
視覚情報処理

visual information processor (VIP)
shikaku jōhō shori sōchi (VIP)
視覚情報処理装置

visual-record printer (VRP)
hyōji rekōdo-purinta (VRP)
表示レコード・プリンタ

visual scanner
kōgakushiki sōsa kikō
光学式走査機械

visual scanning
kōgakushiki sōsa
光学式走査

visual search
shikakuteki tansaku
視覚的探索

VLSI (very large scale integration)
VLSI (chōdai kibo shūsekika)
超大規模集積化

voice
onsei
音声

voice band
onsei tai'iki
音声帯域

voice frequency
onsei shūha
音声周波

voice-grade channel
onsei tai'iki chaneru
音声帯域チャネル

voice-grade line
onsei tai'iki kaisen
音声帯域回線

voice input
onsei nyūryoku
音声入力

voice input device
onsei nyūryoku sōchi
音声入力装置

voice input module
onsei nyūryoku mojyūru
音声入力モジュール

voice recognition
onsei ninshiki
音声認識

voice response
onsei ōtō
音声応答

voice synthesis
koe gōsei; onsei gōsei
声合成；音声合成

voice synthesis card
onsei gōsei kādo
音声合成カード

voice unit (VU)
onsei tan'i (VU)
音声単位

VOL (volume)
VOL (boryūmu)
ボリューム

volatile
hijikyū; kihatsu
非持久；揮発

volatile memory
hijikyū kioku; kihatsusei kioku
非持久記憶；揮発性記憶

volatile storage
hijikyū kioku; kihatsusei kioku
非持久記憶；揮発性記憶

volatility
hijikyūsei; kihatsusei
非持久性；揮発性

volt (v)
boruto (v)
ボルト

voltage
den'atsu
電圧

voltage-controlled oscillator (VCO)
den'atsu seigyo hasshinki (VCO)
電圧制御発振器

voltage regulating
den'atsu chōsei
電圧調整

voltage regulator (VR)
den'atsu anteiki (VR)
電圧安定器

volume (VOL)
boryūmu (VOL); onryō; ryō
ボリューム；音量；量

volume header label
boryūmu midashi raberu
ボリューム見出しラベル

volume identifier
boryūmu shikibetsushi
ボリューム識別子

volume label
boryūmu-raberu
ボリューム・ラベル

volume sequence number
boryūmu junjo bangō
ボリューム順序番号

volume serial number
boryūmu tōshi bangō
ボリューム通し番号

volume table of contents (VTOC)
boryūmu mokuroku (VTOC)
ボリューム目録

volume test
boryūmu-tesuto
ボリューム・テスト

volume trailer label
boryūmu atogaki raberu
ボリューム後書きラベル

volume unit (VU)
onryō tan'i (VU)
音量単位

von Neumann computer
fuon-Noimangata konpyūta
フォン・ノイマン型コンピュータ

VR (voltage regulator)
VR (den'atsu anteiki)
電圧安定器

VRC (vertical redundancy check)
VRC (suichoku jōchō kensa)
垂直冗長検査

VRC (visible-record computer)
VRC (hyōji rekōdo-konpyūta)
表示レコード・コンピュータ

VRP (visual-record printer)
VRP (hyōji rekōdo-purinta)
表示レコード・プリンタ

VSAM (virtual storage access method)
VSAM (kasō kioku akusesu hōshiki)
仮想記憶アクセス方式

VT (vertical tabulation; vertical tabulation character)
VT (suichoku tabu; suichoku tabu moji)
垂直タブ；垂直タブ文字

VTAM (virtual telecommunications access method)
VTAM (kasō tsūshin akusesu hōshiki)
仮想通信アクセス方式

VTL (variable threshold logic)
VTL (kahen shikii chi ronri)
可変敷居値論理

VTOC (volume table of contents)
VTOC (boryūmu mokuroku)
ボリューマ目録

VU (voice unit)
VU (onsei tan'i)
音声単位

VU (volume unit)
VU (onryō tan'i)
音量単位

W

W (word)
W (go; tango; wādo)
語；単語；ワード

WADS (wide-area data service)
WADS (kō'iki dēta-sābisu)
広域データ・サービス

wafer
uēfua
ウェーファ

wait
machi
待ち

wait state
machi jōtai
待ち状態

WAIT status
WAIT jōtai
WAIT 状態

waiting-line theory
machiawase riron
待ち合わせ理論

waiting state
machi jōtai
待ち状態

waiting time
machi jikan
待ち時間

walk back
gyaku tanchi
逆探知

WAN (wide-area network)
WAN (kō'iki nettowāku)
広域ネットワーク

wand
wando
ワンド

warm restart
uōmu saisutāto
ウオーム再スタート

warm start
uōmu-sutāto
ウオーム・スタート

warning
keihō; keikoku
警報；警告

warning device
keihōki
警報器

warning message
keikoku messēji
警告メッセージ

waste operation
mudōsa
無動作

watchdog timer (WDT)
uotchidoggu-taima (WDT)
ウオッチドッグ・タイマ

wave
nami
波

waveform
hakei
波形

waveform equalization
hakei tōka
波形等化

waveform generation
hakei seisei
波形生成

waveform regeneration
hakei saisei
波形再生

waveform regeneration circuit
hakei saisei kairo
波形再生回路

waveform shaping
hakei seikei
波形整形

waveform shaping circuit
hakei seikei kairo
波形整形回路

WBLS (wide-band linear synchronization)
WBLS (kōtai'iki senkei dōki)
広帯域線形同期

WCS (writable control storage)
WCS (kakikomikanō seigyo sōchi)
書き込み可能制御装置

WDT (watchdog timer)
WDT (uotchidoggu-taima)
ウオッチドッグ・タイマ

weight
omomi
重み

weight register
omomi rejisuta
重みレジスタ

weighted-bit code
nishin fugōka jisshin hō
2進符号化10進法

weighted code
omomitsuki kōdo
重み付きコード

wheel printer
hoiiru-purinta
ホイール・プリンタ

white noise
hakushoku zatsuon;
howaito-noizu
白色雑音；ホワイト・ノイズ

who are you? (WRU)
anata wa (WRU)
あなたは

wide area
kō'iki
広域

wide-area data service (WADS)
kō'iki dēta-sābisu (WADS)
広域データ・サービス

wide-area network (WAN)
kō'iki nettowāku (WAN)
広域ネットワーク

wide band
kōtai'iki
広帯域

wide-band linear synchronization (WBLS)
kōtai'iki senkei dōki (WBLS)
広帯域線形同期

Williams tube
Uiriamusu kan
ウイリアムス管

Winchester disk drive
Uinchesuta-deisuku-doraibu
ウインチェスタ・ディスク・ドライブ

window
uindō
ウインドー

window concept
uindō-konseputo
ウインドー・コンセプト

wire
waiya
ワイヤ

wire memory
waiya-memori
ワイヤ・メモリ

wire printer
waiya-purinta
ワイヤ・プリンタ

wire storage
waiya kioku
ワイヤ記憶

wired AND
shutsuryoku ketsugō;
waiyādo AND
出力結合；ワイヤードAND

wired OR
shutsuryoku ketsugō;
waiyādo OR
出力結合；ワイヤードOR

wired-program computer
haisenshiki keisanki
配線式計算機

wiring
haisen
配線

wiring board
haisenban
配線盤

word (W)
go; tango; wādo (W)
語；単語；ワード

word address
go adoresu
語アドレス

word boundary
wādo kyōkai
ワード境界

word computer
go keisanki
語計算機

word length
go chō
語長

word line
go sen
語線

word mark
wādo-māku
ワード・マーク

word of two or more characters (Japanese)
jukugo
熟語

word-oriented
go muki
語向き

word processing (WP)
bunsho shori;
wādo-purosesshingu (WP)
文書処理；
ワード・プロセッシング

word processor (WP)
bunsho shori sōchi;
wādo-purosessa (WP)
文書処理装置；
ワード・プロセッサ

word stem
gokan
語幹

word time
go jikan; wādo-taimu
語時間；ワード・タイム

words per minute (WPM)
go/fun (WPM)
語／分

words per second (WPS)
go/byō (WPS)
語／秒

work
sagyō; wāku
作業；ワーク

work area
sagyō iki
作業域

work file
sagyō fuairu
作業ファイル

work load
sagyō fuka
作業負荷

work scheduling
wāku-sukejyūringu
ワーク・スケジューリング

work storage
sagyō'yō kioku'iki
作業用記憶域

work tape
sagyō'yō tēpu; wāku-tēpu
作業用テープ；ワーク・テープ

work track
sagyō torakku
作業トラック

working area
sagyō iki
作業域

working space
sagyō iki
作業域

working station
sagyō tanmatsu
作業端末

working storage
sagyō'yō kioku'iki
作業用記憶域

working tape
sagyō'yō tēpu
作業用テープ

workspace
sagyō ryō'iki
作業領域

workstation (WS)
sagyō tanmatsu; wāku-sutēshon (WS)
作業端末；ワーク・ステーション

workstation keyboard
wāku-sutēshon-kiibōdo
ワーク・ステーション・
キーボード

WP (word processing)
WP (bunsho shori; wādo-purosesshingu)
文書処理；ワード・
プロセッシング

WP (word processor)
WP (bunsho shori sōchi; wādo-purosessa)
文書処理装置；ワード・
プロセッサ

WPM (words per minute)
WPM (go/fun)
語／分

WPS (words per second)
WPS (go/byō)
語／秒

wraparound
junkan; rappu-araundo
循環；ラップ・アラウンド

writable control storage (WCS)
kakikomikanō seigyo sōchi
(WCS)
書き込み可能制御装置

write
kakidasu; kakikomu
書き出す；書き込む

write cycle time
kakikomi saikuru-taimu
書き込みサイクル・タイム

write head
kakikomi heddo
書き込みヘッド

write inhibit
kakikomi kinshi
書き込み禁止

write-inhibit ring
kakikomi kinshi ringu
書き込み禁止リング

write instruction
kakikomi meirei
書き込み命令

write-permit ring
kakikomi kyoka ringu
書き込み許可リング

write protection
kakikomi hogo
書き込み保護

write ring
kakikomi ringu
書き込みリング

writing
kakidashi; kakikomi
書き出し；書き込み

WRU (who are you?)
WRU (anata wa)
あなたは

WS (workstation)
WS (sagyō tanmatsu; wāku-suteshon)
作業端末；ワーク・ステーション

X

X-chart
X-kōshi
X 格子

X-over punch
X-uwakasane senkō
X 上重ねせん孔

X-position
X-pojishon
X ポジション

X-punch
X-senkō
X せん孔

X-Y plotter
X-Y purotta
X-Y プロッタ

xerographic printer
denshi shashinshiki insho sōchi
電子写真式印書装置

XNOR (exclusive-NOR)
XNOR (haitateki hitei ronriwa; haitateki NOR)
XNOR；排他的否定論理和；排他的 NOR

XNOR circuit (exclusive-NOR circuit)
XNOR kairo (haitateki hitei ronriwa kairo; haitateki NOR kairo)
XNOR 回路；排他的否定論理和回路；排他的 NOR 回路

XOR (exclusive-OR)
XOR (haitateki OR; haitateki ronriwa)
XOR；排他的 OR；排他的論理和

XOR circuit (exclusive-OR circuit)
XOR kairo (haitateki OR kairo; haitateki ronriwa kairo)
XOR 回路；排他的 OR 回路；排他的論理和回路

XOR element (exclusive-OR element)
XOR soshi (haitateki OR soshi; haitateki ronriwa soshi)
XOR 素子；排他的 OR 素子；排他的論理和素子

XOR gate (exclusive-OR gate)
XOR gēto (haitateki OR gēto; haitateki ronriwa gēto)
XOR ゲート；排他的 OR ゲート；排他的論理和ゲート

XOR operation (exclusive-OR operation)
XOR enzan (haitateki OR enzan; haitateki ronriwa enzan)
XOR 演算；排他的 OR 演算；排他的論理和演算

Y

Y-over punch
Y-uwakasane senkō
Y上重ねせん孔

Y-position
Y-pojishon
Yポジション

Y-punch
Y-senkō
Yせん孔

Z

zero
rei; zero
零; ゼロ

zero address
zero-adoresu
ゼロ・アドレス

zero-address instruction
zero-adoresu meirei
ゼロ・アドレス命令

zero-address instruction format
zero-adoresu meirei keishiki
ゼロ・アドレス命令形式

zero balance
zero-baransu
ゼロ・バランス

zero-clear
zero ni suru
ゼロにする

zero compression
zero asshuku
ゼロ圧縮

zero condition
zero jōtai
ゼロ状態

zero elimination
zero shōkyo
ゼロ消去

zero-fill
zero jūten
ゼロ充てん

zero-level address
zero-reberu-adoresu
ゼロ・レベル・アドレス

zero output
zero shutsuryoku
ゼロ出力

zero suppression
zero yokusei
ゼロ抑制

zeroize
zero ni suru
ゼロにする

zone
zōn
ゾーン

zone bit
zōn-bitto
ゾーン・ビット

zone digit
zōn-deijitto
ゾーン・ディジット

zone punch
zōn senkō
ゾーンせん孔

zone purification
zōn seisei
ゾーン精製

zone refining
zōn seisei
ゾーン精製

zoned format
zōn keishiki
ゾーン形式

zoning
zōn hōshiki; zōningu
ゾーン方式; ゾーニング

WA-EI
JAPANESE-ENGLISH
和英

A

abeirabiritei
availability
アベイラビリティ

abeirabiritei kijun
availability criteria
アベイラビリティ基準

abeirabiritei ritsu
availability ratio
アベイラビリティ率

ABEND (tasuku no ijō shūryō)
ABEND (abnormal end of task)
タスクの異常終了

abōto suru
abort
アボートする

AC (kōryū)
AC (alternating current)
ＡＣ；交流

AC danpu (kōryū danpu)
AC dump
ＡＣダンプ；交流ダンプ

AC dengen (kōryū dengen)
AC power supply
ＡＣ電源；交流電源

ACK (akku; kōtei ōtō)
ACK (acknowledgment)
アック；肯定応答

ACM (Amerika Keisanki Gakkai)
ACM (Association for Computing Machinery)
アメリカ計算機学会

ACS (jiritsu seigyo shisutemu)
ACS (autonomous control system)
自律制御システム

ACU (enzan seigyo sōchi)
ACU (arithmetic and control unit)
演算制御装置

ACU (jidō yobidashi sōchi)
ACU (automatic calling unit)
自動呼び出し装置

ACW (akusesu seigyo go)
ACW (access control word)
アクセス制御語

A/D (anarogu-deijitaru)
A/D (analog-to-digital)
Ａ／Ｄ；アナログ・ディジタル

A/D henkan (anarogu-deijitaru henkan)
A/D conversion (analog-to-digital conversion)
Ａ／Ｄ変換；
アナログ・ディジタル変換

A/D henkanki (anarogu-deijitaru henkanki; ADC)
A/D converter (analog-to-digital converter; ADC)
Ａ／Ｄ変換器；
アナログ・ディジタル変換器

A/D konbāta (anarogu-deijitaru-konbāta; ADC)
A/D converter (analog-to-digital converter; ADC)
Ａ／Ｄコンバータ；アナログ・
ディジタル・コンバータ

adā
adder
アダー

ADA (jidō dēta shūshū)
ADA (automatic data acquisition)
自動データ収集

adaputa
adapter
アダプタ

ADC (anarogu-deijitaru henkanki; anarogu-deijitaru-konbāta)
ADC (analog-to-digital converter)
アナログ・ディジタル変換器；
アナログ・ディジタル・
コンバータ

ADCCP (adobansudo-dēta tsūshin seigyo tejun)
ADCCP (advanced data communication control procedure)
アドバンス・データ通信
制御手順

ADD (kasan)
ADD (addition)
加算

ado-in-bōdo
add-in board
アド・イン・ボード

ado-in-kādo
add-in card
アド・イン・カード

ado-on
add-on
アド・オン

ado-on-kiibōdo
add-on keyboard
アド・オン・キーボード

ado-on-memori
add-on memory
アド・オン・メモリ

ado-on-mojūru
add-on module
アド・オン・モジュール

ado-tsū-memori
add-to-memory
アド・ツー・メモリ

adobansu
advance
アドバンス

adobansu-dēta tsūshin seigyo tejun (ADCCP)
advanced data communication control procedure (ADCCP)
アドバンス・データ通信制御
手順

adobansu-mōdo
advance mode
アドバンス・モード

adoresshingu
addressing
アドレッシング

adoresshingu-mōdo
addressing mode
アドレッシング・モード

adoresu
address
アドレス

adoresu ayamari
address error
アドレス誤り

adoresu-basu
address bus
アドレス・バス

adoresu bu
address part
アドレス部

adoresu-fuiirudo
address field
アドレス・フィールド

adoresu henkan
address conversion;
address translation
アドレス変換

adoresu henkan tēburu
address-conversion table;
address-translation table
アドレス変換テーブル

adoresu henkō
address modification
アドレス変更

adoresu henkōshi
address modifier
アドレス変更子

adoresu kanri
address management
アドレス管理

adoresu-kaunta
address counter
アドレス・カウンタ

adoresu keisan
address calculation;
address computation
アドレス計算

adoresu keishiki
address format
アドレス形式

adoresu kensa
address check
アドレス検査

adoresu-kii
address key
アドレス・キー

adoresu kōsei yōso
address component
アドレス構成要素

adoresu kūkan
address space
アドレス空間

adoresu kūkan kakuchō
address-space extension
アドレス空間拡張

adoresu kūkan kanri
address-space management
アドレス空間管理

adoresu kūkan shikibetsushi
address-space identifier
アドレス空間識別子

adoresu-mappingu
address mapping
アドレス・マッピング

adoresu-rejisuta
address register
アドレス・レジスタ

adoresu sanshō
address reference
アドレス参照

adoresu sentaku
address selection
アドレス選択

adoresu shikibetsushi
address identifier
アドレス識別子

adoresu shitei
address assignment; addressing
アドレス指定

adoresu shitei kanō
addressable
アドレス指定可能

adoresu shitei kanōsei
addressability
アドレス指定可能性

adoresu (shitei) kanōten
addressable point
アドレス(指定)可能点

adoresu shitei shisutemu
addressing system
アドレス指定システム

adoresu shūshoku
address modification
アドレス修飾

adoresu shūshokushi
address modifier
アドレス修飾子

adoresu-tēburu
address table
アドレス・テーブル

adoresu teishi
address stop
アドレス停止

adoresu teisū
address constant
アドレス定数

adoresu-torakku
address track
アドレス・トラック

adoresu wariate
address assignment
アドレス割り当て

adoresu-zenerēta
address generator
アドレス・ゼネレータ

adoresutsuke funō kioku
nonaddressable memory
アドレス付け不能記憶

ADP (jidō dēta shori)
ADP (automatic data processing)
自動データ処理

ADPS (jidō dēta shori shisutemu)
ADPS (automatic data-processing system)
自動データ処理システム

AF (kachō shūhasū; onsei shūhasū)
AF (audio frequency)
可聴周波数；音声周波数

afure
overflow
溢れ

afure adoresu
overflow address
溢れアドレス

afure hyōshiki
overflow indicator
溢れ標識

afure iki
overflow area
溢れ域

afure rejisuta
overflow register
溢れレジスタ

afure rekōdo
overflow record
溢れレコード

afure tesuto
overflow test
溢れテスト

AGC (jidō ritoku seigyo)
AGC (automatic gain control)
自動利得制御

āgyumento
argument
アーギュメント

AI (jinkō chinō)
AI (artificial intelligence)
人工知能

aikon
icon; ikon
アイコン

aikotoba
password
合い言葉

aikotoba
password
合い詞

aikotoba kimitsu hogo
password security protection
合い言葉機密保護

aimai
ambiguous
曖昧

aimaisei
ambiguity
曖昧性

aimaisei gosa
ambiguity error
曖昧性誤差

airando
island
アイランド

airando-kōdo
island code
アイランド・コード

aite kotei setsuzoku (PVC)
permanent virtual circuit (PVC)
相手固定接続

aite saki shōhyō seizō kaisha (OEM)
original equipment manufacturer (OEM)
相手先商標製造会社

aite sentaku setsuzoku (VC)
virtual call (VC)
相手選択接続

ajienda
agenda
アジェンダ

ākaibaru-memori
archival memory
アーカイバル・メモリ

ākaibu
archive
アーカイブ

ākaibu-fuairu
archived file
アーカイブ・ファイル

akaunteingu
accounting
アカウンティング

akaunteingu bangō
accounting number
アカウンティング番号

akinai
quotient
商

akiryō'iki
space; space area
空き領域

akiryō'iki wariate
space allocation
空き領域割り当て

akiryō'iki wariate rūchin
space allocation routine
空き領域割り当てルーチン

ākitekucha
architecture
アーキテクチャ

akku (ACK; kōtei ōtō)
ACK (acknowledgment)
アック；肯定応答

akuchuēta
actuator
アクチュエータ

akuronimu
acronym
アクロニム

akuseputa
acceptor
アクセプタ

akuseputabiritei
acceptability
アクセプタビリティ

akusesu
access; accessing; memory access
アクセス

akusesu-āmu
access arm
アクセス・アーム

akusesu hō
access method
アクセス法

akusesu hōshiki
access method; access mode
アクセス方式

akusesu jikan
access time
アクセス時間

akusesu kaisen
access line
アクセス回線

akusesu kanō
accessible
アクセス可能

akusesu kanōsei
accessibility
アクセス可能性

akusesu kanri
access management
アクセス管理

akusesu kansū
access function
アクセス関数

akusesu keiro
access path
アクセス経路

akusesu ken
access right
アクセス権

akusesu-kii
access key
アクセス・キー

akusesu-kii hensei
access key organization
アクセス・キー編成

akusesu kikō
access mechanism
アクセス機構

akusesu kyoka
access permission
アクセス許可

akusesu-mōdo
access mode
アクセス・モード

akusesu-reberu
access level
アクセス・レベル

akusesu seigyo
access control
アクセス制御

akusesu seigyo go (ACW)
access control word (ACW)
アクセス制御語

akusesu seigyo jō
access control lock
アクセス制御錠

akusesu seigyo kii
access control key
アクセス制御キー

akusesu seigyo kikō
access control mechanism
アクセス制御機構

akusesu seigyo rejisuta
access control register
アクセス制御レジスタ

akusesu seigyo setsu
access control section
アクセス制御節

akusesu seigyo sōchi
access controller
アクセス制御装置

akusesu seigyo tetsuzuki
access control procedure
アクセス制御手続き

akusesu suru
access (*verb*)
アクセスする

akusesu-taimu
access time
アクセス・タイム

akusesuhan'i
access range
アカウン範囲

akushon
action
アクション

akushon-entori
action entry
アクション・エントリ

akushon-kōdo
action code
アクション・コード

akushon-komando
action command
アクション・コマンド

akushon-kurasuta
action cluster
アクション・クラスタ

akushon shiji
action directive
アクション指示

akushon-sutabu
action stub
アクション・スタブ

akushu
handshake; handshaking
握手

akuteibitei
activity
アクティビティ

akuteibitei hokan'iki (ASA)
activity save area (ASA)
アクティビティ保管域

akuteibitei shikibetsu mei
activity identifier
アクティビティ識別名

akuteibu
active
アクティブ

akuteibu-deisupurei
active display
アクティブ・ディスプレイ

akuteibu jōtai
active state
アクティブ状態

akuteibu-shisutemu
active system
アクティブ・システム

akuteibu-tasuku
active task
アクティブ・タスク

akyumurēta
accumulator
アキュムレータ

akyumurēta-rejisuta
accumulator register
アキュムレータ・レジスタ

ALGOL (arugorizumikku gengo; Arugoru; sampō gengo)
ALGOL (Algorithmic Language)
アルゴリズミック言語；
アルゴル；算法言語

ALU (enzan ronri sōchi; sanjutsu ronri kairo)
ALU (arithmetic and logic unit)
演算論理装置；算術論理回路

AM (shimpuku henchō)
AM (amplitude modulation)
振幅変調

A-M sōsa (jidō-shudō sōsa)
A-M operation (automatic-manual operation)
A-M操作；自動-手動操作

amendomento
amendment
アメンドメント

amendomento-fuairu
amendment file
アメンドメント・ファイル

amendomento-kōdo
amendment code
アメンドメント・コード

amendomento-rekōdo
amendment record
アメンドメント・レコード

amendomento-tēpu
amendment tape
アメンドメント・テープ

Amerika Keisanki Gakkai (ACM)
Association for Computing Machinery (ACM)
アメリカ計算機学会

Amerika Kikaku Kyōkai (ANSI)
American National Standards Institute (ANSI)
アメリカ規格協会

ammoku no
implicit
暗黙の

ammoku no adoresu
implicit address
暗黙のアドレス

ammoku no meirei
implicit instruction
暗黙の命令

235

ammoku no sengen
implicit declaration
暗黙の宣言

ana
hole
孔

anaraiza
analyzer
アナライザ

anarisuto
analyst
アナリスト

anarogu
analog
アナログ

anarogu-chaneru
analog channel
アナログ・チャネル

anarogu-deijitaru (A/D; A-D)
analog to digital (A/D: A-D)
アナログ・ディジタル

anarogu-deijitaru henkan
analog-to-digital conversion
アナログ・ディジタル変換

anarogu-deijitaru henkanki (A/D henkanki; ADC)
analog-to-digital converter (A/D converter; ADC)
アナログ・ディジタル変換器；
A／D 変換器

anarogu-deijitaru-konbāta (A/D konbāta; ADC)
analog-to-digital converter (A/D converter; ADC)
アナログ・ディジタル・
コンバータ；A／D コンバータ

anarogu-dēta
analog data
アナログ・データ

anarogu hyōgen
analog representation
アナログ表現

anarogu kairomō
analog network
アナログ回路網

anarogu kasanki
analog adder
アナログ加算器

anarogu keisanki
analog computer
アナログ計算機

anarogu-konparēta
analog comparator
アナログ・コンパレータ

anarogu-nettowāku
analog network
アナログ・ネットワーク

anarogu nyūryoku
analog input
アナログ入力

anarogu shingō
analog signal
アナログ信号

anarogu shutsuryoku
analog output
アナログ出力

anarogu sōchi
analog device
アナログ装置

anata wa (WRU)
who are you? (WRU)
あなたは

anbandoringu
unbundling
アンバンドリング

anbandoru-pakkēji
unbundled package
アンバンドル・パッケージ

AND
AND
AND

AND enzan
AND operation
AND演算

AND gēto
AND gate
AND ゲート

AND kairo
AND circuit
AND 回路

AND soshi
AND element
AND 素子

anda-danpingu
under damping
アンダ・ダンピング

andafurō
underflow
アンダフロー

andapanchi
underpunch
アンダパンチ

andarain
underline
アンダライン

angō
cipher; cypher
暗号

angō shuhō
cryptographic technique
暗号手法

angōbun
ciphertext; cyphertext
暗号文

angōgaku
cryptology
暗号学

angōhō
cryptography
暗号法

angōka
encryption
暗号化

anpakku
unpack
アンパック

anpakku keishiki
unpacked format
アンパック形式

anpu
amplifier
アンプ

anrōdo
unload
アンロード

ansabakku
answerback
アンサバック

ANSI (Amerika Kikaku Kyōkai)
ANSI (American National Standards Institute)
アメリカ規格協会

anteido
stability
安定度

anteisei
stability; stable
安定性

anzen
safety
安全

anzen (na)
safe
安全(な)

anzen kaiseki
safety analysis
安全解析

anzen kankyō
safe environment
安全環境

anzen kikō
safety mechanism
安全機構

anzen kinō
safety function
安全機能

anzen saitekika
safety optimization
安全最適化

anzen seigyo
safety control
安全制御

anzen seigyo shisutemu
safety control system
安全制御システム

anzen sekkei
safe design
安全設計

anzen shingō
safety signal
安全信号

anzen shisutemu
safety system
安全システム

anzen sōchi
safety device
安全装置

anzen zaiko
safety stock
安全在庫

**AP (apurikēshon-puroguramu;
ōyō puroguramu)**
AP (application program)
アプリケーション・プログラム；
応用プログラム

apachua-kādo
aperture card
アパチュア・カード

**APL (Apuru; Eipiieru;
puroguramingu gengo)**
APL (A Programming Language)
アプル；エイピーエル；
プログラミング言語

appuwādo-konpateibiritei
upward compatibility
アップワード・コンパティビリティ

appuwādo-konpateiburu
upward compatible
アップワード・コンパティブル

APT (jidō sōga)
APT (automatic picture
transmission)
自動送画

apurikēshon
application
アプリケーション

apurikēshon-fuirosofui
application philosophy
アプリケーション・フィロソフィ

apurikēshon-pakkēji
application package
アプリケーション・パッケージ

apurikēshon-purogurama
applications programmer
アプリケーション・プログラマ

apurikēshon-puroguramu (AP)
application program (AP)
アプリケーション・プログラム

apurōchi
approach
アプローチ

Apuru (APL)
A Programming Language (APL)
アプル

arāmu
alarm
アラーム

arei
array
アレイ

arei haibun
array allocation
アレイ配分

arei-konpyūta
array computer
アレイ・コンピュータ

arei-purosessa
array processor
アレイ・プロセッサ

arei shori
array processing
アレイ処理

arokēshon
allocation
アロケーション

arokēta
allocator
アロケータ

arokēto suru
allocate
アロケートする

arufua-maikuro
alpha-micro
アルファ・マイクロ

arufuabetto
alphabet
アルファベット

arufuabetto no
alphabetic
アルファベットの

arufuamerikku
alphameric
アルファメリック

arufuamerikku-kōdo
alphameric code
アルファメリック・コード

arugorizumikku
algorithmic
アルゴリズミック

arugorizumikku gengo (ALGOL)
Algorithmic Language (ALGOL)
アルゴリズミック言語

arugorizumu
algorithm
アルゴリズム

arugorizumu hon'yaku
algorithm translation
アルゴリズム翻訳

arugorizumu kōzō
algorithmic structure
アルゴリズム構造

arugorizumuteki
algorithmic
アルゴリズム的

Arugoru (ALGOL)
Algorithmic Language (ALGOL)
アルゴル

ASA (akuteibitei hokan'iki)
ASA (activity save area)
アクティビティ保管域

asain suru
assign
アサインする

ASCII (Jōhō Kōkan'yō Beikoku Hyōjun Kōdo)
ASCII (American Standard Code for Information Interchange)
情報交換用米国標準コード

asenbura(-puroguramu)
assembler
アセンブラ（・プログラム）

asenbura shiji
assembler directive
アセンブラ指示

asenbura-sōsu-kōdo
assembler source code
アセンブラ・ソース・コード

asenburi
assembly
アセンブリ

asenburi-fuēzu
assembly phase
アセンブリ・フェーズ

asenburi gengo
assembly language
アセンブリ言語

asenburi jikan
assembly time
アセンブリ時間

asenburi-kōdo
assembly code
アセンブリ・コード

asenburi-puroguramu
assembly program
アセンブリ・プログラム

asenburi-risuto
assembly list
アセンブリ・リスト

asenburi-rūchin
assembly routine
アセンブリ・ルーチン

asenburi sōsa
assembly operation
アセンブリ操作

asenburu
assembling
アセンブル

asenburu jikan
assembling time
アセンブル時間

asenburu suru
assemble
アセンブルする

ashiato
footprint
足跡

asobi
slack
遊び

asobi baito
slack byte
遊びバイト

asobi jikan
idle time
遊び時間

asobi moji
idle character
遊び文字

asobi tsūshin mōdo
idle communications mode
遊び通信モード

ASR (jidō sōjushin sōchi)
ASR (automatic send-receive set)
自動送受信装置

asshinki
compandor
圧伸器

asshuku
compaction; compression
圧縮

asshuku jōhō
condensed information
圧縮情報

asshuku kōdo
compressed code
圧縮コード

asshuku mōdo
compress mode
圧縮モード

asshuku suru
depress (keys)
圧縮する

asshukuki
compressor
圧縮器

asupekuto ritsu
aspect ratio
フスペクト率

atai
value
値

atai no bu
value part
値の部

ataitori
call by value
値取り

atenshon
attention
アテンション

atenshon shingō
attention signal
アテンション信号

atenshon warikomi
attention interrupt
アテンション割り込み

atesaki
destination
宛先

atesaki kōdo
destination code
宛先コード

atesaki shitei
call directing
宛先指定

atesaki shitei kōdo (CDC)
call-directing code (CDC)
宛先指定コード

atesaki sutēshon
destination station
宛先ステーション

ato no gyō
continuation line
後の行

atogaki
trailer
後書き

atogaki raberu
trailer label
後書きラベル

atogaki rekōdo
trailer record
後書きレコード

atoire sakidashi (LIFO)
last-in first-out (LIFO)
後入れ先出し

atoire sakidashi hōshiki
push-down method
後入れ先出し方式

atoire sakidashi hyō
push-down list
後入れ先出し表

atoire sakidashi kioku
push-down storage
後入れ先出し記憶

atoire sakidashi kioku sōchi
push-down store
後入れ先出し記憶装置

atoire sakidashi suru
push down
後入れ先出しする

atoire sakidashi sutakku
push-down stack
後入れ先出しスタック

atsu maku
thick film
厚膜

atsu maku shūseki kairo
thick-film integrated circuit
厚膜集積回路

atsudenkōka
piezoelectric effect
圧電効果

atsuteikō
piezoresistance
圧抵抗

AVR (jidō den'atsu chōseiki)
AVR (automatic voltage regulator)
自動電圧調整器

ayamari
erroneous; error; false; fault
誤り

ayamari burokku
erroneous block
誤りブロック

ayamari han'i
error range
誤り範囲

ayamari hassei nai
error-free
誤り発生ない

ayamari hindo
error frequency
誤り頻度

ayamari hyōshiki
error flag; error indicator
誤り標識

ayamari jōtai
error condition
誤り状態

ayamari kaifuku
error recovery
誤り回復

ayamari kaifuku rūchin
error recovery routine
誤り回復ルーチン

ayamari kaiseki
error analysis
誤り解析

ayamari kakuritsu
error probability
誤り確率

ayamari keihō
error warning
誤り警報

ayamari kensa
error check; error checking
誤り検査

ayamari kensa fugō
error-checking code
誤り検査符号

ayamari kensa-teisei
error checking and correction
誤り検査-訂正

ayamari kensa-teisei shisutemu
error-checking and correction system
誤り検査-訂正システム

ayamari kenshutsu
error detection
誤り検出

ayamari kenshutsu fugō
error-detecting code
誤り検出符号

ayamari kenshutsu fugō hōshiki
error-detecting code system
誤り検出符号方式

ayamari kenshutsu hōshiki
error-detecting system
誤り検出方式

ayamari kenshutsu rūchin
error-detecting routine
誤り検出ルーチン

ayamari kenshutsu-teisei
error detection and correction
誤り検出-訂正

ayamari kenshutsu-teisei kikō
error detection and correction device
誤り検出-訂正機構

ayamari kenshutsu-teisei kinō
error detection and correction function
誤り検出-訂正機能

ayamari kōdo
error code
誤りコード

ayamari messēji
error message
誤りメッセージ

ayamari ritsu
error rate
誤り率

ayamari rūchin
error routine
誤りルーチン

ayamari seigyo
error control
誤り制御

ayamari seigyo hōshiki
error control system
誤り制御方式

ayamari seigyo moji
error control character
誤り制御文字

ayamari shindan
error diagnostics
誤り診断

ayamari shindan kōdo
error diagnostics code
誤り診断コード

ayamari shingō
error signal
誤り信号

ayamari shori rūchin
error-handling routine
誤り処理ルーチン

ayamari teisei
error correction
誤り訂正

ayamari teisei fugō (ECC)
error-correcting code (ECC)
誤り訂正符号

ayamari teisei hōshiki
error-correcting system
誤り訂正方式

ayamari teisei rūchin
error-correcting routine
誤り訂正ルーチン

ayamari tejun
error procedure
誤り手順

B

bā-deisupurei
bar display
バー・ディスプレィ

bā inji sōchi
bar printer
バー印字装置

bā-kōdo
bar code
バー・コード

bā-kōdo yomitori sōchi
bar-code scanner
バー・コード読み取り装置

bā-purinta
bar printer
バー・プリンタ

baburu-sōto
bubble sort
バブル・ソート

baffua
buffer
バッファ

baffua iki
buffer area
バッファ域

baffua kioku
buffer storage
バッファ記憶

baffua kioku sōchi
buffer store
バッファ記憶装置

baffua-rejisuta
buffer register
バッファ・レジスタ

baffua seigyo
buffer control
バッファ制御

baffua seigyogo (BCW)
buffer control word (BCW)
バッファ制御語

baffuaringu
buffering
バッファリング

baffuaringu kinō
buffering function
バッファリング機能

baffuatsuki
buffered
バッファ付き

baffuatsuki insho sōchi
buffered printer
バッファ付き印書装置

bagu
bug
バグ

bai chō go
double-length word
倍長語

bai chō rejisuta
double-length register
倍長語レジスタ

bai (kiroku) mitsudo (DD)
double density (DD)
倍(記録)密度

bai mitsudo deisuku
double-density disk
倍密度ディスク

bai parusu
double pulse
倍パルス

bai parusu kiroku hōshiki
double-pulse recording
倍パルス記録方式

bai ritsu
scale factor
倍率

bai seido
double precision
倍精度

bai seido sū
double-precision number
倍精度数

baiasu
bias
バイアス

baiasu ayamari
bias error
バイアス誤り

baiasu hizumi
bias distortion
バイアス歪み

baikai
parameter
媒介

bainari
binary
バイナリ

bainari-choppu
binary chop
バイナリ・チョップ

bainari-deijitto (bitto)
binary digit (bit)
バイナリ・ディジット；ビット

bainari-kādo
binary card
バイナリ・カード

bainari-kaunta
binary counter
バイナリ・カウンタ

bainari-kōdo
binary code
バイナリ・コード

bainari-rōda
binary loader
バイナリ・ローダ

baionikkusu
bionics
バイオニックス

baipasu
bypass
バイパス

baipasu-rekōdo
bypass record
バイパス・レコード

baipōra
bipolar
バイポーラ

baipōra gijutsu
bipolar technology
バイポーラ技術

baipōragata MOS
biMOS (bipolar MOS)
バイポーラ型MOS

baipōragata MOS
bipolar MOS (biMOS)
バイポーラ型MOS

baitai
media; medium
媒体

baitai henkan
medium conversion
媒体変換

baitai shūtan (EM)
end of medium (EM)
媒体終端

baitai shūtan moji
end-of-medium character
媒体終端文字

baito
byte; unit of storage
バイト

baito-adoresu
byte address
バイト・アドレス

baito/byō (BPS)
bytes per second (BPS)
バイト／秒

baito hōshiki
byte mode
バイト方式

baito/inchi (BPI)
bytes per inch (BPI)
バイト／インチ

baito-kaunto
byte count
バイト・カウント

baito-mōdo
byte mode
バイト・モード

baito muki
byte-oriented
バイト向き

baito shori
byte processing
バイト処理

baketto
bucket
バケット

bakku-appu
backup
バック・アップ

bakku-appu-deisuku
backup disk
バック・アップ・ディスク

bakku-appu-fuairu
backup file
バック・アップ・ファイル

bakku-appu kioku
backup storage
バック・アップ記憶

bakku-appu-kopii
backup copy
バック・アップ・コピー

bakku-appu-memori
backup memory
バック・アップ・メモリ

bakku-appu-puroguramu
backup program
バック・アップ・プログラム

bakku-appu-shisutemu
backup system
バック・アップ・システム

bakku-appu sōchi
backup unit
バック・アップ装置

bakku-endo-purosessa
back-end processor
バック・エンド・プロセッサ

bakkuguraundo
background
バックグラウンド

bakkuguraundo-jyobu
background job
バックグラウンド・ジョブ

bakkuguraundo-puroguramu
background program
バックグラウンド・プログラム

bakkuguraundo shori
background processing
バックグラウンド処理

Bakkusu-Naua hō (BNF)
Backus-Naur Form (BNF)
バックス・メウア法

Bakkusu-Naua hyōkihō (BNF)
Backus-Naur Form (BNF)
バックス・メウア表記法

bakkusupēsu (BS)
backspace (BS)
バックスペース

bakyūmu
vacuum
バキューム

bakyūmu kan
vacuum tube
バキューム管

bakyūmu-karamu
vacuum column
バキューム・カラム

BAL (kihon asenbura gengo)
BAL (basic assembler language)
基本アセンブラ言語

241

BAM (kihon akusesu hōshiki)
BAM (basic access method)
基本アクセス方式

ban
number
番

ban
panel
盤

banchi
address
番地

banchi tori
call by reference
番地取り

bando
band
バンド

bando haba
bandwidth
バンド幅

bandoru-pakkēji
bundled package
バンドル・パッケージ

bandoru sōsa
bundling
バンドル操作

bandoshiki insho sōchi
band printer
バンド式印書装置

bangō
number
番号

bangō kigō
number sign
番号記号

banku
bank
バンク

baransu-chekku
balance check
バランス・チェック

barisuta
varistor
バリスタ

baruku kioku
bulk storage
バルク記憶

basho
location
場所

BASIC (Bēshikku)
BASIC (Beginner's All-purpose
Symbolic Instruction Code)
ベーシック

basu
bus
バス

basuta
burster
バスタ

basuto
burst
バスト

basuto ayamari
burst error
バスト誤り

basuto hōshiki
burst mode
バスト方式

basuto-mōdo
burst mode
バスト・モード

batchi
batch
バッチ

batchi bangō
batch number
バッチ番号

batchi densō
batch transmission
バッチ伝送

batchi gōkei
batch total
バッチ合計

batchi insatsu
batch print; batch printing
バッチ印刷

batchi-jyobu
batch job
バッチ・ジョブ

batchi-puroguramu
batch program
バッチ・プログラム

batchi shori
batch processing
バッチ処理

batteri
battery
バッテリ

batteri-bakku-appu
battery backup
バッテリ・バック・アップ

batteri-bakku-appu sōchi
battery backup unit
バッテリ・バック・アップ装置

baundo
bound
バウンド

BCC (burokku kensa moji)
BCC (block-check character)
ブロック検査文字

BCD (nishinka jisshin)
BCD (binary-coded decimal)
2進化10進

BCD kōdo (nishinka jisshin kōdo)
BCD code (binary-coded decimal
code)
BCDコード；2進化10進コード

BCW (baffua seigyo go)
BCW (buffer control word)
バッファ制御語

BDAM (kihon chokusetsu akusesu hōshiki)
BDAM (basic direct-access
method)
基本直接アクセス方式

Beichi zu
Veitch diagram
ベイチ図

beigun kikaku (MIL) (USA)
military specifications (MIL) (USA)
米軍規格

Beikoku Hyōjun Kyoku (NBS)
National Bureau of Standards
(NBS) (USA)
米国標準局

Beikoku Kikaku Kyōkai (USASI)
United States of America
Standards Institute (USASI)
米国規格協会

Beikoku Rempō Jōhō Shori Hyōjun (FIPS)
Federal Information Processing Standards (FIPS) (USA)
米国連邦情報処理標準

Beikoku Rempō Tsūshin I'inkai (FCC)
Federal Communications Commission (FCC) (USA)
米国連邦通信委員会

bekuta
vector
ベクタ

bekuta-gurafuikkusu
vector graphics
ベクタ・グラフィックス

bekuta-konpyūta
vector computer
ベクタ・コンピュータ

bekuta-mōdo
vector mode
ベクタ・モード

bekuta-mōdo hyōji sōchi
vector mode display unit
ベクタ・モード表示装置

Ben zu
Venn diagram
ベン図

benchimāku
benchmark
ベンチマーク

benchimāku mondai
benchmark problem
ベンチマーク問題

benchimāku-puroguramu
benchmark program
ベンチマーク・プログラム

benchimāku-tesuto
benchmark test
ベンチマーク・テスト

berutoshiki purinta
belt printer
ベルト式プリンタ

Bēshikku (BASIC)
Beginner's All-purpose Symbolic Instruction Code (BASIC)
ベーシック

bēsu
base
ベース

bēsu-adoresu
base address
ベース・アドレス

bēsu-bando
base band
ベース・バンド

bēsu-rejisuta (br)
base register (br)
ベース・レジスタ

betsumei
alias
別名

betsumei kijutsukō
alias description entry
別名記述項

betsumei setsu
alias section
別名節

bibun
differential; differentiating; differentiation
微分

bibun dōsa
derivative action
微分動作

bibun jikan
derivative time
微分時間

bibun kairo
differentiating circuit; differentiation circuit; differentiator
微分回路

bibun kaisekiki
differential analyzer
微分解析器

bibun zōfukuki
differentiating amplifier
微分増幅器

bibunki
differentiator
微分器

bideo
video
ビデオ

bideo-deisuku
videodisc
ビデオ・ディスク

bideo-deisuku hōshiki
videodisc system
ビデオ・ディスク方式

bideo-dēta
video data
ビデオ・データ

bideo-dēta tanmatsu sōchi
video data terminal
ビデオ・データ端末装置

bideo-detekuta
video detector
ビデオ・デテクタ

bideo-fuairu
video file
ビデオ・ファイル

bideo-gēmu
video game
ビデオ・ゲーム

bideo hyōji sōchi
video screen
ビデオ表示装置

bideo hyōji sōchi (VDU)
video display unit (VDU)
ビデオ表示装置

bideo hyōji tanmatsu sōchi (VDT)
video display terminal (VDT)
ビデオ表示端末装置

bideo jōhō shori shisutemu
video information processing system
ビデオ情報処理システム

bideo-kasetto
videocassette
ビデオ・カセット

bideo-kasetto-rekōda (VCR)
videocassette recorder (VCR)
ビデオ・カセット・レコーダ

bideo-kasetto sōchi
videocassette player
ビデオ・カセット装置

bideo-konfuerensu
video conference
ビデオ・コンフェレンス

bideo-monita
video monitor
ビデオ・モニタ

bideo RAM
video RAM
ビデオ RAM

bideo shingō
video signal
ビデオ信号

bideo shori sōchi
video processing unit
ビデオ処理装置

bideo-tēpu-rekōda
videotape recorder
ビデオ・テープ・レコーダ

bideo-tēpu sōchi
videotape player
ビデオ・テープ装置

bideotekkusu
videotex
ビデオテックス

biimu henkō
beam deflection
ビーム偏向

biimu-riido
beam lead
ビーム・リード

biimu-riido soshi (BLD)
beam lead device (BLD)
ビーム・リード素子

bijinesu keiei jōhō shisutemu
business management
information system
ビジネス経営情報システム

bijinesu-otomēshon
business automation
ビジネス・オトメーション

bijinesu-shisutemu
business system
ビジネス・システム

bijinesu-shisutemu kaiseki
business system analysis
ビジネス・システム解析

birudeingu-burokku hōshiki
building-block system
ビルディング・ブロック方式

BISAM (kihon sakuin jun akusesu hōshiki)
BISAM (basic indexed sequential access method)
基本索引順アクセス方式

bitto (bainari-deijitto; nishin sūji)
bit (binary digit)
ビット；バイナリ・ディジット；
２進数字

bitto-adoresu
bit address
ビット・アドレス

bitto-adoresu kioku
bit-addressable memory
ビット・アドレス記憶

bitto ayamari ritsu
bit error rate
ビット誤り率

bitto/byō (bps)
bits per second (bps)
ビット／秒

bitto densō sokudo
bit rate
ビット伝送速度

bitto dōki
bit synchronization
ビット同期

bitto ichi
bit position
ビット位置

bitto/inchi (bpi)
bits per inch (bpi)
ビット／インチ

bitto-konbinēshon
bit combination
ビット・コンビネーション

bitto kōsei
bit configuration
ビット構成

bitto kōzō
bit structure
ビット構造

bitto mitsudo
bit density
ビット密度

bitto muki
bit-oriented
ビット向き

bitto-parusuchō
bit pulse length
ビット・パルス長

bitto-patān
bit pattern
ビット・パターン

bitto retsu
bit string
ビット列

bitto ritsu
bit rate
ビット率

bitto sen
bit line
ビット線

bitto-suraisu
bit slice
ビット・スライス

bitto-suraisu-maikuropurosessa
bit-slice microprocessor
ビット・スライス・
マイクロプロセッサ

bitto-sutoriimu
bit stream
ビット・ストリーム

bitto-sutoringu
bit string
ビット・ストリング

bitto-tēburu
bit table
ビット・テーブル

BLD (biimu-riido sōchi)
BLD (beam lead device)
ビーム・リード装置

BNF (Bakkusu-Naua hō; Bakkusu-Naua hyōkihō)
BNF (Backus-Naur Form)
バックス・ナウア法；
バックス・ナウア表記法

bō
baud
ボー

bōdo
board
ボード

Bōdo-kōdo
Baudot code
ボード・コード

bōdo-konpyūta
board computer
ボード・コンピュータ

bōgai
disturbance; interference
妨害

bōgai kenshutsu
interference detection
妨害検出

bōgai kenshutsu saisōteisei hōshiki
request repeat system by
interference detection
妨害検出再送訂正方式

bōgai kenshutsu shisutemu
interference detection system
妨害検出システム

bokansū
generating function
母関数

borō
borrow
ボロー

boruto (v)
volt (v)
ボルト

boryūmu (VOL)
volume (VOL)
ボリューム

boryūmu atogaki raberu
volume trailer label
ボリューム後書きラベル

boryūmu junjo bangō
volume sequence number
ボリューム順序番号

boryūmu midashi raberu
volume header label
ボリューム見出しラベル

boryūmu mokuroku (VTOC)
volume table of contents (VTOC)
ボリューム目録

boryūmu no owari (EOV)
end of volume (EOV)
ボリュームの終り

boryūmu owari raberu
end-of-volume label
ボリューム終りラベル

boryūmu-raberu
volume label
ボリューム・ラベル

boryūmu shikibetsushi
volume identifier
ボリューム識別子

boryūmu-tesuto
volume test
ボリューム・テスト

boryūmu tōshi bangō
volume serial number
ボリューム通し番号

BOS (kihon operēteingu-shisutemu)
BOS (basic operating system)
基本オペレーティング・システム

bosen
bus
母線

BOT (tēpu kaishi; tēpu no hajime; tēpu shitan)
BOT (beginning of tape)
テープ開始；テープの始め；
テープ始端

botomu-appu-apurōchi
bottom-up approach
ボトム・アップ・アプローチ

BPI (baito/inchi)
BPI (bytes per inch)
バイト／インチ

bpi (bitto/inchi)
bpi (bits per inch)
ビット／インチ

BPS (baito/byō)
BPS (bytes per second)
バイト／秒

bps (bitto/byō)
bps (bits per second)
ビット／秒

br (bēsu-rejisuta; kijun rejisuta; kitei rejisuta)
br (base register)
ベース・レジスタ；
基準レジスタ；基底レジスタ

BS (Eikoku Kōgyō Kikaku)
BS (British Standards)
英国工業規格

BS (kōtai)
BS (backspace)
後退

BSAM (kihon junji akusesu hōshiki)
BSAM (basic sequential access method)
基本順次アクセス方式

BSC (nishin dēta dōki tsūshin)
BSC (binary synchronous communication)
2進データ同期通信

BSI (Eikoku Kōgyō Kikaku Kyōkai)
BSI (British Standards Institution)
英国工業規格協会

BTAM (kihon tsūshin akusesu hōshiki)
BTAM (basic telecommunications access method)
基本通信アクセス方式

bu
division; part; section
部

bubun
segment
部分

bubun go
partial word
部分語

bubun jōchōdo
partial redundancy
部分冗長度

bubun jōken bun
IF statement
部分条件文

bubun keta age
partial carry
部分桁止げ

bubun kōmoku
subitem
部分項目

bubun saitekika
suboptimization
部分最適化

bubun seki
partial product
部分積

bubun wa
partial sum
部分和

bubungo enzan
split-word operation
部分語演算

bubunretsu
substring
部分列

bubunteki itchi
partial match
部分的一致

bubunteki shisutemu koshō
partial system failure
部分的システム故障

buhin
component
部品

bummyaku
context
文脈

bummyaku henshū
context editing
文脈編集

bummyaku izon
context-sensitive
文脈依存

bummyaku izon bumpō
context-sensitive grammar
文脈依存文法

bummyaku izon gengo
context-sensitive language
文脈依存言語

bummyaku jiyū
context-free
文脈自由

bummyaku jiyū bumpō
context-free grammar
文脈自由文法

bummyaku jiyū gengo
context-free language
文脈自由言語

bummyaku tansaku
context searching
文脈探索

bun
narrative; statement
文

bun bangō
statement number
文番号

bun mei
statement name
文名

bun no bangō
statement label
文の番号

bun no kakko
statement bracket
文の括弧

bun shikibetsushi
statement identifier
文識別子

bunkai
factoring
分解

bunkai
demarcation
分界

bunkai ten
demarcation point
分界点

bunkainō
resolution
分解能

bunkatsu
fragmentation
分割

bunkatsu seigyo fuiirudo
split control field
分割制御フィールド

bunkatsu suru
divide (*verb*); split (*verb*)
分割する

bunki
branch
分岐

bunki (no)
multidrop; multipoint
分岐(の)

bunki adoresu
branch address
分岐アドレス

bunki banchi
branch address
分岐番地

bunki gentei hō
branch and bound method
分岐限定法

bunki hōshiki
multipoint system
分岐方式

bunki kairo
multipoint circuit
分岐回路

bunki kaisen
multipoint line
分岐回線

bunki meirei
branch instruction
分岐命令

bunki nettowāku
multipoint network
分岐ネットワーク

bunki pointo
branch point
分岐ポイント

bunki sōsa
multipoint operation
分岐操作

bunki suru
branch off (*verb*)
分岐する

bunkiten
branch point
分岐点

bunri
separation
分離

bunri fugō
separator
分離符号

bunri kigō
separator
分離記号

bunri konpairēshon
separate compilation
分離コンパイレーション

bunri moji
separator
分離文字

bunri suru
decollate; isolate; separate (*verb*)
分離する

bunriki
decollator
分離器

bunrui
sequence; sort; sorting
分類

bunrui burokkuka insū
sort blocking factor
分類ブロック化因数

bunrui kii
sort key
分類キー

bunrui-kumiawase
sort-merge
分類-組み合わせ

bunrui-kumiawase puroguramu
sort-merge program
分類-組み合わせプログラム

bunrui puroguramu
sort program
分類プログラム

bunrui sōsa
sort operation
分類操作

bunrui suru
sort (*verb*)
分類する

bunrui yūteiritei
sorting utility
分類ユーティリティ

bunruiki
sorter
分類機

bunruizumi fuairu
sorted file
分類済みファイル

bunsan
scatter; variance
分散

bunsan bunseki
variance analysis
分散分析

bunsan rōdo
scatter load
分散ロード

bunsan yomitori
scatter read
分散読み取り

bunsangata
decentralized; distributed
分散型

bunsangata dēta shori
decentralized data processing;
decentralized processing;
distributed processing
分散型データ処理

bunsangata dēta shori (DDP)
distributed data processing (DDP)
分散型データ処理

bunsangata dēta shori shisutemu
distributed processing system
分散型データ処理システム

bunsangata jōhō shisutemu
decentralized information
system; distributed information
system
分散型情報システム

bunsangata keisanki
decentralized computer
分散型計算機

bunsangata keisankimō
decentralized computer network
分散型計算機網

bunsangata kinō
distributed function
分散型機能

bunsangata konpyūta
decentralized computer
分散型コンピュータ

bunsangata konpyūta-nettowāku
decentralized computer network
分散型コンピュータ・
ネットワーク

bunsangata kōzō
decentralized structure
分散型構造

bunsangata seigyo
decentralized control;
distributed control
分散型制御

bunsangata shisutemu
distributed system
分散型システム

bunsangata shori sōchi
dispersed processing units
分散型処理装置

bunsangata sōchi
decentralized unit
分散型装置

bunsanka
decentralization
分散化

bunseki
analysis
分析

bunsekisha
analyst
分析者

bunsetsu
basic block; paragraph
文節

bunsetsu no tanmatsu bun
block terminal statement
文節の端末文

bunsettōgo
statement prefix
文接頭語

bunsho
document; documentation; text
文書

bunsho bunseki hyō
document analysis form
文書分析表

bunsho shori
text processing
文書処理

bunsho shori (WP)
word processing (WP)
文書処理

bunsho shori sōchi
document processor
文書処理装置

bunsho shori sōchi (WP)
word processor (WP)
文書処理装置

bunshoka
documentation
文書化

bunshū
dividing
分周

bunshūki
divider
分周器

burakku-bokkusu
black box
ブラック・ボックス

buranchi
branch
ブランチ

buranchi meirei
branch instruction
ブランチ命令

buranku
blank
ブランク

buranku gyō
blank line
ブランク行

buranku moji
blank character
ブランク文字

buranku-tēpu
blank tape
ブランク・テープ

burashi kikō
brush station
ブラシ機構

burashi yomitori
brush sensing
ブラシ読み取り

burashi yomitori kikō
brush sensor
ブラシ読み取り機構

bureddobōdo
breadboard
ブレッドボード

burekku-pointo
breakpoint
ブレック・ポイント

burekku-pointo meirei
breakpoint instruction
ブレック・ポイント命令

burokkingu
blocking
ブロッキング

burokkingu hasshinki
blocking oscillator
ブロッキング発振器

burokku
block
ブロック

burokku-adoresu
block address
ブロック・アドレス

burokku ayamari ritsu
block error rate
ブロック誤り率

burokku bangō
block number
ブロック番号

burokku bunrui
block sort
ブロック分類

burokku-chāto
block chart
ブロック・チャート

burokku-chekku
block check
ブロック・チェック

burokku chō
block length
ブロック長

burokku chō hyōshiki
block-length indicator
ブロック長標識

burokku-daiyaguramu
block diagram
ブロック・ダイヤグラム

burokku-gurafuikkusu
block graphics
ブロック・グラフィックス

burokku junjo hyōshiki
block sequence indicator
ブロック順序標識

burokku kaishi (SOB)
start of block (SOB)
ブロック開始

burokku kankaku
block gap
ブロック間隔

burokku-kaunto
block count
ブロック・カウント

burokku kensa
block check
ブロック検査

burokku kensa moji (BCC)
block-check character (BCC)
ブロック検査文字

burokku-kōdeingu
block coding
ブロック・コーディング

burokku-kōdo
block code
ブロック・コード

burokku kōzō
block structure
ブロック構造

burokku mei
block name
ブロック名

burokku midashi
block header
ブロック見出し

burokku no kaishi bun
block initial statement
ブロックの開始文

burokku no owari (EOB)
end of block (EOB)
ブロックの終り

burokku owari māka (EBM)
end-of-block marker (EBM)
ブロック終りマーカ

burokku-rekōdo
block record
ブロック・レコード

burokku-saizu
block size
ブロック・サイズ

burokku settōgo
block prefix
ブロック接頭語

burokku shūketsu (EOB)
end of block (EOB)
ブロック終結

burokku shūketsu māka (EBM)
end-of-block marker (EBM)
ブロック終結マーカ

burokku-sōto
block sort
ブロック・ソート

burokku tensō
block transfer
ブロック転送

burokku torikeshi moji
block cancel character;
block ignore character
ブロック取り消し文字

burokku zu
block diagram
ブロック図

burokkuka
blocking
ブロック化

burokkuka insū
blocking factor
ブロック化因数

burokkuka rekōdo
blocked record
ブロック化レコード

burokkusū
block count
ブロック数

Būru daisū
Boolean algebra
ブール代数

Būru enzan
Boolean operation
ブール演算

Būru enzanshi
Boolean operator
ブール演算子

Būru enzanshiki
Boolean expression
ブール演算式

Būru hensū
Boolean variable
ブール変数

Būru kansū
Boolean function
ブール関数

Būru kasan
Boolean add
ブール加算

Būru ronri
Boolean logic
ブール論理

Būru ronrishiki
Boolean expression
ブール論理式

Būru shoshiki
Boolean format
ブール書式

būto
boot
ブート

būto-appu
boot-up
ブート・アップ

būtosutorappu
bootstrap
ブートストラップ

butosutorappu kairo
bootstrap circuit
ブートストラップ回路

butosutorappu-rekōdo
bootstrap record
ブートストラップ・レコード

butosutorappu-rōda
bootstrap loader
ブートストラップ・ローダ

butsuri fuairu
physical file
物理ファイル

butsuri rekōdo
physical record
物理レコード

butsuriteki burokku
physical block
物理的ブロック

butsuriteki dēta
physical data
物理的データ

butsuriteki dēta no dokuritsu
physical data independence
物理的データの独立

butsuriteki nyūshutsuryoku seigyo shisutemu (PIOCS)
physical input/output control system (PIOCS)
物理的入出力制御システム

butsuriteki sōchi
physical unit; physical device
物理的装置

butsuriteki sōchi bangō
physical device number
物理的装置番号

butsuriteki sōchi burokku (PUB)
physical unit block (PUB)
物理的装置ブロック

butsuriteki sōchi tēburu
physical unit table
物理的装置テーブル

byūdēta
viewdata
ビューデータ

C

CAD (keisanki enjo sekkei; keisanki en'yō sekkei; keisanki riyō sekkei)
CAD (computer-aided design)
計算機援助設計;
計算機援用設計;
計算機利用設計

CADA (keisanki josei dēta kaiseki)
CADA (computer-assisted data analysis)
計算機助成データ解析

CADCAM (keisanki enjo sekkei−keisanki enjo seizō; keisanki en'yō sekkei−keisanki en'yō seizō; keisanki riyō sekkei−keisanki riyō seizō)
CADCAM (computer-aided design−computer-aided manufacture)
計算機援助設計−計算機援助製造;
計算機援用設計−計算機援用製造;
計算機利用設計−計算機利用製造

CAI (keisanki enjo gakushū; keisanki en'yō gakushū; keisanki riyō gakushū)
CAI (computer-aided instruction)
計算機援助学習;
計算機援用学習;
計算機利用学習

CAI'yō gengo (keisanki enjo gakushū gengo; keisanki en'yō gakushū gengo; keisanki riyō gakushū gengo)
CAI language (computer-aided instruction language)
CAI用語語; 計算機援助学習言語;
計算機援用学習言語;
計算機利用学習言語

CAL (keisanki en'yō gakushū; keisanki josei gakushū; keisanki riyō gakushū)
CAL (computer-assisted learning)
計算機援用学習;
計算機助成学習;
計算機利用学習

CAM (keisanki enjo seizō; keisanki en'yō seizō; keisanki riyō seizō)
CAM (computer-aided manufacturing)
計算機援助製造;
計算機援用製造;
計算機利用製造

CAM (rensō kioku)
CAM (content-addressable memory)
連想記憶

CAN (torikeshi)
CAN (cancel)
取り消し

CAW (chaneru-adoresu go; chaneru-adoresu-wādo)
CAW (channel address word)
チャネル・アドレス語;
チャネル・アドレス・ワード

CBL (keisanki bēsu gakushū; keisanki riyō gakushū)
CBL (computer-based learning)
計算機ベース学習;
計算機利用学習

CBT (keisanki bēsu kunren; keisanki riyō kunren)
CBT (computer-based training)
計算機ベース訓練;
計算機利用訓練

CC (kondeishon-kōdo)
CC (condition code)
コンディション・コード

CCB (komando seigyo burokku; shirei seigyo burokku)
CCB (command control block)
コマンド制御ブロック;
指令制御ブロック

CCD (denka ketsugō soshi)
CCD (charge-coupled device)
電荷結合素子

CCE (tsūshin seigyo sōchi)
CCE (communication control equipment)
通信制御装置

CCP (tsūshin seigyo puroguramu)
CCP (communication control program)
通信制御プログラム

CCR (tsūshin seigyo rūchin)
CCR (communication control routine)
通信制御ルーチン

CCU (tsūshin seigyo sōchi)
CCU (communication control unit)
通信制御装置

CCW (chaneru shirei go; chaneru shirei wādo)
CCW (channel command word)
チャネル指令語;
チャネル指令ワード

CCW (shirei seigyo go)
CCW (command control word)
指令制御語

CDC (atesaki shitei kōdo)
CDC (call-directing code)
宛先指定コード

CDL (keisanki sekkei'yō gengo)
CDL (computer design language)
計算機設計用言語

CE (hoshu'in)
CE (custom engineer)
保守員

chado
chad
チャド

chakushin
arrival (of message); receiving
着信

chakushin suru
arrive (message); receive
着信する

chakushin tanmatsu
receiving station
着信端末

chakushin tanmatsu sōchi
receiving terminal
着信端末装置

chakushinka
ready for receiving
着信可

chakushinsha
receiver (person)
着信者

chaneru
channel
チャネル

chaneru-adoresu
channel address
チャネル・アドレス

chaneru-adoresu-fuiirudo
channel address field
チャネル・アドレス・フィールド

chaneru-adoresu go (CAW)
channel address word (CAW)
チャネル・アドレス語

chaneru-adoresu-rejisuta
channel address register
チャネル・アドレス・レジスタ

chaneru-adoresu-wādo (CAW)
channel address word (CAW)
チャネル・アドレス・ワード

chaneru-dēta-chekku
channel data check
チャネル・データ・チェック

chaneru dōki sōchi
channel synchronizer
チャネル同期装置

chaneru fuka
channel load
チャネル負荷

chaneru-intafuēsu
channel interface
チャネル・インタフェース

chaneru jōtai baito
channel status byte
チャネル状態バイト

chaneru jōtai go (CSW)
channel status word (CSW)
チャネル状態語

chaneru-puroguramu
channel program
チャネル・プログラム

chaneru seigyo
channel control
チャネル制御

chaneru seigyo chekku
channel control check
チャネル制御チェック

chaneru seigyo go
channel control word
チャネル制御語

chaneru seigyo rejisuta
channel control register
チャネル制御レジスタ

chaneru seigyo sōchi
channel control unit
チャネル制御装置

chaneru shirei
channel command
チャネル指令

chaneru shirei go (CCW)
channel command word (CCW)
チャネル指令語

chaneru shirei kōdo
channel command code
チャネル指令コード

chaneru shirei rejisuta
channel command register
チャネル指令レジスタ

chaneru shirei wādo (CCW)
channel command word (CCW)
チャネル指令ワード

chaneru shiyōchū
channel busy
チャネル使用中

chaneru shūryō
channel end
チャネル終了

chaneru-sukejyūra
channel scheduler
チャネル・スケジューラ

chaneru warikomi
channel interrupt
チャネル割り込み

chaneru yōryō
channel capacity
チャネル容量

chaneru yūsen kikō
channel priority feature
チャネル優先機構

chanerukan
channel-to-channel
チャネル間

chanerukan adaputa
channel-to-channel adapter
チャネル間アダプタ

chāto
chart
チャート

chāto-rekōda
chart recorder
チャート・レコーダ

chein
chain
チェイン

chein-kōdo
chain code
チェイン・コード

cheinshiki insatsu sōchi
chain printer
チェイン式印刷装置

chekku
check
チェック

chekku-auto-rūchin
checkout routine
チェック・アウト・ルーチン

chekku-auto sōsa
checkout scanning
チェック・アウト走査

chekku-bitto
check bit
チェック・ビット

chekku-bokkusu
check box
チェック・ボックス

chekku-injikēta
check indicator
チェック・インジケータ

chekku-pointo
checkpoint
チェック・ポイント

chekku-pointo-danpu
checkpoint dump
チェック・ポイント・ダンプ

chekku-pointo-rekōdo
checkpoint record
チェック・ポイント・レコード

chekku-pointo-rūchin
checkpoint routine
チェック・ポイント・ルーチン

chekku-pointo-saishidō
checkpoint restart
チェック・ポイント再始動

chekku-samu
check sum
チェック・サム

chi
value
値

chien
deferred; delay; delayed
遅延

chien furippu-furoppu
delay flip-flop
遅延フリップ・フロップ

251

chien hizumi
delay distortion
遅延歪み

chien inshi
delay factor
遅延因子

chien jikan
delay time
遅延時間

chien kairo
delay circuit
遅延回路

chien kioku
delay memory
遅延記憶

chien kōshin
deferred update
遅延更新

chien ōtō
delayed response
遅延応答

chien sen
delay line
遅延線

chien sen kioku sōchi
delay line store
遅延線記憶装置

chien sen kurokku
delay line clock
遅延線クロック

chien sōchi
delay unit
遅延装置

chien soshi
delay element
遅延素子

chien tōka
delay equalization
遅延等化

chien tōkaki
delay equalizer
遅延等化器

chikan
substitute
置換

chikuji
serial
逐次

chikuji
sequence; sequential
逐次

chikuji akusesu
serial access
逐次アクセス

chikuji akusesu-fuairu
serial-access file
逐次アクセス・ファイル

chikuji akusesu kioku
sequential-access memory;
serial-access memory
逐次アクセス記憶

chikuji hensei fuairu
sequential file
逐次編成ファイル

chikuji hikaku
successive approximation
逐次比較

chikuji insho sōchi
serial printer
逐次印書装置

chikuji puroguramingu
sequential programming
逐次プログラミング

chikuji saishiyōkanō
serially reusable
逐次再使用可能

chikuji saishiyōkanō puroguramu
serially reusable program
逐次再使用可能プログラム

chikuji saishiyōkanō rūchin
serially reusable routine
逐次再使用可能ルーチン

chikuji seigyo
sequence control;
sequential control
逐次制御

chikuji seigyo keisūki
sequence control counter
逐次制御計数器

chikuji seigyo rejisuta (SCR)
sequence control register (SCR)
逐次制御レジスタ

chikuji shori
sequential processing;
serial processing
逐次処理

chikuji sōsa
serial operation
逐次操作

chikuji sukejyūra
sequential scheduler
逐次スケジューラ

chikuji sukejyūringu
sequential scheduling
逐次スケジューリング

chikuji sukejyūringu-shisutemu
sequential scheduling system
逐次スケジューリング・システム

chikuji yomitori
serial read
逐次読み取り

chikuji yomitori senkōki
serial read/punch
逐次読み取りせん孔機

chikujidōsagata densō
sequential-type transmission
逐次動作型伝送

chikujishiki fuairu shori
serial file processing
逐次式ファイル処理

chikuseki
accumulation; storage; storing
蓄積

chikuseki kōkan
store-and-forward switching
蓄積交換

chikuseki suru
accumulate; store (*verb*)
蓄積する

chimeiteki ayamari
fatal error
致命的誤り

chimpu na
obsolete
陳腐な

chimpuka
obsolescence
陳腐化

chinō
intelligence; intelligent
知能

chinō tanmatsu (sōchi)
intelligent terminal;
smart terminal
知能端末（装置）

chippu
chip; tip
チップ

chippu hako
chip tray
チップ箱

chippu-soketto
chip socket
チップ・ソケット

chiruto
tilt
チルト

chishiki
knowledge
知識

chishiki bēsu
knowledge base;
knowledge-based
知識ベース

chishiki bēsu-shisutemu
knowledge-based system
知識ベース・システム

chishiki kōgaku
knowledge engineering
知識工学

chisūki
register
置数器

chō(-)
super(-)
超

chō go
long word
長語

chō seido fudō shōsūten
long-precision floating point
長精度浮動小数点

chōbunkai
hyperresolution
超分解

chōdai kibo shūsekika (GSI)
grand-scale integration
超大規模集積化

chōdai kibo shūsekika (VLSI)
very large scale integration (VLSI)
超大規模集積化

chōgengo
metalangue
超言語

chōgengo hensū
metalinguistic variable
超言語変数

chōgengo shiki
metalinguistic formula
超言語式

chōho
start-stop
調歩

chōho dōkishiki
start-stop synchronous system
調歩同期式

chōho kanshi
start-stop supervision
調歩監視

chōhoshiki
start-stop system
調歩式

chōhoshiki densō
start-stop transmission
調歩式伝送

chōjō
superimposed
重畳

chōjō kairo
superimposed circuit
重畳回路

chokketsu
on-line
直結

chokketsugata toranjisuta ronri (DCTL)
direct-coupled transistor logic (DCTL)
直結型トランジスタ論理

chōko
supersmall
超小

chōkogata
micro-
超小形

chōkogata denshi hōshiki
microelectronic system
超小形電子方式

chōkogata denshi kōgaku
microelectronics
超小形電子工学

chōkogata kōsei bubun
microcomponent
超小形構成部分

chōkogata kōzō
microstructure
超小形構造

chōkogata kumitate
microassembly
超小形組み立て

chōkogata soshi
microelement
超小形素子

chokuheiretsu henkan
serial-parallel conversion
直並列変換

chokuheiretsu henkan kairo
serial-parallel converter
直並列変換回路

chokuheiretsu jōzan
serial-parallel multiplication
直並列乗算

chokuheiretsu kasan
serial-parallel addition
直並列加算

chokuretsu
serial
直列

chokuretsu akusesu
serial access
直列アクセス

chokuretsu akusesu-fuairu
serial-access file
直列アクセス・ファイル

chokuretsu akusesu kioku
serial-access memory
直列アクセス記憶

chokuretsu densō
serial transmission
直列伝送

chokuretsu enzan
serial arithmetic
直列演算

253

chokuretsu hensei
serial organization
直列編成

chokuretsu hōshiki kaunto
serial count
直列方式カウント

chokuretsu kōdo
serial code
直列コード

chokuretsu nyūshutsuryoku intafuēsu (SIO)
serial input/output interface (SIO)
直列入出力インタフェース

chokuretsu sōsa
serial operation
直列操作

chokuretsu tensō
serial transfer
直列転送

chokuretsuka
serialization
直列化

chokuretsuka suru
serialize
直列化する

chokuretsushiki keisanki
serial computer
直列式計算機

chokuretsushiki keisanki shisutemu
serial computer system
直列式計算機システム

chokuretsushiki kioku
serial storage
直列式記憶

chokuryū (DC)
direct current (DC)
直流

chokuryū zōfukuki (DC zōfukuki)
direct-current amplifier (DC amplifier)
直流増幅器; D / C 増幅器

chokusenteki kōdeingu
straight-line coding
直線的コーディング

chokusetsu adoresu
direct address
直接アドレス

chokusetsu adoresu meirei
direct address instruction
直接アドレス命令

chokusetsu adoresu saihaichi
direct address relocation
直接アドレス再配置

chokusetsu adoresu shitei
direct addressing
直接アドレス指定

chokusetsu akusesu
direct access; random access
直接アクセス

chokusetsu akusesu (DMA)
direct memory access (DMA)
直接アクセス

chokusetsu akusesu-fuairu
direct-access file;
random-access file
直接アクセス・ファイル

chokusetsu akusesu hōshiki (DAM)
direct-access method (DAM);
direct memory access method
直接アクセス方式

chokusetsu akusesu kanō
immediately accessible
直接アクセス可能

chokusetsu akusesu kioku sōchi (DASD)
direct-access storage device (DASD)
直接アクセス記憶装置

chokusetsu akusesu-memori
direct-access memory
直接アクセス・メモリ

chokusetsu akusesu sōchi
direct-access device
直接アクセス装置

chokusetsu deijitaru seigyo (DDC)
direct digital control (DDC)
直接ディジタル制御

chokusetsu dēta-deisupurei
direct data display
直接データ・ディスプレィ

chokusetsu dēta nyūryoku (DDE)
direct data entry (DDE)
直接データ入力

chokusetsu dēta-setto
direct data set
直接データ・セット

chokusetsu hensei
direct organization
直接編成

chokusetsu kioku
direct-access storage
直接記憶

chokusetsu kioku sōchi
direct-access store
直接記憶装置

chokusetsu kōdeingu
direct coding
直接コーディング

chokusetsu kōdo
direct code
直接コード

chokusetsu meirei
direct instruction
直接命令

chokusetsu mōdo
direct mode
直接モード

chokusetsu nyūryoku
direct input
直接入力

chokusetsu rokēshon-mōdo
direct location mode
直接ロケーション・モード

chokusetsu sakuin
direct index
直接索引

chokusetsu seigyo
direct control
直接制御

chokusetsu seigyo maikuro-puroguramu
direct control microprogram
直接制御マイクロ・プログラム

chokusetsu shutsuryoku
direct output
直接出力

chokusetsu sōnyū
direct insert
直接挿入

chokusetsu sōnyū bunrui
straight-insertion sort
直接挿入分類

chokusetsu sōnyū rūchin
direct insert routine
直接挿入ルーチン

chokusetsu sōnyū saburūchin
direct insert subroutine
直接挿入サブルーチン

chokusetsu tansaku
direct search
直接探索

chokuteisū
literals
直定数

chō'ompa
ultrasonic; ultrasonic wave
超音波

chō'ompa bondeingu
ultrasonic bonding
超音波ボンディング

chō'ompa chien
acoustic delay
超音波遅延

chō'ompa chiensen
acoustic delay line; sonic delay
line; ultrasonic delay line
超音波遅延線

chō'ompa kioku
acoustic storage; acoustic
memory; ultrasonic memory;
ultrasonic storage
超音波記憶

chō'ompa kioku sōchi
acoustic store
超音波記憶装置

chō'ompa kōgaku
ultrasonics
超音波工学

chōsei
adjustment; justification;
reconciliation; regulating; tuning
調整

chōsei suru
adjust; justify; reconcile; regulate
調整する

chōtampa
ultrahigh frequency
超短波

chōtampa (VHF)
very high frequency (VHF)
超短波

chū
remark
注

chū kibo shūseki kairo
medium-scale integrated circuit
中規模集積回路

chū kibo shūsekika (MSI)
medium-scale integration (MSI)
中規模集積化

chūdan
break; interruption
中断

chūdan suru
interrupt
中断する

chūdan teishi
interruption
中断停止

chūkaku
nucleus
中核

chūkaku shoki settei puroguramu (NIP)
nucleus initialization program
(NIP)
中核初期設定プログラム

chūkan
intermediate
中間

chūkan akusesu kioku
intermediate-access storage
中間アクセス記憶

chūkan burokku-chekku
intermediate block check
中間ブロック・チェック

chūkan dokyumento
intermediate document
中間ドキュメント

chūkan gengo
intermediate language
中間言語

chūkan gōkei
intermediate total
中間合計

chūkan kioku
intermediate storage
中間記憶

chūkan shūhasū
intermediate frequency
中間周波数

chūkan shutsuryoku fuairu
intermediate output file
中間出力ファイル

chūkan tanshiban (IDF)
intermediate distributing frame
(IDF)
中間端子盤

chūkei
interchange
中継

chūkei kairo
interchange circuit
中継回路

chūō enzan shori sōchi
central operation processing unit
中央演算処理装置

chūō keisanki
central computer
中央計算機

chūō kyoku
central station
中央局

chūō seigyo sōchi
central control unit
中央制御装置

chūō shisutemu
central system
中央システム

chūō shori sōchi (CPU)
central processing unit (CPU);
central processor
中央処理装置

chūō tanmatsu sōchi
central terminal
中央端末装置

chūshaku
annotation; comment; narrative
注釈

chūshaku gyō
comment line
注釈行

chūshaku ran
comment field
注釈欄

chūshō(ka)
abstraction
抽象（化）

chūshō(teki na)
abstract
抽象（的な）

chūshō kigō
abstract symbol
抽象記号

chūshō kikai
abstract machine
抽象機械

chūshōteki taishō
abstract object
抽象的対象

chūshutsu
extract
抽出

chūshutsu kinō
extract function
抽出機能

chūshutsu meirei
extract instruction
抽出命令

chūshutsu sōsa
extract operation
抽出操作

CIM (konpyūta nyūryoku maikurofuirumu)
CIM (computer input microfilming; computer input on microfilm)
コンピュータ入力マイクロフィルム

CIR (karento meirei rejisuta)
CIR (current instruction register)
カレント命令レジスタ

CMI (keisanki kanri kyōiku)
CMI (computer-managed instruction)
計算機管理教育

CML (denryū mōdo ronri)
CML (current mode logic)
電流モード論理

CML (keisanki kanri gakushū)
CML (computer-managed learning)
計算機管理学習

CMOS (sōhogata mosu)
CMOS (complementary metal oxide semiconductor)
相補型モス；相補型MOS

CMT (kasettogata jiki tēpu)
CMT (cassette magnetic tape)
カセット型磁気テープ

CMT intafuēsu-bōdo
CMT interface board
CMTインタフェース・ボード

COAX (dōkei kēburu)
COAX (coaxial cable)
同軸ケーブル

COBOL (Koboru)
COBOL (Common Business-Oriented Language)
コボル

COM (konpyūta shutsuryoku maikurofuirumu)
COM (computer output microfilming; computer output on microfilm)
コンピュータ出力マイクロフィルム

COM rekōda
COM recorder
COMレコーダ

COM shutsuryoku
COM output
COM出力

CP (kādo senkō sōchi; kādo senkōki)
CP (card punch)
カードせん孔装置；
カードせん孔機

CP (tsūshin'yō purosessa)
CP (communication processor)
通信用プロセッサ

CPE (keisanki seinō hyōka)
CPE (computer performance evaluation)
計算機性能評価

cpi (moji/inchi)
cpi (characters per inch)
文字／インチ

CPM (genkai keiro hō; kurichikaru-pasu hō)
CPM (critical path method)
限界経路法；クリチカル・パス法

CPM (kādo/fun)
CPM (cards per minute)
カード／分

cpm (moji/fun)
cpm (characters per minute)
文字／分

CP/M (maikpuropurosessa'yō seigyo puroguramu)
CP/M (control program for microprocessors)
マイクロプロセッサ
用制御プログラム

cps (moji/byō)
cps (characters per second)
文字／秒

CPU (chūō shori sōchi)
CPU (central processing unit)
中央処理装置

CPU sukejyūra
CPU scheduler
CPUスケジューラ

CR (fukki; kaigyō fukki)
CR (carriage return)
復帰；改行復帰

CR (kādo yomitori sōchi; kādo yomitoriki)
CR (card reader)
カード読み取り装置；
カード読み取り機

CRC (junkai jōchō kensa)
CRC (cyclic redundancy check)
巡回冗長検査

CRMT (kātorijji jiki tēpu)
CRMT (cartridge magnetic tape)
カートリッジ磁気テープ

CRT (inkyokusenkan)
CRT (cathode-ray tube)
CRT；陰極線管

CRT hyōji sōchi (inkyokusenkan hyōji sōchi)
CRT visual display unit (cathode-ray tube visual display unit)
CRT表示装置；
陰極線管表示装置

CRT kioku (inkyokusenkan kioku)
CRT memory (cathode-ray tube memory)
CRT記憶；陰極線管記憶

CSW (chaneru jōtai go)
CSW (channel status word)
チャネル状態語

CTD (denka tensō soshi)
CTD (charge transfer device)
電荷転送素子

CTS (korudo-taipu-shisutemu)
CTS (cold-type system)
コルド・タイプ・システム

CU (seigyo yunitto)
CU (control unit)
制御ユニット

D

DA (bibun kaisekiki)
DA (differential analyzer)
微分解析器

D/A (deijitaru-anarogu)
D/A (digital to analog)
ディジタル-アナログ

D/A henkan (deijitaru-anarogu henkan)
D/A conversion (digital-to-analog conversion)
D / A 変換;
ディジタル・アナログ変換

D/A henkanki (deijitaru-anarogu henkanki)
D/A converter (digital-to-analog converter)
D / A 変換器;
ディジタル・アナログ変換器

D/A konbāta (deijitaru-anarogu-konbāta)
D/A converter (digital-to-analog converter)
D/Aコンバータ;ディジタル・
アナログ・コンバータ

daburu-parusu
double pulse
ダブル・パルス

daburu-parusu yomi
double-pulse reading
ダブル・パルス読み

daburu-wādo
double word
ダブル・ワード

dagā-operēshon
dagger operation
ダガー・オペレーション

dai
unit for counting computers
台

dai kibo
large scale
大規模

dai kibo nettowāku
large-scale network
大規模ネットワーク

dai kibo shisutemu
large-scale system
大規模システム

dai kibo shūseki kairo
large-scale integrated circuit
大規模集積回路

dai kibo shūsekika (LSI)
large-scale integration (LSI)
大規模集積化

dai kioku
mass storage
大記憶

dai kioku kanri shisutemu
mass-storage control system
大記憶管理システム

dai kioku rekōdo
mass-storage record
大記憶レコード

dai yōryō
large capacity
大容量

dai yōryō kioku (LCS)
large-capacity storage (LCS)
大容量記憶

daiaringu
dialing
ダイアリング

daiaringu-adaputa
dialing adapter
ダイアリング・アダプタ

daiaru
dial
ダイアル

daiaru-mōdo
dialing mode
ダイアル・モード

daiaru sōchi
dialing device
ダイアル装置

daiaru tanmatsu sōchi
dial terminal
ダイアル端末装置

daiaru yobidashi
dialing
ダイアル呼び出し

daigo sedai keisanki
fifth-generation computer
第五世代計算機

dai'ichi operando
first operand
第一オペランド

dai'ichi reberu-adoresu
first-level address
第一レベル・アドレス

dai'ichi sedai keisanki
first-generation computer
第一世代計算機

dai'ikkai no teigi
first-level definition
第一階の定義

daikō
alternative
代行

daikō jushin kinō
alternative receiving function
代行受信機能

daikōjushin
intercepting
代行受信

dainamikku
dynamic
ダイナミック

dainamikku-debaggingu-tsūru
dynamic debugging tool
ダイナミック・デバッギング・
ツール

dainamikku kairo
dynamic circuit
ダイナミック回路

dainamikku RAM
dynamic RAM
ダイナミックRAM

dainamikku-sutoppu
dynamic stop
ダイナミック・ストップ

daini
second (*adjective*)
第二

daini sedai keisanki
second-generation computer
第二世代計算機

dainikai no
secondary
第二階の

dainikai no teigi
secondary level definition
第二階の定義

dainyūbun
assignment statement
代入文

daiōdo (DI)
diode (DI)
ダイオード

daiōdo-gēto
diode gate
ダイオード・ゲート

daiōdo kansū hasseiki
diode function generator
ダイオード関数発生器

daiōdo-matorikkusu
diode matrix
ダイオード・マトリックス

daiōdo ronri
diode logic
ダイオード論理

daiōdo-toranjisuta ronri (DTL)
diode-transistor logic (DTL)
ダイオード・トランジスタ論理

dairekutori
directory
ダイレクトリ

dairekutori kanri
directory management
ダイレクトリ管理

dairyō dēta
mass data
大量データ

daisan sedai keisanki
third-generation computer
第三世代計算機

daisū
algebra
代数

daisū shori gengo
algebraic language
代数処理言語

daitai
alternate; alternative
代替

daitai fuairu
alternate file
代替ファイル

daitai keiro
alternate route
代替経路

daitai keiro shitei
alternate routing
代替経路指定

daitai kiki
alternate device
代替機器

daitai shisutemu
alternative system
代替システム

daitai taima
alternate timer
代替タイマ

daitai torakku
alternate track
代替トラック

daiyaguramu
diagram
ダイヤグラム

daiyō
substitute
代用

daiyon sedai keisanki
fourth-generation computer
第四世代計算機

daiyōryō kioku
bulk storage; mass storage
大容量記憶

daiyōryō kioku shisutemu
mass-storage system
大容量記憶システム

daiyōryō kioku sōchi
mass-storage device;
mass-storage unit
大容量記憶装置

daiyōryō naibu kioku
high-capacity internal storage
大容量内部記憶

DAM (chokusetsu akusesu hōshiki)
DAM (direct-access method)
直接アクセス方式

damii
dummy
ダミー

damii-āgyumento
dummy argument
ダミー・アーギュメント

damii meirei
dummy instruction
ダミー命令

dampenka
fragmentation
断片化

dan shifuto
case shift
段シフト

dankai
cycle; phase
段階

dankaizu
phase diagram
段階図

danpingu
dumping
ダンピング

danpu
dump (*noun*)
ダンプ

danpu kaiseki
dump analysis
ダンプ解析

danpu kensa
dump check
ダンプ検査

danpu suru
dump (*verb*)
ダンプする

danraku
paragraph
段落

danraku mei
paragraph name
段落名

danraku midashi
paragraph header
段落見出し

dantori
housekeeping
段取り

dantori sōsa
housekeeping operation
段取り操作

DASD (chokusetsu akusesu kioku sōchi)
DASD (direct-access storage device)
直接アクセス記憶装置

DAT (dōteki adoresu henkanki)
DAT (dynamic address translator)
動的アドレス変換器

datō
valid
妥当

datōsei
validity
妥当性

datōsei kensa
validation; validation check; validity check
妥当性検査

datōsei kensa no puroguramu
validation program
妥当性検査のプログラム

daun-taimu
down time
ダウン・タイム

daunrōdeingu
downloading
ダウンローディング

daunrōdo
download
ダウンロード

dB (deshiberu)
dB (decibel)
デシベル

DBCS (dētabēsu seigyo shisutemu)
DBCS (database control system)
データベース制御システム

DBE (dēta-basu-enēburu)
DBE (data bus enable)
データ・バス・エネーブル

DBMS (dētabēsu kanri shisutemu)
DBMS (database management system)
データベース管理システム

DC (chokuryū)
DC (direct current)
直流

DC (sōchi seigyo)
DC (device control)
装置制御

DC teiden'atsu kairo (chokuryū teiden'atsu kairo)
DC regulated circuit (direct-current regulated circuit)
DC定電圧回路; 直流定電圧回路

DC zōfukuki (chokuryū zōfukuki)
DC amplifier (direct-current amplifier)
DC増幅器; 直流増幅器

DCB (dēta seigyo burokku)
DCB (data control block)
データ制御ブロック

DCS (dēta tsūshin sōchi)
DCS (data communication subsystem)
データ通信装置

DCTL (chokketsugata toranjisuta ronri)
DCTL (direct-coupled transistor logic)
直結型トランジスタ論理

DD (bai mitsudo)
DD (double density)
倍密度

DDA (keisūgata bibun kaisekiki)
DDA (digital differential analyzer)
計数型微分解析器

DDC (chokusetsu deijitaru seigyo)
DDC (direct digital control)
直接ディジタル制御

DDE (chokusetsu dēta nyūryoku)
DDE (direct data entry)
直接データ入力

DDL (dēta kijutsu gengo)
DDL (data description language)
データ記述言語

DDP (bunsangata dēta shori)
DDP (distributed data processing)
分散型データ処理

DDX (deijitaru-dēta kōkanmō)
DDX (digital data exchange)
ディジタル・データ交換網

debaggingu
debugging
デバッギング

debaggingu-eido
debugging aid
デバッギング・エイド

debaggingu-rūchin
debugging routine
デバッギング・ルーチン

debaggu suru
debug
デバッグする

debaisu
device
デバイス

deddo-taimu
dead time
デッド・タイム

deddorokku
deadlock
デッドロック

deguchi
exit
出口

deguchi adoresu
exit address
出口アドレス

deguchi rūchin
exit routine
出口ルーチン

deguchi ten
exit point
出口点

deijii-chein
daisychain
ディジー・チェイン

deijii-hoiiru-purinta
daisywheel printer
ディジー・ホイール・プリンタ

deijitaiza
digitizer
ディジタイザ

deijitaru
digital
ディジタル

deijitaru-anarogu henkan
digital-to-analog conversion
ディジタル・アナログ変換

deijitaru-anarogu henkanki (D/A henkanki)
digital-to-analog converter (D/A converter)
ディジタル・アナログ変換器;
D／A変換器

deijitaru-anarogu-konbāta (D/A konbāta)
digital-to-analog converter (D/A converter)
ディジタル・アナログ・
コンバータ; D／Aコンバータ

deijitaru-deisupurei
digital display
ディジタル・ディスプレィ

deijitaru denshi keisanki
digital electronic computer
ディジタル電子計算機

deijitaru-dēta
digital data
ディジタル・データ

deijitaru-dēta kōkanmō (DDX)
digital data exchange (DDX)
ディジタル・データ交換網

deijitaru-dēta shori sōchi
digital data processor
ディジタル・データ処理装置

deijitaru-fuiruta
digital filter
ディジタル・フィルタ

deijitaru hyōgen
digital representation
ディジタル表現

deijitaru kairo
digital circuit
ディジタル回路

deijitaru keisanki
digital computer
ディジタル計算機

deijitaru kōkan
digital switching
ディジタル交換

deijitaru-kurokku
digital clock
ディジタル・クロック

deijitaru-moderu
digital model
ディジタル・モデル

deijitaru nyūryoku adaputa
digital input adapter
ディジタル入力アダプタ

deijitaru nyūshutsuryoku
digital input/output
ディジタル入出力

deijitaru-purotta
digital plotter
ディジタル・プロッタ

deijitaru-rekōdo
digital record
ディジタル・レコード

deijitaru-shimyurēshon
digital simulation
ディジタル・シミュレーション

deijitaru shingō
digital signal
ディジタル信号

deijitaru-shisutemu
digital system
ディジタル・システム

deijitaru shutsuryoku
digital output
ディジタル出力

deijitaru shutsuryoku adaputa
digital output adapter
ディジタル出力アダプタ

deijitaru shutsuryoku seigyo
digital output control
ディジタル出力制御

deijitaru tsūshin
digital communication
ディジタル信信

deijitaruka
digitization
ディジタル化

deijitaruka shingō
digitized signal
ディジタル化信号

deijitaruka suru
digitize
ディジタル化する

deijitto
digit
ディジット

deipuriishon
depletion
ディプリーション

deipuriishon gata
depletion type
ディプリーション型

deipuriishon MOS (D-MOS)
depletion MOS (D-MOS)
ディプリーションMOS

deisuketto
diskette
ディスケット

deisuku
disk *or* disc
ディスク

deisuku bunrui
disk sort
ディスク分類

deisuku-danpu
disk dump
ディスク・ダンプ

deisuku-doraibu
disk drive
ディスク・ドライブ

deisuku-fuairu
disk file
ディスク・ファイル

deisuku-fuairu hensei
disk file organization
ディスク・ファイル編成

deisuku-kātorijji
disk cartridge
ディスク・カートリッジ

deisuku-kēburu
disk cable
ディスク・ケーブル

deisuku kioku
disk storage
ディスク記憶

deisuku kudō kikō
disk unit
ディスク駆動機構

deisuku kudō kikō
disk drive
ディスク駆動機構

deisuku-operēteingu-shisutemu (DOS)
disk-based operating system (DOS); disk operating system (DOS)
ディスク・オペレーティング・システム

deisuku-pakku
disk pack
ディスク・パック

deisuku-raiburari
disk library
ディスク・ライブラリ

deisuku-raiburarian
disk librarian
ディスク・ライブラリアン

deisuku-rejidento-shisutemu
disk-resident system
ディスク・レジデント・システム

deisuku-sōto
disk sort
ディスク・ソート

deisuku-yunitto
disk unit
ディスク・ユニット

deisukuriminēta
discriminator
ディスクリミネータ

deisukushiki shisutemu
disk-oriented system
ディスク式システム

deisupatcha
dispatcher
ディスパッチャ

deisupatchi suru
dispatch (*verb*)
ディスパッチする

deisupurei
display
ディスプレィ

deisupurei-kōdo
display code
ディスプレィ・コード

deisupurei-konsoru
display console
ディスプレィ・コンソル

deisupurei sōchi
display unit
ディスプレィ装置

dekku
deck
デック

dekōda
decoder
デコーダ

dekōdeingu
decoding
デコーディング

dekōdeingu kairo
decoding circuit
デコーディング回路

dekōdeingu kaisen
decoding circuit
デコーディング回線

dekōdo-saikuru
decode cycle
デコード・サイクル

dekōdo suru
decode
デコードする

dekorēta
decollator
デコレータ

dekuremento
decrement
デクレメント

dekyū
dequeue
デキュー

demando
demand
デマンド

demando-mōdo
demand mode
デマンド・モード

demando shori
demand processing
デマンド処理

dembun
message
電文

dembun hasshin
message despatch
電文発信

dembun ikisaki
message destination
電文行き先

dembun jushin
message reception
電文受信

dembun no nagare
message flow
電文の流れ

dembun saisō
message retransmission
電文再送

dembun sōsa
message operation
電文操作

261

dembun tsūban
message numbering
電文通番

dempa
propagation
伝播

dempa ayamari
propagated error
伝播誤り

dempa chien
propagation delay
伝播遅延

dempa chien jikan
propagation delay time
伝播遅延時間

dempa jikan
propagation time
伝播時間

dempa keiro
propagation path
伝播経路

dempa suru
propagate
伝播する

den'atsu
voltage
電圧

den'atsu anteiki (VR)
voltage regulator (VR)
電圧安定器

den'atsu chōsei
voltage regulating
電圧調整

den'atsu seigyo hasshinki (VCO)
voltage-controlled oscillator
(VCO)
電圧制御発振器

denchi
battery
電池

denchi kudō
battery-driven
電池駆動

dengen
electric power supply; power;
power supply
電源

dengen ijō
electric power failure;
power failure
電源異常

dengen ijō kaifuku
power fail recovery
電源異常回復

dengen ijō saikaishi
power fail recovery
電源異常再開始

dengen seigyo
power control
電源制御

dengen sōchi
power unit
電源装置

dengen suitchi
power switch
電源スイッチ

dengen yōryō
power capacity
電源容量

denka ketsugō soshi (CCD)
charge-coupled device (CCD)
電荷結合素子

denka tensō soshi (CTD)
charge transfer device (CTD)
電荷転送素子

denkai kōka toranjisuta gijutsu (FET)
field effect transistor technology
(FET)
電界効果トランジスタ技術

Denki Denshi Gakkai (IEEE)
Institute of Electrical and
Electronic Engineers (IEEE)
電気電子学会

denki kōgaku
electrical engineering
電気工学

denkishiki kaikeiki (EAM)
electric accounting machine
(EAM)
電気式会計機

denkiteki saikakikomi ROM (EAROM)
electrically alterable read-only
memory (EAROM)
電気的再書き込み ROM

denkiteki shōkyokanō puroguramukanō ROM (EEPROM)
electrically erasable programmable
read-only memory (EEPROM)
電気的消去可能 PROM

denkiteki shōkyokanō ROM (EEROM)
electrically erasable read-only
memory (EEROM)
電気的消去可能 ROM

denryoku
power
電力

denryoku gen
power source
電力源

denryoku haibun sōchi
power distribution system
電力配分装置

denryoku kēburu
electric cable
電力ケーブル

denryoku reberu
power level
電力レベル

denryoku sōchi
power unit
電力装置

denryoku toranjisuta
power transistor
電力トランジスタ

denryū
current (electricity)
電流

denryū mōdo ronri (CML)
current mode logic (CML)
電流モード論理

denryū zōfuku ritsu
current amplification factor
電流増幅率

denshi
electronic; electronics
電子

denshi bibun kaisekiki
electronic differential analyzer
電子微分解析器

denshi biimu kiroku (EBR)
electron beam recording (EBR)
電子ビーム記録

denshi biimu-memori (EBAM)
electron beam addressed
memory (EBAM)
電子ビーム・メモリ

denshi dēta shori (EDP)
electronic data processing (EDP)
電子データ処理

denshi dēta shori kikai (EDPM)
electronic data-processing
machine (EDPM)
電子データ処理機械

denshi dēta shori shisutemu (EDPS)
electronic data-processing
system (EDPS)
電子データ処理システム

denshi fuairingu
electronic filing
電子ファイリング

denshi fuairu
electronic file
電子ファイル

denshi hōhō
electronic method
電子方法

denshi insho sōchi
electronic printer
電子印書装置

denshi jōhō kōkan shisutemu
electronic information exchange
system
電子情報交換システム

denshi jōhō shisutemu
electronic information system
電子情報システム

denshi jōhō shori shisutemu
electronic information-
processing system
電子情報処理システム

denshi kairo
electronic circuit
電子回路

denshi kairo kaiseki puroguramu (ECAP)
electronic circuit analysis
program (ECAP)
電子回路解析プログラム

denshi kaunta
electronic counter
電子カウンタ

denshi keisanki
electronic computer
電子計算機

denshi keisanki shisutemu
electronic computer system
電子計算機システム

denshi kōgyō
electronics
電子工業

Denshi Kōgyō Kai (EIA)
Electronic Industries Association
(EIA)
電子工業会

denshi kōkan
electronic automatic exchange
電子交換

denshi kōkan shisutemu
electronic switching system
電子交換システム

denshi purinta
electronic printer
電子プリンタ

denshi seigyo shisutemu
electronic control system
電子制御システム

denshi shashin
electrophotography
電子写真

denshi shashinshiki insho sōchi
electrophotographic printer;
xerographic printer
電子写真式印書装置

denshi sōchi
electronic device
電子装置

denshi suitchi
electronic switch
電子スイッチ

denshi yūbin
electronic mail
電子郵便

denshin
transmission;
telegraphic communication
伝信

denshin denwa kaisha
common carrier
電信電話会社

denshin injiki
teleprinter; teletype
電信印字機

denshishiki
electronic
電子式

denshishiki dēta shori (EDP)
electronic data processing (EDP)
電子式データ処理

densō
communication; transmission
伝送；電送

densō burokku shūketsu (ETB)
end-of-transmission block (ETB)
伝送ブロック終結

densō burokku shūketsu moji
end-of-transmission block
character
伝送ブロック終結文字

densō erā
transmission error
伝送エラー

densō hōshiki
transmission mode
伝送方式

densō kaisen
transmission circuit
伝送回線

densō saki
destination
伝送先

densō seigyo (TC)
transmission control (TC)
伝送制御

densō seigyo kakuchō (DLE)
data link escape (DLE)
伝送制御拡張

densō seigyo kakuchō moji
data link escape character
伝送制御拡張文字

densō seigyo moji
transmission control character
伝送制御文字

densō seigyo sōchi (TCU)
transmission control unit (TCU)
伝送制御装置

densō sen
transmission line
伝送線

densō setsubi
transmission facilities
伝送設備

densō shūketsu (EOT)
end of transmission (EOT)
伝送終結

densō shūketsu moji
end-of-transmission character
伝送終結文字

densō sokudo
transmission speed
伝送速度

densō sonshitsu
transmission loss
伝送損失

densō suru
transmit
伝送する

densōki
transmitter
伝送機

densōro
transmission channel
伝送路

dentatsu
transfer
伝達

dentatsu inpiidansu
transfer impedance
伝達インピーダンス

deruta
delta
デルタ

deruta henchō
delta modulation
デルタ変調

deruta shingō
delta signal
デルタ信号

deshiberu (dB)
decibel (dB)
デシベル

deshijon
decision
デシジョン

deshijon-tēburu
decision table
デシジョン・テーブル

dēta
data
データ

dēta-adaputa sōchi
data adapter unit
データ・アダプタ装置

dēta-adoresu
data address
データ・アドレス

dēta angōka
data encryption
データ暗号化

dēta asshuku
data compaction;
data compression
データ圧縮

dēta ayamari
data error
データ誤り

dēta-baffua
data buffer
データ・バッファ

dēta baitai
data medium
データ媒体

dēta-basu
data bus
データ・バス

dēta-basu-enēburu (DBE)
data bus enable (DBE)
データ・バス・エネーブル

dēta bu
data division
データ部

dēta bun
data statement
データ文

dēta-chaneru
data channel
データ・チャネル

dēta-chaneru-maruchipurekusa
data channel multiplexer
データ・チャネル・
マルチプレクサ

dēta-chekku
data check
データ・チェック

dēta chō
data length
データ長

dēta chūkei
data interchange
データ中継

dēta chūshōka
data abstraction
データ抽象化

dēta-dairekutori
data directory
データ・ダイレクトリ

dēta dankaika
data staging
データ段階化

dēta datō kensa
data validation
データ妥当検査

dēta datsuraku
data loss
データ脱落

dēta-deisupurei
data display
データ・ディスプレィ

dēta densō
data transmission
データ伝送

dēta densō kaisen
data transmission circuit
データ伝送回線

dēta densō kōritsu
data transmission efficiency
データ伝送効率

dēta densō nettowāku
data transmission network
データ伝送ネットワーク

dēta densō shisutemu
data transmission system
データ伝送システム

dēta densō sōchi
data transmission unit
データ伝送装置

dēta-derimita
data delimiter
データ・デリミタ

dēta dokuritsu
　data independence
　データ独立

dēta-entori
　data entry
　データ・エントリ

dēta-fuairu
　data file
　データ・ファイル

dēta-fuairu asshuku
　data file compaction
　データ・ファイル圧縮

dēta fugōka
　data coding
　データ符号化

dēta gen
　data source
　データ源

dēta gengo
　data language
　データ言語

dēta go
　data word
　データ語

dēta gun
　data constellation
　データ群

dēta hairetsu
　data array
　データ配列

dēta hason
　data corruption
　データ破損

dēta henkan
　data conversion; data translation
　データ変換

dēta henkan kinō
　data conversion feature
　データ変換機能

dēta hensei
　data organization
　データ編成

dēta hogo
　data protection
　データ保護

dēta hoshu
　data maintenance
　データ保守

dēta hyōgen
　data representation
　データ表現

dēta hyōji
　data display
　データ表示

dēta hyōji sōchi
　data display unit
　データ表示装置

dēta idōsei
　data mobility
　データ移動性

dēta imiron
　data semantics
　データ意味論

dēta isō
　data migration
　データ移送

dēta jisho
　data dictionary
　データ辞書

dēta jittaika
　data materialization
　データ実体化

dēta jumbi
　data preparation
　データ準備

dēta jun gengo
　data sublanguage
　データ準言語

dēta-kādo
　data card
　データ・カード

dēta kaisō
　data hierarchy
　データ階層

dēta kanri
　data administration;
　data management
　データ管理

dēta kanri kyōtsū kōdo
　data management common
　code
　データ管理共通コード

dēta kanri rūchin (DMR)
　data management routine (DMR)
　データ管理ルーチン

dēta kanri shisutemu (DMS)
　data management system (DMS)
　データ管理システム

dēta kanri teigi tēburu
　data management define table
　データ管理定義テーブル

dēta kanrisha
　data administrator
　データ管理者

dēta kanzensei
　data integrity
　データ完全性

dēta keiro
　data path
　データ経路

dēta keishiki
　data format; data layout
　データ形式

dēta keishiki kōmoku
　data format item
　データ形式項目

dēta kensa
　data check; data verification;
　data vetting
　データ検査

dēta kensa puroguramu
　data verifying program
　データ検査プログラム

dēta kensaku
　data retrieval
　データ検索

dēta kijutsu
　data description
　データ記述

dēta kijutsu gengo (DDL)
　data description language (DDL)
　データ記述言語

dēta kijutsu kōmoku
　data description entry
　データ記述項目

dēta kijutsu zokusei
　data description attribute
　データ記述属性

dēta kimitsu hogo
　data security
　データ機密保護

dēta kioku
data storage
データ記憶

dēta kiroku
data capture; data recording
データ記録

dēta kiroku yūteiritei
data capture utility
データ記録ユーティリティ

dēta kirokuki
data inscriber; data recorder
データ記録器

dēta-kōdeingu
data coding
データ・コーディング

dēta-kōdo
data code
データ・コード

dēta-kōdoka
data coding
データ・コード化

dēta kōkan
data exchange; data switching
データ交換

dēta kōmoku
data item
データ項目

dēta kōmoku kenshō
data item validation
データ項目検証

dēta kōzō
data structure
データ構造

dēta kōzō sentaku
data structure choice
データ構造選択

dēta kōzō zu
data structure diagram
データ構造図

dēta-kyapucha
data capture
データ・キャプチャ

dēta-kyarya
data carrier
データ・キャリャ

dēta kyōyū
data sharing
データ共有

dēta-mappu
data map
データ・マップ

dēta mei
data name
データ名

dēta-moderu
data model
データ・モデル

dēta-mōdo
data mode
データ・モード

dēta-mojyūru
data module
データ・モジュール

dēta nagare
data flow
データ流れ

dēta nagare bunseki
data flow analysis
データ流れ分析

dēta nagare zu
data flow diagram;
data flowchart
データ流れ図

dēta no datsuraku
loss of data
データの脱落

dēta no hason
corruption of data
データの破損

dēta no kata
data type
データの型

dēta no kimitsu
privacy of data
テータの機密

dēta no owari
end of data
データの終り

dēta no raiburari
library of data
データのライブラリ

dēta no sonshitsu
loss of data
データの損失

dēta nyūryoku
data entry; data input
データ入力

dēta nyūryoku kemban sōchi
data entry keyboard
データ入力鍵盤装置

dēta nyūryoku kiki
data entry machine
データ入力機器

dēta nyūryoku ryōiki
data input area
データ入力領域

dēta nyūryoku suitchi
data entry switch
データ入力スイッチ

dēta nyūryoku sutēshon
data input station
データ入力ステーション

dēta-orijinēshon
data origination
データ・オリジネーション

dēta owari māka
end-of-data marker
データ終りマーカ

dēta-pen
data pen
データ・ペン

dēta-purotta
data plotter
データ・プロッタ

dēta-rekōda
data recorder
データ・レコーダ

dēta-rekōdeingu
data recording
データ・レコーディング

dēta-rekōdo
data record
データ・レコード

dēta rensa
data chain
データ連鎖

dēta-rinku
data link
データ・リンク

dēta-rinku seigyo
data link control
データ・リンク制御

dēta-risuto
data list
データ・リスト

dēta-roga
data logger
データ・ロガ

dēta-rogingu
data logging
データ・ロギング

dēta-sābisu
data service
データ・サービス

dēta-sabu-moderu
data submodel
データ・サブ・モデル

dēta-sabu-setto
data subset
データ・サブ・セット

dēta saikōsei
data restructuring
データ再構成

dēta-segumento
data segment
データ・セグメント

dēta seigōsei
data consistency
データ整合成

dēta seigyo
data control
データ制御

dēta seigyo burokku (DCB)
data control block (DCB)
データ制御ブロック

dēta seigyo sōchi
data control unit
データ制御装置

dēta seiri
data reduction
データ整理

dēta seiri senta (DRC)
data reduction center
(DRC)
データ整理 センタ

dēta-senta
data center
データ・センタ

dēta-seru
data cell
データ・セル

dēta-seru sōchi
data cell drive
データ・セル装置

dēta-setto (DS)
data set (DS)
データ・セット

dēta-setto haibun
data set allocation
データ・セット配分

dēta-setto hensei
data set organization
データ・セット編成

dēta-setto-raberu
data set label
データ・セット・ラベル

dēta-setto-redei (DSR)
data set ready (DSR)
データ・セット・レディ

dēta-setto seigyo burokku (DSCB)
data set control block (DSCB)
データ・セット制御ブロック

dēta shingō sokudo
data signaling rate
データ信号速度

dēta-shinku
data sink
データ・シンク

dēta-shisutemu
data system(s)
データ・システム

dēta shori
data handling
データ処理

dēta shori (DP)
data processing (DP)
データ処理

dēta shori dōsa
data-processing operation
データ処理動作

dēta shori kiki
data-processing equipment
データ処理機器

dēta shori senta (DPC)
data-processing center (DPC)
データ処理センタ

dēta shori shisutemu
data-processing system
データ処理システム

dēta shori sōchi
data processor
データ処理装置

dēta shori sōsa
data-processing operation
データ処理操作

dēta shoshiki
data format
データ書式

dēta shoshiki kōmoku
data format item
データ書式項目

dēta shūshū
data acquisition; data collection;
data gathering; gathering of data
データ収集

dēta shūshū-seigyo shisutemu
data acquisition and control
system
データ収集制御システム

dēta shūshū shisutemu
data acquisition system;
data collection system
データ収集システム

dēta sonshitsu
data loss
データ損失

dēta sōsa
data manipulation
データ操作

dēta sōsa gengo (DML)
data manipulation language
(DML)
データ操作言語

dēta-sutēshon
data station
データ・ステーション

dēta-taburetto
data tablet
データ・タブレット

dēta-taipu
data type
データ・タイプ

dēta tan'i
data unit
データ単位

dēta tan'i seigyo
data unit control
データ単位制御

dēta tanmatsu
data station
データ端末

dēta tanmatsu (sōchi)
data terminal
データ端末(装置)

dēta tanmatsu sōchi
data terminal equipment
データ端末装置

dēta tanmatsu sōchi redei (DTR)
data terminal ready (DTR)
データ端末装置レディ

dēta teigi
data definition
データ定義

dēta teigi sutētomento
data definition statement
データ定義ステートメント

dēta tenken
data cleaning
データ点検

dēta tensō
data transfer
データ転送

dēta tensō sokudo
data transfer rate;
data transfer speed
データ転送速度

dēta-tēpu
data tape
データ・テープ

dēta-tesuto
data test
データ・テスト

dēta-torakku
data track
データ・トラック

dēta tsūshin
data communications
データ通信

dēta tsūshin kiki
data communication equipment
データ通信機器

dēta tsūshin kōkan
data communications exchange
データ通信交換

dēta tsūshin seigyo
data communication control
データ通信制御

dēta tsūshin shisutemu
data communication system
データ通信システム

dēta tsūshin sōchi (DCS)
data communication subsystem
(DCS); data communication unit
データ通信装置

dēta tsūshin tanmatsu (sōchi)
data communication terminal
データ通信端末(装置)

dēta tsūshinro
data transfer channel
データ通信路

dēta yōryō
data capacity
データ容量

dēta yōshi
data sheet
データ用紙

dēta yōso
data element
データ要素

dēta zokusei
data attribute
データ属性

dētabanku
databank
データバンク

dētabēsu
database
データベース

dētabēsu-apurōchi
database approach
データベース・アプローチ

dētabēsu gengo
database language
データベース言語

dētabēsu ichi'imei
database identifier
データベース一意名

dētabēsu ishokusei
database portability
データベース移植性

dētabēsu jōtai shijishi
database status indicator
データベース状態指示子

dētabēsu kanri
database management
データベース管理

dētabēsu kanri shisutemu (DBMS)
database management system
(DBMS)
データベース管理システム

dētabēsu kanrisha
database administrator
データベース管理者

dētabēsu-kii
database key
データベース・キー

dētabēsu kijutsu
database description
データベース記述

dētabēsu kikai
database machine
データベース機械

dētabēsu kōzō
database structure
データベース構造

dētabēsu reigai jōken
database exception condition
データベース例外条件

dētabēsu-sapōto
database support
データベース・サポート

dētabēsu seigyo shisutemu (DBCS)
database control system (DBCS)
データベース制御システム

dētabēsu-shisutemu
database system
データベース・システム

dētabēsu tetsuzuki
database procedure
データベース手続き

dētagata nyūshutsuryoku
data-directed input/output
データ型入出力

dētapen-riida
datapen reader
データペン・リーダ

deyuaru
dual
デュアル

deyuaru-chaneru
dual channel
デュアル・チャネル

deyuaru-furekishiburu-deisuku kudō kikō
dual flexible disk drive
デュアル・フレキシブル・ディスク駆動機構

deyuaru-in-rain (DIL)
dual-in-line (DIL)
デュアル・イン・ライン

deyuaru-in-rain-pakkēji (DIP)
dual-in-line package (DIP)
デュアル・イン・ライン・パッケージ

deyuaru-in-rain-suitchi (DIL suitchi)
dual-in-line switch (DIL switch)
デュアル・イン・ライン・スイッチ；DILスイッチ

deyuaru-indekkusu-mōdo
dual index mode
デュアル・インデックス・モード

deyuaru-mōdo
dual mode
デュアル・モード

deyuaru-purosessa
dual processor
デュアル・プロセッサ

deyuaru-shisutemu
dual system
デュアル・システム

Deyūi jisshin bunruihō
Dewey decimal classification
デューイ10進分類法

deyupurekkusu
duplex
デュプレックス

deyupurekkusu-operēshon
duplex operation
デュプレックス・オペレーション

deyupurekkusu-shisutemu
duplex system
デュプレックス・システム

DI (daiōdo)
DI (diode)
ダイオード

DIL (deyuaru-in-rain)
DIL (dual-in-line)
デュアル・イン・ライン

DIL suitchi (deyuaru-in-rain-suitchi)
DIL switch (dual-in-line switch)
DILスイッチ；デュアル・イン・ライン・スイッチ

DIP (deyuaru-in-rain-pakkēji)
DIP (dual-in-line package)
デュアル・イン・ライン・パッケージ

DLE (densō seigyo kakuchō)
DLE (data link escape)
伝送制御拡張

DMA (chokusetsu akusesu)
DMA (direct memory access)
直接アクセス

DMCL (sōchi baitai seigyo gengo)
DMCL (device media control language)
装置媒体制御言語

DML (dēta sōsa gengo)
DML (data manipulation language)
データ操作言語

D-MOS (deipuriishon MOS)
D-MOS (depletion MOS)
ディプリーション MOS

DMR (dēta kanri rūchin)
DMR (data management routine)
データ管理ルーチン

DMS (dēta kanri shisutemu)
DMS (data management system)
データ管理システム

dō
simultaneous
同

dōchi
equivalence
同値

dōchō
tuning
同調

dōhō tsūshin
broadcast
同報通信

dōji
simultaneous
同時

dōji akusesu
simultaneous access
同時アクセス

dōji densō
simultaneous transmission
同時伝送

dōji DMA
simultaneous DMA
同時 DMA

dōji heikō dōsa
concurrent operation
同時並行動作

dōji heikō no
concurrent
同時並行の

dōji keta age
simultaneous carry
同時桁上げ

dōji shori
concurrent processing;
simultaneous processing
同時処理

dōji sōsa
simultaneous operation
同時操作

dōji tansaku
simultaneous search
同時探索

dōjisei
simultaneity
同時性

dōka
equivalence
同価

dōkei kēburu (COAX)
coaxial cable (COAX)
同軸ケーブル

269

dōki
synchronization
同期

dōki(ka) suru
synchronize
同期(化)する

dōki(shiki)
synchronous
同期(式)

dōki(shiki) kairo
synchronous circuit
同期(式)回路

dōki(shiki) kikai
synchronous machine
同期(式)機械

dōki densō
synchronous transmission
同期伝送

dōki dōsa
synchronous operation
同期動作

dōki gosa
synchronization error
同期誤差

dōki mōdo
synchronous mode
同期モード

dōki parusu
synchronization pulse;
synchronizing pulse
同期パルス

dōki shingō (SYN)
synchronous idle (SYN)
同期信号

dōki shisutemu tsūshin
synchronous system
communication
同期システム通信

dōki shori
synchronous processing
同期処理

dōki shori shisutemu
synchronous processing system
同期処理システム

dōki shisutemu
synchronous system
同期システム

dōki sōchi
synchronizer
同期装置

dōki sōsa
synchronous operation
同期操作

dōki tsūshin
synchronous communication
同期通信

dōkihōshiki
synchronous system
同期方式

dōkika
synchronization
同期化

dōkishiki
synchronous system
同期式

dōkishiki dēta-rinku seigyo (SDLC)
synchronous data link control
(SDLC)
同期式データ・リンク制御

dōkishiki keisanki
synchronous computer
同期式計算機

dokuritsu
independent
独立

dokuritsu(gata)
stand-alone
独立(型)

dokuritsu(gata) keisanki
stand-alone computer
独立(型)計算機

dokuritsu(gata) kikai
stand-alone machine
独立(型)機械

dokuritsu(gata) puroguramu
stand-alone program
独立(型)プログラム

dokuritsu(gata) shisutemu
stand-alone system
独立(型)システム

dokuritsu(gata) shori shisutemu
stand-alone processing system
独立(型)処理システム

dokuritsu(gata) sōsataku
stand-alone console
独立(型)操作卓

dokuritsu hensū
independent variable
独立変数

dokuritsu kōmoku
noncontiguous item
独立項目

dokuritsu sagyō basho
noncontiguous working storage
独立作業場所

dokuritsu tejun
independent procedure
独立手順

dokuritsu yūteiritei
independent utility
独立ユーティリティ

dokuritsu yūteiritei-puroguramu
independent utility program
独立ユーティリティ・プログラム

dokuritsugata
stand-alone type
独立型

dokyumentēshon
documentation
ドキュメンテーション

dokyumentēshon-shisutemu
documentation system
ドキュメンテーション・システム

dokyumento
document
ドキュメント

dokyumento kensaku
document retrieval
ドキュメント検索

dokyumento-riida
document reader
ドキュメント・リーダ

doraibu
drive
ドライブ

doramu
drum
ドラム

doramushiki insho sōchi
drum printer
ドラム式印書装置

doramushiki purotta
drum plotter
ドラム式プロッタ

doramushiki shisutemu
drum-oriented system
ドラム式システム

dorifuto
drift
ドリフト

doroppo-auto
drop-out
ドロッポ・アウト

doroppo-in
drop-in
ドロッポ・イン

dōryoku
power
動力

dōryoku sen
power line
動力線

dōryoku sen kēburu
power line cable
動力線ケーブル

DOS (deisuku-operēteingu-shisutemu)
DOS (disk-based operating system; disk operating system)
ディスク・オペレーティング・システム

dōsa
action; activity; operation (action)
動作

dōsa funō
inoperable
動作不能

dōsa jikan
operating time
動作時間

dōsa jōtai
active state
動作状態

dōsa ritsu
operating ratio
動作率

dōsa saikuru
operation cycle
動作サイクル

dōsa shirei
operating instructions
動作指令

dōshiki
synchronous system
同式

dōshitsu
homogeneity
同質

dōshitsu no
homogeneous
同質の

dōshutsu
derivation
導出

dōteki
dynamic
動的

dōteki adoresu henkanki (DAT)
dynamic address translator (DAT)
動的アドレス変換器

dōteki baffuaringu
dynamic buffering
動的バッファリング

dōteki danpu
dynamic dump
動的ダンプ

dōteki furippu-furoppu
dynamic flip-flop
動的フリップ・フロップ

dōteki kairo
dynamic circuit
動的回路

dōteki keikakuhō (DP)
dynamic programming (DP)
動的計画法

dōteki kioku
dynamic storage
動的記憶

dōteki kioku sōchi
dynamic store
動的記憶装置

dōteki kioku'iki wariate
dynamic memory allocation; dynamic storage allocation
動的記憶域割り当て

dōteki kōzō
dynamic structure
動的構造

dōteki moderu
dynamic model
動的モデル

dōteki parameta
dynamic parameter
動的パラメタ

dōteki puroguramu-rōdeingu
dynamic program loading
動的プログラム・ローディング

dōteki puroguramu saihaichi
dynamic program relocation
動的プログラム再配置

dōteki rejisuta
dynamic register
動的レジスタ

dōteki saburūchin
dynamic subroutine
動的サブルーチン

dōteki saihaichi
dynamic relocation
動的再配置

dōteki saikōsei
dynamic restructuring
動的再構成

dōteki seigyo
dynamic control
動的制御

dōteki shigen haibun
dynamic resource allocation
動的資源配分

dōteki sōchi saikōsei
dynamic device reconfiguration
動的装置再構成

dōteki wariate
dynamic allocation
動的割り当て

dōtokusei
dynamic characteristics
動特性

dotto
dot
ドット

dotto hōshiki
dot method
ドット方式

dotto-matorikkusu
dot matrix
ドット・マトリックス

dotto-matorikkusu moji
dot matrix character
ドット・マトリックス文字

dotto-matorikkusu-purinta
dot matrix printer
ドット・マトリックス・プリンタ

dotto-patān
dot pattern
ドット・パターン

dotto-patān hasseiki
dot pattern generator
ドット・パターン発生器

dotto-pitchi
dot pitch
ドット・ピッチ

dotto-purinta
dot printer
ドット・プリンタ

dotto seisei
dot generation
ドット生成

dottoshiki insho sōchi
dot printer
ドット式印書装置

dotto shūki
dot cycle
ドット周期

DP (dēta shori)
DP (data processing)
データ処理

DP (dōteki keikakuhō)
DP (dynamic programming)
動的計画法

DPC (dēta shori senta)
DPC (data-processing center)
データ処理センタ

DRC (dēta seiri senta)
DRC (data reduction center)
データ整理センタ

DRO (hakai yomidashi)
DRO (destructive readout)
破壊読み出し

DS (dēta-setto)
DS (data set)
データ・セット

DSCB (dēta-setto seigyo burokku)
DSCB (data set control block)
データ・セット制御ブロック

DSR (dēta-setto-redei)
DSR (data set ready)
データ・セット・レディ

DSS (ishi kettei shien shisutemu)
DSS (decision support system)
意思決定支援システム

DTL (daiōdo-toranjisuta ronri)
DTL (diode transistor logic)
ダイオード・トランジスタ論理

DTR (dēta tanmatsu sōchi redei)
DTR (data terminal ready)
データ端末装置レディ

E

EAM (denkishiki kaikeiki)
EAM (electrical accounting machine)
電気式会計機

EAROM (denkiteki saikakikomi ROM)
EAROM (electrically alterable read-only memory)
電気的再書き込みROM

EBAM (denshi biimu-memori)
EBAM (electron-beam addressed memory)
電子ビーム・メモリ

EBCDIC (kakuchō nisshinka jisshin kōdo)
EBCDIC (extended binary-coded decimal interchange code)
拡張2進化10進コード

EBM (burokku owari māka; burokku shūketsu māka)
EBM (end-of-block marker)
ブロック終りマーカ；
ブロック終結マーカ

EBR (denshi biimu kiroku)
EBR (electron-beam recording)
電子ビーム記録

ECAP (denshi kairo kaiseki puroguramu)
ECAP (electronic circuit analysis program)
電子回路解析プログラム

ECB (jishō seigyo burokku)
ECB (event control block)
事象制御ブロック

ECC (ayamari teisei fugō)
ECC (error-correcting code)
誤り訂正符号

ECL (emitta ketsugōgata ronri)
ECL (emitter-coupled logic)
エミッタ結合型論理

ECMA (Ōshū Denshi Keisanki Seizō Gyōsha Kyōkai)
ECMA (European Computer Manufacturers' Association)
欧州電子計算機製造業者協会

edeita
editor
エディタ

edeittogata nyūshutsuryoku
edit-directed input/output
EDIT型入出力

EDP (denshi dēta shori; denshishiki dēta shori)
EDP (electronic data processing)
電子データ処理;
電子式データ処理

EDPM (denshi dēta shori kikai)
EDPM (electronic data-processing machine)
電子データ処理機械

EDPS (denshi dēta shori shisutemu)
EDPS (electronic data-processing system)
電子データ処理システム

EDS (kōkankanō deisuku kioku sōchi)
EDS (exchangeable disk store)
交換可能ディスク記憶装置

EEPROM (denkiteki shōkyokanō puroguramukanō ROM)
EEPROM (electrically erasable programmable read-only memory)
電気的消去可能プログラム可能ROM

EEROM (denkiteki shōkyokanō ROM)
EEROM (electrically erasable read-only memory)
電気的消去可能ROM

EFM (fuiirudo owari māka)
EFM (end-of-field marker)
フィールド終りマーカ

efuekuta
effector
エフェクタ

eguzekuteibu
executive
エグゼクティブ

eguzekuteibu-rikuesuto (ER)
executive request (ER)
エグゼクティブ・リクェスト

eguzekuteibu-rūchin
executive routine
エグゼクティブ・ルーチン

eguzekuteibu-shisutemu
executive system
エグゼクティブ・システム

EIA (Denshi Kōgyō Kai)
EIA (Electronic Industries Association)
電子工業会

eiji
alphabet; alphabetic;
alphabetical; alphabetical
character; letter (character)
英字

eiji kōdo
alphabetic code
英字コード

eiji retsu
alphabetic string
英字列

eiji shifuto (LTRS)
letter shift (LTRS)
英字シフト

Eikoku Kōgyō Kikaku (BS)
British Standards (BS)
英国工業規格

Eikoku Kōgyō Kikaku Kyōkai (BSI)
British Standards Institution (BSI)
英国工業規格協会

eikyū
permanent
永久

eikyū ayamari
permanent error
永久誤り

Eipiieru (APL)
A Programming Language (APL)
エイピーエル

eisei
statellite
衛星

eisei keisanki
satellite computer
衛星計算機

eisei shori sōchi
satellite processor
衛星処理装置

eisei tsūshin
satellite communication
衛星通信

eisūji
alphameric; alphameric
character; alphanumeric
character
英数字

eisūji (no)
alphanumeric
英数字の

eisūji dēta
alphanumeric data
英数字データ

eisūji dēta-kōdo
alphanumeric data code
英数字データ・コード

eisūji kemban sōchi
alphanumeric keyboard
英数字鍵盤装置

eisūji kiibōdo
alphanumeric keyboard
英数字キーボード

eisūji kōdo
alphameric code;
alphanumeric code
英数字コード

eisūji kōdo-setto
alphanumeric coded character set
英数字コード・セット

eisūji setto
alphanumeric character set
英数字セット

eizō
image
映像

eizō hyōji sōchi (VDU)
video display unit (VDU)
映像表示装置

eizō shingō
video signal
映像信号

eizō shori
image processing
映像処理

eizoku
permanent
永続

eizoku fuairu
permanent file
永続ファイル

ejji
edge
エッジ

ejji-kādo
edge card; edge-punched card
エッジ・カード

ejji-konekuta
edge connector
エッジ・コネクタ

ejji senkō kādo
edge-punched card
エッジせん孔カード

eki
duty; function (feature)
役

ekishō
liquid crystal
液晶

ekishō deisupurei (LCD)
liquid-crystal display (LCD)
液晶ディスプレイ

ekkusupāto-shisutemu
expert system
エックスパート・システム

ekō
echo
エコー

ekō-chekku
echo check
エコー・チェック

ekō-chekku hōshiki
echo-checking system
エコー・チェック方式

ekō yokuseiki
echo suppressor
エコー抑制器

ekusutento
extent
エクステント

ekusutento-tēburu
extent table
エクステント・テーブル

ekusutento yōkyū burokku (ERB)
extent request block (ERB)
エクステント要求ブロック

EM (baitai no owari; baitai shūtan)
EM (end of medium)
媒体の終わり；媒体終端

emitta
emitter
エミッタ

emitta-fuōrowa
emitter follower
エミッタ・フォーロワ

emitta-fuōrowa-daiōdo-toranjisuta ronri
emitter-follower diode transistor logic
エミッタ・フォーロワ・ダイオード・ドランジスタ論理

emitta-fuōrowa ronri kairo
emitter-follower logic circuit
エミッタ・フォーロワ論理回路

emitta ketsugōgata ronri (ECL)
emitter-coupled logic (ECL)
エミッタ結合型論理

EMOS (enhansumentogata MOS)
EMOS (enhancement MOS)
エンハンスメント型MOS

emyurēshon
emulation
エミュレーション

emyurēta
emulator
エミュレータ

emyurēta-puroguramu
emulator program
エミュレータ・プログラム

enbosu suru
emboss
エンボスする

enbosumento
embossment
エンボスメント

endo
end
エンド

endo gyō
END line
エンド行

endo-māku
end mark
エンド・マーク

endo-yūza
end user
エンド・ユーザ

enēburu
enable
エネーブル

enhansu suru
enhance
エンハンスする

enhansumento
enhancement
エンハンスメント

enhansumentogata MOS (EMOS)
enhancement MOS (EMOS)
エンハンスメント型MOS

enkaku(chi)
remote
遠隔(地)

enkaku(chi) dēta shori sōchi
remote data processor
遠隔(地)データ処理装置

enkaku akusesu
remote access
遠隔アクセス

enkaku akusesu keisanki shisutemu
remote-access computer system
遠隔アクセス計算機システム

enkaku debaggingu
remote debugging
遠隔デバッギング

enkaku jyobu nyūryoku (RJE)
remote job entry (RJE)
遠隔ジョブ入力

enkaku keisan (shori)
remote computing
遠隔計算(処理)

enkaku keisan (shori) shisutemu
remote computing system
遠隔計算(処理)システム

enkaku keisanki
remote computer
遠隔計算機

enkaku keisanki shisutemu
remote computer system
遠隔計算機システム

enkaku keishiki
remote format
遠隔形式

enkaku kyoku
remote station
遠隔局

enkaku operēteingu sōchi
remote operating unit
遠隔オペレーティング装置

enkaku sagyō kyoku
remote workstation
遠隔作業局

enkaku sagyō tanmatsu
remote workstation
遠隔作業端末

enkaku seigyo
remote control
遠隔制御

enkaku seigyo kinō
remote control function
遠隔制御機能

enkaku seigyo sōchi
remote controller
遠隔制御装置

enkaku shisutemu
remote system
遠隔システム

enkaku shōkai
remote inquiry
遠隔照会

enkaku shōkai sōchi
remote inquiry unit
遠隔照会装置

enkaku shoshiki
remote format
遠隔書式

enkaku sokutei
telemetering
遠隔測定

enkaku sōsa
remote operation
遠隔操作

enkaku sōsataku
remote console
遠隔操作卓

enkaku tanmatsu
remote location; remote station
遠隔端末

enkaku tanmatsu sōchi
remote terminal
遠隔端末装置

enkaku toiawase
remote inquiry
遠隔問い合わせ

enkaku tsūshin kinō
remote communication facility
遠隔通信機能

enkaku tsūshin sōchi
remote communication unit
遠隔通信装置

enkakuchi batchi
remote batch
遠隔地バッチ

enkakuchi batchi shori
remote batch processing
遠隔地バッチ処理

enkakuchi dēta shori
remote data processing
遠隔地データ処理

enkōda
encoder
エンコーダ

enkōdo-tēburu
encode table
エンコード・テーブル

ENQ (toiawase)
ENQ (enquiry)
問い合わせ

entō inji sōchi
barrel printer
円筒印字装置

entori
entry
エントリ

enzan
computing; operation (math)
演算

enzan/fun
operations per minute
演算／分

enzan jikan
computing time; operation time
演算時間

enzan kairo
arithmetic circuit
演算回路

enzan rejisuta
arithmetic register
演算レジスタ

enzan ronri sōchi (ALU)
arithmetic and logic unit (ALU)
演算論理装置

enzan saburūchin
arithmetic subroutine
演算サブルーチン

enzan saikuru
operation cycle
演算サイクル

enzan seigyo sōchi (ACU)
arithmetic and control unit (ACU)
演算制御装置

enzan sōchi
arithmetic unit
演算装置

enzan sokudo
computing speed; operation speed
演算速度

enzan zōfukuki
OP-amp; operational amplifier
演算増幅器

enzanjō no imi
operational semantics
演算上の意味

enzanshi
operator
演算子

enzanshi jun'i
hierarchy of operators
演算子順位

enzanshi no yūsen jun'i
operator precedence
演算子の優先順位

enzansū
operand
演算数

EOB (burokku no owari; burokku shūketsu)
EOB (end of block)
ブロックの終り；ブロック終結

EOF (fuairu no owari)
EOF (end of file)
ファイルの終り

EOJ (jyobu no owari; jyobu shūryō)
EOJ (end of job)
ジョブの終り；ジョブ終了

EOM (messēji no owari; messēji shūketsu)
  EOM (end of message)
  メッセージの終り；
  メッセージ終結

EOT (densō shūketsu)
  EOT (end of transmission)
  伝送終結

EOT (tēpu no owari; tēpu shūtan)
  EOT (end of tape)
  テープの終り；テープ終端

EOV (boryūmu no owari)
  EOV (end of volume)
  ボリュームの終り

epitakushi
  epitaxy
  エピタクシ

EPOC (iichi-pasu-oun-kōdo)
  EPOC (each-pass own code)
  イーチ・パス・オウン・コード

EPROM (shōkyokanō puroguramukanō ROM)
  EPROM (erasable programmable read-only memory)
  消去可能プログラム可能ROM

EQ (tōka)
  EQ (equivalence)
  等価

EQ gēto (tōka gēto)
  EQ gate (equivalence gate)
  EQゲート；等価ゲート

ER (eguzekuteibu-rikuesuto)
  ER (executive request)
  エグゼクティブ・リクェスト

erā
  error
  エラー

erā-chekku
  error check
  エラー・チック

erā-messēji
  error message
  エラー・メッセージ

erā-ripōto
  error report
  エラー・リポート

erā-risuto
  error list
  エラー・リスト

erā-rūchin
  error routine
  エラー・ルーチン

erā shingō
  error signal
  エラー信号

ERB (ekusutento yōkyū burokku)
  ERB (extent request block)
  エクステント要求ブロック

erekutoronikkusu
  electronic; electronics
  エレクトロニックス

erekutoronikkusu-ofuisu
  electronic office
  エレクトロニックス・オフィス

eremento
  element
  エレメント

eremento ayamari ritsu
  element error rate
  エレメント誤り率

eremento-fuairu
  element file
  エレメント・ファイル

ERM (rekōdo owari māka)
  ERM (end-of-record marker)
  レコード終りマーカ

ESC (kakuchō)
  ESC (escape)
  拡張

ETB (densō burokku shūketsu)
  ETB (end-of-transmission block)
  伝送ブロック終結

ETX (tekisuto shūketsu)
  ETX (end of text)
  テキスト終結

F

F (fuōmatto; keishiki; shoshiki; yōshiki)
  F (format)
  フォーマット；形式；書式；様式

FAX (fuakushimiri; mosha densō)
  FAX (facsimile)
  ファクシミリ；模写電送

FCB (fuairu seigyo burokku)
  FCB (file control block)
  ファイル制御ブロック

FCC (Beikoku Rempō Tsūshin I'inkai)
  FCC (Federal Communications Commission) (USA)
  米国連邦通信委員会

FCT (fuairu seigyo tēburu)
  FCT (file control table)
  ファイル制御テーブル

FD (furoppi-deisuku)
  FD (floppy disk)
  フロッピ・ディスク

FD (zen nijū)
  FD (full duplex)
  全二重

FDM (shūhasū bunkatsu tajū hōshiki; shūhasū bunkatsu tajū hōshiki sōchi)
  FDM (frequency division multiplexing; frequency division multiplexer)
  周波数分割多重方式；
  周波数分割多重方式装置

FDM (yūgen sabumpō)
  FDM (finite difference method)
  有限差分法

FDOS (furoppi-deisuku-operēteingu-shisutemu)
  FDOS (floppy-disk operating system)
  フロッピ・ディスク・
  オペレーティング・システム

FDX (zen nijū)
  FDX (full duplex)
  全二重

FE (shoshiki seigyo moji)
  FE (format effector)
  書式制御文字

FEM (yūgen yōso hō)
FEM (finite element method)
有限要素法

FEP (furonto-endo-purosessa)
FEP (front-end processor)
フロント・エンド・プロセッサ

FET (denkai kōka toranjisuta gijutsu)
FET (field effect transistor technology)
電界効果トランジスタ技術

FF (shoshiki okuri)
FF (form feed)
書式送り

FFT (kōsoku Fūrie henkan)
FFT (fast Fourier transform)
高速フーリェ変換

FIFO (saki ire saki dashi)
FIFO (first-in first-out)
先入れ先出し

FIGS (sūji shifuto)
FIGS (figure shift)
数字シフト

FILO (saki ire ato dashi)
FILO (first-in last-out)
先入れ後出し

FIPS (Beikoku Rempō Jōhō Shori Hyōjun)
FIPS (Federal Information-Processing Standards) (USA)
米国連邦情報処理標準

FLOPS (fudō shōsūten enzan/byō)
FLOPS (floating-point operations per second)
浮動小数点演算／秒

FM (shūhasū henchō)
FM (frequency modulation)
周波数変調

FM dēta-rekōda
FM data recorder
FMデータ・レコーダ

FORTRAN (Fuōtoran)
FORTRAN (Formula Translation)
フォートラン

FP (fudō shōsūten)
FP (floating point)
浮動小数点

FPP (fudō shōsūten pakkēji)
FPP (floating-point package)
浮動小数点パッケージ

fr (fudō shōsūten rejisuta)
fr (floating-point register)
浮動小数点レジスタ

FS (fuairu bunri moji)
FS (file separator)
ファイル分離文字

FSK (shūhasū hen'i hōshiki)
FSK (frequency shift keying)
周波数変位方式

FSX (gaikokugo shisutemu kakuchō)
FSX (foreign [non-Japanese] language system extension)
外国語システム拡張

fu
negative
負

fuaiba-oputeikkusu
fiber optics
ファイバ・オプティックス

fuaiba-oputeikkusu densō
fiber-optics transmission
ファイバ・オプティックス伝送

fuairingu
filing
ファイリング

fuairingu-shisutemu
filing system
ファイリング・システム

fuairu
file
ファイル

fuairu-ākaibu
file archive
ファイル・アーカイブ

fuairu-akusesu-mōdo
file access method
ファイル・アクセス・モード

fuairu atogaki raberu
file trailer label
ファイル後書きラベル

fuairu atogaki raberu gun
file trailer label group
ファイル後書きラベル群

fuairu bunri moji (FS)
file separator (FS)
ファイル分離文字

fuairu bunseki
file analysis
ファイル分析

fuairu bunsekihyō
file analysis form
ファイル分析表

fuairu-danpu
file dumping
ファイル・ダンプ

fuairu fukkyū
file reconstitution
ファイル復旧

fuairu fukugen
file reconstitution
ファイル復元

fuairu hajime raberu
beginning of file label
ファイル始めラベル

fuairu hakidashi
file dumping
ファイル掃き出し

fuairu henkan
file conversion
ファイル変換

fuairu henkō
file amendment
ファイル変更

fuairu hensei
file organization
ファイル編成

fuairu hogo
file protection; file security
ファイル保護

fuairu hogo ringu
file protection ring
ファイル保護リング

fuairu hoshu
file maintenance
ファイル保守

fuairu hozon
file archive
ファイル保存

fuairu hozon kikan
file retention period
ファイル保存期間

fuairu iji
file maintenance
ファイル維持

fuairu-indekkusu
file index
ファイル・インデックス

fuairu in'yō
file reference
ファイル引用

fuairu junjo
file sequence
ファイル順序

fuairu junjo bangō
file sequence number
ファイル順序番号

fuairu kaifuku
file recovery
ファイル回復

fuairu kanri
file management
ファイル管理

fuairu kanri shisutemu
file management system
ファイル管理システム

fuairu kensaku
file inquiry
ファイル検索

fuairu ketsugō
file coupling
ファイル結合

fuairu kijutsu
file description
ファイル記述

fuairu kijutsu kōmoku
file description entry
ファイル記述項目

fuairu kijutsushi
file descriptor
ファイル記述子

fuairu kioku sōchi
filestore
ファイル記憶装置

fuairu-konbāta
file converter
ファイル・コンバータ

fuairu kōshin
file cleanup; file update;
file updating
ファイル更新

fuairu kōzō
file structure
ファイル構造

fuairu kubunka
file partitioning
ファイル区分化

fuairu kyōyō
file sharing
ファイル共用

fuairu mei
file name
ファイル名

fuairu midashi
file header
ファイル見出し

fuairu midashi raberu (HDR)
file header label (HDR)
ファイル見出しラベル

fuairu midashi raberu gun
file header label group
ファイル見出しラベル群

fuairu naiyō
file contents
ファイル内容

fuairu no owari (EOF)
end of file (EOF)
ファイルの終り

fuairu-ōbafurō
file overflow
ファイル・オーバフロー

fuairu owari māka
end-of-file marker
ファイル終りマーカ

fuairu owari raberu
end-of-file label
ファイル終りラベル

fuairu-purinto
file print
ファイル・プリント

fuairu-raberu
file label
ファイル・ラベル

fuairu-reiauto
file layout
ファイル・レイアウト

fuairu-rekōdo shiyō
file record specification
ファイル・レコード仕様

fuairu-rōdeingu
file loading
ファイル・ローディング

fuairu-sāba
file server
ファイル・サーバ

fuairu sanshō
file reference
ファイル参照

fuairu-sapōto
file support
ファイル・サポート

fuairu seigyo
file control
ファイル制御

fuairu seigyo burokku (FCB)
file control block (FCB)
ファイル制御ブロック

fuairu seigyo tēburu
file control table
ファイル制御テーブル

fuairu sekkei
file layout
ファイル設計

fuairu sengen bun
file declaration statement
ファイル宣言文

fuairu-setto
file set
ファイル・セット

fuairu-setto shikibetsumei
file set identifier
ファイル・セット識別名

fuairu-sheāringu
file sharing
ファイル・シェアーリング

fuairu shijisho
file specification form
ファイル指示書

fuairu shikibetsu
file identification
ファイル識別

fuairu shikibetsumei
file identifier
ファイル識別名

fuairu shitei
file designation
ファイル指定

fuairu shiyō ritsu
file activity ratio; hit rate
ファイル使用率

fuairu shori
file processing
ファイル処理

fuairu shūryō kiroku
end file record
ファイル終了記録

fuairu sōsa
file scan
ファイル走査

fuairu tansaku
file search
ファイル探索

fuairu teigi mei
file definition name
ファイル定義名

fuairu tensō
file transfer
ファイル転送

fuairu tensō yūteiritei
file transfer utility
ファイル転送ユーティリティ

fuairu tōgō
file consolidation
ファイル統合

fuairu tōgō adaputa
integrated file adapter
ファイル統合アダプタ

fuairu tōgō kōzō
integrated file structure
ファイル統合構造

fuairu yōshiki
file layout
ファイル様式

fuairu zokusei
file attribute
ファイル属性

fuairukan kankei
interfile relationship
ファイル間関係

fuairusutōa
filestore
ファイルストーア

fuakushimiri (FAX)
facsimile (FAX)
ファクシミリ

fuāmuuea
firmware
ファームウェア

fuan-auto
fan-out
ファン・アウト

fuan-in
fan-in
ファン・イン

fuantei
instability; unstable
不安定

fuanzen
unsafe
不安全

fuasuto-pasu-oun-kōdo (FPOC)
first-pass own code (FPOC)
ファスト・パス・オウン・コード

fudō adoresu
floating address
浮動アドレス

fudō heddo
floating head; flying head
浮動ヘッド

fudō moji
floating character
浮動文字

fudō okikae moji
floating replacement character
浮動置き換え文字

fudō shōsūten (FP)
floating point (FP)
浮動小数点

fudō shōsūten enzan
floating-point arithmetic
浮動小数点演算

fudō shōsūten enzan/byō (FLOPS)
floating-point operations per second (FLOPS)
浮動小数点演算／秒

fudō shōsūten hōshiki keisanki
floating-point computer
浮動小数点方式計算機

fudō shōsūten hyōji
floating-point representation
浮動小数点表示

fudō shōsūten hyōkihō
floating-point notation
浮動小数点表記法

fudō shōsūten kisū
floating-point base;
floating-point radix
浮動小数点基数

fudō shōsūten pakkēji (FPP)
floating-point package (FPP)
浮動小数点パッケージ

fudō shōsūten rejisuta (fr)
floating-point register (fr)
浮動小数点レジスタ

fudō shōsūten rūchin
floating-point routine
浮動小数点ルーチン

fudō shōsūten sū
floating-point number
浮動小数点数

fudō shōsūten teisū
floating-point constant
浮動小数点定数

fuēdo-auto
fade out
フェード・アウト

fuēdo-in
fade in
フェード・イン

fueiru-sēfu
fail-safe
フェイル・セーフ

fueiru-sēfu sekkei
fail-safe design
フェイル・セーフ設計

fueiru-sēfu-shisutemu
fail-safe system
フェイル・セーフ・システム

fueiru-sēfu tejun
fail-safe procedure
フェイル・セーフ手順

fueiru-sēfu tetsuzuki
fail-safe procedure
フェイル・セーフ手続き

fueiru-sofuto
fail-soft
フェイル・ソフト

fueiru-sofuto-shisutemu
fail-soft system
フェイル・ソフト・システム

fueraito
ferrite
フェライト

fueraito jishin
ferrite core
フェライト磁心

fueraito-koa
ferrite core
フェライト・コア

fueraito-roddo
ferrite rod
フェライト・ロッド

fuēsu
face
フェース

fuēsu-bondeingu
face bonding
フェース・ボンディング

fuēsu-daun-bondeingu
face-down bonding
フェース・ダウン・ボンディング

fuetchi
fetch (*noun*)
フェッチ

fuetchi suru
fetch (*verb*)
フェッチする

fuēzu
phase
フェーズ

fuēzu-erā
phase error
フェーズ・エラー

fuēzu mei
phase name
フェーズ名

fuēzu-rokku-rūpu
phase-locked loop
フェーズ・ロック・ループ

fuēzu-tēburu
phase table
フェーズ・テーブル

fugō
code; sign
符号

fugō bitto
sign bit
符号ビット

fugō dempa
sign propagation
符号伝播

fugō hyō
code table
符号表

fugō ichi
sign position
符号位置

fugō jōken
sign condition
符号条件

fugō keta
sign position
符号桁

fugō keta sūji
sign digit
符号桁数字

fugō moji
sign character
符号文字

fugō nai
unsigned
符号ない

fugō nai messēji
unsigned message
符号ないメッセージ

fugō nai nishinsū
unsigned binary
符号ない2進数

fugō nai seisū
unsigned integer
符号ない整数

fugō seigyo furippu-furoppu
sign control flip-flop
符号制御フリップ・フロップ

fugō tesuto
sign test
符号テスト

fugō zettaichi
sign magnitude
符号絶対値

fugō zettaichi hyōkihō
sign magnitude notation
符号絶対値表記法

fugōka
coding; encoding
符号化

fugōka hyōji
coded representation
符号化表示

fugōka jisshinhō
coded decimal notation
符号化10進法

fugōka jisshinsū
coded decimal
符号化10進数

fugōka moji
coded character
符号化文字

fugōka moji setto
coded character set
符号化文字セット

fugōka puroguramu
coded program
符号化プログラム

fugōka riron
coding theory
符号化理論

fugōka suru
encode
符号化する

fugōki
encoder
符号器

fugōtsuki fuiirudo
signed field
符号付きフィールド

fugōtsuki kō
signed term
符号付き項

fugōtsuki nishinsū
signed binary
符号付き2進数

fugōtsuki seisū
signed integer
符号付き整数

fugōtsuki teisū
signed constant
符号付き定数

fuheikō gosa
unbalanced error
不平衡誤差

fuhen gengo teigi (ULD)
universal language definition (ULD)
普遍言語定義

Fuibonatchi sūretsu
Fibonacci series
フィボナッチ数列

Fuibonatchi tansaku
Fibonacci search
フィボナッチ探索

fuiido
feed
フィード

fuiido-fuōwādo
feed forward
フィード・フォーワード

fuiido-fuōwādo seigyo
feed forward control
フィード・フォーワード制御

fuiido-hoppa
feed hopper
フィード・ホッパ

fuiido-pitchi
feed pitch
フィード・ピッチ

fuiido sokudo
feed rate
フィード速度

fuiidobakku
feedback
フィードバック

fuiidobakku-rūpu
feedback loop
フィードバック・ループ

fuiidobakku seigyo
feedback control
フィードバック制御

fuiidobakku-shisutemu
feedback system
フィードバック・システム

fuiijibiritei kenkyū
feasibility study
フィージビリティ研究

fuiirudo
field
フィールド

fuiirudo-chekku
field check
フィールド・チック

fuiirudo chō
field length
フィールド長

fuiirudo kaihatsu puroguramu
field-developed program
フィールド開発プログラム

fuiirudo kijutsushi
field descriptor
フィールド記述子

fuiirudo no nagasa
field length
フィールドの長さ

fuiirudo no owari
end of field
フィールドの終り

fuiirudo owari māka (EFM)
end-of-field marker (EFM)
フィールド終りマーカ

fuiirudo seigyo
field control
フィールド制御

fuiirudo seigyo chekku
field control check
フィールド制御チェック

fuiirudo sentaku
field selection
フィールド選択

fuiirudo-shiikensu
field sequence
フィールド・シーケンス

fuiirudo teigi
field definition
フィールド定義

fuirumu
film
フィルム

fuirumu kiroku sōchi
film recorder
フィルム記録装置

fuirumu sōsa kikō
film scanner
フィルム走査機構

fuirumu yomitori sōchi
film reader
フィルム読み取り装置

fuiruta
filter
フィルタ

fuisshu
fiche
フィッシュ

fuitchi
mismatch
不一致

fuka
load (LOAD)
負荷

fuka bunsan
load distribution
負荷分散

fuka bunseki
load analysis
負荷分析

fuka mitsudo
load density
負荷密度

fukihassei
nonvolatile
不揮発性

fukihassei kioku
nonvolatile memory
不揮発性記憶

fukikan (NFB)
negative feedback (NFB)
負帰還

fukki
return
復帰

fukki (CR)
carriage return (CR)
復帰

fukki kikō
return mechanism
復帰機構

fukki meirei
return instruction
復帰命令

fukki moji
carriage-return character
復帰文字

fuku
multi-
複

fuku
secondary
副

fuku hyōjun tēpu
secondary reference tape
副標準テープ

fuku kijutsukō
subentry
副記述項

fuku kinō
subfunction
副機能

fuku puroguramu
subprogram
副プログラム

fuku ringu-fuairu
multiring file
複リング・ファイル

fuku saikuru bunrui
multicycle sort
複サイクル分類

fukuchō
demodulation
複調

fukuchōki
demodulator
複調器

fukugen
reconstitution (of files)
復元

fukugen suru
restore
復元する

fukugō
decoding
復号

fukugō buhin
composite part
複合部品

fukugō bumpu
composite distribution
複合分布

fukugō bun
compound statement
複合文

fukugō fuairu
composite file
複合ファイル

fukugō hō
composite algorithm
複合法

fukugō jōken
compound condition
複合条件

fukugō keisanki shisutemu
multicomputer system
複合計算機システム

fukugō mōdo
compound mode
複合モード

fukugō ritoku
composite gain
複合利得

fukugō sekkei
composite design
複合設計

fukugō shiki
compound expression
複合式

fukugō suru
decode
復号する

fukugōki
decoder
復号器

fukuryū
double current
複流

fukuryū densō
double current transmission
複流伝送

fukusayō
side effect
副作用

fukusei
duplication
複製

fukusei suru
duplicate (*verb*); reproduce
複製する

fukusha mojyūru
copy module
複写モジュール

fukusha raiburari
copy library
複写ライブラリ

fukusha senkōki
reproducing punch
複写せん孔機

fukusha suru
copy (*verb*); reproduce
複写する

fukuso
complex
複素

fukuso dēta
complex data
複素データ

fukuso kukan
complex interval
複素区間

fukuso sū
complex number
複素数

fukuso sūkei
complex numeral expression
複素数形

fukuso teisū
complex constant
複素定数

fukusū
multi-; multiple
複数

fukusū adoresu
multiaddress; multiple address
複数アドレス

fukusū adoresu-kōdo
multiple-address code
複数アドレス・コード

fukusū adoresu meirei
multiaddress instruction;
multiple-address instruction
複数アドレス命令

fukusū adoresu-messēji
multiaddress message
複数アドレス・メッセージ

fukusū boryūmu
multivolume
複数ボリューム

fukusū boryūmu-fuairu
multivolume file
複数ボリューム・ファイル

fukusū fuairu
multifile; multiple file
複数ファイル

fukusū fuairu-boryūmu
multifile volume
複数ファイル・ボリューム

fukusū fuēzu
multiphase
複数フェーズ

fukusū kaisen
multiple line
複数回線

fukusū ran
multifield
複数欄

fukusū ran sakuin
multifield index
複数欄索引

fukusū riiru
multireel
複数リール

fukusū riiru-fuairu
multireel file
複数リール・ファイル

fukusū shisutemu
multisystem
複数システム

fukusū yunitto
multiunit
複数ユニット

———— funō
failure of ————; failure to
————不能

fuoaguraundo
foreground
フォアグラウンド

fuoaguraundo-jyobu
foreground job
フォアグラウンド・ジョブ

fuoaguraundo-puroguramu
foreground program
フォアグラウンド・プログラム

fuōmatto (F)
format (F)
フォーマット

fuōmu
form (document)
フォーム

fuōmu-sutakka
form stacker
フォーム・スタッカ

fuōmu-sutoppu
form stop
フォーム・ストップ

fuon-Noimangata konpyūta
von Neumann computer
フォン・ノイマン型コンピュータ

fuonto
font
フォント

Fuōsu
FORTH
フォース

fuoto-daiōdo
photodiode
フォト・ダイオード

fuoto-etchingu
photoetching
フォト・エッチング

Fuōtoran (FORTRAN)
Formula Translation (FORTRAN)
フォートラン

furaggu
flag
フラッグ

furagu-bitto
flag bit
フラッグ・ビット

furaingu-supotto sōsa kikō
flying spot scanner
フライング・スポット走査機構

furatto-kēburu
flat cable
フラット・ケーブル

furatto-pakkēji
flat package
フラット・パッケージ

furatto-pakku
flat pack
フラット・パック

furatto-sukuriin
flat screen
フラット・スクリーン

furekishiburu-deisuku
flexidisk; flexible disk
フレキシブル・ディスク

furekishiburu-deisuku-rekōda
flexible-disk recorder
フレキシブル・ディスク・
レコーダ

furekishiburu-deisuku sōchi
flexible-disk unit
フレキシブル・ディスク装置

furēmu
frame
フレーム

furēmu dōki
frame synchronization
フレーム同期

furēmu-kaunto-erā
frame count error
フレーム・カウント・エラー

furēmu shiji
framing
フレーム指示

furēmu shiji bitto
framing bit
フレーム指示ビット

Fūrie henkan
Fourier transform
フーリエ変換

furii-akusesu
free access
フリー・アクセス

furii-fuōmatto
free format
フリー・フォーマット

furii kioku
free storage
フリー記憶

furippu-furoppu
flip-flop
フリップ・フロップ

furō
flow
フロー

furoa-sutando
floor stand
フロア・スタンド

furōchāteingu
flowcharting
フローチャーティング

furonri
negative logic
負論理

furonto-endo
front end
フロント・エンド

furonto-endo-purosessa (FEP)
front-end processor (FEP)
フロント・エンド・プロセッサ

furonto-paneru
front panel (of console)
フロント・パネル

furoppi-deisuku
floppy disk
フロッピ・ディスク

furoppi-deisuku-operēteingu-shisutemu (FDOS)
floppy-disk operating system (FDOS)
フロッピ・ディスク・オペレーティング・システム

fusei
abnormal; negative
不正；負性

fusei teikō
negative resistance
負性抵抗

fuseiki kansū
abnormal function
不正規関数

futei
undefined
不定

futei keishiki
undefined format
不定形式

futei keishiki rekōdo
undefined record
不定形式レコード

futei yōshiki
unformatted
不定様式

futei yōshiki dēta
unformatted data
不定様式データ

futei yōshiki hyōji
unformatted display
不定様式表示

futei yōshiki messēji
unformatted message
不定様式メッセージ

futō
invalid
不当

futō dēta
invalid data
不当データ

futō junjo
invalid sequence
不当順序

futō kii
invalid key
不当キー

futō namae
invalid name
不当名前

futō senkō
invalid punch
不当せん孔

futōka (NEQ)
nonequivalence (NEQ)
不等価

futōka gēto (NEQ gēto)
nonequivalence gate (NEQ gate)
不等価ゲート；NEQゲート

futōka soshi (NEQ soshi)
nonequivalence element (NEQ element)
不等価素子；NEQ素子

fuyō jōhō
garbage
不要情報

G

G (giga-)
G (giga-)
ギガ

gābejji
garbage
ガーベッジ

gābejji-in-gābejji-auto (GIGO)
garbage-in garbage-out (GIGO)
ガーベッジ・イン・ガーベッジ・アウト；ギゴ

gābejji-korekushon
garbage collection
ガーベッジ・コレクション

gaibu
external
外部

gaibu baitai
external medium
外部媒体

gaibu bunrui
external sort
外部分類

gaibu dōki
external synchronization
外部同期

gaibu iriguchi ten
external entry point
外部入り口点

gaibu kankyō jōhō
external environment information
外部環境情報

gaibu kansū
external function
外部関数

gaibu kansū in'yō
external function reference
外部関数引用

gaibu kigō
external symbol
外部記号

gaibu kioku
external storage
外部記憶

gaibu kioku sōchi
external store
外部記憶装置

gaibu kumiawase
external merge
外部組み合わせ

gaibu mei
external name
外部名

gaibu puroguramu-parameta
external program parameter
外部プログラム・パラメタ

gaibu saburūchin
external subroutine
外部サブルーチン

gaibu sanshō
external reference
外部参照

gaibu sanshō rekōdo
external reference record
外部参照レコード

gaibu seigyo
external control
外部制御

gaibu shingō
external signal
外部信号

gaibu sukiima
external schema
外部スキーマ

gaibu teigi
external definition
外部定義

gaibu teigi rekōdo
external definition record
外部定義レコード

gaibu tetsuzuki
external procedure
外部手続き

gaibu warikomi
external interrupt
外部割り込み

gaibu warikomi jōtai go
external interrupt status word
外部割り込み状態語

gaibu zokusei
external attribute
外部属性

gaido
guide
ダイド

gaido-ejji
guide edge
ダイド・エッジ

gaido-mājin
guide margin
ダイド・マージン

gaikokugo
foreign (non-Japanese) language
外国語

gaikokugo shisutemu kakuchō (FSX)
foreign (non-Japanese) language system extension (FSX)
外国語システム拡張

gainen
concept; conceptual
概念

gairan
disturbance
外乱

gairyaku
schema; schematic
概略

gakushū
learning
学習

gakushū kikai
learning machine
学習機械

gakushū shisutemu
learning system
学習システム

gakushūsha
learner
学習者

gamen
picture
画面

gamen idō
scroll; scrolling
画面移動

Gan-daiōdo
Gunn diode
ガン・ダイオード

Gan kōka
Gunn effect
ガン効果

gan'i
IF THEN; implication
含意

gappei
union
合併

garupu
gulp
ガルプ

gaso
picture element; pixel
画素

Gausugata parusu
Gaussian pulse
ガウス型パルス

gazō
image; picture
画像

gazō kaiseki
image analysis
画像解析

gazō patān ninshiki
pictorial pattern recognition
画像パターン認識

gazō shori
image processing;
picture processing
画像処理

GCR (gurūpu-kōdeiddo-rekōdeingu)
GCR (group-coded recording)
グループ・コーディッド・
レコーディング

GD (gurafuikku-deisupurei; zukei hyōji)
GD (graphic display)
グラフィック・ディスプレイ;
図形表示

gembun
decrement
減分

gēmu
game
ゲーム

gēmu riron
game theory
ゲーム理論

gen
origin
原

gengo
language
言語

gengo bunseki
language analysis
言語分析

gengo henkan
language conversion
言語変換

gengo henkan puroguramu
language conversion program
言語変換プログラム

gengo hon'yaku
language translation
言語翻訳

gengo hon'yaku puroguramu
language translator
言語翻訳プログラム

gengo keishiki
language form; language type
言語形式

gengo kōchiku
language construction
言語構築

gengo ninshiki
language recognition
言語認識

gengo no fukusatsusei
language complexity
言語の複雑性

gengo riron
language theory
言語理論

gengo seisei
language generation
言語生成

gengo shori
language processing
言語処理

gengo shori puroguramu
language processor
言語処理プログラム

gengo suijun
language level
言語水準

gengo sutētomento
language statement
言語ステートメント

gengo teigi
language definition
言語定義

genkai
margin
限界

genkai keiro
critical path
限界経路

genkai keiro hō (CPM)
critical path method (CPM)
限界経路法

genkai kensa
marginal check
限界検査

genkei
prototype
原型

genketsugō
decoupling
減結合

genketsugō suru
decouple
減結合する

genshi
original; source
原始

genshi bunsho
original document
原始文書

genshi dekku
source deck
原始デック

genshi dēta
raw data; source data
原始データ

genshi gengo
source language
原始言語

genshi kādo
source card
原始カード

genshi kōdeingu
source coding
原始コーディング

genshi kōdo
source code
原始コード

genshi konpyūta
source computer
原始コンピュータ

genshi mojyūru
source module
原始モジュール

genshi puroguramu
source program
原始プログラム

genshi raiburari
source library
原始ライブラリ

genshi rekōdo
source record
原始レコード

genshi rekōdo sakusei
source recording
原始レコード作成

genshi rūchin
source routine
原始ルーチン

genshi seigyo bun
source control statement
原始制御文

genshi shorui
source document
原始書類

genshi sutētomento
source statement
原始ステートメント

gensui
attenuation; damping; decay
減衰

gensui hizumi
attenuation distortion
減衰歪み

gensui jikan
damping time; decay time
減衰時間

gensui shindō
damping oscillation
減衰振動

gensui tōka
attenuation equalization
減衰等化

gensuiki
attenuator
減衰器

gentei shiyō
restricted use
限定使用

genzai
current (present)
現在

genzai ichi
current position
現在位置

genzai rekōdo
current record
現在レコード

genzan
subtraction
減算

genzanki
subtracter
減算器

GET
GET
GET

gēto
gate
ゲート

gēto kairo
gate circuit
ゲート回路

gēto-matorikkusu
gate matrix
ゲート・マトリックス

gēto-parusu
gate pulse
ゲート・パルス

gēto seigyo
gate control
ゲート制御

gētouei
gateway
ゲートウェイ

gētouei-konpyūta
gateway computer
ゲートウェイ・コンピュータ

Gibuson-mikkusu
Gibson mix
ギブソン・ミックス

giga (G)
giga- (G)
ギガ

giga-saikuru
gigacycle
ギガ・サイクル

GIGO (gābejji-in-gābejji-auto)
GIGO (garbage-in garbage-out)
ギゴ；ガーベッジ・イン・
ガーベッジ・アウト

giji
dummy; pseudo-
疑似

giji akuteibitei
dummy activity
疑似アクティビティ

giji asenburi gengo
pseudoassembly language
疑似アセンブリ言語

giji hensū
pseudovariable
疑似変数

giji kōdo
pseudocode
疑似コード

giji meirei
pseudoinstruction
疑似命令

giji nyūryoku
dummy entry
疑似入力

giji randamu-kōdo
pseudorandom codes
疑似ランダム・コード

giji ransū
pseudorandom numbers
疑似乱数

giji ransū retsu
pseudorandom sequence of
numbers
疑似乱数列

giji rejisuta
pseudoregister
疑似レジスタ

giji sōsa
pseudooperation
疑似操作

gijutsu
technology
技術

gijutsu(teki)
technical
技術(的)

gijutsu hyōjun
technical standards
技術標準

gijutsu jōhō
technical information
技術情報

gijutsu jōhō shori shisutemu
technical information processing
system
技術情報処理システム

gijutsu shiyō
technical specifications
技術仕様

gijutsuteki seigyo
technical control
技術的制御

**GIS (han'yō jōhō shisutemu;
ippanka jōhō shisutemu)**
GIS (generalized information
system)
汎用情報システム；
一般化情報システム

go (W)
computer word; word (W)
語

go adoresu
word address
語アドレス

go/byō (WPS)
words per second (WPS)
語／秒

go chō
word length
語長

go/fun (WPM)
words per minute (WPM)
語／分

go jikan
word time
語時間

go keisanki
word computer
語計算機

go muki
word-oriented
語向き

go sen
word line
語線

go tan'i fugō
five-level code
5 単位符号

GO TO (goto; tobikoshi)
GO TO
GO TO；ゴト；飛び越し

GO TO bun
GO TO statement
GO TO文；ゴト文

gobitto-baito
quintet
5 ビット・バイト

godōsa
malfunction
誤動作

godōsa ichi
malfunction location
誤動作位置

godōsa keihō
malfunction warning
誤動作警報

gōfubōru
golfball
ゴーフボール

gōfubōru-purinta
golfball printer
ゴーフボール・プリンタ

goji
character error
誤字

gojiritsu
character error rate
誤字率

gojōhō
misinformation
誤情報

gokan
word stem
語幹

gokansei
compatibility
互換性

gokansei ga aru
compatible
互換性がある

gokansei kensa
compatibility check
互換性検査

gōkei
sum; total
合計

gōkei kādo
summary card
合計カード

gōkei kensa
sum check; summation check
合計検査

gōkei senkō
summary punch
合計せん孔

gosa
error
誤差

gosa suitei
error estimation
誤差推定

gōsei
synthesis
合成

gōsei adoresu
synthetic address
合成アドレス

gōsei gengo
synthetic language;
synthetic voice
合成言語

gōsei gihō
synthesis technique
合成技法

gōsei tejun
synthesis procedure
合成手順

goshikku-fuonto
gothic font
ゴシック・フォント

goshinhō
quinary
5 進法

gosōsa
misoperation
誤操作

gosōsa kenshutsu
misoperation detection
誤操作検出

gosōsa kenshutsu kinō
misoperation detection function
誤操作検出機能

GPSS (han'yō shimyurēshon-shisutemu)
GPSS (general-purpose simulation system)
汎用シミュレーション・システム

gr (han'yō rejisuta)
gr (general register)
汎用レジスタ

GS (gurūpu bunri moji)
GS (group separator)
グループ分離文字

GSI (chōdai kibo shūsekika)
GSI (grand-scale integration)
超大規模集積化

gun
group
群

gun chien
group delay
群遅延

gun fugō
group code
群符号

gun ron
group theory
群論

gurafu
graph
グラフ

gurafu kōzō
graph structure
グラフ構造

gurafu-purotta
graph plotter
グラフ・プロッタ

gurafu riron
graph algorithm;
theory of graphs
グラフ理論

gurafu shori
graph manipulation
グラフ処理

gurafuikku
graphic; graphical
グラフィック

gurafuikku-bōdo
graphic board
グラフィック・ボード

gurafuikku-deisupurei (GD)
graphic display (GD)
グラフィック・ディスプレィ

gurafuikku-deisupurei seigyo
graphic display control
グラフィック・ディスプレィ制御

gurafuikku-dēta
graphic data
グラフィック・データ

gurafuikku-dēta-deisupurei
graphic data display
グラフィック・データ・
ディスプレィ

gurafuikku-dēta shori
graphic data processing
グラフィック・データ処理

gurafuikku hyōshiki
graphic indicator
グラフィック標識

gurafuikku-paneru
graphic panel
グラフィック・パネル

gurafuikku-shisutemu
graphic system
グラフィック・システム

gurafuikkusu
graphics
グラフィックス

gurafuikkusu-bōdo
graphics board
グラフィックス・ボード

gurafuikkusu-deisupurei
graphics display
グラフィックス・ディスプレィ

gurafuikkusu-kādo
graphics card
グラフィックス・カード

gurafuikkusu keikaku shisutemu
graphic planning system
グラフィックス計画システム

gurafuikkusu-operēteingu-shisutemu
graphics operating system
グラフィックス・
オペレーティング・システム

gurafuikkusu-shisutemu
graphics system
グラフィックス・システム

gurafuikkusu-shisutemu sekkei
graphics system design
グラフィックス・システム設計

gurafuikkusu shori
graphic manipulation
グラフィックス処理

gurafuikkusu shori tanmatsu sōchi
graphics terminal
グラフィックス処理端末装置

gurafuikkusu-taburetto
graphics tablet
グラフィックス・タブレット

gurafuikkusu'yō gengo
graphic language
グラフィックス用言語

guranpu sōsa
gramping
グランプ操作

Gurei-kōdo
Gray code
グレイ・コード

guriin-deisupurei
green display
グリーン・ディスプレィ

gurōbaru
global
グローバル

gurōbaru hensū
global variable
グローバル変数

gurōbaru-setto kigō
global set symbol
グローバル・セット記号

gurūpu
group; grouped
グループ

gurūpu bangō
group number
グループ番号

gurūpu bunri moji (GS)
group separator (GS)
グループ分離文字

gurūpu bunrui
group classification
グループ分数

gurūpu bunrui kōdo
group classification code
グループ分数コード

gurūpu(ka) dembun
grouped messages
グループ（化）電文

gurūpu hyōji
group indicate
グループ表示

gurūpu insatsu
group printing
グループ印刷

gurūpu kensa
group check
グループ検査

gurūpu keta age
group carry
グループ桁上げ

gurūpu-kōdeiddo-rekōdeingu (GCR)
group-coded recording (GCR)
グループ・コーディッド・
レコーディング

gurūpu kōmoku
group item
グループ項目

gurūpu-māka
group marker
グループ・マーカ

gurūpu-māku
group mark
グループ・マーク

gurūpu mei
group name
グループ名

gurūpu-purinto
group printing
グループ・プリント

gurūpu-raiburari
group library
グループ・ライブラリ

gurūpu-rekōdo
group record
グループ・レコード

gurūpu(ka) rekōdo
grouped records
グループ（化）レコード

gurūpuka
grouped; grouping
グループ化

gūsū kensa
even check
偶数検査

gūsū paritei
even parity
偶数パリティ

gūsū paritei-chekku
even-parity check
偶数パリティ・チェック

gyaku
reverse
逆

gyaku asenbura
disassembler
逆アセンブラ

gyaku bunrui
inverse sort
逆分類

gyaku chaneru
backward channel;
reverse channel
逆チャネル

gyaku den'atsu
reverse voltage
逆電圧

gyaku fuairu
inverted file
逆ファイル

gyaku hōkō
backward direction;
reverse direction
逆方向

gyaku hōkō insatsu
backward printing
逆方向印刷

gyaku hōkō no nagare
reverse direction flow
逆方向の流れ

gyaku junjo
inverse sequence
逆順序

gyaku Pōrando kihō (RP)
reverse Polish (RP)
逆ポーランド記法

gyaku sōsa
reverse operation
逆操作

gyaku tanchi
walk back
逆探知

gyaku yomi
backward read
逆読み

gyappu
gap
ギャップ

gyappu no baratsuki
gap scatter
ギャップのばらつき

gyō
line (text); row
行

gyō bangō
line number
行番号

gyō/fun (LPM)
lines per minute (LPM)
行／分

gyō hyōji
line indicator
行表示

gyō inji sōchi
line printer (LP)
行印字装置

gyō insatsu
line printing
行印刷

gyō masshō
line deletion
行抹消

gyō nishin kādo
row-binary card
行2進カード

gyō okuri
line spacing
行送り

gyōmu keisanki
office computer
業務計算機

gyōmu no jikkō
transaction
業務の実行

gyōretsu
matrix; queue; queuing
行列

gyōretsu hyōgen
matrix representation
行列表現

H

H (kō'i; kō reberu)
H (high)
高位; 高レベル

haba
range
幅

habu
hub
ハブ

hachi bitto eisūji kōdo
eight-bit alphameric code
8ビット英数字コード

hachi tan'i kōdo
eight-level code
8単位コード

hachijū ran kādo
eighty-column card
80欄カード

hādo-deisuku (HD)
hard disk (HD)
ハード・ディスク

hādo-deisuku-intafuēsu-kādo
hard-disk interface card
ハード・ディスク・
インタフェース・カード

hādo-deisuku-konekuta
hard-disk connector
ハード・ディスク・コネクタ

hādo-kopii
hard copy
ハード・コピー

hādo-kopii-rogu
hard-copy log
ハード・コピー・ログ

hādo-sekuta-deisuku
hard-sectored disk
ハード・セクタ・ディスク

hādo-sekutoringu
hard-sectoring
ハード・セクトリング

hādo-shisutemu
hard system
ハード・システム

hādouea
hardware
ハードウェア

hādouea-chekku
hardware check
ハードウェア・チック

hādouea jōjosan
hardware multiply/divide
ハードウェア乗除算

hādouea kanri
hardware management
ハードウェア管理

hādouea kensa
hardware check
ハードウェア検査

hādouea kijutsu
hardware description
ハードウェア記述

hādouea kōsei
hardware configuration
ハードウェア構成

hādouea moji seisei
hardware character generation
ハードウェア文字生成

hādouea seigyo
hardware control
ハードウェア制御

hādouea-sofutouea kōsei
hardware-software configuration
ハードウェア・ソフトウェア構成

hāfu-wādo
half word
ハーフ・ワード

haibun
allocation
配分

haiburiddo
hybrid
ハイブリッド

haiburiddo-chaneru
hybrid channel
ハイブリッド・チャネル

haiburiddo IC
hybrid IC
ハイブリッドIC

haiburiddo-intafuēsu
hybrid interface
ハイブリッド・インタフェース

haiburiddo jissō
hybrid package
ハイブリッド実装

haiburiddo kairo
hybrid circuit
ハイブリッド回路

haiburiddo keisanki
hybrid computer
ハイブリッド計算機

haiburiddo-koiru
hybrid coil
ハイブリッド・コイル

haiburiddo-konpyūta
hybrid computer
ハイブリッド・コンピュータ

haiburiddo-moderu
hybrid model
ハイブリッド・モデル

haiburiddo-shisutemu
hybrid system
ハイブリッド・システム

haichi
layout
配置

haichi keikaku
layout planning
配置計画

haichi sekkei
layout design
配置設計

haidenki
power distribution system
配電機

haikei
background
背景

haikei jyobu
background job
背景ジョブ

haikei puroguramu
background program
背景プログラム

haikei shori
background processing
背景処理

haireberu-dēta-rinku seigyo (HDLC)
high-level data link control (HDLC)
ハイレベル・データ・リンク制御

haireberu-dēta-rinku seigyo tejun
high-level data link control
procedure
ハイレベル・データ・
リンク制御手順

hairetsu
array; arrangement; ordering;
rank
配列

hairetsu bunkatsu
array partitioning
配列分割

hairetsu gengo
array language
配列言語

hairetsu haibun
array allocation
配列配分

hairetsu junkyo no kiibōdo
standard keyboard
配列準拠のキーボード

hairetsu mei
array name
配列名

hairetsu segumento
array segment
配列セグメント

hairetsu sengenshi
array declarator
配列宣言子

hairetsu sengenshi bun
array declarator statement
配列宣言子文

hairetsu yōso
array element
配列要素

haisen
hard-wired; wiring
配線

haisen ronri
hard-wired logic
配線論理

haisenban
patchboard; plugboard;
terminal board; wiring board
配線盤

haisenshiki keisanki
wired-program computer
配線式計算機

haita
exclusion
排他

haitateki
exclusive
排他的

haitateki enzan
exclusion operation
排他的演算

haitateki hitei ronriwa (XNOR)
exclusive-NOR (XNOR)
排他的否定論理和；XNOR

haitateki hitei ronriwa kairo (XNOR kairo)
exclusive-NOR circuit (XNOR circuit)
排他的否定論理和回路；
XNOR回路

haitateki NOR (XNOR)
exclusive-NOR (XNOR)
排他的NOR；XNOR

haitateki NOR kairo (XNOR kairo)
exclusive-NOR circuit (XNOR circuit)
排他的NOR回路；XNOR回路

haitateki OR
exclusive-OR
排他的OR

haitateki OR enzan (XOR enzan)
exclusive-OR operation (XOR operation)
排他的OR演算；XOR演算

haitateki OR gēto (XOR gēto)
exclusive-OR gate (XOR gate)
排他的OR ゲート；XOR ゲート

haitateki OR kairo (XOR kairo)
exclusive-OR circuit (XOR circuit)
排他的OR回路；XOR回路

haitateki OR soshi (XOR soshi)
exclusive-OR element (XOR element)
排他的OR素子；XOR素子

haitateki ronriwa
OR ELSE; exclusive-OR
排他的論理和

haitateki ronriwa enzan (XOR enzan)
exclusive-OR operation (XOR operation)
排他的論理和演算；XOR演算

haitateki ronriwa gēto (XOR geto)
exclusive-OR gate (XOR gate)
排他的論理和ゲート；
XOR ゲート

haitateki ronriwa kairo (XOR kairo)
exclusive-OR circuit (XOR circuit)
排他的論理和回路；XOR回路

haitateki ronriwa soshi (XOR soshi)
exclusive-OR element (XOR element)
排他的論理和素子；XOR素子

haitateki sanshō
exclusive reference
排他的参照

haitateki segumento
exclusive segment
排他的セグメント

haitateki seigyo
exclusive control
排他的制御

haiuei
highway
ハイウェイ

hajikidashi
ejection
弾き出し

hakai
destruction; destructive
破壊

hakai kasan
destructive addition
破壊加算

hakai kioku
destructive storage
破壊記憶

hakai shiken
destructive test(ing)
破壊試験

hakai yomidashi
destructive reading
破壊読み出し

hakai yomidashi (DRO)
destructive readout (DRO)
破壊読み出し

hakei
waveform
波形

hakei saisei
waveform regeneration
波形再生

hakei saisei kairo
waveform regeneration circuit
波形再生回路

hakei seikei
waveform shaping
波形整形

hakei seikei kairo
waveform shaping circuit
波形整形回路

hakei seisei
waveform generation
波形生成

hakei tōka
waveform equalization
波形等化

hakka
hacker
ハッカ

hakken
heuristics
発見

hakken(teki)
heuristic
発見(的)

hakkenteki apurōchi
heuristic approach
発見的アプローチ

hakkenteki puroguramu
heuristic program
発見的プログラム

hakkenteki tansaku
heuristic search
発見的探索

hakkingu
hacking
ハッキング

hakkō daiōdo (LED)
light-emitting diode (LED)
発光ダイオード

hakōchi (P-P)
peak to peak (P-P)
波高値

haku maku
thin film
薄膜

haku maku shūseki kairo
thin-film integrated circuit
薄膜集積回路

hakushoku zatsuon
white noise
白色雑音

hakyū
ripple
波及

Hamingu-kōdo
Hamming code
ハミング・コード

Hamingu kyori
Hamming distance
ハミング距離

hampuku
iteration; iterative; recursion;
repeat; repetition; repetitive
反復

hampuku meirei
repetition instruction
反復命令

hampuku suru
iterate
反復する

hampukusū
repeat count
反復数

han gensanki
half subtracter
半減算器

han go
half word
半語

han'i
range
範囲

han'i chōseiki
range finder
範囲調整器

han'i kensa
range check
範囲検査

han kasanki
half adder
半加算器

han nijū (HDX)
half duplex (HDX)
半二重

han nijū densō (HDX)
half-duplex transmission (HDX)
半二重伝送

han nijū tsūshin shisutemu
half-duplex communication
system
半二重通信システム

han nijū tsūshinro
half-duplex channel
半二重通信路

han sentaku kakikomi parusu
half-write pulse
半選択書き込みパルス

hanchi
mesial
半値

hanchi ten
mesial point
半値点

handan
decision; judgment
判断

handan jikan
judgment time
判断時間

handan kigō
decision box; decision symbol
判断記号

handan kinō
judgment function
判断機能

handan meirei
decision instruction;
discrimination instruction
判断命令

hando-panchi
hand punch
ハンド・パンチ

handora
handler
ハンドラ

handoringu
handling
ハンドリング

handoringu jikan
handling time
ハンドリング時間

handoru suru
handle (*verb*)
ハンドルする

handōtai
semiconductor
半導体

handōtai kioku
semiconductor memory
半導体記憶

handōtai seiryūki
semiconductor rectifier
半導体整流器

handōtai shūseki kairo (SIC)
semiconductor integrated circuit
(SIC)
半導体集積回路

hanjidō
semiautomatic
半自動

hanjidō kōkan kyoku
semiautomatic switching center
半自動交換局

hanjidō seigyo
semiautomatic control
半自動制御

hankyō
echo
反響

hankyō kensa
echo check
反響検査

hankyō yokuseiki
echo suppressor
反響抑制器

hansha
reflectance; reflection
反射

hansha keisū
reflection coefficient
反射係数

hansha māka
reflective marker
反射マーカ

hansha māku
reflective mark
反射マーク

hansha ritsu
reflectance ratio
反射率

hansō shisutemu
carrier system
搬送システム

hansōha
carrier
搬送波

hansōha kyōdō
common carrier
搬送波共同

hantei
decision
判定

hantei kikan hōshiki
decision feedback system
判定帰還方式

hanteingu
hunting
ハンティング

hanten
inversion
反転

hanten suru
invert (*verb*)
反転する

han'yō
general-purpose; general-use;
generalized; universal
汎用

han'yō bunrui-kumiawase
puroguramu
generalized sort-merge program
汎用分類-組み合わせプログラム

han'yō hidōki sōjushin kairo
(UART)
universal asynchronous
receiver-transmitter (UART)
汎用非同期送受信回路

han'yō intafuēsu
general interface;
general-purpose interface
汎用インタフェース

han'yō jōhō shisutemu (GIS)
generalized information system
(GIS)
汎用情報システム

han'yō keisanki
all-purpose computer;
general-purpose computer
汎用計算機

han'yō keisanki shisutemu
general-purpose computer
system
汎用計算機システム

han'yō konpyūta
general-purpose computer
汎用コンピュータ

han'yō meirei setto
universal instruction set
汎用命令セット

han'yō moji setto
universal character set
汎用文字セット

han'yō mojyūru
module for general use
汎用モジュール

han'yō operēteingu-shisutemu
general-purpose operating
system
汎用オペレーティング・システム

han'yō puroguramu
general-purpose program
汎用プログラム

han'yō rejisuta (gr)
general-purpose register;
general register (gr)
汎用レジスタ

han'yō rūchin
generalized routine
汎用ルーチン

han'yō shimyurēshon
general-purpose simulation
汎用シミュレーション

han'yō shimyurēshon-shisutemu (GPSS)
general-purpose simulation system (GPSS)
汎用シミュレーション・システム

han'yō shori sōchi
universal processing unit
汎用処理装置

han'yō sōgō shisutemu
general-purpose integrated system
汎用総合システム

hasei dēta kōmoku
derived data item
派生データ項目

hasei rekōdo
derived record
派生レコード

hashi
edge
端

hason sareta dēta
corrupted data
破損されたデータ

hassei suru
generate; set off; trigger off
発生する

hasseiki
generator
発生器

hasshin
octal
8進

hasshin
oscillating
発振

hasshin
sending
発信

hasshin hō
octal notation;
octal number system
8進法

hasshin ran kijutsu
octal field description
8進欄記述

hasshin sū
octal number
8進数

hasshin sūji
octal digit
8進数字

hasshin suru
send
発信する

hasshin tanmatsu (sōchi)
sending terminal
発信端末（装置）

hasshin teisū
octal constant
8進定数

hasshingu
hashing
ハッシング

hasshinki
oscillator
発振器

hasshinsha
sender
発信者

hasshu
hash
ハッシュ

hasshu gōkei
hash total
ハッシュ合計

hasshu-kōdeingu
hash coding
ハッシュ・コーディング

hasshu-tēburu
hash table
ハッシュ・テーブル

hatsuban suru
issue a number
発番する

hausukiipingu
housekeeping
ハウスキーピング

hausukiipingu-rūchin
housekeeping routine
ハウスキーピング・ルーチン

hausukiipingu sōsa
housekeeping operation
ハウスキーピング 操作

hazādo
hazard
ハザード

hazādo haijo
hazard elimination
ハザード排除

hazādo kaiseki
hazard analysis
ハザード解析

hazādo ritsu
hazard rate
ハザード率

hazādo seigyo
hazard control
ハザード制御

HCI (ningen-keisanki intafuēsu)
HCI (human-computer interface)
人間-計算機インタフェース

HD (hādo-deisuku)
HD (hard disk)
ハード・ディスク

HDLC (haireberu-dēta-rinku seigyo; kōreberu-dēta-rinku seigyo)
HDLC (high-level data link control)
ハイレベル・データ・リンク制御; 高レベル・データ・リンク制御

HDR (fuairu midashi raberu)
HDR (file header label)
ファイル見出しラベル

HDX (han nijū; han nijū densō)
HDX (half duplex; half-duplex transmission)
半二重; 半二重伝送

hedda
header
ヘッダ

heddeingu
heading
ヘッディング

heddeingu kaishi (SOH)
start of heading (SOH)
ヘッディング開始

heddeingu kaishi moji
start-of-heading character
ヘッディング開始文字

heddo
head
ヘッド

heddo-gyappu
head gap
ヘッド・ギャップ

heddo ichi settei
head positioning
ヘッド位置設定

heddo kankaku
head gap
ヘッド間隔

heddo shōtotsu
head crash
ヘッド衝突

heichokuretsu kōkan kairo
deserializer
並直列交換回路

heigō
merging
併合

heikatsu
smooth
平滑

heikatsuka
smoothing
平滑化

heikin
average; mean
平均

heikin akusesu jikan
mean access time
平均アクセス時間

heikin densō sokudo
average transmission speed
平均伝送速度

heikin dōsa jikan
average operation time
平均動作時間

heikin enzan jikan
average operation time
平均演算時間

heikin hoshu kankaku (MTBM)
mean time between
maintenance (MTBM)
平均保守間隔

heikin jōhō ryō
average information content;
mean information content
平均情報量

heikin koshō kankaku (MTBF)
mean time between failures
(MTBF)
平均故障間隔

heikin shoki koshō jikan (MTTF)
mean time to failure (MTTF)
平均初期故障時間

heikin shūfuku jikan (MTTR)
mean time to repair (MTTR)
平均修復時間

heikin yobidashi jikan
average access time
平均呼び出し時間

heikō
overlap; parallel
並行

heikō dōsa
concurrent operation
並行動作

heikō heigō
parallel merging
並行併合

heikō (shori) kikai
parallel machine
並行(処理)機械

heikō mōdo densō
parallel mode transmission
並行モード伝送

heikō no
concurrent
並行の

heikō puroguramingu
parallel programming
並行プログラミング

heikō sekkei
concurrent design
並行設計

heikō shori
concurrent processing; overlap
processing; parallel processing
並行処理

heikō shori kenshutsu
parallelism detection
並行処理検出

heikō sōsa
parallel operation
並行操作

heikō tansaku
parallel search
並行探索

heikō unten
parallel running
並行運転

heimen purotta
flatbed plotter
平面プロッタ

heiretsu
parallel
並列

heiretsu akusesu
parallel access
並列アクセス

heiretsu densō
parallel transmission
並列伝送

heiretsu dēta densō
parallel data transmission
並列データ伝送

heiretsu enzan
parallel arithmetic
並列演算

heiretsu kasan
parallel addition
並列加算

heiretsu kasanki
parallel adder
並列加算器

heiretsu kioku
parallel storage
並列記憶

heiretsu seigyo
parallel control
並列制御

heiretsu shisutemu
parallel system
並列システム

heiretsu shori
parallel processing
並列処理

heiretsu sōsa
parallel operation
並列操作

heiretsu tansaku
parallel search
並列探索

heiretsu tansaku kioku
parallel search storage
並列探索記憶

heiretsushiki keisanki
parallel computer
並列式計算機

heisa
closure
閉鎖

heishi
closure
閉止

heisoku
congestion; engaged (line)
閉塞

hen'i
displacement
変位

henchō
modulation
変調

henchō sōchi
modulator
変調装置

henchō sokudo
modulation rate
変調速度

hendō
fluctuation
変動

henfukuchō sōchi
modem (modulator-
demodulator)
変復調装置

henkan
conversion; converting;
translation
変換

henkan kigō
conversion code
変換記号

henkan kikō
convert feature
変換機構

henkan puroguramu
conversion program
変換プログラム

henkan suru
convert (*verb*); translate
変換する

henkan teigi gengo (TDL)
translation definition language
(TDL)
変換定義言語

henkanki
converter; transducer
変換器

henkei
deformation; transformation
変形

henkei suru
transform (*verb*)
変形する

henkō
alteration; amendment; change;
modification
変更

henkō
deflection
偏向

henkō ban
deflection plate
偏向板

henkō bitto
change bit
変更ビット

henkō kairo
deflection circuit
偏向回路

henkō(yō) suitchi
alteration switch
変更(用)スイッチ

henkō suru
amend; modify
変更する

henkō'iki danpu
change dump
変更域ダンプ

henkōshi
modifier
変更子

henryūki
transformer
変流器

hensa
deviation
偏差

hensei
organization
編成

hensei fuairu
organization file
編成ファイル

hensei kōzō
organization structure
編成構造

henshū
editing
編集

henshū kinō
editing function
編集機能

henshū mōdo
edit mode
編集モード

henshū puroguramu
edit program; editor
編集プログラム

henshū rūchin
edit routine
編集ルーチン

henshū seigyo moji
edit control character
編集制御文字

henshū shiji densō
edit-directed transmission
編集指示伝送

henshū suru
edit (*verb*)
編集する

henshū'yō fugō
editing sign control character
編集用符号

henshū'yō kigō
editing symbol
編集用記号

henshū'yō moji
editing character
編集用文字

hensō shōgō
loop checking
返送照合

297

hensō shōgō hōshiki
  loop checking system
  返送照合方式

hensū
  variable
  変数

hensū fuiirudo
  variable field
  変数フィールド

hensū mei
  variable name
  変数名

hentō
  answer; answerback; answering
  返答

herutsu (Hz)
  hertz (Hz)
  ヘルツ

HEX (jūrokushin hō)
  HEX (hexadecimal notation)
  16進法

hiantei
  astable
  非安定

hiburokkuka
  deblocking; unblocked;
  unblocking
  非ブロック化

hiburokkuka rekōdo
  unblocked records
  非ブロック化レコード

hiburokkuka suru
  deblock
  非ブロック化する

hichokketsu
  off-line; off-lining
  非直結

hidari shifuto
  left shift
  左シフト

hidari tsume
  left justify
  左詰め

hidari yose
  left justify
  左寄せ

hidō
  asynchronous
  非同

hidōki
  asynchronous
  非同期

hidōki densō
  asynchronous transmission
  非同期伝送

hidōki dēta densō
  asynchronous data transmission
  非同期データ伝送

hidōki dōsa
  asynchronous working
  非同期動作

hidōki maruchi-puroguramingu
  asynchronous multiprogramming
  非同期マルチ・プログラミング

hidōki(shiki) mōdo
  asynchronous mode
  非同期(式)モード

hidōki seigyo
  asynchronous control
  非同期制御

hidōki shisutemu
  asynchronous system
  非同期システム

hidōki shori
  asynchronous processing
  非同期処理

hidōki sōsa
  asynchronous operation
  非同期操作

hidōki tsūshin
  asynchronous communication
  非同期通信

hidōkishiki
  asynchronous;
  asynchronous system
  非同期式

hidōkishiki kairo
  asynchronous circuit
  非同期式回路

hidōkishiki keisanki
  asynchronous computer
  非同期式計算機

hidōkishiki sōchi
  asynchronous device
  非同期式装置

higensū
  minuend
  被減数

hihaitateki
  nonexclusive
  非排他的

hihakai yomidashi (NDRO)
  nondestructive readout (NDRO)
  非破壊読み出し

hihakai yomidashi kioku
  NDRO storage; nondestructive
  readout memory
  非破壊読み出し記憶

hihyōjun
  nonstandard
  非標準

hijikkō
  nonexecutable
  非実行

hijikkō bun
  nonexecutable statement
  非実行文

hijikkō meirei
  nonexecutable instruction
  非実行命令

hijikyū
  volatile
  非持久

hijikyū kioku
  volatile memory; volatile storage
  非持久記憶

hijikyūsei
  volatility
  非持久性

hijōchū
  nonresident; transient
  非常駐

hijōchū rūchin
  nonresident routine
  非常駐ルーチン

hijōchū ryō'iki
  transient area
  非常駐領域

hijōsū
multiplicand
被乗数

hikaku
comparison; relation
比較

hikaku (dēta no)
comparing (of data)
比較（データの）

hikaku enzanshi
relative operator
比較演算子

hikaku jōken
relation condition
比較条件

hikaku kensa
comparator check
比較検査

hikaku kikō
comparing unit
比較機構

hikaku moji
relation character
比較文字

hikaku sayōso
relational operator
比較作用素

hikaku shiki
comparison expression
比較式

hikaku suru
compare (*verb*)
比較する

hikaku tesuto
relation test
比較テスト

hikakuki
comparator
比較器

hikakushiki
relational
比較式

hikanji
non-Chinese character
非漢字

hikari
optical
光

hikari denkan
photocell
光電管

hikari fuaiba
optical fiber
光ファイバ

hikari fuaiba kan (OFT)
optical fiber tube (OFT)
光ファイバ管

hikari kenshutsu kikō
photodetector
光検出機構

hikasū
augend
被加数

hikatsudō
inactive
非活動

hikatsudō kaisen
inactive line
非活動回線

hikatsudō puroguramu
inactive program
非活動プログラム

hikatsudō tanmatsu
inactive station
非活動端末

hikeisangata
noncomputational
非計算型

hiketsugō
unconnected
非結合

hiketsugō tanmatsu (sōchi)
unconnected terminal
非結合端末（装置）

hiketteisei
nondeterminacy
非決定性

hiketteisei shisutemu
nondeterministic system
非決定性システム

hiketteiteki keikakuhō
nondeterministic programming
非決定的計画法

hikinobashi
stretching
引き伸し

hikinobasu
stretch
引き伸す

hikisū
argument
引き数

hiko hyōji
calling indicator
被呼表示

hiko kyoku
called station
被呼局

hikyokushoteki
nonlocal
非局所的

hikyokushoteki sūchi hensū
nonlocal variable
非局所的数値変数

hindo
frequency
頻度

hinshitsu
quality
品質

hinshitsu hoshō
quality assurance
品質保証

hinshitsu jōhō shisutemu
quality information system
品質情報システム

hinshitsu kanri
quality control
品質管理

hinshitsu shisutemu
quality system
品質システム

hipakettogata tanmatsu
non-packed-mode terminal
非パケット型端末

hiraita
open
開いた

hiraita fukupuroguramu
open subprogram
開いた副プログラム

hiraita kairo
open circuit
開いた回路

hiraita saburūchin
open subroutine
開いたサブルーチン

hiraita shisutemu
open system
開いたシステム

hirei seigyo dōsa
proportional control action
比例制御動作

hiritsu
rate; ratio
比率

hiritsu seigyo
ratio control
比率制御

hisenkei
nonlinear
非線形

hisenkei kairo
nonlinear circuit
非線形回路

hisenkei keikakuhō
nonlinear programming
非線形計画法

hisenkei nettowāku
nonlinear network
非線形ネットワーク

hisenkei saitekika
nonlinear optimization
非線形最適化

hisenkei tōka
nonlinear equalization
非線形等化

hisen'yō
nondedicated
非専用

hisen'yō tanmatsu (sōchi)
nondedicated terminal
非専用端末 (装置)

hishikii chi ronri (NTL)
nonthreshold logic (NTL)
非敷居値論理

hishōgekishiki inji sōchi
nonimpact printer
非衝撃式印字装置

hishūshoku
unmodified
非修飾

hishūshoku meirei
unmodified instruction
非修飾命令

hisuterishisu
hysteresis
ヒステリシス

hisuterishisu-rūpu
hysteresis loop
ヒステリシス・ループ

hisuterishisu son
hysteresis loss
ヒステリシス損

hitei
negation; negative
否定

hitei AND
NAND; negative AND
否定AND

hitei enzan
NOT operation
否定演算

hitei gēto
ignore gate; NOT gate
否定ゲート

hitei kairo
NOT circuit
否定回路

hitei ōtō (NAK; nakku)
negative acknowledgment (NAK)
否定応答; ナック

hitei ōtō moji
negative acknowledgment
character
否定応答文字

hitei ronriwa
neither-NOR
否定論理和

hitei ronriwa enzan
neither-NOR operation
否定論理和演算

hitei soshi
negator; NOT element
否定素子

hitei suru
negate
否定する

hiteironriseki
NAND; negative AND; NOT AND
否定論理積

hiteironriseki enzan
alternative denial; NAND
operation; NOT-AND operation
否定論理積演算

hiteironriseki gēto
NAND gate; NOT-AND gate
否定論理積ゲート

hiteironriseki kairo
NAND circuit; NOT-AND circuit
否定論理積回路

hiteironriseki soshi
NAND element;
NOT-AND element
否定論理積素子

hiteironriwa
NOT-OR
否定論理和

hiteironriwa enzan
NOT-OR operation
否定論理和演算

hiteiseki (NAND)
inverted AND (NAND)
否定積

hiteiseki enzan
inverted AND operation;
NAND operation
否定積演算

hiteiseki gēto
inverted AND gate; NAND gate
否定積ゲート

hiteiseki kairo
inverted AND circuit;
NAND circuit
否定積回路

hiteiseki soshi
inverted AND element;
NAND element
否定積素子

hiteiwa (NOR)
inverted OR (NOR)
否定和

hiteiwa enzan
inverted OR operation;
NOR operation
否定和演算

hiteiwa gēto
inverted OR gate; NOR gate
否定和ゲート

hiteiwa kairo
inverted OR circuit; NOR circuit
否定和回路

hiteiwa soshi
inverted OR element;
NOR element
否定和素子

hitejun(teki)
nonprocedural
非手順(的)

hitejunteki gengo
nonprocedural language
非手順的言語

hitetsuzuki
nonprocedural
非手続き

hitetsuzuki muki gengo
nonprocedural language
非手続き向き言語

hitokken meirei
nonprivilege instruction
非特権命令

hiyō
cost
費用

hiyō bunseki
cost analysis
費用分析

hiyō jōhō
cost information
費用情報

hiyō saishōka
cost minimization
費用最小化

hiyō seinō
cost-performance
費用性能

hiyō teigen
cost reduction
費用低減

hiyō yūkō
cost-effective
費用有効

hiyō yūkōsei
cost-effectiveness
費用有効性

hizero fukki (NRZ)
nonreturn to zero (NRZ)
非ゼロ復帰

hizero fukki henka kiroku hōshiki
nonreturn-to-zero change
recording
非ゼロ復帰変化記録方式

hizero fukki kiroku hōshiki
nonreturn-to-zero recording
非ゼロ復帰記録方式

hizero fukki māku kiroku hōshiki
nonreturn-to-zero mark
recording
非ゼロ復帰マーク記録方式

hizero modori (NRZ)
nonreturn to zero (NRZ)
非ゼロ戻り

hizumi
distorted; distortion
歪み

hizumi jōhō
distorted information
歪み情報

hizumi ritsu
distortion rate
歪み率

hizumu
distort
歪む

hō
distribution (of messages)
報

hō
method
法

hoan'yō setchi
protective ground
保安用接地

hobiisuto
hobbyist
ホビースト

hōganteki NOR
inclusive NOR
包含的NOR

hōganteki NOR kairo
inclusive NOR circuit
包含的NOR回路

hōganteki OR
inclusive OR
包含的OR

hōganteki OR enzan
inclusive OR operation
包含的OR演算

hōganteki OR kairo
inclusive OR circuit
包含的OR回路

hōganteki ronriwa
either-OR; inclusive OR
包含的論理和

hōganteki ronriwa enzan
either-OR operation;
inclusive OR operation
包含的論理和演算

hōganteki ronriwa kairo
inclusive OR circuit
包含的論理和回路

hogo
protection
保護

hogo iki
protected location
保護域

hogo keta
guard digit
保護桁

hogo kii
protection key
保護キー

hogo kikō
protecting mechanism
保護機構

hogo kioku (ryō)iki
protected location
保護記憶(領)域

hogo mōdo
guard mode
保護モード

hogo moji
protection character
保護文字

hogo sareta
protected
保護された

hogo sareta dēta
protected data
保護されたデータ

hogo sareta fuiirudo
protected field
保護されたフィールド

hogo sareta rekōdo
protected record
保護されたレコード

hogo shingō
guard signal
保護信号

hogo sōchi
protecting device
保護装置

hogo suru
protect
保護する

hōhō
approach; method
方法

hōhōron
methodology
方法論

hoiiru-purinta
wheel printer
ホイール・プリンタ

hoji
hold(ing)
保持

hoji kairo
holding circuit
保持回路

hoji meirei
hold instruction
保持命令

hoji rejisuta
holding register
保持レジスタ

hojo
auxiliary; backup; secondary
補助

hojo hyōjishi
secondary indicator
補助表示子

hojo kioku
auxiliary memory; auxiliary
storage; backup memory;
backup storage; secondary
memory; secondary storage
補助記憶

hojo kioku sōchi
auxiliary memory unit; auxiliary
store; backing storage device;
backing store; secondary store
補助記憶装置

hojo sōchi
auxiliary equipment
補助装置

hojo sōsa
auxiliary operation
補助操作

hojū jōhō
supplementary information
補充情報

hokan
interpolation
補間

hokan'iki
save area
保管域

hokan kairo
interpolation circuit; interpolator
補間回路

hōkei parusu
rectangular pulse
方形パルス

hōkeiha
square wave
方形波

hōki suru
abort
放棄する

hōkō
direction
方向

hōkoku(sho)
report
報告(書)

hōkoku fuairu
report file
報告ファイル

hōkokusho kijutsu yōshi
report description form
報告書記述用紙

hōkokusho no yōshiki
report layout
報告書の様式

hōkokusho sakusei
report generation
報告書作成

hōkokusho sakusei kinō
report writer feature
報告書作成機能

**hōkokusho sakusei puroguramu
(RPG)**
report generator; report program
generator (RPG)
報告書作成プログラム

hōkokusho setsu
report section
報告書節

homban tesuto
production test
本番テスト

homban unten
production run
本番運転

hombun
text
本文

homeosutashisu
homeostasis
ホメオスタシス

hōmu-adoresu
home address
ホーム・アドレス

hōmu-erekutoronikkusu
home electronics
ホーム・エレクトロニックス

hōmu-konpyūta
home computer
ホーム・コンピュータ

hōmu-mōdo
home mode
ホーム・モード

hōmu-pojishon
home position
ホーム・ポジション

hōmu-rekōdo
home record
ホーム・レコード

honegumi
skeleton
骨組み

honegumi kōdo
skeletal code
骨組みコード

honrai no
original; originating
本来の

honrai no tanmatsu (sōchi)
original terminal
本来の端末(装置)

hontai
mainframe
本体

hon'yaku
compilation; interpreting;
translation
翻訳

hon'yaku arugorizumu
translating algorithm
翻訳アルゴリズム

hon'yaku ayamari
compilation error
翻訳誤り

hon'yaku jikan
compilation time; compile time;
translate duration; translating
time
翻訳時間

hon'yaku puroguramu
translating program;
translator program
翻訳プログラム

hon'yaku shiji meirei
compiler-directing statement
翻訳指示命令

hon'yaku suru
interpret; translate
翻訳する

hon'yakuki
interpreter; translator
翻訳器

hoppa
hopper
ホッパ

Horerisu-kādo
Hollerith card
ホレリス・カード

Horerisu-kōdo
Hollerith code
ホレリス・コード

horogurafui
holography
ホログラフィ

horogurafuikku kioku
holographic memory
ホログラフィック記憶

hōru
hole
ホール

hōru-sōto
hole sort
ホール・ソート

hōrudo
hold
ホールド

hōrudo-fuairu
hold file
ホールド・ファイル

horyū jikan
holding time
保留時間

horyū machigyōretsu
hold queue
保留待ち行列

horyū shingō
hold signal
保留信号

horyū suru
hold (*verb*)
保留する

hosei
correction
補正

hōshiki
approach; method; mode;
system
方式

hōshiki bitto
mode bit
方式ビット

hōshiki gokansei
mode compatibility
方式互換性

hoshō
compensation
補償

hoshu
maintenance
保守

hoshu(yō) puroguramu
maintenance program
保守(用)プログラム

hoshu'in (CE)
custom engineer (CE)
保守員

hoshu jikan
maintenance time
保守時間

hoshu keiyaku
maintenance contract
保守契約

hoshu rūchin
maintenance routine
保守ルーチン

hoshu sābisu
maintenance service
保守サービス

hoshu shisutemu
maintenance system
保守システム

hoshusei
maintainability
保守性

hosū
complement(ary)
補数

hosū enzan
complementary operation
補数演算

hosū enzanshi
complementary operator
補数演算子

hosū kairo
complementer
補数回路

hosū no soko
complement base
補数の底

hosūki
complementer
補数器

hosuto
host
ホスト

hosuto-konpyūta
host computer
ホスト・コンピュータ

hosuto-purosessa
host processor
ホスト・プロセッサ

hosuto-purosesshingu
host processing
ホスト・プロセッシング

hosuto-shisutemu
host system
ホスト・システム

hōwa
saturation
飽和

hōwagata
saturated
飽和型

howaito-noizu
white noise
ホワイト・ノイズ

hozen
integrity
保全

hozensei
maintainability
保全性

hozon
storage
保存

hozon kikan
retention period
保存期間

hozon kioku
archival memory
保存記憶

hozon suru
deposit (*verb*)
保存する

HSI (ningen-shisutemu-intafuēsu)
HSI (human-system interface)
人間‐システム・インタフェース

HT (suihei tabu; suihei tabu moji)
HT (horizontal tabulation;
horizontal tabulation character)
水平タブ；水平タブ文字

HTL (kōshikiichi ronri)
HTL (high-threshold logic)
高敷居値論理

hyō
list; table
表

hyōdai
title
表題

hyōdai no shoshiki
title format
表題の書式

hyōgen
expression; form; representation
表現

hyōhon
sample
標本

hyōhon heikin
sample mean
標本平均

hyōhon hoji
sample hold
標本保持

hyōhon oyobi hoji (S/H)
sample and hold (S/H)
標本及び保持

hyōhonchi
sampled value
標本値

hyōhonka
sampling
標本化

hyōhonka kairo
sampling circuit
標本化回路

hyōhonka parusu
sampling pulse
標本化パルス

hyōhonka ritsu
sampling rate
標本化率

hyōhonka shūhasū
sampling frequency
標本化周波数

hyōji
display; indication;
representation; sentinel
表示

hyōji gamen
display screen; screen
表示画面

hyōji jōhō
display information
表示情報

hyōji kan
display tube
表示管

hyōji keihō
displayed warning
表示警報

hyōji kiki
indicating device
表示機器

hyōji kikō
indicator
表示機構

hyōji kinō
indicating function
表示機能

hyōji kishin
pointing device
表示器針

hyōji mitsudo
display density
表示密度

hyōji mōdo
display mode
表示モード

hyōji paneru
display panel
表示パネル

hyōji ranpu
indicator lamp
表示ランプ

hyōji rejisuta
indicator register
表示レジスタ

hyōji rekōdo-konpyūta (VRC)
visible-record computer (VRC)
表示レコード・コンピュータ

hyōji rekōdo-purinta (VRP)
visual-record printer (VRP)
表示レコード・プリンタ

hyōji seigyo
display control
表示制御

hyōji sōchi
display; display unit; visual display
表示装置

hyōji sōchi (VDU)
visual display unit (VDU)
表示装置

hyōji sōchi keihō shingō
VDU warning signal
表示装置警報信号

hyōji sōchi shingō
VDU signal
表示装置信号

hyōji sōchi shutsuryoku
visual display output
表示装置出力

hyōji sōsataku
display console
表示操作卓

hyōji suru
indicate; point (*verb*)
表示する

hyōjimen
screen
表示面

hyōjishi
indicator
表示子

hyōji'yō tanmatsu (sōchi)
display terminal
表示用端末（装置）

hyōjun
standard
標準

hyōjun deisuku sōchi
standard disk unit
標準ディスク装置

hyōjun dēta keishiki
standard data format
標準データ形式

hyōjun fuairu
standard file
標準ファイル

hyōjun gata
standard form
標準型

hyōjun haichi
standard layout
標準配置

hyōjun hensa
standard deviation
標準偏差

hyōjun intafuēsu
standard interface
標準インタフェース

hyōjun jiki tēpu
standard reference tape
標準磁気テープ

hyōjun kakin tan'i (SUA)
standard unit of accounting (SUA)
標準課金単位

hyōjun keishiki
standard format
標準形式

hyōjun kikō
standard feature
標準機構

hyōjun kinō
standard function
標準機能

hyōjun meirei
standard command
標準命令

hyōjun meirei setto
standard instruction set
標準命令セット

hyōjun moji
standard characters
標準文字

hyōjun nyūshutsuryoku intafuēsu
standard input/output interface
標準入出力インタフェース

hyōjun pakkēji
standard package
標準パッケージ

hyōjun raberu
standard label
標準ラベル

hyōjun rūchin
standard routine
標準ルーチン

hyōjun saburūchin
standard subroutine
標準サブ・ルーチン

hyōjun shisutemu-tēpu
standard system tape
標準システム・テープ

hyōjun shori tan'i (SUP)
standard unit of processing (SUP)
標準処理単位

hyōjun shoshiki
standard format
標準書式

hyōjun sōbi
standard equipment
標準装備

hyōjun sōsa tejun (SOP)
standard operating procedure (SOP)
標準操作手順

hyōjun tempu
standard attachment
標準添付

hyōjun tēpu
standard tape
標準テープ

hyōjun tetsuzuki
standard procedure
標準手続き

hyōjungai
nonstandard
標準外

hyōjunka
standardization
標準化

hyōjunka suru
standardize
標準化する

hyōka
evaluation
評価

hyōka shisutemu
evaluation system
評価システム

hyōkihō
notation
表記法

hyōmei
indication
表明

hyōmei gengo
assertion language
表明言語

hyōmen
surface
表面

hyōmen danseiha (SAW)
surface acoustic waves (SAW)
表面弾性波

hyōmen deisuku
surface disk
表面ディスク

hyōmen purotto
surface plot
表面プロット

hyōshiki
flag; indicator; marker; sentinel; tag
標識

hyōtei
assessment
評定

Hz (herutsu)
Hz (hertz)
ヘルツ

I

IACK (warikomi kōtei ōtō shingō)
IACK (interrupt acknowledge signal)
割り込み肯定応答信号

IAR (meirei adoresu-rejisuta)
IAR (instruction address register)
命令アドレス・レジスタ

IAS (sokuji akusesu kioku; sokuji akusesu kioku sōchi)
IAS (immediate-access storage; immediate-access store)
即時アクセス記憶;
即時アクセス記憶装置

ibento
event
イベント

IBG (burokkukan kankaku)
IBG (interblock gap)
ブロック間間隔

IC (shūseki kairo)
IC (integrated circuit)
集積回路

IC soketto
IC socket
ICソケット

ICA (Kokusai Tsūshin Kyōkai)
ICA (International Communications Association)
国際通信協会

ICC (Kokusai Keisan Senta)
ICC (International Computation Center)
国際計算センタ

ichi
location; position
位置

ichi adoresu
one address; single address
1アドレス

ichi adoresu-kōdo
one-address code
1アドレス・コード

ichi adoresu meirei
one-address instruction; single-address instruction
1アドレス命令

ichi chippu
single chip
1チップ

ichi chōsei
justification
位置調整

ichi doraibu
one drive
1ドライブ

ichi furekishiburu-deisuku kudō kikō
single flexible disk drive
1フレキシブル・
ディスク駆動機構

ichi hōkō
one way
一方向

ichi hōkō tsūshin
one-way communication
一方向通信

ichi hyōji kikō
cursor
位置表示機構

ichi hyōshiki
position indicator
位置標識

ichi jōhō
data; information
位置情報

ichi jōtai
one state
1状態

ichi kenshutsuki
connection interface
位置検出器

ichi mitsudo (SD)
single density (SD)
一密度

ichi mitsudo deisuku
single-density disk
一密度ディスク

ichi no hosū
complement on one; one's complement
1の補数

ichi o chōsei suru
justify
位置を調整する

ichi o shitei suru
locate
位置を指定する

ichi purasu ichi adoresu
one-plus-one address
1＋1アドレス

ichi purasu ichi adoresu meirei
one-plus-one address instruction
1＋1アドレス命令

ichi reberu
one level
1レベル

ichi reberu-adoresu
one-level address
1レベル・アドレス

ichi reberu kioku
one-level storage
1レベル記憶

ichi reberu kioku sōchi
one-level store
1レベル記憶装置

ichi reberu-saburūchin
one-level subroutine
1レベル・サブルーチン

ichi sakitori adoresu shitei
one-ahead addressing
1先取リアドレス指定

ichi seigyo
position control
位置制御

ichi settei
position setting
位置設定

ichi settei kijutsushi
position setting descriptor
位置設定記述子

ichi shitei
locate
位置指定

ichi shitei mōdo
locate mode
位置指定モード

ichi tai ichi
one-for-one
1対1

ichi tai ichi asenbura
one-to-one assembler
1対1アセンブラ

ichi tai ichi hon'yakuki
one-to-one translator
1対1翻訳器

ichiawase
alignment
位置合わせ

ichiawase māku
alignment mark
位置合わせマーク

ichiawaseru
align
位置合わせる

ichi'i mei
identifier
一意名

ichiji
first order
一次

ichiji(teki)
backup; temporary
一時（的）

ichiji CPU
primary CPU
一次CPU

ichiji(teki) fuairu
temporary file
一時（的）ファイル

ichiji(teki) hensū
temporary variable
一時（的）変数

ichiji(teki) kioku
backup memory; backup
storage; temporary memory;
temporary storage
一時（的）記憶

ichiji kioku sōchi
primary store
一時（的）記憶装置

ichiji kyoku
primary station
一次局

ichiji rejisuta
temporary register
一時レジスタ

ichiji saburūchin
first-order subroutine
一次サブルーチン

ichiji seigyo
first-order control
一次制御

ichiji shisutemu
first-order system
一次システム

ichiji teishi
pause
一時停止

ichiji teishi meirei
pause instruction
一時停止命令

ichijiteki yūza
casual user
一時的ユーザ

ichikime
positioning; registration
位置決め

ichikime gosa
positioning error
位置決め誤差

ichikime jikan
positioning time
位置決め時間

ichikime seigyo
positioning control
位置決め制御

ichikime seigyo shisutemu
positioning control system
位置決め制御システム

ichiren
contiguous; sequence
一連

ichiren bangō
sequence number; serial number
一連番号

ichisūji kasanki
one-digit adder
1数字加算器

ICM (shūseki kairo kioku)
ICM (integrated circuit memory)
集積回路記憶

ID (indasutoriaru-dainamikkusu)
ID (industrial dynamics)
インダストリアル・ダイナミックス

ID (shikibetsu)
ID (identification)
識別

IDCS (intarakuteibu-deisutoribyūshon seigyo shisutemu)
IDCS (interactive distribution control system)
インタラクティブ・ディストリビューション制御システム

IDF (chūkan tanshiban)
IDF (intermediate distributing frame)
中間端子盤

idō
shift
移動

idō heikin
moving average
移動平均

idō meirei
move instruction
移動命令

idō mōdo
move mode
移動モード

idō mokuhyō
moving target
移動目標

idō suru
move (verb)
移動する

idōshiki
mobile; movable
移動式

idōshiki heddo
movable head
移動式ヘッド

IDP (shūchū dēta shori; sōgō dēta shori)
IDP (integrated data processing)
集中データ処理；総合データ処理

IDPS (shūchū dēta shori shisutemu; sōgō dēta shori shisutemu)
IDPS (integrated data-processing system)
集中データ処理システム；
総合データ処理システム

IE (indasutoriaru-enjiniaringu)
IE (industrial engineering)
インダストリアル・
エンジニアリング

IEC (Kokusai Denki Hyōjun Kaigi)
IEC (International Electrotechnical Commission)
国際電気標準会議

IEEE (Denki Denshi Gakkai)
IEEE (Institute of Electrical and Electronic Engineers)
電気電子学会

IFAC (Kokusai Jidō Seigyo Rengō)
IFAC (International Federation for Automatic Control)
国際自動制御連合

IFIP (Kokusai Jōhō Shori Rengō)
IFIP (International Federation for Information Processing)
国際情報処理連合

ifu-zen
IF THEN
IF-THEN

IGDM (iriigaru-gādo-mōdo)
IGDM (illegal guard mode)
イリーガル・ガード・モード

ihō
illegal
違法

ihō kōdo
illegal code
違法コード

ihō komando
illegal command
違法コマンド

ihō meirei
illegal instruction
違法命令

ihō moji
illegal character
違法文字

ihō sōsa
illegal operation
違法操作

iichi-pasu-oun-kōdo (EPOC)
each-pass own code (EPOC)
イーチ・パス・オウン・コード

iji
maintenance
維持

ijō
abnormality; fault
異常

ijō (na)
abnormal; faulty
異常（な）

ijō dembun
faulty message
異常電文

ijō na shūryō
abnormal termination
異常な終了

iki
threshold
閾

ikisaki
destination
行き先

ikisaki adoresu
destination address
行き先アドレス

ikisaki shiki
designational expression
行き先式

ikkatsu
batch
一括

ikkatsu chekku
batch checking
一括チェック

ikkatsu densō
batch transmission
一括伝送

ikkatsu insatsu
batch print; batch printing
一括印刷

ikkatsu jyobu
batch job
一括ジョブ

ikkatsu pōru
general poll
一括ポール

ikkatsu shori
batch processing
一括処理

ikō
conversion
移行

imēji
image
イメージ

imēji-dēta
image data
イメージ・データ

imēji-enhansumento
image enhancement
イメージ・エンハンスメント

imēji-mōdo
image mode
イメージ・モード

imēji-sensa
image sensor
イメージ・センサ

imēji shori
image processing
イメージ処理

imēji shori shisutemu
image-processing system
イメージ処理システム

imēji sōsa
image scanning
イメージ走査

imēji sōsa kikō
image scanner
イメージ走査機構

imēji-sukyana
image scanner
イメージ・スキャナ

imi
semantics
意味

imi (teki)
semantic
意味 (的)

imi ketsugōmō
semantic net
意味結合網

imi memori
semantic memory
意味メモリ

imi seisei
semantic generation
意味生成

imijō no senkō
semantic preference
意味上の選好

imiron
semantics
意味論

imiron(teki)
semantic
意味論 (的)

imironteki hyōgen
semantic representation
意味論的表現

imironteki hyōka
semantic evaluation
意味論的評価

imironteki kaiseki
semantic analysis
意味論的解析

imiteki dēta dokuritsusei
semantic data independence
意味的データ独立性

IMP (intafuēsu-messēji-purosessa)
IMP (interface message processor)
インタフェース・メッセージ・プロセッサ

IMS (jōhō kanri shisutemu)
IMS (information management system)
情報管理システム

in
hidden; implicit
陰

in dēta
hidden data
陰データ

in-hausu
in-house
イン・ハウス

in-pointa
implicit pointer
陰ポインタ

in-rain
in-line
イン・ライン

in-rain-saburūchin
in-line subroutine
イン・ライン・サブルーチン

in-rain-shisutemu
in-line system
イン・ライン・システム

in-rain shori
in-line processing
イン・ライン処理

in-rain tejun
in-line procedure
イン・ライン手順

inbāta
inverter
インバータ

indekkusshingu
indexing
インデックシング

indekkusu
index
インデックス

indekkusu(do)
indexed
インデックス (ド)

indekkusu bumpō
indexed grammar
インデックス文法

indekkusu-fuairu
index file
インデックス・ファイル

indekkusu gengo
indexed language
インデックス言語

in'ei
shading
陰影

infuikkusu hyōkihō
infix notation
インフィックス表記法

infuomachikkusu
informatics
インフォマチックス

inhibitto
inhibit
インヒビット

inhibitto-rain
inhibit line
インヒビット・ライン

i'nin
delegation
委仕

inji
print
印字

inji hamma
print hammer
印字ハンマ

inji heddo
print(ing) head
印字ヘッド

inji hoiiru
print wheel
印字ホイール

inji shutsuryoku
printout; printed output
印字出力

inji sōchi
printer
印字装置

inji sōchi setsuzoku kikō
printer attachment
印字装置接続機構

inji sōchi tempu
printer attachment
印字装置添付

inji waiya
print wire
印字ワイヤ

inji yokusei
nonprint
印字抑制

inji yōshi
stationary
印字用紙

inku
ink
インク

inku-jietto-purinta
ink jet printer
インク・ジェット・プリンタ

inku-misuto-purinta
ink mist printer
インク・ミスト・プリンタ

inku no hamidashi
ink smudge
インクのはみ出し

inku no hansharitsu
ink reflectance
インクの反射率

inku no kasure
ink squeeze-out
インクのかすれ

inku no kin'itsusei
ink uniformity
インクの均一性

inku-ribon
ink ribbon
インク・リボン

inku-ribon-kātorijji
ink ribbon cartridge
インク・リボン・カートリッジ

inkurimentaru
incremental
インクリメンタル

inkurimentaru-danpu
incremental dump
インクリメンタル・ダンプ

inkurimentaru-konpaira
incremental compiler
インクリメンタル・コンパイラ

inkurimentaru-purotta
incremental plotter
インクリメンタル・プロッタ

inkurimentaru-rekōda
incremental recorder
インクリメンタル・レコーダ

inkyoku
negative pole
陰極

inkyokusenkan (CRT)
cathode-ray tube (CRT)
陰極線管

inkyokusenkan hyōji sōchi (CRT hyōji sōchi)
cathode-ray-tube visual display unit (CRT visual display unit)
陰極線管表示装置;
CRT表示装置

inkyokusenkan kioku (CRT kioku)
cathode-ray-tube memory (CRT memory)
陰極線管記憶; CRT記憶

inmen jokyo
hidden-surface removal
陰面除去

inpakuto
impact
インパクト

inpakuto hyōka
impact evaluation
インパクト評価

inpakuto-purinta
impact printer
インパクト・プリンタ

inpakuto-rain-dotto-purinta
impact line dot printer
インパクト・ライン・ドット・プリンタ

inparesu
impulse
インパレス

inparesu ōtō
impulse response
インパレス応答

inpiidansu
impedance
インピーダンス

insatsu
print; printing
印刷

insatsu gyō
print line
印刷行

insatsu haisen kairo (PC)
printed circuit (PC)
印刷配線回路

insatsu haisenban (PCB)
printed circuit board (PCB)
印刷配線板

insatsu ichi
print position
印刷位置

insatsu kikō
print station
印刷機構

insatsu machigyōretsu
print queue
印刷待ち行列

insatsu seigyo moji
print control character
印刷制御文字

insatsu seigyo sōchi
print control unit
印刷制御装置

insatsu senkōki
printing card proof punch;
printing card punch
印刷せん孔機

insatsu senmeido
print contrast ratio
印刷鮮明度

insatsu shūdan
printable group
印刷集団

insatsu shutsuryoku
printout; printed output
印刷出力

insatsu sōchi
printer
印刷装置

insatsu sokudo
printing speed
印刷速度

insatsu yōshiki
printing format
印刷様式

insatsuki
printing machine
印刷機

insatsushi
printing paper; stationery
印刷紙

insen
hidden line
陰線

insen jokyo
hidden-line removal
陰線除去

inshi
factor
因子

inshi bunseki
factor analysis
因子分析

insho
print
印書

insho fuairu
print file
印書ファイル

insho gyō
print line
印書行

insho ichi
print position
印書位置

insho'iki
print area
印書域

insho imēji
print image
印書イメージ

insho sōchi
printer
印書装置

insū
factor
因数

intabaru
interval
インタバル

intafuēshingu ronri
interfacing logic
インタフェーシング論理

intafuēsu
interface
インタフェース

intafuēsu-bōdo
interface board
インタフェース・ボード

intafuēsu-kādo
interface card
インタフェース・カード

intafuēsu keisanki
interface computer
インタフェース計算機

intafuēsu-messēji-purosessa (IMP)
interface message processor (IMP)
インタフェース・メッセージ・プロセッサ

intafuēsu-mojyūru
interface module
インタフェース・モジュール

intafuēsu-rūchin
interface routine
インタフェース・ルーチン

intafuēsu seigyo
interface control
インタフェース制御

intafuēsu seigyo chekku
interface control check
インタフェース制御チェック

intafuēsu shūtan
interface termination
インタフェース終端

intafuēsu-yunitto
interface unit
インタフェース・ユニット

intapurita
interpreter
インタプリタ

intapuriteibu
interpretive
インタプリティブ

intarakushon
interaction
インタラクション

intarakuteibu
interactive
インタラクティブ

intarakuteibu-deisutoribyūshon seigyo shisutemu (IDCS)
interactive distribution control system (IDCS)
インタラクティブ・ディストリビューション制御システム

intariibu suru
interleave
インタリーブする

intarokku
interlock
インタロック

intasekushon
intersection
インタセクション

integurēshon
integration
インテグレーション

interijiento
intelligent
インテリジェント

interijiento tanmatsu (sōchi)
intelligent terminal
インテリジェント端末(装置)

in'yō
reference
引用

in'yō suru
access (*verb*); refer (*verb*)
引用する

I/O (nyūshutsuryoku)
I/O (input/output)
入出力

IOCS (nyūshutsuryoku seigyo shisutemu)
IOCS (input/output control system)
入出力制御システム

IOM (nyūshutsuryoku mojyūru)
IOM (input/output module)
入出力モジュール

IOP (nyūshutsuryoku shori sōchi)
IOP (input/output processor)
入出力処理装置

IPL (shoki puroguramu-rōda)
IPL (initial program loader)
初期プログラム・ローダ

ippan(ka)
generalized
一般（化）

ippan (no)
general
一般（の）

ippan dēta shori
general data processing
一般データ処理

ippan jōhō
general information
一般情報

ippan jōhō nettowāku
general information network
一般情報ネットワーク

ippan keishiki
general format
一般形式

ippan no teisū
generic constant
一般の定数

ippan shisutemu
general system
一般システム

ippan tsūshin shisutemu
general communication system
一般通信システム

ippanka
generalization
一般化

ippanka jōhō shisutemu (GIS)
generalized information system (GIS)
一般化情報システム

IR (jōhō kensaku)
IR (information retrieval)
情報検索

ir (meirei rejisuta)
ir (instruction register)
命令レジスタ

ireko
nest; nesting
入れ子

ireko kankei
nest relation
入れ子関係

ireko kioku sōchi
nesting store
入れ子記憶装置

ireko kōzō
nested structure
入れ子構造

ireko rūpu
nesting loop
入れ子ループ

ireko saburūchin
nesting subroutine
入れ子サブルーチン

IRG (rekōdokan kankaku)
IRG (Interrecord gap)
レコード間間隔

iriguchi
entry
入り口

iriguchi jōken
entry conditions
入り口条件

iriguchi mei
entry name
入り口名

iriguchi ten
entry point
入り口点

iriigaru
illegal
イリーガル

iriigaru-gādo-mōdo (IGDM)
illegal guard mode (IGDM)
イリーガル・ガード・モード

iriigaru-operēshon
illegal operation
イリーガル・オペレーション

iriketsugōshi
inconnector
入り結合子

iro
color
色

iro kōdeingu
color coding
色コーディング

iro kōdo
color code
色コード

IRQ (warikomi yōkyū)
IRQ (interrupt request; interruption request)
割り込み要求

IS (jōhō bunri moji)
IS (information separator)
情報分離文字

IS-R (jōhō chikuseki-kensaku)
IS-R (information storage and retrieval)
情報蓄積－検索

ISAM (sakuin junji akusesu hōshiki)
ISAM (indexed sequential access method)
索引順次アクセス方式

ISFMS (sakuin junji fuairu kanri shisutemu)
ISFMS (indexed sequential file management system)
索引順次ファイル管理システム

ishi kettei
decision making
意思決定

ishi kettei katei
decision-making process
意思決定過程

ishi kettei kinō
decision-making capability
意思決定機能

ishi kettei riron
decision-making theory
意思決定理論

ishi kettei senryaku
decision-making strategy
意思決定戦略

ishi kettei shien shisutemu (DSS)
decision support system (DSS)
意思決定支援システム

ishi kettei shisutemu
decision-making system
意思決定システム

ishitsu (no)
heterogeneous
異質（の）

ishoku
portable
移植

ishokusei
portability
移植性

ISI mōdo
ISI mode
ISIモード

isō
phase
位相

isō
transport
移送

ISO (Kokusai Hyōjunka Kikō)
ISO (International Organization
for Standardization; International
Standards Organization)
国際標準化機構

isō henchō
phase modulation
位相変調

isō hizumi
phase distortion
位相歪み

isō kikō
transport mechanism;
transport station
移送機構

ISO kōdo
ISO code
ISOコード

isō kōdoka hōshiki (PE)
phase encoding (PE)
位相コード化方式

ISO suisen kikakuan
draft ISO recommendation;
ISO recommendation
ISO推選規格案

ISP (meirei setto-purosessa)
ISP (instruction set processor)
命令セット・プロセッサ

IT (jōhō gijutsu)
IT (information technology)
情報技術

itarikku-fuonto
italic font
イタリック・フォント

itchi
coincidence; consistency
一致

itchi gēto
coincidence gate
一致ゲート

itchi jikan
coincidence duration
一致時間

itchi kairo
coincidence circuit
一致回路

itomakigata hizumi
pincushion distortion
糸巻型歪み

itsuwari
false
偽り

itsuwari kōdo
false code
偽りコード

ITU (Kokusai Denki Tsūshin Rengō)
ITU (International
Telecommunication Union)
国際電気通信連合

J

JCB (jyobu seigyo burokku)
JCB (job control block)
ジョブ制御ブロック

JCL (jyobu seigyo gengo)
JCL (job control language)
ジョブ制御言語

JEIDA (Nihon Denshi Kōgyō Shinkō Kyōkai)
JEIDA (Japanese Electronic
Industry Development
Association)
日本電子工業振興協会

jibunkatsu
time sharing
時分割

jibunkatsu monita-shisutemu
time-sharing monitor system
時分割モニタ・システム

jibunkatsu nyūshutsuryoku shisutemu
time-shared input/output system
時分割入出力システム

jibunkatsu opushon (TSO)
time-sharing option (TSO)
時分割オプション

jibunkatsu shisutemu (TSS)
time-sharing system (TSS)
時分割システム

jibunkatsu suru
time-share
時分割する

jibunkatsu tajū akusesu (TDMA)
time-division multiple access
(TDMA)
時分割多重アクセス

jibunkatsu tajū hōshiki (TDM)
time-division multiplexing (TDM)
時分割多重方式

jibunkatsu tajū sōchi
time-division multiplexer
時分割多重装置

jibunkatsu tajū tsūshin
time-division multiplex
communication
時分割多重通信

jidō
automatic; built-in
自動

jidō(teki na)
automatic
自動 (的な)

jidō ayamari kenshutsu
automatic error detection
自動誤り検出

jidō ayamari kenshutsu-teisei kinō
automatic error detection and
correction
自動誤り検出 - 訂正機能

jidō ayamari teisei
automatic error correction
自動誤り訂正

jidō bunrui
automatic sort
自動分類

jidō daiaru
automatic dialing
自動ダイアル

jidō daiaru sōchi
automatic dialing unit
自動ダイアル装置

jidō debaggingu
automatic debugging
自動デバッギング

jidō den'atsu chōseiki (AVR)
automatic voltage regulator
(AVR)
自動電圧調整器

jidō dēta kōkan
automatic data switching
自動データ交換

jidō dēta shori (ADP)
automatic data processing (ADP)
自動データ処理

jidō dēta shori shisutemu (ADPS)
automatic data-processing
system (ADPS)
自動データ処理システム

jidō dēta shori sōchi
automatic data-processing
equipment; automatic data
processor
自動データ処理装置

jidō dēta shūshū (ADA)
automatic data acquisition (ADA)
自動データ収集

jidō fukki kikō
automatic return mechanism
自動復帰機構

jidō gengo hon'yaku
automatic language translation
自動言語翻訳

jidō gyōbangōka
automatic line numbering
自動行番号化

jidō hādouea-danpu
automatic hardware dump
自動ハードウェア・ダンプ

jidō hentō
automatic answering
自動返答

jidō ishi kettei
automatic decision making
自動意思決定

jidō jisho
automatic dictionary
自動辞書

jidō jōhō kōsei shisutemu
automatic information
organization system
自動情報構成システム

jidō keisanki
automatic computer
自動計算機

jidō kensa
automatic check
自動検査

jidō kido chōsetsu
automatic brightness control
自動輝度調節

jidō kikō
automechanism
自動機構

jidō kōdeingu
autocoding; automatic coding
自動コーディング

jidō kōkan
automatic exchange
自動交換

jidō kumitate shisutemu
automatic assembling system
自動組み立てシステム

jidō monita
automonitor
自動モニタ

jidō ninshiki
automatic recognition
自動認識

jidō ōtō
automatic answering
自動応答

jidō puroguramingu
automatic programming
自動プログラミング

jidō puroguramu
autoprogramming
自動プログラム

jidō rensō hōshiki
automatic repetition system
自動連送方式

jidō ritoku seigyo (AGC)
automatic gain control (AGC)
自動利得制御

jidō rōda
autoloader
自動ローダ

jidō rokku
autolock
自動ロック

jidō saishidō
automatic restart
自動再始動

jidō sakuin
autoindex; automatic indexing
自動索引

jidō seigyo
automatic control
自動制御

jidō seizu
autodraft
自動製図

jidō senkō
automatic punch
自動せん孔

jidō setsudan
automatic disconnection
自動切断

jidō shidō
autostart; automatic start
自動始動

jidō shiken shisutemu
automatic test system
自動試験システム

jidō shindan
automatic diagnosis
自動診断

jidō shindan kinō
automatic diagnostic function
自動診断機能

jidō shokuji
automatic typesetting
自動植字

jidō shōroku
autoabstract; automatic abstract
自動抄録

jidō-shudō sōsa (A-M sōsa)
automatic-manual operation
(A-M operation)
自動-手動操作；A-M操作

jidō sōga (APT)
automatic picture transmission
(APT)
自動送画

jidō sōjushin sōchi (ASR)
automatic send-receive set (ASR)
自動送受信装置

jidō teishi
automatic stop
自動停止

jidō tojita rūpu-shisutemu
automatic closed-loop system
自動閉じたループ・システム

jidō warikomi
autointerrupt
自動割り込み

jidō yobidashi
autocall; automatic calling
自動呼び出し

jidō yobidashi sōchi
automatic calling equipment
自動呼び出し装置

jidō yobidashi sōchi (ACU)
automatic calling unit (ACU)
自動呼び出し装置

jidōka
automated; automation
自動化

jidōka dēta kaiseki
automated data analysis
自動化データ解析

jidōka dēta shūshū shisutemu
automated data collection
system
自動化データ収集システム

jidōka jōhō shisutemu
automated information system
自動化情報システム

jigen
dimension
次元

jigen meireibun
dimension statement
次元命令文

jigen zokusei
dimension attribute
次元属性

jigo bunseki
postmortem
事後分析

jigo bunseki danpu
postmortem dump
事後分析ダンプ

jigo bunseki rūchin
postmortem routine
事後分析ルーチン

jigo henshū
postedit
事後編集

jihen
time variable; time-varying
時変

jijitsu
fact
事実

jijitsu jōhō
factual information
事実情報

jijitsu kensaku
fact retrieval
事実検索

jikan
duration; time
時間

jikan bēsu
time base
時間ベース

jikan dokuritsu
time independence;
time-independent
時間独立

jikan izon
time dependence;
time-dependent
時間依存

jikan kankaku
time interval
時間間隔

jikan okure
time delay; time lag
時間遅れ

jikan waritsuke
time allocation
時間割り付け

jikei
typeface
字形

jikeiretsu
time series
時系列

jikeiretsu kaiseki
time series analysis
時系列解析

jiki
magnetic
磁気

jiki baburu
magnetic bubble
磁気バブル

jiki baburu kioku
bubble memory
磁気バブル記憶

jiki chien sen
magnetic delay line
磁気遅延線

jiki deisuku
magnetic disk
磁気ディスク

jiki deisuku kioku
magnetic-disk storage
磁気ディスク記憶

jiki deisuku-pakku
magnetic-disk pack
磁気ディスク・パック

jiki deisuku sōchi
magnetic-disk unit
磁気ディスク装置

jiki doramu
drum; magnetic drum
磁気ドラム

jiki doramu kioku
drum storage;
magnetic-drum storage
磁気ドラム記憶

jiki doramu sōchi
magnetic-drum unit
磁気ドラム装置

jiki fuairu
magnetic file
磁気ファイル

jiki fugōki shutsuryoku
magnetically encoded output
磁気符号器出力

jiki fuirumu
magnetic film
磁気フィルム

jiki gengo
magnetic language
磁気言語

jiki haku maku
magnetic thin film
磁気薄膜

jiki haku maku kioku
magnetic thin film memory;
magnetic thin film storage
磁気薄膜記憶

jiki heddo
magnetic head
磁気ヘッド

jiki hojo kioku sōchi
magnetic backing store
磁気補助記憶装置

jiki inku
magnetic ink
磁気インク

jiki inku moji
magnetic-ink character
磁気インク文字

jiki inku moji bunruiki
magnetic-ink character sorter
磁気インク文字分類機

jiki inku moji fugōka
magnetic-ink character encoding
磁気インク文字符号化

jiki inku moji kenshō
magnetic-ink character
verification
磁気インク文字検証

jiki inku moji kirokuki
magnetic-ink character inscriber
磁気インク文字記録機

jiki inku moji kōdoka
magnetic-ink character encoding
磁気インク文字コード化

jiki inku moji ninshiki (MICR)
magnetic-ink character
recognition (MICR)
磁気インク文字認識

**jiki inku moji yomitori sōchi
(MICR)**
magnetic-ink character reader
(MICR)
磁気インク文字読み取り装置

jiki kādo
magnetic card
磁気カード

jiki kādo kioku
magnetic-card memory;
magnetic-card storage
磁気カード記憶

jiki kādo sōchi
magnetic-card unit
磁気カード装置

jiki kioku
magnetic memory
磁気記憶

jiki koa
magnetic core
磁気コア

jiki koa kioku
magnetic-core memory;
magnetic-core storage
磁気コア記憶

jiki koa-matorikkusu
magnetic-core matrix
磁気コア・マトリックス

jiki moji
magnetic character
磁気文字

jiki moji ninshiki (MCR)
magnetic-character recognition
(MCR)
磁気文字認識

jiki moji yomitori/bunruiki
magnetic-character reader/sorter
磁気文字読み取り／分類機

jiki moji yomitori sōchi (MCR)
magnetic-character reader (MCR)
磁気文字読み取り装置

jiki sutoraipu
magnetic stripe
磁気ストライプ

jiki tēpu (MT)
magnetic tape (MT)
磁気テープ

jiki tēpu-dekku
magnetic-tape deck
磁気テープ・デック

jiki tēpu-enkōda
magnetic-tape encoder
磁気テープ・エンコーダ

jiki tēpu-kasetto
magnetic tape cassette
磁気テープ・カセット

jiki tēpu-kasetto sōchi
magnetic tape cassette handler;
magnetic tape cassette unit
磁気テープ・カセット装置

jiki tēpu kioku
magnetic-tape storage
磁気テープ記憶

jiki tēpu-kōdo
magnetic-tape code
磁気テープ・コード

jiki tēpu kudō kikō
magnetic-tape drive
磁気テープ駆動機構

jiki tēpu-raberu
magnetic-tape label
磁気テープ・ラベル

jiki tēpu sōchi
magnetic-tape handler
磁気テープ装置

jiki tēpu sōchi (MTU)
magnetic-tape unit (MTU);
tape unit
磁気テープ装置

jiki waiya kioku sōchi
magnetic wire store
磁気ワイヤ記憶装置

jikken'yō mokei
breadboard
実験用模型

jikkō
computer run; execution; run
実行

jikkō(kanō)
executable
実行（可能）

jikkō adoresu
effective address
実行アドレス

jikkō ayamari
execution error
実行誤り

jikkō bun
executable statement
実行文

jikkō dankai
execution cycle; run phase;
running phase
実行段階

jikkō funō
nonexecutable
実行不能

jikkō funō puroguramu
nonexecutable program
実行不能プログラム

jikkō jikan
effective time; execution time;
run duration; running time
実行時間

jikkō jikan kaunta
running-time counter
実行時間カウンタ

jikkō jōtai
running state
実行状態

jikkō junjo
effective order
実行順序

jikkō meirei
actual instruction; effective
instruction; effective order
実行命令

jikkō nagarezu
run chart
実行流れ図

jikkō ritoku
effective gain
実行利得

jikkō ryō'iki
execution area
実行領域

jikkō saikuru
execution cycle
実行サイクル

jikkō seigyo bun
execute statement
実行制御文

jikkō sokudo
effective speed
実行速度

jikkō suru
execute
実行する

jikkō suteppu
execution step
実行ステップ

jikkō tan'i
executable unit
実行単位

jikkōchū no
active
実行中の

jikkōchū no jyobu
active job
実行中のジョブ

jikkōchū no puroguramu
active program
実行中のプログラム

jikkōgata makuro
imperative macro
実行型マクロ

jikkōgata makuro meirei
imperative macroinstruction
実行型マクロ命令

jikkōji
object time; run time
実行時

jikkōji ayamari
run-time error
実行時誤り

jikkōji shisutemu
run-time system
実行時システム

jikkōji sofutouea
run-time software
実行時ソフトウェア

jikkōji tōkei
run-time statistics
実行時統計

jikkōkanō puroguramu
executable program
実行可能プログラム

jikkōyō keisanki
object computer
実行用計算機

jikō
fact
事項

jiko
failure; fault; faulty; incident
事故

jiko anteika
self-stabilization
自己安定化

jiko chōsei
self-adapting; self-regulating
自己調整

jiko chōsei shisutemu
self-regulating system
自己調整システム

jiko dembun
faulty message
事故電文

jiko dōchō
self-tuning
自己同調

jiko hensei
self-organizing
自己編成

jiko hensei shisutemu
self-organizing system
自己編成システム

317

jiko hozen
self-maintenance
自己保全

jiko iji
self-maintaining;
self-maintenance
自己維持

jiko kanshi
self-monitoring
自己監視

jiko kensa
self-checking
自己検査

jiko kensa bangō
self-checking number;
self-checking numeral
自己検査番号

jiko kensa bangō hassei kikō
self-checking number generator
自己検査番号発生機構

jiko kensa hōshiki
self-checking system
自己検査方式

jiko kensa kōdo
self-checking code
自己検査コード

jikō kensaku
fact retrieval
事項検索

jiko kijutsu
self-describing
自己記述

jiko kijutsusei
self-description
自己記述性

jiko risetto-rūpu
self-resetting loop
自己リセット・ループ

jiko rōdeingu
self-loading
自己ローディング

jiko saihaichi
self-relocation
自己再配置

jiko saihaichikanō
self-relocatable
自己再配置可能

jiko shidō puroguramu
self-triggering program
自己始動プログラム

jiko shindan
self-diagnosis; self-diagnostics
自己診断

jiko shokika
self-initialize
自己初期化

jiko shūfuku
self-repair
自己修復

jiko sōkan
auto-correlation
自己相関

jiko sōtai adoresu
self-relative address
自己相対アドレス

jiko sōtai adoresu shitei
self-relative addressing
自己相対アドレス指定

jiko teigi
self-defining
自己定義

jiko teigi chi
self-defining value
自己定義値

jiko teigi kō
self-defining term
自己定義項

jiko teisei
self-correcting
自己訂正

jiko teisei hōshiki
self-correcting system
自己訂正方式

jiko tekiō
self-adapting
自己適応

jiko umekomi
self-embedding
自己埋め込み

jiko yomikomi
self-load
自己読み入み

jiku
magnetic domain
磁区

jikyū
nonvolatile
持久

jikyū kioku
nonvolatile memory
持久記憶

jimu jidōka
business automation
事務自動化

jimu kanri dēta shori
administrative data processing
事務管理データ処理

jimu kikai
business machine
事務機械

jimu shisutemu
business system
事務システム

jimu (dēta) shori
business data processing
事務 (データ) 処理

jinkō chinō (AI)
artificial intelligence (AI)
人工知能

jinkō gengo
artificial language
人工言語

JIPDEC (Nihon Jōhō Shori Kaihatsu Kyōkai)
JIPDEC (Japan Information-Processing Development Center)
日本情報処理開発協会

jiritsu
autonomous
自律

jiritsu dōsa
autonomous working
自律動作

jiritsu keipabiritei
autonomous capability
自律ケィパビリティ

jiritsu keisan
autonomous computing
自律計算

jiritsu seigyo shisutemu (ACS)
autonomous control system (ACS)
自律制御システム

jiritsu shisutemu
autonomous system
自律システム

jiryoku
self-actuated; self-operating
自力

JIS (Nihon Kōgyō Hyōjun Kikaku)
JIS (Japanese Industrial Standards)
日本工業標準規格

JIS kiibōdo
JIS keyboard
JIS キーボード

jisage
indentation
字下げ

JISC (Nihon Kōgyō Hyōjun Chōsakai)
JISC (Japanese Industrial Standards Committee)
日本工業標準調査会

jisei hakumaku kioku
thin-film memory; thin-film storage
磁性薄膜記憶

jishin
core; magnetic
磁心

jishin arei
core array
磁心アレイ

jishin baitai
magnetic media; magnetic medium
磁心媒体

jishin kioku
core memory; core storage; magnetic-core memory; magnetic-core storage
磁心記憶

jishin kioku sōchi
core store
磁心記憶装置

jisho
dictionary
辞書

jishō
event
事象

jishō hensū
event variable
事象変数

jishō seigyo burokku (ECB)
event control block (ECB)
事象制御ブロック

jishō shiikensu
event sequence
事象シーケンス

jishō shimyurēshon
event simulation
事象シミュレーション

jishō sōsa
event scanning
事象走査

jishō sōsa kikō
event scanning mechanism
事象走査機構

jisoku
flux
磁束

jisoku hanten
flux transition
磁束反転

jisoku mitsudo
flux density
磁束密度

jissai no shōsūten
actual decimal point
実際の小数点

jisshin
decimal
10進

jisshin adoresu
decimal address
10進アドレス

jisshin enzan
decimal arithmetic; decimal operation
10進演算

jisshin enzan kikō
decimal arithmetic function; decimal feature
10進演算機構

jisshin enzanshi
decimal operator
10進演算子

jisshin hō
decimal notation; decimal number system; decimal numeration system; decimal system
10進法

jisshin kaunta
decimal counter
10進カウンタ

jisshin keta afure
decimal overflow
10進桁溢れ

jisshin keta afure reigai
decimal overflow exception
10進桁溢れ例外

jisshin kisū
decimal radix
10進基数

jisshin kōdo
decimal code
10進コード

jisshin-nishin henkan
decimal-to-binary conversion
10進-2進変換

jisshin seikika
decimal normalization
10進正規化

jisshin shōsūten
decimal point
10進小数点

jisshin sū
decimal number; decimal numeral
10進数

jisshin sū shoshiki
decimal number format
10進数書式

jisshin sūji
decimal digit
10進数字

jisshō
demonstration
実証

jissō
package
実装

jissō mitsudo
packaging density
実装密度

319

jissō yōryō
packaging capacity
実装容量

jissū
real number
実数

jitai
face; font
字体

jitai henkan moji
font change character
字体変換文字

jitai henkō moji
face change character
字体変更文字

jiteisū
time constant
時定数

jitsu adoresu
actual address; real address
実アドレス

jitsu genshi
actual source
実原始

jitsu hensū
real variable
実変数

jitsu hikisū
actual argument
実引き数

jitsu jikan
real time
実時間

jitsu jikan dōsa
real-time operation
実時間動作

jitsu jikan jōhō shori
real-time information processing
実時間情報処理

jitsu jikan jyobu
real-time job
実時間ジョブ

jitsu jikan keisanki
real-time computer
実時間計算機

jitsu jikan nyūryoku
real-time input
実時間入力

jitsu jikan operēteingu-shisutemu
real-time operating system
実時間オペレーディング・
システム

jitsu jikan OS
real-time OS
実時間OS

jitsu jikan seigyo
real-time control
実時間制御

jitsu jikan shimyurēshon
real-time simulation
実時間シミュレーション

jitsu jikan shisutemu
real-time system
実時間システム

jitsu jikan shori
real-time processing
実時間処理

jitsu jikan shutsuryoku
real-time output
実時間出力

jitsu jikan tokei (RTC)
real-time clock (RTC)
実時間時計

jitsu kekka
actual result
実結果

jitsu kioku('iki)
real storage
実記憶（域）

jitsu kōdeingu
actual coding
実コーディング

jitsu kōdo
actual code
実コード

jitsu kukan
real interval
実区間

jitsu parameta
actual parameter
実パラメタ

jitsu parameta bu
actual parameter part
実パラメタ部

jitsu parameta no narabi
actual parameter list
実パラメタの並び

jitsu teisū
real constant
実定数

jitsugen
implementation; realization
実現

jitsugen kanōsei kentō
implementation feasibility study
実現可能性検討

jitsugen keikaku
implementation planning
実現計画

jitta
fluctuation; jitter
ジッタ

jiyū keishiki
free form
自由形式

jiyū shoshiki
free format
自由書式

jizen insatsu
preprinted
事前印刷

jizen insatsu yōshi
preprinted form; printed form
事前印刷用紙

jizen senkō
prepunch
事前せん孔

jizoku jikan
duration
持続時間

jōbu kami okuri
upper paper feed
上部紙送り

jōchō
redundant
冗長

jōchō bitto
redundant bit
冗長ビット

jōchō dēta
redundant data
冗長データ

jōchō fugō
redundancy code;
redundant code
冗長符号

jōchō hōshiki
redundancy system
冗長方式

jōchō jōhō
redundant information
冗長情報

jōchō keisan
redundant computation
冗長計算

jōchō kensa
redundancy check
冗長検査

jōchō moji
redundant character
冗長文字

jōchō shisutemu
redundant system
冗長システム

jōchōdo
redundancy
冗長度

jōchū
permanent; resident
常駐

jōchū eremento
resident element
常駐エレメント

jōchū iki
resident area
常駐域

jōchū kanshi puroguramu
resident supervisor program
常駐監視プログラム

jōchū mojyūru
resident module
常駐モジュール

jōchū rōda
resident loader
常駐ローダ

jōchū rūchin
resident routine
常駐ルーチン

jōchū segumento
permanent segment
常駐セグメント

jōchū seigyo puroguramu
resident control program
常駐制御プログラム

jōhō
information
情報

jōhō bitto
information bit
情報ビット

jōhō bunri moji (IS)
information separator (IS)
情報分離文字

jōhō chikuseki
information storage
情報蓄積

jōhō chikuseki-kensaku (IS/R)
information storage and retrieval
(IS/R)
情報蓄積-検索

jōhō densō
information transmission
情報伝送

jōhō dentatsu
information transfer
情報伝達

jōhō fuiidobakku
information feedback
情報フィードバック

jōhō gen
information source
情報源

jōhō gijutsu (IT)
information technology (IT)
情報技術

jōhō gōsei
information synthesis
情報合成

jōhō hogo
information protection
情報保護

jōhō hyōji
information display
情報表示

jōhō hyōji sōchi
information display unit
情報表示装置

jōhō hyōka
information evaluation
情報評価

jōhō hyōshiki
information flag
情報標識

jōhō ikisaki
information destination
情報行き先

jōhō kagaku
information science
情報科学

jōhō kanri shisutemu (IMS)
information management system
(IMS)
情報管理システム

jōhō kensaku (IR)
information retrieval (IR)
情報検索

jōhō kensaku shisutemu
information retrieval system
情報検索システム

jōhō kikan
information feedback
情報帰還

jōhō kikan hōshiki
information feedback system
情報帰還方式

jōhō kōkan
information interchange
情報交換

Jōhō Kōkan'yō Beikoku Hyōjun Kōdo (ASCII)
American Standard Code for
Information Interchange (ASCII)
情報交換用米国標準コード

Jōhō Kōkan'yō Beikoku Hyōjun Kōdo (USASCII)
United States of America
Standards Code for Information
Interchange (USASCII)
情報交換用米国標準コード

jōhō kōmoku
information item
情報項目

jōhō kōzō
information structure
情報構造

jōhō nagare
information flow
情報流れ

jōhō nagare kaiseki
information flow analysis
情報流れ解析

jōhō nagare seigyo
information flow control
情報流れ制御

jōhō nagarezu
information flowchart
情報流れ図

jōhō nettowāku
information network
情報ネットワーク

jōhō nettowāku seigyo
information network control
情報ネットワーク制御

jōhō no datsuraku
loss of information
情報の脱落

jōhō no sentaku haifu (SDI)
selective dissemination of
information (SDI)
情報の選択配布

jōhō no sonshitsu
loss of information
情報の損失

jōhō riron
information theory
情報理論

jōhō ryō
amount of information;
information content
情報量

jōhō seigyo
information control
情報制御

jōhō seigyo shisutemu
information control system
情報制御システム

jōhō sentaku
information selection
情報選択

jōhō shien shisutemu
information support system
情報支援システム

jōhō shigen
information resource
情報資源

jōhō shisutemu
information system
情報システム

jōhō shisutemu kagaku
information systems science
情報システム科学

jōhō shori
information processing
情報処理

Jōhō Shori Gakkai (Nihon)
Information Processing Society of
Japan
情報処理学会（日本）

jōhō shori gengo
information-processing language
情報処理言語

jōhō shori ryō
information-processing load
情報処理量

jōhō shori senta
information-processing center
情報処理センタ

jōhō shori shisutemu
information-processing system
情報処理システム

jōhō shori sōchi
information processor
情報処理装置

jōhō shūshū
information collection
情報収集

jōhō sonshitsu
information loss
情報損失

jōhō tōgō
information integration
情報統合

jōhō tsūshinro
information channel
情報通信路

jōhōmō
information network
情報網

jōi
host
上位

jōi CPU
host CPU
上位CPU

jōi gengo
host language
上位言語

jōi keisanki
host computer
上位計算機

jōi konpyūta
host computer
上位コンピュータ

jōi no
significant
上位の

jōi no dēta
significant data
上位のデータ

jōi ruisanki (UA)
upper accumulator (UA)
上位累算器

jōi shisutemu
host system
上位システム

jōi shisutemu jumbi kinō
host preparation facility
上位システム準備機能

jōihan
superior print
上位版

jōken
condition; conditional
条件

jōken bun
conditional statement
条件文

jōken entori
condition entry
条件エントリ

jōken hensū
conditional variable
条件変数

jōken hyōshiki
condition indicator
条件標識

jōken kōdo
condition code
条件コード

jōken mei
condition name
条件名

jōken meirei
conditional statement
条件命令

jōken rejisuta
condition(al) register
条件レジスタ

jōken shiki
conditional expression
条件式

jōken sutabu
condition stub
条件スタブ

jōkentsuki
conditional
条件付き

jōkentsuki asenburi meirei
conditional assembly instruction
条件付きアセンブリ命令

jōkentsuki bunki
conditional branch
条件付き分岐

jōkentsuki bunki meirei
conditional branch instruction
条件付き分岐命令

jōkentsuki tobikoshi
conditional jump;
conditional transfer
条件付き飛び越し

jōkentsuki tobikoshi meirei
conditional jump instruction;
conditional transfer instruction
条件付き飛び越し命令

jokyo
elimination
除去

jokyo suru
eliminate; remove
除去する

josan
division (operation)
除算

jōshōgata apurōchi
bottom-up approach
上昇型アプローチ

jōshōgata kaiseki
bottom-up parsing
上昇型解析

josū
dividend
除数

jōsū
multiplier; multiplier factor
乗数

jōtai
state; status
状態

jōtai go
status word
状態語

jōtai hōkoku
status report
状態報告

jōtai hyōshiki
status flag; status indicator
状態標識

jōtai jōhō
status information
状態情報

jōtai kirikae
status switching
状態切り換え

jōtai sen'i zu
state transition diagram
状態遷移図

jōtai toiawase
status inquiry
状態問い合わせ

jōtai zu
state diagram
状態図

jōyo
remainder; residue
剰余

jōyo chekku
remainder check
剰余チェック

jōyo kensa
residue check
剰余検査

jōzan
multiplication
乗算

jōzan suru
multiply
乗算する

jū no hosū
complement on ten;
ten's complement
10の補数

judō
passive
受動

judō kairo
passive circuit
受動回路

judō shisutemu
passive system
受動システム

judō soshi
passive element
受動素子

judō tanmatsu
passive station
受動端末

jūichi senkō
eleven punch
11せん孔

jukugo
word of two or more characters
(Japanese)
熟語

jumbi (PREP)
housekeeping; preparation (PREP)
準備

jumbi jikan
setup time
準備時間

jumbi kigō
preparation symbol
準備記号

jumbi rūchin
housekeeping routine
準備ルーチン

jumbi sōsa
 housekeeping operation
 準備操作

jumyō
 life span
 寿命

jun
 sequence; sequential
 順

jun(ji) adoresu shitei
 sequential addressing
 順(次)アドレス指定

jun(ji) akusesu
 sequential access
 順(次)アクセス

jun(ji) akusesu-deisuku
 sequential-access disk
 順(次)アクセス・ディスク

jun(ji) akusesu-fuairu
 sequential-access file
 順(次)アクセス・ファイル

jun(ji) akusesu hōshiki (SAM)
 sequential-access method (SAM)
 順(次)アクセス方式

jun(ji) akusesu kioku
 sequential-access memory/
 storage
 順(次)アクセス記憶

jun bunrui
 forward sort
 順分類

jun dēta-setto
 sequential data set
 順(次)データ・セット

jun(ji) hensei fuairu
 sequential file
 順(次)編成ファイル

jun kōzō
 sequential structure
 順構造

jun nagare
 sequential flow
 順流れ

jun nishin hō
 pure binary notation
 純2進法

jun nishin kisūhō
 pure binary numeration system
 純2進記数法

jun risuto
 sequential list
 順リスト

jun risuto kōzō
 sequential list structure
 順リスト構造

jun(ji) yobidashi
 sequential access
 順(次)呼び出し

jun yomi
 forward read(ing)
 順読み

junhōkō
 forward direction
 順方向

junhōkō chaneru
 forward channel
 順方向チャネル

jun'i
 order (sequence); precedence;
 rank; sort
 順位

jūni inchi-deisupurei
 twelve-inch display
 12インチ・ディスプレイ

jun'i reberu
 precedence level
 順位レバル

jun'i seigyo kii
 sort control key
 順位制御キー

jun'i seigyo kōmoku
 sort control item
 順位制御項目

jūni senkō
 twelve punch
 12せん孔

jūnishin(hō)
 duodecimal
 12進(法)

jūnishin sū
 duodecimal number
 12進数

jun'itsuke
 ranking; sequencing
 順位付け

jun'itsuke kii
 sequencing key
 順位付けキー

junji
 sequence; sequential
 順次

junji dēta-setto
 sequential data set
 順次データ・セット

junji dōsa
 sequential operation
 順次動作

junji kensaku
 sequential retrieval
 順次検索

junji seigyo
 sequential control
 順次制御

junji shori keisanki
 sequential computer
 順次処理計算機

junji sukejyūra
 sequential scheduler
 順次スケジューラ

junji sukejyūringu
 sequential scheduling
 順次スケジューリング

junji sukejyūringu-shisutemu
 sequential scheduling system
 順次スケジューリング・システム

junjo
 order (sequence); sequence;
 sequential
 順序

junjo ayamari
 sequence error
 順序誤り

junjo kairo
 sequential circuit
 順序回路

junjo kensa
 sequence check(ing)
 順序検査

junjo kōdo
sequence code
順序コード

junjo ronri
sequential logic
順序論理

junjo ronri kairo
sequential logical circuit
順序論理回路

junjo ronri soshi
sequential logic element
順序論理素子

junjo seigyo
sequence control
順序制御

junjotsuke
sequencing
順序付け

junkai fugō
cyclic code
巡回符号

junkai jōchō kensa (CRC)
cyclic redundancy check (CRC)
巡回冗長検査

junkai jōchō kensa moji
cyclic redundancy check
character
巡回冗長検査文字

junkan
wraparound
循環

junkan keta age
end-around carry
循環桁上げ

junkan keta idō
end-around shift; ring shift
循環桁移動

junkan keta okuri
cyclic shift
循環桁送り

junkan kioku
circulating memory; circulating
storage; cyclic storage
循環記憶

junkan rejisuta
circulating register
循環レジスタ

junkan shifuto
circular shift; cyclic shift
循環シフト

junkanteki kōzō
cyclic structure
循環的構造

junkyo
standard
準拠

jūretsu
column
縦列

jūrokushin
hexadecimal; sexadecimal
16進

jūrokushin adoresu
hexadecimal address
16進アドレス

jūrokushin chi
hexadecimal value
16進値

jūrokushin hō
hexadecimal number system;
hexadecimal representation;
sexadecimal notation
16進法

jūrokushin hō (HEX)
hexadecimal notation (HEX)
16進法

jūrokushin kōdo
hexadecimal code
16進コード

jūrokushin sū
hexadecimal number;
hexadecimal numeral;
sexadecimal number;
sexadecimal numeral
16進数

jūrokushin sūji
hexadecimal digit;
sexadecimal digit
16進数字

jushin
receiving
受信

jushin chūdan
receive interrupt(ion)
受信中断

jushin dembun
incoming message
受信電文

jushin dēta
received data
受信データ

jushin mōdo
receive mode
受信モード

jushin sentaku
select receive
受信選択

jushin sen'yō
receive-only
受信専用

jushin shingō eremento-taimingu
receiver signal element timing
受信信号エレメント・タイミング

jushin suru
receive
受信する

jushin tanmatsu
accepting station;
receiving station
受信端末

jushin tanmatsu sōchi
receiving terminal
受信端末装置

jushinki
receiver (equipment)
受信機

jūten
fill
充てん

jūten moji
fill character
充てん文字

jūtēpu sōchi
slave tape unit
従テープ装置

juyōki
receptor
受容器

jūzoku
dependence; dependent
従属

jūzoku hensū
dependent variable
従属変数

jūzoku risuto
dependence list
従属リスト

jūzoku segumento
dependent segment
従属セグメント

jyakku
jack
ジャック

jyakku-paneru
jack panel
ジャック・パネル

jyakku-puragu
jack plug
ジャック・プラグ

jyakkugata haisenban
jack panel
ジャック型配線盤

jyamu
jam
ジャム

jyamu kenshutsu
jam detection
ジャム検出

jyamu kenshutsu sōchi
jam detection device
ジャム検出装置

jyānaru
journal
ジャーナル

jyānaru insatsu
journal printing
ジャーナル印刷

jyānaru-rōru-riida
journal roll reader
ジャーナル・ロール・リーダ

jyobu
job
ジョブ

jyobu-dekku
job deck
ジョブ・デック

jyobu-fairu
job file
ジョブ・ファイル

jyobu-fairu no sakuin
job file index
ジョブ・ファイルの索引

jyobu kaikei
job accounting
ジョブ会計

jyobu kaikei rūchin
job accounting routine
ジョブ会計ルーチン

jyobu kanri
job management
ジョブ管理

jyobu machigyōretsu
job queue
ジョブ待ち行列

jyobu-mikkusu
job mix
ジョブ・ミックス

jyobu nagare
job flow; job stream
ジョブ流れ

jyobu nagare seigyo
job flow control
ジョブ流れ制御

jyobu no hōki
job abort
ジョブの放棄

jyobu no owari (EOJ)
end of job (EOJ)
ジョブの終り

jyobu nyūryoku
job entry
ジョブ入力

jyobu-raiburari
job library
ジョブ・ライブラリ

jyobu-rogingu
job logging
ジョブ・ロギング

jyobu seigyo
job control
ジョブ制御

jyobu seigyo bun
job control statement
ジョブ制御文

jyobu seigyo burokku (JCB)
job control block (JCB)
ジョブ制御ブロック

jyobu seigyo gengo (JCL)
job control language (JCL)
ジョブ制御言語

jyobu seigyo puroguramu
job control program
ジョブ制御プログラム

jyobu seigyo sutētomento
job control statement
ジョブ制御ステートメント

jyobu-shoppu-operēshon
job shop operation
ジョブ・ショップ・
オペレーション

jyobu-shoppu-shimyurēshon
job shop simulation
ジョブ・ショップ・
シミュレーション

jyobu-shoppu-sukejyūringu
job shop scheduling
ジョブ・ショップ・
スケジューリング

jyobu shūryō (EOJ)
end of job (EOJ)
ジョブ終了

jyobu-sukejyūra
job scheduler
ジョブ・スケジューラ

jyobu-sukejyūringu
job scheduling
ジョブ・スケジューリング

jyobu-sutakku
job stack
ジョブ・スタック

jyobu-suteppu
job step
ジョブ・ステップ

jyobu-sutētomento
job statement
ジョブ・ステートメント

jyobu-sutoriimu
job stream
ジョブ・ストリーム

jyobu-taimu-rimitto
job time limit
ジョブ・タイム・リミット

jyobu yūsen jun'i
job priority
ジョブ優先順位

jyoi-suteikku
joy stick
ジョイ・スティック

K

k (kiro-) (10³ or 1,000)
k (kilo-) (10³ or 1,000)
k；キロ

K (kiro-) (2¹⁰ or 1,024)
K (kilo-) (2¹⁰ or 1,024)
K；キロ

kabu kami okuri
lower paper feed
下部紙送り

kachi
value
価値

kachi bunseki
value analysis
価値分析

kachi shisutemu
value system
価値システム

kachō keihō
alarm tone; audible alarm
可聴警報

kachō shūhasū (AF)
audio frequency (AF)
可聴周波数

kādo
card
カード

kadō
operation (action)
稼動

kado
transient
過渡

kādo bunruiki
card sorter
カード分類機

kādo-deisuku
card-to-disk
カード・ディスク

kādo-deisuku henkan
card-to-disk conversion
カード・ディスク変換

kādo-deisuku henkanki
card-to-disk converter
カード・ディスク変換器

kādo-dekku
card deck
カード・デック

kādo-fuairu
card file
カード・ファイル

kādo-fuēsu
card face
カード・フェース

kādo-fuiido
card feed
カード・フィード

kādo-fuiirudo
card field
カード・フィールド

kādo/fun (CPM)
cards per minute (CPM)
カード / 分

kādo-gēji
card gauge
カード・ゲージ

kādo-hoppa
card hopper
カード・ホッパ

kādo-imēji
card image
カード・イメージ

kadō jikan
operating time
稼動時間

kādo-jyamu
card jam
カード・ジャム

kādo keishiki
card format
カード形式

kādo kenkō
card verifying
カード検孔

kādo kenkōki
card verifier
カード検孔機

kādo-kōdo
card code
カード・コード

kādo no fuchi
card edge
カードの縁

kādo no keta
card column
カードの桁

kādo no kōen
card trailing edge
カードの後縁

kādo no omote
card face
カードの表

kādo no tsukiawase
card matching
カードの突き合わせ

kādo no zen'en
card leading edge
カードの前縁

kādo nyūryoku
card input
カード入力

kādo okuri
card feed
カード送り

kādo osae
card weight
カード押さえ

kado ōtō
transient response
過渡応答

kādo ran
card field
カード欄

kadō ritsu
operating ratio
稼動率

kādo-rō
card row
カード・ロー

kādo sekkei
card design
カード設計

kādo senkō
card punching
カードせん孔

kādo senkō sōchi (CP; PCM)
card punch (CP);
punch-card machine (PCM)
カードせん孔装置

kādo senkōki (CP; PCM)
card punch (CP);
punch-card machine (PCM)
カードせん孔機

kādo-shisutemu
card systems
カード・システム

kādo-sōta
card sorter
カード・ソータ

kādo-sutakka
card stacker
カード・スタッカ

kādo-tēpu
card-to-tape
カード・テープ

kādo-tēpu henkan
card-to-tape conversion
カード・テープ変換

kādo-tēpu henkanki
card-to-tape converter
カード・テープ変換器

kādo yomitori sōchi (CR)
card reader (CR)
カード読み取り装置

kādo yomitoriki (CR)
card reader (CR)
カード読み取り機

kafuka
overload; overloading
過負荷

kafuka kanshi
overload monitor
過負荷監視

kagaku keisan
scientific calculation
科学計算

kagaku keisan meirei setto
scientific instruction set
科学計算命令セット

kagakuteki dēta shori
scientific data processing
科学的データ処理

kagakuteki jōhō shisutemu
scientific information system
科学的情報システム

kagakuteki kanri
scientific management
科学的管理

kagaku'yō gengo
scientific language
科学用言語

kagaku'yō keisanki
scientific computer
科学用計算機

kagaku'yō shisutemu
scientific system
科学用システム

kagen enzanshi
adding operator
加減演算子

kagenzanki
adder-subtracter
加減算器

kagenzanki jikkō
adder-subtracter execution
加減算器実行

kagenzanki jikkō jikan
adder-subtracter execution time
加減算器実行時間

kagenzanki meirei
adder-subtracter instruction
加減算器命令

kagyaku(sei)
reversible
可逆(性)

kagyaku kaunta
reversible counter
可逆カウンタ

kagyakusei
reversibility
可逆性

kahen
variable
可変

kahen adoresu
variable address
可変アドレス

kahen burokku chō
variable block length
可変ブロック長

kahen chō
variable length
可変長

kahen chō adoresu shitei
variable-length addressing
可変長アドレス指定

kahen chō dēta
variable-length data
可変長データ

kahen chō fuiirudo
variable-length field
可変長フィールド

kahen chō go
variable-length word;
variable word
可変長語

kahen chō keishiki
variable format
可変長形式

kahen chō rekōdo
variable-length record
可変長レコード

kahen go chō
variable word length
可変語長

kahen-kahen burokku
variable-variable block
可変可変ブロック

kahen kansū zenerēta
variable function generator
可変関数ゼネレータ

kahen ketsugōshi
variable connector
可変結合子

kahen kigō
variable symbol
可変記号

kahen kotei burokku
variable fixed block
可変固定ブロック

kahen kōzō
variable structure
可変構造

kahen renketsu
variable binding
可変連結

kahen ronri
variable logic
可変論理

kahen seido
variable precision
可変精度

kahen shikii chi ronri (VTL)
variable threshold logic (VTL)
可変敷居値論理

kahen shōsūten
variable point
可変小数点

kahen shōsūten hyōji
variable-point representation
可変小数点表示

kahen shōsūten hyōji hō
variable-point representation
system
可変小数点表示法

kahen shūhasū hasshinki (VFO)
variable frequency oscillator
(VFO)
可変周波数発振器

kahen sokudo
variable speed
可変速度

kai
open
開

ka'i gainen
narrower term
下位概念

ka'i no
insignificant
下位の

ka'i no dēta
insignificant data
下位のデータ

ka'i no sūji
insignificant digit
下位の数字

kai rūpu
open loop
開ループ

kai rūpu seigyo
open-loop control
開ループ制御

kai rūpu-shisutemu
open-loop system
開ループ・システム

kaidan
step
階段

kaidanha
staircase
階段波

kaidoku
decoding
解読

kaidoku suru
decode
解読する

kaidokuki
decoder
解読器

kaifuku
recovery
回復

kaifuku kanri
recovery management
回復管理

kaifuku kanri sapōto (RMS)
recovery management support
(RMS)
回復管理サポート

kaifuku tejun
recovery procedure
回復手順

kaifuku ten
recovery point
回復点

kaifukufunō
unrecoverable
回復不能

kaifukufunō ayamari
unrecoverable error
回復不能誤り

kaifukukanō
recoverable
回復可能

kaifukukanō ayamari
recoverable error
回復可能誤り

kaifukusei
recoverability; recoverable
回復性

kaigai no tsūshin
overseas telecommunications
海外の通信

kaigi
conferencing
会議

kaigyō (LF)
line feed (LF)
改行

kaigyō fukki (CR)
carriage return (CR)
改行復帰

kaigyō fukki moji (NL)
new-line character (NL)
改行復帰文字

kaihatsu
development
開発

kaiheiki
circuit breaker
開閉器

kaihen
disintegration
壊変

kaihō
release
解放

kaijo
cancellation
解除

kaikei
accounting
会計

kaikei jōhō
accounting information
会計情報

kaikei rūchin
accounting routine
会計ルーチン

kaikei shisutemu
accounting system
会計システム

kaikeiki
accounting machine
会計機

kaiketa afure
underflow
下位桁溢れ

kaiketsu
solution
解決

kaiketsu funō
unsolvable
解決不能

kaiki
regression
回帰

kaiki bunseki
regression analysis
回帰分析

kaiki kyokusen
regression curve
回帰曲線

kainyū (operēta no)
intervention (from operator)
介入（オペレータの）

kainyū yōkyū
intervention required
介入要求

kairo
circuit
回路

kairo bōdo
circuit board
回路ボード

kairo kaiseki
circuit analysis
回路解析

kairo ronri
circuit logic
回路論理

kairomō
network
回路網

kairyō
amelioration
改良

kaiseki
analytic(al); analysis
解析

kaiseki kansū
analytical function
解析関数

kaiseki kansū zenerēta
analytical function generator
解析関数ゼネレータ

kaiseki moderu
analytical model
解析モデル

kaiseki shisutemu
analysis system
解析システム

kaisekihō
analysis method
解析法

kaisekiki
analyzer
解析器

kaisen
circuit; line (communication)
回線

kaisen adaputa
line adapter
回線アダプタ

kaisen bōdo
circuit board
回線ボード

kaisen bunseki
line analysis
回線分析

kaisen fuka
circuit load; line load
回線負荷

kaisen gurūpu
line group
回線グループ

kaisen hogo
line protection
回線保護

kaisen hogo sōchi
circuit protection device;
line protection device
回線保護装置

kaisen inpiidansu
line impedance
回線インピーダンス

kaisen intafuēsu
circuit interface; line interface
回線インタフェース

kaisen kōkan
circuit switching; line switching
回線交換

kaisen kōkan shisutemu
line-switching system
回線交換システム

kaisen kōkanmō
circuit-switched network;
line-switched network
回線交換網

kaisen no shurui
circuit grade
回線の種類

kaisen seigyo
line control
回線制御

kaisen seigyo burokku (LCB)
line control block (LCB)
回線制御ブロック

kaisen shūtan sōchi
line terminal
回線終端装置

kaisen sokudo
line speed
回線速度

kaisendan kenshutsu
line detection
回線断検出

kaisenmō
network
回線網

kaisenmō sōsain
network operator
回線網操作員

kaisetsu
decoding
解説

kaisetsu suru
decode
解説する

kaisetsu suru (fairu o)
open (a file) (*verb*)
開設する(ファイルを)

kaisetsusho
instruction book; manual
解説書

kaishaku
interpretive
解釈

kaishaku rūchin
interpretive routine
解釈ルーチン

kaishaku suru
interpret
解釈する

kaishi
initial; start
開始

kaishi adoresu
start address
開始アドレス

kaishi bun
initial statement
開始文

kaishi gyō
initial line
開始行

kaishi puroguramu
initiator
開始プログラム

kaishi puroguramu-shūshi puroguramu
initiator/terminator
開始プログラム-終止プログラム

kaishi shingō
start signal
開始信号

kaishi tasuku
initiating task
開始タスク

kaisō
hierarchy
階層

kaisō bunrui
hierarchical classification
階層分類

kaisō keisanki
hierarchical computer
階層計算機

kaisō kioku
hierarchical storage
階層記憶

kaisō kōzō
hierarchical structure
階層構造

kaisō shisutemu
hierarchy system
階層システム

kaisū
frequency; ratio
回数

kaitei
revised; revision
改訂

kaitei bangō
revision number
改訂番号

kaitei suru
revise
改訂する

kaiten
rotation
回転

kaiten machi jikan
latency time
回転待ち時間

kaiten suru
rotate
回転する

kaiwa(gata)
conversational
会話(型)

kaiwa mōdo
conversational mode
会話モード

kaiwagata
interactive
会話型

kaiwagata gengo
conversational language;
interactive language
会話型言語

kaiwagata gurafuikkusu
interactive graphics
会話型グラフィックス

kaiwagata jōhō shisutemu
interactive information system
会話型情報システム

kaiwagata konpaira
conversational compiler
会話型コンパイラ

kaiwagata mōdo
conversational/interactive mode
会話型モード

kaiwagata puroguramingu
interactive programming
会話型プログラミング

kaiwagata purosessa
interactive processor
会話型プロセッサ

kaiwagata shisutemu
interactive system
会話型システム

kaiwagata shori
conversational processing;
interactive processing
会話型処理

kaiwagata tanmatsu (sōchi)
interactive terminal
会話型端末（装置）

kaiwagata tasuku
interactive task
会話型タスク

kaiwagata yūteiritei
conversational utility
会話型ユーティリティ

kaiwagata zukei
interactive graphics
会話型図形

kaizōdo
resolution
解像度

kakidashi
writing
書き出し

kakidasu
write
書き出す

kakikomi
writing
書き込み

kakikomi heddo
write head
書き込みヘッド

kakikomi hogo
write protection
書き込み保護

kakikomi kinshi
write inhibit
書き込み禁止

kakikomi kinshi ringu
write-inhibit ring
書き込み禁止リング

kakikomi kyoka
enable
書き込み許可

kakikomi kyoka ringu
enable ring; write-permit ring
書き込み許可リング

kakikomi meirei
write instruction
書き込み命令

kakikomi ringu
write ring
書き込みリング

kakikomi saikuru taimu
write cycle time
書き込みサイクル・タイム

kakikomikanō seigyo sōchi (WCS)
writable control storage (WCS)
書き込み可能制御装置

kakikomu
write
書き込む

kakin
accounting
課金

kakin shori
accounts processing
課金処理

kakinaoshi
overwriting
書き直し

kakinaosu
overwrite
書き直す

kakōgata apurōchi
top-down approach
下降型アプローチ

kakōgata kaiseki
top-down parsing
下降型解析

kakōgata sekkei
top-down design
下降型設計

kaku
kernel
核

kakuchō
expansion; extended; extension
拡張

kakuchō (ESC)
escape (ESC)
拡張

kakuchō BASIC
extended BASIC
拡張 BASIC

kakuchō bunrui
extension sort
拡張分類

kakuchō gengo
extended language
拡張言語

kakuchō intafuēsu
expansion interface
拡張インタフェース

kakuchō kikō
expansion feature
拡張機構

kakuchō kioku
extended storage
拡張記憶

kakuchō moji
escape character
拡張文字

**kakuchō nisshinka jisshin kōdo
(EBCDIC)**
extended binary-coded decimal
interchange code (EBCDIC)
拡張 2 進化10進コード

kakuchō seido
extended precision
拡張精度

kakuchō seigyo
extended control
拡張制御

kakuchō sōto
extension sort
拡張ソート

kakuchō tan'i
extension unit
拡張単位

kakuchō yunitto
extension unit
拡張ユニット

kakuchōkanō
extensible; open-ended
拡張可能

kakuchōkanō gengo
extensible language
拡張可能言語

kakuchōkanō sekkei
open-ended design
拡張可能設計

kakunō dēta teigi gengo (SDDL)
stored data definition language
(SDDL)
格納データ定義言語

kakuritsu
probability
確率

kakuritsu katei
stochastic process
確率過程

kakuritsu kensa
probability check
確率検査

kakuritsu mitsudo kansū
probability density function
確率密度関数

kakuritsu otōmaton
probabilistic automaton
確率オートマトン

kakuritsu ron
probability theory
確率論

kakuritsuteki arugorizumu
probabilistic algorithm
確率的アルゴリズム

kakuritsuteki keikakuhō
stochastic programming
確率的計画法

kakuritsuteki kensaku
stochastic retrieval
確率的検索

kakuritsuteki kettei katei
stochastic decision process
確率的決定過程

kakuritsuteki shimyurēshon
stochastic simulation
確率的シミュレーション

kakuritsuteki shisutemu
probabilistic system
確率的システム

kakusan
diffusion
拡散

kakutei
defined; definition
確定

kakutei(teki)
deterministic
確定(的)

kakutei suru
define
確定する

kakuteiteki katei
deterministic process
確定的過程

kakuteiteki kensaku
deterministic retrieval
確定的検索

kakuteiteki moderu
deterministic model
確定的モデル

kakuteiteki shimyurēshon
deterministic simulation
確定的シミュレーション

kakuteiteki shisutemu
deterministic system
確定的システム

kami okuri
paper feed
紙送り

kami okuri kikō
carriage; paper feed mechanism
紙送り機構

kami okuri seigyo
carriage control
紙送り制御

kami okuri seigyo tēpu
carriage-control tape
紙送り制御テープ

kami tēpu
paper tape
紙送りテープ

kami tēpu kenkō
paper-tape verifying
紙テープ検孔

kami tēpu kenkōki
paper-tape verifier
紙テープ検孔機

kami tēpu-kōdo
paper-tape code
紙テープ・コード

kami tēpu-panchi (PTP)
paper-tape punch (PTP)
紙テープ・パンチ

kami tēpu-rūpu
paper loop; paper-tape loop
紙テープ・ループ

kami tēpu senkō sōchi (PTP)
paper-tape punch (PTP)
紙テープせん孔装置

kami tēpu senkōki (PTP)
paper-tape punch (PTP)
紙テープせん孔機

kami tēpu sōchi
paper-tape unit
紙テープ装置

kami tēpu yomitori sōchi (PTR)
paper-tape reader (PTR)
紙テープ読み取り装置

kami tēpu yomitoriki (PTR)
paper-tape reader (PTR)
紙テープ読み取り機

kami tobashiokuri
paper throw
紙飛ばし送り

kana
kana (Japanese characters)
仮名

kanamono
hardware
金物

kanamono hyōgen
hardware representation
金物表現

kando
sensitivity
感度

kangen
reduction
還元

kangen ritsu
reduction ratio
還元率

kan'i
spreadsheet
簡易

kan'i puroguramu
spreadsheet program
簡易プログラム

kanji
kanji (Chinese characters)
漢字

kanji denshin injiki
Chinese-character teleprinter
漢字電信印字機

kanji purinta
Chinese-character printer
漢字プリンタ

kanji terepurinta
Chinese-character teleprinter
漢字テレプリンタ

kanjō keisūki
ring counter
環状計数機

kanjō kōzō
ring structure
環状構造

kankaku
gap; interval; pitch; space;
spacing
間隔

kankaku keiji kikō
interval timer
間隔計時機構

kankaku keiji kikō warikomi
interval timer interruption
間隔計時機構割り込み

kankaku moji (SP)
space character (SP)
間隔文字

kankei
relation; relational
関係

kankei daisū
relational algebra
関係代数

kankei enzan
relational calculus
関係演算

kankei enzanshi
relational operator
関係演算子

kankei kōzō
relational structure
関係構造

kankei shiki
relational expression
関係式

kanketsu
intermittent
間欠

kanketsu ayamari
intermittent error
間欠誤り

kanketsu dōsa
intermittent action
間欠動作

kankyō
environment
環境

kankyō bu
environment division
環境部

kankyō ku
environment clause
環境句

kankyō shiken
environmental test
環境試験

kankyō shiyō
environment specification
環境仕様

kannetsushiki insho sōchi
thermal printer
感熱式印書装置

kanō
function (feature)
可能

kanren
relation; relational
関連

kanren dētabēsu
relational database
関連データベース

kanren gainengo
related term
関連概念語

kanri
control; management;
monitoring
管理

kanryaku kioku kigō
mnemonic symbol
簡略記憶記号

kanryaku kioku kōdo
mnemonic code
簡略記憶コード

kanryaku kiokugō
mnemonics
簡略記憶号

kanryaku mei
mnemonic name
簡略名

kanryaku meirei kōdo
mnemonic instruction code;
mnemonic operation codes
簡略命令コード

kanryō
completion
完了

kansa
auditing; audits
監査

kansa shisutemu
auditing system
監査システム

kansei
completion
完成

kansetsu
indirect
間接

kansetsu adoresu
indirect address
間接アドレス

kansetsu adoresu shitei
indirect addressing
間接アドレス指定

kansetsu meirei
indirect instruction
間接命令

kansetsu seigyo
indirect control
間接制御

kansetsu shutsuryoku
indirect output
間接出力

kanshi
control; executive; monitoring
監視

kanshi kōdo
monitor code
監視コード

kanshi mōdo
monitor mode
監視モード

kanshi moji
supervisory character
監視文字

kanshi puroguramu
executive program; monitor;
monitoring program; supervisor
(equipment); supervisory program
監視プログラム

kanshi puroguramu warikomi
monitor interrupt
監視プログラム割り込み

kanshi rūchin
monitor routine;
supervisory routine
監視ルーチン

kanshi seigyo
monitoring
監視制御

kanshi shisutemu
executive system; monitor(ing)
system; supervisory control
system; supervisory system
監視システム

kanshi sōsain
supervisor (person)
監視操作員

kanshi suru
control (*verb*); monitor (*verb*)
監視する

kanshi tanmatsu
monitor station
監視端末

kanshi'yō insho sōchi
monitor printer
監視用印書装置

kanshō
buffer
緩衝

kanshō kioku
buffer storage
緩衝記憶

kanshō kioku sōchi
buffer store
緩衝記憶装置

kanshō ryō'iki
buffer area
緩衝領域

kanshō shuhō
buffering
緩衝手法

kansoku
observation
観測

kansoku gyōretsu
observation matrix
観測行列

kansū
function (arithmetic)
関数

kansū hassei puroguramu
function generator
関数発生プログラム

kansū hasseiki
function generator
関数発生器

kansū hyō
function table
関数表

kansū hyōka
function evaluation
関数評価

kansū izon
functional dependence
関数依存

kansū kūkan
function space
関数空間

kansū sabupuroguramu
function subprogram
関数サブプログラム

kansū tēburu
function table
関数テーブル

kanyū
registration; subscription
加入

kanyūsen
subscriber's line
加入線

kanyūsha
subscriber
加入者

kanzensei
integrity
完全性

kapura
coupler
カプラ

karā
color
カラー

kara (NUL)
null (NUL)
空

karā-deisupurei
color display
カラー・ディスプレィ

karā-dekōda
color decoder
カラー・デコーダ

karā-kōdeingu
color coding
カラー・コーディング

karā-kōdo
color code
カラー・コード

karamu
column
カラム

karamu-bainari
column binary
カラム・バイナリ

karenda-kurokku
calendar clock
カレンダ・クロック

karento meirei rejisuta (CIR)
current instruction register (CIR)
カレント命令レジスタ

kari
borrow
借り

kari parameta
formal parameter
仮パラメタ

kasan (ADD)
addition (ADD)
加算

kasan hyō
addition table
加算表

kasan jikan
add time
加算時間

kasan suru
add
加算する

kasanegaki
overwriting
重ね書き

kasanegaku
overwrite
重ね書く

kasanki
adder; adding machine
加算器

kasetto
cassette
カセット

kasetto-doraibu
cassette drive
カセット・ドライブ

kasetto-rekōda
cassette recorder
カセット・レコーダ

kasetto sōchi
cassette handler
カセット装置

kasettogata jiki tēpu (CMT)
cassette magnetic tape (CMT)
カセット型磁気テープ

kasho
station; unit (office)
箇所

kashūri
repairable
可修理

kasō adoresu (VADR)
virtual address (VADR)
仮想アドレス

kasō adoresu kūkan
virtual address space
仮想アドレス空間

kasō adoresu shitei
virtual addressing
仮想アドレス指定

kasō kairo
virtual circuit
仮想回路

kasō keiro
virtual route
仮想経路

kasō keisanki
virtual machine
仮想計算機

kasō keisanki gijutsu
virtual machine technology
仮想計算機技術

kasō keisanki shisō
virtual machine philosophy
仮想計算機思想

kasō kekka
virtual result
仮想結果

kasō kioku
virtual memory; virtual storage
仮想記憶

kasō kioku akusesu hōshiki (VSAM)
virtual storage access method (VSAM)
仮想記憶アクセス方式

kasō kioku sōchi
virtual store
仮想記憶装置

kasō operēteingu-shisutemu
virtual operating system
仮想オペレーティング・システム

kasō tsūshin akusesu hōshiki (VTAM)
virtual telecommunications access method (VTAM)
仮想通信アクセス方式

kasoku
acceleration
加速

kasoku jikan
acceleration time
加速時間

kāsoru
cursor
カーソル

kāsoru-adoresu shitei
cursor addressing
カーソル・アドレス指定

kāsoru-kii
cursor key
カーソル・キー

kāsoru no ichi
cursor position
カーソルの位置

kasū
addend
加数

kasū
mantissa
仮数

kasukēdo bunrui
cascade sort
カスケード分類

kasukēdo seigyo
cascade control
カスケード制御

kasukēdoshiki keta age
cascaded carry
カスケード式桁上げ

kasutamu LSI
custom LSI
カスタム LSI

kasutamu-puroguramu
custom program
カスタム・プログラム

kata
model; type
型 / 形

kataji
superscript
肩字

katakōzō zu
skeleton structure diagram
型構造図

katarogu
catalog
カタログ

katayori
bias
偏り

katei
process (*noun*)
過程

kātorijji
cartridge
カードリッジ

kātorijji-deisuku
cartridge disk
カードリッジ・ディスク

kātorijji jiki tēpu (CRMT)
cartridge magnetic tape (CRMT)
カードリッジ磁気テープ

kātorijji yomitori sōchi
cartridge reader
カードリッジ読み取り装置

katsu jikei
type font
活字形

katsudō
active; activity
活動

katsudō fuairu
active file
活動ファイル

katsudō puroguramu
active program
活動プログラム

katsudō shiken
live testing
活動試験

katsudō sōsa
live operation
活動操作

katsudō tanmatsu
active station
活動端末

katsudō tasuku
active task
活動タスク

katsudō unten
live run
活動運転

katsudōka suru
activate
活動化する

katsudōsei
activity
活動性

katsuyō
activity
活用

katsuyōka
activation
活用化

katsuyōka suru
activate
活用化する

kaunta
counter
カウンタ

kaunto
count
カウント

kayōsei
availability
可用性

Kb (Kbitto; kirobitto)
Kb (kilobit)
Kb; K ビット; キロビット

KB (kirobaito)
KB (kilobyte)
KB; キロバイト

KB/s (kirobaito/byō)
KB/s (kilobytes per second)
KB/s; キロバイト / 秒

Kbitto (Kb)
kilobit (Kb)
K ビット

kēburu
cable
ケーブル

——— **ni tempu suru kēburu**
cable attached to ———
——— に添付するケーブル

keidenki
relay
継電器

kei'ei
management
経営

kei'ei jōhō
management information
経営情報

kei'ei jōhō (kanri) shisutemu (MIS)
management information system (MIS)
経営情報（管理）システム

kei'ei muki
management-oriented
経営向き

kei'ei sapōto-shisutemu
management support system
経営サポート・システム

keihō
alarm; warning
警報

keihō hyōji
alarm display
警報表示

keihō shisutemu
alarm system
警報システム

keihōki
warning device
警報器

keijikikō
timer
計時機構

keijō
shape
形状

keijō gōsei
shape synthesis
形状合成

keijō kōdo
shape code
形状コード

keijō tēburu
shape table
形状テーブル

keika jikan
elapsed time
経過時間

keika taima
elapsed timer
経過タイマ

keikaku
planning; project; schedule; scheduled
計画

keikaku hoshu
scheduled maintenance
計画保守

keikaku jōhō
planning information
計画情報

keikaku kagaku
planning science
計画科学

keikaku kettei
planning decision
計画決定

keikaku moderu
planning model
計画モデル

keikaku senryaku
planning strategy
計画戦略

keikaku shisutemu
planning system
計画システム

keikakuhō
programming
計画法

keikō
fluorescence
蛍光

keikoku
alarm; warning
警告

keikoku hyōji
alarm display
警告表示

keikoku messēji
warning message
警告メッセージ

keipabiritei
capability
ケイパビリティ

keipabiritei hyōtei shisū
capability rating index
ケイパビリティ評定指数

keipabiritei kikō
capability mechanism
ケイパビリティ機構

keiro
path; route
経路

keiro kaiseki
path analysis
経路解析

keiro kōzō
path structure
経路構造

keiro no nagasa
path length
経路の長さ

keiro saishitei
rerouting
経路再指定

keiro seigyo
path control
経路制御

keiro seigyo (RTC)
routing control (RTC)
経路制御

keiro sentaku
routing
経路選択

keiro shitei
routing
経路指定

keisan
calculation; computation;
computing
計算

keisan gosa
computing error
計算誤差

keisan junjo
computation sequence
計算順序

keisan kanō
computable
計算可能

keisan kanōsei
computability
計算可能性

keisan kii
calculation key
計算キー

keisan riron
theory of computation
計算理論

keisan suru
calculate; compute
計算する

keisangata
computational
計算型

keisanki
calculator
計算器

keisanki
computer
計算機

keisanki bēsu
computer-based
計算機ベース

keisanki bēsu gakushū (CBL)
computer-based learning (CBL)
計算機ベース学習

keisanki bēsu gakushū shisutemu
computer-based learning system
計算機ベース学習システム

keisanki bēsu jidōka
computer-based automation
計算機ベース自動化

keisanki bēsu jōhō-seigyo shisutemu
computer-based information and control system
計算機ベース情報-制御システム

keisanki bēsu kaigi shisutemu
computer-based conference system
計算機ベース会議システム

keisanki bēsu kanri shisutemu
computer-based management system
計算機ベース管理システム

keisanki bēsu-konsarutanto-shisutemu
computer-based consultant system
計算機ベース・コンサルタント・システム

keisanki bēsu kunren (CBT)
computer-based training (CBT)
計算機ベース訓練

keisanki bēsu kunren shisutemu
computer-based training system
計算機ベース訓練システム

keisanki bēsu seigyo
computer-based control
計算機ベース制御

keisanki bēsu seigyo-tsūshin shisutemu
computer-based control and communication system
計算機ベース制御-通信システム

keisanki bēsu seisan kanri shisutemu
computer-based production control system
計算機ベース生産管理システム

keisanki bēsu tsūshin shisutemu
computer-based communication system
計算機ベース通信システム

keisanki enjo gakushū (CAI)
computer-aided instruction (CAI)
計算機援助学習

keisanki enjo gakushū gengo (CAI'yō gengo)
computer-aided instruction language (CAI language)
計算機援助学習言語; CAI用言語

keisanki enjo seizō (CAM)
computer-aided manufacturing (CAM)
計算機援助製造

keisanki enjo sekkei (CAD)
computer-aided design (CAD)
計算機援助設計

keisanki enjo sekkei−keisanki enjo seizō (CADCAM)
computer-aided design−computer-aided manufacture (CADCAM)
計算機援助設計-計算機援助製造

keisanki en'yō gakushū (CAI)
computer-aided instruction (CAI)
計算機援用学習

keisanki en'yō gakushū (CAL)
computer-assisted learning (CAL)
計算機援用学習

keisanki en'yō gakushū gengo (CAI'yō gengo)
computer-aided instruction language (CAI language)
計算機援用学習言語; CAI用言語

keisanki en'yō kyōiku
computer-assisted teaching
計算機援用教育

keisanki en'yō seizō (CAM)
computer-aided manufacturing (CAM)
計算機援用製造

keisanki en'yō sekkei (CAD)
computer-aided design (CAD)
計算機援用設計

keisanki en'yō sekkei−keisanki en'yō seizō (CADCAM)
computer-aided design−computer-aided manufacture (CADCAM)
計算機援用設計-計算機援用製造

keisanki fukugōtai
computer complex
計算機複合体

keisanki gakushū
computer learning
計算機学習

keisanki gengo
computer language
計算機言語

keisanki izon gengo
computer-dependent language
計算機依存言語

keisanki jōhō
computer information
計算機情報

keisanki jōhō shien shisutemu
computer information support system
計算機情報支援システム

keisanki jōhō shisutemu
computer information system
計算機情報システム

keisanki josei dēta hyōka
computer-assisted data evaluation
計算機助成データ評価

keisanki josei dēta kaiseki (CADA)
computer-assisted data analysis (CADA)
計算機助成データ解析

keisanki josei gakushū (CAL)
computer-assisted learning (CAL)
計算機助成学習

keisanki josei kyōiku
computer-assisted teaching
計算機助成教育

keisanki kagaku
computer science
計算機科学

keisanki kanren
computer-related
計算機関連

keisanki kanren kagaku
computer-related science
計算機関連科学

keisanki kanri gakushū (CML)
computer-managed learning (CML)
計算機管理学習

keisanki kanri kyōiku (CMI)
computer-managed instruction (CMI)
計算機管理教育

keisanki kōdo
computer code
計算機コード

keisanki kōsei
computer configuration
計算機構成

keisanki meirei
computer instruction
計算機命令

keisanki moderu
computer model
計算機モデル

keisanki nettowāku
computer network
計算機ネットワーク

keisanki nettowāku gijutsu
computer networking technology
計算機ネットワーク技術

keisanki ōyō
computer application
計算機応用

keisanki puroguramu
computer program
計算機プログラム

keisanki riyō
computer application; computer-based
計算機利用

keisanki riyō gakushū (CAI)
computer-aided instruction (CAI)
計算機利用学習

keisanki riyō gakushū (CAL)
computer-assisted learning (CAL)
計算機利用学習

keisanki riyō gakushū (CBL)
computer-based learning (CBL)
計算機利用学習

keisanki riyō gakushū gengo (CAI'yō gengo)
computer-aided instruction language (CAI language)
計算機利用学習言語; CAI用言語

keisanki riyō kunren (CBT)
computer-based training (CBT)
計算機利用訓練

keisanki riyō kyōiku
computer-assisted teaching
計算機利用教育

keisanki riyō seizō (CAM)
computer-aided manufacturing (CAM)
計算機利用製造

keisanki riyō sekkei (CAD)
computer-aided design (CAD)
計算機利用設計

keisanki riyō sekkei–keisanki riyō seizō (CADCAM)
computer-aided design–computer-aided manufacture (CADCAM)
計算機利用設計-計算機利用製造

keisanki riyō shisutemu
computer application system
計算機利用システム

keisanki seigyo
computer control
計算機制御

keisanki seigyo (no)
computer-controlled
計算機制御(の)

keisanki seinō hyōka (CPE)
computer performance evaluation (CPE)
計算機性能評価

keisanki sekkei'yō gengo (CDL)
computer design language (CDL)
計算機設計用言語

keisanki setchi
computer installation
計算機設置

keisanki shimyurēshon
computer simulation
計算機シミュレーション

keisanki shisutemu
computer system
計算機システム

keisanki sōsa
computer operation
計算機操作

keisanki sōsain
computer operator
計算機操作員

keisanki tetsuzuki nagarezu
computer procedure flowchart
計算機手読き流れ図

keisanki wādo
computer word
計算機ワード

keisankika
computerized
計算機化

keisankika ishi kettei shisutemu
computerized decision-making system
計算機化意思決定システム

keisankika jōhō
computerized information
計算機化情報

keisankika jōhō shisutemu
computerized information system
計算機化情報システム

keisankika kei'ei jōhō shisutemu
computerized management information system
計算機化経営情報システム

keisankimō
computer network
計算機網

keisankimuki gengo
computer-oriented language
計算機向き言語

keisha
ramp
傾斜

keisha hichokusen hizumi
ramp nonlinearity
傾斜非直線歪み

keishiki
expression; form; formal
形式

keishiki (F)
format (F)
形式

keishiki gengo
formal language
形式言語

keishiki kōmoku
format item
形式項目

keishiki ronri
formal logic
形式論理

keishiki shiyō
formal specification
形式仕様

keishiki teigi
formal definition
形式定義

keisoku
instrumentation
計測

keisoku bunseki
instrumentation analysis
計測分析

keisoku kōgaku
instrumentation technology
計測工学

keisoku seigyo intafuēsu-kādo
instrumentation control interface card
計測制御インタフェース・カード

keisoku seigyo intafuēsu-mojyūru
instrumentation control interface module
計測制御インタフェース・モジュール

keisoku shisutemu
instrumentation system
計測システム

keisū
coefficient
係数

keisūgata
digital
計数型

keisūgata bibun kaisekiki (DDA)
digital differential analyzer (DDA)
計数型微分解析器

keisūgata keisanki
digital computer
計数型計算機

keisūka
digitization; digitized
計数化

keisūka suru
digitize
計数化する

keisūki
counter
計数器

keitai
form (expression; shape)
形態

keitai('yō)
portable
携帯（用）

keitaisei
portability
携帯性

keitai'yō dēta baitai
portable data medium
携帯用データ媒体

keitai'yō kēsu
carrying case
携帯用ケース

keitai'yō tanmatsu (sōchi)
portable remote terminal
携帯用端末（装置）

keitō gosa
systematic error
系統誤差

keitōteki
systematic
系統的

keiyaku puroguramingu
contract programming
契約プログラミング

keizoku
continuation
継続

keizoku gyō
continuation line
継続行

keizoku hyōji keta
continuation column
継続表示桁

kekka
result
結果

kekka tori
call by result
結果取り

kekkan
defect; fault
欠陥

kekkan no aru
defective
欠陥のある

kemban
keyboard
鍵盤

kemban hyōji sōchi
keyboard display
鍵盤表示装置

kemban insatsu sōchi
keyboard printer
鍵盤印刷装置

kemban nyūryoku
keyboard entry
鍵盤入力

kemban senkōki
key punch; keyboard perforator;
keyboard punch
鍵盤せん孔機

kemban sōjushin (KSR)
keyboard send/receive (KSR)
鍵盤送受信

kemban sōjushin sōchi
keyboard send/receive device
鍵盤送受信装置

kemban toiawase
keyboard inquiry
鍵盤問い合わせ

kempa
detection
検波

kempa suru
detect
検波する

kenkō
verification; verifying
検孔

kenkō suru
verify
検孔する

kenkōki
verifier
検孔機

kenkyū
research
研究

kensa
check (*noun*); inspection; test;
verification
検査

kensa ayamari
inspection error
検査誤り

kensa bitto
check bit
検査ビット

kensa gōkei
check sum
検査合計

kensa hōshiki
check system
検査方式

kensa kigō
check symbol
検査記号

kensa kinō
checking feature
検査機能

kensa moji
check character
検査文字

kensa puroguramu
checking program
検査プログラム

kensa rūchin
checking routine
検査ルーチン

kensa sūji
check digit
検査数字

kensa sūji keisan
check-digit calculation
検査数字計算

kensa sūji kenshō
check-digit verification
検査数字検証

kensa suru
verify
検査する

kensa tejun
inspection routine
検査手順

kensaku
interrogation; retrieval
検索

kensaku (ENQ)
enquiry (ENQ); inquiry
検索

kensaku kinō
retrieval function
検索機能

kensaku suru
retrieve
検索する

kensaku tanmatsu (sōchi)
interrogation terminal
検索端末（装置）

kenshō
verification; verifying
検証

kenshō gihō
verification technique
検証技法

kenshō katei
verification process
検証過程

kenshō suru
verify
検証する

kenshutsu
detection
検出

kenshutsu fugō
detecting code
検出符号

kenshutsu fugō saisōteisei hōshiki
request repeat system with
error-detecting code
検出符号再送訂正方式

kenshutsu hōshiki
detection system
検出方式

kenshutsu intafuēsu
connection interface
検出インタフェース

kenshutsu kairo
detection circuit
検出回路

kenshutsu suru
detect; identify (error); sense
(*verb*)
検出する

kenshutsuki
detector; sensor
検出器

kēsu-sutētomento
case statement
ケース・ステートメント

keta
column; digit
桁

keta age
carry
桁上げ

keta age hyōjishi
carry indicator
桁上げ表示子

keta age jikan
carry time
桁上げ時間

keta age kanryō shingō
carry complete signal
桁上げ完了信号

keta asshuku
digit compression
桁圧縮

keta hyōjiki
column indicator
桁表示器

keta ichi
digit position
桁位置

keta idō
shift
桁移動

keta idō kaunta
shift counter
桁移動カウンタ

keta idō meirei
shift instruction
桁移動命令

keta idō sū
shift count
桁移動数

keta okuri
shift
桁送り

ketsugō
association; coupling; union
結合

ketsugō asenburi
joint assembly
結合アセンブリ

ketsugōshi
connective; connector
結合子

kettei
decision
決定

kettei hyō
decision table
決定表

kettei kaiseki
decision analysis
決定解析

kettei katei
decision process
決定過程

kettei kijun
decision criteria
決定基準

kettei kikō
decision mechanism
決定機構

kettei riron
decision theory
決定理論

kettei seigyo
decision control
決定制御

kettei senryaku
decision strategy
決定戦略

ketteisei
deterministic
決定性

ketteisei gengo
deterministic language
決定性言語

ki
tree
木

ki kōzō
tree structure
木構造

ki kōzō gengo
tree-form language
木構造言語

kiban
board
基盤

kiban
substrate
基板

kibo
scale
規模

kichi jōhō
known information
既知情報

kichi kōzō
known structure
既知構造

kido
brightness
輝度

kidō
activation; start
起動

kidō botan
start button
起動ボタン

kidō jikan
starting time
起動時間

kidō kii
start key
起動キー

kidō saseru
activate
起動させる

kidō shingō
seizing signal
起動信号

kidō shisutemu
starter system
起動システム

kidō-teishi
start-stop
起動-停止

kidō-teishi jikan
start-stop time
起動-停止時間

kidōchū no
active
起動中の

kidōchū no burokku
active block
起動中のブロック

kigō
symbol
記号

kigō adoresu
symbolic address
記号アドレス

kigō adoresu shitei
symbolic addressing
記号アドレス指定

kigō gengo
symbolic language
記号言語

kigō hyō
symbol table
記号表

kigō hyōgen
symbolic representation
記号表現

kigō kōdeingu
symbolic coding
記号コーディング

kigō kōdo
symbolic code
記号コード

kigō mei
symbolic name
記号名

kigō meirei
symbolic instruction
記号命令

kigō no kihonretsu
proper string
記号の基本列

kigō operando
symbolic operand
記号オペランド

kigō puroguramingu
symbolic programming
記号プログラミング

kigō ronri
symbolic logic
記号論理

kigō shiki
notational system
記号式

kigō shori
symbol manipulation;
symbolic manipulation
記号処理

kigō shori gengo
symbol manipulation language
記号処理言語

kigō sutoringu
symbolic string
記号ストリング

kigōretsu hyōgen
string representation
記号列表現

kigōretsu shori
string processing
記号列処理

kigū
parity
奇偶

kigū kensa
even-odd check; odd-even
check; parity check
奇偶検査

kigū kensa ayamari
parity error
奇偶検査誤り

kigū kensa bitto
parity bit
奇偶検査ビット

kigyōnai jōhō tsūshinmō (LAN)
  local-area network (LAN)
  企業内情報通信網

kihatsu
  volatile
  揮発

kihatsusei
  volatility
  揮発性

kihatsusei kioku
  volatile memory; volatile storage
  揮発性記憶

kihon
  basic; master
  基本

kihon akusesu hōshiki (BAM)
  basic access method (BAM)
  基本アクセス方式

kihon asenbura
  basic assembler
  基本アセンブラ

kihon asenbura gengo (BAL)
  basic-assembler language (BAL)
  基本アセンブラ言語

kihon chokusetsu akusesu hōshiki (BDAM)
  basic direct-access method (BDAM)
  基本直接アクセス方式

kihon dēta go chō
  basic data word length
  基本データ語長

kihon fuairu
  master file
  基本ファイル

kihon gaibu kansū
  basic external function
  基本外部関数

kihon go chō
  basic word length
  基本語長

kihon hensū
  basic variable
  基本変数

kihon jitsu teisū
  basic real constant
  基本実定数

kihon junji akusesu hōshiki (BSAM)
  basic sequential access method (BSAM)
  基本順次アクセス方式

kihon kādo
  master card
  基本カード

kihon kigō
  basic symbol
  基本記号

kihon kii
  primary key
  基本キー

kihon kōmoku
  elementary item
  基本項目

kihon kōmoku tenki
  elementary item posting
  基本項目転記

kihon meirei
  basic instruction
  基本命令

kihon meirei setto
  basic-instruction set
  基本命令セット

kihon operēteingu-shisutemu (BOS)
  basic operating system (BOS)
  基本オペレーティング・システム

kihon renketsu
  basic linkage
  基本連結

kihon saikuru
  basic cycle
  基本サイクル

kihon sakuin jun akusesu hōshiki (BISAM)
  basic indexed sequential access method (BISAM)
  基本索引順アクセス方式

kihon sōsa
  elementary operation
  基本操作

kihon tsūshin akusesu hōshiki (BTAM)
  basic telecommunications access method (BTAM)
  基本通信アクセス方式

kihonbun
  basic statement
  基本文

kii
  key
  キー

kii-āgyumento
  key argument
  キー・アーギュメント

kii asshuku
  key depression
  キー圧縮

kii-entori
  key entry
  キー・エントリ

kii-entori iki
  key entry area
  キー・エントリ域

kii-fuiirudo
  key field
  キー・フィールド

kii hairetsu
  key arrangement
  キー配列

kii henkan
  key transformation
  キー変換

kii-in suru
  key in (*verb*)
  キー・インする

kii jun
  key sequence
  キー順

kii kenkō
  key verify
  キー検孔

kii-kurikka
  key click
  キー・クリッカ

kii-memori
  key memory
  キー・メモリ

kii no nai rekōdo
  unkeyed record
  キーのないレコード

kii no ryakujika
  key abbreviation
  キーの略字化

kii-panchi
key punch
キー・パンチ

kii-parusu
key pulse
キー・パルス

kii-rōōba
key rollover
キー・ローオーバ

kii seisei
key generation
キー生成

kii sū
key number
キー数

kii-sutēshon
key station
キー・ステーション

kii-tsū-deisuketto
key-to-diskette
キー・ツー・ディスケット

kii-tsū-deisuku
key-to-disk
キー・ツー・ディスク

kii-tsū-deisuku sōchi
key-to-disk unit
キー・ツー・ディスク装置

kii-tsū-furoppi-deisuku
key-to–floppy disk
キー・ツー・フロッピ・ディスク

kii-tsū-kasetto
key-to-cassette
キー・ツー・カセット

kii-tsū-tēpu
key-to-tape
キー・ツー・テープ

kii ware
key break
キー割れ

kiibōdo
keyboard
キーボード

kiibōdo-dēta
keyboard data
キーボード・データ

kiibōdo kaikeiki
keyboard accounting machine
キーボード会計機

kiibōdo-konekuta
keyboard connector
キーボード・コネクタ

kiipaddo
keypad
キーパッド

kiiwādo
keyword
キーワード

kijihō
notation
記示法

kijō kensa
dry run
机上検査

kijun
base; criteria; criterion; reference
基準

kijun adoresu
base address
基準アドレス

kijun adoresu-rejisuta
base address register
基準アドレス・レジスタ

kijun'en
reference edge
基準縁

kijun gengo
reference language
基準言語

kijun hakei
reference waveform
基準波形

kijun jikai
reference field
基準磁界

kijun noizu
reference noise
基準ノイズ

kijun nyūryoku
reference input
基準入力

kijun onryō
reference volume
基準音量

kijun reberu
reference level
基準レベル

kijun rejisuta (br)
base register (br)
基準レジスタ

kijunka
scale; scaling
基準化

kijunka insū
scale factor
基準化因数

kijutsu
description
記述

kijutsukō
entry
記述項

kijutsushi
descriptor
記述子

kijutsuteki parameta
descriptive parameter
記述的パラメタ

kikai
machine; mechanical
機械

kikai ayamari
machine error
機械誤り

kikai chekku
machine check
機械チェック

kikai chekku warikomi
machine-check interruption
機械チェック割り込み

kikai chinō
machine intelligence
機械知能

kikai enjo
machine-aided
機械援助

kikai enjo ninchi
machine-aided cognition
機械援助認知

kikai gakushū
machine learning
機械学習

kikai gengo
machine language
機械言語

345

kikai go
machine word
機械語

kikai godōsa
machine malfunction
機械誤動作

kikai hōhō
mechanical method
機械方法

kikai hon'yaku
machine translation;
mechanical translation
機械翻訳

kikai ishi kettei
machine decision
機械意思決定

kikai izon
machine dependence;
machine-dependent
機械依存

kikai kadoku
machine-sensible
機械可読

kikai kadoku baitai
machine-readable medium
機械可読媒体

kikai kadoku hō
machine-sensible form
機械可読法

kikai kadoku jōhō
machine-sensible information
機械可読情報

kikai kara dokuritsu
machine independence;
machine-independent
機械から独立

kikai kijutsu go
machine description language
機械記述語

kikai kōdo
machine code
機械コード

kikai kōsei
machine configuration
機械構成

kikai muki gengo
machine-oriented language
機械向き言語

kikai puroguramu
machine program
機械プログラム

kikai ronri
machine logic
機械論理

kikai saikuru
machine cycle
機械サイクル

kikai seigyo
machine control;
machine monitoring
機械制御

kikai sōsa
machine operation
機械操作

kikai sōsa'in
machine operator
機械操作員

kikaigo
absolute language;
machine language
機械語

kikaigo adoresu
machine address
機械語アドレス

kikaigo kōdeingu
machine language coding
機械語コーディング

kikaigo meirei
absolute instruction;
machine instruction
機械語命令

kikaigo puroguramingu
absolute programming
機械語プログラミング

kikaika
mechanization
機械化

kikaika mondai
mechanization problem
機械化問題

kikaiteki shisutemu
mechanistic system
機械的システム

kikan
feedback
帰還

kikan hōshiki
feedback system
帰還方式

kiken
critical
危険

kiken chi'iki
critical section
危険地域

kiken ryō'iki
critical region
危険領域

kiki
equipment; function (feature)
機器

kiki (no) gokansei
equipment compatibility
機器(の)互換性

kiki kensa
equipment check
機器検査

kiki koshō
equipment failure
機器故障

kiki seigyo kōdo
function code
機器制御コード

kikō
feature; function; station
機構

kikō kanri
facilities management
機構管理

kiko kyoku
calling station
起呼局

kimatta dēta mei
fixed data name
決まったデータ名

kimitsu
privacy
機密

kimitsu hogo
computer security; security
機密保護

kimitsu hoji
security protection
機密保持

kimitsu jō
privacy lock
機密錠

kimitsu jō tetsuzuki
privacy lock procedure
機密錠手続き

kimitsu kii
privacy key
機密キー

kimitsu no dankai
security class
機密の段階

kinissei
uniformity
均一性

kinitsu
uniformity
均一

kinji
approximation
近似

kinkyū
emergency; urgent
緊急

kinkyū dōsa
emergency action
緊急動作

kinkyū hoshu
emergency maintenance
緊急保守

kinkyū shingō
emergency signal
緊急信号

kinkyū teishi
emergency shutdown
緊急停止

kinō
capability; facility; feature;
function (feature)
機能

kinō burokku
functional block
機能ブロック

kinō debaisu
functional device
機能デバイス

kinō hyō
function table
機能表

kinō hyōjishi
role indicator
機能表示子

kinō jōhō
functional information
機能情報

kinō jōhō shisutemu
functional information system
機能情報システム

kinō kii
function key
機能キー

kinō kyarakuta
functional character
機能キャラクタ

kinō makuro meirei
functional macroinstruction
機能マクロ命令

kinō mokuteki
functional objective
機能目的

kinō sekkei
functional design
機能設計

kinō shindan tesuto
diagnostic function test
機能診断テスト

kinō shisutemu
functional system
機能システム

kinō soshi
function element
機能素子

kinō tēburu
function table
機能テーブル

kinō teishi
stall
機能停止

kinō tesuto
functional test
機能テスト

kinō zu
function(al) diagram
機能図

kinōsei
functionality
機能性

kinshi
inhibit
禁止

kinshi kumiawase
forbidden combination
禁止組み合わせ

kinshi moji fugō
forbidden character code
禁止文字符号

kinshi shingō
inhibiting signal
禁止信号

kinyū
entry
記入

kinyū baffua
entry buffer
記入バッファ

kioku
storing
記憶

kioku (sōchi)
memory; storage
記憶(装置)

kioku adoresu-rejisuta (MAR)
memory address register (MAR)
記憶アドレス・レジスタ

kioku asshuku
memory compaction
記憶圧縮

kioku ayamari
memory error
記憶誤り

kioku ayamari hyōjishi
memory-error indicator
記憶誤り表示子

kioku baitai
storage medium
記憶媒体

kioku basho
memory location;
storage location
記憶場所

kioku bōdo
memory board
記憶ボード

kioku burokku
storage block
記憶ブロック

kioku chizu
memory map
記憶地図

kioku danpu
storage dump
記憶ダンプ

kioku dēta
stored data
記憶データ

kioku dēta-rejisuta
memory data register
記憶データ・レジスタ

kioku('iki) hogo
memory protection;
storage protection
記憶(域)保護

kioku hogo kii
storage protection key
記憶保護キー

kioku hogo kikō
storage protection feature
記憶保護機構

kioku hōshiki
memory system; storage system
記憶方式

kioku ichi
location; store location
記憶位置

kioku ichi kaunta
location counter
記憶位置カウンタ

kioku'iki
area; memory area; storage area
記憶域

kioku'iki hensei
memory constitution
記憶域編成

kioku'iki kanri
memory management
記憶域管理

kioku'iki rokku-auto
memory lockout
記憶域ロック・アウト

kioku'iki sairiyō
storage reclaim
記憶域再利用

kioku'iki shiyō ni tai suru kakin
memory usage accounting
記憶域使用に対する課金

kioku'iki shōtotsu
memory interference
記憶域衝突

kioku'iki sōdatsu
memory contention
記憶域争奪

kioku'iki teigi
area definition
記憶域定義

kioku'iki teigi bun
define storage statement
記憶域定義文

kioku jōchū operēteingu-shisutemu
memory-resident operating
system
記憶常駐オペレーティング・
システム

kioku kādo
memory card
記憶カード

kioku kaisō
memory hierarchy
記憶階層

kioku kii
storage key
記憶キー

kioku kōkan shisutemu
memory switching system
記憶交換システム

kioku kūkan
storage space
記憶空間

kioku mappingu
memory mapping
記憶マッピング

kioku mitsudo
recording density
記憶密度

kioku mojyūru
memory module
記憶モジュール

kioku rejisuta
memory register; storage register
記憶レジスタ

kioku rejisuta (MBR)
memory buffer register (MBR)
記憶レジスタ

kioku ryō'iki
memory area; storage area
記憶領域

kioku saikuru
memory cycle; storage cycle;
store cycle
記憶サイクル

kioku saikuru jikan
storage cycle time
記憶サイクル時間

kioku saikuru-taimu
store cycle time
記憶サイクル・タイム

kioku saisei
regeneration
記憶再生

kioku seigyo
storage control
記憶制御

kioku seigyo no
memory-controlled
記憶制御の

kioku seru
memory cell
記憶セル

kioku shazō
memory mapping
記憶写像

kioku shien
memory support
記憶支援

kioku shien shisutemu
memory support system
記憶支援システム

kioku sōchi
memory system; storage device;
storage equipment; storage unit;
store (*noun*)
記憶装置

kioku sokudo
storage speed
記憶速度

kioku sōsa
storage operation
記憶操作

kioku soshi
storage element
記憶素子

kioku suru
store (*verb*)
記憶する

kioku sutakku
storage stack
記憶スタック

kioku('iki) wariate
memory allocation;
storage allocation
記憶(域)割り当て

kioku wariatezu
storage map
記憶割り当て図

kioku('iki) waritsuke
storage allocation
記憶(域)割り付け

kioku yōryō
memory capacity; memory size;
storage capacity
記憶容量

kioku zokusei
storage attribute
記憶属性

kiriage
rounding up
切り上げ

kiriageru
round up (*verb*)
切り上げる

kirihanashi
disconnection
切り離し

kirihanasu
disconnect
切り離す

kirikae
switch; switching
切り換え

kirikae jikan
switching time
切り換え時間

kirikae sokudo
switching speed
切り換え速度

kirikaeru
switch over (*verb*)
切り換える

kirisute
rounding down; truncation
切り捨て

kirisute gosa
truncation error
切り捨て誤差

kirisuteru
round down (*verb*)
切り捨てる

kiro (k) (10³ or 1,000)
kilo (k) (10³ or 1,000)
k; キロ

kiro (K) (2¹⁰ or 1,024)
kilo (K) (2¹⁰ or 1,024)
K; キロ

kirobaito (KB)
kilobyte (KB)
KB; キロバイト

kirobaito/byō (KB/s)
kilobytes per second (KB/s)
KB/s; キロバイト／秒

kirobitto (Kb)
kilobit (Kb)
Kb; キロビット

kirobō
kilobaud
キロボー

kiroku
archive; archiving; log; record;
recording
記録

kiroku baitai
recording medium
記録媒体

kiroku heddo
recording head
記録ヘッド

kiroku mitsudo
packing density;
recording density
記録密度

kiroku suru
record (*verb*)
記録する

kiroku torakku
recording track
記録トラック

kiroku'yō tēpu
recording tape
記録用テープ

kirokuki
inscriber; recorder
記録機

kirosaikuru
kilocycle
キロサイクル

kisetsu hendō
seasonal variation
季節変動

kisū
base number; basic number;
radix
基数

kisū henkan
radix conversion
基数変換

kisū hyōkihō
base notation; radix notation;
radix numeration system
基数表記法

kisū kensa
odd check
基数検査

kisū mainasu ichi no hosū
radix-minus-one complement
基数マイナス1の補数

kisū no hosū
radix complement
基数の補数

kisū paritei
odd parity
基数パリティ

kisū paritei kensa
odd-parity check
基数パリティ検査

349

kisūhō
number representation system;
number system; numeration
system
基数法

kisūhō bunrui
radix sort
基数法分類

kitai chi
expected value
期待値

kitai ōtō
expected response
期待応答

kitei
base
基底

kitei
defined; definition; predefined
規定

kitei adoresu
base address
基底アドレス

kitei adoresu-rejisuta
base-address register
基底アドレス・レジスタ

kitei rejisuta (br)
base register (br)
基底レジスタ

kitei suru
define
規定する

kiteikai
basic solution
基底解

kiteitsuki kioku'iki
based storage
基底付き記憶域

kiten
origin; radix point
基点

kiyaku
protocol
規約

ko
member
子

kō
term
項

ko no jōken
member condition
子の条件

kō reberu (H)
high (H)
高レベル

ko rekōdo
member record
子レコード

koa
core
コア

koa-danpu
core dump
コア・ダンプ

koa-imēji
core image
コア・イメージ

koa-purein
core plane
コア・プレィン

kōban nishin kōdo
reflected binary code
交番2進コード

kobetsu
single
個別

kobetsu asenburi
separate assembly
個別アセンブリ

kobetsu buhin
discrete component;
discrete part
個別部品

kobetsu dembun
individual message
個別電文

kobetsu dēta kōzō kijutsukō
subschema description entry;
subschema entry
個別データ構造記述項

kobetsu dēta kōzō kijutsumei
subschema name
個別データ構造記述名

kobetsu dēta kōzō kijutsusetsu
subschema section
個別データ構造記述節

kobetsu messēji dōhō
simultaneous distribution of
single messages
個別メッセージ同報

Koboru (COBOL)
Common Business-Oriented
Language (COBOL)
コボル

Koboru moji
COBOL character
コボル文字

kōbun
syntax
構文

kōbun ayamari
syntax error
構文誤り

kōbun kaiseki
syntax analysis
構文解析

kōbun kaisekizu
syntax diagram
構文解析図

kōchigata keisanki
back-end computer
後置型計算機

kōchigata purosessa
back-end processor
後置型プロセッサ

kōchiku suru
build (a system) (*verb*)
構築する

kōda
coder
コーダ

kōdeingu
coding
コーディング

kōdeingu gyō
coding line
コーディング行

kōdeingu yōshi
coding sheet
コーディング用紙

kōdeingu-yunitto
coding unit
コーディング・ユニット

kōdenshiki yomitori sōchi
photoelectric reader
光電式読み取り装置

kōdo
advanced (development)
高度

kōdō
behavior
行動

kōdo
code
コード

kōdo-bukku
code book
コード・ブック

kōdo-chekku
code check
コード・チェック

kōdo chi
code value
コード値

kōdo henkan
code conversion
コード変換

kōdo henkanki
code converter
コード変換器

kōdo hon'yaku
code translation
コード翻訳

kōdo hyō
code table
コード表

kōdo-imēji
code image
コード・イメージ

kōdo-imēji yomitori
code image read
コード・イメージ読み取り

kōdo jōhō shisutemu
advanced information system(s)
高度情報システム

kōdo kakuchō moji
code extension character
コード拡張文字

kōdo kyori
code distance
コード距離

kōdo seigyo
advanced control
高度制御

kōdo seigyo shisutemu
advanced control system
高度制御システム

kōdo-setto
code set
コード・セット

kōdo shisutemu
advanced system(s)
高度システム

kōdo shisutemu gijutsu
advanced system technology
高度システム技術

kōdo shisutemu kaihatsu
advanced system development
高度システム開発

kōdo taikei
coding system
コード体系

kōdo yōso
code element
コード要素

kōdoka
coding; encoding
コード化

kōdoka jisshinhō
coded decimal notation
コード化10進法

kōdoka jisshinsū
coded decimal
コード化10進数

kōdoka suru
encode
コード化する

koe gōsei
voice synthesis
声合成

kōen
trailing edge
後縁

kōfu
breakdown
降伏

kōgaku bā-kōdo yomitori sōchi
optical bar-code reader
光学バー・コード読み取り装置

kōgaku taipu fuonto
optical type font
光学タイプ・フォント

kōgakushiki
optical
光学式

kōgakushiki deisuku
optical disk
光学式ディスク

kōgakushiki kioku shisutemu
optical memory system
光学式記憶システム

kōgakushiki māku
optical mark
光学式マーク

kōgakushiki māku fugōka
optical mark encoding
光学式マーク符号化

kōgakushiki māku-kōdoka
optical mark encoding
光学式マーク・コード化

kōgakushiki māku ninshiki (OMR)
optical mark recognition (OMR)
光学式マーク認識

kōgakushiki māku yomitori
optical mark reading
光学式マーク読み取り

kōgakushiki māku yomitori sōchi (OMR)
optical mark reader (OMR)
光学式マーク読み取り装置

kōgakushiki moji
optical character
光学式文字

kōgakushiki moji fugōka
optical character encoding
光学式文字符号化

kōgakushiki moji kenshō
optical character verification
光学式文字検証

kōgakushiki moji kōdoka
optical character encoding
光学式文字コード化

kōgakushiki moji ninshiki (OCR)
optical character recognition (OCR)
光学式文字認識

kōgakushiki moji yomitori sōchi (OCR)
optical character reader (OCR)
光学式文字読み取り装置

kōgakushiki sōsa
optical scanning; visual scanning
光学式走査

kōgakushiki sōsa kikō
optical scanner; visual scanner
光学式走査機構

kōgakushiki yomitori sōchi
optical reader
光学式読み取り装置

kogataka
miniaturization
小形化

kōgo
alternate
交互

kōgu
tool
工具

kōgyō otomēshon
industrial automation
工業オトメーション

kōgyō otomēshon-shisutemu
industrial automation system
工業オトメーション・システム

kōgyō'yō dēta shori
industrial data processing
工業用データ処理

kōgyō'yō jōhō shisutemu
industrial information system
工業用情報システム

kōgyō'yō keisanki
industrial computer
工業用計算機

kōgyō'yō keisanki shisutemu
industrial computer system
工業用計算機システム

kōgyō'yō shisutemu
industrial system
工業用システム

kōi (H)
high (H)
高位

kō'iki
wide area
広域

kō'iki dēta-sābisu (WADS)
wide-area data service (WADS)
広域データ・サービス

kō'iki nettowāku (WAN)
wide-area network (WAN)
広域ネットワーク

kojin
personal
個人

kojin kōdo
personal code
個人コード

kojin shikibetsu bangō (PIN)
personal identification number (PIN)
個人識別番号

kojin shikibetsu sōchi (PID)
personal identification device (PID)
個人識別装置

kojinka
personalization
個人化

kojinka dētabēsu-shisutemu
personalized database system
個人化データベース・システム

kōjun
descending order
降順

kōkaizōdo
high resolution
高解像度

kōkaizōdo zukei
high-resolution graphics
高解像度図形

kōkan
exchange; interchange; switching
交換

kōkan hōshiki
exchange system
交換方式

kōkan kaisen
switched line
交換回線

kōkan kaisenmō
switched circuit
交換回線網

kōkan kanōsei
interchangeability
交換可能性

kōkan kanshō hōshiki
exchange buffering
交換緩衝方式

kōkan kikō
switching device
交換機構

kōkan rejisuta
exchange register
交換レジスタ

kōkan riron
switching theory
交換理論

kōkan sābisu
exchange service
交換サービス

kōkankanō
interchangeable
交換可能

kōkankanō deisuku
exchangeable disk
交換可能ディスク

kōkankanō deisuku kioku sōchi (EDS)
exchangeable disk store (EDS)
交換可能ディスク記憶装置

kōkankanō jiki deisuku
exchangeable magnetic disk
交換可能磁気ディスク

kōkankyoku
exchange; switching center
交換局

kōkanmō
switched network
交換網

kōkanmō seigyo
switched-network control
交換網制御

kōketsugō
tight coupling
硬結合

kokuji parusu
clock pulse
刻時パルス

kokuji rejisuta
clock register
刻時レジスタ

kokuji sōchi
clock
刻時装置

kokuji sōsa
clock scan
刻時走査

kokusai(teki)
universal
国際(的)

Kokusai Denki Hyōjun Kaigi (IEC)
International Electrotechnical
Commission (IEC)
国際電気標準会議

Kokusai Denki Tsūshin Rengō (ITU)
International Telecommunication
Union (ITU)
国際電気通信連合

Kokusai Hyōjunka Kikō (ISO)
International Organization for
Standardization; International
Standards Organization (ISO)
国際標準化機構

Kokusai Jidō Seigyo Rengō (IFAC)
International Federation for
Automatic Control (IFAC)
国際自動制御連合

kokusai jisshin bunruihō (UDC)
universal decimal classification
(UDC)
国際10進分類法

Kokusai Jōhō Shori Rengō (IFIP)
International Federation for
Information Processing (IFIP)
国際情報処理連合

komando
command
コマンド

komando gengo
command language
コマンド言語

kōmoku
entry; item
項目

kōnai
local
構内

kōnai sōsa
local operation
構内操作

kōnai tanmatsu
local station
構内端末

kōnai tanmatsu (sōchi)
local terminal
構内端末(装置)

konbāta
converter
コンバータ

kondeishon-kōdo (CC)
condition code (CC)
コンディション・コード

kondensa
capacitor
コンデンサ

kondensa kioku
capacitor storage
コンデンサ記憶

kondensa kioku sōchi
capacitor store
コンデンサ記憶装置

konekuta
connector
コネクタ

konekuta-pin
connector pins
コネクタ・ピン

kongō enzan
mixed-mode operation
混合演算

kongō kisū
mixed radix
混合基数

kongō kisū hyōkihō
mixed-base notation; mixed-base
numeration system; mixed-radix
notation
混合基数表記法

kongō mōdo
mixed mode
混合モード

kongō sanjutsu shiki
mixed-type arithmetic expression
混合算術式

kongō seisū keikakuhō (MIP)
mixed integer programming (MIP)
混合整数計画法

konnyū suru
erā ga shisutemu ni konnyū suru
get into
an error gets into a system
混入する
エラーがシステムに混入する

konpaira
compiler
コンパイラ

konpaira gengo
compiler language
コンパイラ言語

konpaira-konpaira
compiler-compiler
コンパイラ・コンパイラ

konpaira ni yoru saitekika
compiler optimization
コンパイラによる最適化

konpaira-zenerēta
compiler generator
コンパイラ・ゼネレータ

konpairēshon
compilation
コンパイレーション

konpairēshon ayamari
compilation error
コンパイレーション誤り

konpairēshon-ran
compilation run
コンパイレーション・ラン

konpairingu
compiling
コンパイリング

konpairingu keisanki
compiling computer
コンパイリング計算機

konpairingu-shisutemu
compiling system
コンパイリング・システム

353

konpairu jikan
compilation time; compile time
コンパイル時間

konpairu suru
compile
コンパイルする

konpateibiritei
compatibility
コンパティビリティ

konpojitto-bideo
composite video
コンポジット・ビデオ

konponento
component
コンポーネント

konpyūta
computer
コンピュータ

konpyūta-ākitekucha
computer architecture
コンピュータ・アーキテクチャ

konpyūta-animēshon
computer animation
コンピュータ・アニメーション

konpyūta-āto
computer art
コンピュータ・アート

konpyūta-byūrō
computer bureau
コンピュータ・ビューロー

konpyūta-gurafuikkusu
computer graphics
コンピュータ・グラフィックス

konpyūta-gurafuikkusu-shimyurēshon
computer graphics simulation
コンピュータ・グラフィックス・
シミュレーション

konpyūta-hobiisuto
computer hobbyist
コンピュータ・ホビースト

konpyūta-kōdo
computer code
コンピュータ・コード

konpyūta nyūryoku maikurofuirumu (CIM)
computer input microfilming;
computer input on microfilm (CIM)
コンピュータ入力マイクロフィルム

konpyūta-operēta
computer operator
コンピュータ・オペレータ

konpyūta-ran
computer run
コンピュータ・ラン

konpyūta-ran-chāto
computer run chart
コンピュータ・ラン・チャート

konpyūta shutsuryoku maikurofuirumu (COM)
computer output microfilming;
computer output on microfilm (COM)
コンピュータ出力マイクロフィルム

konpyūta-yūteiritei
computer utility
コンピュータ・ユーティリティ

konpyūtauea
computerware
コンピュータウェア

konsatsu
congestion
混雑

konsei
hybrid
混成

konsei IC
hybrid IC
混成 IC

konsei jissō
hybrid package
混成実装

konsei kairo
hybrid circuit
混成回路

konsei shūseki kairo
hybrid integrated circuit
混成集積回路

konsoru
console
コンソル

kontenshon
contention
コンテンション

kontorasuto
contrast
コントラスト

kopii suru
copy (verb)
コピーする

kopurosessa
coprocessor
コプロセッサ

kōreberu-dēta-rinku seigyo (HDLC)
high-level data link control (HDLC)
高レベル・データ・リンク制御

kōreberu-dēta-rinku seigyo tejun
high-level data link control procedure
高レベル・データ・リンク制御手順

kōreberu gengo
high-level language
高レベル言語

kōreberu ishi kettei
high-level decision making
高レベル意思決定

korekuta
collector
コレクタ

kōritsu
efficiency
効率

koritsu
isolation
孤立

koritsu kioku ichi
isolated locations
孤立記憶位置

koritsu shita dēta
orphan
孤立したデータ

kōru
call
コール

kōru-bakku
call-back
コール・バック

kōru meirei
call instruction
コール命令

korūchin
coroutine
コルーチン

korudo-sutāto
cold start
コルド・スタート

korudo-taipu-shisutemu (CTS)
cold-type system (CTS)
コルド・タイプ・システム

kōrui
category
項類

koryō
traffic intensity
呼量

kōryū (AC)
alternating current (AC)
交流

kōsa
intersection
交差

kōsei
configuration
構成

kōsei yōso
component
構成要素

kōshi
chart; grid
格子

kōshi seigyo
grid control
格子制御

kōshikiichi ronri (HTL)
high-threshold logic (HTL)
高敷居値論理

kōshin
communication
交信

kōshin
updating
更新

kōshin bangō
update number
更新番号

kōshin ran
update run
更新ラン

kōshin rūchin
update routine
更新ルーチン

kōshin suru
update (*verb*)
更新する

kōshinraido
high reliability
高信頼度

kōshinraisei
high reliability
高信頼性

koshō
breakdown; failure; fault
故障

koshō bunri
fault isolation
故障分離

koshō hakken
fault finding; fault location
故障発見

koshō hakken mondai
fault location problem
故障発見問題

koshō jikan
downtime; fault time
故障時間

koshō jōchō(do)
fault redundancy
故障冗長(度)

koshō kakuritsu
failure probability
故障確率

koshō kenchisei
fault detectability
故障検知性

koshō kikō
failure mechanism
故障機構

koshō kyoyō
fault tolerance
故障許容

koshō kyoyō shisutemu
fault-tolerant system
故障許容システム

koshō mōdo dōsa
crippled mode operation;
graceful degradation
故障モード動作

koshō ritsu
failure rate
故障率

koshō saishōka
failure minimization
故障最小化

koshō seigyo
fault monitoring
故障制御

koshō shikibetsu
failure identification
故障識別

kōshū dēta mō
public data network
公衆データ網

kōsoku(do)
high speed
高速(度)

kōsoku akusesu
fast access; high-speed access
高速アクセス

kōsoku bosen
high-speed bus
高速母線

kōsoku Fūrie henkan (FFT)
fast Fourier transform (FFT)
高速フーリェ変換

kōsoku insho sōchi
high-speed printer
高速印書装置

kōsoku keta age
high-speed carry
高速桁上げ

kōsoku kioku
fast-access memory; fast-access
storage; high-speed memory;
high-speed storage
高速記憶

kōsoku ōtō jikan
quick response time
高速応答時間

kōsoku sen
fast line
高速線

kōsoku shori
high-speed processing
高速処理

kōsoku yobidashi
fast access
高速呼び出し

kōsuea
courseware
コースウェア

kōsuijun gengo
high-level language
高水準言語

kōsuijun gengo kikai
high-level-language machine
高水準言語機械

kosuto
cost
コスト

kosuto-pafuōmansu
cost-performance
コスト・パフォーマンス

kōtai (BS)
backspace (BS)
後退

kōtai dainyū
back substitution
後退代入

kōtai'iki
broadband; wide band
広帯域

kōtai'iki senkei dōki (WBLS)
wide-band linear synchronization
(WBLS)
広帯域線形同期

kotai kairo
solid-state circuit
固体回路

kotai kairo keisanki
solid-state computer
固体回路計算機

kōtai moji
backspace character
後退文字

kotai ronri gijutsu
solid-logic technology
固体論理技術

kotai sōchi
solid-state device
固体装置

kotai soshi
solid-state component
固体素子

kotei burokku chō
fixed-block length
固定ブロック長

kotei chō fuiirudo
fixed-length field
固定長フィールド

kotei chō go
fixed-length word
固定長語

kotei chō keishiki
fixed-length format
固定長形式

kotei chō rekōdo
fixed-length record
固定長レコード

kotei deisuku
fixed disk
固定ディスク

kotei deisuku kioku sōchi
fixed-disk store
固定ディスク記憶装置

kotei fuiirudo
fixed field
固定フィールド

kotei go chō
fixed word length
固定語長

kotei go chō keisanki
fixed-word-length computer
固定語長計算機

kotei heddo
fixed head
固定ヘッド

kotei heddo-deisuku
fixed-head disk
固定ヘッド・ディスク

kotei heddo kioku
fixed-head storage
固定ヘッド記憶

kotei jisshin shōsūten
fixed decimal point
固定10進小数点

kotei-kahen
fixed-variable
固定-可変

kotei-kahen chō
fixed-variable length
固定-可変長

kotei-kahen chō fuiirudo
fixed-variable-length field
固定-可変長フィールド

kotei keishiki
fixed format
固定形式

kotei keishiki messēji
fixed-format message
固定形式メッセージ

kotei kioku
fixed memory; fixed storage;
permanent memory; permanent
storage
固定記憶

kotei kioku (ROM)
read-only memory (ROM)
固定記憶

kotei kioku (ROS)
read-only storage (ROS)
固定記憶

kotei kioku sōchi
read-only storage unit;
read-only store
固定記憶装置

kotei kisū hyōkihō
fixed-radix notation
固定基数表記法

kotei konekuta
fixed connector
固定コネクタ

kotei-kotei burokku
fixed-fixed block
固定-固定ブロック

kōtei ōtō (ACK; Akku)
acknowledgment (ACK);
positive acknowledgment
肯定応答

kōtei ōtō moji
acknowledgment character
肯定応答文字

kotei rūchin
fixed routine
固定ルーチン

kotei shōsūten
fixed point
固定小数点

kotei shōsūten chi
fixed-point value
固定小数点値

kotei shōsūten enzan
fixed-point arithmetic
固定小数点演算

kotei shōsūten hōshiki keisanki
fixed-point computer
固定小数点方式計算機

kotei shōsūten hyōji
fixed-point representation
固定小数点表示

kotei shōsūten hyōkihō
fixed-point notation; fixed-point
representation system
固定小数点表記法

kotei shōsūten nishinsū
fixed-point binary
固定小数点 2 進数

kotei shōsūten seisū
fixed-point integer
固定小数点整数

kotei shōsūten sū
fixed-point number
固定小数点数

koteichō
fixed length
固定長

kōteiteki
positive
肯定的

kōtsū
traffic
交通

kōtsū seigyo
traffic control
交通制御

kōyō
utility
効用

koyū chi
eigenvalue
固有値

koyū dēta kōzō kijutsukō
schema entry
固有データ構造記述項

koyū dēta kōzō kijutsumei
schema name
固有データ構造記述名

koyū dēta kōzō kijutsuzu
schema chart
固有データ構造記述図

kōzō
structure
構造

kōzō(teki)
structural
構造(的)

kōzō bu
structure division
構造部

kōzō(teki) dēta
structural data
構造(的)データ

kōzō(teki) dēta kankei
structural data relationships
構造(的) データ関係

kōzō kaiseki
structural analysis
構造解析

kōzō sekkei
structural design
構造設計

kōzō shiki
structural expression
構造式

kōzō zu
structure diagram
構造図

kōzōka
structured; structuring
構造化

kōzōka puroguramingu
structured programming
構造化プログラミング

kōzōka uōkusurū
structured walkthrough
構造化ウオークスルー

KSR (kemban sōjushin)
KSR (keyboard send/receive)
鍵盤送受信

ku
clause
句

kū (NUL)
null (NUL)
空

kū baitai
empty medium
空媒体

kū dēta'iki
null data area
空データ域

kū fuairu
empty file; null file
空ファイル

ku iki
region
区域

ku ikinai adoresu
regional address
区域内アドレス

kū retsu
null string
空列

kū shūgō
empty set; null set
空集合

kū sutoringu
empty string
空ストリング

kubun
partition; partitioned; segment
区分

kūbun
dummy statement
空文

kubun bangō
segment number
区分番号

kubun dēta-setto
partitioned data set
区分データ・セット

kubun fuairu
partitioned file
区分ファイル

kubun hensei
partitioned organization
区分編成

357

kubun mei
segment name
区分名

kubun puroguramu
segmented program
区分プログラム

kubunka
partitioning
区分化

kubunteki senkei kinji
piecewise linear approximation
区分的線形近似

kudō kikō
drive; transport
駆動機構

kudō parusu
drive pulse
駆動パルス

kugiri kigō
delimiter
区切り記号

kugiri moji
delimiter
区切り文字

kugiri sutētomento
delimiter statement
区切りステートメント

kugiriten
breakpoint
区切点

kugiriten meirei
breakpoint instruction
区切り点命令

kugiriten suitchi
breakpoint switch
区切り点スイッチ

kugiriten teishi
breakpoint halt
区切り点停止

kugiru
delimit
区切る

kūhaku
blank
空白

kūhaku (NUL)
null (NUL)
空白

kūhaku gyō
blank line
空白行

kūhaku moji
blank character; null character
空白文字

kūhaku tēpu
blank tape
空白テープ

kuikku (KWIC)
keyword in context (KWIC)
クイック

kuikku-akusesu-memori
quick-access memory
クイック・アクセス・メモリ

kuikku-rukku
quick look
クイック・ルック

kuikku-sutāto
quick start
クイック・スタート

kukaku
partition
区画

kūkan
interval; space
空間

kūkan bunkatsu
space sharing
空間分割

kūkan enzan
interval arithmetic
空間演算

kūkan kakuchō
space extension
空間拡張

kukei parusu
rectangular pulse
矩形パルス

kukei parusu haba
rectangular pulse duration
矩形パルス幅

kumi
suite
組

kumiawase
combination; merge; merging
組み合わせ

kumiawase-bunrui
merge-sort
組み合わせ分類

kumiawase kairo
combinational circuit
組み合わせ回路

kumiawase pasu
merge pass
組み合わせパス

kumiawase ronri
combinational logic
組み合わせ論理

kumiawaseru
merge (*verb*)
組み合わせる

kumikomi
built-in
組み込み

kumikomi kansū
built-in function;
intrinsic function
組み込み関数

kumikomi kensa
built-in check
組み込み検査

kumikomi kinō
built-in function
組み込み機能

kumikomi seigyo
built-in control
組み込み制御

kumitate
assembling; assembly
組み立て

kumitate rain
assembly line
組み立てライン

kumitate shisutemu
assembling system
組み立てシステム

kunren
training
訓練

kuoddo-in-rain
quad in line
クオッド・イン・ライン

kuokku (KWOC)
keyword out of context (KWOC)
クオック

kuraidori
scale; scaling
位取り

kuraidori kisūhō
positional notation;
positional representation
位取り記数法

kuranpu
clamp
クランプ

kuranpu kairo
clamping circuit
クランプ回路

kurasuta
cluster
クラスタ

kurasuta seigyo
cluster control
クラスタ制御

kurasutaringu
clustering
クラスタリング

kuria
clear
クリア

kuria suru
clear (*verb*)
クリアする

kurichikaru
critical
クリチカル

kurichikaru-pasu
critical path
クリチカル・パス

kurichikaru-pasu hō (CPM)
critical-path method (CPM)
クリチカル・パス法

kūrie-fuonto
courier font
クーリェ・フォント

kurikaeshi
iteration; iterative; repeat;
repetition; repetitive
繰り返し

kurikaeshi bun
FOR statement
繰り返し文

kurikaeshi enzan
repeat operation;
repetitive operation
繰り返し演算

kurikaeshi kaunta
repeat counter
繰り返しカウンタ

kurikaeshi kinō
repeat function
繰り返し機能

kurikaeshi kōmoku
repeating item
繰り返し項目

kurikaeshi meirei
repeat instruction;
repetition instruction
繰り返し命令

kurikaeshi shūdan
repeating group
繰り返し集団

kurikaeshi sōsa
repeat operation;
repetitive operation
繰り返し操作

kurikaeshisei
repeatability
繰り返し性

kurikaesu
iterate; repeat
繰り返す

kurippingu
clipping
クリッピング

kurippu kairo
clipper; clipping circuit
クリップ回路

kurokku
clock
クロック

kurokku-parusu
clock pulse
クロック・パルス

kurokku-reito
clock rate
クロック・レイト

kurokku-sābisu
clock service
クロック・サービス

kurokku shingō
clock signal
クロック信号

kurokku shingō hasshinki
clock signal generator
クロック信号発振器

kurokku shūhasū
clock frequency
クロック周波数

kurokku sokudo
clock rate
クロック速度

kurokku-tēburu
clock table
クロック・テーブル

kurokku-torakku
clock track
クロック・トラック

kurokku-zenerēta
clock generator
クロック・ゼネレータ

kurosu-asenbura
cross-assembler
クロス・アセンブラ

kurosu-chekku
cross-check
クロス・チェック

kurosu-konpaira
cross-compiler
クロス・コンパイラ

kurozudo-shoppu
closed-shop
クロズド・ショップ

kurozudo-shoppu-puroguramingu
closed-shop programming
クロズド・ショップ・
プログラミング

kutō
punctuation
句読

kutō kigō
punctuation mark
句読記号

kutō moji
punctuation character
句読文字

kutōten
punctuation mark
句読点

KWIC (kuikku)
KWIC (keyword in context)
クイック

KWIC indekkusu
KWIC index
クイック・インデックス

KWOC (kuokku)
KWOC (keyword out of context)
クオック

kyapusutan
capstan
キャプスタン

kyarakuta
character
キャラクタ

kyarakuta-adoresu kanō
character addressable
キャラクタ・アドレス可能

kyarakuta-burokku
character block
キャラクタ・ブロック

kyarakuta-deisupurei
character display
キャラクタ・ディスプレィ

kyarakuta-emitta
character emitter
キャラクタ・エミッタ

kyarakuta-enkōdeingu
character encoding
キャラクタ・エンコーディング

kyarakuta-kii
character key
キャラクタ・キー

kyarakuta-kōdo
character code
キャラクタ・コード

kyarakuta-paritei
character parity
キャラクタ・パリティ

kyarakuta-purinta
character printer
キャラクタ・プリンタ

kyarakuta-setto
character set
キャラクタ・セット

kyari
carry
キャリ

kyari-deijitto
carry digit
キャリ・ディジット

kyaria
carrier
キャリァ

kyaria kenshutsu
carrier detector
キャリァ検出

kyaria-shisutemu
carrier system
キャリァ・システム

kyasshu-memori
cache-memory
キャッシュ・メモリ

kyōchō
enhancement
強調

kyōchō suru
enhance
強調する

kyodō
behavior
挙動

kyohi
reject; rejection
拒否

kyōkai
boundary
境界

kyōkai awase
boundary alignment
境界合わせ

kyōkai chi
boundary value
境界値

kyōkai chi mondai
boundary-value problem
境界値問題

kyōkai hikisū
boundary argument
境界引き数

kyōkai jōken
boundary condition
境界条件

kyōkai makuro meirei
delimiter macroinstruction
境界マクロ命令

kyōkai shitei suru
delimit
境界指定する

kyoku
station
局

kyokubu kioku
local storage
局部記憶

kyokubu kioku rejisuta
local storage register
局部記憶レジスタ

kyoku'ikinai seigyo
local control
局域内制御

kyoku'ikinai shori
local processing
局域内処理

kyokusen
curve; curved line
曲線

kyokusen kenshutsu
curve detection
曲線検出

kyokusen patān
curve-pattern
曲線パターン

kyokusen patān asshuku
curve-pattern compaction
曲線パターン圧縮

kyokushosei
locality
局所性

kyokushoteki
local
局所的

kyokushoteki shori sōchi
local processor
局所的処理装置

kyokushoteki sūchi hensū
local variable
局所的数値変数

kyori
distance
距離

kyōsei haijo
preemption
強制排除

kyōtai'iki
narrow band
狭帯域

kyōtsū bubun
intersection
共通部分

kyōtsū bubun gēto
intersection gate
共通部分ゲート

kyōtsu bubun shiki
common subexpression
共通部分式

kyōtsū burokku
common block
共通ブロック

kyōtsū fuiirudo
common field
共通フィールド

kyōtsū gengo
common language
共通言語

kyōtsū hensū
common variable
共通変数

kyōtsū iki
common area
共通域

kyōtsū kioku ryō'iki
common storage area
共通記憶領域

kyōtsū kōdo
common code
共通コード

kyōtsū saburūchin
common subroutine
共通サブルーチン

kyōtsū segumento
common segment
共通セグメント

kyōtsū shiki
common expression
共通式

kyōtsū yūza-nettowāku
common user network
共通ユーザ・ネットワーク

kyōyō adoresu
shared address
共用アドレス

kyōyō fuairu
shared file
共用ファイル

kyōyō funō
nonshareable
共用不能

kyoyō genkai
tolerance
許容限界

kyōyō kioku
shared storage
共用記憶

kyōyō kioku'iki
shared memory
共用記憶域

kyōyō nyūshutsuryoku sōchi
shared input/output device
共用入出力装置

kyōyō purosessa
shared processor
共用プロセッサ

kyōyō ronri
shared logic
共用論理

kyōyō sabuchaneru
shared subchannel
共用サブチャネル

kyōyō seigyo sōchi
shared control unit
共用制御装置

kyōyō shigen
shared resources
共用資源

kyōyō shisutemu
shared system
共用システム

kyōyō shu kioku
shared main storage
共用主記憶

kyōyō tanmatsu (sōchi)
shared terminal
共用端末(装置)

kyōyōkanō
shareable
共用可能

kyōyōkanō sōchi
shareable device
共用可能装置

kyōyū fuairu
public file
共有ファイル

kyū no hosū
complement on nine;
nine's complement
9の補数

kyū torakku jiki tēpu
nine-track magnetic tape
9トラック磁気テープ

kyūjōyo kensa
nines check
9剰余検査

kyūjū ran kādo
ninety-column card
90欄カード

kyūrai no
conventional
旧来の

kyūsekihō
quadrature
求積法

kyūshi jikan
downtime
休止時間

kyūshi jōtai
dormant state
休止状態

kyūshichū
inactive
休止中

kyūshichū fuairu
inactive file
休止中ファイル

kyūyo
allowance; compensation
給与

L

LA (raboratori-otomēshon)
LA (laboratory automation)
ラボラトリ・オトメーション

LAN (kigyōnai jōhō tsūshinmō)
LAN (local-area network)
企業内情報通信網

LCB (kaisen seigyo burokku)
LCB (line control block)
回線制御ブロック

LCD (ekishō deisupurei)
LCD (liquid-crystal display)
液晶ディスプレイ

LCS (dai yōryō kioku)
LCS (large-capacity storage)
大容量記憶

LDB (ronriteki dētabēsu)
LDB (logical database)
論理的データベース

LED (hakkō daiōdo)
LED (light-emitting diode)
発光ダイオード

LED deisupurei
LED display
LEDディスプレイ

LF (kaigyō)
LF (line feed)
改行

LIFO (atoire sakidashi)
LIFO (last-in first-out)
後入れ先出し

LISP (risuto shori gengo)
LISP (list-processing language)
リスト処理言語

LOAD (fuka; rōdo)
LOAD (load)
負荷；ロード

LP (gyō inji sōchi; rain-purinta)
LP (line printer)
行印字装置；ライン・プリンタ

LP (senkei keikakuhō)
LP (linear programming)
線形計画法

LPC (suihei paritei kensa)
LPC (longitudinal parity check)
水平パリティ検査

LPM (gyō/fun)
LPM (lines per minute)
行／分

LPOC (rasuto-pasu-oun-kōdo)
LPOC (last-pass own code)
ラスト・パス・オウン・コード

LRC (suihei jōchō kensa)
LRC (longitudinal redundancy check)
水平冗長検査

LSB (saika'i no bitto)
LSB (least significant bit)
最下位のビット

LSC (saika'i no moji)
LSC (least significant character)
最下位の文字

LSD (saika'i no sūji)
LSD (least significant digit)
最下位の数字

LSI (dai kibo shūsekika)
LSI (large-scale integration)
大規模集積化

LTRS (eiji shifuto)
LTRS (letter shift)
英字シフト

M

m (miri-)
m (milli-)
ミリ

MAC (tajū akusesu keisanki)
MAC (multiaccess computer)
多重アクセス計算機

machi
wait
待ち

machi jikan
latency; waiting time
待ち時間

machi jōtai
wait(ing) state
待ち状態

machiawase
queuing
待ち合わせ

machiawase riron
queuing theory; waiting-line theory
待ち合わせ理論

machigyōretsu
queue; queuing
待ち行列

machigyōretsu nettowāku
queuing network
待ち行列ネットワーク

machigyōretsu risuto
queuing list
待ち行列リスト

machigyōretsu seigyo
queue control
待ち行列制御

machigyōretsu seigyo burokku (QCB)
queue control block (QCB)
待ち行列制御ブロック

machigyōretsu shisutemu
queuing system
待ち行列システム

mae okuri
forward space
前送り

maeshori (PREP)
preparation (PREP)
前処理

maikuro
micro-
マイクロ

maikuro byō
microsecond
マイクロ秒

maikuro-doraibu
microdrive
マイクロ・ドライブ

maikuro-doraibu-kātorijji
microdrive cartridge
マイクロ・ドライブ・カートリッジ

maikuro-furoppi-deisuku
micro–floppy disk
マイクロ・フロッピ・ディスク

maikuro gochō
micro–word length
マイクロ語長

maikuro kairo
microcircuit
マイクロ回路

maikuro-kasetto
microcassette
マイクロ・カセット

maikuro-kōdo
microcode
マイクロ・コード・

maikuro kogataka
microminiaturization
マイクロ小形化

maikuro-konpyūta
microcomputer
マイクロ・コンピュータ

maikuro-kontorōra
microcontroller
マイクロ・コントローラ

maikuro-māketto
micromarket
マイクロ・マーケット

maikuro-meinfurēmu
micromainframe
マイクロ・メインフレーム

maikuro-meinfurēmu-rinku
micromainframe link
マイクロメインフレーム・リンク

maikuro meirei
microcommand/instruction
マイクロ命令

maikuro-mojyūru
micromodule
マイクロ・モジュール

maikuro-mojyūru gijutsu
micromodule technique
マイクロ・モジュール技術

maikuro nami
microwave
マイクロ波

maikuro OS
micro-OS
マイクロ OS

maikuro shindan
microdiagnostics
マイクロ診断

maikuro sōsa
microoperation
マイクロ操作

maikuro-suitchi
microswitch
マイクロ・スイッチ

maikurofuirumu
microfilm
マイクロ・フィルム

maikurofuisshu
microfiche
マイクロ・フィッシュ

maikurofuisshu hyōjiki
microfiche viewer
マイクロフィッシュ表示器

maikurokonpyūta'yō puroguramingu gengo (PL/M)
program language for microcomputers (PL/M)
マイクロコンピュータ用プログ
ラミング言語

maikuropuroguramingu
microprogramming
マイクロプログラミング

maikuropuroguramu
microprogram
マイクロプログラム

maikuropurosessa
microprocessor
マイクロプロセッサ

maikuropurosessa sōchi (MPU)
microprocessor unit (MPU)
マイクロプロセッサ装置

maikuropurosessa'yō seigyo puroguramu (CP/M)
control program for microprocessors (CP/M)
マイクロプロセッサ用制御
プログラム

Maira
Mylar
マイラ

māji
merge
マージ

māji-pasu
merge pass
マージ・パス

māji-sōto
merge-sort
マージ・ソート

māji suru
merge (*verb*)
マージする

māka
marker
マーカ

makimodoshi
rewind
巻戻し

makimodoshi jikan
rewind time
巻戻し時間

makimodosu
rewind (*verb*)
巻戻す

maku
film
膜

māku
mark
マーク

māku-enkōdeingu
mark encoding
マーク・エンコーディング

māku fugōka
mark encoding
マーク符号化

363

māku-horudo
mark hold
マーク・ホルド

māku-kādo
mark card
マーク・カード

māku kensa
mark verification
マーク検査

māku kenshō
mark verification
マーク検証

māku-kōdoka
mark encoding
マーク・コード化

māku-senshingu
mark sensing
マーク・センシング

māku-sensu
mark sense
マーク・センス

māku-sensu-kādo
mark-sensed card
マーク・センス・カード

māku yomitori
mark reading; mark sensing
マーク読み取り

māku yomitori kādo
mark-sensing card
マーク読み取りカード

māku yomitori kikō
mark-reading station
マーク読み取り機構

māku yomitori senkōki
mark-sensing punch
マーク読み取りせん孔機

māku yomitori sōchi
mark reader
マーク読み取り装置

makuro-asenbura
macro assembler
マクロ・アセンブラ

makuro-asenburi
macro assembly
マクロ・アセンブリ

makuro-asenburi-puroguramu
macroassembly program
マクロ・アセンブリ・プログラム

makuro-dairekutori
macrodirectory
マクロ・ダイレクトリ

makuro gengo
macrolanguage
マクロ言語

makuro genkei
macroprototype
マクロ原型

makuro-kōdeingu
macrocoding
マクロ・コーディング

makuro-kōdo
macrocode
マクロ・コード

makuro-komando
macrocommand
マクロ・コマンド

makuro-kōru
macrocall
マクロ・コール

makuro meirei
macroinstruction
マクロ命令

makuro-raiburari
macrolibrary
マクロ・ライブラリ

makuro seigyo
macrocontrol
マクロ制御

makuro seigyo bun
macrocontrol statement
マクロ制御文

makuro seisei
macrogeneration
マクロ生成

makuro seisei puroguramu
macrogenerating program;
macrogenerator
マクロ生成プログラム

makuro sengen
macrodeclaration
マクロ宣言

makuro shindan
macrodiagnostics
マクロ診断

makuro shirei
macrocommand
マクロ指令

makuro teigi
macrodefinition
マクロ定義

makuro tenkai
macroexpansion
マクロ展開

makuro yobidashi
macrocall
マクロ呼び出し

makuro yōso
macroelement
マクロ要素

makuropuroguramingu
macroprogramming
マクロプログラミング

makuropuroguramu
macroprogram
マクロプログラム

makuropurosessa
macroprocessor
マクロプロセッサ

manyuaru
manual (≠automatic)
マニュアル

mappingu
mapping
マッピング

mappingu kinō
mapping function
マッピング機能

mappingu-shisutemu
mapping system
マッピング・システム

mappu
map
マップ

mappu-rejisuta (mr)
map register (mr)
マップ・レジスタ

MAR (kioku adoresu-rejisuta)
MAR (memory address register)
記憶アドレス・レジスタ

maruchi-
multi-
マルチ

maruchi-akusesu
multiaccess
マルチ・アクセス

maruchi-akusesu-shisutemu
multiaccess system
マルチ・アクセス・システム

maruchi-basu
multibus
マルチ・バス

maruchi-chippu
multichip
マルチ・チップ

maruchi-jyobu
multijob
マルチ・ジョブ

maruchi-jyobu-operēshon
multijob operation
マルチ・ジョブ・オペレーション

maruchi-pēji
multipage
マルチ・ページ

maruchi-pointo
multipoint
マルチ・ポイント

maruchi-pureito-deisuku
multiplate disk
マルチ・プレイト・ディスク

maruchi-puroguramingu
multiprogramming
マルチ・プログラミング

maruchi-purosessa
multiprocessor
マルチ・プロセッサ

maruchi-purosessa-shisutemu
multiprocessor system
マルチ・プロセッサ・システム

maruchi-sutēshon
multistation
マルチ・ステーション

maruchi-tasuku
multitask
マルチ・タスク

maruchi-yūza
multiuser
マルチ・ユーザ

maruchi-yūza-shisutemu
multiuser system
マルチ・ユーザ・システム

maruchibaiburēta
multivibrator
マルチバイブレータ

maruchipurekusa (MUX)
multiplexer (MUX)
マルチプレクサ

maruchipurekusa-chaneru
multiplexer channel
マルチプレクサ・チャネル

maruchipurekusa-mōdo
multiplexer mode
マルチプレクサ・モード

maruchipurekusu
multiplex
マルチプレクス

maruchipurekusu-adaputa
multiplex adapter
マルチプレクス・アダプタ

maruchipurekusu-mōdo
multiplex mode
マルチプレクス・モード

marume
rounding; rounding off
丸め

marume gosa
round-off error; rounding error
丸め誤差

marumeru
round off (*verb*)
丸める

masatsu
friction
摩擦

masatsu okuri
friction feed
摩擦送り

masatsu sokudo
friction speed
摩擦速度

mashin
machine
マシン

massatsu suru
erase
抹殺する

masshō
deletion; erasure
抹消

masshō moji
delete character
抹消文字

masshō suru
delete; erase
抹消する

masu-dēta
mass data
マス・データ

masuku
mask
マスク

masuku awase
mask alignment
マスク合わせ

masuku-bitto
mask bit
マスク・ビット

masuku fukanō warikomi
nonmaskable interrupt
マスク不可能割り込み

masuku jōtai
masked state
マスク状態

masuku-rejisuta
mask register
マスク・レジスタ

masuku ROM
masked ROM
マスクROM

masuta
master
マスタ

masuta-fuairu
master file
マスタ・ファイル

masuta-fuairu-dairekutori
master file directory
マスタ・ファイル・ダイレクトリ

masuta-insutorakushon-tēpu (MIT)
master instruction tape (MIT)
マスタ・インストラクション・
テープ

masuta-kādo
master card
マスタ・カード

masuta-kurokku
master clock
マスタ・クロック

masuta-menyū
master menu
マスタ・メニュー

masuta-rekōdo
master record
マスタ・レコード

masuta seigyo puroguramu
master control program
マスタ制御プログラム

masuta-sukejyūra
master scheduler
マスタ・スケジューラ

masuta/surēbu-shisutemu
master/slave system
マスタ/スレーブ・システム

masuta-sutēshon
master station
マスタ・ステーション

masuta-tēpu
master tape
マスタ・テープ

matorikkusu
matrix
マトリックス

matorikkusu-deisupurei
matrix display
マトリックス・ディスプレィ

matorikkusu kaiseki
matrix analysis
マトリックス解析

matorikkusu kioku
matrix storage
マトリックス記憶

matorikkusu-matchingu
matrix matching
マトリックス・マッチング

matorikkusu-purinta
matrix printer
マトリックス・プリンタ

mausu
mouse
マウス

mausu-doriiben
mouse driven
マウス・ドリーベン

mausu-intafuēsu
mouse interface
マウス・インタフェース

mausu-konekuta
mouse connector
マウス・コネクタ

mausu-setto
mouse set
マウス・セット

mazā-bōdo
mother board
マサー・ボード

MB (megabaito)
MB (megabyte)
メガバイト

Mb (megabitto)
Mb (megabit)
メガビット

MBR (kioku baffua-rejisuta)
MBR (memory buffer register)
記憶バッファ・レジスタ

MCR (jiki moji ninshiki)
MCR (magnetic-character recognition)
磁気文字認識

MCR (jiki moji yomitori sōchi)
MCR (magnetic-character reader)
磁気文字読み取り装置

megabaito (MB)
megabyte (MB)
メガバイト

megabitto (Mb)
megabit (Mb)
メガビット

megaherutsu (MHz)
megahertz (MHz)
メガヘルツ

mei
name
名

meido
brightness
明度

meimoku sokudo
nominal speed
名目速度

mein-memori
main memory
メイン・メモリ

meinfurēmu(-konpyūta)
mainframe
メインフレーム(・コンピュータ)

meinfurēmu-maikuro
mainframe micro
メインフレーム・マイクロ

meirei
command; instruction; order
命令

meirei adoresu
instruction address
命令アドレス

meirei adoresu-rejisuta (IAR)
instruction address register (IAR)
命令アドレス・レジスタ

meirei banku
instruction bank
命令バンク

meirei bu
instruction part; operation part; operator part
命令部

meirei bunkai
primitive resolution
命令分解

meirei chō
instruction length
命令長

meirei chō kōdo
instruction length code
命令長コード

meirei chōfuku
instruction overlap
命令重複

meirei dankai
instruction phase
命令段階

meirei dekōda
instruction decoder; operation decoder
命令デコーダ

meirei dekōdo
instruction decode
命令デコード

meirei fuetchi
instruction fetch
命令フェッチ

meirei fuetchi-saikuru
instruction fetch cycle
命令フェッチ・サイクル

meirei fuiirudo
instruction field; operation field
命令フィールド

meirei go
instruction word
命令語

meirei jikan
instruction time
命令時間

meirei jikkō
execution; instruction execution
命令実行

meirei jikkō dankai
execution cycle; execution phase
命令実行段階

meirei jikkō jikan
instruction execution time
命令実行時間

meirei jikkō saikuru
instruction execution cycle
命令実行サイクル

meirei kaidoku
instruction decode
命令解読

meirei kaidokuki
operation decoder
命令解読器

meirei kaunta
instruction counter
命令カウンタ

meirei keishiki
instruction format
命令形式

meirei kōdo
instruction code
命令コード

meirei kōdo (opu-kōdo)
operation code (op code)
命令コード; オプ・コード

meirei ran
operation field
命令欄

meirei rejisuta (ir)
instruction register (ir)
命令レジスタ

meirei repātori
instruction repertoire
命令レパートリ

meirei saikuru
instruction cycle
命令サイクル

meirei sakitori
instruction prefetch
命令先取り

meirei setto
instruction set
命令セット

meirei setto-purosessa (ISP)
instruction set processor (ISP)
命令セット・プロセッサ

meirei shori sōchi
instruction processing unit
命令処理装置

meirei sū
instruction number
命令数

meirei toridashi
instruction fetch
命令取り出し

meirei toridashi dankai
fetch cycle
命令取り出し段階

meirei toridashi jikan
fetch time
命令取り出し時間

meirei toridashi-jikkō
fetch-execute
命令取り出し実行

meirei toridashi-jikkō dankai
fetch-execute cycle
命令取り出し実行段階

meirei toridashi saikuru
instruction fetch cycle
命令取り出しサイクル

meireibun
statement
命令文

meisai fuairu
detail file
明細ファイル

meisai kādo
detail card
明細カード

meisai rekōda
detail record
明細レコーダ

meisai tēpu
detail tape
明細テープ

meishi adoresu
explicit address
明示アドレス

meishi sengen
explicit declaration
明示宣言

memori
memory
メモリ

memori-danpu
memory dump
メモリ・ダンプ

memori-intariibu
memory interleave
メモリ・インタリーブ

memori-mappu
memory map
メモリ・マップ

memori-mappudo I/O
memory-mapped I/O
メモリ・マップド I/O

memori-ōbarei
memory overlays
メモリ・オーバレイ

memori-saikuru
memory cycle
メモリ・サイクル

memori-sapōto-shisutemu
memory support system
メモリ・サポート・システム

menba
member
メンバ

menseki
escape
免責

menseki tetsuzuki
escape procedure
免責手続き

menyū
menu
メニュー

menyū kudōgata sofutouea
menu-driven software
メニュー駆動型ソフトウェア

menyū sentaku
menu selection
メニュー選択

messēji
message
メッセージ

messēji dōhō
simultaneous distribution of
messages
メッセージ同報

messēji gen
message source
メッセージ源

messēji-gurūpu dōhō
simultaneous distribution of
grouped messages
メッセージ・グループ同報

messēji henshū
message editing
メッセージ編集

messēji issei dōhō
simultaneous distribution of
single and grouped messages
メッセージ一斉同報

messēji kaishi
start of message
メッセージ開始

messēji keiro shitei
message routing
メッセージ経路指定

messēji kōkan
message switching
メッセージ交換

messēji kōkan shisutemu
message-switching system
メッセージ交換システム

messēji kōkanmō
switched-message network
メッセージ交換網

messēji machigyōretsu
message queuing
メッセージ待ち行列

messēji no owari (EOM)
end of message (EOM)
メッセージの終り

messēji-pariti
message parity
メッセージ・パリティ

messēji-segumento
message segment
メッセージ・セグメント

messēji seigyo puroguramu
message control program
メッセージ制御プログラム

messēji shori
message processing
メッセージ処理

messēji shori puroguramu
message-processing program
メッセージ処理プログラム

messēji shūketsu (EOM)
end of message (EOM)
メッセージ終結

MHz (megaherutsu)
MHz (megahertz)
メガヘルツ

MICR (jiki inku moji ninshiki)
MICR (magnetic-ink character
recognition)
磁気インク文字認識

**MICR (jiki inku moji yomitori
sōchi)**
MICR (magnetic-ink character
reader)
磁気インク文字読み取り装置

midashi
header; heading; identity
見出し

midashi bu
identification division
見出し部

midashi burokku
header block
見出しブロック

midashi gyō
heading line
見出し行

midashi kādo
header card
見出カード

midashi kōmoku
header entry
見出項目

midashi raberu
header label
見出しラベル

midashi rekōdo
header record
見出しレコード

midashi ryō'iki
key area
見出し領域

midashi seru
header cell
見出しセル

midashi tēburu
header table
見出しテーブル

migi shifuto
right shift
右シフト

migi tsume
right justify
右詰め

migi yose
right justify
右寄せ

mihari
sentinel
見張り

mikan kōdo
incomplete code
未完コード

mikan messēji
incomplete message
未完メッセージ

mikan rūchin
incomplete routine
未完ルーチン

MIL (beigun kikaku) (USA)
MIL (military specifications) (USA)
米軍規格

mini-deisuketto
minidiskette
ミニ・ディスケット

mini-deisuku
minidisk
ミニ・ディスク

mini-furoppi
miniflopy
ミニ・フロッピ

mini-furoppi-deisuku
mini floppy disk
ミニ・フロッピ・ディスク

mini-konpyūta
minicomputer
ミニ・コンピュータ

mini-makkusu hō
minimax method
ミニ・マックス法

mini-makkusu kinji
minimax approximation
ミニ・マックス近似

minimaikuro-konpyūta
minimicro
ミニマイクロ・コンピュータ

minogashi
residual; undetected
見逃し

minogashi ayamari
residual error; undetected error
見逃し誤り

minogashi ayamari ritsu
residual error rate;
undetected error rate
見逃し誤り率

MIP (kongō seisū keikakuhō)
MIP (mixed integer programming)
混合整数計画法

miri- (m)
milli- (m)
ミリ

miribyō (ms)
millisecond (ms)
ミリ秒

miribyō sokudo haba
millisecond speed range
ミリ秒速度幅

MIS (kei'ei jōhō kanri shisutemu; kei'ei jōhō shisutemu)
MIS (management information system)
経営情報管理システム；
経営情報システム

mishiyō baitai
virgin medium
未使用媒体

MIT (masuta-insutorakushon-tēpu)
MIT (master instruction tape)
マスタ・インストラクション・テープ

miteigi
undefined
未定義

miteigi kigō
undefined symbol
未定義記号

miteigi meirei
undefined instruction
未定義命令

mitsudo
density
密度

MMI (ningen-kikai intafuēsu)
MMI (man-machine interface)
人間-機械インタフェース

mō
network
網

modemu
modulator-demodulator (modem)
モデム

moderingu-pakkēji
modeling package
モデリング・パッケージ

moderu
model
モデル

moderu jikkō gengo
model-running language
モデル実行言語

moderu kōsei gengo
model-building language
モデル構成言語

mōdo
mode
モード

mōdo gokansei
mode compatibility
モード互換性

modori
return
戻り

modori adoresu
return address
戻りアドレス

modori adoresu meirei
return-address instruction
戻りアドレス命令

modori kii
return key
戻りキー

modori kōdo
return code
戻りコード

modori kōdo-rejisuta
return-code register
戻りコード・レジスタ

modori meirei
return instruction
戻り命令

moji
character; letter
文字

moji/byō (cps)
characters per second (cps)
文字／秒

moji dōki
character synchronization
文字同期

moji hasseiki
character generator
文字発生器

moji henkō
character change
文字変更

moji hyōji
character display
文字表示

moji ichi
character position
文字位置

moji/inchi (cpi)
characters per inch (cpi)
文字／インチ

moji inji sōchi
inscriber
文字印字装置

369

moji jūten
character fill
文字充てん

moji kankaku
character pitch; character space
文字間隔

moji kaunto
character count
文字カウント

moji kensa
character check
文字検査

moji kōdo
character code
文字コード

moji kōdoka
character encoding
文字コード化

moji kyōkai
character boundary
文字境界

moji mitsudo
character density
文字密度

moji muki
character-oriented
文字向き

moji ninshiki
character recognition
文字認識

moji no kumi
character set
文字の組

moji paritei
character parity
文字パリティ

moji pikucha
character picture
文字ピクチャ

moji ran kijutsushi
Hollerith field descriptor
文字欄記述子

moji retsu
character string
文字列

moji rinkaku
character outline
文字輪郭

moji sabusetto
character subset
文字サブセット

moji sakujo
character deletion
文字削除

moji setto
character set
文字セット

moji shiki
character expression
文字式

moji shori
character manipulation;
character processing
文字処理

moji sōnyū
character insertion
文字挿入

moji teisū
Hollerith constant
文字定数

moji yomitori sōchi
character reader
文字読み取り装置

mojigata
Hollerith type
文字型

mojyūra
modular
モジューラ

mojyūra keisanki shisutemu
modular computer system
モジューラ計算機システム

mojyūra kōzō
modular structure
モジューラ構造

mojyūra-puroguramingu
modular programming
モジューラ・プログラミング

mojyūra sekkei
modular design
モジューラ設計

mojyūra-shisutemu
modular system
モジューラ・システム

mojyūra-shisutemu-puroguramu
modular system program
モジューラ・システム・プログラム

mojyūra-shisutemu seigyo
modular system control
モジューラ・システム制御

mojyūraka
modularization
モジューラ化

mojyūrasei
modularity
モジューラ性

mojyūro
modulo
モジューロ

mojyūro enzan
modulo arithmetic
モジューロ演算

mojyūro *n* jōyo
modulo *n* residue
モジューロ n 剰余

mojyūro *n* kaunta
modulo *n* counter
モジューロ n カウンタ

mojyūro *n* kensa
modulo *n* check
モジューロ n 検査

mojyūru
module
モジュール

mojyūru kōzō
module structure
モジュール構造

mojyūru mei
module name
モジュール名

mokuhyō
target
目標

mokuhyō dēta kōmoku
target data item
目標データ項目

mokuhyō shikibetsu
target identification
目標識別

mokuhyōchi
set point
目標値

mokuroku
menu
目録

mokuteki
objective; target
目的

mokuteki gengo
object language; target language
目的言語

mokuteki gengo puroguramu
object language program
目的言語プログラム

mokuteki kansū
objective function
目的関数

mokuteki keisanki
object computer;
target computer
目的計算機

mokuteki kikai
object machine
目的機械

mokuteki kōdo
object code
目的コード

mokuteki mojyūru
object module
目的モジュール

mokuteki puroguramu
object program; target program
目的プログラム

mokuteki rūchin
object routine
目的ルーチン

mondai
problem
問題

mondai bunseki
problem analysis
問題分析

mondai hakken
problem location
問題発見

mondai hyōka
problem evaluation
問題評価

mondai jōtai
problem state
問題状態

mondai kaiketsu
problem solving
問題解決

mondai kijutsu
problem description
問題記述

mondai kijutsu bunseki
problem statement analysis
問題記述分析

mondai kijutsu kaiwa
problem statement dialogue
問題記述会話

mondai muki gengo
problem-oriented language
問題向き言語

mondai puroguramu
problem program
問題プログラム

mondai seigyo
problem control
問題制御

mondai shikibetsu
problem identification
問題識別

mondai shindan
problem diagnosis
問題診断

mondai teigi
problem definition
問題定義

monita
monitor
モニタ

monita-rūchin
monitor routine
モニタ・ルーチン

monita-shisutemu
monitor system
モニタ・システム

monokuro
monochrome
モノクロ

monorishikku
monolithic
モノリシック

monorishikku-puroguramingu
monolithic programming
モノリシック・プログラミング

monorishikku shūseki kairo
monolithic integrated circuit
モノリシック集積回路

MOS (mosu)
MOS (metal-oxide
semiconductor)
モス

**MOSFET (mosu denkai kōka
toranjisuta gijutsu)**
MOSFET (metal-oxide
semiconductor field effect
transistor technology)
モス電界効果トランジスタ技術

MOSgata IC
metal-oxide semiconductor IC
MOS型IC; モス型IC

MOSgata ROM
metal-oxide semiconductor ROM
MOS型ROM; モス型ROM

mosha densō (FAX)
facsimile (FAX)
模写伝送

MOST (mosu-toranjisuta)
MOST (metal-oxide
semiconductor transistor)
モス・トランジスタ

mosu (MOS)
metal-oxide semiconductor
(MOS)
モス

**mosu denkai kōka toranjisuta
gijutsu (MOSFET)**
metal-oxide semiconductor field
effect transistor technology
(MOSFET)
モス電界効果トランジスタ技術

mosu IC
metal-oxide semiconductor IC
モスIC

mosu ROM
metal-oxide semiconductor ROM
モスROM

mosu shūseki kairo
metal-oxide semiconductor
integrated circuit
モス集積回路

mosu-toranjisuta (MOST)
metal-oxide semiconductor transistor (MOST)
モス・トランジスタ

motomeru
seek
求める

MP (sūri keikakuhō)
MP (mathematical programming)
数理計画法

MP/M
MP/M
ＭＰ／Ｍ

MPU (maikuropurosessa sōchi)
MPU (microprocessor unit)
マイクロプロセッサ装置

mr (mappu-rejisuta)
mr (map register)
マップ・レジスタ

ms (miribyō)
ms (millisecond)
ミリ秒

MSB (saijō'i no bitto)
MSB (most significant bit)
最上位のビット

MSC (saijō'i no moji)
MSC (most significant character)
最上位の文字

MSD (saijō'i no sūji)
MSD (most significant digit)
最上位の数字

MSI (chū kibo shūsekika)
MSI (medium-scale integration)
中規模集積化

MT (jiki tēpu)
MT (magnetic tape)
磁気テープ

MTBF (heikin koshō kankaku)
MTBF (mean time between failures)
平均故障間隔

MTBM (heikin hoshu kankaku)
MTBM (mean time between maintenance)
平均保守間隔

MTTD (shindan made no heikin jikan)
MTTD (mean time to diagnosis)
診断までの平均時間

MTTF (heikin shoki koshō jikan)
MTTF (mean time to failure)
平均初期故障時間

MTTR (heikin shūfuku jikan)
MTTR (mean time to repair)
平均修復時間

MTU (jiki tēpu sōchi)
MTU (magnetic-tape unit)
磁気テープ装置

muadoresu meirei
no-address instruction
無アドレス命令

mudōsa
waste operation
無動作

mudōsa (no-opu)
no operation (no op)
無動作；ノ・オプ

mudōsa meirei
do-nothing instruction;
no-op instruction;
nonoperation instruction
無動作命令

mugen pado hōshiki
infinite-pad method
無限パド方式

mugen rūpu
infinite loop
無限ループ

muhogo
unprotected
無保護

mujin
unmanned
無人

mujin sōsa
unattended operation;
unmanned operation
無人操作

mujin tanmatsu
unmanned station
無人端末

mujōken
unconditional
無条件

mujōken bun
unconditional statement
無条件文

mujōken bunki
unconditional branch
無条件分岐

mujōken bunki meirei
unconditional branch instruction
無条件分岐命令

mujōken GO TO bun
unconditional GO TO statement
無条件 GO TO 文

mujōken meirei
imperative statement
無条件命令

mujōken tensō
unconditional transfer
無条件転送

mujōken tobikoshi
unconditional jump;
unconditional transfer
無条件飛び越し

mujōken tobikoshi meirei
unconditional jump instruction;
unconditional transfer instruction
無条件飛び越し命令

mujun
inconsistency
矛盾

muki
oriented
向き

mukō
invalid
無効

mukō jikan
ineffective time
無効時間

MUX (maruchipurekusa; tajū hōshiki sōchi)
MUX (multiplexer)
マルチプレクサ；多重方式装置

N

N-chaneru MOS (NMOS)
N-channel metal-oxide
semiconductor (NMOS)
N-チャネルMOS

n **kō enzan**
n-adic operation
n項演算

n **kō kankei**
n-ary relation
n項関係

n **koa/bittoshiki kioku**
n-core-per-bit storage
nコア/ビット式記憶

n **reberu-adoresu**
n-level address
nレベル・アドレス

n **reberu ronri**
n-level logic
nレベル論理

nafuda
label
名札

nafuda no nai
unlabeled
名札のない

nafuda no nai burokku
unlabeled block
名札のないブロック

nafuda no nai kihon bun
unlabeled basic statement
名札のない基本文

nagare
flow
流れ

nagare kaiseki
flow analysis
流れ解析

nagare nettowāku
flow network
流れネットワーク

nagare no muki
flow direction
流れの向き

nagare seigyo
flow control
流れ制御

nagare sen
flow line
流れ線

nagare shisutemu
flow system
流れシステム

nagare zu
flow diagram; flowchart
流れ図

nagarezu ketsugōshi
flowchart connector
流れ図結合子

nagarezu kigō
flowchart symbols
流れ図記号

nagarezu sakusei
flowcharting
流れ図作成

nagasa
length
長さ

nagasa no keisū
length factor
長さの係数

nai
internal
内

naibu
internal
内部

naibu bunrui
internal sort
内部分類

naibu doraibu
internal drive
内部ドライブ

naibu kankyō jōhō
internal environment information
内部環境情報

naibu kinō rejisuta
internal function register
内部機能レジスタ

naibu kioku
internal memory; internal storage
内部記憶

naibu kioku sareta puroguramu
internally stored program
内部記憶されたプログラム

naibu kioku sōchi
internal store
内部記憶装置

naibu kōdo
internal code
内部コード

naibu kurokku
internal clocking
内部クロック

naibu mei
internal name
内部名

naibu puroguramu
internally stored program;
stored program
内部プログラム

naibu rejisuta
internal register
内部レジスタ

naibu sagyōyō kioku
internal working memory
内部作業用記憶

naibu tetsuzuki
internal procedure
内部手続き

naibu warikomi
internal interrupt
内部割り込み

naibu warikomi shisutemu
internal interrupt system
内部割り込みシステム

naigan gēto
implication gate
内含ゲート

naihō gēto
inclusion gate
内包ゲード

naiyō
content(s)
内容

naiyō bunseki
contents analysis
内容分析

naiyō dokuritsu adoresu
content-independent address
内容独立アドレス

naiyō kanshi
contents supervision
内容監視

naiyō kensaku
contents retrieval
内容検索

naizō
built-in; internal
内蔵

naizō doraibu
internal drive
内蔵ドライブ

naizō puroguramu
stored program
内蔵プログラム

naizō ROM
internal ROM
内蔵ROM

NAK (hitei ōtō; nakku)
NAK (negative acknowledgment)
ナック；否定応答

nakku (hitei ōtō; NAK)
NAK (negative acknowledgment)
ナック；否定応答

nama dēta
raw data
生データ

namae
identifier; name
名前

namae fuiirudo
name field
名前フィールド

namaekae
call by name
名前変え

namaetsuki kyōtsū burokku
named common block
名前付き共通ブロック

namaetsuki teisū
named constant
名前付き定数

nami
wave
波

nana segumento-deisupurei
seven-segment display
7セグメント・ディスプレイ

nana torakku jiki tēpu
seven-track magnetic tape
7トラック磁気テープ

nanabitto-baito
septet
7ビット・バイト

NAND (hiteiseki; hitei AND; hiteironriseki)
NAND (inverted AND; negative AND; NOT AND)
NAND；否定積；
否定AND；否定論理積

NAND enzan
inverted AND operation;
NAND operation
NAND演算

NAND gēto
inverted AND gate; NAND gate
NANDゲート

NAND kairo
inverted AND circuit;
NAND circuit
NAND回路

NAND soshi
inverted AND element;
NAND element
NAND素子

nano-
nano-
ナノ

nanobyō (ns)
nanosecond (ns)
ナノ秒

nanobyō sokudo haba
nanosecond speed range
ナノ秒速度幅

nanopurosessa
nanoprocessor
ナノプロセッサ

NBS (Beikoku Hyōjun Kyoku)
NBS (National Bureau of Standards) (USA)
米国標準局

NC (sūchi seigyo)
NC (numerical control)
数値制御

NCU (nettowāku seigyo sōchi)
NCU (network control unit)
ネットワーク制御装置

NDRO (hihakai yomidashi)
NDRO (nondestructive readout)
非破壊読み出し

NDU (nettowāku-dēta tan'i)
NDU (network data unit)
ネットワーク・データ単位

NEQ (futōka)
NEQ (nonequivalence)
不等価

NEQ gēto (futōka gēto)
NEQ gate (nonequivalence gate)
NEQゲート；不等価ゲート

NEQ soshi (futōka soshi)
NEQ element (nonequivalence element)
NEQ素子；不等価素子

nesuteingu
nesting
ネスティング

nesuto
nest
ネスト

netsuden kōka
thermoelectric effect
熱電効果

netsudendō
heat conduction
熱伝導

netsudendō kaiseki
heat conduction analysis
熱伝導解析

netsuteikō
thermal resistance
熱抵抗

nettowāku
network
ネットワーク

nettowāku-adoresu
network address
ネットワーク・アドレス

nettowāku-anaraiza
network analyzer
ネットワーク・アナライザ

nettowāku-anarogu
network analog
ネットワーク・アナログ

nettowāku-dēta tan'i (NDU)
network data unit (NDU)
ネットワーク・データ単位

nettowāku kaiseki
network analysis
ネットワーク解析

nettowāku kaisekiki
network analyzer
ネットワーク解析器

nettowāku kōzō
network structure
ネットワーク構造

nettowāku-puroguramingu
network programming
ネットワーク・プログラミング

nettowāku seigyo
network control
ネットワーク制御

nettowāku seigyo sōchi (NCU)
network control unit (NCU)
ネットワーク制御装置

nettowāku-shisutemu
network system
ネットワーク・システム

NFB (fukikan)
NFB (negative feedback)
負帰還

ni adoresu
double address; two-address
2アドレス

ni adoresu meirei
two-address instruction
2アドレス命令

ni dankai tantai hō
two-phase simplex method
二段階単体法

ni doraibu
two-drive
2ドライブ

ni doraibu-rekōda
two-drive recorder
2ドライブ・レコーダ

ni go shin(hō)
biquinary
2-5進(法)

ni go shin(hō) fugō
biquinary code
2-5進(法)符号

ni go shin(hō) kōdo
biquinary code
2-5進(法)コード

ni go shinhō
biquinary notation
2-5進法

ni go shinsū
biquinary; biquinary number
2-5進数

ni jōtai
two-state
二状態

ni jōtai hensū
two-state variable
二状態変数

ni no hosū
two's complement
2の補数

ni purasu ichi adoresu
two-plus-one address
2＋1アドレス

ni reberu-saburūchin
two-level subroutine
2レベル・サブルーチン

ni shigen kioku
two-dimensional storage
2次元記憶

ni tēpu hōhō
two-tape method
2テープ方法

niantei
bistable
二安定

niantei kairo
bistable circuit
二安定回路

nibai chōsū
double-length number
二倍長数

nibai seido
double precision
二倍精度

nibai seido enzan
double-precision arithmetic
二倍精度演算

nibun tansaku
binary search;
dichotomizing search
二分探索

nibunhō
dichotomy
二分法

niburu
nibble
ニブル

nichi
binary
2値

nichi hensū
binary variable
2値変数

nichi ronri
binary logic
2値論理

nichi ronri soshi
binary logic element
2値論理素子

nichi soshi
binary cell
2値素子

nichitenkan densō
point-to-point transmission
二地点間伝送

nichitenkan hōshiki
point-to-point system
二地点間方式

Nihon Denshi Kōgyō Shinkō Kyōkai (JEIDA)
Japanese Electronic Industry Development Association (JEIDA)
日本電子工業振興協会

Nihon Jōhō Shori Kaihatsu Kyōkai (JIPDEC)
Japan Information Processing Development Center (JIPDEC)
日本情報処理開発協会

Nihon Kōgyō Hyōjun Chōsakai (JISC)
Japanese Industrial Standards Committee (JISC)
日本工業標準調査会

Nihon Kōgyō Hyōjun Kikaku (JIS)
Japanese Industrial Standards (JIS)
日本工業標準規格

375

Nihongo jōhō shisutemu (NIS)
Japanese-language information
system (NIS)
日本語情報システム

Nihongo rain-purinta (NLP)
Japanese-language line printer
(NLP)
日本語ライン・プリンタ

Nihongo shiriaru-purinta (NSP)
Japanese-language serial printer
(NSP)
日本語シリアル・プリンタ

Nihongo wādo-purosessa (NWP)
Japanese-language word
processor (NWP)
日本語ワード・プロセッサ

niji
secondary
二次

niji keikakuhō (QP)
quadratic programming (QP)
二次計画法

niji kioku
secondary storage
二次記憶

niji kioku sōchi
secondary store
二次記憶装置

niji kyoku
secondary station
二次局

niji saburūchin
second-order subroutine
二次サブルーチン

niji sakuin hensei
secondary index organization
二次索引編成

niji sentaku hōshiki
quadratic selection
二次選択方式

nijū
duplex
二重

nijū ayamari
double error
二重誤り

nijū baffuaringu
double buffering
二重バッファリング

nijū densō
duplex transmission
二重伝送

nijū kaisen
duplex line
二重回線

nijū kanshō shuhō
double buffering
二重緩衝手法

nijū kensa
duplication check
二重検査

nijū seigyo
dual control
二重制御

nijū senkō
double punching
二重せん孔

nijū shisutemu
duplex system
二重システム

nijū teigi raberu
duplicate label
二重定義ラベル

nijū tsūshin hōshiki
duplex communication system
二重通信方式

nijū tsūshinro
duplex channel
二重通信路

nikkeru chien sen
nickel delay line
ニッケレ遅延線

nikō
binomial
2項

nikō bumpu
binomial distribution
2項分布

nikō Būru enzan
dyadic Boolean operation
2項ブール演算

nikō Būru enzanshi
dyadic Boolean operator
2項ブール演算子

nikō enzan
dyadic operation
2項演算

nikō enzanshi
binary operator
2項演算子

ningen-keisanki intafuēsu (HCI)
human-computer interface (HCI)
人間-計算機インタフェース

ningen-kikai
man-machine
人間-機械

ningen-kikai intafuēsu (MMI)
man-machine interface (MMI)
人間-機械インタフェース

ningen-kikai shisutemu
man-machine system
人間-機械システム

ningen-kikai sōgokankei
man-machine interaction
人間-機械相互関係

**ningen-shisutemu-intafuēsu
(HSI)**
human-system interface (HSI)
人間-システム・インタフェース

nin'i
optional
任意

nin'i junjo keisanki
arbitrary sequence computer
任意順序計算機

nin'i mojyūru
optional module
任意モジュール

nin'i no tanmatsu (sōchi)
optional terminal
任意の端末(装置)

nin'i raberu
optional label
任意ラベル

nin'i sentaku
option; optional
任意選択

nin'i sentaku kikō
optional feature
任意選択機構

nin'i sentaku kinō
optional feature
任意選択機能

nin'i teishi meirei
optional stop instruction
任意停止命令

nin'igata kii-in
unsolicited key-in
任意型キー・イン

ninshiki
recognition
認識

NIP (chūkaku shoki settei puroguramu)
NIP (nucleus initialization program)
中核初期設定プログラム

NIS (Nihongo jōhō shisutemu)
NIS (Japanese-language information system)
日本語情報システム

nisen shiki
two-wire system
二線式

nisenshiki chaneru
two-wire channel
二線式チャネル

nisenshiki kaisen
two-wire circuit
二線式回線

nishin
binary
2進

nishin Būru enzan
binary Boolean operation
2進ブール演算

nishin dēta dōki tsūshin (BSC)
binary synchronous communication (BSC)
2進データ同期通信

nishin enkōdeingu
binary encoding
2進エンコーディング

nishin enzan
binary arithmetic operation; binary operation
2進演算

nishin fugōka jisshin hō
weighted-bit code
2進符号化10進法

nishin genzanki
binary subtractor
2進減算器

nishin hankasanki
binary half-adder
2進半加算器

nishin hensū
binary variable
2進変数

nishin hikaku
binary comparison
2進比較

nishin hikaku kairo
binary comparator
2進比較回路

nishin hō
denary notation
2進法

nishin hyōgen
binary representation
2進表現

nishin hyōjihō
binary representation
2進表示法

nishin jisshin henkan
binary-to-decimal conversion
2進10進変換

nishin ju
binary tree
2進樹

nishin kairo
binary circuit
2進回路

nishin kasanki
binary adder
2進加算器

nishin kaunta
binary counter
2進カウンタ

nishin kisū
binary radix
2進基数

nishin kōdo
binary code
2進コード

nishin moji
binary character
2進文字

nishin sanjutsu enzan
binary arithmetic operation
2進算術演算

nishin seisū
binary integer
2進整数

nishin shingō
binary signaling
2進信号

nishin shisutemu
binary system
2進システム

nishin shōsū
binary fraction
2進小数

nishin shōsūten
binary point
2進小数点

nishin sūji (bitto)
binary digit (bit)
2進数字（ビット）

nishin tan'i
binary unit
2進単位

nishin tansaku
binary search
2進探索

nishin tansaku ju
binary-search tree
2進探索樹

nishin yōso
binary element
2進要素

nishin yōso retsu
binary element string
2進要素列

nishin zōbun hyōjihō
binary incremental representation
2進増分表示法

nishinhō
binary form; binary notation; binary representation
2進法

nishinka hyōkihō
binary-coded notation
2進化表記法

nishinka jisshin (BCD)
binary-coded decimal (BCD)
2進化10進

nishinka jisshin hyōjihō
binary-coded-decimal
representation
2進化10進表示法

nishinka jisshin kōdo (BCD kōdo)
binary-coded-decimal code (BCD
code)
2進化10進コード；BCDコード

nishinka jisshinhō
binary-coded-decimal notation
2進化10進法

nishinka moji
binary-coded character
2進化文字

nishinsū
binary; binary number;
binary numeral
2進数

nishinsū kādo
binary card
2進数カード

nishinsū shisutemu
binary number system
2進数システム

NL (kaigyō fukki moji)
NL (new-line character)
改行復帰文字

NLP (Nihongo rain-purinta)
NLP (Japanese-language line
printer)
日本語ライン・プリンタ

NMOS (N-chaneru MOS)
NMOS (N-channel metal-oxide
semiconductor)
N-チャネルMOS

no-opu (mudōsa)
no op (no operation)
ノ・オプ；無動作

no-opu meirei
no-op instruction
ノ・オプ命令

nōdaru-purosessa
nodal processor
ノーダル・プロセッサ

nōdo
node
ノード

nōdō
active
能動

nōdō soshi
active element
能動素子

noizu
noise
ノイズ

noizu bōshiki
noise killer
ノイズ防止器

noizu-mōdo
noisy mode
ノイズ・モード

noizu ritsu
noise ratio
ノイズ率

noizu yō'in
noise factor
ノイズ要因

nokogirigata parusu
sawtooth pulse
のこぎり型パルス

NOR (hiteiwa; hitei OR; hiteironriwa)
NOR (inverted OR; neither-nor;
NOR OR)
NOR；否定和；否定 OR；
否定論理和

NOR enzan
inverted OR operation;
NOR operation
NOR演算

NOR gēto
inverted OR gate; NOR gate
NORゲート

NOR kairo
inverted OR circuit; NOR circuit
NOR回路

NOR soshi
inverted OR element;
NOR element
NOR素子

nōryoku
capacity
能力

NOT-AND (hitei AND; hiteironriseki)
NOT-AND (NAND; negative
AND)
NOT-AND；否定 AND；
否定論理積

NOT-AND enzan
NOT-AND operation
NOT-AND演算

NOT-AND gēto
NOT-AND gate
NOT-ANDゲート

NOT-AND kairo
NOT-AND circuit
NOT-AND回路

NOT-AND soshi
NOT-AND element
NOT AND素子

NOT enzan
NOT operation
NOT演算

NOT gēto
NOT gate
NOTゲート

NOT kairo
NOT circuit
NOT回路

NOT soshi
NOT element
NOT素子

NRZ (hizero fukki; hizero modori; NRZ hōshiki)
NRZ (nonreturn to zero)
非ゼロ復帰；非ゼロ戻り；
NRZ方式

NRZI (NRZI hōshiki)
NRZI (nonreturn-to-zero inverted)
NRZI方式

NRZI hōshiki (NRZI)
nonreturn-to-zero inverted (NRZI)
NRZI方式

ns (nanobyō)
ns (nanosecond)
ナノ秒

NSP (Nihongo shiriaru-purinta)
NSP (Japanese-language serial printer)
日本語シリアル・プリンタ

NTL (hishikii chi ronri)
NTL (nonthreshold logic)
非敷居値論理

NUL (kūhaku)
NUL (null)
空白

NWP (Nihongo wādo-purosessa)
NWP (Japanese-language word processor)
日本語ワード・プロセッサ

nyūryoku
entry; input
入力

nyūryoku baffua
input buffer
入力バッファ

nyūryoku baitai
input medium
入力媒体

nyūryoku burokku
input block
入力ブロック

nyūryoku burokkuka insū
input blocking factor
入力ブロック化因数

nyūryoku chaneru
input channel
入力チャネル

nyūryoku dēta
input data
入力データ

nyūryoku dēta kenshō
input data validation
入力データ検証

nyūryoku eremento
input element
入力エレメント

nyūryoku gen
input source
入力源

nyūryoku haichi
input layout
入力配置

nyūryoku hensū
input variable
入力変数

nyūryoku hoppa
input hopper
入力ホッパ

nyūryoku hosū
input complement
入力補数

nyūryoku iki
input area
入力域

nyūryoku jōtai
input state
入力状態

nyūryoku jun
entry sequence
入力順

nyūryoku jyobu-sutoriimu
input job stream
入力ジョブ・ストリーム

nyūryoku kii
enter key
入力キー

nyūryoku kiibōdo
input keyboard
入力キーボード

nyūryoku kiki
input device
入力機器

nyūryoku machigyōretsu
input queue
入力待ち行列

nyūryoku magajin
input magazine
入力マガジン

nyūryoku meirei
input instruction
入力命令

nyūryoku mōdo
enter mode
入力モード

nyūryoku nagare
input stream
入力流れ

nyūryoku puroguramu
input program
入力プログラム

nyūryoku reiauto
input layout
入力レイアウト

nyūryoku rūchin
input routine
入力ルーチン

nyūryoku sagyō machigyōretsu
input work queue
入力作業待ち行列

nyūryoku saki
destination
入力先

nyūryoku seigyo
input control
入力制御

nyūryoku seigyo sōchi
input control unit
入力制御装置

nyūryoku shingō
input signal
入力信号

nyūryoku shiyō
input specification
入力仕様

nyūryoku shiyōsho
input specification sheet
入力仕様書

nyūryoku shori
input processing
入力処理

nyūryoku-shutsuryoku apurōchi
input-to-output approach
入力-出力アプローチ

nyūryoku sōchi
input device; input unit
入力装置

nyūryoku sokudo
speed of input
入力速度

nyūryoku suru
enter; input (*verb*)
入力する

nyūryoku sutoriimu
input stream
入力ストリーム

nyūryoku tetsuzuki
input procedure
入力手続き

nyūshutsuryoku (I/O)
input/output (I/O)
入出力

nyūshutsuryoku baffua
input/output buffers
入出力ブッファ

nyūshutsuryoku baitai
input/output medium
入出力媒体

nyūshutsuryoku basu
input/output bus
入出力バス

nyūshutsuryoku bun
input/output statement
入出力文

nyūshutsuryoku chaneru
input/output channel
入出力チャネル

nyūshutsuryoku chippu
input/output chip
入出力チップ

nyūshutsuryoku dēta
input/output data
入出力データ

nyūshutsuryoku fuairu
input/output file
入出力ファイル

nyūshutsuryoku intafuēsu
input/output interface
入出力インタフェース

nyūshutsuryoku kankei
input/output relationship
入出力関係

nyūshutsuryoku kiki
input/output equipment
入出力機器

nyūshutsuryoku kyōyō fuairu
combined file
入出力共用ファイル

nyūshutsuryoku meirei
input/output instruction
入出力命令

nyūshutsuryoku mojyūru (IOM)
input/output module (IOM)
入出力モジュール

nyūshutsuryoku narabi
input/output list
入出力並び

nyūshutsuryoku pōto
input/output port
入出力ポート

nyūshutsuryoku pōto-baffua
input/output port buffer
入出力ポート・バッファ

nyūshutsuryoku rejisuta
input/output register
入出力レジスタ

nyūshutsuryoku rūchin
input/output routine
入出力ルーチン

nyūshutsuryoku ryō'iki
input/output area
入出力領域

nyūshutsuryoku seigen
input/output restrictions
入出力制限

nyūshutsuryoku seigyo
input/output control
入出力制御

nyūshutsuryoku seigyo shingō
input/output control signal
入出力制御信号

nyūshutsuryoku seigyo shisutemu (IOCS)
input/output control system (IOCS)
入出力制御システム

nyūshutsuryoku seigyo sōchi
input/output control unit;
input/output controller
入出力制御装置

nyūshutsuryoku sekushon
input/output section
入出力セクション

nyūshutsuryoku shirei
input/output command
入出力指令

nyūshutsuryoku shisutemu
input-output system
入出力システム

nyūshutsuryoku shori
input-output processing
入出力処理

nyūshutsuryoku shori sōchi (IOP)
input-output processor (IOP)
入出力処理装置

nyūshutsuryoku sōchi
input/output device;
input/output unit
入出力装置

nyūshutsuryoku sōsa
input/output operation
入出力操作

nyūshutsuryoku taipuraita
input/output typewriter
入出力タイプライタ

nyūshutsuryoku tanmatsu (sōchi)
input/output terminal
入出力端末(装置)

nyūshutsuryoku tetsuzuki
input-output procedure
入出力手続き

nyūshutsuryoku warikomi
input/output interruption
入出力割り込み

O

O and M (soshiki-hōshiki)
O and M (organization and methods)
O and M; OアンドM;組織-方式

OA (ofuisu-otomēshon)
OA (office automation)
オフィス・オトメーション

ōbafurō
overflow
オーバフロー

ōbaheddo
overhead
オーバヘッド

ōbaheddo-bitto
overhead bit
オーバヘッド・ビット

ōbaheddo-taimu
overhead time
オーバヘッド・タイム

ōbaintegurēshon
overintegration
オーバインテグレーション

ōbapanchi
overpunch
オーバパンチ

ōbaran
overrun
オーバラン

ōbarei
overlay
オーバレィ

ōbarei kanshi puroguramu
overlay supervisor
オーバレィ監視プログラム

ōbarei kōzō
overlay structure
オーバレィ構造

ōbarei-puroguramu
overlay program
オーバレィ・プログラム

ōbarei-rōdo-mojyūru
overlay load module
オーバレィ・ロード・モジュール

ōbarei-segumento
overlay segment
オーバレィ・セグメント

O/C (ōpun-korekuta)
O/C (open collector)
オープン・コレクタ

OCR (kōgakushiki moji ninshiki)
OCR (optical character recognition)
光学式文字認識

OCR (kōgakushiki moji yomitori sōchi)
OCR (optical character reader)
光学式文字読み取り装置

OEM (aite sakishōhyō seizō kaisha)
OEM (original equipment manufacturer)
相手先商標製造会社

OFT (hikari fuaiba kan)
OFT (optical fiber tube)
光ファイバ管

ofu
off
オフ

ofu-hukku
off-hook
オフ・フック

ofu-rain
off-line
オフ・ライン

ofu-rain-dēta densō
off-line data transmission
オフ・ライン・データ伝送

ofu-rain dōsa
off-line operation;
off-line working
オフ・ライン動作

ofu-rain kiki
off-line equipment
オフ・ライン機器

ofu-rain kikō
off-line feature
オフ・ライン機構

ofu-rain kinō
off-line feature
オフ・ライン機能

ofu-rain kioku
off-line storage
オフ・ライン記憶

ofu-rain seigyo
off-line control
オフ・ライン制御

ofu-rain-shisutemu
off-line system
オフ・ライン・システム

ofu-rain shori
off-line processing
オフ・ライン処理

ofu-rain sōchi
off-line equipment
オフ・ライン装置

ofu-rain sōsa
off-line operation
オフ・ライン操作

ofu-rainingu
off-lining
オフ・ライン・ライニング

ofu senkō
off-punch
オフせん孔

ofuisu-konpyūta
office computer
オフィス・コンピュタ

ofuisu-otomēshon (OA)
office automation (OA)
オフィス・オトメーション

ofusetto
offset
オフセット

ofusetto-sutakka
offset stacker
オフセット・スタッカ

okikae
replacement; substitute;
substitution
置き換え

okikae hōhō
substitution method
置き換え方法

okikae moji (SUB)
substitute character (SUB)
置き換え文字

okikaeru
replace
置き換える

ōkisa
size
大きさ

okure
delay; lag; time delay
遅れ

okuri
feed; shift
送り

okuri ana
feed holes; sprocket holes
送り孔

okuri ayamari
feed error; misfeed
送り誤り

okuri hoppa
feed hopper
送りホッパ

okuri kankaku
feed pitch
送り間隔

okuri rejisuta
shift register
送りレジスタ

okuri sokudo
feed rate
送り速度

okuridashi
sending
送り出し

okuridasu
send
送り出し

okuru
feed (*verb*)
送る

OLRT (on-rain-riaru-taimu)
OLRT (on-line real time)
オン・ライン・リアル・タイム

OLRT shisutemu (on-rain-riaru-taimu-shisutemu)
OLRT system (on-line real-time system)
オン・ライン・リアル・タイム・システム；OLRTシステム

OLRT sōsa (on-rain-riaru-taimu sōsa)
OLRT operation (on-line real-time operation)
オン・ライン・リアル・タイム操作；OLRT操作

omomi
significance; weight
重み

omomi rejisuta
weight register
重みレジスタ

omomitsuki kōdo
weighted code
重み付きコード

omote okuri
face-up feed
表送り

OMR (kōgakushiki māku ninshiki)
OMR (optical mark recognition)
光学式マーク認識

OMR (kōgakushiki māku yomitori sōchi)
OMR (optical mark reader)
光学式マーク読み取り装置

on
on
オン

on-hukku
on-hook
オン・フック

on-ofu dōsa
on-off action
オン・オフ動作

on-ofu-seigyo
on-off control
オン・オフ制御

on-ofu-shisutemu
on-off system
オン・オフ・システム

on-rain
on-line
オン・ライン

on-rain chūō fuairu
on-line central file
オン・ライン中央ファイル

on-rain-debaggingu
on-line debugging
オン・ライン・デバッギング

on-rain-dēta densō
on-line data transmission
オン・ライン・データ伝送

on-rain-dēta nyūryoku
on-line data entry
オン・ライン・データ入力

on-rain-dēta shūshū
on-line data acquisition;
on-line data gathering
オン・ライン・データ収集

on-rain dōsa
on-line operation;
on-line working
オン・ライン動作

on-rain jōhō
on-line information
オン・ライン情報

on-rain jōhō kensaku
on-line information retrieval
オン・ライン情報検索

on-rain keisan hōshiki
on-line computing
オン・ライン計算方式

on-rain kensaku
on-line interrogation
オン・ライン検索

on-rain kiki
on-line equipment
オン・ライン機器

on-rain kioku
on-line storage
オン・ライン記憶

on-rain-riaru-taimu (OLRT)
on-line real time (OLRT)
オン・ライン・リアル・タイム

on-rain-riaru-taimu-shisutemu (OLRT shisutemu)
on-line real-time system (OLRT system)
オン・ライン・リアル・タイム・システム；OLRTシステム

on-rain-riaru-taimu sōsa (OLRT sōsa)
on-line real-time operation (OLRT operation)
オン・ライン・リアル・タイム操作；OLRT操作

on-rain seigyo
on-line control
オン・ライン制御

on-rain shiken
on-line testing
オン・ライン試験

on-rain shindan
on-line diagnosis
オン・ライン診断

on-rain-shisutemu
on-line system
オン・ライン・システム

on-rain shori
on-line processing
オン・ライン処理

on-rain sōchi
on-line equipment
オン・ライン装置

on-rain tanmatsu (sōchi)
on-line terminal
オン・ライン端末(装置)

on-rain-tēpu-panchi
on-line tape punch
オン・ライン・テープ・パンチ

on-rain-tesuteingu
on-line testing
オン・ライン・テスティング

on-rain toiawase
on-line interrogation
オン・ライン問い合わせ

on-rain tsūshin
on-line communication
オン・ライン通信

on-rain tsūshin shisutemu
on-line communication system
オン・ライン通信システム

on-saito
on-site
オン・サイト

ON yunitto
ON unit
ONユニット

ondo
temperature
温度

onkyō
acoustics
音響

onkyō fuiidobakku
acoustic feedback
音響フィードバック

onkyō kapura
acoustic coupler
音響カプラ

onkyō ketsugō sōchi
acoustic coupler
音響結合装置

onkyō kōka
acoustic efficiency
音響効果

onkyō shingō
acoustic signal
音響信号

onkyōteki chūjissei
acoustic fidelity
音響的忠実性

onryō
volume
音量

onryō tan'i (VU)
volume unit (VU)
音量単位

onsei
speech; voice
音声

onsei gōsei
speech synthesis; voice synthesis
音声合成

onsei gōsei kādo
voice synthesis card
音声合成カード

onsei gōseiki
speech synthesizer
音声合成器

onsei hassei
speech generation
音声発生

onsei hasseiki
speech generation device
音声発生器

onsei ninshiki
speech recognition;
voice recognition
音声認識

onsei nyūryoku
voice input
音声入力

onsei nyūryoku mojyūru
voice input module
音声入力モジュール

onsei nyūryoku sōchi
voice input device
音声入力装置

onsei ōtō
audio-response; verbal response;
voice response
音声応答

onsei ōtō sōchi
audio-response unit
音声応答装置

onsei rikai
speech understanding
音声理解

onsei shori
speech processing
音声処理

onsei shūha
voice frequency
音声周波

onsei shūhasū (AF)
audio frequency (AF)
音声周波数

onsei tai'iki
voice band
音声帯域

onsei tai'iki chaneru
voice grade channel
音声帯域チャネル

onsei tai'iki kaisen
voice grade line
音声帯域回線

onsei tan'i (VU)
voice unit (VU)
音声単位

operando
operand
オペランド

operando bu
operand part
オペランド部

operando-fuiirudo
operand field
オペランド・フィールド

operando kaiseki
parse
オペランド解析

operando no nagasa
operand length
オペランドの長さ

operando ran
operand field
オペランド欄

operando shitei
operand addressing
オペランド指定

operēshon
operation
オペレーション

operēshon kaiseki
operations analysis
オペレーション解析

operēshon keikaku
operation(al) planning
オペレーション計画

operēshon keikaku jōhō
operational planning information
オペレーション計画情報

operēshon-rejisuta
operation register
オペレーション・レジスタ

operēshon-risāchi (OR)
operations research (OR)
オペレーション・リサーチ

operēta
operator
オペレータ

operēta-erā
operator error
オペレータ・エラー

operēta-gaido
operator's guide
オペレータ・ガイド

operēta-konsoru
operator console
オペレータ・コンソル

operēta seigyo
operator control
オペレータ制御

operēta seigyoban
operator's control panel
オペレータ制御盤

operēta shirei
operator command
オペレータ指令

operēteingu-mōdo
operating mode
オペレーティング・モード

operēteingu-shisutemu (OS)
operating system (OS)
オペレーティング・システム

operēteingu-shisutemu-fuāmuuea
operating system firmware
オペレーティング・システム・
ファームウェア

operēteingu-yunitto
operating unit
オペレーティング・ユニット

opu-kōdo
op code (operation code)
オプ・コード

ōpun
open
オープン

ōpun-endo
open end
オープン・エンド

ōpun-korekuta (O/C)
open collector (O/C)
オープン・コレクタ

ōpun-rūchin
open routine
オープン・ルーチン

ōpun-rūpu
open loop
オープン・ループ

ōpun-saburūchin
open subroutine
オープン・サブルーチン

ōpun-shoppu
open-shop
オープン・ショップ

ōpun-shoppu-puroguramingu
open-shop programming
オープン・ショップ・
プログラミング

opushon
option
オプション

opushon-kādo
option card
オプション・カード

opushon meirei
optional command
オプション命令

opushonaru
optional
オプショナル

opushonaru kikō
optional feature
オプショナル機構

opushonaru kinō
optional feature;
optional function
オプショナル機能

opushonaru teishi meirei
optional stop instruction
オプショナル停止命令

oputo-erekutoronikkusu
optoelectronics
オプト・エレクトロニックス

OR (operēshon-risāchi)
OR (operations research)
オペレーション・リサーチ

OR
OR
OR

OR enzan
OR operation
OR演算

OR gēto
OR gate
OR ゲート

OR kairo
OR circuit
OR回路

OR soshi
OR element
OR 表子

orientēshon
orientation
オリエンテーション

orijinēta
originator
オリジネータ

OS (operēteingu-shisutemu)
OS (operating system)
オペレーティング・システム

oshi
push
押し

oshi botan-daiaru hōshiki
touch-tone dialing
押しボタン・ダイアル方式

oshi kando sōchi
touch-sensitive device
押し感度装置

oshipado
touchpad
押しパッド

oshirēta
oscillator
オシレータ

oshirēteingu
oscillating
オシレーティング

oshirēteingu bunrui
oscillating sort
オシレーティング分類

oshirosukopu
oscilloscope
オシロスコプ

Ōshū Denshi Keisanki Seizō Gyōsha Kyōkai (ECMA)
European Computer Manufacturers' Association (ECMA)
欧州電子計算機製造業者協会

ōtō
answer; response
応答

ōto-fuiido
autofeed
オート・フィード

oto gōseiki
sound synthesizer
音合成器

ōtō jikan
response time
応答時間

ōto-kōdeingu
autocoding
オート・コーディング

ōto-kōdo
autocode
オート・コード

ōtō on
answer tone
応答音

ōtōgata kii-in
solicited key-in
応答型キー・イン

otōmata
automata
オトーマタ

otōmaton
automaton
オトーマトン

otomēshon
automation
オトメーション

oun-kōdeingu
own coding
オウン・コーディング

oun-kōdeingu-rūchin
own coding routine
オウン・コーディング・ルーチン

oun-kōdo
own code
オウン・コード

oya
host; owner; parent
親

oya gengo
host language
親言語

oya gengo dētabēsu
host language database
親言語データベース

oya pointa
owner pointer
親ポインタ

oya rekōdo
owner record
親レコード

oya shisutemu
host system
親システム

oyako kankei
set membership
親子関係

oyako ketsugō shūgō
owner-coupled set
親子結合集合

oyako shūgō
set (*noun*)
親子集合

oyako shūgō fuku kijutsukō
set subentry
親子集合副記述項

oyako shūgō junjo kijun
set-ordering criteria
親子集合順序基準

oyako shūgō kijutsukō
set-description entry
親子集合記述項

oyako shūgō kō
set entry
親子集合項

oyako shūgō sentaku
set selection
親子集合選択

oyako shūgō setsu
set section
親子集合節

ōyō
application; practical application
応用

ōyō dēta shori
applied data processing
応用データ処理

ōyō jōhō gijutsu
applied information technology
応用情報技術

ōyō kei'ei jōhō shisutemu
applied management information system
応用経営情報システム

ōyō keisanki kagaku
applied computer science
応用計算機科学

ōyō kenkyū
application study
応用研究

ōyō operēshon-risāchi
applied operations research
応用オペレーション・リサーチ

ōyō purogurama
applications programmer
応用プログラマ

ōyō puroguramu (AP)
application program (AP)
応用プログラム

ōyō shisō
application philosophy
応用思想

ōyō shisutemu
application system
応用システム

ōyō shisutemu kenkyū
applied systems research
応用システム研究

P

p-chaneru MOS
p-channel metal-oxide
semiconductor; p-channel MOS
p-チャネルMOS

PAD (paketto kumitate/bunkai)
PAD (packet assembly/
disassembly)
パケット組み立て/分解

paddeingu
padding
パッディング

paddo
pad
パッド

paddo suru
pad (*verb*)
パッドする

paipu-rain-shisutemu
pipeline system
パイプ・ライン・システム

pairotto-moderu
pilot model
パイロット・モデル

pairotto-shisutemu
pilot system
パイロット・システム

paketto
packet
パケット

paketto kōkan
packet switching
パケット交換

paketto kōkanmō
packet-switching network
パケット交換網

paketto kumitate/bunkai (PAD)
packet assembly/disassembly
(PAD)
パケット組み立て/分解

pakettogata tanmatsu (sōchi)
packed-mode terminal
パケット型端末(装置)

pakkēji
package
パッケージ

pakkēji-puroguramu
package program
パッケージ・プログラム

pakkingu
packing
パッキング

pakku
pack
パック

pakku jisshinsū
packed decimal
パック10進数

PAM (parusu shimpuku henchō)
PAM (pulse amplitude
modulation)
パルス振幅変調

pancha
puncher; punching machine
パンチャ

panchi
punch
パンチ

panchi-operēta
punch operator
パンチ・オペレータ

panchi suru
punch (*verb*)
パンチする

panchingu
punching
パンチング

paneru
panel
パネル

paneru-deisupurei
panel display
パネル・ディスプレイ

panikku-danpu
panic dump
パニック・ダンプ

parameta
parameter
パラメタ

parameta go
parameter word
パラメタ語

parameta-kādo
parameter card
パラメタ・カード

parameta kudōgata
parameter-driven
パラメタ駆動型

parameta-tēburu
parameter table
パラメタ・テーブル

parametagata gengo
parametric language
パラメタ型言語

parametoron
parametron
パラメトロン

paritei
parity
パリティ

paritei-bitto
parity bit
パリティ・ビット

paritei-chekku
parity check
パリティ・チェック

paritei-erā
parity error
パリティ・エラー

parusu
pulse
パルス

parusu-bēsu
pulse base
パルス・ベース

parusu-bēsu chūōten
pulse base center point
パルス・ベース中央点

parusu-bēsu hizumi
pulse base distortion
パルス・ベース歪み

parusu-bēsu shimpuku
pulse base magnitude
パルス・ベース振幅

parusu chūōten
pulse center point
パルス中央点

parusu fugō henchō (PCM)
pulse code modulation (PCM)
パルス符号変調

parusu haba
pulse duration; pulse length;
pulse width
パルス幅

parusu haba henchō
pulse duration modulation;
pulse length modulation
パルス幅変調

parusu haba hizumi
pulse duration distortion;
pulse length distortion;
pulse width distortion
パルス幅歪み

parusu hakei
pulse waveform
パルス波形

parusu hasseiki
pulse generator
パルス発生器

parusu henchō
pulse modulation
パルス変調

parusu ichi
pulse position
パルス位置

parusu ichi henchō
pulse position modulation
パルス位置変調

parusu isō henchō
pulse phase modulation
パルス位相変調

parusu jihenchō
pulse time modulation
パルス時変調

parusu kankaku
pulse separation
パルス間隔

parusu kankaku hizumi
pulse separation distortion
パルス間隔歪み

parusu kei
pulse shape
パルス形

parusu keisei
pulse forming
パルス形成

parusu keisei kairo
pulse-forming circuit
パルス形成回路

parusu kurikaeshi ritsu
pulse repetition rate
パルス繰り返し率

parusu kurikaeshi shūhasū
pulse repetition frequency
パルス繰り返し周波数

parusu kurikaeshi shūhasū jitta
pulse repetition frequency
fluctuation; pulse repetition
frequency jitter
パルス繰り返し周波数ジッタ

parusu kurikaeshi shūki
pulse repetition period
パルス繰り返し周期

parusu kurikaeshi shūki jitta
pulse repetition period
fluctuation; pulse repetition
period jitter
パルス繰り返し周期ジッタ

parusu no okure
pulse delay time
パルスの遅れ

parusu no susumi
pulse advance
パルスの進み

parusu ōtō
pulse response
パルス応答

parusu retsu
pulse train
パルス列

parusu saisei
pulse regeneration
パルス再生

parusu saisei kairo
pulse regeneration circuit
パルス再生回路

parusu seikei
pulse shaping
パルス整形

parusu seikei kairo
pulse shaping circuit
パルス整形回路

parusu shimpuku
pulse amplitude;
pulse magnitude
パルス振幅

parusu shimpuku henchō (PAM)
pulse amplitude modulation (PAM)
パルス振幅変調

parusu shimpuku jitta
pulse magnitude fluctuation; pulse magnitude jitter
パルス振幅ジッタ

parusu shūhasū henchō
pulse frequency modulation
パルス周波数変調

parusu sūhenchō
pulse number modulation
パルス数変調

parusu tachiagari jikan
pulse rise time
パルス立ち上り時間

parusu tachisagari jikan
pulse fall time
パルス立ち下り時間

parusu-toppu
pulse top
パルス・トップ

parusu-toppu chūōten
pulse top center point
パルス・トップ中央点

parusu-toppu hizumi
pulse top distortion
パルス・トップ歪み

parusu-toppu shimpuku
pulse top magnitude
パルス・トップ振幅

pāshingu
parsing
パーシング

pāshingu-tēburu
parsing table
パーシング・テーブル

pāsokon (PC)
personal computer (PC)
パーソコン

pāsokon gamen
personal computer picture
パーソコン画面

pāsonaru
personal
パーソナル

pāsonaru CP/M
personal CP/M
パーソナルCP／M

pāsonaru-konpyūta (PC)
personal computer (PC)
パーソナル・コンピュータ

pasu
pass; path
パス

pasu asshuku
path compression
パス圧縮

Pasukaru
PASCAL
パスカル；Pascal

pasuwādo
password
パスワード

patān
pattern
パターン

patān-deisupurei
pattern display
パターン・ディスプレイ

patān kaiseki
pattern analysis
パターン解析

patān ninshiki
pattern recognition
パターン認識

patān riron
pattern theory
パターン理論

patān seigyo
pattern control
パターン制御

patān-shisutemu
pattern system
パターン・システム

patchi
patch
パッチ

patchi-paneru
patch panel
パッチ・パネル

pāto (PERT; puroguramu hyōka-kanri gihō)
program evaluation and review technique (PERT)
パート；プログラム評価-管理技法；PERT

pāza
parser
パーザ

pāza kōchiku
parser construction
パーザ構築

pāza-zenerēta
parser generator
パーザ・ゼネレータ

pāzu
parse
パーズ

pāzu ki
parse tree
パーズ木

PC (insatsu haisen kairo)
PC (printed circuit)
印刷配線回路

PC (pāsokon; pāsonaru-konpyūta)
PC (personal computer)
パーソコン；パーソナル・コンピュータ

PCB (insatsu haisenban; purinto kiban)
PCB (printed circuit board)
印刷配線板；プリント基板

PCB (puroguramu renraku burokku)
PCB (program communication block)
プログラム連絡ブロック

PCM (kādo senkō sōchi; kādo senkōki)
PCM (punch-card machine)
カードせん孔装置；カードせん孔機

PCM (parusu fugō henchō)
PCM (pulse code modulation)
パルス符号変調

PCS (senkō kādo-shisutemu)
PCS (punch-card system)
せん孔カード・システム

PDU (pōto-dēta tan'i)
 PDU (port data unit)
 ポート・データ単位

PE (isō kōdoka hōshiki; PE hōshiki)
 PE (phase encoding)
 位相コード化方式；PE 方式

PE hōshiki (PE)
 phase encoding (PE)
 PE 方式

PEEK (piiku)
 PEEK (peek)
 ピーク

pēji
 page
 ページ

pēji-adoresu
 page address
 ページ・アドレス

pēji afure
 page overflow
 ページ溢れ

pēji ashigaki
 page footer; page footing
 ページ脚書き

pēji atamagaki
 page heading
 ページ頭書き

pēji-auto
 page-out
 ページ・アウト

pēji bangō
 page number
 ページ番号

pēji fuzai
 page fault
 ページ不在

pēji-in
 page-in
 ページ・イン

pēji insho sōchi
 page printer
 ページ印書装置

pēji midashi
 page header
 ページ見出し

pēji-saizu
 page size
 ページ・サイズ

pēji shōgai
 page fault
 ページ障害

pēji shōgai hindo (PFF)
 page fault frequency (PFF)
 ページ障害頻度

pēji-tēburu
 page table
 ページ・テーブル

pēji waku
 page frame
 ページ枠

pēji yomitori sōchi
 page reader
 ページ読み取り装置

pējingu
 paging
 ページング

pējingu-arugorizumu
 paging algorithm
 ページング・アルゴリズム

pējingu gihō
 paging technique
 ページング技法

pējingu kikai
 paging machine
 ページング機械

pējingu ritsu
 paging rate
 ページング率

pējingu-shisutemu
 paging system
 ページング・システム

pējingu sōchi
 paging device
 ページング装置

pen-purotta
 pen plotter
 ペン・プロッタ

PERT (pāto; puroguramu hyōka-kanri gihō)
 PERT (program evaluation and review technique)
 パート；プログラム評価-管理技法

PFB (seikikan)
 PFB (positive feedback)
 正帰還

PFC (pōto nagare seigyo)
 PFC (port flow control)
 ポート流れ制御

PFF (pēji shōgai hindo)
 PFF (page fault frequency)
 ページ障害頻度

PI (puroguramu gakushū)
 PI (programmed instruction)
 プログラム学習

pibotto enzan
 pivot operation; pivoting
 ピボット演算

PID (kojin shikibetsu sōchi)
 PID (personal identification device)
 個人識別装置

pigibakku-shisutemu
 piggy-back system
 ピギバック・システム

piiku (PEEK)
 peek (PEEK)
 ピーク

piiku-dēta tensō sokudo
 peak data transfer rate
 ピーク・データ転送速度

piiku fuka
 peak load
 ピーク負荷

piikupiiku (P-P)
 peak to peak (P-P)
 ピークピーク

piikupiiku chi
 peak-to-peak value
 ピークピーク値

piikupiiku shimpuku
 peak-to-peak magnitude
 ピークピーク振幅

pikobyō (ps)
 picosecond (ps)
 ピコ秒

pikucha
 picture
 ピクチャ

pikucha-dēta
 picture data
 ピクチャ・データ

pikucha kensa
picture check
ピクチャ検査

pikucha shori
picture processing
ピクチャ処理

pikuseru
pixel
ピクセル

pin
pin
ピン

PIN (kojin shikibetsu bangō; PIN bangō)
PIN (personal identification number)
個人識別番号；PIN番号

PIN bangō (PIN)
personal identification number (PIN)
PIN番号

pin-fuiido
pin feed
ピン・フィード

pin-hedda
pin header
ピン・ヘッダ

pinbōdo
pinboard
ピンボード

pinchi-ofu
pinch-off
ピンチ・オフ

pinchi-rōra
pinch roller
ピンチ・ローラ

PIOCS (butsuriteki nyūshutsuryoku seigyo shisutemu)
PIOCS (physical input/output control system)
物理的入出力制御システム

pitchi
pitch
ピッチ

PL/M (maikurokonpyūta'yō puroguramingu gengo)
PL/M (program language for microcomputers)
マイクロコンピュータ用プログラミング言語

PL/1 (puroguramingu gengo/ichi)
PL/1 (programming language/one)
プログラミング言語/1；PL/1

PLOT (purotta)
PLOT (plotter)
プロッタ

PM (yobō hoshu)
PM (preventive maintenance)
予防保守

PMOS (p-chaneru MOS)
PMOS (p-channel metal-oxide semiconductor; p-channel MOS)
p-チャネルMOS

pointa
pointer
ポインタ

pointa-arei
pointer array
ポインタ・アレイ

pointa-dēta
pointer data
ポインタ・データ

pointa hensū
pointer variable
ポインタ変数

pointo tai pointo hōshiki
point-to-point system
ポイント対ポイント方式

POKE (pōku)
POKE (poke)
ポーク

pōku (POKE)
poke (POKE)
ポーク

poppu
pop
ポップ

Pōrando kihō
Polish notation
ポランド記法

porifuēzu bunrui
polyphase sort
ポリフェーズ分類

pōringu
polling
ポーリング

pōringu-risuto
polling list
ポーリング・リスト

pōru
poll
ポール

POS (posu)
POS (point of sales)
ポス；POS

POS tanmatsu sōchi (posu tanmatsu sōchi)
POS terminal (point-of-sales terminal)
ポス端末装置；POS端末装置

posu (POS)
point of sales (POS)
ポス；POS

posu tanmatsu sōchi (POS tanmatsu sōchi)
point-of-sales terminal (POS terminal)
ポス端末装置；POS端末装置

posuto-purosessa
postprocessor
ポスト・プロゼッサ

posuto-riido-sutēshon
postread station
ポスト・リード・ステーション

posutoanburu-burokku
postamble block
ポストアンブル・ブロック

pōto
port
ポート

pōto-dēta tan'i (PDU)
port data unit (PDU)
ポート・データ単位

pōto nagare seigyo (PFC)
port flow control (PFC)
ポート流れ制御

pōto teiji sābisu (PPS)
port presentation service (PPS)
ポート提示サービス

P-P (hakōchi; piiku-piiku)
P-P (peak to peak)
波高値；ピーク・ピーク

PPS (pōto teiji sābisu)
PPS (port presentation service)
ポート提示サービス

PREP (maeshori)
PREP (preparation)
前処理

PROM (puroguramukanō yomidashi sen'yō kioku; puroguramukanō yomitori sen'yō kioku)
PROM (programmable read-only memory; programmable ROM)
プログラム可能読み出し専用記憶；
プログラム可能読み取り専用記憶

PROM purogurama
PROM programmer
PROM プログラマ

ps (pikobyō)
ps (picosecond)
ピコ秒

PSR (purosessa jōtai rejisuta)
PSR (processor state register)
プロセッサ状態レジスタ

PSW (puroguramu jōtai go)
PSW (program status word)
プログラム状態語

PSWR (puroguramu jōtai go rejisuta)
PSWR (program status word register)
プログラム状態語レジスタ

PTP (kami tēpu-panchi; kami tēpu senkō sōchi; kami tēpu senkōki)
PTP (paper-tape punch)
紙テープ・パンチ；紙テープ
せん孔装置；紙テープせん孔機

PTR (kami tēpu yomitoriki; kami tēpu yomitori sōchi)
PTR (paper-tape reader)
紙テープ読み取り機
紙テープ読み取り装置

PUB (butsuriteki sōchi burokku)
PUB (physical unit block)
物理的装置ブロック

puragu gokansei
plug compatible
プラグ互換性

puragu-in
plug-in
プラグ・イン

puragu-in hōshiki
plug-in system
プラグ・イン方式

puragu-in tanshi
plug-in terminal
プラグ・イン端子

puragu-in-yunitto
plug-in unit
プラグ・イン・ユニット

puraten
platen
プラテン

puri-asain-memori
preassigned memory
プリ・アサイン・メモリ

puri-purosessa
preprocessor
プリ・プロセッサ

puri-risuto
prelist
プリ・リスト

puri-setto
preset
プリ・セット

puri-setto-parameta
preset parameter
プリ・セット・パラメタ

purianburu-burokku
preamble block
プリアンブル・ブロック

purimiteibu
primitive
プリミティブ

purinta
printer
プリンタ

purinta-intafuēsu
printer interface
プリンタ・インタフェース

purinta-kēburu
printer cable
プリンタ・ケーブル

purinta-kiibōdo
printer keyboard
プリンタ・キーボード

purinta-konekuta
printer connector
プリンタ・コネクタ

purinto
print
プリント

purinto-auto
printout
プリント・アウト

purinto-heddo
print head
プリント・ヘッド

purinto-hoiiru
print wheel
プリント・ホイール

purinto kiban (PCB)
printed circuit board (PCB)
プリント基板

purinto-sāba
print server
プリント・サーバ

purinto-sutēshon
print station
プリント・ステーション

purinto-waiya
print wire
プリント・ワイヤ

purōbu
probe
プローブ

purodakuto
product
プロダクト

purofuairu
profile
プロファイル

purogurama
programmer
プログラマ

purogurama teigi makuro meirei
programmer-defined macroinstruction
プログラマ定義マクロ命令

puroguramingu
programming
プログラミング

puroguramingu ayamari
programming error
プログラミング誤り

puroguramingu gengo
programming language
プログラミング言語

puroguramingu gengo (APL)
A Programming Language (APL)
プログラミング言語；APL

puroguramingu gihō
programming technique
プログラミング技法

puroguramingu hyōjun
programming standards
プログラミング標準

puroguramingu kankyō
programming environment
プログラミング環境

puroguramingu kihon meirei
programming primitive
プログラミング基本命令

puroguramingu-mojyūru
programming module
プログラミング・モジュール

puroguramingu nagarezu
programming flow diagram;
programming flowchart
プログラミング流れ図

puroguramingu-shisutemu
programming system
プログラミング・システム

puroguramu
program
プログラム

puroguramu-adoresu-kaunta
program address counter
プログラム・アドレス・カウンタ

puroguramu bubun
program part
プログラム部分

puroguramu bun kaiseki
program statement analysis
プログラム文解析

puroguramu bunshoka
program documentation
プログラム文書化

puroguramu-chekku
program check
プログラム・チェック

puroguramu dōki
program synchronization
プログラム同期

puroguramu-fuairu
program file
プログラム・ファイル

puroguramu gakushū
programmed learning
プログラム学習

puroguramu gakushū (PI)
programmed instruction (PI)
プログラム学習

puroguramu gengo
program language
プログラム言語

puroguramu henkan
program transformation
プログラム変換

puroguramu henkō
program modification
プログラム変更

puroguramu henshū
program editing
プログラム編集

puroguramu hikaku
program comparison
プログラム比較

puroguramu hontai
program body
プログラム本体

puroguramu hoshu
program maintenance
プログラム保守

puroguramu hyōjun
program standards
プログラム標準

**puroguramu hyōka-kanri gihō
(pāto; PERT)**
program evaluation and review
technique (PERT)
プログラム評価-管理技法；‘
パート；PERT

puroguramu ichiji teishi
program pause
プログラム一時停止

puroguramu jōtai go (PSW)
program status word (PSW)
プログラム状態語

**puroguramu jōtai go rejisuta
(PSWR)**
program status word register
(PSWR)
プログラム状態語レジスタ

puroguramu jōtai rejisuta
program status register
プログラム状態レジスタ

puroguramu jumbi
program preparation
プログラム準備

puroguramu-kādo
program card
プログラム・カード

puroguramu kaihatsu jikan
program development time
プログラム開発時間

puroguramu kaiseki
program analysis
プログラム解析

puroguramu-kaunta
program counter
プログラム・カウンタ

puroguramu kenshō
program certification
プログラム検証

puroguramu kijutsu
program description
プログラム記述

puroguramu kiokushiki
stored program
プログラム記憶式

puroguramu kōritsu
program efficiency
プログラム効率

puroguramu-kurasshi
program crash
プログラム・クラッシ

puroguramu mei
program identifier;
program name
プログラム名

puroguramu meirei
program instruction;
programmed instruction
プログラム命令

puroguramu-mikkusu
program mix
プログラム・ミックス

puroguramu-moderuka
program modeling
プログラム・モデル化

puroguramu-mojyūru
program module
プログラム・モジュール

puroguramu-monita
program monitor
プログラム・モニタ

puroguramu nagarezu
program flowchart
プログラム流れ図

puroguramu naizōshiki
stored program
プログラム内蔵式

puroguramu naizōshiki keisanki
stored-program computer
プログラム内蔵式計算機

puroguramu ni yoru kensa
programmed check
プログラムによる検査

puroguramu ni yoru teishi
programmed halt
プログラムによる停止

puroguramu no datōsei kensa
program validation
プログラムの妥当性検査

puroguramu no gokansei
program compatibility
プログラムの互換性

puroguramu no imiron
program semantics
プログラムの意味論

puroguramu no jikkō
program execution
プログラムの実行

puroguramu no kenshō
program verification
プログラムの検証

puroguramu no kōdō
program behavior
プログラムの行動

puroguramu no seitōsei
program correctness
プログラムの正当性

puroguramu nyūryoku
program input
プログラム入力

puroguramu-ōbarei
program overlay
プログラム・オーバレイ

puroguramu-pakkēji
program package
プログラム・パッケージ

puroguramu-parameta
program parameter
プログラム・パラメタ

puroguramu-raiburari
program library
プログラム・ライブラリ

puroguramu reigai
program exception
プログラム例外

puroguramu reigai warikomi
program exception interrupt
プログラム例外割り込み

puroguramu-rejisuta
program register
プログラム・レジスタ

puroguramu renraku burokku (PCB)
program communication block (PCB)
プログラム連絡ブロック

puroguramu rikai
program comprehension
プログラム理解

puroguramu-rinkēji
program linkage
プログラム・リンケージ

puroguramu-risuto
program listing
プログラム・リスト

puroguramu-rōda
program loader
プログラム・ローダ

puroguramu-rōdo
program load
プログラム・ロード

puroguramu-rokku-rejisuta
program lock register
プログラム・ロック・レジスタ

puroguramu-rūpu
program loop
プログラム・ループ

puroguramu saikōsei
program restructuring
プログラム再構成

puroguramu saitekika
program optimization
プログラム最適化

puroguramu sakusei
program composition
プログラム作成

puroguramu-segumento
program segment
プログラム・セグメント

puroguramu seigyo
program control
プログラム制御

puroguramu seigyo dēta
program control data
プログラム制御データ

puroguramu seigyo ni yoru warikomi
program-controlled interrupt
プログラム制御による割り込み

puroguramu sekkei
program design
プログラム設計

puroguramu shiyō
program specification
プログラム仕様

puroguramu shori
program manipulation
プログラム処理

puroguramu-suitchi
program switch
プログラム・スイッチ

puroguramu-suteppu
program step
プログラム・ステップ

puroguramu tan'i
program unit
プログラム単位

puroguramu teigi
program definition
プログラム定義

puroguramu-tēpu
program tape
プログラム・テープ

puroguramu-tesuto
program test
プログラム・テスト

puroguramu warikomi
program interrupt(ion)
プログラム割り込み

puroguramu yōshi
program sheet
プログラム用紙

puroguramu yūsen jun'i
program priority
プログラム優先順位

puroguramu yūsendo
program priority
プログラム優先度

puroguramu-zenerēta
program generator
プログラム・ゼネレータ

puroguramudo-danpu
programmed dump
プログラムド・ダンプ

**puroguramudo nyūshutsuryoku
(puroguramudo I/O)**
programmed input/output
(programmed I/O)
プログラムド入出力；
プログラムドI/O

puroguramudo ronri
programmed logic
プログラムド論理

puroguramudo-suitchi
programmed switch
プログラムド・スイッチ

puroguramukan renraku
interprogram communication
プログラム間連絡

puroguramukanō jōhō
programmable information
プログラム可能情報

puroguramukanō maruchipurekusa
programmable multiplexer
プログラム可能マルチプレクサ

**puroguramukanō yomidashi sen'yō
kioku (PROM)**
programmable read-only
memory; programmable ROM;
PROM
プログラム可能読み出し専用記憶

**puroguramukanō yomitori sen'yō
kioku (PROM)**
programmable read-only
memory; programmable ROM;
PROM
プログラム可能読み取り専用記憶

purokon
process computer
プロコン

puronputeingu
prompting
プロンプティング

puronputo
prompt (*noun*)
プロンプト

purosessa
processor
プロセッサ

purosessa-baundo
processor-bound
プロセッサ・バウンド

purosessa-chippu
processor chips
プロセッサ・チップ

purosessa jōtai rejisuta (PSR)
processor state register (PSR)
プロセッサ状態レジスタ

purosessa kyōyū
processor sharing
プロセッサ共有

purosessa seigyotaku
processor control console
プロセッサ制御卓

purosessa yobidashi seigyobun
processor call statement
プロセッサ呼び出し制御文

purosessakan baffua
interprocessor buffer
プロセッサ間バッファ

purosesu-baundo
process-bound
プロセス・バウンド

purosesu-chāto
process chart
プロセス・チャート

purosesu dōki
process synchronization
プロセス同期

purosesu-konpyūta
process computer
プロセス・コンピュータ

purosesu nagarezu
process chart
プロセス流れ図

**purosesu nyūshutsuryoku
(purosesu I/O)**
process input/output (process
I/O)
プロセス入出力；プロセスI/O

**purosesu nyūshutsuryoku sōchi
(purosesu I/O sōchi)**
process input/output unit
(process I/O unit)
プロセス入出力装置；
プロセスI/O装置

purosesu seigyo
process control
プロセス制御

purosesu seigyo keisanki
process control computer
プロセス制御計算機

purotokoru
protocol
プロトコル

purototaipu
prototype
プロトタイプ

purotta (PLOT)
plotter (PLOT)
プロッタ

puru-auto-deisuku
pull-out disk
プル・アウト・ディスク

puru-auto-deisuku sōchi
pull-out disk unit
プル・アウト・ディスク装置

purūfu-risuto
proof list
プルーフ・リスト

pusshu
push
プッシュ

PVC (aite kotei setsuzoku)
PVC (permanent virtual circuit)
相手固定接続

Q

Q-A (shitsumon-kaitō)
Q-A (question and answer)
質問-回答

QCB (machigyōretsu seigyo burokku)
QCB (queue control block)
待ち行列制御ブロック

QISAM (taiki sakuin junji akusesu hōshiki)
QISAM (queued indexed sequential-access method)
待機索引順次アクセス方式

QP (niji keikakuhō)
QP (quadratic programming)
二次計画法

QSAM (taiki junji akusesu hōshiki)
QSAM (queued sequential-access method)
待機順次アクセス方式

QTAM (taiki tsūshin akusesu hōshiki)
QTAM (queued telecommunications access method)
待機通信アクセス方式

QUICKTRAN
QUICKTRAN
QUICKTRAN

QWERTY kiibōdo
QWERTY keyboard
QWERTYキーボード

R

r (rejisuta)
r (register)
レジスタ

raberu
label
ラベル

raberu bangō
label number
ラベル番号

raberu-chekku
label check
ラベル・チェック

raberu gun
label group
ラベル群

raberu-gurūpu
label group
ラベル・グループ

raberu hensū
label variable
ラベル変数

raberu hyōjun reberu
label standard level
ラベル標準レベル

raberu kensa
label check
ラベル検査

raberu ran
label field
ラベル欄

raberu-rekōdo
label record
ラベル・レコード

raberu-rūchin
label routine
ラベル・ルーチン

raberu-setto
label set
ラベル・セット

raberu shikibetsushi
label identifier
ラベル識別子

raberu shori
label handling
ラベル処理

raberu shori rūchin
label-handling routine
ラベル処理ルーチン

raberu teisū
label constant
ラベル定数

raberutsuki
labeled
ラベル付き

raboratori-otomēshon (LA)
laboratory automation (LA)
ラボラトリ・オトメーション

raiburari
library
ライブラリ

raiburari-fuairu
library file
ライブラリ・ファイル

raiburari-fuairu shijishi
library file designator
ライブラリ・ファイル指示子

raiburari henshū puroguramu
library editor
ライブラリ編集プログラム

raiburari hoshu
library maintenance
ライブラリ保守

raiburari kanri
library management
ライブラリ管理

raiburari kansū
library function
ライブラリ関数

raiburari kōshin
library update
ライブラリ更新

raiburari kōzō
library structure
ライブラリ構造

raiburari mei
library name
ライブラリ名

raiburari-puroguramu
library program
ライブラリ・プログラム

raiburari-rūchin
library routine
ライブラリ・ルーチン

raiburari-saburūchin
library subroutine
ライブラリ・サブルーチン

raiburari seigyo
library control
ライブラリ制御

raiburari-sofutouea
library software
ライブラリ・ソフトウェア

raiburari-tēpu
library tape
ライブラリ・テープ

raiburarian
librarian
ライブラリアン

raiburarian-puroguramu
librarian program
ライブラリアン・プログラム

raibuuea
liveware
ライブウェア

rain
line (communication); line (text)
ライン

rain-edeita
line editor
ライン・エディタ

rain okuri
line feed (LF)
ライン送り

rain-purinta (LP)
line printer (LP); train printer
ライン・プリンタ

rain-segumento
line segment
ライン・セグメント

raito-gaido
light guide
ライト・ガイド

raito-pen
light pen
ライト・ペン

raito-pen-intafuēsu
light-pen interface
ライト・ペン・インタフェース

raito-pen-konekuta
light-pen connector
ライト・ペン・コネクタ

rakku
rack
ラック

rakkugata
rack type
ラック型

**RAM (randamu-akusesu kioku;
randamu-akusesu-memori)**
RAM (random-access memory)
ランダム・アクセス記憶;
ランダム・アクセス・メモリ

RAM bōdo
RAM board
RAM ボード

RAM chippu
RAM chip
RAM チップ

RAMPS (ranpusu)
RAMPS (resource allocation in
multiple-project scheduling)
ランプス

ran
field
欄

ran
run
ラン

ran
random
乱

ran akusesu
random access
乱アクセス

ran akusesu-fuairu
random-access file
乱アクセス・ファイル

ran akusesu kanō
randomly accessible
乱アクセス可能

ran-chāto
run chart
ラン・チャート

ran dēta
random data
乱データ

ran hensei
random organization
乱編成

ran hensei fuairu
random file
乱編成ファイル

ran kugiri
field separator
欄区切り

ran okuri (TAB)
tabulation
欄送り

ran okuri kankaku
tab spacing; tabulation spacing
欄送り間隔

ran owari
end of run
ラン終り

ran shūryō
end of run
ラン終了

ran-sutoriimu
run stream
ラン・ストリーム

ran-taima
run timer
ラン・タイマ

ran-taima-sapōto-pakkēji
run-timer support package
ラン・タイマ・サポート・
パッケージ

ran-taimu
run time
ラン・タイム

ran-taimu-erā
run-time error
ラン・タイム・エラー

ran-taimu-shisutemu
run-time system
ラン・タイム・システム

ran toiawase
random inquiry
乱問い合わせ

ran yobidashi
random access
乱呼び出し

ran-yunitto
run unit
ラン・ユニット

ranchō
hunting
乱調

randamu
random
ランダム

randamu-akusesu
random access
ランダム・アクセス

randamu-akusesu-fuairu
random-access file
ランダム・アクセス・ファイル

randamu-akusesu kanō
randomly accessible
ランダム・アクセス可能

randamu-akusesu kioku (RAM)
random-access memory (RAM);
random-access storage
ランダム・アクセス記憶

randamu-akusesu-memori (RAM)
random-access memory (RAM)
ランダム・アクセス・メモリ

randamu-akusesu sōchi
random-access device
ランダム・アクセス装置

randamu-fuairu
random file
ランダム・ファイル

randamu kensaku
random retrieval
ランダム検索

randamu-parusu retsu
random pulse train
ランダム・パルス列

randamu shori
random processing
ランダム処理

randamu sōsa
random scan
ランダム走査

randamu tansaku
random search
ランダム探索

randamu-uōku hō
random-walk method
ランダム・ワオーク法

randamuka
randomizing
ランダム化

ranpu
ramp
ランプ

ranpu hichokusen hizumi
ramp nonlinearity
ランプ非直線歪み

ranpu ōtō
ramp response
ランプ応答

ranpusu (RAMPS)
resource allocation in multiple-
project scheduling (RAMPS)
ランプス

ransū
random number(s)
乱数

ransū hairetsu
random number sequence
乱数配列

ransū hassei
random number generation
乱数発生

ransū hasseiki
random number generator
乱数発生器

rappu-araundo
wraparound
ラップ・アラウンド

rasuta
raster
ラスタ

rasuta hyōji sōchi
raster display
ラスタ表示装置

rasuta-purotta
raster plotter
ラスタ・プロッタ

rasuta sōsa
raster scan; raster scanning
ラスタ走査

rasuto-pasu
last pass
ラスト・パス

rasuto-pasu-oun-kōdo (LPOC)
last-pass own code (LPOC)
ラスト・パス・オウン・コード

RB (RB hōshiki)
RB (return to bias)
RB 方式

RB hōshiki (RB)
return to bias (RB)
RB 方式

RB kiroku
return-to-bias recording
RB 記録

RB rekōdeingu
return-to-bias recording
RB レコーディング

RC (rimōto-konsentorēta)
RC (remote concentrator)
リモート・コンセントレータ

reberu
level
レベル

reberu bangō
level number
レベル番号

reberu-daiyaguramu
level diagram
レベル・ダイヤグラム

reberu hyōshiki
level indicator
レベル標識

reberu-shifuta
level shifter
レベル・シフタ

reberu-shifuto
level shift
レベル・シフト

reddo-tēpu
red tape
レッド・テープ

reddo-tēpu sōsa
red-tape operation
レッド・テープ操作

redei
ready
レディ

redei jōtai
ready condition; ready status
レディ状態

redei jōtai go
ready status word
レディ状態語

refuarensu
reference
レファレンス

refuarensu-kii
reference key
レファレンス・キー

refuarensu tsūban
reference number
レファレンス通番

rei
zero
零

reiauto
layout
レイアウト

reigai
exception
例外

reigai hōkoku
exception reporting
例外報告

reigai hōshiki
exception principle system
例外方式

reigai kanri
management by exception
例外管理

reinji
range
レインジ

reinji-chekku
range check
レインジ・チェック

rejisuta (r)
register (r)
レジスタ

rejisuta chō
register length
レジスタ長

rejisuta kioku
register memory
レジスタ記憶

rejisuta-setto
register set
レジスタ・セット

rejisuta tensō
register transfer
レジスタ転送

rejisuta wariate
register assignment
レジスタ割り当て

rekōda
recorder
レコーダ

rekōdo
record
レコード

rekōdo bunri moji (RS)
record separator (RS)
レコード分離文字

rekōdo-burokku
record block
レコード・ブロック

rekōdo-burokkuka
record blocking
レコード・ブロック化

rekōdo chō
record length
レコード長

rekōdo chō hyōshiki
record length indicator
レコード長標識

rekōdo densō
record-oriented transmission
レコード伝送

rekōdo fukukijutsukō
record subentry
レコード副記述項

rekōdo haichi
record position
レコード配置

rekōdo kaihō
record release
レコード解放

rekōdo kankaku
record gap
レコード間隔

rekōdo-kaunto
record count
レコード・カウント

rekōdo keishiki
record format
レコード形式

rekōdo kensa
record checking
レコード検査

rekōdo-kii
record key
レコード・キー

rekōdo kijutsu
record description
レコード記述

rekōdo kijutsukō
record description entry;
record entry
レコード記述項

rekōdo-māku
record mark
レコード・マーク

rekōdo mei
record name
レコード名

rekōdo nai
no record found
レコードない

rekōdo no owari
end of record
レコードの終り

rekōdo-okarensu
record occurrence
レコード・オカレンス

rekōdo owari go
end-of-record word
レコード終り語

rekōdo owari māka (ERM)
end-of-record marker (ERM)
レコード終りマーカ

rekōdo-reiauto
record layout
レコード・レイアウト

rekōdo-saizu
record size
レコード・サイズ

rekōdo-segumento
record segment
レコード・セグメント

rekōdo sentaku
record selection
レコード選択

rekōdo-shiikensu-oun-kōdo
record sequence own code
レコード・シーケンス・オウン・
コード

rekōdo shikibetsu
record identification
レコード識別

rekōdo suru
record (*verb*)
レコードする

rekōdo yōshiki
record layout
レコード様式

rekōdokan kankaku (IRG)
interrecord gap (IRG)
レコード間間隔

renkei
link; linkage
連係

renkei henshū puroguramu
link editor; linkage editor
連係編集プログラム

renkei jōhō
link information
連係情報

renkei mei
linkage name
連係名

renkei raiburari
link library
連係ライブラリ

renketsu
binding; concatenation; link;
linkage
連結

renketsu adoresu
link address
連結アドレス

renketsu dēta-setto
concatenated data set
連結データ・セット

renketsu enzanshi
concatenation operator
連結演算子

renketsu henshū puroguramu
link editor; linkage editor
連結編集プログラム

renketsu jōhō
link information
連結情報

renketsu mei
linkage name
連結名

renketsu moji
concatenation character
連結文字

renketsu raiburari
link library
連結ライブラリ

renketsu shiki
concatenation expression
連結式

renketsu suru
concatenate
連結する

renketsugo
connective
連結語

renketsusei
connectivity
連結性

renketsuzumi mojyūru
bound module
連結済みモジュール

renraku
communication
連絡

rensa
chain; chaining
連鎖

rensa adoresu
chaining address
連鎖アドレス

rensa afure
chaining overflow
連鎖溢れ

rensa chekku
chaining check
連鎖チェック

rensa fuairu
chained file
連鎖ファイル

rensa kōdo
chain code
連鎖コード

rensa rekōdo
chained record
連鎖レコード

399

rensa risuto
chained list
連鎖リスト

rensa shirei
chained command
連鎖指令

rensa tansaku
catenated search;
chaining search
連鎖探索

renshi
string
連糸

rensō
association
連想

rensō adoresu
associated address
連想アドレス

rensō kankei
associative relation
連想関係

rensō kensaku
associative retrieval
連想検索

rensō kioku
associative memory; associative
storage; search memory
連想記憶

rensō kioku (CAM)
content-addressable memory
(CAM)
連想記憶

rensō kioku sōchi
associative store;
content-addressable store
連想記憶装置

rensō purosessa
associative processor
連想プロセッサ

renzoku
consecutive; continuous; serial;
series
連続

renzoku bangō
consecutive number
連続番号

renzoku bumpu
continuous distribution
連続分布

renzoku dōsa
continuous action
連続動作

renzoku fuairu
consecutive file
連続ファイル

renzoku inji yōshi
continuous stationery
連続印字用紙

renzoku insatsushi
continuous stationery
連続印刷紙

renzoku jōhō
continuous information
連続情報

renzoku jōhō gen
continuous information source
連続情報源

renzoku kioku
consecutive storage
連続記憶

renzoku rekōdo
continuous record
連続レコード

renzoku shisutemu
continuous system
連続システム

renzoku shisutemu-shimyurēshon
continuous system simulation
連続システム・シミュレーション

renzoku shori
consecutive processing;
continuous processing
連続処理

renzoku shori shisutemu
continuous processing system
連続処理システム

renzoku sōsa
continuous operation
連続操作

renzoku unten
continuous running
連続運転

renzoku yōshi ukedai
form stacker
連続用紙受け台

renzokuban
serial number
連続番

renzokushiki jyobu shori
stacked job processing
連続式ジョブ処理

REP (sainyūkanō purosessa)
REP (reentrant processor)
再入可能プロセッサ

rēsu-kādo
laced card
レース・カード

rēsu senkō
lace punch
レースせん孔

resukyū-danpu
rescue dump
レスキュー・ダンプ

rēsuuei
raceway
レースウェイ

retsu
string
列

retsu kansū
string functions
列関数

retsuka
degradation
劣化

retsukyohō
enumeration
列挙法

rēza kiroku
laser recording
レーザ記録

rēza-memori
laser memory
レーザ・メモリ

rēza-purinta
laser printer
レーザ・プリンタ

riaru-taimu
real time
リアル・タイム

riaru-taimu dōsa
real-time operation
リアル・タイム動作

riaru-taimu-konpyūta
real-time computer
リアル・タイム・コンピュータ

riaru-taimu-kurokku (RTC)
real-time clock (RTC)
リアル・タイム・クロック

riaru-taimu-operēteingu-shisutemu
real-time operating system
リアル・タイム・
オペレーティング・システム

riaru-taimu OS
real-time OS
リアル・タイム OS

riaru-taimu-shisutemu
real-time system
リアル・タイム・システム

riaru-taimu shori
real-time processing
リアル・タイム処理

ribāsu
reverse
リバース

ribāsu-bideo
reverse video
リバース・ビデオ

ribāsu hyōji
reverse indicator
リバース表示

ribon
ribbon
リボン

ribon-kēburu
ribbon cable
リボン・ケーブル

rifuresshingu
refreshing
リフレッシング

rifuresshu
refresh
リフレッシュ

rifuresshu-deisupurei
refreshed display
リフレッシュ・ディスプレィ

rifuresshu-rēto
refresh rate
リフレッシュ・レート

rifuresshu-saikuru
refresh cycle
リフレッシュ・サイクル

riibūto
reboot
リーブート

riida
reader
リーダ

riido-auto
readout
リード・アウト

riiru
reel
リール

riiru bangō
reel number
リール番号

riiru no owari
end of reel
リールの終り

riiru shūtan
end of reel
リール終端

riishingu
leasing
リーシング

rijiekuto
reject
リジェクト

rijiekuto kinō
reject function
リジェクト機能

rimeinda
remainder
リメインダ

rimeinda-chekku
remainder check
リメインダ・チェック

rimitta
limiter
リミッタ

rimitto
limit
リミット

rimitto-chekku
limit check
リミット・チェック

rimōto
remote
リモート

rimōto-batchi
remote batch
リモート・バッチ

rimōto-batchi shori
remote batch processing
リモート・バッチ処理

rimōto-batchi tanmatsu
remote batch terminal
リモート・バッチ端末

rimōto-konsentorēta (RC)
remote concentrator (RC)
リモート・コンセントレータ

rimōto sōchi
remote unit
リモート装置

ringu-kaunta
ring counter
リング・カウンタ

ringu kōzō
ring structure
リング構造

ringu-nettowāku
ring network
リング・ネットワーク

ringu-shifuto
ring shift
リング・シフト

rinka
linker
リンカ

rinkēji
linkage
リンケージ

rinku
link
リンク

rinku-adoresu
link address
リンク・アドレス

rinku-rōda
link loader
リンク・ローダ

rinkuto-risuto
linked list
リンクト・リスト

rinkuto-saburūchin
linked subroutine
リンクト・サブルーチン

ripōto
report
リポート

ripōto-puroguramu
report program
リポート・プログラム

ripōto-puroguramu-zenerēta (RPG)
report program generator (RPG)
リポート・プログラム・
ゼネレータ

riran
rerun
リラン

riran-pointo
rerun point
リラン・ポイント

rirē
relay
リレー

rirēshon
relation
リレーション

rirēshonaru(gata)
relational
リレーショナル(型)

ririisu
release
リリース

rirokēshon
relocation
リロケーション

rirokēshon-rejisuta
relocation register
リロケーション・レジスタ

rirokētaburu
relocatable
リロケータブル

rirokētaburu-eremento
relocatable element
リロケータブル・エレメント

rirokēto suru
relocate
リロケートする

riron
theory
理論

riron(teki)
theoretical
理論(的)

rironteki sekkei
theoretical design
理論的設計

rironteki shisutemu
theoretical system
理論的システム

risanteki dēta
discrete data
離散的データ

risanteki hyōgen
discrete representation
離散的表現

risanteki jishō
discrete event
離散的事象

risanteki jishō shimyurēshon
discrete event simulation
離散的事象シミュレーション

risanteki shimyurēshon
discrete simulation
離散的シミュレーション

risetto (suru)
reset (*verb*)
リセット(する)

risetto-kii
reset key
リセット・キー

risetto-parusu
reset pulse
リセット・パルス

risōteki shisutemu
ideal system
理想的システム

risuteingu
listing
リスティング

risuto
list
リスト

risuto asshuku
list compacting
リスト圧縮

risuto henshū puroguramu
list editor
リスト編集プログラム

risuto hyōgen
list representation
リスト表現

risuto idō
list moving
リスト移動

risuto kōzō
list structure
リスト構造

risuto seisei
list generation
リスト生成

risuto shiji densō
list-directed transmission
リスト指示伝送

risuto shori
list processing
リスト処理

risuto shori gengo
list manipulation language
リスト処理言語

risuto shori gengo (LISP)
list-processing language (LISP)
リスト処理言語

risuto-sukejyūringu
list scheduling
リスト・スケジューリング

risutokei nyūshutsuryoku
list-directed input/output
リスト形入出力

riteraru
literals
リテラル

riteraru-operando
literal operand
リテラル・オペランド

riteraru teisū
literal constant
リテラル定数

ritoku
gain
利得

ritsu
rate; ratio
率

riyō
application; use
利用

riyō bun'ya
application field
利用分野

riyō hōhō
application method
利用方法

riyō jittai
conditions of application
利用実態

riyō kanō jikan
accountable time;
available machine time
利用可能時間

riyō kanōdo
availability
利用可能度

riyō keitai
form of application
利用形態

riyōsha
user
利用者

riyōsha atogaki raberu (UTL)
user trailer label (UTL)
利用者後書きラベル

riyōsha boryūmu midashi raberu
user volume header label
利用者ボリューム見出しラベル

riyōsha enjo shisutemu
user-friendly system
利用者援助システム

riyōsha fuairu midashi raberu (UHL)
user header label (UHL)
利用者ファイル見出しラベル

riyōsha muki shisutemu
user-oriented system
利用者向きシステム

riyōsha yūsen jun'i
user priority
利用者優先順位

RJE (enkaku jyobu nyūryoku)
RJE (remote job entry)
遠隔ショブ入力

RMS (kaifuku kanri sapōto)
RMS (recovery management support)
回復管理サポート

RO (yomidashi sen'yō)
RO (read only)
読み出し専用

RO (yomitori sen'yō)
RO (read only)
読み取り専用

rōda
loader
ローダ

roddo-memori
rod memory
ロッド・メモリ

rōdeingu
loading
ローディング

rōdo (LOAD)
load (LOAD)
ロード

rōdo-ando-gō
load-and-go
ロード・アンド・ゴー

rōdo meirei
loading instruction
ロード命令

rōdo-mojyūru
load module
ロード・モジュール

rōdo-pointo
load point
ロード・ポイント

rōdo-pointo hyōshiki
load-point indicator
ロード・ポイント標識

rōdo-pointo-māka
load-point marker
ロード・ポイント・マーカ

rōdo-rūchin
loading routine
ロード・ルーチン

rōdo-shearingu
load sharing
ロード・シェアリング

roga
logger
ロガ

rogingu
logging
ロギング

rogingu-auto
logging-out
ロギング・アウト

rogingu-in
logging-in
ロギング・イン

rogu
log
ログ

rogu-auto
log out
ログ・アウト

rōgu chi
rogue value
ローグ値

rogu-in
log in
ログ・イン

rogu-ofu
log off
ログ・オフ

rogu-on
log on
ログ・オン

rōkaru
local
ローカル

rōkaru-mōdo
local mode
ローカル・モード

rōkaru shori
local processing
ローカル処理

rōkaru shori sōchi
local processor
ローカル処理装置

rōkaru-tesuto
local test
ローカル・テスト

rokēshon
location
ロケーション

rokēta
locator
ロケータ

rokēta shūshokushi
locator qualifier
ロケータ修飾子

rokku
lock
ロック

rokku-auto
lockout
ロック・アウト

rokku-auto tejun
lockout procedure
ロック・アウト手順

rokku-kii
lock key
ロック・キー

rokku-mōdo
lock mode
ロック・モード

rokku-opushon
lock option
ロック・オプション

rokku-risuto
lock list
ロック・リスト

roku bitto eisūji kōdo
six-bit alphameric code
6ビット英数字コード

rokubitto-baito
sextet
6ビット・バイト

rokuga
picture recording
録画

ROM (kotei kioku; rōmu; yomidashi sen'yō kioku; yomitori sen'yō kioku)
ROM (read-only memory)
固定記憶; ローム;
読み出し専用記憶;
読み取り専用記憶

ROM chippu
read-only memory chip
ROMチップ

ROM kātorijji
ROM cartridge
ROMカートリッジ

rōmaji
roman character
ローマ字

rōmu (ROM)
read-only memory (ROM)
ローム

ronri
logic
論理

ronri(teki)
logical
論理(的)

ronri adoresu
logical address
論理アドレス

ronri anaraiza
logic analyzer
論理アナライザ

ronri ayamari
logical error
論理誤り

ronri bunseki
logic analysis
論理分析

ronri burokku
logical block
論理ブロック

ronri chi
logical value
論理値

ronri dēta
logical data
論理データ

ronri enzan
logic(al) operation
論理演算

ronri enzanshi
logical operator
論理演算子

ronri erā
logical error
論理エラー

ronri fuairu
logical file
論理ファイル

ronri gata
logical type
論理型

ronri gēto
logic gate
論理ゲート

ronri handan
logical judgment
論理判断

ronri hensū
logic variable; logical variable
論理変数

ronri hikaku
logical comparison
論理比較

ronri hyō
logical table
論理表

ronri ichijishi
logical primary
論理一次子

ronri IF bun
logical IF statement
論理IF文

ronri inshi
logical factor
論理因子

ronri jōhō shisutemu
logic information system
論理情報システム

ronri kairo
logic(al) circuit
論理回路

ronri kansū
logic(al) function
論理関数

ronri kasan
Boolean add
論理加算

ronri keta okuri
logic(al) shift
論理桁送り

ronri ketsugōshi
logical connectives
論理結合子

ronri kigō
functional symbol; logic symbol
論理記号

ronri kōseitai
logical entity
論理構成体

ronri mei
logical name
論理名

ronri meirei
logic(al) instruction
論理命令

ronri nagarezu
logical flowchart
論理流れ図

ronri nettowāku
logic network
論理ネットワーク

ronri nyūryoku
fan-in
論理入力

ronri operando
logical operand
論理オペランド

ronri pōto
logical port
論理ポート

ronri rekōdo
logical record
論理レコード

ronri sa
logical difference
論理差

ronri sayōso
logical operator
論理作用素

ronri seki
logical product
論理積

ronri sekkei
logic(al) design
論理設計

ronri shifuto
logic(al) shift
論理シフト

ronri shiki
logical expression
論理式

ronri shisutemu
logic system
論理システム

ronri shisutemu sekkei
logic system design
論理システム設計

ronri shoshiki
Boolean format
論理書式

ronri shutsuryoku
fan-out
論理出力

ronri shutsuryoku nai
fan-out free
論理出力ない

ronri(teki) sōchi
logic unit; logical unit
論理(的)装置

ronri(teki) sōchi bangō
logical device number;
logical unit number
論理(的)装置番号

ronri(teki) sōchi mei
logical unit name
論理(的)装置名

ronri(teki) sōchi tēburu
logical unit table
論理(的)装置テーブル

ronri soshi
decision element;
logic(al) element
論理素子

ronri tan'i
logical unit
論理単位

ronri tansaku
logic seeking
論理探索

ronri teisū
logical constant
論理定数

ronri wa
logical add; logical sum
論理和

ronri zu
logic diagram
論理図

ronriseki
AND
論理積

ronriseki enzan
AND operation
論理積演算

ronriseki gēto
AND gate
論理積ゲート

ronriseki kairo
AND circuit
論理積回路

ronriseki soshi
AND element
論理積素子

ronriteki dēta no dokuritsu
logical data independence
論理的データの独立

ronriteki dētabēsu (LDB)
logical database (LDB)
論理的データベース

ronriteki nyūshutsuryoku seigyo shisutemu
logical I/O control system
論理的入出力制御システム

ronriwa
OR
論理和

ronriwa enzan
OR operation
論理和演算

ronriwa gēto
buffer gate; OR gate
論理和ゲート

ronriwa kairo
OR circuit
論理和回路

ronriwa soshi
OR element
論理和素子

rōru-auto
roll out
ロール・アウト

rōru-bakku
roll back
ロール・バック

rōru-in
roll in
ロール・イン

rōru kami horuda
paper-roll holder
ロール紙ホルダ

rōru yōshi okuri
　roll paper feed
　ロール用紙送り

rōru yōshi okuri kikō
　roll paper feeder
　ロール用紙送り機構

ROS (kotei kioku; yomidashi sen'yō kioku; yomitori sen'yō kioku)
　ROS (read-only storage)
　固定記憶；読み出し専用記憶；
　読み取り専用記憶

rōwa
　cross-talk
　漏話

RP (gyaku Pōrando kihō)
　RP (reverse Polish)
　逆ポーランド記法

RPG (hōkokusho sakusei puroguramu; ripōto-puroguramu-zenerēta)
　RPG (report program generator)
　報告書作成プログラム
　リポート・プログラム・
　ゼネレータ

RS (rekōdo bunri moji)
　RS (record separator)
　レコード分離文字

RTC (jitsu jikan tokei; riaru-taimu-kurokku)
　RTC (real-time clock)
　実時間時計；リアル・タイム・
　クロック

RTC (keiro seigyo)
　RTC (routing control)
　経路制御

RTL (teikō toranjisuta ronri)
　RTL (resistor transistor logic)
　抵抗トランジスタ論理

rūchin
　routine
　ルーチン

rūchin hoshu
　routine maintenance
　ルーチン保守

ruibetsu
　classification
　類別

ruibetsu suru
　classify
　類別する

ruisan
　accumulation
　累算

ruisan suru
　accumulate
　累算する

ruisanki
　accumulator
　累算器

ruisanki rejisuta
　accumulator register
　累算器レジスタ

ruiseki
　cumulative
　累積

ruiseki ritsu
　cumulative percentage
　累積率

ruiseki sakuintsuke
　cumulative indexing
　累積索引付け

ruiseki saritsu
　cumulative remainder
　累積差率

rukku-appu
　look up
　ルック・アップ

rukku-appu-tēburu
　look-up table
　ルック・アップ・テーブル

rūpu
　loop
　ループ

rūpu-bokkusu
　loop box
　ループ・ボックス

rūpu-kaunta
　loop counter
　ループ・カウンタ

rūpu-nettowāku
　loop network
　ループ・ネットワーク

rūto-fuēzu
　root phase
　ルート・フェーズ

rūto-segumento
　root segment
　ルート・セグメント

R-W (yomikaki; yomitori kakikomi)
　R-W (read-write)
　読み書き；読み取り書き込み

ryakuseigo
　acronym
　略成語

ryō
　quantity; volume
　量

ryō'iki
　area; domain; realm; region
　領域

ryō'iki dēta kōmoku
　realm data item
　領域データ項目

ryō'iki idō
　domain movement
　領域移動

ryō'iki kijutsukō
　realm description entry
　領域記述項

ryō'iki kukakuka
　region partitioning
　領域区画化

ryō'iki mei
　realm name
　領域名

ryō'iki setsu
　realm section
　領域節

ryō'iki tansaku
　area search
　領域探索

ryōhōkō kaunta
　reversible counter
　両方向カウンタ

ryōkyokusei
　bipolar
　両極性

ryōkyokusei parusu
　bipolar pulse
　両極性パルス

ryōkyokusei shingō
　bipolar signal
　両極性信号

ryōshi
quantum
量子

ryōshika
quantization
量子化

ryōshika gosa
quantize error
量子化誤差

ryōshika hizumi
quantize distortion
量子化歪み

ryōshika suru
quantize
量子化する

ryōshika zatsuon
quantize noise
量子化雑音

ryōtori
call by quantity
量取り

RZ (RZ hōshiki; zero fukki; zero modori)
RZ (return to zero)
RZ方式；ゼロ復帰；ゼロ戻り

RZ hōshiki
return to zero (RZ)
RZ方式

RZM (zero fukki māku; zero modori māku)
RZM (return-to-zero mark)
ゼロ復帰マーク；ゼロ戻りマーク

RZM hōshiki
RZM method
RZM方式

S

s (byō)
s (second)
秒

sa
difference
差

sābisu
function (feature)
サービス

sābisu-bitto
service bit
サービス・ビット

sābisu jikan
service time
サービス時間

sābisu-puroguramu
service program
サービス・プログラム

sābisu-purosessa (SVP)
service processor (SVP)
サービス・プロセッサ

sābisu-rūchin
service routine
サービス・ルーチン

sābo
servo
サーボ

sābo jōzanki
servomultiplier
サーボ乗算器

sābo kikō
servomechanism
サーボ機構

sābo sekibunki
servo integrator
サーボ積分器

sābo-shisutemu
servo system
サーボ・システム

sabu-ākitekucha-intafuēsu (SAI)
subarchitecture interface (SAI)
サブ・アーキテクチャ・
インタフェース

sabu-chaneru
subchannel
サブ・チャネル

sabu-nettowāku
subnetwork
サブ・ネットワーク

sabu-puroguramu
subprogram
サブ・プログラム

sabu-rūchin
subroutine
サブ・ルーチン

sabu-rūchin-raiburari
subroutine library
サブ・ルーチン・ライブラリ

sabu-rūchin-sabu-puroguramu
subroutine subprogram
サブ・ルーチン・サブ・
プログラム

sabu-rūchin yobidashi
subroutine call
サブ・ルーチン呼び出し

sabu-shisutemu
subsystem
サブ・システム

sabu-sukiima
subschema
サブ・スキーマ

sabu-sukiima kijutsukō
subschema description entry;
subschema entry
サブ・スキーマ記述項

sabu-sukiima mei
subschema name
サブ・スキーマ名

sabu-sukiima setsu
subschema section
サブ・スキーマ節

sabu-tasuku
subtask
サブ・タスク

sabun
differential
差分

sabun shingō
differential signal
差分信号

sabusetto
subset
サブセット

sabusutoringu
substring
サブストリング

sadō
differential
差動

sadō
operation (action)
作動

sadō jōtai
operating state
作動状態

sadō zōfukuki
differential amplifier
差動増幅器

sadōkanō
ready
作動可能

sadōkanō jōtai
ready condition
作動可能状態

sagu
sag
サグ

sagyō
activity; operation (action); work
作業

sagyō fuairu
work file
作業ファイル

sagyō fuka
work load
作業負荷

sagyō iki
work area; working area;
working space
作業域

sagyō ryō'iki
workspace
作業領域

sagyō tanmatsu (WS)
workstation; working station
(WS)
作業端末

sagyō torakku
work track
作業トラック

sagyō'yō kioku'iki
work(ing) storage
作業用記憶域

sagyō'yō tēpu
work tape; working tape
作業用テープ

sahyō
listing
作表

SAI (sabu-ākitekucha-intafuēsu)
SAI (subarchitecture interface)
サブ・アーキテクチャ・
インタフェース

saibaneteikku seigyo
cybernetic control
サイバネティック制御

saibaneteikku-shisutemu
cybernetic system
サイバネティック・システム

saibaneteikkusu
cybernetics
サイバネティックス

saiburokkuka
reblock; reblocking
再ブロック化

saidai burokku chō
maximum block length
最大ブロック長

saidai fuka
maximum load
最大負荷

saidai insatsu sokudo
maximum printing speed
最大印刷速度

saidai tsūshin sokudo
maximum communication speed
最大通信速度

saidai yōryō
maximum capacity
最大容量

saigenritsu
recall factor
再現率

saigensei
repeatability
再現性

saihaibun
reallocation
再配分

saihaichi
relocation
再配置

saihaichi deikushonari
relocation dictionary
再配置ディクショナリ

saihaichi funō
nonrelocatable
再配置不能

saihaichi rekōdo
relocation record
再配置レコード

saihaichi suru
relocate
再配置する

saihaichikanō
relocatable
再配置可能

saihaichikanō adoresu
relocatable address
再配置可能アドレス

saihaichikanō eremento
relocatable element
再配置可能エレメント

saihaichikanō iki
relocatable area
再配置可能域

saihaichikanō kigō
relocatable symbol
再配置可能記号

saihaichikanō kōdo
relocatable code
再配置可能コード

saihaichikanō mei
relocatable name
再配置可能名

saihaichikanō puroguramu
relocatable program
再配置可能プログラム

saihaichikanō puroguramu-rōda
relocatable program loader
再配置可能プログラム・ローダ

saihaichikanō raiburari
relocatable library
再配置可能ライブラリ

saihaichikanō rōda
relocatable loader
再配置可能ローダ

saihaichikanō rūchin
relocatable routine
再配置可能ルーチン

saihaichikanō shiki
relocatable expression
再配置可能式

saihaichikanōsei
relocatability
再配置可能性

saihensei
reorganization
再編成

saihensei suru
reorganize
再編成する

saihyōka
reevaluation
再評価

saijikkō
rerun
再実行

saijikkō rūchin
rerun routine
再実行ルーチン

saijikkō ten
rerun point
再実行点

saijōi no bitto (MSB)
most significant bit (MSB)
最上位のビット

saijōi no moji (MSC)
most significant character (MSC)
最上位の文字

saijōi no sūji (MSD)
most significant digit (MSD)
最上位の数字

saikai no bitto (LSB)
least significant bit (LSB)
最下位のビット

saikai no moji (LSC)
least significant character (LSC)
最下位の文字

saikai no sūji (LSD)
least significant digit (LSD)
最下位の数字

saikaishi
restart
再開始

saikaiten
rescue point
再開点

saikakikomi
rewrite (*verb*)
再書き込み

saiki
recursive
再帰

saiki yobidashi
recursive call
再帰呼び出し

saikiteki
recursive
再帰的

saikiteki kansū
recursive function
再帰的関数

saikiteki puroguramu
recursive program
再帰的プログラム

saikiteki rūchin
recursive routine
再帰的ルーチン

saikiteki saburūchin
recursive subroutine
再帰的サブルーチン

saikiteki teigi
recursive definition
再帰的定義

saikōsei
reconfiguration; restructuring
再構成

saikōsei gijutsu
restructuring technique
再構成技術

saikuru
cycle
サイクル

saikuru/byō
cycles per second
サイクル／秒

saikuru-chekku
cycle check
サイクル・チェック

saikuru-indekkusu
cycle index
サイクル・インデックス

saikuru jikan
cycle time
サイクル時間

saikuru-kaunta
cycle counter
サイクル・カウンタ

saikuru-kaunto
cycle count
サイクル・カウント

saikuru-taima
cycle timer
サイクル・タイマ

saikuru-taimu
cycle time
サイクル・タイム

sain-ofu
sign off
サイン・オフ

sain-on
sign on
サイン・オン

sainyū
reentry
再入

sainyūkanō
reenterable; reentrant
再入可能

sainyūkanō kōdo
reentrant code
再入可能コード

sainyūkanō puroguramu
reenterable program;
reentrant program
再入可能プログラム

sainyūkanō purosessa (REP)
reentrant processor (REP)
再入可能プロセッサ

sainyūkanō rōdo-mojyūru
reenterable load module
再入可能ロード・モジュール

sainyūkanō rūchin
reentrant routine
再入可能ルーチン

sainyūten
reentry point
再入点

saipuroguramuka
reprogrammability
再プログラム化

saipuroguramukanō
reprogrammable
再プログラム可能

sairisuta
thyristor
サイリスタ

sairōdeingu jikan
reloading time
再ローディング時間

sairōdo
reload
再ロード

saisatan
high-order end
最左端

saisei
refreshing; regeneration
再生

saisei kioku
regenerative storage
再生記憶

saisei kioku sōchi
regenerative store
再生記憶装置

saisei shūki
regeneration period
再生周期

saisei torakku
regenerative track
再生トラック

saisei yomidashi
regenerative reading
再生読み出し

saisekkei
redesign
再設計

saishidō
restart
再始動

saishidō jōken
restart conditions
再始動条件

saishidō meirei
restart instruction
再始動命令

saishikō
retry
再試行

saishiyōfunō
nonreusable
再使用不能

saishiyōkanō
reusable
再使用可能

saishiyōkanō puroguramu
reusable program
再使用可能プログラム

saishiyōkanō rūchin
reusable routine
再使用可能ルーチン

saishiyōkanōsei
reusability
再使用可能性

saishō
minimal; minimum
最小

saishō akusesu-kōdeingu
minimum access coding
最小アクセス・コーディング

saishō akusesu-kōdo
minimum access code
最小アクセス・コード

saishō burokku chō
minimum block length
最小ブロック長

saishō chien kōdo
minimum delay code
最小遅延コード

saishō hiyō
minimum cost
最小費用

saishō kyori kōdo
minimum distance code
最小距離コード

saishō machijikan kōdeingu
minimum latency coding
最小待ち時間コーディング

saishō machijikan kōdo
minimum latency code
最小待ち時間コード

saishō ryō'iki
minimum area
最小領域

saishō tsūshin sokudo
minimum communication speed
最小通信速度

saishō yobidashi kōdeingu
minimum access coding
最小呼び出しコーディング

saishō yobidashi kōdo
minimum access code
最小呼び出しコード

saishū riyōsha
end user
最終利用者

saisō
retransmission
再送

saisōteisei hōshiki
request repeat system
再送訂正方式

saitan jikan
minimum time
最短時間

saitan keiro
shortest route
最短経路

saitan keiro mondai
shortest-route problem
最短経路問題

saiteigi
redefinition
再定義

saitei'i no sūji
low-order digit
最低位の数字

saiteki
optimal; optimum
最適

saiteki keikakuhō
optimum programming
最適計画法

saiteki kōdeingu
optimum coding
最適コーディング

saiteki kōdo
optimum code
最適コード

saiteki puroguramingu
optimum programming
最適プログラミング

saiteki seigyo
optimal control;
optimum control
最適制御

saitekika
optimization
最適化

saitekika gihō
optimization technique
最適化技法

saitekika konpaira
optimizing compiler
最適化コンパイラ

saitekika puroguramu
optimization program
最適化プログラム

saitekika seigyo
optimizing control
最適化制御

saitekika senryaku
optimization strategy
最適化戦略

saitekika suru
optimize
最適化する

saitekikai
optimal solution
最適解

saiutan
low-order end
最右端

saiyomitori
reread
再読み取り

saizu
size
サイズ

sakiire atodashi (FILO)
first-in last-out (FILO)
先入れ後出し

sakiire sakidashi (FIFO)
first-in first-out (FIFO)
先入れ先出し

sakiire sakidashi hōshiki
push-up method
先入れ先出し方式

sakiire sakidashi hyō
push-up list
先入れ先出し表

sakiire sakidashi kioku
push-up storage
先入れ先出し記憶

sakiire sakidashi kioku sōchi
push-up store
先入れ先出し記憶装置

sakiire sakidashi suru
push up (*verb*)
先入れ先出しする

sakimawari seigyo
advanced control
先回り制御

sakimawari seigyo shisutemu
advanced control system
先回り制御システム

sakitori
prefetch
先取り

sakuhyō
table look-up
索表

sakuin
index
索引

sakuin chizu
index map
索引地図

sakuin hyō
index table
索引表

sakuin junji
index sequential
索引順次

sakuin junji akusesu
index sequential access
索引順次アクセス

sakuin junji akusesu-deisuku
index sequential-access disk
索引順次アクセス・ディスク

sakuin junji akusesu hōshiki (ISAM)
indexed sequential-access
method (ISAM)
索引順次アクセス方式

sakuin junji dēta-setto
indexed sequential data set
索引順次データ・セット

sakuin junji fuairu
indexed sequential file
索引順次ファイル

sakuin junji fuairu kanri shisutemu (ISFMS)
indexed sequential file
management system (ISFMS)
索引順次ファイル管理システム

sakuin junji hensei
indexed sequential organization
索引順次編成

sakuin junji kōzō
index sequential structure
索引順次構造

sakuin kōmoku
index item
索引項目

sakuin kōzō
index structure
索引構造

sakuin ryō'iki
index domain
索引領域

sakuintsuke
indexing
索引付け

sakuintsuki
indexed
索引付き

sakuintsuki adoresu
indexed address
索引付きアドレス

sakuintsuki adoresu shitei
indexed addressing
索引付きアドレス指定

sakuintsuki fuairu
indexed file
索引付きファイル

sakuintsuki oyako shūgō
indexed set
索引付き親子集合

411

sakujo
deletion
削除

sakujo suru
delete
削除する

sakusei
creation
作成

sakuseisha
implementor
作成者

sakuzu
graph
作図

sakuzu ban
plotting board
作図盤

sakuzu purotta
graph plotter
作図プロッタ

sakuzu sōchi (PLOT)
plotter (PLOT)
作図装置

sakuzu suru
plot (*verb*)
作図する

SAM (junji akusesu hōshiki)
SAM (sequential-access method)
順次アクセス方式

sāmisuta
thermistor
サーミスタ

sampō
algorithm
算法

sampō gengo (ALGOL)
Algorithmic Language (ALGOL)
算法言語

san adoresu
three-address
3アドレク

san adoresu meirei
three-address instruction
3アドレス命令

san purasu ichi adoresu
three-plus-one address
3＋1アドレス

sanbitto-baito
triplet
3ビット・バイト

sangyō otomēshon
industrial automation
産業オトメーション

sangyō otomēshon-shisutemu
industrial automation system
産業オトメーション・システム

sangyō'yō dēta shori
industrial data processing
産業用データ処理

sangyō'yō jōhō shisutemu
industrial information system
産業用情報システム

sangyō'yō keisanki
industrial computer
産業用計算機

sangyō'yō keisanki shisutemu
industrial computer system
産業用計算機システム

sangyō'yō shisutemu
industrial system
産業用システム

sanjutsu enzan
arithmetic operation
算術演算

sanjutsu enzanshi
arithmetic operator
算術演算子

sanjutsu heikin
arithmetic mean
算術平均

sanjutsu kaiketa afure
arithmetic underflow
算術下位桁溢れ

sanjutsu kensa
arithmetic check
算術検査

sanjutsu keta afure
arithmetic overflow
算術桁溢れ

sanjutsu keta okuri
arithmetic shift
算術桁送り

sanjutsu meirei
arithmetic instruction
算術命令

sanjutsu ronri kairo (ALU)
arithmetic and logic unit (ALU)
算術論理回路

sanjutsu sayōso
arithmetic operator
算術作要素

sanjutsu shifuto
arithmetic shift
算術シフト

sanjutsu shiki
arithmetic expression
算術式

sanjutsu sutētomento
arithmetic statement
算術ステートメント

sanjutsu wa
arithmetic sum
算術和

sankaku
triangular
三角

sankaku parusu
triangular pulse
三角パルス

sanpuringu
sampling
サンプリング

sanpuringu shūki
sampling period
サンプリング周期

sanpuru
sample
サンプル

sanpuruchi dēta seigyo
sampled data control
サンプル値データ制御

sanshin
ternary
3進

sanshin hō
ternary notation
3進法

sanshin zōbun hyōjihō
ternary incremental
representation
3進増分表示法

sanshō
look up; reference
参照

sanshō fuairu
reference file
参照ファイル

sanshō kōdo
reference code
参照コード

sanshō suru
access (*verb*)
参照する

sanshō'yō tēburu
look-up table
参照用テーブル

sapōto
support
サポート

sapōto-shisutemu
support system
サポート・システム

sapōto-yūteiritei
support utility
サポート・ユーティリティ

sashikomishiki
plug-in
さし込み式

sashikomishiki buhin
plug-in unit
さし込み式部品

sateraito
satellite
サテライト

sateraito-konpyūta
satellite computer
サテライト・コンピュータ

sateraito-purosessa
satellite processor
サテライト・プロセッサ

sateraito-shisutemu
satellite system
サテライト・システム

sateraito-sutēshon
satellite station
サテライト・ステーション

saundo-bōdo
sound board
サウンド・ボード

SAW (hyōmen danseiha)
SAW (surface acoustic waves)
表面弾性波

SBASIC (Sutorakuchādo-Bēshikku)
SBASIC (Structured BASIC)
ストラクチャード・ベーシック

SBC (shinguru-bōdo-konpyūta)
SBC (single-board computer)
シングル・ボード・コンピュータ

SCR (chikuji seigyo rejisuta)
SCR (sequence control register)
逐次制御レジスタ

SCW (segumento seigyo go)
SCW (segment control word)
セグメント制御語

SD (ichi mitsudo)
SD (single density)
一密度

SDDL (kakunō dēta teigi gengo)
SDDL (stored-data definition
language)
格納データ定義言語

SDI (jōhō no sentaku haifu)
SDI (selective dissemination of
information)
情報の選択配布

SDLC (dōkishiki dēta-rinku seigyo)
SDLC (synchronous data link
control)
同期式データ・リンク制御

SE (shisutemu-enjinia)
SE (systems engineer)
システム・エンジニア

sedai
generation
世代

sedai bangō
generation number
世代番号

sedai gihō
generation technique
世代技法

sedai hō
generation technique
世代法

sedai hōshiki
generation system
世代方式

sedai kōshin bangō
generation version number
世代更新番号

sedaibetsu dēta-gurūpu
generation data group
世代別データ・グループ

segumentēshon
segmentation
セグメンテーション

segumento
segment
セグメント

segumento bangō
segment number
セグメント番号

segumento mei
segment name
セグメント名

segumento-puroguramu
segmented program
セグメント・プログラム

segumento seigyo go (SCW)
segment control word (SCW)
セグメント制御語

segumento tansaku insū (SSA)
segment search argument (SSA)
セグメント探索引数

seidenshiki insho sōchi
electrostatic printer
静電式印書装置

seidenshiki kioku
electrostatic storage
静電式記憶

seidenshiki purinta
electrostatic printer
静電式プリンタ

seido
precision
精度

seifu fugō
sign
正負符号

seigen
limit; restriction
制限

seigen suru
restrict
制限する

413

seigō
adjustable; adjustment
整合

seigyo
control; monitoring
制御

seigyo arugorizumu
control algorithm
制御アルゴリズム

seigyo ban
control panel
制御盤

seigyo basu
control bus
制御バス

seigyo bun
control statement
制御文

seigyo burokku
control block
制御ブロック

seigyo chūshōka
control abstraction
制御抽象化

seigyo fuiirudo
control field
制御フィールド

seigyo gihō
control technique
制御技法

seigyo go
control word
制御語

seigyo hensa
control error
制御偏差

seigyo i'inkai
steering committee
制御委員会

seigyo ikō
control transfer
制御移行

seigyo intafuēsu
control interface
制御インタフェース

seigyo jōhō
control information
制御情報

seigyo kādo
control card
制御カード

seigyo kairo
control circuit
制御回路

seigyo kaisō
control hierarchy
制御階層

seigyo kaunta
control counter
制御カウンタ

seigyo kii
control key
制御キー

seigyo kikō
control mechanism
制御機構

seigyo kinō
control function
制御機能

seigyo kioku
control storage
制御記憶

seigyo kioku sōchi
control store
制御記憶装置

seigyo kōzō
control structure
制御構造

seigyo kyoku
control station
制御局

seigyo meirei
control instruction
制御命令

seigyo meirei rejisuta
control instruction register
制御命令レジスタ

seigyo mōdo
control mode
制御モード

seigyo moji
control character
制御文字

seigyo no kireme
control break
制御の切れ目

seigyo no nagare
control flow
制御の流れ

seigyo puroguramu
control program
制御プログラム

seigyo purosessa
control processor
制御プロセッサ

seigyo reberu
control level
制御レベル

seigyo rejisuta
control register
制御レジスタ

seigyo rūchin
control routine
制御ルーチン

seigyo rūpu
control loop
制御ループ

seigyo ryō
controlled variable
制御量

seigyo senkō
control hole; control punch;
function punch
制御せん孔

seigyo setsu
control section
制御節

seigyo shiikensu
control sequence
制御シーケンス

seigyo shingō
control signal
制御信号

seigyo shirei
control command
制御指令

seigyo shisutemu
control system
制御システム

seigyo shisutemu sōsa
control system operation
制御システム操作

seigyo shoshiki
control format
制御書式

seigyo sōchi
control unit; controller
制御装置

seigyo sōsa
control operation
制御操作

seigyo suru
control (*verb*)
制御する

seigyo taishō
controlled system
制御対象

seigyo taku
control desk; console unit;
operator console
制御卓

seigyo tanmatsu
control station
制御端末

seigyo tanmatsu (sōchi)
control terminal
制御端末(装置)

seigyo tetsuzuki
control procedure
制御手続き

seigyo wādo
control word
制御ワード

seigyo yunitto (CU)
control unit (CU)
制御ユニット

seigyo'yō keisanki
control computer
制御用計算機

seihensū
integer variable
整変数

seihōkō no nagare
normal direction flow
正方向の流れ

seihōkō okuri
feed forward
正方向送り

seihōkō pointa
next pointer
正方向ポインタ

seihyō (TAB)
tabulation (TAB)
製表

seihyō kigō
tabulation mark
製表記号

seihyō suru
tabulate
製表する

seihyōki
tabulator
製表機

seijō
normal
正常

seijō kyodō
normal behavior
正常挙動

seijō ōtō
normal answer/response
正常応答

seijō shūryō
normal termination
正常終了

seijōgata nettowāku
star network
星状型ネットワーク

seikakudo
accuracy
正確度

seikakudo seigyo
accuracy control
正確度制御

seikakudo seigyo moji
accuracy control character
正確度制御文字

seikakudo seigyo shisutemu
accuracy control system
正確度制御システム

seiki
normal
正規

seiki gata
normal form
正規型

seiki kansū
normal function
正規関数

seikika
normalization
正規化

seikika suru
normalize
正規化する

seikikan (PFB)
positive feedback (PFB)
正帰還

seinō
performance
性能

seinō hyōka
performance evaluation
性能評価

seinō shiken
performance test
性能試験

seinōteika
degradation
性能低下

seinōteika insū
degradation factor
性能低下因数

seiretsu
alignment
整列

seiri henshū
reduction
整理編集

seironri
positive logic
正論理

seiryū
rectification
整流

seiryūki
rectifier
整流器

seisan
production
生産

seisan jikan
production time
生産時間

415

seisan kanri
production control
生産管理

seisan rain
production line
生産ライン

seisan rain kanri
production line monitoring
生産ライン管理

seisan shisutemu
production system
生産システム

seisei
generated; generating;
generation; production
生成

seisei adoresu
generated address
生成アドレス

seisei gengo
production language
生成言語

seisei gihō
generation technique
生成技法

seisei hō
generation technique
生成法

seisei hōshiki
generation system
生成方式

seisei kansū
generating function
生成関数

seisei puroguramu
generating program; generator
生成プログラム

seisei rūchin
generating routine;
generation routine
生成ルーチン

seisei suru
generate
生成する

seisei takōshiki
generating function
生成多項式

seishika kikō
staticizer
静止化機構

seishika suru
staticize
静止化する

seisoku
regular
正則

seisoku gengo
regular language
正則言語

seisoku hyōgen
regular expression
正則表現

seisū
integer; integral number
整数

seisū BASIC
integer BASIC
整数 BASIC

seisū bu
integer division
整数部

seisū enzan
integer arithmetic
整数演算

seisū keikakuhō
integer programming
整数計画法

seisū zokusei
integer attribute
整数属性

seisūgata
integer type
整数型

seiteisū
integer constant
整定数

seiteki
static
静的

seiteki arokēshon
static allocation
静的アロケーション

seiteki danpu
static dump
静的ダンプ

seiteki kairo
static circuit
静的回路

seiteki kioku
static storage
静的記憶

seiteki kioku sōchi
static store
静的記憶装置

seiteki RAM
static RAM
静的 RAM

seiteki saihaichi
static relocation
静的再配置

seiteki shisutemu
static system
静的システム

sekando-sōsu
secondary source
セカンド・ソース

seki
product
積

sekibun
integration
積分

sekibun hōteishiki
integral equation
積分方程式

sekibun kairo
integrating circuit
積分回路

sekibun seigyo
integral control
積分制御

sekibun seigyo dōsa
integral control action
積分制御動作

sekibunki
integrator
積分器

sekkei
design
設計

sekkei jidōka
design automation
設計自動化

sekkei mokuteki
design objective
設計目的

sekkei riron
design theory
設計理論

sekkei shisō
design philosophy
設計思想

sekushon
section
セクション

sekushon mei
section name
セクション名

sekushon midashi
section header
セクション見出し

sekuta
sector
セクタ

sekuta-adoresu
sector address
セクタ・アドレス

sekuta machigyōretsu
sector queuing
セクタ待ち行列

sekuta-mōdo
sector mode
セクタ・モード

sekutoringu
sectoring
セクトリング

semanteikku
semantic
セマンティック

semanteikku-matorikkusu
semantic matrix
セマンティック・マトリックス

semanteikkusu
semantics
セマンティックス

sembetsu
selecting; selection; selective
選別

sembetsu suitchi
selection switch
選別スイッチ

sembetsu suru
select (*verb*)
選別する

sembetsu sutakka
selective stacker
選別スタッカ

sen
line (communication)
線

sengen
declaration
宣言

sengen bun
declarative statement;
specification statement
宣言文

sengen makuro meirei
declarative macroinstruction
宣言マクロ命令

sengenshi
declarator
宣言子

sen'i
transition
遷移

sen'i jikan
transition duration
遷移時間

sen'i kādo
transition card
遷移カード

sen'i tēburu
transition table
遷移テーブル

sen'i zu
transition diagram
遷移図

senjutsu seigyo jōhō
tactical control information
戦術制御情報

senkei
linear
線形

senkei hōteishiki
linear equation
線形方程式

senkei kairo
linear circuit
線形回路

senkei keikakuhō (LP)
linear programming (LP)
線形計画法

senkei kōzō
linear structure
線形構造

senkei risuto
linear list
線形リスト

senkei saitekika
linear optimization
線形最適化

senkei sentaku
linear selection
線形選択

senkei tōka
linear equalization
線形等化

senkiroku mitsudo
track recording density
線記録密度

senkō
preference
先行

senkō
hole; perforation; punching
せん孔

senkō ichi
punch(ing) position
せん孔位置

senkō jikan
lead time
先行時間

senkō kādo
punched card
せん孔カード

senkō kādo-intapurita
punched-card interpreter
せん孔カード・インタプリタ

senkō kādo kenkō
punched-card verifying
せん孔カード検孔

senkō kādo kenkōki
punched-card verifier
せん孔カード検孔機

senkō kādo-kōdo
punched-card code
せん孔カード・コード

senkō kādo-shisutemu (PCS)
punched-card system (PCS)
せん孔カード・システム

senkō kādo shori
punched-card processing
せん孔カード処理

senkō kādo yomitori sōchi
punched-card reader
せん孔カード読み取り装置

senkō kādo yomitoriki
punched-card reader
せん孔カード読み取り機

senkō kami tēpu
perforated paper tape
せん孔紙テープ

senkō kansū
precedence function
先行関数

senkō kikō
punch station
せん孔機構

senkō kuzu
chad
せん孔くず

senkō machigyōretsu
punch queue
せん孔待ち行列

senkō moji
leading character;
leading graphics
先行文字

senkō patān
hole pattern
せん孔パターン

senkō shutsuryoku
punched output
せん孔出力

senkō sōchi
perforator; punch; puncher;
punching machine
せん孔装置

senkō sokudo
perforation rate; punch rate
せん孔速度

senkō sōsa
punching
せん孔操作

senkō suru
perforate; punch (*verb*)
せん孔する

senkō tagu
punched tag
せん孔タグ

senkō tēpu
perforated tape; punched tape
せん孔テープ

senkōki
perforator; punch; puncher;
punching machine
せん孔機

senkōsū ayamari
hole count error
せん孔数誤り

senkōsū kensa
hole count check
せん孔数検査

senren
refinement
洗練

senryaku
strategy
戦略

senryaku keikaku jōhō
strategic planning information
戦略計画情報

sensa
sensor
センサ

sensa-bēsu keisanki
sensor-based computer
センサ・ベース計算機

sensu-anpu
sense amplifier
センス・アンプ

sensu-baito
sense byte
センス・バイト

sensu-dēta
sense data
センス・データ

sensu kikō
sense station
センス機構

sensu-suitchi
sense switch
センス・スイッチ

sensu suru
sense (*verb*)
センスする

sensu-waiya
sense wire
センス・ワイヤ

sensu zōfukuki
sense amplifier
センス増幅器

sentaku
selecting; selection; selective
選択

sentaku chaneru
selector channel
選択チャネル

sentaku kensa
selection check
選択検査

sentaku kinō
optional function;
selecting ability
選択機能

sentaku sahyō
selective listing
選択作表

sentaku sakiyomi
preselection
選択先読み

sentaku seigyo
selection control
選択制御

sentaku suitchi
selection switch
選択スイッチ

sentaku suru
select (*verb*)
選択する

sentaku yobidashi
selective calling
選択呼び出し

sentakuhō bunrui
selection sort
選択法分類

sentakusei
selectivity
選択性

sentakuteki
selective
選択的

sentakuteki jōhō kensaku (SIR)
selective information retrieval
(SIR)
選択的情報検索

sentakuteki tansaku
selective search
選択的探索

sentakuteki tsuiseki
selective trace
選択的追跡

sentanteki
advanced (development)
先端的

sentanteki jidōka
advanced automation
先端的自動化

sentanteki jidōka shisutemu
advanced automation system
先端的自動化システム

sentei
selecting; selection
選定

sentei suru
select (*verb*)
選定する

sen'yō
dedicated; private
専用

sen'yō kaisen
dedicated line; leased line;
private line
専用回線

sen'yō kaisenmō
leased-line network
専用回線網

sen'yō kaisen sābisu
private line service
専用回線サービス

sen'yō keisanki
dedicated computer;
special-purpose computer
専用計算機

sen'yō puroguramu
specially written program
(≠package)
専用プログラム

sen'yō sen
leased line
専用線

sen'yō shisutemu
dedicated system
専用システム

sen'yū
private
専有

sen'yū fuairu
private file
専有ファイル

sen'yū raiburari
private library
専有ライブラリ

serekuta
selector
セレクタ

serekuta-chaneru
selector channel
セレクタ・チャネル

serekuteingu kinō
selecting ability
セレクティング機能

seru
cell
セル

sesshon
session
セッション

sesshon seigyo
session control
セッション制御

setchi
installation
設置

setchi kijitsu
installation date
設置期日

setchi suru
install
設置する

setsu
section
節

setsubi
facility
設備

setsubi kanri
facilities management
設備管理

setsudan
disconnection
切断

setsudan mōdo
disconnect mode
切断モード

setsudan shingō
disconnect signal
切断信号

setsudan suru
cut off (*verb*); disconnect
切断する

setsugō
junction
接合

setsugō daiōdo
junction diode
接合ダイオード

setsugō toranjisuta
junction transistor
接合トランジスタ

setsumeisho
instruction manual; manual
説明書

setsuzoku
connection
接続

setsuzoku gyōretsu
incidence matrix
接続行列

setsuzoku jikan
connect time
接続時間

setsuzoku kikō
attachment
接続機構

setsuzoku nai
no connection
接続ない

setsuzoku suru
attach; connect
接続する

setsuzokukanō
connectable
接続可能

setsuzokuyō kēburu
connection cable
接続用ケーブル

settei
setting
設定

settei suru
set (*verb*)
設定する

setten
point of contact
接点

settō
prefix
接頭

setto
set
セット

setto-appu
setup
セット・アップ

setto-appu-daiyaguramu
setup diagram
セット・アップ・ダイヤグラム

setto-appu jikan
setup time
セット・アップ時間

settō enzanshi
prefix operator
接頭演算子

settō hyōkihō
prefix notation
接頭表記法

setto kijutsu
set description
セット記述

setto kijutsukō
set description entry
セット記述項

setto mei
set name
セット名

setto-menba
set member
セット・メンバ

setto-okarensu
set occurrence
セット・オカレンス

setto-ouna
set owner
セット・オウナ

setto-parusu
set pulse
セット・パルス

setto-rokēshon-mōdo
set location mode
セット・ロケーション・モード

setto seigyo kii
set control key
セット制御キー

setto sentaku kijun
set selection criteria
セット選択基準

setto setsu
set section
セット節

setto shikibetsu
set identification
セット識別

setto shikibetsushi
set identifier
セット識別子

setto suru
set (*verb*)
セットする

SG (shingō'yō setchi; tsūshin'yō āsu)
SG (signal ground)
信号用接地; 通信用アース

S/H (hyōhon oyobi hoji)
S/H (sample and hold)
標本及び保持

shadan
shutdown
遮断

shadou insatsu
shadow printing
シャドウ印刷

shanaimō
internal company network
社内網

shashin kioku
photographic storage
写具記憶

shashin shokuji
photographic typesetting
写具植字

shashin shokujiki
photographic typesetting equipment
写具植字機

shazō
map; mapping
写像

shazō bu
mapping division
写像部

shazō suru
map (*verb*)
写像する

shibun kukan
quadrant
四分区間

shichō hasshinki
relaxation oscillator
し張発振器

shidō
start
始動

shien
support
支援

shien shigen
support resources
支援資源

shien shisutemu
support system
支援システム

shien sofutouea
support software
支援ソフトウェア

shifuto
shift
シフト

shifuto-auto (SO)
shift-out (SO)
シフト・アウト

shifuto-auto moji (SO moji)
shift-out character (SO character)
シフト・アウト文字; SO文字

shifuto-in (SI)
shift-in (SI)
シフト・イン

shifuto-in moji (SI moji)
shift-in character (SI character)
シフト・イン文字; SI文字

shifuto-kaunta
shift counter
シフト・カウンタ

shifuto-kaunto
shift count
シフト・カウント

shifuto-kii
shift key
シフト・キー

shifuto-kōdo
shift code
シフト・コード

shifuto-parusu
shift pulse
シフト・パルス

shifuto-rejisuta
shift register
シフト・レジスタ

shigen
resource
資源

shigen haibun
resource allocation
資源配分

shigen kanri
resource management
資源管理

shigen keikaku
resource planning
資源計画

shigen kyōyō
resource sharing
資源共用

shihyō
index
指標

shihyō bu
index part
指標部

shihyō dēta kōmoku
index data item
指標データ項目

shihyō go
index word
指標語

shihyō henkō
index modification
指標変更

shihyō hensū
index variable
指標変数

shihyō mei
index name
指標名

shihyō parameta
index parameter
指標パラメタ

shihyō rejisuta
index register; modifier register
指標レジスタ

shihyōtsuke
indexing
指標付け

shihyōtsuki adoresu
indexed address
指標付きアドレス

shihyōtsuki dēta kōmoku
indexed data item
指標付きデータ項目

shiikensa
sequencer
シーケンサ

shiikensu
sequence
シーケンス

shiiku
seek
シーク

shiiku bunri
seek separation
シーク分離

shiiku jikan
seek time
シーク時間

shiiku ryō'iki
seek area
シーク領域

shiito
sheet
シート

shiito-fuiida
sheet feeder
シート・フィーダ

shiji
command; directive; indication; instruction
指示

shiji suru
indicate
指示する

shijishi
designator
指示子

shijisho
instruction manual; manual
指示書

shijiteki shōroku
indicative abstract
指示的抄録

shikaku jōhō shori
visual information processing
視覚情報処理

shikaku jōhō shori sōchi (VIP)
visual information processor (VIP)
視覚情報処理装置

shikaku kensa
sight check
視覚検査

shikaku senkō kensa
peek-a-boo check; sight check
視覚せん孔検査

shikakuteki hyōji sōchi (VDU)
visual display unit (VDU)
視覚的表示装置

shikakuteki kenshutsu
visual detection
視覚的検出

shikakuteki tansaku
 visual search
 視覚的探作

shiken
 test; testing
 試験

shiken ban
 test board
 試験盤

shiken tejun
 test procedure
 試験手順

shiki
 expression; form; system
 式

shiki no hyōka
 evaluation of expression
 式の評価

shikibetsu
 discrimination
 識別

shikibetsu (ID)
 identification (ID)
 識別

shikibetsu adoresu
 identification address
 識別アドレス

shikibetsu bangō
 identification number
 識別番号

shikibetsu kairo
 discrimination circuit
 識別回路

shikibetsu kōdo
 identification code
 識別コード

shikibetsu reberu
 decision level;
 discrimination level
 識別レベル

shikibetsu suru
 identify
 識別する

shikibetsumei
 name
 識別名

shikibetsushi
 identifier
 識別子

shikiiichi
 threshold; threshold level
 敷居値

shikiiichi ronri
 threshold logic
 敷居値論理

shikiiichi soshi
 threshold element
 敷居値素子

shikō kasho
 operating station; operating unit
 施工箇所

shikō suru
 operate
 施工する

shikyū
 urgent
 至急

shikyū dembun
 urgent message
 至急電文

shimei
 dispatching
 指名

shimei jun'i
 dispatching priority
 指名順位

shimei suru
 dispatch (*verb*)
 指名する

shimpuku
 amplitude; magnitude
 振幅

shimpuku henchō (AM)
 amplitude modulation (AM)
 振幅変調

shimpuku hikaku
 magnitude comparison
 振幅比較

shimpuku hizumi
 amplitude distortion
 振幅歪み

shimpuku seigen
 amplitude limiting
 振幅制限

shimpuku seigenki
 amplitude limiter
 振幅制限器

shimpuku seigyo
 amplitude control
 振幅制御

shimpuku sen'i
 magnitude transition
 振幅遷移

shimyurēshon
 simulation
 シミュレーション

shimyurēshon-eguzekuteibu
 simulation executive
 シミュレーション・
 エグゼクティブ

shimyurēshon gengo
 simulation language
 シミュレーション言語

shimyurēshon-moderu
 simulation model
 シミュレーション・モデル

shimyurēta
 simulator
 シミュレータ

shimyurēta-puroguramu
 simulator program
 シミュレータ・プログラム

shimyurēta-rūchin
 simulator routine
 シミュレータ・ルーチン

shimyurēteddo-atenshon
 simulated attention
 シミュレーテッド・アテンション

shimyurēto suru
 simulate
 シミュレートする

shin nishin hyōkihō
 true binary notation
 真2進表記法

shin no hosū
 true complement
 真の補数

shinbionto
 symbiont
 シンビオント

shinbionto seigyo
symbiont control
シンビオント制御

shinbubun shūgō
proper subset
真部分集号

shinchō
expansion
伸長

shinchōki
expander
伸長器

shindan
diagnosis; diagnostics
診断

shindan kensa
diagnostic check
診断検査

shindan made no heikin jikan (MTTD)
mean time to diagnosis (MTTD)
診断までの平均時間

shindan puroguramu
diagnostic program
診断プログラム

shindan rūchin
diagnostic routine
診断ルーチン

shindan shisutemu
diagnostic system
診断システム

shindan tansaku
diagnostic search
診断探索

shindan tesuto
diagnostic test
診断テスト

shingō
sign; signal
信号

shingō hinshitsu kenshutsuki
signal quality detector
信号品質検出器

shingō hōshiki
signaling system
信号方式

shingō kenshutsu
signal detection
信号検出

shingō kyori
signal distance
信号距離

shingō parameta
signal parameter
信号パラメタ

shingō reberu
signal level
信号レベル

shingō saisei
signal regeneration
信号再生

shingō shikibetsu
signal recognition
信号識別

shingō tai zatsuon hi (S/N)
signal-to-noise ratio (S/N)
信号対雑音比

shingōsen kēburu
signal cable
信号線ケーブル

shingō'yō setchi (SG)
s-earth; signal ground (SG)
信号用接地

shinguru
single
シングル

shinguru-bōdo-konpyūta (SBC)
single-board computer (SBC)
シングル・ボード・コンピュタ

shinguru-shotto sōsa
single-shot operation
シングル・ショット操作

shinguru-suteppu sōsa
single-step operation
シングル・ステップ操作

shinkōhakan (TWT)
traveling-wave tube (TWT)
進行波管

shinkū
vacuum
真空

shinkū jōchaku
vacuum evaporation
真空蒸着

shinpurekkusu
simplex
シンプレックス

shinpurekkusu hōhō
simplex method
シンプレックス方法

shinpurekkusu-operēshon
simplex operation
シンプレックス・オペレーション

shinpurekkusu-shisutemu
simplex system
シンプレックス・システム

shinraido
reliability
信頼度

shinraisei
reliability; reliable
信頼性

shinraisei hyōtei
reliability assessment
信頼性評定

shinraisei kaiseki
reliability analysis
信頼性解析

shinri chihyō
truth table
真理値表

shirei
command; instruction; order
指令

shirei adoresu
command address
指令アドレス

shirei gengo
command language
指令言語

shirei kōdo
command code
指令コード

shirei kyohi
command rejection
指令拒否

shirei mōdo
command mode
指令モード

shirei parusu
command pulse
指令パルス

423

shirei rensa
command chaining
指令連鎖

shirei saishikō
command retry
指令再識行

shirei seigyo burokku (CCB)
command control block (CCB)
指令制御ブロック

shirei seigyo go (CCW)
command control word (CCW)
指令制御語

shirei shori
command processing
指令処理

shirei warikomi
command interrupt
指令割り込み

shiriaru
serial
シリアル

shiriaru-dotto-purinta
serial dot printer
シリアル・ドット・プリンタ

shiriaru-purinta
serial printer
シリアル・プリンタ

shiriizu
series
シリーズ

shirikon
silicon
シリコン

shirikon-chippu
silicon chip
シリコン・チップ

shirikon-daiōdo
silicon diode
シリコン・ダイオード

shirikon-deisuku
silicon disk
シリコン・ディスク

shirikon-on-safuaia (SOS)
silicon on sapphire (SOS)
シリコン・オン・サファイア

shirinda
cylinder
シリンダ

shirinda afure
cylinder overflow
シリンダ溢れ

shirinda sōsa
cylinder operation
シリンダ操作

shiruku-sukuriiningu
silk-screening
シルク・スクリーニング

shisetsu
private
私設

shisetsu
facility
施設

shisetsu kaisen
privately owned line
私設回線

shisetsu kanri
facilities management
施設管理

shisetsu tsūshinmō
privately owned communication
network
私設通信網

shishō
breakdown
支障

shisū
exponent
指数

shisū andafurō
exponent underflow
指数アンダフロー

shisū bu
exponent part
指数部

shisū bumpu
exponential distribution
指数分布

shisū ka'i keta afure
exponent underflow
指数下位桁溢れ

shisū kansū
exponential function
指数関数

shisū keta afure
exponent overflow
指数桁溢れ

shisū ōbafurō
exponent overflow
指数オーバフロー

shisūka
exponentiation
指数化

shisutemu
system
システム

shisutemu-ākitekucha
system architecture
システム・アーキテクチャ

shisutemu-akusesu
system access
システム・アクセス

shisutemu-anarisuto
systems analyst
システム・アナリスト

shisutemu anzen
system safety
システム安全

shisutemu anzen hoshu
system security
システム安全保守

shisutemu bunseki
system(s) analysis
システム分析

shisutemu bunsekisha
systems analyst
システム分析者

shisutemu-chāto
system chart
システム・チャート

shisutemu-chekku
system check
システム・チェック

shisutemu chōsei
system tuning
システム調整

shisutemu-danpu
system dump
システム・ダンプ

shisutemu-daun
system down
システム・ダウン

shisutemu-dēta
system data
システム・データ

shisutemu-dēta-fuairu keishiki
system data file format
システム・データ・ファイル形式

shisutemu dōchō
system tuning
システム同調

shisutemu-enjinia (SE)
systems engineer (SE)
システム・エンジニア

shisutemu-eremento
system element
システム・エレメント

shisutemu gairyaku
system outline
システム概略

shisutemu gengo
system language
システム言語

shisutemu genkei
system prototype
システム原型

shisutemu gensoku
system slowdown
システム減速

shisutemu gokansei
systems compatibility
システム互換性

shisutemu gosa
system error
システム誤差

shisutemu haichi
system layout
システム配置

shisutemu han'i
system scope
システム範囲

shisutemu-hausu
system house
システム・ハウス

shisutemu henkō
system modification
システム変更

shisutemu hiyō
system cost
システム費用

shisutemu hōhōron
systems methodology
システム方法論

shisutemu hozen
system integrity;
system maintenance
システム保全

shisutemu hyōka
system evaluation
システム評価

shisutemu hyōtei
system assessment
システム評定

shisutemu iji
system(s) maintenance
システム維持

shisutemu jiritsusei
system autonomy
システム自律性

shisutemu jisshō
system demonstration
システム実証

shisutemu jitsugen
system implementation
システム実現

shisutemu jō no ichiji kioku'iki (SYSPOOL)
system temporary storage pool (SYSPOOL)
システム上の一時記憶域

shisutemu jōchū
system residence
システム常駐

shisutemu jōchū boryūmu
system residence volume;
system-resident volume
システム常駐ボリューム

shisutemu jōchū deisuku-pakku
system-resident disk pack
システム常駐ディスク・パック

shisutemu jōchū kanshi puroguramu
system-resident executive program
システム常駐監視プログラム

shisutemu jōchū kioku
system-resident storage
システム常駐記憶

shisutemu jōchū sōchi
system-resident device
システム常駐装置

shisutemu kaifuku jikan
system recovery time
システム回復時間

shisutemu kaihatsu
system development
システム開発

shisutemu kaisō
system hierarchy
システム階層

shisutemu kanren
system-related
システム関連

shisutemu kanri
system management
システム管理

shisutemu keika kiroku
system log
システム経過記録

shisutemu keikaku
system planning
システム計画

shisutemu keishiki
system format
システム形式

shisutemu kensa
system verification
システム検査

shisutemu kentō
system study
システム検討

shisutemu kijutsu
system description
システム記述

shisutemu kijutsu gengo
system description language
システム記述言語

shisutemu kikō
system mechanism
システム機構

shisutemu kinō
system function
システム機能

shisutemu kinō zu
system function diagram
システム機能図

shisutemu-kōdo
system code
システム・コード

shisutemu kōgaku
systems engineering
システム工学

shisutemu kōgyō
systems engineering
システム工業

shisutemu-konponento
system component
システム・コンポネント

shisutemu kōritsu
system efficiency
システム効率

shisutemu kōsei
system composition;
system configuration
システム構成

shisutemu kōsei kiki
system component
システム構成機器

shisutemu kōsei zu
system composition diagram
システム構成図

shisutemu koshō
system failure
システム故障

shisutemu kōzō
system structure
システム構造

shisutemu-makuro meirei
system macroinstruction
システム・マクロ命令

shisutemu-moderu
system model
システム・モデル

shisutemu mokuhyō
system goal
システム目標

shisutemu mokuteki
system objective
システム目的

shisutemu-monita
system monitor
システム・モニタ

shisutemu muki
systems-oriented
システム向き

shisutemu nagarezu
system flowchart
システム流れ図

shisutemu-nettowāku-ākitekucha
system network architecture
システム・ネットワーク・
アーキテクチャ

shisutemu no jitsugen
systems implementation
システムの実現

shisutemu no jumyō
system life cycle
システムの寿命

shisutemu nyūryoku sōchi
system input device
システム入力装置

shisutemu ōtō
system response
システム応答

shisutemu ōtō jikan
system response time
システム応答時間

shisutemu ōyō
system application
システム応用

shisutemu-pakkēji
system package
システム・パッケージ

shisutemu-purogurama
systems programmer
システム・プログラマ

shisutemu-puroguramingu
systems programming
システム・プログラミング

shisutemu-puroguramu
system program
システム・プログラム

shisutemu-raiburari
system library
システム・ライブラリ

shisutemu-raifu-saikuru
system life cycle
システム・ライフ・サイクル

shisutemu rinkaku
system outline
システム輪郭

shisutemu riron
systems theory
システム理論

shisutemu-risetto
system reset
システム・リセット

shisutemu-rōda
system loader
システム・ローダ

shisutemu ronri
system logic
システム論理

shisutemu saishidō
system restart
システム再始動

shisutemu saitekika
system optimization
システム最適化

shisutemu sakusei
systems implementation
システム作成

shisutemu sakusei gengo
systems implementation
language
システム作成言語

shisutemu-sapōto
system support
システム・サポート

shisutemu seigyo
system control
システム制御

shisutemu seigyo ban
system control panel
システム制御盤

shisutemu seigyo sōchi
system controller
システム制御装置

shisutemu seinō
system performance
システム性能

shisutemu seisansei
system productivity
システム生産性

shisutemu seisei (SYSGEN)
systems generation (SYSGEN)
システム生成

shisutemu sekkei
system(s) design
システム設計

shisutemu sekkei kōgaku
system design engineering
システム設計工学

shisutemu sekkeisha
systems designer
システム設計者

shisutemu setchi
system installation
システム設置

shisutemu shien
system support
システム支援

shisutemu shigen
system resources
システム資源

shisutemu-shimyurēshon
system simulation
システム・シミュレーション

shisutemu shinraisei
system reliability
システム信頼性

shisutemu shiyō
system specification
システム仕様

shisutemu shoki settei
system initialization
システム初期設定

shisutemu shoki settei puroguramu
system initialization program
システム初期設定プログラム

shisutemu shokika
system initialization
システム初期化

shisutemu shokika puroguramu
system initialization program
システム初期化プログラム

shisutemu shoriryō
system throughput
システム処理量

shisutemu shoryakuji kaishaku
system default
システム省略時解釈

shisutemu shutsuryoku sōchi
system output device
システム出力装置

shisutemu-sofutouea
system(s) software
システム・ソフトウェア

shisutemu sōsain
system operator
システム操作員

shisutemu sōsataku
system console
システム操作卓

shisutemu-sūpabaiza
system supervisor
システム・スーパバイザ

shisutemu tagei
system versatility
システム多芸

shisutemu teigi
system definition
システム定義

shisutemu tekiōsei
system adaptability
システム適応性

shisutemu-tēpu
system tape
システム・テープ

shisutemu-tesuto
system test
システム・テスト

shisutemu tōgō
system integration
システム統合

shisutemu tokusei
system characteristics
システム特性

shisutemu uchi ni chikuseki suru
accumulate in a system
システム内に蓄積する

shisutemu unten teishi
system shutdown
システム運転停止

shisutemu yōkyū
system requirements
システム要求

shisutemu yōryō
system capacity
システム容量

shisutemukan tsūshin
intersystem communication
システム間通信

shisutemu'yō seigyo kioku
control storage for system
システム用制御記憶

shitei
selecting; selective; specification
指定

shitei'iki danpu
selective dump
指定域ダンプ

shitei yōshi
specification sheet
指定用紙

shitsumon
query; question
質問

shitsumon-kaitō (Q-A)
question and answer (Q-A)
質問-回答

shitsumon-kaitō shisutemu
question-and-answer system
質問-回答システム

shitsumon keishikika
query formation
質問形式化

shiyō
personal; private
私用

shiyō
activity; use
使用

shiyō(gaki)
specification
仕様(書き)

shiyō jōken
conditions of use
使用条件

shiyō kanō jikan
accountable time; available
machine time; serviceable time;
up time
使用可能時間

shiyō kijutsu gengo
specification language
使用記述言語

427

shiyō kinshi
disable; disabling
使用禁止

shiyō raiburari
private library
私用ライブラリ

shiyō ritsu
activity ratio; utilization ratio
使用率

shiyōchū (no)
active; busy
使用中（の）

shiyōchū no fuairu
active file
使用中のファイル

shiyōkanō
enable; enabled; enabling;
serviceable
使用可能

shiyōkanō banku
active bank
使用可能バンク

shiyōkanō shingō
enabling signal
使用可能信号

shiyōkanōdo
availability
使用可能度

shiyōkanōsei
serviceability
使用可能性

shiyōkyū
request; requesting
旨要求

shiyōkyū tanmatsu sōchi
requesting terminal
旨要求端末装置

shiyōsei
usability
使用性

shiyōsha
user
使用者

shizen gengo
natural language
自然言語

shizen junjo
natural sequence
自然順序

shizen kansū zenerēta
natural-function generator;
natural-law function generator
自然関数ゼネレータ

shizen sū
natural number
自然数

shizen taisū
natural logarithm
自然対数

shō kibo shūseki kairo (SSIC)
small-scale integrated circuit
(SSIC)
小規模集積回路

shō kibo shūsekika (SSI)
small-scale integration (SSI)
小規模集積化

shō rejisuta
quotient register
商レジスタ

shōgai
breakdown; fault
障害

shōgai kenshutsu
fault detection
障害検出

shōgai tankyū
troubleshooting
障害探究

shōgai tsuikyū
troubleshooting
障害追求

shōgeki
impact
衝撃

shōgekishiki insho sōchi
impact printer
衝撃式印書装置

shōgō
collating
照合

shōgō junjo
collating sequence
照合順序

shōgō sōsa
collating operation
照合操作

shōgō suru
collate
照合する

shōgōki
collator
照合機

shōjun
ascending order
昇順

shōkai (ENQ)
enquiry (ENQ); inquiry
照会

shōkai sōchi
enquiry system; inquiry system
照会装置

shōkai'yō tanmatsu (sōchi)
enquiry station; enquiry terminal;
inquiry station; inquiry terminal
照会用端末（装置）

shoki
initial
初期

shoki chi
initial value
初期値

shoki jōken
initial condition
初期条件

shoki koshō
initial failure
初期故障

shoki meirei
initial instructions
初期命令

shoki mōdo
initial mode
初期モード

shoki puroguramu-rōda (IPL)
initial program loader (IPL)
初期プログラム・ローダ

shoki puroguramu-rōdeingu
initial program loading
初期プログラム・ローディング

shoki rōdo
initial load
初期ロード

shoki setsuzoku
handshake
初期接続

shoki setsuzoku tejun
handshaking
初期接続手順

shoki settei
initialization
初期設定

shoki settei mōdo
initialization mode
初期設定モード

shoki settei suru
initialize
初期設定する

shokichi settei
initialization
初期値設定

shokichi settei fukupuroguramu
block-data subprogram;
specification subprogram
初期値設定副プログラム

shokichi settei suru
initialize
初期値設定する

shokuji
typesetting
植字

shokuji shisutemu
typesetting system
植字システム

shōkyo
clear
消去

shōkyo funō
nonerasable
消去不能

shōkyo funō kioku
nonerasable storage
消去不能記憶

shōkyo heddo
erase head
消去ヘッド

shōkyo meirei
clear instruction
消去命令

shōkyo moji
erase character
消去文字

shōkyo suru
clear (*verb*); erase
消去する

shōkyokanō
erasable
消去可能

shōkyokanō kioku
erasable storage
消去可能記憶

shōkyokanō puroguramukanō ROM (EPROM)
erasable programmable read-
only memory (EPROM)
消去可能プログラム可能ROM

shōkyoki
erasing device
消去器

shōmi jikan
net time
正味時間

shōrai jōhō
futuristic information
将来情報

shori
manipulation
処理

shori (sōsa)
processing
処理(操作)

shori fuka
processing load
処理負荷

shori genkai
processing limits
処理限界

shori gihō
processing technique(s)
処理技法

shori hōhō
processing technique(s)
処理方法

shori jikan
processing time
処理時間

shori kiki
processing equipment
処理機器

shori kinō
processing capability
処理機能

shori nōryoku
throughput
処理能力

shori puroguramu
processing program
処理プログラム

shori rūchin
processing routine
処理ルーチン

shori sareta dēta
processed data
処理されたデータ

shori sareta jōhō
processed information
処理された情報

shori seiyaku
process bound
処理制約

shori shisutemu
processing system
処理システム

shori sōchi
processing equipment;
processing unit; processor
処理装置

shori sokudo
processing speed
処理速度

shori suru
process (*verb*)
処理する

shoriryō
throughput
処理量

shorui
document
書類

shoryaku
abbreviation
省略

shoryakuji kaishaku
default; default assumption
省略時解釈

shoryakuji no atai
default value
省略時の値

shoryakuji opushon
default option
省略時オプション

shōsai
detailed
詳細

shoshiki
form (document)
書式

shoshiki (F)
format (F)
書式

shoshiki kijutsu
format description
書式記述

shoshiki kōdo
format code
書式コード

shoshiki nai
unformatted
書式ない

shoshiki nai raito bun
unformatted WRITE statement
書式ない WRITE 文

shoshiki nai riido bun
unformatted READ statement
書式ない READ 文

shoshiki okuri
form advance
書式送り

shoshiki okuri (FF)
form feed (FF)
書式送り

shoshiki okuri moji
form feed character
書式送り文字

shoshiki sakusei
formatting
書式作成

shoshiki seigyo
form control; format control
書式制御

shoshiki seigyo kādo
format control card
書式制御カード

shoshiki seigyo moji (FE)
format effector (FE);
layout character
書式制御文字

shoshiki shiyō
format specification
書式仕様

shoshiki tsuke
formatting
書式付け

shoshiki tsuki
formatted
書式付き

shoshikitsuki raito bun
formatted WRITE statement
書式付き WRITE 文

shoshikitsuki riido bun
formatted READ statement
書式付き READ 文

shōshūki
minor cycle
小周期

shōsū
fraction
小数

shōsūbu
fixed-point part; fractional part
小数部

shōsūten
radix point
小数点

shōtotsu
crash
衝突

Shottokii-daiōdo
Schottky diode
ショットキー・ダイオード

Shottokii-toranjisuta ronri (STL)
Schottky transistor logic (STL)
ショットキー・トランジスタ論理

shoyūken o shuchō dekiru puroguramu
proprietary program
所有権を主張できるプログラム

shoyūken o shuchō dekiru sofutouea
proprietary software
所有権を主張できるソフトウェア

shoyūsha
owner
所有者

shoyūsha shikibetsumei
owner identifier
所有者識別名

shu
manual (≠automatic)
手

shu
master
主

shu bōdo
main board; mother board
主ボード

shu fuairu
main file
主ファイル

shu gun
master group
主群

shu kioku
main internal memory;
main memory
主記憶

shu kioku'iki
main storage
主記憶域

shu kioku'iki danpu
main storage dump
主記憶域ダンプ

shu kioku ryō'iki
main storage
主記憶領域

shu kioku sōchi
main internal memory unit
主記憶装置

shu kokuji kikō
master clock
主刻時機構

shu puroguramu
main program
主プログラム

shu purosessa
main processor
主プロセッサ

shu rūchin
main routine; master routine
主ルーチン

shu seigyo
main control
主制御

shu seigyo sōchi
main control unit
主制御装置

shu shisutemu
main system; primary system
主システム

shu sōsa
manual operation
手操作

shu sōsataku
primary console
主操作卓

shu tanmatsu
master station
主端末

shu tasuku
main task
主タスク

shu torakku
primary track
主トラック

shubetsu
classification
種別

shūchū
integrated
集中

shūchū(gata)
centralized
集中(型)

shūchū dēta-shisutemu
integrated data system
集中データ・システム

shūchū dēta shori
centralized data processing
集中データ処理

shūchū dēta shori (IDP)
integrated data processing (IDP)
集中データ処理

shūchū dēta shori shisutemu
centralized data-processing
system
集中データ処理システム

shūchū dēta shori shisutemu (IDPS)
integrated data-processing
system (IDPS)
集中データ処理システム

shūchū dētabēsu
integrated database
集中データベース

shūchū han'yō rejisuta
integrated general register
集中汎用レジスタ

shūchū hōshiki
centralized system
集中方式

shūchū jōhō kōzō
centralized information structure
集中情報構造

shūchū jōhō shisutemu
centralized information system
集中情報システム

shūchū kei'ei jōhō shisutemu
integrated management
information system
集中経営情報システム

shūchū seigyo
centralized control
集中制御

shūchū sōsa
centralized operation
集中操作

shūchūgata konpyūta
centrally located computer
集中型コンピュータ

shūchūgata konpyūta-nettowāku
centralized computer network
集中型コンピュータ・
ネットワーク

shūchūka
centralization
集中化

shūdan senkō
gang punch
集団せん孔

shudō (no)
manual (≠automatic)
手動(の)

shudō bakku-appu
manual backup
手動バック・アップ

shudō hōhō
manual method
手動方法

shudō keisanki
hand-operated calculator
手動計算器

shudō nyūryoku
manual input
手動入力

shudō nyūryoku rejisuta
manual input register
手動入力レジスタ

shudō nyūryoku sōchi
manual input unit
手動入力装置

shudō seigyo
manual control
手動制御

shudō shisutemu
manual system
手動システム

shudō sōsa
manual operation
手動操作

shudō tojita rūpu shisutemu
manual closed-loop system
手動閉じたループ・システム

shudōshiki
hand-operated; manual
手動式

shudōshiki senkōki
hand punch
手動式せん孔機

shudōteki mōdo
manual mode
手動的モード

shūgō
set (*noun*)
集合

431

shūgō kakidashi
gather write
集合書き出し

shūgō kansū
aggregation function
集合関数

shūgō sōsa
set operation
集合操作

shūgō taishiki
aggregate expression
集合体式

shūgōron
set theory
集合論

shūgōtai no kata
aggregate type
集合体の型

shūhasū
frequency
周波数

shūhasū bembetsu
frequency discrimination
周波数弁別

shūhasū bunkatsu tajū hōshiki (FDM)
frequency division multiplexing (FDM)
周波数分割多重方式

shūhasū bunkatsu tajū hōshiki sōchi (FDM)
frequency division multiplexer (FDM)
周波数分割多重方式装置

shūhasū henchō (FM)
frequency modulation (FM)
周波数変調

shūhasū hen'i
frequency shift
周波数変位

shūhasū hen'i hōshiki (FSK)
frequency shift keying (FSK)
周波数変位方式

shūhasū ōtō
frequency response
周波数応答

shūhasū tai'iki
frequency band
周波数帯域

shūhen intafuēsu
peripheral interface
周辺インタフェース

shūhen intafuēsu-chaneru
peripheral interface channel
周辺インタフェース・チャネル

shūhen kiki
peripheral device; peripheral equipment; peripherals
周辺機器

shūhen kiki ni yoru seigen
peripheral-limited
周辺機器による制限

shūhen kiki seigyo
peripherals control
周辺機器制御

shūhen LSI chippu
peripheral LSI chip
周辺LSIチップ

shūhen seigyo sōchi
peripheral control unit
周辺制御装置

shūhen sōchi
peripheral device; peripheral equipment; peripheral unit; peripherals
周辺装置

shūhen sōchikan dēta tensō
peripheral transfer
周辺装置間データ転送

shūkeihyō (TAB)
tabulation
集計表

shūketsu
conclusion; end; termination
終結

shūki
cycle; period
周期

shūki(teki)
periodic
周期(的)

shūki kensa
cycle check
周期検査

shūkiteki gairan
periodic disturbance
周期的外乱

shūkiteki parusu retsu
periodic pulse train
周期的パルス列

shukutai
degeneracy
縮退

shukutai (shita)
degenerate
縮退(した)

Shumitto kairo
Schmitt circuit
シュミット回路

Shumitto-toriga kairo
Schmitt trigger circuit
シュミット・トリガ回路

shūri
repair
修理

shūri chien jikan
repair delay time
修理遅延時間

shūri hoshu
corrective maintenance
修理保守

shūri jikan
repair time
修理時間

shūrifunō
unrepairable
修理不能

shūryō
completion; end; termination
終了

shūsa
aberration
収差

shūsei
correction
修正

shūsei(ka)
modification
修正(化)

shūsei reberu
modification level
修正レベル

shūseika adoresu
modified address
修正化アドレス

shūseikanōsei
modifiability
修正可能性

shūseki
integrated; integration
集積

shūseki kairo (IC)
integrated circuit (IC)
集積回路

shūseki kairo kioku (ICM)
integrated circuit memory (ICM)
集積回路記憶

shūsekika
integration
集積化

shūshi
end
終止

shūshi keta
end column
終止桁

shūshoku
modifier
修飾

shūshoku(ka)
modification
修飾(化)

shūshoku bitto
modifier bit
修飾ビット

shūshoku sareta namae
qualified name
修飾された名前

shūshoku suru
modify
修飾する

shūshokushi
qualifier
修飾子

shūsoku
convergence
収束

shutai
subject
主体

shūtan (TE)
end; trailing end (TE)
終端

shūtan (sōchi)
terminal
終端(装置)

shūtan kigō
terminal symbol
終端記号

shūtan ryō'iki
termination environment
終端領域

shūtan senro
terminated line
終端線路

shūtankan kakunin
end-to-end acknowledgment
終端間確認

shutsu ketsugōshi
out connector
出結合子

shutsugen
occurrence
出現

shutsunyūryoku apurōchi
output-to-input approach
出入力アプローチ

shutsunyūryoku hōhō
output-to-input approach
出入力方法

shutsuryoku
output
出力

shutsuryoku baffua
output buffer
出力バッファ

shutsuryoku baitai
output medium
出力媒体

shutsuryoku basu
output bus
出力バス

shutsuryoku burokku
output block
出力ブロック

shutsuryoku burokkuka insū
output blocking factor
出力ブロック化因数

shutsuryoku chaneru
output channel
出力チャネル

shutsuryoku chūdan
output break
出力中断

shutsuryoku dēta
output data
出力データ

shutsuryoku fuairu
output file
出力ファイル

shutsuryoku hensū
output variable
出力変数

shutsuryoku iki
output area
出力域

shutsuryoku jyānaru
output journal
出力ジャーナル

shutsuryoku ketsugō
wired AND; wired OR
出力結合

shutsuryoku kōritsu
output efficiency
出力効率

shutsuryoku machigyōretsu
output queue
出力待ち行列

shutsuryoku puroguramu
output program
出力プログラム

shutsuryoku reiauto
output layout
出力レイアウト

shutsuryoku rūchin
output routine
出力ルーチン

shutsuryoku ryō'iki
output area
出力領域

shutsuryoku sagyō machigyōretsu
output work queue
出力作業待ち行列

shutsuryoku senkōki
output punch
出力せん孔機

shutsuryoku shingō
output signal
出力信号

shutsuryoku shitei
output specifications
出力指定

shutsuryoku (yōshiki) shiyōgaki
output format specification
出力（様式）仕様書き

shutsuryoku shori
output processing
出力処理

shutsuryoku sōchi
out device; output device;
output unit
出力装置

shutsuryoku sokudo
speed of output
出力速度

shutsuryoku soshi
output element
出力素子

shutsuryoku suru
output (*verb*)
出力する

shutsuryoku sutakka
output stacker
出力スタッカ

shutsuryoku taipuraita
output typewriter
出力タイプライタ

shutsuryoku tetsuzuki
output procedure
出力手続き

shutsuryoku yōshiki
output format
出力様式

shūyō
capacity
収容

SI (shifuto-in)
SI (shift-in)
シフト・イン

SI moji (shifuto-in moji)
SI character (shift-in character)
シフト・イン文字；SI文字

SIC (handōtai shūseki kairo)
SIC (semiconductor integrated
circuit)
半導体集積回路

SIO (chokuretsu nyūshutsuryoku intafuēsu)
SIO (serial input/output interface)
直列入出力インタフェース

SIR (sentakuteki jōhō kensaku)
SIR (selective information
retrieval)
選択的情報検索

S/N (shingō tai zatsuon hi)
S/N (signal-to-noise ratio)
信号対雑音比

SO (shifuto-auto)
SO (shift-out)
シフト・アウト

sō bitto
dibit
双ビット

SO moji (shifuto-auto moji)
SO character (shift-out
character)
シフト・アウト文字；SO文字

sōantei
bistable
双安定

sōantei kairo
bistable circuit;
bistable trigger circuit
双安定回路

sōantei soshi
bistable element
双安定素子

sōantei toriga kairo
bistable trigger circuit
双安定トリガ回路

SOB (burokku kaishi)
SOB (start of block)
ブロック開始

sōbi
equipment
装備

sōchi
device; equipment; unit
装置

sōchi adaputa
device adapter
装置アダプタ

sōchi adoresu
device address
装置アドレス

sōchi baitai seigyo gengo (DMCL)
device media control language
(DMCL)
装置媒体制御言語

sōchi bangō
device number; unit number
装置番号

sōchi dokuritsu
device independence;
device-independent
装置独立

sōchi dokuritsu akusesu hōshiki
device-independent access
method
装置独立アクセス方式

sōchi dōsa funō
device inoperable
装置動作不能

sōchi izon
device dependence
装置依存

sōchi jōtai go
device status word
装置状態語

sōchi kensa
equipment check
装置検査

sōchi seigyo (DC)
device control (DC)
装置制御

sōchi seigyo burokku (UCB)
unit control block (UCB)
装置制御ブロック

sōchi seigyo go
unit control word
装置制御語

sōchi seigyo moji
device control character
装置制御文字

sōchi shikibetsu
device identification
装置識別

sōchi shikibetsushi
device identifier
装置識別子

sōchi shindan puroguramu
device diagnostic program
装置診断プログラム

sōchi shiyōchū
device busy
装置使用中

sōchi tai'ō hyō
device correspondence table
装置対応表

sōchi taipu
device type
装置タイプ

sōchi wariate
device allocation
装置割り当て

soeji
subscript
添え字

soeji iki
subscript bound
添え字域

soeji risuto
subscript list
添え字リスト

soeji shiki
subscript expression
添え字式

soejitsuki
subscripted
添え字付き

soejitsuki hensū
subscripted variable
添え字付き変数

sofu fuairu
grandfather file
祖父ファイル

sofuto-kiibōdo
soft keyboard
ソフト・キーボード

sofuto-kopii
soft copy
ソフト・コピー

sofuto-sekuta
soft-sectored
ソフト・セクタ

sofuto-sekuta-deisuku
soft-sectored disk
ソフト・セクタ・ディスク

sofuto-sekutoringu
soft-sectoring
ソフト・セクトリング

sofuto-shisutemu
soft system
ソフト・システム

sofutouea
software
ソフトウェア

sofutouea-hausu
software house
ソフトウェア・ハウス

sofutouea hoshu
software maintenance
ソフトウェア保守

sofutouea kagaku
software science
ソフトウェア科学

sofutouea kaihatsu
software development
ソフトウェア開発

sofutouea keisoku
software instrumentation
ソフトウェア計測

sofutouea kijutsu
software description
ソフトウェア記述

sofutouea kōgaku
software engineering
ソフトウェア工学

sofutouea-pakkēji
software package
ソフトウェア・パッケージ

sofutouea seigyo
software control
ソフトウェア制御

sofutouea sekkei
software design
ソフトウェア設計

sofutouea-shisutemu
software system
ソフトウェア・システム

sofutouea sokutei
software measurement
ソフイウェア測定

sofutouea tōgō
software integration
ソフトウェア統合

sofutouea tōgō tesuto
software integration test
ソフトウェア統合テスト

sofutouea-tsūru
software tool
ソフトウェア・ツール

sōgō
integrated
総合

sōgō dēta-shisutemu
integrated data system
総合データ・システム

sōgō dēta shori (IDP)
integrated data processing (IDP)
総合データ処理

sōgō dēta shori shisutemu (IDPS)
integrated data-processing system (IDPS)
総合データ処理システム

sōgō dētabēsu
integrated database
総合データベース

sōgō haijo
mutual exclusion
相互排除

sōgō jōhō
mutual information
相互情報

sōgō jōhō shisutemu
integrated information system
総合情報システム

sōgō kaiki
mutual recursion
相互回帰

sōgō kei'ei jōhō shisutemu
integrated management information system
総合経営情報システム

sōgō keisanki shisutemu
integrated computer system
総合計算機システム

sōgō ofuisu-shisutemu
integrated office system
総合オフィス・システム

sōgo sanshō
cross-reference
相互参照

sōgo sanshō hyō
cross-reference list;
corss-reference table
相互参照表

sōgo shisutemu
integrated system
総合システム

sōgo sōkan
cross-correlation
相互相関

sōgokankei
interaction; interactive;
interrelated
相互関係

sōgokanren
interaction; interactive;
interrelated
相互関連

sōgoketsugō
interconnected; interconnecting
相互結合

sōgoketsugō akuteibitei
interconnecting activities
相互結合アクティビティ

sōgoketsugō eremento
interconnecting elements
相互結合エレメント

sōgoketsugō nettowāku
interconnecting network
相互結合ネットワーク

sōgosayō
interaction; interactive
相互作用

sōgosayō hōshiki
interactive method
相互作用方式

sōgosayō mōdo
interactive mode
相互作用モード

sōgosayō shisutemu
interactive system
相互作用システム

sōgosetsuzoku
interconnected; interconnecting;
interconnection
相互接続

sogyōretsu
sparse matrix
疎行列

SOH (heddeingu kaishi)
SOH (start of heading)
ヘッディング開始

sōhan bumpu
reciprocal distribution
相反分布

sōhogata
complementary
相補型

sōhogata kairo
complementary circuit
相補型回路

sōhogata mosu (CMOS)
complementary metal oxide
semiconductor (CMOS)
相補型モス；相補型MOS

sōhogata seigyo sōchi
complementary controller
相補型制御装置

sōhōkō insho sōchi
bidirectional printer
双方向印書装置

sōhōkō nagare
bidirectional flow
双方向流れ

sōhōkō sōsa
bidirectional operation
双方向操作

sōhoteki
complementary
相補的

sōhoteki puroguramingu
complementary programming
相補的プログラミング

sōjigata
analog
相似型

sōjushin
transmission
送受信

sōjushin sōchi
transmitter-receiver
送受信装置

sōkan
correlation
相関

sōkan kaiseki
correlation analysis
相関解析

sokuchi adoresu
immediate address
即値アドレス

sokuchi adoresu shitei
immediate addressing
即値アドレス指定

sokuchi dēta
immediate data
即値データ

sokuchi endo
immediate AND
即値AND

sokuchi meirei
immediate instruction
即値命令

sokuchi operando
immediate operand
即値オペランド

sokudo
measurement
測度

sokudo
speed; velocity
速度

sokudo haba
speed range
速度幅

sokudo han'i
speed range
速度範囲

sokudo zōka
speed enhancement
速度増加

sokudo zōka kikō
speed enhancer
速度増加機構

sokuhatai
sideband
側波帯

sokuji akusesu
immediate access
即時アクセス

sokuji akusesu kioku (IAS)
immediate-access storage (IAS)
即時アクセス記憶

sokuji akusesu kioku sōchi (IAS)
immediate-access store (IAS)
即時アクセス記憶装置

sokuji kaitō shisutemu
on-demand system
即時回答システム

sokuji seigyo
immediate control
即時制御

sokuji shirei
immediate command
即時指令

sokuji shori
immediate processing
即時処理

sokuji sōsa
immediate operation
即時操作

sokuji sukippu
immediate skip
即時スキップ

sokuji sutētasu
immediate status
即時ステータス

sokuji yobidashi
random access
即時呼び出し

sokuji yobidashi fuairu
random-access file
即時呼び出しファイル

sokuōgata hōshiki
transparent mode
即応型方式

sokutei suru
measure (*verb*)
測定する

sōnyū
insertion
挿入

sōnyū no retsu
insertion sequence
挿入の列

sōnyū rekōdo
inserted record
挿入レコード

sōnyū suru
insert (*verb*)
挿入する

sōnyūhō bunrui
insertion sort
挿入法分類

sonzai
existence
存在

sonzai kenshō
existence verification
存在検証

SOP (hyōjun sōsa tejun)
SOP (standard operating procedure)
標準操作手順

soroe
justification
揃え

soroeru
justify
揃える

SOS (shirikon-on-safuaia)
SOS (silicon on sapphire)
シリコン・オン・サファイア

sōsa
scan; scanning
走査

sōsa
operation (action)
操作

sōsa ban
console panel; control panel
操作盤

sōsa bu
function part
操作部

sōsa hōhō
scan method
走査方法

sōsa jikan
scanning time
走査時間

sōsa kaisetsusho
operation manual
操作解説書

sōsa kemban
operator console
操作鍵盤

sōsa kikō
scanner
走査機構

sōsa nagarezu
operational flowchart
操作流れ図

sōsa seigyoban
operator control panel
操作制御盤

sōsa sen
operating line
操作線

sōsa setsumeisho
operation manual
操作説明書

sōsa shijisho
operation manual
操作指示書

sōsa sokudo
scanning rate
走査速度

sōsa sōsa
scanning operation
走査操作

sōsa suru
operate
操作する

sōsa suru
scan (*verb*)
走査する

sōsa tēburu
scan table
走査テーブル

sōsain
operator
操作員

sōsain akusesu kōdo
operator's access code
操作員アクセス・コード

sōsain ID
operator ID
操作員 ID

sōsain kainyū
operator's intervention
操作員介入

437

sōsain seigyo
operator control
操作員制御

sōsain seigyoban
operator's control panel
操作員制御盤

sōsain shikibetsu kādo
operator identity card
操作員識別カード

sōsain shirei
operator command
操作員指令

sōsakanō
operational
操作可能

sōsaki
scanner
走査器

sōsasen
scanning spot
走査線

sōsataku
console (unit); operating station;
operator console
操作卓

sōsataku hyōji sōchi
console display
操作卓表示装置

sōsataku messēji
console message
操作卓メッセージ

sōsenkei
bilinear
双線形

sōsenkei shisutemu
bilinear system
双線形システム

soshi
element
素子

soshiki
organization; system
組織

soshiki-hōshiki (O and M)
organization and methods
(O and M)
組織-方式；O アンド M；
O and M

sōshin
sending; transmission
送信

sōshin chūdan
transmission interruption
送信中断

sōshin o zokkō suru
resume transmission (*verb*)
送信を続行する

sōshin sentaku
select transmit
送信選択

sōshin suru
send; transmit
送信する

sōshin tochū
during transmission
送信途中

sōshin yōkyū
request to send
送信要求

sōshinka
ready for sending
送信可

sōshinki
transmitter
送信機

sōshō(teki) dēta
generic data
総称(的)データ

sōshō mei
generic name
総称名

sōshō(teki) tetsuzuki
generic procedure
総称(的)手続き

sōsu
source
ソース

sōsu-kōdo
source code
ソース・コード

sosū seisei
prime number generation
素数生成

sōta
sorter
ソータ

sōtai
dual
双対

sōtai
relative
相対

sōtai adoresu
relative address
相対アドレス

sōtai adoresu shitei
relative addressing
相対アドレス指定

sōtai dēta
relative data
相対データ

sōtai enzan
dual operation
双対演算

sōtai fuairu
relative file
相対ファイル

sōtai gosa
relative error
相対誤差

sōtai hensei
relative organization
相対編成

sōtai hensei fuairu
relative file
相対編成ファイル

sōtai kii
relative key
相対キー

sōtai kōdeingu
relative coding
相対コーディング

sōtai kōdo
relative code
相対コード

sōtai puroguramingu
relative programming
相対プログラミング

sōtai rekōdo ban
relative record number
相対レコード番

sōtai shihyōtsuke
relative indexing
相対指標付け

sōtatsu
delivery (of message)
送達

sōtei shita shōsūten
assumed decimal point
想定した小数点

sōto
sort
ソート

sōto-puroguramu
sort program
ソート・プログラム

sōto suru
sort (*verb*)
ソートする

sōto-yūteiritei
sort utility
ソート・ユーティリティ

sōzō shisutemu
creative system
創造システム

SP (kankaku moji)
SP (space character)
間隔文字

SSA (segumento tansaku insū)
SSA (segment search argument)
セグメント探索引数

SSB (tansoku hatai)
SSB (single sideband)
単測波帯

SSI (shō kibo shūsekika)
SSI (small-scale integration)
小規模集積化

SSIC (shō kibo shūseki kairo)
SSIC (small-scale integrated circuit)
小規模集積回路

STL (Shottokii-toranjisuta ronri)
STL (Schottky transistor logic)
ショットキー・トランジスタ論理

STX (tekisuto kaishi)
STX (start of text)
テキスト開始

sū
number; numeral
数

sū no hyōgen
number representation;
numeric representation
数の表現

sū no kurancha
number cruncher
数のクランチャ

sū zokusei
number attribute
数属性

SUA (hyōjun kakin tan'i)
SUA (standard unit of accounting)
標準課金単位

SUB (okikae moji)
SUB (substitute character)
置き換え文字

sūchi
numeric; numeric value;
numerical
数値

sūchi dēta-purosessa
numerical data processor
数値データ・プロセッサ

sūchi dēta shori sōchi
numerical data processor
数値データ処理装置

sūchi hensū
variable (*noun*)
数値変数

sūchi kaiseki
numerical analysis
数値解析

sūchi keisan'yō sofutouea
mathematical software
数値計算用ソフトウェア

sūchi kiipaddo
numeric keypad
数値キーパッド

sūchi paddo
numerical pad
数値パッド

sūchi seigyo (NC)
numerical control (NC)
数値制御

sueoki
deferred
据え置き

sueoki deguchi
deferred exit
据え置き出口

sueoki iriguchi
deferred entry
据え置き入り口

sūgakuteki kensa
mathematical check
数学的検査

sūgakuteki moderu
mathematical model
数学的モデル

sūhyōji
numeric representation
数表示

suichoku
vertical
垂直

suichoku dōki
vertical synchronization
垂直同期

suichoku jōchō kensa (VRC)
vertical redundancy check (VRC)
垂直冗長検査

suichoku kensa
vertical check
垂直検査

suichoku kigū kensa
vertical parity check
垂直奇偶検査

suichoku okuri
vertical feed
垂直送り

suichoku sen
vertical line
垂直線

suichoku shoshiki
vertical format
垂直書式

suichoku sōsa
vertical scanning
垂直走査

suichoku tabu (VT)
vertical tabulation (VT)
垂直タブ

suichoku tabu moji (VT)
vertical tabulation character (VT)
垂直タブ文字

suigin chien sen
mercury delay line
水銀遅延線

suigin kioku
mercury storage
水銀記憶

suigin setten keidenki
mercury-wetted relay
水銀接点継電器

suigin setten rirē
mercury contact relay
水銀接点リレー

suihei(gata)
horizontal
水平(型)

suihei jōchō kensa (LRC)
longitudinal redundancy check (LRC)
水平冗長検査

suihei jōchō kensa moji
longitudinal redundancy check character
水平冗長検査文字

suihei kensa
horizontal check;
longitudinal check
水平検査

suihei kigū
horizontal parity
水平奇偶

suihei kigū kensa
horizontal parity check
水平奇偶検査

suihei okuri
horizontal feed
水平送り

suihei pariti
horizontal parity;
longitudinal parity
水平パリティ

suihei pariti-chekku
horizontal parity check
水平パリティ・チェック

suihei pariti kensa (LPC)
longitudinal parity check (LPC)
水平パリティ検査

suihei shoshiki
horizontal format
水平書式

suihei sōsa
horizontal scanning
水平走査

suihei tabu (HT)
horizontal tabulation (HT)
水平タブ

suihei tabu moji (HT)
horizontal tabulation character (HT)
水平タブ文字

suiheigata maikuropuroguramu
horizontal microprogram
水平型マイクロプログラム

suijun
horizontal; level
水準

suijun kanji
horizontal Chinese characters
水準漢字

suiron
inference
推論

suishō
quartz crystal
水晶

suitchi
switch
スイッチ

suitchi-risuto
switch list
スイッチ・リスト

suitchi-sutētomento
switch statement
スイッチ・ステートメント

suitchingu
switching
スイッチング

suitchingu-daiōdo
switching diode
スイッチング・ダイオード

suitei
estimation
推定

sūji
digit; figure; numeral; numeric; numeric character; numeric digit; numerical; numerical character
数字

sūji deisupurei
numeric display
数字ディスプレィ

sūji dēta
numeric data
数字データ

sūji dēta-purosessa
numeric data processor
数字データ・プロセッサ

sūji dēta shori sōchi
numeric data processor
数字データ処理装置

sūji fuiirudo
numeric field
数字フィールド

sūji go
numeric word
数字語

sūji hyōji (sōchi)
digital display
数字表示(装置)

sūji ichi
digit position
数字位置

sūji kemban kikō
numeric keyboard
数字鍵盤機構

sūji kōdeingu
numeric coding
数字コーディング

sūji kōdo
numeric code
数字コード

sūji kōmoku
numeric item
数字項目

sūji ronri
digital logic
数字論理

sūji senkō
digit punch; numeric punching
数字せん孔

sūji sentaku moji
digit select character
数字選択文字

sūji setto
numeric character set
数字セット

sūji shifuto
numeric shift
数字シフト

sūji shifuto (FIGS)
figure shift (FIGS)
数字シフト

sukejyūra
scheduler
スケジューラ

sukejyūringu
scheduling
スケジューリング

sukejyūringu-arugorizumu
scheduling algorithm
スケジューリング・アルゴリズム

sukejyūringu-moderu
scheduling model
スケジューリング・モデル

sukejyūru
schedule
スケジュール

sukēru
scale
スケール

sukēru henkōshi
scale modifier
スケール変更子

sukiima
schema
スキーマ

sukiima kō
schema entry
スキーマ項

sukiima mei
schema name
スキーマ名

sukiima zu
schema chart
スキーマ図

sukippu
skip
スキップ

sukippu hyōshiki
skip flag
スキップ標識

sukippu meirei
skip instruction
スキップ命令

sukōringu
scrolling
スコーリング

sukuranburingu
scrambling
スクランブリング

sukuratchi-fuairu
scratch file
スクラッチ・ファイル

sukuratchi-paddo
scratch pad
スクラッチ・パッド

sukuratchi-paddo-memori
scratch pad memory
スクラッチ・パッド・メモリ

sukuratchi-tēpu
scratch tape
スクラッチ・テープ

sukuriin
screen
スクリーン

sukuriin-danpu
screen dump
スクリーン・ダンプ

sukuriin-edeita
screen editor
スクリーン・エディタ

sukuriin-tātaru
screen turtle
スクリーン・タータル

sukuriiningu
screening
スクリーニング

sukuriiningu-tesuto
screening test
スクリーニング・テスト

sukurōru
scroll
スクロール

sukyāna
scanner
スキャーナ

sukyū
skew
スキュー

sunappu-shotto
snapshot
スナップ・ショット

sunappu-shotto-danpu
snapshot dump
スナップ・ショット・ダンプ

sunappu-shotto-deisupurei
snapshot display
スナップ・ショット・
ディスプレイ

sunappu-shotto-puroguramu
snapshot program
スナップ・ショット・プログラム

SUP (hyōjun shori tan'i)
SUP (standard unit of processing)
標準処理単位

sūpa-konpyūta
supercomputer
スーパ・コンピュータ

sūpabaiza
supervisor
スーパバイザ

sūpabaiza jōtai
supervisor state
スーパバイザ状態

sūpabaiza-kōru meirei
supervisor call instruction
スーパバイザ・コール命令

sūpabaiza-mōdo
supervisor mode
スーパバイザ・モード

sūpabaiza-rejisuta
supervisor register
スーパバイザ・レジスタ

sūpabaiza yobidashi
supervisor call
スーパバイザ呼び出し

sūpabaiza yobidashi meirei
supervisor call instruction
スーパバイザ呼び出し命令

sūpainpōzu
superimposed
スーパインポーズ

sūpainpōzu-bōdo
superimposed board
スーパインポーズ・ボード

sūpainpōzu-yunitto
superimposed unit
スーパインポーズ・ユニット

supan
span
スパン

supan shijishi
spanning indicator
スパン指示子

supando-fuairu
spanned file
スパンド・ファイル

supando-rekōdo
spanned record
スパンド・レコード

suparaisa
splicer
スパライサ

suparaishingu
splicing
スパライシング

supāsu-matorikkusu
sparse matrix
スパース・マトリックス

supattaringu
sputtering
スパッタリング

supēsu
space
スペース

supēsu-kii
space key
スペース・キー

supotto-panchi
spot punch
スポット・パンチ

supurain
spline
スプライン

supurain kinō
spline function
スプライン機能

supūringu
spooling
スプーリング

supūru
spool
スプール

supūru-auto
spool out
スプール・アウト

supūru-in
spool in
スプール・イン

suraisa
slicer
スライサ

suraisu
slice
スライス

suraisu kairo
slicing circuit
スライス回路

suraisu-reberu
slice level
スライス・レベル

surasshingu
thrashing
スラッシング

surededdo-kōdo
threaded code
スレデッド・コード

sūri kaiseki
mathematical analysis
数理解析

sūri keikakuhō (MP)
mathematical programming (MP)
数理計画法

surotto
slot
スロット

surūputto
throughput
スループット

sūshiki shori
formula manipulation
数式処理

sūshiki shori gengo
formula manipulation language
数式処理言語

sūshiki teisū
expression constant
数式定数

sutabu
stub
スタブ

sutakka
stacker
スタッカ

sutakku
stack
スタック

sutakku haibun
stack allocation
スタック配分

sutakku hyōjishi
stack indicator
スタック表示子

sutakku kikai
stack machine
スタック機械

sutakku-memori
stacked memory
スタック・メモリ

sutakku-pointa
stack pointer
スタック・ポインタ

sutāto
start
スタート

sutāto-bitto
start bit
スタート・ビット

sutāto-bitto-taimu
start interval
スタート・ビット・タイム

sutāto-eremento
start element
スタート・エレメント

sutāto-parusu
start pulse
スタート・パルス

suteppu
step
ステップ

suteppu-bai-suteppu
stey by step
ステップ・バイ・ステップ

suteppu-bai-suteppu hōshiki
step-by-step system
ステップ・バイ・ステップ方式

suteppu-bai-suteppu sōsa
step-by-step operation
ステップ・バイ・ステップ操作

suteppu-kaunta
step counter
ステップ・カウンタ

suteppu ōtō
step response
ステップ応答

sutēshon
station
ステーション

sutētasu
status
ステータス

sutētomento
statement
ステートメント

sutoppu
stop
ストップ

sutoppu-bitto
stop bit
ストップ・ビット

sutoppu-bitto-taimu
stop interval
ストップ・ビット・タイム

sutoppu-eremento
stop element
ストップ・エレメント

sutoppu-kōdo
stop code
ストップ・コード

sutoppu-parusu
stop pulse
ストップ・パルス

Sutorakuchādo-Bēshikku (SBASIC)
Structured BASIC (SBASIC)
ストラクチャード・ベーシック

sutoriimu
stream
ストリーム

sutoringu
string
ストリング

sutoringu-dēta
string data
ストリング・データ

sutoringu shori
string manipulation;
string processing
ストリング処理

sutoringu-sōto
string sort
ストリング・ソート

sutorōbu
strobe
ストローブ

sutorōbu kairo
strobing circuit
ストローブ回路

sutorōbu-parusu
strobe pulse
ストローブ・パルス

sutorōku
stroke
ストローク

sutorōku chūshin sen
stroke center line
ストローク中心線

sutorōku fuchi
stroke edge
ストローク縁

sutorōku haba
stroke width
ストローク幅

sutorōku hōshiki
stroke method
ストローク方式

suwappingu
swapping
スワッピング

suwappu-auto
swap out
スワップ・アウト

suwappu-in
swap in
スワップ・イン

SVP (sābisu-purosessa)
SVP (service processor)
サービス・プロセッサ

SYN (dōki shingō)
SYN (synchronous idle)
同期信号

SYSGEN (shisutemu seisei)
SYSGEN (systems generation)
システム生成

SYSPOOL (shisutemu jō no ichiji kioku'iki)
SYSPOOL (system temporary storage pool)
システム上の一時記憶域

443

ta
multi-
多

TA (tekunoroji-asesumento)
TA (technology assessment)
テクノロジ・アセスメント

TAB (ran okuri; seihyō; shūkeihyō; tabu; tabyurēshon)
TAB (tabulation)
欄送り；製表；集計表；タブ；
タビュレーション

tabai seido
multiple precision
多倍精度

tabai seido enzan
multiprecision arithmetic;
multiple precision arithmetic
多倍精度演算

tabaichō enzan
multilength arithmetic
多倍長演算

tabaichō shori
multilength working
多倍長処理

tabaichō sū
multilength number;
multiple-length number
多倍長数

tabu (TAB)
tabulation (TAB)
タブ

tabu-fuairu
tab file
タブ・ファイル

tabu setteiten
tab position
タブ設定点

taburetto
tablet
タブレット

tabyura gengo
tabular language
タビュラ言語

tabyurēshon (TAB)
tabulation (TAB)
タビュレーション

tachaneru
multichannel
多チャネル

tachiagari jikan
rise time
立ち上り時間

tachisagari jikan
fall time
立ち下り時間

tadankai
multistage
多段階

tagei
versatility
多芸

tageisei
versatile
多芸性

tāgetto
target
ターゲット

tāgetto dankai
target phase
ターゲット段階

tāgetto-konfuigyurēshon
target configuration
ターゲット・コンフィギュ
レーション

tagu
tag
タグ

tagu bunrui
tag sort
タグ分類

tagu-kādo
tag card
タグ・カード

tagu keishiki
tag format
タグ形式

tagu-riida
tag reader
タグ・リーダ

tagu senkōki
tag marker
タグせん孔機

tagu-shisutemu
tag system
タグ・システム

tagu-sōto
tag sort
タグ・ソート

tagu yomitori senkōki
tag reader
タグ読み取りせん孔機

tahensū
multivariable
多変数

tahōkō akusesu
multiway access
多方向アクセス

tahōkō henkan
multiway conversion
多方向変換

tai'iki
band
帯域

tai'iki (no; teki)
global
大域(の；的)

tai'iki asshuku
band compression
帯域圧縮

tai'iki haba
bandwidth
帯域幅

tai'ikiteki hensū
global variable
大域的変数

tai'ikiteki nagare kaiseki
global flow analysis
大域的流れ解析

tai'ikiteki purosessa
global processor
大域的プロセッサ

tai'ikiteki saitekika
global optimization
大域的最適化

taiji
delayed
待時

taiji hōshiki
delayed time system
待時方式

taiji toranzakushon
delayed transaction
待時トランザクション

taikei
system
体系

taiki
standby
待機

taiki akusesu
queued access
待機アクセス

taiki akusesu hōshiki
queued access method
待機アクセス方式

taiki jikan
standby time
待機時間

taiki jōchō
standby redundancy
待機冗長

taiki junji akusesu hōshiki (QSAM)
queued sequential-access method (QSAM)
待機順次アクセス方式

taiki kikai
standby machine
待機機械

taiki ryō'iki
standby area
待機領域

taiki sakuin junji akusesu hōshiki (QISAM)
queued indexed sequential-access method (QISAM)
待機索引順次アクセス方式

taiki shisutemu
standby system
待機システム

taiki shori
standby processing
待機処理

taiki tsūshin akusesu hōshiki (QTAM)
queued telecommunications access method (QTAM)
待機通信アクセス方式

taikyūsei
durability
耐久性

taima (kikō)
timer
タイマ（機構）

taima-kaunta
timer counter
タイマ・カウンタ

taima-sābisu
timer service
タイマ・サービス

taima seigyo
timer control
タイマ制御

taima shori
timer processing
タイマ処理

taima warikomi
timer interrupt
タイマ割り込み

taimingu
timing
タイミング

taimingu-chāto
timing chart
タイミング・チャート

taimingu-erā
timing error
タイミング・エラー

taimingu-parusu
timing pulse
タイミング・パルス

taimingu-torakku
timing track
タイミング・トラック

taimu
time
タイム

taimu-auto
time out
タイム・アウト

taimu-chāto
time chart
タイム・チャート

taimu-shiearingu
time sharing
タイム・シェアリング

taimu-shiearingu-shisutemu (TSS)
time-sharing system (TSS)
タイム・シェアリング・システム

taimu-suraishingu
time slicing
タイム・スライシング

taimu-suraisu
time slice
タイム・スライス

taimu-suraisu no chi
time slicing value
タイム・スライスの値

Taini BASIC
Tiny BASIC
タイニ BASIC

Taini-Bēshikku
Tiny BASIC
タイニ・ベーシック

taipu
type
タイプ

taipu-bā
type bar
タイプ・バー

taipu-hoiiru
type wheel
タイプ・ホイール

taipu-hoiiru insho sōchi
type wheel printer
タイプ・ホイール印書装置

taipu-in
type in
タイプ・イン

taipu sengen(bun)
type declaration
タイプ宣言（文）

taipuraita
typewriter
タイプライタ

taipuraita sōsataku
typewriter console
タイプライタ操作卓

taipuraita-tāminaru
typewriter terminal
タイプライタ・ターミナル

tairyū
accumulation; conservation; maintenance
滞留

taishō jun'i
total precedence
対称順位

taishō rekōdo
object record
対象レコード

taisū
logarithm
対数

taiwa
dialogue; interaction
対話

taiwa(gata; shiki)
conversational; interactive
対話（型；式）

taiwa hōshiki
interactive method
対話方式

taiwa mōdo
interactive mode
対話モード

taiwagata gurafuikkusu
interactive graphics
対話型グラフィックス

taiwagata zukei
interactive graphics
対話型図形

taiwashiki gurakuikkusu
interactive graphics
対話式グラフィックス

tajigen
multidimensional
多次元

tajigen shisutemu
multidimensional system
多次元システム

tajū
multi-; multiple
多重

tajū akusesu
multiple access
多重アクセス

tajū akusesu keisanki (MAC)
multiaccess computer (MAC)
多重アクセス計算機

tajū ayamari
multiple error
多重誤り

tajū chaneru
multiplexer channel
多重チャネル

tajū dainyūbun
multiple-assignment statement
多重代入文

tajū heisa
multiple closure
多重閉鎖

tajū hōshiki
multiplex(ing) mode
多重方式

tajū hōshiki sōchi (MUX)
multiplexer (MUX)
多重方式装置

tajū jōtai
multistate
多重状態

tajū jyobu
multijob
多重ジョブ

tajū jyobu sōsa
multijob operation
多重ジョブ操作

tajū jyobu-sukejyūringu
multijob scheduling
多重ジョブ・スケジューリング

tajū machigyōretsu
multiqueue
多重待ち行列

tajū puroguramingu
multiprogramming
多重プログラミング

tajū puroguramingu dōsa
multiprogramming operations
多重プログラミング動作

tajū puroguramingu-shisutemu
multiprogramming system
多重プログラミング・システム

tajū puroguramingu sōsa
multiprogramming operations
多重プログラミング操作

tajū purosessa
multiprocessor
多重プロセッサ

tajū purosessa-shisutemu
multiprocessor system
多重プロセッサ・システム

tajū purosesu dōki
multiprocess synchronization
多重プロセス同期

tajū reberu
multilevel
多重レベル

tajū reberu-adoresu
multilevel address
多重レベル・アドレス

tajū reberu keikaku
multilevel planning
多重レベル計画

tajū reberu keisanki
multilevel computer
多重レベル計算機

tajū reberu kōzō
multilevel structure
多重レベル構造

tajū reberu-shisutemu
multilevel system
多重レベル・システム

tajū renketsu risuto
multilinked list
多重連結リスト

tajū rūpu
multiloop
多重ループ

tajū sengen
multiple declaration
多重宣言

tajū senkō
multiple punch(ing)
多重せん孔

tajū shisutemu
multisystem
多重システム

tajū shisutemu sōsa
multisystem operation
多重システム操作

tajū shori
multiprocessing;
multiple processing
多重処理

tajū shori shisutemu
multiprocessing system;
multiple processing system
多重処理システム

tajū sōsa
multiplex operation
多重操作

tajū sutētomento
multiple statement
多重ステートメント

tajū tanmatsu
multiple terminals
多重端末

tajū tasuku
multitask
多重タスク

tajū tasuku sōsa
multitask operation
多重タスク操作

tajū torakku
multiple track
多重トラック

tajū torakku ayamari
multiple-track error
多重トラック誤り

tajū yobidashi
multiaccess; multiple access
多重呼び出し

tajū yobidashi shisutemu
multiaccess system
多重呼び出しシステム

tajū yōkyū
multiple-request
多重要求

tajūka
multiplexing
多重化

takaisō
multilevel
多階層

takaisō sakuin
multilevel index
多階層索引

taken
keying
打鍵

takijun
multicriteria
多基準

takinō
multifunction
多機能

takinō bōdo
multifunction board
多機能ボード

takinō kādo
multifunction card
多機能カード

takinōteki
multifunctional
多機能的

takujōgata keisanki
desk-top computer
卓上型計算機

takujōgata kensa
desk checking
卓上型検査

tameshi
trial
試し

tamesu
test (*verb*)
試す

tāminaru
terminal
ターミナル

tāminaru-sukuriin
terminal screen
ターミナル・スクリーン

tamokuteki
multiobjective;
multiple objective
多目的

tamokuteki kādo
multiple-use card
多目的カード

tampatsu sōsa
one-shot operation
単発操作

tān-araundo-dokyumento
turnaround document
ターン・アラウンド・
ドキュメント

tān-araundo jikan
turnaround time
ターン・アラウンド時間

tan burokku
short block; truncated block
短ブロック

tān-kii sōsa
turnkey operation
ターン・キー操作

tān-ofu
turn off
ターン・オフ

tān-ofu jikan
turn-off time
ターン・オフ時間

tān-on
turn on
ターン・オン

tān-on jikan
turn-on time
ターン・オン時間

tan seido
short precision
短精度

tan'antei
monostable
単安定

tan'antei kairo
monostable circuit;
monostable trigger circuit
単安定回路

tan'antei maruchibaiburēta
monostable multivibrator
単安定マルチバイブレータ

tan'antei soshi
monostable element
単安定素子

tan'antei toriga kairo
monostable trigger circuit
単安定トリガ回路

tanchi
detection
探知

tanchiki
detector
探知器

tandemu
tandem
タンデム

tandemu-purosessa
tandem processor
タンデム・プロセッサ

tandemu-shisutemu
tandem system
タンデム・システム

tandemu sōsa
tandem operation
タンデム操作

tandoku no
independent
単独の

tandoku seigyo shisutemu
independent control system
単独制御システム

tango (W)
word (W)
単語

tanhōkō
unidirectional
単方向

tan'i
unit
単位

tan'i inparusu
unit impulse
単位インパルス

tan'i inparusu ōtō
unit impulse response
単位インパルス応答

tan'i kankaku
unit interval
単位間隔

tan'i renshi
unit string
単位連糸

tan'i suteppu
unit step
単位ステップ

tan'i suteppu ōtō
unit step response
単位ステップ応答

tan'i sutoringu
unit string
単位ストリング

tan'inshi
elementary divisor
単因子

taninsū seigyo
multiperson control
多人数制御

tan'itsu
single
単一

tan'itsu adoresu
single address
単一アドレス

tan'itsu adoresu meirei
single-address instruction
単一アドレス命令

tan'itsu akusesu kikō
single-access mechanism
単一アクセス機構

tan'itsu ayamari
single error
単一誤り

tan'itsu boryūmu-fairu
single-volume file
単一ボリューム・ファイル

tan'itsu jyobu-sukejyūringu
single-job scheduling
単一ジョブ・スケジューリング

tan'itsu oyako shūgō
singular set
単一親子集合

tan'itsu parusu
single pulse
単一パルス

tan'itsu purosessa
uniprocessor; unit processor
単一プロセッサ

tan'itsu riiru
single reel
単一リール

tan'itsu torakku
single track
単一トラック

tan'itsu yunitto
single unit
単一ユニット

tanjun baffuaringu
simple buffering
単純バッファリング

tanjun enzan shiki
simple arithmetic expression
単純演算式

tanjun hensū
simple variable
単純変数

tanjun jōken
simple condition
単純条件

tanjun jōken shiki
simple conditional expression
単純条件式

tanjun junjo kōzō
simple sequence structure
単純順序構造

tanjun kanshō shuhō
simple buffering
単純緩衝手法

tanjun kōzō
simple structure
単純構造

tanjun mei
simple name
単純名

tanjun ronrishiki
simple Boolean expression
単純論理式

tanjun shiki
simple expression
単純式

tanjun shisutemu
simple system
単純システム

tanjun sutētomento
simple statement
単純ステートメント

tanjun zettai shiki
simple absolute expression
単純絶対式

tanjunka
simplification
単純化

tankō
monadic; simplex; unary
単項

tankō Būru enzanshi
monadic Boolean operator
単項ブール演算子

tankō enzan
monadic operation;
unary operation
単項演算

tankō enzanshi
monadic operator;
unary operator
単項演算子

tankyokusei
unipolar
単極性

tankyokusei parusu
unipolar pulse
単極性パルス

tankyokusei shingō
unipolar signal
単極性信号

tanmatsu
station
端末

tanmatsu (sōchi)
terminal
端末(装置)

tanmatsu bōdo
terminal board
端末ボード

tanmatsu kanri
terminal management
端末管理

tanmatsu kiibōdo
terminal keyboard
端末キーボード

tanmatsu kiki
terminal equipment
端末機器

tanmatsu ni chakushin
arrival of message at terminal
端末に着信

tanmatsu riyōsha
terminal user
端末利用者

tanmatsu seigyo
terminal control
端末制御

tanmatsu sōchi
terminal control unit
端末装置

tanmatsu yūza
terminal user
端末ユーザ

tanō
multifunction; multipurpose
多能

tanryū
single current
単流

tanryūshiki densō
neutral transmission;
single-current transmission
単流式伝送

tansaku
look up; search; searching
探索

tansaku hōhō
search method
探索方法

tansaku insū
search argument
探索引数

tansaku jikan
search time
探索時間

tansaku kii
search key
探索キー

tansaku kii-rokku
search key lock
探索キー・ロック

tansaku senryaku
search strategy
探索戦略

tansaku shūki
search cycle
探索周期

tansaku sōsa
look-up operation
探索操作

tanseido
single precision
単精度

tansen
edge
端線

tansen kenshutsu
edge detection
端線検出

tanshi
terminal
端子

tanshin
simplex
単信

tanshin densō
simplex transmission
単信伝送

tanshin kaisen
simplex circuit
単信回線

tanshin tsūshin
simplex communication
単信通信

tanshin tsūshin shisutemu
simplex communication system
単信通信システム

tanshin tsūshinro
simplex channel
単信通信路

tansoku hatai (SSB)
single sideband (SSB)
単測波帯

tansoku hatai densō
single-sideband transmission
単測波帯伝送

tansoku hatai henchō
single-sideband modulation
単測波帯変調

tasō
multilayer
多層

tasō insatsu haisen kiban
multilayer printed circuit board
多層印刷配線基板

tasokudo
multispeed
多速度

tasūketsu
majority
多数決

tasūketsu enzan
majority operation
多数決演算

tasūketsu ronri
majority logic
多数決論理

tasūketsu soshi
majority decision element;
majority element
多数決素子

tasuku
task
タスク

tasuku kaiseki
task analysis
タスク解析

tasuku kaishi
task initiation
タスク開始

tasuku kanri
task management
タスク管理

tasuku kansei
task completion
タスク完成

tasuku kijutsu
task description
タスク記述

tasuku machigyōretsu
task queue
タスク待ち行列

tasuku no ijō shūryō (ABEND)
abnormal end of task (ABEND)
タスクの異常終了

tasuku no owari
end of task
タスクの終り

tasuku seigyo
task control
タスク制御

tasuku seigyo burokku (TCB)
task control block (TCB)
タスク制御ブロック

tasuku sentaku
task selection
タスク選択

tasuku-shiikensu
task sequence
タスク・シーケンス

tasuku shikibetsu
task identification
タスク識別

tasuku shimei
task dispatch
タスク技名

tasuku shimei puroguramu
task dispatcher
タスク技名プログラム

tasuku shūryō
end of task
タスク終了

tasuku teigi
task definition
タスク定義

tasuku yūsen jun'i
task priority
タスク優先順位

tātaru-gurafuikkusu
turtle graphics
タータル・グラフィックス

tatchikando sōchi
touch-sensitive device
タッチ感度装置

TC (densō seigyo)
TC (transmission control)
伝送制御

TCAM (tsūshin akusesu hōshiki)
TCAM (telecommunications
access method)
通信アクセス方式

TCB (tasuku seigyo burokku)
TCB (task control block)
タスク制御ブロック

TCU (densō seigyo sōchi)
TCU (transmission control unit)
伝送制御装置

**TDG (tesuto-dēta seisei
puroguramu)**
TDG (test data generator)
テスト・データ生成プログラム

TDL (henkan teigi gengo)
TDL (translation definition
language)
変換定義言語

TDM (jibunkatsu tajū hōshiki)
TDM (time division multiplexing)
時分割多重方式

TDMA (jibunkatsu tajū akusesu)
TDMA (time division multiple
access)
時分割多重アクセス

TE (shūtan)
TE (trailing end)
終端

tēburu
table
テーブル

tēburu chokusetsu sakuin
table look-at
テーブル直接索引

tēburu kensaku
table search
テーブル検索

tēburu kudōgata konpaira
table-driven compiler
テーブル駆動型コンパイラ

tēburu kudōgata puroguramu
table-driven program
テーブル駆動型プログラム

tēburu sakuin
table look-up
テーブル索引

tēburu sakuin meirei
table look-up instruction
テーブル索引命令

tēburu yōso
table element
テーブル要素

tei
base
底

tei banchi kioku ryō'iki
low-order memory;
low-order storage
低番地記憶領域

tei chi hyōjishi
low indicator
低値表示子

tei reberu
low level
低レベル

tei reberu gengo
low-level language
低レベル言語

tei reberu-kōdo
low-level code
低レベル・コード

tei shūha
low frequency
低周波

tei soku(do)
low speed
低速(度)

tei suijun
low level
低水準

tei suijun gengo
low-level language
低水準言語

teichi seigyo
constant value control;
fixed-command control
定値制御

teigi
definition
定義

teigi(sumi)
defined
定義(済み)

teigi suru
define
定義する

teigisumi
predefined
定義済み

teigisumi jiki
predefined period
定義済み時期

teigisumi meirei
defined instruction;
predefined instruction
定義済み命令

teigisumi shori
predefined processing
定義済み処理

tei'i no seigyo henkō
minor control change
低位の制御変更

tei'ichi parameta
positional parameter
定位置パラメタ

teijō
stationary; steady
定常

teijō jōhō gen
stationary information source
定常情報源

teijō jōtai
stationary state
定常状態

teikaku
rated
定格

teikaku sokudo
rated speed
定格速度

teikankaku jikan seigyo hōshiki
fixed-clock time control
定間隔時間制御方式

teikō
resistor
抵抗

teikō toranjisuta ronri (RTL)
resistor transistor logic (RTL)
抵抗トランジスタ論理

teiritsu kōdo
constant ratio code
定率コード

teiryōteki
quantitative
定量的

teiryōteki jōhō
quantitative information
定量的情報

teisei
correction
訂正

teiseiteki
qualitative
定性的

teiseiteki jōhō
qualitative information
定性的情報

teishi
presentation
提示

teishi
halt; hang up; stop
停止

teishi jikan
stop time
停止時間

teishi kii
stop key
停止キー

teishi meirei
halt instruction; stop instruction
停止命令

teishi shingō
stop signal
停止信号

teisoku(do)
slow
低速(度)

teisoku ōtō jikan
slow response time
低速応答時間

teisū
constant (*noun*)
定数

teisū teigi bun
define constant statement
定数定義文

teiyōshiki
formatted; preformatted
定様式

teiyōshiki dēta
formatted data
定様式データ

teiyōshiki hyōji
formatted display
定様式表示

teiyōshiki messēji
formatted message
定様式メッセージ

tejun
procedure; routine
手順

tejun bunseki
procedure analysis
手順分析

tejun gengo
procedural language
手順言語

tejun mei
routine name
手順名

tejunmuki gengo
procedure-oriented language
手順向き言語

tekaki
hand-written
手書き

tekaki moji ninshiki
hand-written character recognition
手書き文字認識

tekaki sūji ninshiki
hand-written numeral recognition
手書き数字認識

tekigō
adaptation; compatible
適合

tekigō keiro sentaku
adaptive routing
適合経路選択

tekigō ritsu
relevance ratio
適合率

tekigō shisutemu
adaptive system
適合システム

tekiō
adaptation
適応

tekiō kanō
adaptable
適応可能

tekiō kinō
adaptive function
適応機能

tekiō kōzō
adaptive structure
適応構造

tekiō ōtō
adaptive response
適応応答

tekiō seigyo
adaptive control
適応制御

tekiō seigyo shisutemu
adaptive-control system
適応制御システム

tekiō shisutemu
adaptive system
適応システム

tekiōsei
adaptability
適応性

tekisuto
text
テキスト

tekisuto asshuku
text compression
テキスト圧縮

tekisuto-edeita
text editor
テキスト・エディタ

tekisuto henshū
text editing
テキスト編集

tekisuto henshū puroguramu
text editor
テキスト編集プログラム

tekisuto hyōji
text indicator
テキスト表示

tekisuto kaishi
beginning of text
テキスト開始

tekisuto kaishi (STX)
start of text (STX)
テキスト開始

tekisuto kaishi moji
start-of-text character
テキスト開始文字

tekisuto no hajime
beginning of text
テキストの始め

tekisuto shitan
beginning of text
テキスト始端

tekisuto shori
text processing
テキスト処理

tekisuto shūketsu (ETX)
end of text (ETX)
テキスト終結

tekisuto shūketsu moji
end-of-text character
テキスト終結文字

tekiyō
application
適用

tekunoroji
technology
テクノロジ

tekunoroji-asesumento (TA)
technology assessment (TA)
テクノロジ・アセスメント

TELEX (terekkusu; teretaipu kōkan)
TELEX (teleprinter exchange)
テレックス；テレタイプ交換

tempu
attachment
添付

tempu suru
attach
添付する

——— ni tempu
attached to ———
———に添付

tenaoshi
debugging
手直し

tenaosu
debug
手直す

tenki
transcription
転記

tenki suru
copy (*verb*); transcribe
転記する

tenpurēto
template
テンプレート

tenpurēto tsukiawase
template-matching
テンプレート突き合わせ

tensha
transcription
転写

tensha suru
transcribe
転写する

tensō
transfer; transport
転送

tensō jikan
transfer time
転送時間

tensō kensa
transfer check
転送検査

tensō meirei
transfer instruction
転送命令

tensō nettowāku (TN)
transport network (TN)
転送ネットワーク

tensō nettowāku seigyo (TNC)
transport network control (TNC)
転送ネットワーク制御

tensō ritsu
transfer rate
転送率

tensō seigyo
transfer control
転送制御

tensō seigyo tejun
transfer control procedure
転送制御手順

tensō sokudo
transfer rate
転送速度

tensō sōsa
transfer operation
転送操作

tensō suru
transfer (*verb*)
転送する

tensōkanō
transferable
転送可能

tentō suru
light up (*verb*)
点灯する

tēpu
tape
テープ

tēpu bunrui
tape sort
テープ分類

tēpu-burokku
tape block
テープ・ブロック

tēpu-chaneru
tape channel
テープ・チャネル

tēpu-danpu
tape dump
テープ・ダンプ

tēpu-fuairu
tape file
テープ・ファイル

tēpu-kādo henkan
tape-to-card conversion
テープ・カード変換

tēpu-kādo henkanki
tape-to-card converter
テープ・カード変換器

tēpu kaishi (BOT)
beginning of tape (BOT)
テープ開始

tēpu kaishi māka
beginning-of-tape marker
テープ開始マーカ

tēpu-kasetto
tape cassette
テープ・カセット

tēpu-kātorijji
tape cartridge
テープ・カートリッジ

tēpu keishiki
tape format
テープ形式

tēpu kenkō
tape verifying
テープ検孔

tēpu kenkōki
tape verifier
テープ検孔機

tēpu-kōdo
tape code
テープ・コード

tēpu-kōdo sembetsu suitchi
tape code selection switch
テープ・コード選別スイッチ

tēpu-kōdo sentaku suitchi
tape code selection switch
テープ・コード選択スイッチ

tēpu kudō kikō
tape drive; tape transport
テープ駆動機構

tēpu-māka
tape marker
テープ・マーカ

tēpu makitori riiru
take-up reel
テープ巻き取りリール

tēpu-māku (TM)
tape mark (TM)
テープ・マーク

tēpu no hajime (BOT)
beginning of tape (BOT)
テープの始め

tēpu no hajime māka
beginning-of-tape marker
テープの始めマーカ

tēpu no owari (EOT)
end of tape (EOT)
テープの終り

tēpu okuri
tape feed
テープ送り

tēpu-operēteingu-shisutemu (TOS)
tape-operating system (TOS)
テープ・オペレーティング・システム

tēpu owari māka
end-of-tape marker
テープ終りマーカ

tēpu-panchi
tape punch
テープ・パンチ

tēpu-panchi setsuzoku kikō
tape punch attachment
テープ・パンチ接続機構

tēpu-raberu
tape label
テープ・ラベル

tēpu-raberu-shisutemu (TLS)
tape-labeling system (TLS)
テープ・ラベル・システム

tēpu-raiburari
tape library
テープ・ライブラリ

tēpu-riiru
tape reel
テープ・リール

tēpu seigyoshiki kyarijji
tape-controlled carriage
テープ制御式キャリッジ

tēpu senkōki
  tape punch
  テープせん孔機

tēpu shitan
  beginning of tape (BOT)
  テープ始端

tēpu shitan māka
  beginning-of-tape marker
  テープ始端マーカ

tēpu shūtan (EOT)
  end of tape (EOT)
  テープ終端

tēpu shūtan māka
  end-of-tape marker
  テープ終端マーカ

tēpu shūtan yokoku
  end-of-tape warning
  テープ終端予告

tēpu sōchi
  tape deck
  テープ装置

tēpu-sōto
  tape sort
  テープ・ソート

tēpu-sutēshon
  tape station
  テープ・ステーション

tēpu-sutoriima
  tape streamer
  テープ・ストリーマ

tēpu-suwappu
  tape swap
  テープ・スワップ

tēpu-tēpu henkan
  tape-to-tape conversion
  テープ・テープ変換

tēpu-tēpu henkanki
  tape-to-tape converter
  テープ・テープ変換器

tēpu yomitori sōchi
  tape reader
  テープ読み取り装置

terebi (TV)
  television (TV)
  テレビ

terekanfuerenshingu
  teleconferencing
  テレカンフェレンシング

terekkusu (TELEX)
  teleprinter exchange (TELEX)
  テレックス

teremēta
  telemeter
  テレメータ

teremētaringu
  telemetering
  テレメータリング

terepurinta
  teleprinter
  テレプリンタ

terepurosesshingu
  teleprocessing
  テレプロセッシング

terepyūta
  teleputer
  テレピュータ

teresofutouea
  telesoftware
  テレソフトウェア

teretaipu
  teletype
  テレタイプ

teretaipu kōkan (TELEX)
  teleprinter exchange (TELEX)
  テレタイプ交換

teretaipuraita
  teletypewriter
  テレタイプライタ

teretaipuraita kōkan sābisu (TWX)
  teletypewriter exchange service (TWX)
  テレタイプライタ交換サービス

teretekisuto
  teletext
  テレテキスト

teretekkusu
  teletex
  テレテックス

terewāka
  teleworker
  テレワーカ

tesuteingu
  testing
  テスティング

tesuto
  test
  テスト

tesuto-dēta
  test data
  テスト・データ

tesuto-dēta seisei puroguramu (TDG)
  test data generator (TDG)
  テスト・データ生成プログラム

tesuto jōken
  test conditions
  テスト条件

tesuto-kēsu
  test case
  テスト・ケース

tesuto-mōdo
  test mode
  テスト・モード

tesuto-pakku
  test pack
  テスト・パック

tesuto-puroguramu
  test program
  テスト・プログラム

tesuto-ran
  test run
  テスト・ラン

tesuto-tsūru
  test tool
  テスト・ツール

tetsuzuki
  procedure
  手続き

tetsuzuki bu
  procedure division
  手続き部

tetsuzuki bun
  procedure narrative;
  procedure statement
  手続き文

tetsuzuki chāto
  procedure chart
  手続きチャート

tetsuzuki chūshaku
  procedure narrative
  手続き注釈

tetsuzuki fukupuroguramu
procedure subprogram
手続き副プログラム

tetsuzuki kansū
procedure function
手続き関数

tetsuzuki mei
procedure identifier;
procedure name
手続き名

tetsuzuki modori
procedure return
手続き戻り

tetsuzuki no sengen
procedure declaration
手続きの宣言

tetsuzuki taipu
procedure type
手続きタイプ

tetsuzuki teigi
procedure definition
手続き定義

tetsuzukigata gengo
procedural language
手続き型言語

TLS (tēpu-raberu-shisutemu)
TLS (tape-labeling system)
テープ・ラベル・システム

TM (tēpu-māku)
TM (tape mark)
テープ・マーク

TN (tensō nettowāku)
TN (transport network)
転送ネットワーク

TNC (tensō nettowāku seigyo)
TNC (transport network control)
転送ネットワーク制御

tobikoshi
jump
飛び越し

tobikoshi bun
GO TO statement
飛び越し文

tobikoshi meirei
jump instruction
飛び越し命令

tōchi hyōjishi
equal indicator
等値表示子

tōchō
tapping
盗聴

tochū
place of interruption
途中

tōgō
integrated
統合

tōgō(gata) deisuku
integrated disk
統合(型)ディスク

tōgō(gata) deisuku sōchi
integrated disk unit
統合(型)ディスク装置

tōgō dētabēsu
combined database
統合データベース

tōgō emyurēshon
integrated emulation
統合エミュレーション

tōgō emyurēta
integrated emulator
統合エミュレータ

tōgō(gata) sofutouea
integrated software
統合(型)ソフトウェア

tōgōka
integration
統合化

toguru
toggle
トグル

toguru-furippu-furoppu
toggle flip-flop
トグル・フリップ・フロップ

toguru-suitchi
toggle switch
トグル・スイッチ

toiawase
inquiry; interrogation; query
問い合わせ

toiawase (ENQ)
enquiry (ENQ)
問い合わせ

toiawase moji
enquiry character
問い合わせ文字

toiawase ōtō shisutemu
query-answering system
問い合わせ応答システム

toiawase shisutemu
enquiry system; inquiry system
問い合わせシステム

toiawase shori
query processing
問い合わせ処理

toiawase sōchi
inquiry unit; interrogator
問い合わせ装置

toiawase tanmatsu (sōchi)
inquiry station
問い合わせ端末(装置)

toiawase yūteiritei
enquiry utility
問い合わせユーティリティ

tōjigo
acronym
頭辞語

tojita hairetsu
closed array
閉じた配列

tojita rūchin
closed routine
閉じたルーチン

tojita rūpu
closed loop
閉じたループ

tojita rūpu-shisutemu
closed-loop system
閉じたループ・システム

tojita saburūchin
closed subroutine
閉じたサブルーチン

tojita shisutemu
closed system
閉じたシステム

tōka
equalization
等化

tōka (EQ)
equivalence (EQ)
等価

tōka gēto (EQ gēto)
equivalence gate (EQ gate)
等価ゲート；EQ ゲート

tōka nishin sūji
equivalent binary digit
等価 2 進数字

tōkaki
equalizer
等化器

tōkei
statistics
統計

tōkeiteki
statistical
統計的

tōken
token
トークン

tokken meirei
privileged instruction
特権命令

tokken meirei reigai
privileged operation exception
特権命令例外

tokken mōdo
privileged mode
特権モード

tokken sōsa
privileged operation
特権操作

tokken yūza
privileged user
特権ユーザ

tokkenteki akusesu
privileged access
特権的アクセス

tōkō sen
contour line
等高線

tōkō senzu
contour map
等高線図

tokuchō
feature; main features
特徴

toku'i chi kaiseki
singular value analysis
特異値解析

tokusei
characteristic; property
特性

tokusei
characteristics
特性

tokusei bunrui
property sort
特性分類

tokusei hizumi
characteristic distortion
特性歪み

tokusei inpiidansu
characteristic impedance
特性インピーダンス

tokusen
special line
特線

tokushu kikō
special feature
特殊機構

tokushu kinō
special function
特殊機能

tokushu moji
additional characters;
special characters
特殊文字

tokushu na sōchi
special equipment
特殊な装置

tokushu rejisuta
special register
特殊レジスタ

tokushu seigyo moji
special control character
特殊制御文字

tokutei
specific
特定

tokutei gyōmumuki gengo
applications-oriented language
特定業務向き言語

tokutei gyōmuyō tanmatsu (sōchi)
job-oriented terminal
特定業務用端末（装置）

tokuyū
specific
特有

tokuyū adoresu
specific address
特有アドレス

tokuyū kōdo
specific code
特有コード

tōnamento
tournament
トーナメント

tōnamento sentaku hōshiki
tournament selection
トーナメント選択方式

tōnamento sentakuhō bunrui
tournament sort
トーナメント選択法分類

toporojii
topology
トポロジー

toppu-daun-apurōchi
top-down approach
トップ・ダウン・アプローチ

toppu-daun sekkei
top-down design
トップ・ダウン設計

torakkingu
tracking
トラッキング

torakkingu-erā
tracking error
トラッキング・エラー

torakku
track
トラック

torakku-adoresu
track address
トラック・アドレス

torakku afure
track overflow
トラック溢れ

torakku hogo
track hold
トラック保護

torakku jōken tēburu
track condition table
トラック条件テーブル

torakku kan no kyori
track pitch
トラック間の距離

torakku sentaku
track selection
トラック選択

torakuta-fuiido
tractor feed
トラクト・フィード

toranjisuta
transistor
トランジスタ

toranjisuta-toranjisuta ronri (TTL)
transistor-transistor logic (TTL)
トランジスタ・トランジスタ論理

toranku
trunk
トランク

toranku seigyo
trunk control
トランク制御

toranshiiba
transceiver
トランシーバ

toransuparento-dēta
transparent data
トランスパレント・データ

toransurēta
translator
トランスレータ

toransurēta sakusei shisutemu
translator writing system
トランスレータ作成システム

toranzakushon
transaction
トランザクション

toranzakushon-dēta
transaction data
トランザクション・データ

toranzakushon-fuairu
transaction file
トランザクション・ファイル

toranzakushon-kādo
transaction card
トランザクション・カード

toranzakushon-rekōdo
transaction record
トランザクション・レコード

toranzakushon shori
transaction(-driven) processing
トランザクション処理

torappu
trap
トラップ

torēra
trailer
トレーラ

torēsa
tracer
トレーサ

torēsabiritei
traceability
トレーサビリティ

torēsu
trace
トレース

toridashi
fetch
取り出し

toridashi bōshi
fetch protection
取り出し防止

toridasu
fetch (*verb*)
取り出す

toriga
trigger; triggering
トリガ

toriga kairo
trigger circuit
トリガ回路

toriga-parusu
trigger pulse
トリガ・パルス

torihazushikanō deisuku
removable disk
取り外し可能ディスク

torihazushikanō deisuku-pakku
removable disk pack
取り外し可能ディスク・パック

torihazusu
remove (*verb*)
取り外す

torihiki
transaction
取り引き

torihiki fuairu
transaction file
取り引きファイル

torihiki kādo
transaction card
取り引きカード

torikae
replacement
取り替え

torikae mondai
replacement problem
取り替え問題

torikaeru
replace
取り替える

torikeshi (CAN)
cancel (CAN); cancellation
取り消し

torikeshi hyōji
cancel indicator
取り消し表示

torikeshi moji
cancel character;
ignore character
取り消し文字

torikesu
cancel (*verb*)
取り消す

tōroku
registration
登録

tōrokubo
directory
登録簿

TOS (tēpu-operēteingu-shisutemu)
TOS (tape-operating system)
テープ・オペレーティング・
システム

tōsaku
piracy
盗作

tōsha
projection
投射

tōshi bangō
sequence number; serial number
通し番号

457

tōshi kōdo
serial code
通しコード

tōtaru jōhō
total information
トータル情報

tōtaru jōhō shisutemu
total information system
トータル情報システム

tōtaru-shisutemu
total system
トータル・システム

tōtaru-shisutemu-apurōchi
total systems approach
トータル・システム・アプローチ

TSO (jibunkatsu opushon)
TSO (time-sharing option)
時分割オプション

TSS (taimu-shiearingu-shisutemu)
TSS (time-sharing system)
タイム・シェアリング・システム

tsūban ga tsukeru
issue a number
通番が付ける

tsui kensa
twin check
対検査

tsuijū seigyo
follow-up control
追従制御

tsuika
additional
追加

tsuika dēta kioku
additional data storage
追加データ記憶

tsuika fuairu
additional file
追加ファイル

tsuika kioku
additional storage
追加記憶

tsuika kōmoku
additional item
追加項目

tsuika kudō kikō
additional drive
追加駆動機構

tsuika moji
additional characters
追加文字

tsuika on-rain-dēta yōryō
additional on-line data capacity
追加オン・ライン・データ容量

tsuika rekōdo
additional record
追加レコード

tsuika ryō'iki
additional area
追加領域

tsuika sōchi
additional unit
追加装置

tsuiseki
trace
追跡

tsuiseki mōdo
trace mode
追跡モード

tsuiseki puroguramu
trace program; tracer;
tracing program
追跡プログラム

tsuiseki rūchin
tracing routine
追跡ルーチン

tsuiseki shisutemu
tracking system
追跡システム

tsuiseki tēburu
trace table
追跡テーブル

tsuisuta kioku
twister storage
ツイスタ記憶

tsuisuto-pea
twisted pair
ツイスト・ペア

tsūjō
normal
通常

tsūjō mōdo
normal mode
通常モード

tsūjō nagare
normal flow
通常流れ

tsūjō no (dembun)
ordinary (≠urgent message)
通常の（電文）

tsūjō ōtō
normal response
通常応答

tsukiawase (dēta no)
matching (of data)
突き合わせ（データの）

tsukiawase kii
match key
突き合わせキー

tsukiawaseru
match (*verb*)
突き合わせる

tsume
justification
詰め

tsumeru
justify
詰める

tsunagi risuto
threaded list
つなぎリスト

tsūshin
communication(s);
telecommunication(s)
通信

tsūshin akusesu hōshiki (TCAM)
telecommunications access
method (TCAM)
通信アクセス方式

tsūshin bōdo
communication board
通信ボード

tsūshin chaneru
communication channel
通信チャネル

tsūshin eisei
communication satellite
通信衛星

tsūshin eremento
communication element
通信エレメント

tsūshin gengo
communications language
通信言語

tsūshin hojo sōchi
communication auxiliary
equipment
通信補助装置

tsūshin kādo
communication card
通信カード

tsūshin kagaku
communication science
通信科学

tsūshin kaisen
communication line;
telecommunication line
通信回線

tsūshin keiro
communication path
通信経路

tsūshin kinō
communication function;
communication facility;
telecommunication facility
通信機能

tsūshin rinku
communication link
通信リンク

tsūshin riron
communication theory
通信理論

tsūshin seigyo
communication control
通信制御

tsūshin seigyo adaputa
communications control adapter
通信制御アダプタ

tsūshin seigyo moji
communication control
character
通信制御文字

tsūshin seigyo puroguramu (CCP)
communication control program
(CCP)
通信制御プログラム

tsūshin seigyo rūchin (CCR)
communication control routine
(CCR)
通信制御ルーチン

tsūshin seigyo sōchi
communication controller
通信制御装置

tsūshin seigyo sōchi (CCE)
communication control
equipment (CCE)
通信制御装置

tsūshin seigyo sōchi (CCU)
communication control unit
(CCU)
通信制御装置

tsūshin seigyo taku
communication console
通信制御卓

tsūshin setsubi
communication equipment;
communication facilities
通信設備

tsūshin shisutemu
communication system;
telecommunication system
通信システム

tsūshin shori shisutemu
communication processing
system
通信処理システム

tsūshin sōchi
communication device
通信装置

tsūshin sokudo
communication speed
通信速度

tsūshin tanmatsu (sōchi)
communication terminal
通信端末(装置)

tsūshin tōgō adaputa
integrated communication
adapter
通信統合アダプタ

tsūshin warikomi
communication interrupt
通信割り込み

tsūshin'yō āsu (SG)
s-earth; signal ground (SG)
通信用アース

tsūshin'yō adaputa
communications adapter
通信用アダプタ

tsūshin'yō baffua
communication buffer
通信用バッファ

tsūshin'yō intafuēsu
communications interface
通信用インタフェース

tsūshin'yō purosessa (CP)
communication processor (CP)
通信用プロセッサ

tsūshin'yō sāba
communication server
通信用サーバ

tsūshin'yō shori sōchi
communications processor
通信用処理装置

tsūshin'yō sofutouea
communication(s) software
通信用ソフトウェア

tsūshin'yō tanmatsu
communications terminal
通信用端末

tsūshinki
transmitter
通信機

tsūshinmō
communication network;
telecommunication network
通信網

tsūshinro
channel; communication
channel
通信路

tsūshinryō
traffic
通信量

tsūyaku
interpreting; interpretive
通訳

tsūyaku kōdo
interpretive code
通訳コード

tsūyaku puroguramingu
interpretive programming
通訳プログラミング

tsūyaku rūchin
interpreter; interpretive routine
通訳ルーチン

459

tsūyaku suru
interpret
通訳する

tsūyō
application
通用

TTL (toranjisuta-toranjisuta ronri)
TTL (transistor-transistor logic)
トランジスタ・トランジスタ論理

TV (terebi)
TV (television)
テレビ

TWT (shinkōhakan)
TWT (traveling-wave tube)
進行波管

TWX (teretaipu kōkan sābisu)
TWX (teletypewriter exchange
service)
テレタイプ交換サービス

U

UA (jōi ruisanki)
UA (upper accumulator)
上位累算器

**UART (han'yō hidōki sōjushin
kairo)**
UART (universal asynchronous
receiver-transmitter)
汎用非同期送受信回路

UCB (sōchi seigyo burokku)
UCB (unit control block)
装置制御ブロック

uchikiru
abort
打ち切る

UDC (kokusai jisshin bunruihō)
UDC (universal decimal
classification)
国際10進分類法

udegi shingō
semaphore
腕木信号

uēfua
wafer
ウェーファ

**UHL (riyōsha fuairu midashi
raberu)**
UHL (user header label)
利用者ファイル見出しラベル

UHP (yunibāsaru-hosuto-purosessa)
UHP (universal host processor)
ユニバーサル・ホスト・
プロセッサ

Uiinshiki teigi gengo (VDL)
Vienna definition language (VDL)
ウイーン式定義言語

Uinchesuta-deisuku-doraibu
Winchester disk drive
ウインチェスタ・ディスク・
ドライブ

uindō
window
ウインドー

uindō-konseputo
window concept
ウインドー・コンセプト

Uiriamusu kan
Williams tube
ウイリアムス管

ukai
deviation
迂回

ukaisen
deviation line
迂回線

ukeire kensa
acceptance inspection
受け入れ検査

ukeire shiken
acceptance test
受け入れ試験

uketori
receiving
受け取り

uketoru
receive
受け取る

ULD (fuhen gengo teigi)
ULD (universal language
definition)
普遍言語定義

umekomi
pad (*noun*)
埋め込み

umekomi keisanki
embedded computer
埋め込み計算機

umekomi keisanki shisutemu
embedded computer system
埋め込み計算機システム

umekomi moji
pad character
埋め込み文字

umekomi sōsa
padding
埋め込み操作

umekomu
pad (*verb*)
埋め込む

UNIX (Yunikkusu)
UNIX
ユニックス；UNIX

unten
operation (action); run
運転

V

unten teishi
shutdown
運転停止

uōmu-saisutāto
warm restart
ウオーム再スタート

uōmu-sutāto
warm start
ウオーム・スタート

uotchidoggu-taima (WDT)
watchdog timer (WDT)
ウオッチドッグ・タイマ

ura okuri
face-down feed
裏送り

USASCII (Jōhō Kōkan'yō Beikoku Hyōjun Kōdo)
USASCII (USA Standards Code for Information Interchange)
情報交換用米国標準コード

USASI (Beikoku Kikaku Kyōkai)
USASI (USA Standards Institute)
米国規格協会

UTL (riyōsha atogaki raberu)
UTL (user trailer label)
利用者後書きラベル

uwamuki no gokansei
upward compatibility
上向きの互換性

uwamuki no gokansei no
upward compatible
上向きの互換性の

v (boruto)
v (volt)
ボルト

VADR (kasō adoresu)
VADR (virtual address)
仮想アドレス

VC (aite sentaku setsuzoku)
VC (virtual call)
相手選択接続

VCO (den'atsu seigyo hasshinki)
VCO (voltage-controlled oscillator)
電圧制御発振器

VCR (bideo-kasetto-rekōda)
VCR (videocassette recorder)
ビデオ・カセット・レコーダ

VDL (Uiinshiki teigi gengo)
VDL (Vienna definition language)
ウイーン式定義言語

VDT (bideo hyōji tanmatsu sōchi)
VDT (video display terminal)
ビデオ表示端末装置

VDU (bideo hyōji sōchi; eizō hyōji sōchi)
VDU (video display unit)
ビデオ表示装置；映像表示装置

VDU (hyōji sōchi; shikakuteki hyōji sōchi)
VDU (visual display unit)
表示装置；視覚的表示装置

VENUS (biinasu)
VENUS (valuable and efficient network utility service)
ビーナス；VENUS

VFO (kahen shūhasū hasshinki)
VFO (variable frequency oscillator)
可変周波数発振器

VHF (chōtampa)
VHF (very high frequency)
超短波

VIP (hyōji jōhō sōchi)
VIP (visual information processor)
表示情報装置

VLSI (chōdai kibo shūsekika)
VLSI (very large scale integration)
超大規模集積化

VOL (boryūmu)
VOL (volume)
ボリューム

VR (den'atsu anteiki)
VR (voltage regulator)
電圧安定器

VRC (hyōji rekōdo-konpyūta)
VRC (visible-record computer)
表示レコード・コンピュータ

VRC (suichoku jōchō kensa)
VRC (vertical redundancy check)
垂直冗長検査

VRP (hyōji rekōdo-purinta)
VRP (visual-record printer)
表示レコード・プリンタ

VSAM (kasō kioku akusesu hōshiki)
VSAM (virtual storage access method)
仮想記憶アクセス方式

VT (suichoku tabu; suichoku tabu moji)
VT (vertical tabulation; vertical tabulation character)
垂直タブ；垂直タブ文字

VTAM (kasō tsūshin akusesu hōshiki)
VTAM (virtual telecommunications access method)
仮想通信アクセス方式

VTL (kahen shikii chi ronri)
VTL (variable threshold logic)
可変敷居値論理

VTOC (boryūmu mokuroku)
VTOC (volume table of contents)
ボリューム目録

VU (onryō tan'i)
VU (volume unit)
音量単位

VU (onsei tan'i)
VU (voice unit)
音声単位

W

W (go; tango; wādo)
W (word)
語；単語；ワード

wa
sum
和

wādo (W)
computer word; word (W)
ワード

wādo kyōkai
word boundary
ワード境界

wādo-māku
word mark
ワード・マーク

wādo-purosessa (WP)
word processor (WP)
ワード・プロセッサ

wādo-purosesshingu (WP)
word processing (WP)
ワード・プロセッシング

wādo-taimu
word time
ワード・タイム

WADS (kōʼiki dēta-sābisu)
WADS (wide-area data service)
広域データ・サービス

WAIT jōtai
WAIT status
WAIT 状態

waiya
wire
ワイヤ

waiya kioku
wire storage
ワイヤ記憶

waiya-memori
wire memory
ワイヤ・メモリ

waiya-purinta
wire printer
ワイヤ・プリンタ

waiyādo AND
wired AND
ワイヤード AND

waiyādo OR
wired OR
ワイヤード OR

wāku
work
ワーク

wāku-sukejyūringu
work scheduling
ワーク・スケジューリング

wāku-sutēshon (WS)
workstation (WS)
ワーク・ステーション

wāku-sutēshon-kiibōdo
workstation keyboard
ワーク・ステーション・
キーボード

wāku-tēpu
work tape
ワーク・テープ

WAN (kōʼiki nettowāku)
WAN (wide-area network)
広域ネットワーク

wan-chippu CPU
one-chip CPU
ワン・チップ CPU

wan-chippu-konpyūta
one-chip computer
ワン・チップ・コンピュータ

wan-shotto-maruchibaiburēta
one-shot multivibrator
ワン・ショット・
マルチバイブレータ

wando
wand
ワンド

wariate
allocation; assignment
割り当て

wariateru
allocate; assign
割り当てる

warifu
tally
割り符

warikomi
interruption; trap
割り込み

warikomi dōsa
interrupt action
割り込み動作

warikomi gen
interrupt source
割り込み原

warikomi I/O
interrupt I/O
割り込み I/O

warikomi jikan
interrupt time
割り込み時間

warikomi jōken
interrupt condition
割り込み条件

warikomi jōtai go
interruption status word
割り込み状態語

warikomi kaiseki
interrupt analysis
割り込み解析

warikomi kanō
interrupt enable
割り込み可能

warikomi kaunta
interrupt counter
割り込みカウンタ

warikomi kinō
interrupt function
割り込み機能

warikomi kinshi
interrupt inhibit
割り込み禁止

warikomi kōdo
interruption code
割り込みコード

warikomi kōtei ōtō shingō (IACK)
interrupt acknowledge signal
(IACK)
割り込み肯定応答信号

warikomi machi
interruption pending
割り込み待ち

warikomi machigyōretsu
interruption queue
割り込み待ち行列

warikomi masuku
interrupt mask
割り込みマスク

warikomi reberu
　interrupt level; interruption level
　割り込みレベル

warikomi rokku auto
　interrupt lockout
　割り込みロック・アウト

warikomi rūchin
　interruption routine
　割り込みルーチン

warikomi saburūchin
　interruption subroutine
　割り込みサブルーチン

warikomi seigyo
　interrupt control
　割り込み制御

warikomi seigyo jōtai
　interrupt control state
　割り込み制御状態

warikomi shingō
　interrupt signal
　割り込み信号

warikomi shokika tejun
　interrupt initialization procedure
　割り込み初期化手順

warikomi shori rūchin
　interrupt handler;
　interruption handling routine
　割り込み処理ルーチン

warikomi yōkyū (IRQ)
　interrupt request;
　interruption request (IRQ)
　割り込み要求

warikomi yōkyū shingō
　interruption request signal
　割り込み要求信号

warikomi yūsen kyoka shingō
　interrupt priority signal
　割り込み優先許可信号

warikomi yūsendo
　interrupt priority
　割り込み優先度

warikomikanō jōtai
　interruptible state
　割り込み可能状態

warikomu
　interrupt (*verb*)
　割り込む

waritsuke
　allocation
　割り付け

waritsuke rūchin
　allocation routine
　割り付けルーチン

waritsukeru
　allocate
　割り付ける

WBLS (kōtai'iki senkei dōki)
　WBLS (wide-band linear
　synchronization)
　広帯域線形同期

WCS (kakikomikanō seigyo sōchi)
　WCS (writable control storage)
　書き込み可能制御装置

WDT (uotchidoggu-taima)
　WDT (watchdog timer)
　ウオッチドック・タイマ

**WP (bunsho shori sōchi; wādo-
purosessa)**
　WP (word processor)
　文書処理装置; ワード・
　プロセッサ

**WP (bunsho shori; wādo-
purosesshingu)**
　WP (word processing)
　文書処理; ワード・
　プロセッシング

WPM (go/fun)
　WPM (words per minute)
　語／分

WPS (go/byō)
　WPS (words per second)
　語／秒

WRU (anata wa)
　WRU (who are you?)
　あなたは

**WS (sagyō tanmatsu; wāku-
sutēshon)**
　WS (workstation)
　作業端末; ワーク・ステーション

X

X-kōshi
　X-chart
　X 格子

X-pojishon
　X-position
　X ポジション

X-senkō
　X-punch
　X せん孔

X-uwakasane senkō
　X-over punch
　X 上重ねせん孔

X-Y purotta
　X-Y plotter
　X-Y プロッタ

**XNOR (haitateki hitei ronriwa;
haitateki NOR)**
　XNOR (exclusive-NOR)
　XNOR; 排他的否定論理和;
　排他的 NOR

**XNOR kairo (haitateki hitei ronriwa
kairo; haitateki NOR kairo)**
　XNOR circuit (exclusive-NOR
　circuit)
　XNOR回路;
　排他的否定論理和回路;
　排他的NOR回路

**XOR (haitateki OR; haitateki
ronriwa)**
　XOR (exclusive-OR)
　XOR; 排他的OR; 排他的論理和

**XOR enzan (haitateki OR enzan;
haitateki ronriwa enzan)**
　XOR operation (exclusive-OR
　operation)
　XOR 演算; 排他的 OR 演算;
　排他的論理和演算

**XOR gēto (haitateki OR gēto;
haitateki ronriwa gēto)**
　XOR gate (exclusive-OR gate)
　XOR ゲート; 排他的 OR ゲート;
　排他的論理和ゲート

**XOR kairo (haitateki OR kairo;
haitateki ronriwa kairo)**
　XOR circuit (exclusive-OR circuit)
　XOR 回路; 排他的 OR 回路;
　排他的論理和回路

XOR soshi (haitateki OR soshi; haitateki ronriwa soshi)
XOR element (exclusive-OR element)
XOR 素子；排他的 OR 素子；排他的論理和素子

Y

Y-pojishon
Y-position
Y ポジション

Y-senkō
Y-punch
Y せん孔

Y-uwakasane senkō
Y-over punch
Y 上重ねせん孔

yakumemei
role name
役目名

yakuwari
role
役割り

yasen kii
arrow key
矢線キー

yasenzu
arrow diagram
矢線図

yobi
preliminary
予備

yobi sekkei
preliminary design
予備設計

yobi tēpu
spare tape
予備テープ

yobidashi
access; accessing; call; calling
呼び出し

yobidashi go
call word
呼び出し語

yobidashi hyōji
calling indicator
呼び出し表示

yobidashi jikan
access time; latency time
呼び出し時間

yobidashi keiretsu
calling sequence
呼び出し系列

yobidashi meirei
call instruction
呼び出し命令

yobidashi puroguramu
calling program
呼び出しプログラム

yobidashi risuto
calling list
呼び出しリスト

yobidasu
access (*verb*)
呼び出す

yobō
prevention; protection
予防

yobō hoshu (PM)
preventive maintenance (PM)
予防保守

yobō suru
prevent; protect
予防する

yōgo sakuin
concordance
用語索引

yōgojiten
glossary
用語辞典

yōgoshū
glossary
用語集

yō'in
factor
要因

yōken
requirement(s)
要件

yokoyomi
row-by-row reading
横読み

yokusei
suppression
抑制

yokusei suru
suppress
抑制する

yokushi (suru)
inhibit
抑止（する）

yokushi gēto
inhibit gate
抑止ゲート

yokushi kairo
inhibit circuit
抑止回路

yokushi parusu
inhibit pulse
抑止パルス

yokushi sen
inhibit line
抑止線

yōkyū
demand; request; requesting;
requirement(s)
要求

yōkyū bunseki
requirements analysis
要求分析

yōkyū gengo
requirements language
要求言語

yōkyū shiyō
requirements specification
要求仕様

yōkyū teigi
requirements definition
要求定義

yōkyū teigi gijutsu
requirements engineering
要求定義技術

yōkyūji pējingu
demand paging
要求時ページング

yomibun
read statement
読み文

yomidashi
readout; reading
読み出し

yomidashi bun
read statement
読み出し文

yomidashi parusu
read pulse
読み出しパルス

yomidashi sen
sense line
読み出し線

yomidashi sen'yō (RO)
read only (RO)
読み出し専用

yomidashi sen'yō chippu
read-only chip
読み出し専用チップ

yomidashi sen'yō kioku (ROM)
read-only memory (ROM)
読み出し専用記憶

yomidashi sen'yō kioku (ROS)
read-only storage (ROS)
読み出し専用記憶

yomidasu
read (*verb*)
読み出す

yomikaki (R-W)
read-write (R-W)
読み書き

yomikaki heddo
read-write head
読み書きヘッド

yomikaki kensa
read-write check
読み書き検査

yomikaki kioku
read-write memory
読み書き記憶

yomitori
reading
読み取り

yomitori ayamari
read error
読み取り誤り

yomitori bun
read statement
読み取り文

yomitori chekku
read-back check
読み取りチェック

yomitori heddo
read head
読み取りヘッド

yomitori kakikomi (R-W)
read-write (R-W)
読み取り書き込み

yomitori kakikomi chaneru
read-write channel
読み取り書き込みチャネル

yomitori kakikomi hogo
read-write protection
読み取り書き込み保護

yomitori kakikomi kioku
read-write memory
読み取り書き込み記憶

yomitori kikō
read station
読み取り機構

yomitori meirei
read instruction
読み取り命令

yomitori saikuru-taimu
read cycle time
読み取りサイクル・タイム

yomitori sen'yō (RO)
read only (RO)
読み取り専用

yomitori sen'yō kioku (ROM)
read-only memory (ROM)
読み取り専用記憶

yomitori sen'yō kioku (ROS)
read-only storage (ROS)
読み取り専用記憶

yomitori sōchi
reader
読み取り装置

yomitori sokudo
read rate
読み取り速度

yomitorikanō kaisū
read-around ratio
読み取り可能回数

yomitoru
read (*verb*)
読み取る

yomu
read (*verb*)
読む

yon adoresu
four-address
4アドレス

yon adoresu meirei
four-address instruction
4アドレス命令

yon purasu ichi adoresu
four-plus-one address
4＋1アドレス

yonbaicho rejisuta
quadruple-length register
四倍長レジスタ

yonbitto-baito
quartet
4 ビット・バイト

yonsenshiki
four-wire system
4 線式

yonsenshiki kaisen
four-wire circuit
4 線式回線

yonsenshiki tsūshinro
four-wire channel
4 線式通信路

yorigonomi
preference
選り好み

yōryō
capacity
容量

yōryō kakuchō
capacity expansion
容量拡張

yōryō kakuchō mondai
capacity expansion problem
容量拡張問題

yōryō keikaku
capacity planning
容量計画

yōryō kōyō kansū
capacity utility function
容量効用関数

yose
justification
寄せ

yoseru
justify
寄せる

yōshi
form (document); sheet
用紙

yōshi fusoku hyōji
"paper low" indicator
用紙不足表示

yōshi no jyamu
paper jam
用紙のジャム

yōshi no jyamu kenshutsu
paper jam detection
用紙のジャム検出

yōshi no jyamu kenshutsu kikō
paper jam detector
用紙のジャム検出機構

yōshi okuri kikō
sheet feeder
用紙送り機構

yōshi sumpō
paper size
用紙寸法

yōshiki
layout
様式

yōshiki (F)
format (F)
様式

yōshiki zu
format chart
様式図

yōso
element
要素

yosō kekka
potential result
予想結果

yosoku
forecasting
予測

yosoku gihō
forecasting technique
予測技法

yotei
schedule
予定

yōto
use
用途

yōyaku
summary
要約

yoyaku go
reserved word
予約語

yoyaku suru
reserve (*verb*)
予約する

yūgen jōtai
finite state
有限状態

yūgen jōtai gengo
finite-state language
有限状態言語

yūgen jōtai kikai
finite-state machine
有限状態機械

yūgen otōmaton
finite automaton
有限オートマトン

yūgen sabumpō (FDM)
finite difference method (FDM)
有限差分法

yūgen yōso hō (FEM)
finite element method (FEM)
有限要素法

yūi ayamari
significant error
有意誤り

yūi jishō
significant event
有意事象

yūi jōtai
significant conditions
有意状態

yūi kankaku
significant interval
有意間隔

yūi no
significant
有意の

yūi shunkan
significant instant
有意瞬間

yūisei
significance
有意性

yūjin
manned
有人

yūjin dōsa
manned operation
有人動作

yukauegata
free-standing
床上型

yukauegata kudō kikō
free-standing drive
床上型駆動機構

yūkitai shisutemu
organic system
有機体システム

yūkō
significant
有効

yūkō
effectiveness
有効

yūkō adoresu
effective address
有効アドレス

yūkō bubun
significant part
有効部分

yūkō dēta densō ritsu
data transmission utilization ratio
有効データ伝送率

yūkō dēta tensō sokudo
effective data transfer rate
有効データ転送速度

yūkō han'i
scope
有効範囲

yūkō jikan
accountable time
有効時間

yūkō keta kaishi moji
significance start character
有効桁開始文字

yūkō shisutemu
effective system
有効システム

yūkō sūji
significant digit; significant figure
有効数字

yūkō sūji enzan
significant-digit arithmetic
有効数字演算

yūkōka
enabling
有効化

yunibāsaru
universal
ユニバーサル

yunibāsaru-bōdo
universal board
ユニバーサル・ボード

yunibāsaru-hosuto-purosessa (UHP)
universal host processor (UHP)
ユニバーサル・ホスト・
プロセッサ

yunibāsaru-mojyūru
universal module
ユニバーサル・モジュール

yunibasu
unibus
ユニバス

yunibasu renketsu
unibus link
ユニバス連結

yunibasu-rinku
unibus link
ユニバス・リンク

Yunikkusu (UNIX)
UNIX
ユニックス；UNIX

yunitto
unit
ユニット

yunitto bunri moji (US)
unit separator (US)
ユニット分離文字

yunitto-rekōdo
unit record
ユニット・レコード

yunitto-rekōdo-fuairu
unit record file
ユニット・レコード・ファイル

yunitto-rekōdo-rūchin
unit record routine
ユニット・レコード・ルーチン

yūrisū
rational number
有理数

yūsen
priority
優先

——— **yori yūsen sareru**
to have priority over ———
———より優先される

yūsen bangō
priority number
優先番号

yūsen dembun
priority communication
優先電文

yūsen hyōshiki
priority indicator
優先標識

yūsen jun'i
order of precedence;
precedence; priority;
priority level
優先順位

yūsen jun'i tēburu
precedence table
優先順位テーブル

yūsen junjo
precedence
優先順序

yūsen kensaku
priority retrieval
優先検索

yūsen reberu
priority level
優先レベル

yūsen sābisu
priority service
優先サービス

yūsen shori
priority processing
優先処理

yūsen sukejyūra
priority scheduler
優先スケジューラ

yūsen sukejyūringu
priority scheduling
優先スケジューリング

yūsen tsūshin
priority communication
優先通信

yūsen warikomi
priority interrupt
優先割り込み

yūsendo
precedence; priority
優先度

yūsendo kansū
precedence function
優先度関数

yūteiritei
utility
ユーティリティ

yūteiritei-puroguramu
utility program
ユーティリティ・プログラム

yūteiritei-purosessa
utility processor
ユーティリティ・プロセッサ

yūteiritei-rūchin
utility routine
ユーティリティ・ルーチン

yūza
user
ユーザ

yūza bunsho
user documentation
ユーザ文書

yūza-fuairu
user file
ユーザ・ファイル

yūza-gurūpu
user group
ユーザ・グループ

yūza-intafuēsu
user interface
ユーザ・インタフェース

yūza-opushon
user option
ユーザ・オプション

yūza-pōto
user port
ユーザ・ポート

yūza-purofuairu
user profile
ユーザ・プロファイル

yūza-puroguramu
user program
ユーザ・プログラム

yūza shikibetsu
user identification
ユーザ識別

yūza tanmatsu (sōchi)
user terminal
ユーザ端末(装置)

yūza teigikanō kii
user-definable key
ユーザ定義可能キー

yūza teigisumi moji
user-defined character
ユーザ定義済み文字

yūza'yō seigyo kioku
control storage for user
ユーザ用制御記憶

Z

zahyō
coordinate (math)
座標

zahyō kei
coordinate system
座標系

zahyō kōshi
coordinate grid
座標格子

zaiko
stock
在庫

zaiko jōhō shisutemu
inventory information system
在庫情報システム

zaiko kanri
inventory control; stock control
在庫管理

zaiko keikaku
inventory planning
在庫計画

zatsuon
noise
雑音

zatsuon hasseiki
noise generator
雑音発生器

zatsuon no aru
noisy
雑音のある

zatsuon no nai
noiseless
雑音のない

zatsuon shisū
noise figure
雑音指数

zatsuon yokuatsu
noise suppression
雑音抑圧

zatsuon yoyū
noise margin
雑音余裕

zen genzanki
full subtractor
全減算器

zen go
full word
全語

zen kasanki
full adder
全加算器

zen keta age
complete carry
全桁上げ

zen nijū (FDX)
full duplex (FDX)
全二重

zen nijū densō
full-duplex transmission
全二重伝送

zen nijū hōshiki
full-duplex system
全二重方式

zen nijū tsūshin
full-duplex communication
全二重通信

zen nijū tsūshinro
full-duplex channel
全二重通信路

zen sentaku yomidashi parusu
full-read pulse
全選択読み出しパルス

zenchi
front end
前置

zenchi shisutemu
front-end system
前置システム

zen'en
leading edge
前縁

zenerēta
generator
ゼネレータ

zenkei
foreground
前景

zenkei jyobu
foreground job
前景ジョブ

zenkei puroguramu
foreground program
前景プログラム

zenkei shori
foreground processing
前景処理

zensettei
preset; presetting
前設定

zensettei puroguramu
preprepared program
前設定プログラム

zensū tansaku
exhaustive search
全数探索

zentai shisutemu
overall system
全体システム

zentei
prerequisite
前提

zero
zero
ゼロ

zero-adoresu
zero address
ゼロ・アドレス

zero-adoresu meirei
zero-address instruction
ゼロ・アドレス命令

zero-adoresu meirei keishiki
zero-address instruction format
ゼロ・アドレス命令形式

zero asshuku
zero compression
ゼロ圧縮

zero-baransu
zero balance
ゼロ・バランス

zero fukki (RZ)
return to zero (RZ)
ゼロ復帰

zero fukki māku (RZM)
return-to-zero mark (RZM)
ゼロ復帰マーク

zero jōtai
nought state; zero condition
ゼロ状態

zero jūten
zero-fill
ゼロ充てん

zero modori (RZ)
return to zero (RZ)
ゼロ戻り

zero modori māku (RZM)
return-to-zero mark (RZM)
ゼロ戻りマーク

zero ni suru
clear (*verb*); zero-clear; zeroize
ゼロにする

zero-reberu-adoresu
zero-level address
ゼロ・レベル・アドレス

zero shōkyo
zero elimination
ゼロ消去

zero shutsuryoku
zero output
ゼロ出力

zero yokusei
zero suppression
ゼロ抑制

zetsuentai
insulator
絶縁体

zettai adoresshingu
absolute addressing
絶対アドレッシング

zettai adoresu
absolute address
絶対アドレス

zettai adoresu shitei
absolute addressing
絶対アドレス指定

zettai chi
absolute value; magnitude
絶対値

zettai chi keikakuhō
absolute-value programming
絶対値計画法

zettai chi keisanki
absolute-value computer
絶対値計算機

zettai eremento
absolute element
絶対エレメント

zettai gosa
absolute error
絶対誤差

zettai hyōgen keishiki
absolute expression
絶対表現形式

zettai jikkō ryō'iki
  absolute execution area
  絶対実行領域

zettai kōdeingu
  absolute coding
  絶対コーディング

zettai kōdo
  absolute code
  絶対コード

zettai puroguramu-rōda
  absolute program loader
  絶対プログラム・ローダ

zettai rōda
  absolute loader
  絶対ローダ

zettai rōda-rūchin
  absolute loader routine
  絶対ローダ・ルーチン

zettai shiki
  absolute expression
  絶対式

zōbun
  increment; incremental
  増分

zōbun asshuku
  incremental compaction
  増分圧縮

zōbun bekuta
  incremental vector
  増分ベクタ

zōbun hyōjihō
  incremental representation
  増分表示法

zōbun keisanki
  incremental computer
  増分計算機

zōbun nishin hyōjihō
  incremental binary
  representation
  増分 2進表示法

zōbun sekibunki
  incremental integrator
  増分積分器

zōfuku
  amplification
  増幅

zōkukuki
  amplifier
  増幅器

zokusei
  attribute
  属性

zokusei chi
  property value
  属性値

zokusei chi shūgō
  property value set
  属性値集合

zōn
  zone
  ゾーン

zōn-bitto
  zone bit
  ゾーン・ビット

zōn-deijitto
  zone digit
  ゾーン・ディジット

zōn hōshiki
  zoning
  ゾーン方式

zōn keishiki
  zoned format
  ゾーン形式

zōn seisei
  zone purification; zone refining
  ゾーン精製

zōn senkō
  zone punch
  ゾーンせん孔

zōningu
  zoning
  ゾーニング

zu
  diagram
  図

zuhyō
  diagram; graphic; graphic form;
  graphical; graphics
  図表

zukei
  graphics
  図形

zukei dēta
  graphic data
  図形データ

zukei dēta shori
  graphic data processing
  図形データ処理

zukei (shori) gengo
  graphic language
  図形(処理)言語

zukei hyōji
  graphic data display
  図形表示

zukei hyōji (GD)
  graphic display (GD)
  図形表示

zukei hyōji puroguramu
  graphic display program
  図形表示プログラム

zukei hyōji seigyo
  graphic display control
  図形表示制御

zukei hyōji sōchi
  graphic data display unit;
  graphic display unit
  図形表示装置

zukei moji
  graphic character
  図形文字

zukei shori
  graphics processing
  図形処理

zukei shori tanmatsu sōchi
  graphics terminal
  図形処理端末装置

zukei shutsuryoku
  graphic(al) output
  図形出力

zukei shutsuryoku sōchi
  graphic output unit
  図形出力装置

zukigō
  graphic symbol
  図記号